Publications
Of
The Colonial Society of Massachusetts

VOLUME LXXIII

The Papers of Francis Bernard

Governor of Colonial Massachusetts, 1760-69

❧❧❧ ❧❧❧

VOLUME 1: 1759-1763

Sir Francis Bernard. By permission of Robert Spencer Bernard. Photograph by Charles Crisp, A.B.I.P.P.

EDITED BY COLIN NICOLSON

The Papers of Francis Bernard

Governor of Colonial Massachusetts, 1760-69

❧❧❧ ❧❧❧

VOLUME 1: 1759-1763

Research Assistant
Stuart Salmon

BOSTON   THE COLONIAL SOCIETY OF MASSACHUSETTS   2007
Distributed by the University of Virginia Press

DEDICATION

To Catherine, Catriona, and Kristen

CONTENTS

APPENDICES

ILLUSTRATIONS

ACKNOWLEDGEMENTS

The *Bernard Papers* project commenced in February 2000 as my writing of *The 'Infamas Govener': Francis Bernard and the Origins of the American Revolution* drew to a close. The project's origins lie partly in my own conviction that historians ought to do more to publish their sources, but more to the vision of John Tyler, publications editor of the Colonial Society of Massachusetts and editor of the *Select Correspondence of Thomas Hutchinson*. The project would not have been undertaken without his encouragement and would not have been possible without generous funding from the Society.

I am indebted to many others. First of all, I am delighted to thank John Catanzariti, former editor of the Jefferson Papers, who put aside his own projects in order to read a draft of this volume in its entirety; it is far, far better for his guidance and the detailed advice he kindly proffered, particularly concerning editorial method. Stephen Conway was another selfless reader whose comments enhanced the draft. Stuart Salmon proved an able and willing research assistant, adept at digitizing materials, fact-checking, and ferreting useful information, and who displayed commendable patience during double-proofreading procedures. My thanks also to Oron Joffe for helping me to develop an electronic file of source texts. Key support came from the University of Stirling's Faculty of Arts and Department of History by way of expensive equipment, sabbatical leave, and a reduced teaching load. Annabelle Hopkins and the late Marjory Clarkson ably assisted with the management of the project's finances. For advice on sources and editorial method I am grateful to Deborah Andrews, David Bebbington, Anne Decker Cecere, Owen Dudley Edwards, Jennifer Fauxsmith, Susan Halpert, James Lewis, Malcolm Freiberg, James Knowles, Robin Law, Margaret Newell, George Peden, Robert Spencer Bernard, Celeste Walker, Matthew Ward, and Conrad E. Wright. My colleagues Emma Macleod, Ben Marsh, Richard Oram, and Michael Rapport willingly gave their time to answer a host of questions. Photography was undertaken by Charles Crisp and Peter Hoare, graphic work by Laura Brown and Leanne Hogg, and the spendid book design by Jeanne Abboud.

I am conscious of my reliance upon the numerous librarians and archivists of the following North American repositories who responded gracefully and efficiently to enquiries made in person and by correspondence: the American Antiquarian Society; the Boston Athenaeum; the Bostonian Society; Bowdoin College Museum of Art; Detroit Institute of Arts; the Episcopal Diocese of Massachusetts; the Fogg Art Museum; Harvard Archives; the Historical Society of Pennsylvania; the Hollis Library, Harvard University; the Houghton Library, Harvard University; the Library Company of Philadelphia; Maine Historical Society; Maine State Library; Maryland State Archives; Massachusetts Archives; Massachusetts Historical Society; the Morgan Library; the Museum of Fine Arts, Boston; the National Archives of Canada; the National Gallery of Art; New Brunswick Museum; the New England Historic Genealogical Society; the Centre for Newfoundland Studies; New Jersey Historical Society; New Jersey State Archives; New-York Historical Society; New York Public Library; Peabody Essex Museum; Princeton University Library; Propietary House, Perth Amboy; Rosenbach Museum and Library; Rutgers University Library; the Smith College Museum of Art; the Smithsonian Institution; the Swett Library; the Library of Congress; University of Minnesota Libraries; University of Chicago Library; University of Virginia Library; the William L. Clements Library; Yale Center for British Art; Yale University Libraries.

My thanks also to the staff of several British repositories: Berkshire Record Office; the Bodleian Library; the British Library; Cardiff Central Library; the Centre for Buckinghamshire Studies; Christ Church College, Oxford University; Dalkeith House; Derby Record Office; East Sussex Record Office; the House of Lords Library; Lambeth Palace Library; Leeds Public Libraries; the Lewis Walpole Library; Lichfield Record Office; Lincolnshire Archives; the Metropolitan Museum of Art; the National Archives: Public Record Office; the National Archives of Scotland; the National Gallery of Scotland; the National Library of Scotland; the National Maritime Museum; Oxfordshire Record Office; the Royal Artillery Institution; the Royal Society for the Encouragement of Arts, Manufactures & Commerce; Sheffield Archives; Staffordshire Record Office; Suffolk County Council Archives; West Yorkshire Archive Service. Information Services staff at the University of Stirling assisted the project throughout, especially Marilyn Scott and Andrew Monteith of the computing advisory team and Linda Cameron of the document delivery service.

Permission to publish edited transcripts from various manuscript collections is herewith acknowledged: the Massachusetts Archives Collection, courtesy of Massachusetts Archives; the private collections of Robert Spencer Bernard; the Cadwallader Colden Papers at the New-York Historical Society; the Dartmouth Papers courtesy of Staffordshire Record Office; Material Relating to America, 1754-1806, in the Royal Society for the Encouragement of Arts, Manufactures & Commerce; William L. Clements Library, University of Michigan, for the Gage Papers; the Records of the Board of Overseers II, courtesy of Harvard Archives; the

Bernard Papers, Sparks MS 4 are reproduced by permission of Houghton Library, Harvard University. Transcript **No. 28** is reproduced courtesy of the Massachusetts Historical Society.

My last debts are the greatest: to my dear wife Catherine and my wonderful daughters, Catriona and Kristen, for their forbearance when the lives of historical others intrude upon the present.

LIST OF ABBREVIATIONS

Acts and Resolves	*The Acts and Resolves, Public and Private of the Province of Massachusetts Bay, 1692-1776.* 21 Vols. Boston, 1896-1922.
ADM 1/482	Papers of Admirals Colvill and Saunders, 1759-1766. Records of the Admiralty, Naval Forces, Royal Marines, Coastguard, and Related Bodies. ADM 1/482, PRO.
American Papers, Dartmouth Papers	American Papers, Dartmouth Papers. D(W)1778. Staffordshire Record Office.
APC	W. L. Grant and James Munro, eds., *Acts of the Privy Council of England: Colonial Series, 1613-1783.* 6 Vols. Vols. 4-6. London, 1909-1912.
Barrington-Bernard	Edward Channing and Archibald Cary Coolidge, eds., *The Barrington-Bernard Correspondence and Illustrative Matter, 1760-1770. Harvard Historical Studies Series.* Vol. 17. Cambridge, Mass., 1912.
Boston Gazette	*Boston Gazette and Country Journal.*
BP	Bernard Papers, 13 Vols. Sparks Papers, MS 4. Houghton Library, Harvard University.
CO 5	Colonial Office Records, Colonial Office Series. The National Archives of the UK: Public Record Office, London.
CO 5/7	Despatches and Misc.: Correspondence, Original-Secretary of State, 1755-1779. CO 5/7. PRO.

CO 5/19	Despatches, 1759-1760. CO 5/19. PRO.
CO 5/20	Despatches and Misc.: Correspondence, Original-Secretary of State, 1760-1761. CO 5/20. PRO.
CO 5/755	Original Correspondence of Secretary of State, 1761-1766. CO 5/755. PRO.
CO 5/850	Shipping Returns, 1752-1765. CO 5/850. PRO.
CO 5/851	Shipping Returns, 1756-1762. CO 5/851. PRO.
CO 5/891	New England, Original Correspondence of Board of Trade, 1760-1766. CO 5/891. PRO.
CO 5/897	New England, Draft Correspondence of Board of Trade, 1731-1774. CO 5/897. PRO.
CO 5/920	Instructions, Board of Trade Correspondence New England, 1760-1774. CO 5/920. PRO.
CO 5/998	Commissions, Instructions, Board of Trade Correspondence E, 1758-1760. CO 5/998. PRO.
Colden Papers	Cadwallader Colden Papers, 1677-1832. New-York Historical Society.
DNB	Sir Leslie Stephen and Sir Sidney Lee, eds., *The Dictionary of National Biography*. 22 Vols. London, 1964.
FB	Francis Bernard.
Gage	Gage Papers. William L. Clements Library.
Hutchinson, *History of Massachusetts*	Thomas Hutchinson, *The History of the Colony and Province of Massachusetts-Bay* 3 vols. (1764, 1767, 1828: Cambridge, Mass., 1936), ed. Lawrence Shaw Mayo.
JBT	*Journal of the Commissioners for Trade and Plantations*. 14 Vols. London, 1920-1938.

JHRM	*The Journals of the House of Representatives of Massachusetts, 1715-1776.* 55 Vols. Boston, 1919-1990.
King's	Official Transcripts of Reports (In-Letters) on the State of the British Colonies in North America and the West Indies. King's Manuscripts, King's, 205-206. The British Library
Labaree, *Royal Instructions*	Leonard Woods Labaree, ed., *Royal Instructions to British Colonial Governors, 1670-1776.* 2 Vols. London, 1935.
Mass. Archs.	Massachusetts Archives Collection, Records, 1629-1799. 328 Vols. SC1-45x. Massachusetts Archives.
MHS	Massachusetts Historical Society.
MP	Member of Parliament.
NAS	The National Archives of Scotland, Edinburgh.
ODNB-e	*Oxford Dictionary of National Biography Online.* London, 2004-2006, http://www.oxforddnb.com.
OED	*Oxford English Dictionary Online.* London 2004-2006, http://dictionary.oed.com.
PRO	The National Archives of the UK: Public Record Office, London.
PROB 11	Will Registers, Probate Records of the Prerogative Court of Canterbury. PROB 11. PRO.
Prov. Sec. Letterbooks	Province Secretary's Letterbooks, 1755-74, Secretary's Letterbooks, 1701-1872. 4 Vols., SC1-117x. [Vols. 1, 2, 2A, & 3]. Massachusetts Archives.
RSA	The Royal Society for the Encouragement of Arts, Manufactures & Commerce, London.

Select Letters	[Francis Bernard], *Select Letters on the Trade and Government of America; and the Principles of Law and Polity, Applied to the American Colonies Written by Governor Bernard in the Years 1763, 4, 5, 6, 7, and 8.* London, 1774.
Spencer Bernard Papers	Spencer Bernard Papers. D/SB. Centre for Buckinghamshire Studies, Aylesbury, Eng.
WMQ	*The William and Mary Quarterly: A Magazine of Early American History and Culture,* 3d ser.
WO 34/26	Letters from Governors of Massachusetts, Jan. 1760-Oct. 1763. Amherst Papers/Official Correspondence of Commander in Chief, 1760-1763. War Office Records. WO 34/26. PRO
WO 34/27	Letters to Governors of Massachusetts, Aug. 1756-Oct. 1763. Amherst Papers/Official Correspondence of Commander in Chief, 1756-1763. WO 34/27. PRO.

INTRODUCTION

The *Bernard Papers* is a comprehensive selection of the correspondence and other papers of Sir Francis Bernard (1712-79), governor of colonial Massachusetts between 1760 and 1769. This volume is the first of a projected three volumes of edited transcripts concerning his administration in Massachusetts and will be followed by a calendar of documents covering his life and career. The project aims to address a lacuna in published documentary resources pertaining to Massachusetts on the eve of the American Revolution.[1] The erratic publication of colonial records may not have appreciably hindered scholarship on this period yet comparative studies of colonial government during the imperial crisis remain logistically awkward and very expensive for scholars conducting transatlantic research. Massachusetts is a case in point: the province's legislative proceedings are available in series, but the vast majority of manuscripts generated by the provincial executive are not, including the governors' official correspondence.

Bernard's papers, which are held by repositories in both Great Britain and the United States, are a fecund resource, for his administration coincided with the onset of sustained opposition to British colonial policies. While much of Bernard's time was taken up by routine governmental matters rarely is the historical record he bequeathed ever mundane. His correspondence discusses, *inter alia*, the dissipation of the good feelings in Massachusetts that heralded victory over the French in 1763, long-running disputes with the provincial legislature over Crown requisitions, and the emergence of colonial radicalism in 1765. Bernard's letters home were a major source of information for British policymakers, particularly with regard to the decision to send regular soldiers to Boston in 1768 to quell riots and protests.[2] While historians have rarely failed to read Bernard's letters uncritically, often they have worked with a limited range of materials: his unpublished letter-books mainly (these are described below), some contemporary editions of official letters,[3] and a reliable edition of his private correspondence with Lord Barrington.[4] These account for a fraction of the available sources.

The project has collected, catalogued, and imaged facsimiles of more than four thousand source texts. To date, items authored or authorized by Bernard include over five hundred holographs; over thirteen hundred scribal copies of letters; and over four hundred and fifty printed versions of letters, speeches, and other official documents bearing his signature; there are also references to over four hundred non-extant letters. The largest single archival collection is the Bernard Papers in Sparks MS 4 at Houghton Library, Harvard University. The thirteen bound volumes contain over 1,680 documents: there are eight letterbooks of copies of private and official correspondence (vols. 1-8) that were largely maintained by clerks; three volumes of original in-letters and occasional autograph drafts (vols. 9-12), and one volume of royal instructions (vol. 13).[5]

The legibility of Bernard's letterbooks and their accessibility to New England-based scholars likely dissuaded anyone from editing the governor's official correspondence. Bernard's original letters to British ministers and officials are in the National Archives: Public Record Office, the main repository for British state papers. The Colonial Office Records (CO 5) and the War Office Records (WO 34) contain nearly six hundred unpublished letters and manuscripts, none of which are included in the only major serial of British state papers of the American Revolution.[6] The documents in CO 5 and WO 34 are well-preserved; while some pieces, such as CO 5/755, are torn at the edges, all are largely intact and in the same order as they were in the eighteenth century. In contrast, the Massachusetts Archives Collection in the State Archives (SC1-45x) was reorganized by subject in the nineteenth century. This particular collection, spread over 328 volumes, contains hundreds of official documents generated by Bernard's administration, including some correspondence; many are fragile and the microfilm copies are difficult to read.[7] Bernard's papers can also be found elsewhere—in the Massachusetts Historical Society and in English local archives, particularly the Centre for Buckingham Studies and the Lincolnshire Archives; and among the papers of correspondents like Thomas Hutchinson[8] or third parties, including British ministers, who received copies of his letters.[9]

It is not practical or feasible to publish transcripts of all of Bernard's correspondence, and in selecting items for publication priority has been given to his official letters dealing with colonial government and imperial administration. Most of Bernard's 175 correspondents were acting in an official or semi-official capacity, but precedence has been accorded his communications with the Board of Trade, the secretary of state, and the commander-in-chief of British forces in North America. Throughout, I have tried to present Bernard's correspondence as a dialogue. The volume of correspondence between Bernard and General Amherst, however, necessitated a further round of pruning; items that have not been transcribed, Amherst's out-letters in the main, are occasionally quoted in the source notes and endnotes. The transcripts published here deal mainly with government affairs, but passages wherein Bernard discusses family or personal affairs have not been excised for they are integral to the dialogue. Some previously published material, and maps and enclosures to which Bernard refers in his letters, are included in this and later volumes, but legislative proceedings, warrants, certificates, accounts, proclamations, and record book entries have been omitted. All transcripts have been allocated a number **in bold**. The source notes and endnotes contain cross-references to transcripts together with references to and occasional extracts from unpublished letters. There is also a back-of-book list to this volume of all extant outgoing and incoming correspondence pertinent to the first three years of his administration in Massachusetts (**Appendix 3**).

Francis Bernard was born in the parish of Brightwell, Berkshire, in June or July 1712, the only child of the rector, the Rev. Francis Bernard, and his much younger wife, Margery Winlowe of Lewknor, the daughter of an Oxfordshire squire. Francis's childhood was punctured by tragedy: his father died before he was three years old, and shortly thereafter his mother, Margery, married the incoming rector, the Rev. Anthony Alsop, a noted Latin scholar and Tory; tragically she succumbed to the smallpox just three years later. The trauma and the disruption young Francis indubitably endured were alleviated by Alsop's attentiveness and the ministrations of Francis's maternal aunt Sarah Terry and her husband, Moses, a lawyer, who raised him at their home in the ancient market town of Lincoln.

Bernard's prospects were not impressive, however. The Rev. Bernard possessed modest estates, which he had acquired upon marriage, that were already mortgaged by his wife Margery; all he could leave his son, Francis, was an annuity of £30, £50 on his sixteenth birthday, and the small rents of Margery's estates. Alsop did not add to his stepson's income, though he certainly fostered his education and entry both to Westminster School and Christ Church, Oxford.[10] Francis Bernard duly sought a profession, as did many other sons of impecunious clerics. Instead of entering the church, however, he studied law at the Middle Temple and was admitted to the bar in 1737. He came to embody the nascent professionalism and acquisitiveness of England's growing band of skilled lawyers. He obtained several middle-ranking offices in the Church of England and local government, where he exercised his talents as an accountant, a procurator, and a judge.[11] While Bernard fully embraced the patronage of the local Whig elites, on which his advancement rested, his economic dependency likely strengthened feelings of insecurity.

A propitious marriage, however, brought domestic contentment and stability, and in due course opportunities for advancement beyond local administration. In December 1741, Bernard married Amelia Offley, the daughter of Stephen Offley, the squire of Norton Hall near Sheffield and the high sheriff of Derbyshire. Francis's marriage to Amelia did not bring him any property,[12] but instead ten healthy children and valuable political connections to the Shute Barringtons through Stephen Offely's second wife, Ann Shute. As far as can be ascertained, Francis and Amelia had a

Francis Bernard, c.1741. This portrait was probably commissioned soon after his marriage to Amelia Offley. By permission of Robert Spencer Bernard. Photograph by Charles Crisp, A.B.I.P.P.

Amelia Bernard, c.1741. By permission of Robert Spencer Bernard. Photograph by Charles Crisp, A.B.I.P.P.

loving and close relationship. They were rarely apart for more than two weeks at a time during their thirty-seven years of marriage, and consequently there is no surviving correspondence between them.[13] Nor do the Bernard family papers and estate papers proffer much material of relevance to Bernard's personal life: Bernard is rarely mentioned by his children in the Spencer Bernard Papers (D/SB) at the Centre for Buckinghamshire Studies. The family home, Nether Winchendon House, Bucks., has several portraits of family members, some of which have been reproduced.[14]

By the mid-1750s—when Bernard was in his mid-forties with a large and growing family to support—his career aspirations were contingent upon the patronage of his wife's cousin William Wildman Barrington, the second viscount Barrington.[15] The *Barrington-Bernard Correspondence*[16] is a fount of information about family affairs and their patron-client relationship. Barrington provided Bernard with a conduit into the decision-making process in London, albeit one that the reality of British high politics determined would be opened and closed on a minister's whim. Through his connection with Prime Minister Thomas Pelham Holles, the duke of Newcastle, Barrington was able to obtain for Bernard the governorship of New Jersey. Bernard was appointed governor on 27 Jan. 1758, and he, his wife, and four of their children arrived at Perth Amboy in April.[17] For the most part, New Jersey was an enjoyable experience for the family, and Bernard's administration was generally successful in as much as it was characterized by an absence of bitter disputes between himself and the colonists or their assembly.[18] Bernard often mused that his prospects would be better in another colony, and news that he was to be offered Massachusetts after just eighteen months in post was a welcome surprise.

As Lord Barrington put it, the death of the governor of Jamaica occasioned a "general promotion" of the American governors (**No. 4**). Bernard was to replace his erstwhile Lincolnshire neighbor, Thomas Pownall, who was generally regarded as having had a very successful administration in the Bay colony.[19] On 27 Nov. 1759, the Privy Council approved the Board of Trade's draft commission for Bernard together with warrants requiring the king's signature for issuing a patent with the royal seal.[20] Two sets of instructions were normally issued to colonial governors: the first outlined his duties and responsibilities under the commission generally, while the other made detailed references to the trade laws. Bernard's instructions were considered by the Privy Council on 16 Jan.1760, and signed and dated on 18 Mar. (**Appendices 1** and **2**).[21]

As might be expected, Bernard and his family's readjustment to their new life figures prominently in his correspondence. Bernard regretted having to leave the tranquility and fine climate of Perth Amboy (**No. 5**), and supposed that one day he might retire there. After a first extremely cold winter in Boston, the Bernards enjoyed summers spent in the refurbished apartments at the newly-rebuilt Castle William out in the harbor, where the children had more freedom to roam, but where

Bernard had a "narrow escape" in some unspecified incident (**No. 89**). When the General Court granted Bernard Mount Desert Island (**No. 91**) off the coast of Maine, in February 1762, he saw it as an opportunity to develop an American estate and permanent residence. Even so, he was careful not to lose touch with influential old friends such as Thomas Pownall (**No. 67**), Bishop William Warburton (**No. 50**), and the lawyer Randle Wilbraham (**Nos. 30** and **106**), whose assistance he might require if and when he returned to England. Bernard freely discussed his aspirations in his letters to Barrington (**No. 9** etc), but also—surprisingly—in those to British acquaintances such as William Bollan (**No. 22**) and Richard Jackson (**Nos. 167, 206, 220,** and **228**). For sure, Barrington, Bollan, Jackson, and the Pownalls were, to varying degrees, potential champions of Bernard's interests, but the candor that typified his correspondence may have stemmed from anxiety: that the goodwill of others was dependent upon them receiving detailed and regular reports. In the fullness of time, however, Bollan and Thomas Pownall, with good reason, turned against Bernard, and John Pownall—perhaps his most loyal friend— lectured him on political realities; even Barrington's letters, dispatched from his fashionable home in Cavendish Square, London, often proved disappointing.

Frequently, Bernard's ruminations disclose a gloomy disposition, probably because Massachusetts was failing to yield what he had hoped. With an annual salary of £1,500, payable by provincial grant, and the governor's entitlement to a one-third share of prosecutions and fees, Bernard had supposed that he might be able to recoup some of the expenses he had incurred in acquiring his two commissions under George II. Unfortunately, the king's death on 25 Oct.1760 and the succession of George III entailed a further round of costs for a third commission that virtually wiped out his personal savings; a request for reimbursement was refused (**Nos. 22, 24,** and **34**). Sources of income other than his provincial salary were hard to come by. The pursuit of smugglers, some of whom were well-to-do merchants, exposed the governor to accusations of avarice, while his share of seizures was jeopardized by the commissions to apprehend smugglers given Royal Navy officers on vessels cruising American waters (**Nos. 255** and **257**).

While Bernard fretted over the family finances he also worried about the three children who had remained in England (albeit in the capable hands of the Terrys and his cousin Jane Beresford). Bernard's efforts to compensate for being an absent father were clumsy; attentive though he was to settling his sons' career paths, the boys probably thought their father's endeavors overbearing regardless how much they benefited. Bernard labored to reserve the Massachusetts Naval Office for his sons (**Nos. 32, 34, 65, 82,** and **166**) and insisted that they join him in Boston. John was placed with a Boston merchant, where he learned the inner workings of the counting house, before opening his own business in the town (**Nos. 34** and **89**). Bernard also thought that Francis Jr. (or Frank) should be "settled in business" after Oxford University, but the "interview" they had in Boston opened a rift between them: Frank ignored his father's pleas to settle on a profession and took off for Philadelphia, from whence he ventured to the back country of Pennsylvania and Virginia (see **Nos. 168, 246,** and **250**).

As royal governor, Bernard was both the province's chief executive and the king's representative, for which the extant documentation is extensive and comprehensive in its coverage. As chief executive, the governor was part of the General Court, along with the House of Representatives and the Council. He addressed in person and sent messages to the assembly of the House and Council during legislative sessions, and presided over the executive meetings of the Governor's Council; he approved legislation, issued warrants and certificates, received petitions, and generally functioned as the head of a limited executive.[22] Province secretary Andrew Oliver[23] routinely forwarded state papers, including accounts and legislative proceedings, to the secretary of the Board of Trade, John Pownall,[24] upon which Bernard commented in his own letters (**Nos. 98, 109, 114,** and **123**) and to which the Board responded (**Nos. 43** and **87**). The province secretary was also responsible for maintaining regular correspondence with the province agent, although Bernard frequently wrote to agents William Bollan[25] and Richard Jackson,[26] but rarely to Jasper Mauduit,[27] whom he regarded as a tool of his critics in the assembly (**Nos. 105** and **191**).

The Massachusetts royal governor was the king's captain general and vice admiral and exercised by proxy Crown prerogatives in imperial administration. He was accountable in the first instance to the Lords Commissioners for Trade and Plantations, known as the Board of Trade, from whom royal governors received an initial set of instructions supplemented by directives and occasional circulars from the secretary of state. The Board, established in 1696, had considerable influence on colonial policymaking, but never possessed full executive power and remained, strictly speaking, an advisory body to the secretary of state. It was the secretary of state for the Southern Department who was ultimately responsible for the execution of colonial policy, until the creation of the American Department in 1768.[28] Bernard was obliged to communicate regularly with the Board of Trade, reserving to the secretary of state only those matters requiring his "immediate direction" (**No. 214**n2).[29] (In 1766, however, in the wake of the Stamp Act crisis, the secretary of state assumed direct control of all channels of communication with the governors, who henceforth merely copied letters to the Board.[30]) In short, Bernard was expected to provide ministers and officials in London with regular and relevant reports on the state of the province and to ensure that all royal commissions were being obeyed.

There were three British administrations between 1759 and 1763: the Pitt-Newcastle ministry (29 Jun. 1757–26 May 1762),[31] which led Britain to victory over France in the Seven Years War, the short-lived Bute ministry (27 May 1762–9 Apr. 1763),[32] which negotiated the peace treaty; and the Grenville ministry (16 Apr. 1763–10 Jul. 1765),[33] which instituted the reforms that would spark opposition in the American colonies. Bernard's correspondence touches upon these and other major issues. His letters to secretaries of state William Pitt and the earl of Egremont,[34] though formal in style, were never formulaic, and written with considerable confidence. Bernard was not shy to ask favors of Pitt for his sons (**No. 66**). His early declamation that Massachusetts merchants were not trading with the enemy proved an embarrassing mistake, however (**No. 18**); a desire to make amends could account for the zeal with which in subsequent letters to Pitt (**No. 75**) and Egremont (**No. 240**) he promised to enforce the trade laws. Bernard's relationship with the earl of Halifax, one of the most influential British colonial policymakers,[35] is not in itself of singular significance in this volume, but it laid the foundations for the transmission in 1764 of controversial ideas on the reform of colonial government and imperial administration.

More important at this juncture was Bernard's correspondence with John Pownall, of which there are thirty-two letters in this volume. Bernard wrote candidly to a knowledgeable and respected friend, and trusted Pownall's judgment implicitly. Pownall referred Bernard's letters and enclosures to Board meetings, where occasionally the details were discussed, as when provincial legislation raised points of law requiring advice from Sir Matthew Lamb, K.C.[36] Legally contentious items or letters raising policy issues were decided by the Privy Council,[37] such as when Bernard requested confirmation of provincial land grants (**Nos. 177** and **248**, and below).

Bernard's sanguine expectations for his new posting in part derived from his determination to make a name for himself as a conciliating governor above partisan politics (**Nos. 118, 122,** and **123**). The roots of Bernard's nonpartisanship lie in English politics, where the Pitt-Newcastle ministry had embarked on a "broad bottom" and the young George III embraced "Britons" without the distinction of party labels. Inevitably, however, Bernard's emulatory agenda was compromised by the exigencies of wartime and the practicalities of provincial politics. While Bernard was often later criticized for lacking guile and acumen, he was no stranger to political management and intrigue.

In the coming years, Bernard benefited from the advice of Thomas Hutchinson, his long-serving deputy and eventual successor. Unfortunately, he never did explain why he promised Hutchinson the chief justice's office (**No. 19**), thereby alienating the Otis family, but the appointment indubitably ensured Hutchinson's loyalty. There is no surviving correspondence between Bernard and Hutchinson for the period covered by this volume, save one minor letter, but Bernard undoubtedly trusted Hutchinson's advice on politics, public finance, and a host of other matters. He evidently read a draft of the first volume of Hutchinson's *History of*

Thomas Hutchinson. Oil on canvas by Edward Truman, 1741.
Massachusetts Historical Society. Courtesy of the Massachusetts Historical Society.

Massachusetts, published in 1764 (see **Nos. 216** and **234**). The two men were probably wary of each other at first. They subsequently disagreed on many issues, not least of which were the reform of colonial government and the Anglicization of colonial law—both firmly advocated by Bernard. Understanding how their relationship developed is integral to understanding how their respective administrations fashioned responses to the imperial crisis.[38]

With Hutchinson behind him, Bernard thought his prospects for an "easy administration" augured well. It was not to be, of course. Bernard's *bête noire*, James Otis Jr., appears often in the governor's missives, in which he is portrayed as a resentful but highly effective and intelligent partisan dedicated to "the declared purpose of raising a flame in the government" (**No. 192**). (See also **Nos. 85, 186, 191,** and **220**.) By the spring of 1762, Bernard convinced himself that it was rare for the assembly to engage in "free deliberation uninfluenced by any motives but a sense of their duty to his Majesty" (**No. 102**). Thereafter, Bernard's letters are a vital source in following partisanship, for he began to enumerate internal divisions in both houses (**No. 191**), a practice he continued for the remainder of his administration.

When Bernard shed his naiveté he cast a perceptive eye on his surroundings. His observations on the differences in judicial procedure between the colonies and England are still informative (**No. 175**). One lengthy report for the Board of Trade, compiled after three years residence in Massachusetts, also contains valuable information on the law, meteorology, geography, and demography. Those sections wherein he mentions how few families there were left among the indigenous Abenaki tribes of the Penobscot region was as much a surprise to him as it is today enlightening of the destructive consequences of cultural encounters on the frontier (**No. 234**). The Abenakis' predicament stands in marked contrast to the Mashpees' successful struggle for autonomy and the remarkable exploits of Rueben Cognehew (**No. 45**). There are other nuggets too, such as the sympathy Bernard evinced for those lower-order Bostonians "least able to bear" the socio-economic consequences of the Great Fire of March 1760 (**No. 26**); another remark alludes to the rise in labor costs due to the labor shortage occasioned by the recruitment drive for the provincial and regular regiments (**No. 68**).

Bernard's early successes owed much to the fact that his arrival in the colony coincided with a favorable turning point in the French and Indian War of 1754-63. A royal governor's military responsibilities were restricted to the province in which he served, and in operational matters concerning the British Army he was subordinate to the commanders-in-chief of North American forces: Gen. Sir Jeffery Amherst, 1758-63, and Gen. Sir Thomas Gage, 1763-75. Bernard's early letters describe the successful British campaign of 1760 to take Montréal (**Nos. 10, 12-14**). Transcript **No. 20** is Pitt's notable circular to the colonial governors requesting further resources to finish the job. Bernard was already fully aware of how much the province had contributed in terms of manpower and financial resources, and he was soon obliged to engage in often protracted, discomfiting negotiations with the assembly over Crown requisitions (**Nos. 35, 36, 41, 103,** etc.). While Amherst, as any general might, fretted over getting the provincials ready for battle, Bernard dwelt on the practical and political difficulties he encountered in trying to persuade the province to raise recruits for the provincial and regular regiments. Bounty jumping seems to have been a particular problem after the province was obliged to raise bounties in order to attract volunteers (**Nos. 56** and **92**). Bernard provides details of the mechanics of mustering the regiments (**Nos. 42, 72,** etc.) and notable cases of unsuitable recruits (**Nos. 27** and **149**). There is mention, too, of desertion and mutiny among the provincials stationed at Halifax, Nova Scotia, despondent as they were by Amherst's decision to extend their service and alarmed by the prospect of being sent to the West Indies, where few would have expected to survive beyond the six-month "seasoning" (**Nos. 15, 217,** and **221**). Bernard was not unconcerned by his soldiers' welfare, as is indicated by his lack of enthusiasm for crushing the mutiny, his determination to prevent officers suttling to their own men at exorbitant prices (**Nos. 70** and **71**), and his enthusiasm for spruce beer as an alternative to contaminated water and strong rum (**No. 69**).

Bernard, however, was frustrated by Amherst's lack of understanding of colonial politics and economics. While both strove to root out abuses in the flag of truce trade with the French colonies (**Nos. 18, 47, 49, 112,** and **115**), the governor was irritated by the general's initial inflexibility in enforcing an embargo on coastal trade that was damaging to the colonial merchants (**Nos. 107, 110, 111, 113,** and **121**). Disagreements over seemingly peripheral matters—such as Amherst's reluctance to supply the province with certificates attesting to how many Massachusetts men served in the campaigns of 1758-60 (**No. 55**)—betray underlying concerns about the province's ability to service its war debts. While the American colonies had received parliamentary subsidies totaling £200,000 between 1758 and 1760, the subsidy for 1761 was reduced to £133,333. Eventually, Massachusetts was to incur the largest debt of all the colonies—nearly £500,000. The stabilization of the public finances probably would not have been achieved without the close cooperation of the assembly and the governor: both agreed on the necessity of sinking the debt by 1765, even though this required provincial taxes being raised to unprecedented levels and other special measures being adopted.[39]

As the war drew to a close, one worrisome episode was the French capture of St. John's, Newfoundland, in the summer of 1762, a diversionary action to British maneuvers in the West Indies. Leaving Brest on 8 May, a French expeditionary force comprising two ships of the line and two frigates, with over five hundred fusiliers on board, arrived at the Bay of Bulls on 23 Jun.; Fort William at St. John's was quickly captured, and on the 27th the French proceeded to burn British settlements and disable some 460 ships of the fishing fleet—inflicting damage purportedly worth £1 million. Bernard was able to alert Vice-Admiral Sir George Pocock (**No. 135**), in charge of the British campaign against Havana (which the British took on 13 Aug. after a two-month siege). He also provides a valuable glimpse of what ordinary British soldiers thought of the surrender of Fort William (**No. 151**). The capture of St. John's sparked a short-lived "alarm" in Massachusetts: there may not have been any prospect of a French invasion—Bernard did not call the militia to arms—but the disruption to shipping, on top of the recent embargo, was deeply troubling (**No. 153**). In the event, Col. William Amherst, the general's brother, landed his force at Torbay on 13 Sept.; he encountered fierce resistance from the French for several days, but after taking the high ground in the battle of Signal Hill and bombarding Fort William, the French capitulated on 18 Sept.[40]

Military issues aside, Bernard's correspondence provides much documentation on the displacement of Nova Scotia's French-speaking population. Perhaps as many as 13,000 Acadians, or French Neutrals as they were known by New Englanders, were forcibly evacuated from Nova Scotia from 1755 onwards, in which business the Massachusetts regiments were given a leading role. The majority of Acadian refugees were Catholics and were relocated to other British colonies in North America, but 1,105 were sent to Massachusetts. The General Court made substantial provision to alleviate the Acadians' distress (£9,563 by 1763), with variable success, and distributed them throughout the province. The New Englanders' initial hostility, which was fuelled by anti-Catholicism and suspicions as to the Acadians' "neutrality," was soon diluted by genuine compassion and daily contact. Bernard supposed they would integrate with little difficulty, largely because they proved, ironically, to embody the Protestant work ethic (**No. 227**). Even so, there was little enthusiasm to establish a permanent settlement for the refugees or extend a welcome to the six hundred deported from Nova Scotia by Lt. Gov. Jonathan Belcher in August 1762 (see **Nos. 152, 155, 159, 160, 231, 233, and 235**). Eventually, the Acadians set out for France, as Bernard mentions, as well as England and Louisiana, while others managed to return to Nova Scotia; the destitution of the remaining Acadians led the Board of Trade to relocate them to Quebec in 1766 at the invitation of Gov. James Murray.

Another material consequence of the warfare and imperial diplomacy that ordained the Acadians' displacement was that Massachusetts and Nova Scotia were left to squabble over their boundary line, and the territory in between known as Sagadahoc. Massachusetts claimed the St. Croix River as the boundary whereas Nova Scotia set the boundary further west at the Penobscot River (**No. 154**). Bernard was an effective advocate of the province's claim, largely because of rather than in spite of his own interests in the matter (**Nos. 178, 201, and 216**). A royal instruction to the Nova Scotia governor Montague Wilmot in October 1763 established the St. Croix rather than the Penobscot River as the western boundary of Nova Scotia, thus effectively quashing that province's claims to Sagadahoc. However, the confusion surrounding the identification of the St. Croix was not resolved, and the Crown delayed confirming any provincial grant in Sagadahoc.[41]

Bernard's lucid contribution to the boundary dispute was undoubtedly self-interested. The carrot dangled by the province was Mount Desert Island, for which Bernard was obliged to seek confirmation by the Crown. Bernard's initial optimism that confirmation would be straightforward bordered on arrogance, and the realization that his enjoyment of the island depended on Britain's recognition of Massachusetts's title to Sagadahoc was probably more painful than he admits. Moreover, Bernard was also obliged to assist the province to obtain Crown approval for twelve townships to be established on the Penobscot River (**Nos. 90, 172, 180,** and **212**). By way of encouragement, on 12 Jun. 1762 the General Court commended Gov. Bernard for his attentiveness but also resolved to establish a joint boundary commission with Nova Scotia.[42] The township grants alarmed Lt. Gov. Belcher, who alerted the Board of Trade to the proposed commission, and in due course Bernard was censured for having consented to the grants and thereby inadvertently traducing Crown prerogatives to settle boundaries (**No. 181**). When the joint commission failed to meet, the General Court published in February 1763 the committee report setting forth Massachusetts's claims.[43]

Bernard was not blinded by his disappointment, and he also began thinking of ways and means to develop Mount Desert Island. He made three voyages to Mount Desert and the Penobscot coast: the journal of the first voyage 28 Sept.-15 Oct. 1762 is printed in full (**No. 161**); his second visit took place between c.15 Sept. and c.7 Oct. 1763; and the third between 27 Aug. and c.28 Sept. 1764. After surveying the land, Bernard was confident that in time he could establish a viable community of settlers from New England and Europe; they could make their living from lumber, fishing, and the production of hemp and potash, in which matters he sought expert assistance (**Nos. 176, 178, 179,** and **232**). However, Bernard was unable to persuade the British to break the linkage between the provincial boundary disputes and any of the contested provincial land grants, including his own. As the British procrastinated over the Nova Scotia and Quebec boundary lines, the grants were referred back and forth between the Board of Trade and the Privy Council, until 1771, when they were finally confirmed.[44]

As a chief executive, Bernard did not fare at all badly in defending the province's interests, but his correspondence is also notable for what it reveals about growing opposition. Critics of the governor seemed to emerge from all quarters, even Harvard College, when Bernard toyed with the idea of chartering a new college in the west of the province. Bernard promptly withdrew his support for the scheme after protests by the Board of Overseers, though this likely cost him the goodwill and loyalty of its most powerful champion, Col. Israel Williams (**Nos. 95, 97,** and **98**). Bernard himself championed the "little Seminary" at Cambridge in a condescending fashion (**Nos. 130** and **133**), but his inattentiveness to the interests of the province's Congregationalists—as well as his sense of cultural superiority—did not augur well. New Englanders, troubled by talk of the establishment of an American episcopate, thought that the governor's staunch Anglicanism belied his claims to be above sectarianism; early in 1762 they set about engineering the replacement of the province agent William Bollan, an Anglican, with Jasper Mauduit, a Dissenter. Bernard could ill afford to remain aloof from the contest and duly strove to obtain the appointment of Richard Jackson, an Anglican, as Mauduit's solicitor, even though it meant alienating Bollan (**Nos. 105, 106, 185,** and **186**). Equally troublesome was the dispute between the Customhouse and an unmanageable officer, Benjamin Barons, on which Bernard commented upon at length. The suits brought against customs officers by Barons, the merchant John Erving, and the province treasurer, if successful, would have undermined the Customhouse's ability to enforce the trade laws. On these and other issues, Bernard called upon the Crown to exert itself far more in defense of its imperial servants (see **Nos. 60, 62, 64, 67, 85,** and **88**). It was advice that mostly fell on deaf ears, even when ministers began to consider how to increase colonial revenues—whether by raising duties or improving their collection, or by a combination of the two methods.

Hitherto, Bernard had been loath to criticize British colonial policy (**No. 75**). After the Barons affair, he seemed less reticent, perhaps because he was more attuned to the grumblings of the merchants. Bernard was obliged to supply Britain with key information about imports and exports of molasses (**No. 203**) prior to the renewal of the 1733 Molasses Act. The prospect of a hefty tax was "Very alarming" (**No. 229**), and would do nothing to discourage smuggling, he warned: like the Boston merchants, Bernard argued for a duty of between 1d and 1 ½ d per gallon in any prospective revenue act. He pressed the merchants' case upon Jackson (**Nos. 229** and **245**) and also raised it directly with the Board of Trade (**No. 256**). His louche observation that customs officers normally turned a blind eye to contraband lemons, oil, and Madeira wine (**Nos. 240** and **241**) probably did not go down too well with officials in London—and certainly not with Surveyor General John Temple, who in 1764 pursued Bernard for corruption.

By the end of the period covered by this volume, Gov. Francis Bernard had adjusted to the vicissitudes of governing a fractious province like Massachusetts. Many of the disputes briefly discussed here have been examined by historians trying to figure out why it was that Massachusetts's politics experienced upheaval in the decade that followed the peace of 1763.[45] Some answers may be found in Bernard's correspondence. At the beginning of his administration, Bernard was able to embrace the ideal of rising above partisanship, only to find out that the governance of empire was rather more difficult than he expected. When key groups, such as the merchants and the House of Representatives, started criticising British colonial policies, Bernard's abiding refrain was for them to be patient and wait for the peace. As he confided to Barrington, "the merchants here want redress in regard to several of the Laws of trade: but they don't use proper means nor take the proper time. I tell 'em again & again that they must wait for the conclusion of peace before they can ask the Ministry to set about civil regulations: and Assure them that at such time I will Assist them to the Utmost of my power" (**No. 89**). The colonists' response was no better than lukewarm, and might have been rather more hostile had they known that Bernard hoped to be involved in a British-led "general disquisition of the constitutions of the several Governments" (**No. 74**). Bernard himself began working on plans to reform colonial government, but reform of that nature was never attempted by subsequent British administrations; instead, ministers continued with their revenue-raising measures without ever properly addressing the colonists' grievances with the trade laws. A modernizing, centralist agenda and unfulfilled expectations on a grand scale are the fuel of colonial rebellions, and evidence for these abounds in Bernard's papers. In time, Bernard would lament a missed opportunity to avert a crisis in imperial relations, though whether such an opportunity ever really existed is quite another matter. Subsequent volumes will reveal much more about how Bernard's administration in Massachusetts struggled to cope with the emergence of colonial radicalism and the upsurge in popular protests.

EDITORIAL APPARATUS

✸✸✸ ✦✦✦

Editorial policy has aimed to preserve the integrity of manuscripts, printing them in full (except where noted) and depicting their content as accurately as possible with limited editorial intervention. To these ends, it is important to distinguish four processes in Bernard's epistolary record that have influenced editorial method.

The first is the mode of composition. His "way of doing the public business," Bernard noted, was "wholly by my own hands using my Secretaries in nothing but Copying" (**No. 167**). Bernard generally wrote his own out-letters, official as well as personal, in a clear and distinctive hand, making corrections to them before they were sealed and posted. He did not routinely work from loose-file drafts. When he did do so, for example in preparing a riposte to a censure by the Board of Trade (**Nos. 200** and **201**), he filed the annotated drafts (in BP, 10) and had his clerks enter fair versions in a letterbook (BP, 3); then, as he said in **No. 214**, he "authenticated" the out-going receiver's copy (**RC**) by comparing it with the letterbook entry (**LbC**). Bernard was a diligent rather than a prolific correspondent: there are 114 extant autograph out-letters for his first three and one half years in office, an average of one letter every eleven days.

The second process is the preservation of letterbook copies of out-letters. As Bernard mentions, he delegated this task to his secretaries, and in later years he engaged his son Thomas as an amanuensis and probably other family members too. Chirographical analysis of Bernard's letterbooks revealed that the 329 entries for the period 1 Aug. 1760 to 31 Dec. 1763 were produced by seven different hands. Bernard himself was responsible for around 14 percent of entries. One scribe, who copied only two letters before 1763, may have been Amelia Bernard, but the examination of the samples proved inconclusive. Two other scribal hands produced one letter each (clerks nos. 5 and 6). Unfortunately, the identities of the most important scribes—the secretaries whom Bernard employed—are not known. "Clerk no. 1," who copied 53 percent of entries, worked for Bernard in New Jersey and came with him to Boston. "Clerk no. 2" (16 percent) made frequent copies from May 1762 onwards and continued working until 1768. "Clerk no. 3" (9 percent), who

*Bernard holograph, 1741. The earliest known Bernard holograph, in MON 25/2/97.
By permission of Lincolnshire Archives.*

favour me with, to his Friends, that You'll think me a Person not entirely unworthy of being recommended to Your Brother My Lord.

As M[r] Gylby's Death will occasion a Vacancy in the City, I should be very proud of My Lords Orders in what Manner He would have me apply. If His Lordship shall think me a proper Person for the Recordership, I shall be very thankful for It, e very punctual in the Duties thereof. But If M[r] Reynolds shall be approved of for that office, I shall be very much obliged for the favour of being recommended to the Stewardy. I don't propose taking any publick Steps herein, till I am favour'd by a Line of what will be most agreable to his Lordship: By whose favour e also yours I am desirous of Succeeding.

I beg your Indulgence in this e that I may assure you that I am S[r] Y[r] most faithful
e most Obedt Servt

Fra: Bernard

If You favour me with an Answer please to direct to me at Joseph Offley Esq's at Norton near Sheffield Yorkshire, whom I am going for part of the Holydays

Lincoln Dec. 19 1741

Bernard holograph, 1763. Bernard writes to the Royal Society of Arts to promote Levi Willard's method of manufacturing potash. RSA, London. PR.GE/110/14/114.

He is very communicative &
willing to assist any one who will
undertake the same business. As I
have intended to set up potash works
upon an Island (which has been gran-
-ted to me by the General Court of this
Province & is now submitted to the King
for his confirmation) this Gentleman
has engaged to give me full instruc-
-tions to provide Utensils & lend me
one of his best hands. I have the
greatest hopes that this business
will be well understood in this Country:
and it is to encourage & propagate
it only that I propose to engage
in it. I shall write to you soon
again on the same subject & am
        Sr Your most faithful &
    obedient Servant Fra Bernard

had the neatest handwriting, produced only two entries before November 1762, after which he or she was particularly busy over a two-month period when Bernard was preparing documentation in support of his claim to Mount Desert Island (see illustrations on pp. 23-25).[46] The three principal clerks copied all manner of private and official correspondence and were not allocated specific areas; nor did Bernard reserve for himself the job of copying up correspondence with any particular person. These clerks continued to work for Bernard; others were also employed, and their role will be discussed in subsequent volumes.[47]

The clerks generally made letterbook copies from Bernard's autograph out-letters before they were dispatched. Systematic comparison of letterbook copies with autographs revealed little variation in content and insignificant accidental differences and grammatical inconsistencies. The clerks also made fair copies of autograph drafts when required (as with **No. 75**). Bernard occasionally made emendations to the letterbooks, of which **No. 256** is an example, but usually left the clerks to correct errors themselves—no doubt confident that they would do so satisfactorily. For example, a misreading of Admiral Sir George Pocock's surname, rather than a garbled dictation, probably accounts for the scribal emendations in **No. 137**, represented thus, "Admiral ~~Pocke~~ ^Pococke^." Patterns of emendation are highly ambiguous sources of evidence, and the possibility that Bernard dictated to his clerks and then prepared his autographs from the letterbook entry should not be wholly disregarded (especially in those cases where letterbook copies with idiosyncratic spelling cannot be compared with originals). By and large, however, the letterbooks comprise copies of complete originals minus the closure.

The third process—the storage of in-letters—might be thought unworthy of further comment, but there are some significant gaps in the record of incoming correspondence. At the Houghton Library, volumes 9-12 of the Bernard Papers constitute as near a complete record of Bernard's official correspondence as can be expected, but the receivers' copies of letters from the province agents are missing (nor can they be found in the Massachusetts Archives). What Bernard did with these letters is a mystery. It would be helpful to know in particular what William Bollan thought of Bernard in the wake of his dismissal from the agency, given that Bollan was later instrumental in destroying Bernard's reputation,[48] or how Richard Jackson regarded Bernard's transparently self-vaunting promotion of the Mount Desert grant (**No. 131**) and his specious characterization of the Mauduit brothers, Jackson's rivals for the agency (**No. 186**). No doubt Jackson pondered whether the brouhaha over his (unsalaried) appointment as solicitor to the agent was worth the trouble (**No. 226**), though in 1765 he was elected province agent.

The last process concerns the carriage of Bernard's mail. Bernard routinely dispatched official letters by the regular transatlantic mail packet operating once a month between New York and Falmouth, England, and by the war-time packet

Bernard's Letterbooks. A scribal entry by clerk no. 1: BP, 1: 272. By permission of the Houghton Library, Harvard University.

Bernard's Letterbooks. A scribal entry by clerk no. 2: BP, 3: 76. By permission of the Houghton Library, Harvard University.

255

interested. And yet if they had one Agent, it should be previously settled what part he should act in Cases of dispute between them. To answer this in your own Case, it is certain that you cannot be desired by this Province to relinquish the defence of the right of Connecticut to the Townships which you have already undertaken: on the contrary other hand Connecticut could not take exception if this Province should expect, as the Superior, to have your assistance in such other Matters of controversy as shall hereafter arise: especially as it is not easy to foresee that any such will arise. What you say in Your Letter of the dispute concerning the Townships seems to amount to this: but I should be glad to be allowed to make such a Stipulation in positive terms if it should be expedient.

Febry 1.

Since I wrote the foregoing, Mr Mauduits friend Mr Otis (a Gentleman of great Warmth of Temper & much indiscretion) has workt himself into such a passion by his disappointment, that none but the most violent measures are pursued by him & his friends. On Saturday last (on the Mornings of which, as on Monday Evenings, the House is always very thin) there being but 45 in the House, he intro: duced a Letter in the Name of the House to Mr Mauduit, apologising for their not having complied with his request, & assigning for reason their not

Bernard's Letterbooks. The main text of letter is in the hand of clerk no. 3, while the postscript dated 1 Feb. 1763 is in that of clerk no. 2. Bernard criticizes James Otis Jr. for his "warmth of Temper." BP, 2: 255. By permission of the Houghton Library, Harvard University.

between Boston and Bristol. Duplicates and (sometimes triplicates) were dispatched to the same destinations in separate vessels, usually merchant-men sailing out of Boston or Portsmouth, N.H. Urgent letters went direct from Boston by the first available merchant ship sailing for England. Delays were inevitable, however, and transatlantic mail could take anything between six weeks and three months to reach the addressee. Getting mail to and from New York by land or sea could also be troublesome: the twice-weekly courier service by the post road did not always deliver as promised, as Bernard notes in the postscript to **No. 186**, and delays to the coastal vessels sailing out of Boston were commonplace, judging by the preponderance of postscripts to the letters printed in this volume. Two express riders were employed at the province's expense to carry letters intended for the New York packet-boat (**No. 21**) and to facilitate communications between Bernard and Gen. Amherst at New York: Jonathan Lowder and David Wyer. Wyer, as Bernard told Deputy Postmaster-General Benjamin Franklin, was "quite a Master of the road" (**No. 250**), yet still it took five days to travel from Boston to New York (**Nos. 158 and 159**). (Bernard evidently thought highly of Wyer, having two years previously appointed him a suttler to the provincial regiments at Halifax.)

Confidentiality was another problem. During the Barons affair, when Bernard was accused of deriding the Boston merchants as smugglers in his letters to London, he became anxious that his correspondence was being tampered with. At the time, he wrote that his concerns "accordingly prescribe to me a reserve, particularly in regard to the politicks of this place" (**No. 57**). Secret or private letters were kept back for a "safe conveyance," usually a trusted merchant-mariner or Royal Navy captain (**No. 29**). Long before some of his letters were sensationally published in Boston, Bernard fretted that his enemies were somehow privy to his correspondence, but there is no clear evidence that he mistrusted his clerks.

The processes described above have influenced the selection of documents for publication. Whenever possible, autograph out-letters and in-letters have been used as authoritative texts—the actual manuscripts upon which the transcripts are based. When the receiver's copy (**RC**) or its duplicate were not extant, contemporary copies were substituted from the preserved record in the receiver's or author's letterbook (**RLbC** and **LbC**), and are accompanied with editorial commentaries clarifying scribal involvement. In the absence of a letterbook, the transcript was based on a copy of an original made by a third party; printed versions were used in the last resort—contemporary imprints before modern imprints and transcriptions. The authoritative texts have been systematically collated with extant variants. Generally, textual comparison did not reveal substantive differences in content between the author's drafts (**ADft**) and letterbook copies (**LbC**), (**Nos. 75, 200 and 201**), or between these types and the **RC** (**Nos. 176** and **177**). In the cases just mentioned, the corrections made to the draft were incorporated in the fair

LbCs and **RCs**. Major differences in content are discussed in the footnotes and source notes.

Transcripts are presented in chronological order, according to the first given date. Non-epistolary enclosures follow the covering letter, while letters that were themselves enclosures have been placed in sequence by date. With letters bearing the same date, out-letters take precedence over in-letters (unless the out-letter is a reply to the in-letter); thereafter, out-letters are sorted by the likely order of composition (for which Bernard's letterbooks provide a rough guide); date of receipt has been used to sort in-letters; the remainder have been sorted alphabetically by correspondent. For example, the in-letters **No. 1** and **No. 2** were enclosed in **No. 3** but precede that letter in the order of presentation: **No. 1** was composed one day before the other two, while **No. 2** would have had to have been written before **No. 3** in order for the author to take receipt of the original and prepare a copy for transmission.

Editorial practice is to show the whole text plus any substantive emendations made by the author—the person(s) on whose authority a document was prepared or under whose signature it was sent—and by any clerk who drafted or copied the document. (Non-contemporaneous annotations on manuscripts have been excluded.) Obvious slips of the pen have been ignored; minor emendations are not shown, such as corrections of oversights and grammatical errors. Generally, original emendations, including scribal corrections, are reconstituted when this might help to illuminate authorial intention or when the additions suggest ambiguity or invite alternative interpretations: the representations follow the editorial apparatus set out in Table 1. For example, irrespective of the fact that emendations to **No. 186** are in a clerk's hand (and there is no way of knowing if Bernard dictated the revision) they are nevertheless suggestive of the governor's growing antipathy toward James Otis Jr. Otis is described as "A Gentleman of ~~much~~ ^great^ warmth of Temper & much indiscretion." Conversely, it has been necessary to present Bernard's first set of general instructions from 1760 as a clear text transcript, since the only extant source is a draft of that date containing annotations and emendations added in 1771 (**Appendix 1**).

Grammar and spelling were transcribed with limited modernization. Orthographical idiosyncrasies have been retained, save for the kind of transparent mistakes mentioned above. Abbreviations, contractions, and terminal punctuation follow the manuscript, as does capitalization, when the writer's intention can be determined, and the underlining of dates. Emphasis is rendered in italics. Superscripts have been preserved but with all accompanying punctuation lowered to the line. Accidentally conjoined words have been separated. Eighteenth-century spelling, such as "highth" for "height," is readily understood; however, instances confusing to the reader are clarified by an interpolation or an appended note. Original forms have been reproduced, such as the ampersand (&) and the thorn ("y" for "th"), but not the long "s." Confusing punctuation in numbers has been silently corrected, with period separators being replaced by commas (thus "20.000" becomes "20,000"). Where symbols are used in the original to indicate pounds sterling, they are lowered to the line, and silently corrected to "£. s. d." Clarification on currency and monetary values is provided in endnotes.

The layout of the transcripts has preserved some common features of manuscripts and standardized others. The location and punctuation of salutations and datelines have been preserved, but placed in one line; the addressee's name is at the end of the closure (where it usually is) and above the postscript regardless of its location in the manuscript. Original lineation has not been retained but paragraphing sequencing has. Epigraphs and postscripts have been formatted. Closures have been centered, except those running-on from the last paragraph of a letter. Tabulated information is presented in a form as close to the original as possible. Quotation marks placed at the beginning of every line of quoted material have been silently relocated to the beginning and end; block quotations have been indented. Flourishes have been omitted, as have brackets in dockets and closures. All transcripts have been given a caption; original titles have been transcribed and placed with the main body of text except entrybook titles, which are given in the source note.

The source note at the end of each transcript provides information about the provenance and location of the authoritative text. Table 2 is a list of descriptive acronyms used to indicate the typology of authoritative texts. The acronyms representing manuscript collections and archives are explained in the List of Abbreviations, above. (Pagination, folio, and volume descriptors have not been provided for any citations, unless required by the citation style recommended by the repository.) Where possible, the source note provides some clarification as to the processes of composition and preservation, noting among other things differences in handwriting styles, the extent of authorial emendation, and the location of variant texts. Endorsements added by the recipient confirming receipt and dockets added by the sender have been transcribed in accordance with editorial method. (When FB marked a letter with "r" he meant "received" and with "a" "answered".) Extant enclosures are briefly described, and should be assumed to be manuscript copies (usually third-party copies) unless otherwise indicated. Relevant historical and administrative information is provided at the end of the source note. Guidance is given as to where to find any replies and rejoinders. Numbered endnotes to source notes follow in sequence those for the transcript.

Endnotes aim to clarify obscurities in the transcript and direct the reader to additional material. Cross-references to transcripts published in this volume are indicated by bold numerals, thus, **No. 3**. Citations of manuscripts not printed here establish the location of the authoritative version, although in many cases there is only one extant manuscript: thus Jeffery Amherst to FB, New York, 16 Nov.1761,

WO 34/27, p. 233. (The typology can be checked in the back-of-book list). "Not found" is used to signal the absence of a manuscript. Biographical information is given at the first mention of a person in the correspondence; rare sources are cited but standard reference works are not.[49] Francis Bernard is referred to throughout as "FB." Provincial legislation and acts of the English, Scottish, and British parliaments are cited according to regnal year, with dates where appropriate, and with modernized titles; the index provides both the dates and a short-title.

Throughout the project I have tried to record information and transcribe manuscripts as accurately as possible. It is inevitable that there will errors in this volume. I am grateful to all those who have helped me to correct them, and I take full responsibility for those that remain.

TABLE 1
EDITORIAL SYMBOLS

The following symbols have been used to represent emendation:

Additions (insertions, interlineations, and substitutions) are marked with carets "^"at the intended location. When it is necessary to distinguish different hands or differentiate between insertions and substitutions the following will be used: ↑roman↓.

Bold type or heavily-inked letters are set in **bold**.

Canceled text is shown in ~~strikethrough font~~.

Confusing passages are described "thus in manuscript" in an endnote.

Conjectured readings for illegible material that can be inferred from the source text are in [roman text within square brackets]; there is a question mark before the closing bracket if there is considerable doubt as to the accuracy of the reading, [roman?].

Editorial interpolations have been italicized and placed in square brackets, [*editor's comment*].

Ellipses signify material that is either illegible or missing. The number of suspension points corresponds to the number of missing letters or numbers, e.g. [. . .] for three letters missing. Missing words are rendered thus, [_ _ _].

Emphasis is conveyed by *italics* and double underlining by SMALL CAPITALS.

Lacunae are represented by [*blank*].

Passages marked for deletion are indicated by <angled brackets>.

Underlining in authorial tables, numbers, dates, and punctuation has been retained.

TABLE 2
SOURCE TEXT TYPOLOGY

❯❯❯ ❰❰❰

The first set of acronyms in table 2 describes the nature of the authoritative text on which the transcript is based. The second set categorizes documents by their administrative history and preservation.

ADft   Author's Draft Manuscript.

AL   Autograph Letter (text in the hand of the author, but unsigned).

ALS   Autograph Letter Signed (text and signature in the hand of the author).

AMs   Autograph Manuscript (text in the hand of the author but unsigned).

AMsS   Autograph Manuscript Signed (text and signature in the hand of author).

Dft   Draft.

dup/trip duplicate/triplicate.

extract   An extract of a source text.

L   Letter (text not in the hand of the author and unsigned).

LS   Letter Signed (text not in the hand of the author but signed by the author).

Ms   Manuscript.

MsS   Manuscript Signed.

noted   A documentary record of the existence of a nonextant source text.

Prt   Contemporary Printed version of manuscript.

AC   Author's Copy (loose file or bound copies usually found in a personal collection).

Copy   Third Party Copy.

LbC   Author's Letterbook or Entry-Book

PC   Published Copy.

RbC   Recordbook Copy.

RC   Receiver's Copy.

RLbC   Receiver's Letterbook Copy.

ENDNOTES

❧❧❧ ❧❧❧

1. The Colonial Society of Massachusetts is also publishing the *Select Correspondence* of FB's deputy and successor Thomas Hutchinson, edited by John Tyler.

2. See Colin Nicolson, *The 'Infamas Govener': Francis Bernard and the Origins of the American Revolution* (Boston, 2001).

3. [Francis Bernard], *Select Letters on the Trade and Government of America; and the Principles of Law and Polity, Applied to the American Colonies Written by Governor Bernard in the Years 1763, 4, 5, 6, 7, and 8* (London, 1774); John Almon, *A Collection of Interesting, Authentic Papers, Relative to the Dispute Between Great Britain and America; Shewing the Causes and Progress of That Misunderstanding, From 1764 to 1775* (London, 1777).

4. Edward Channing and Archibald Cary Coolidge, eds., *The Barrington-Bernard Correspondence and Illustrative Matter, 1760-1770, Harvard Historical Studies Series*, vol. 17 (Cambridge, Mass., 1912). Extracts of FB's correspondence can be found in rare family histories: Sir Thomas Bernard, *Life of Sir Francis Bernard* (London, 1790); Mrs. Sophie Elizabeth Napier Higgins, *The Bernards of Abington and Nether Winchendon: A Family History,* 4 vols. (London, 1903-04).

5. Prof. Jared Sparks donated the Bernard Papers to Harvard in the mid-nineteenth century. Nicolson, *The 'Infamas Govener'*, 7. A useful guide is Justin Winsor, *Catalogue of the Bound Historical Manuscripts Collected by Jared Sparks and Now Deposited in the Library of Harvard University* (Cambridge, Mass., 1871), 4-6. The entire Sparks Collection can be searched using Harvard University Library, Oasis: Online archival Search Information System (http://oasis.harvard.edu:10080/oasis/deliver/deepLink?_collection=oasis&uniqueId=hou01999).

6. K. G. Davies, ed., *Documents of the American Revolution, 1770-1783,* 21 vols. (Shannon, 1972-81).

7. There are copies of ten of FB's out-letters in Letters, 1756-74, Mass. Archives, vol. 56. There are over 180 in-letters in volumes 4, 5, 6, 22, 25-27, 33, and 46. Warrants and certificates bearing FB's signature, and depositions and petitions received by him are scattered throughout the collection.

8. Thomas Hutchinson Letterbooks, Mass. Archs., vols. 25-27. See also Malcolm Freiberg, ed., Transcripts of the Letterbooks of Massachusetts Governor Thomas Hutchinson, vols. 25-27 (Originals in the Massachusetts Archives Collection) MHS.

9. These include Transcripts of Official Correspondence of the colonial governors with the Board of Trade about the Stamp Act crisis, 1764-1766, Stowe Ms, 264-265, British Library. In the papers of Charles Watson-Wentworth, the marquis of Rockingham and prime minister (1765-66), are early notifications of the Stamp Act Riots in Boston of Aug. 1765: Letters to the Marquis of Rockingham, Fitzwilliam (Wentworth Woodhouse) Muniments, Sheffield Archives. Charles Townshend, a president of the Board of Trade, maintained a file of FB's letters, mainly extracts, relating to items placed before Parliament during debates on the Stamp Act in Jan. 1766: Charles Townshend Papers, Buccleuch Muniments, RH4/98, Dalkeith House, microfilm by Microform; Charles Townshend Papers, RH4/99, the William L. Clements Library. Charles Jenkinson, a lord commissioner of Customs, and later first earl of Liverpool, kept copies of correspondence relating to the Liberty Riot in Boston of Jun. 1768: Official American Papers, Liverpool Papers, British Library Manuscript Collection, Add 38340. William Legge, the second earl of Dartmouth, received several autograph manuscripts on the reform of the Massachusetts Council, in American Papers, Dartmouth Papers, D(W)1778, Staffordshire Record Office.

10. Probate of the will of the Rev. Francis Bernard, 8 May 1716, PROB 11/552, ff 18-20; Probate of the will of the Rev. Anthony Alsop, 22 Feb. 1720, PROB 11/615, f 92.

11. Nicolson, *The 'Infamas Govener'*, 24-42. Lincolnshire Archives holds twenty-eight documents that illuminate FB's career in Lincoln between 1738, when he obtained his first local office, and 1758, when he left for America. Most of the manuscripts concern the official business of the Dean and Chapter

of Lincoln and the Diocese of Lincoln. As a church lawyer, FB prosecuted cases (CC85/313734) and kept visitation books (L.C./XX/C) and day-books (Cj/40), while as a deputy registrar he maintained accounts and ledgers (R/Ac). There are no extant records for the period in which FB was commissioner of bails for the Midlands Assizes, nor any concerning his activities in private practice save acting as an agent and accountant for proprietors of the Lincoln Assembly Rooms, 1745-52 (2 Anc 10/6). FB's correspondence with Charles Monson (1741-42), the Whig MP for Lincoln (1734-54) and recorder of Lincoln, are the earliest surviving personal letters (Mon 25/2/97-99), and reveal FB's unsuccessful attempts to become Monson's deputy. Modern transcripts mention FB's duties as recorder of Boston, Lincs., Betty Coy, et al., *Transcription of the Minutes of the Corporation of Boston* (Boston, Lincs., 1993). Other items include a subscription list, signed by FB, to raise a Loyalist regiment during the Jacobite rebellion of 1745-46 (Mon 7/10/17-18).

12. The Derbyshire estates of Joseph Offley (1702-51), Amelia Bernard's half-brother, comprised the family home of Norton Hall and properties in the parishes of Bamford, Coal Aston, and Dronfield and Greenhill (plus land in other counties). The bulk of the property was held in trust for Joseph's son Edmund who, on reaching his majority in 1754, alienated much of the estate to an Edinburgh clergyman and died shortly thereafter. Amelia and FB assisted in the legal recovery of the estates for Joseph's daughters Urith (1736-81) and Hannah. Probates of the wills of Joseph Offley and Edmund Offley, 9 Dec. 1754, PROB 11/812: 262-65; Napier Higgins, *The Bernards,* 1: 210-212.

13. Their longest separation was for eighteen months after FB returned to England in Aug. 1769. Any correspondence that was maintained during their separation may have been left behind when Amelia finally left Boston on 25 Dec. 1770, or, more likely, was lost at sea when the family's luggage was swept overboard during a storm.

14. In Nicolson, *The 'Infamas Govener'.*

15. William Wildman Barrington (1717-93) was the scion of an English Presbyterian family of the Irish peerage. He was the eldest of the five sons of John Shute Barrington (1678-1734), the first viscount Barrington, whose sister, Ann Shute, was Amelia Offley's mother. Barrington was Amelia Offley's cousin and godfather to her eldest son. He succeeded his father to the peerage and entered the Irish House of Lords in 1745. In the British parliament, he was an MP for Berwick-upon-Tweed from 1740 to Mar. 1754, and thereafter for Plymouth until 1778. He served as secretary at war from 1755 to Mar. 1761 (and again from 19 Jul. 1765 to 1778); as chancellor of the Exchequer in Mar. 1761; and treasurer of the Navy from May 1762 to 1765. Sir Lewis Namier and John Brooke, *The House of Commons, 1754-1790,* 3 vols. (London, 1964), 1: 55; Dylan E. Jones, "Barrington, William Wildman, second Viscount Barrington (1717-1793)," in *ODNB-e* (http://www.oxforddnb.com/view/article/1535, accessed 12 Nov., 2004); Nicolson, *The 'Infamas Govener',* 33-34, 41.

16. The letters have been re-transcribed from BP, vols. 1-12 for inclusion in *The Bernard Papers.* This is not on account of any major deficiencies in the 1912 edition, but because their correspondence, private though it was, was also an important facet of FB's communications with the British government. (Colonial governors were not obliged to write the secretary at war in an official capacity.) FB's original letters to Lord Barrington have not been found among Barrington's papers in Additional MSS, British Library, or in the secretary of war's papers (WO 1 and WO 4) at the PRO.

17. The baby William, the infants Amelia and Shute, and seven-year-old Thomas traveled with their parents; eleven-year old Jane and thirteen-month old Frances Elizabeth (Fanny) remained in England with the Terrys or Jane Beresford; Francis Jr. and John were still at school in England. Scrope (b.Oct 1758) and Julia were (b.19 Nov. 1759) were born in Perth Amboy. The Bernards first-born son, Joseph, was a baby when he died in the late 1740s. I am grateful to Jonathan Fowler for correcting a previous error regarding Thomas Bernard's arrival in America. Biographies of all the Bernard children can be found in Higgins, *The Bernards,* 4 vols., *passim.*

18. Jordan D. Fiore, "Francis Bernard, Colonial Governor," Unpublished Ph.D Diss., Boston Univ. (1950), 27-63, 454-458; Donald L. Kemmerer, *Path to Freedom: The Struggle for Self-Government in Colonial New Jersey, 1703-1776* (Cos Cob, Conn., 1968), 256-266; Nicolson, *The 'Infamas Govener',* 43-44. The project does not intend to issue FB's New Jersey papers. His out-letters are in New Jersey Original Correspondence of Board of Trade, 1754-1760, CO 5/977; there are letterbook copies in BP, vols. 1-2

and receiver letterbook copies in Original Correspondence of Board of Trade: Despatches to Governors and others, 1759-1763, CO 5/214. The in-letters are in BP, 9. Extracts of FB's official correspondence have been published along with the many of the colony's official records. William A. Whitehead, ed., *Documents relating to the Colonial History of the State of New Jersey*, 42 vols.: vol. 9 (1757-67), eds. Frederick W. Ricord and William Nelson (Newark, 1885).

19. Thomas Pownall (1722-1805) had been lieutenant governor and acting governor of New Jersey, 1753-57, and governor of Massachusetts, 1757-60.

20. Orders in Council, 1755-1759, CO 5/22, f 204, and *mutatis mutandis* for the other governors involved, ff 208-211, 214.

21. *APC*, 4: 777.

22. FB sent holographs and copies of his speeches, messages, and addresses to the Council and the House of Representatives to Britain. They are in Assembly, Massachusetts, 1761-1768, CO 5/842-CO 5/843, and CO 5/844. The Council's record books are Council Executive Records, 1760-1769, CO 5/823 and CO 5/827; there is also a set of nineteenth-century transcripts in Council Executive Records, 1692-1774, 13 vols. [vols. 2-14], GC3-327, vols. 15-16, Massachusetts Archives. There are two contemporaneous sets of the Council's legislative records. One was kept in Boston and is in Council Legislative Records, 1692-1774, 24 vols., GC3-1701x, vols. 23-28, Massachusetts Archives. The other was sent to London: Council in Assembly, Massachusetts, 1760-1769, CO 5/820-CO 5/828.

23. Andrew Oliver (1706-74) was one of the most experienced of provincial legislators and officeholders. He was a member of the Governor's Council, 1746-65, and province secretary, 1756-70.

24. John Pownall (1724/5-95), brother of Thomas Pownall and secretary to the Board of Trade, 1745-68. See Franklin B. Wickwire, "John Pownall and British Colonial Policy," *WMQ* 20 (1963): 543-554.

25. William Bollan (1705-82), Massachusetts province agent, 1743-62. See Malcolm Freiberg, "William Bollan, Agent of Massachusetts," *More Books: The Bulletin of the Boston Public Library* 23 (1948): 43-53, 90-100, 135-146, 212-220.

26. Richard Jackson (1721/2-87), politician and barrister and MP for Weymouth and Melcombe Regis, 1762-68. He was secretary to the chancellor of the Exchequer and first lord of the Treasury, George Grenville during his administration of 1763-65, and counsel to the Board of Trade, 1770-82. A friend of Benjamin Franklin, Jackson took a keen interest in American affairs, and was provincial agent for Connecticut (1760–70), Pennsylvania (1763–70), and Massachusetts (1765–67). See W. P. Courtney, 'Jackson, Richard (1721/2-1787)', rev. J.-M. Alter, *ODNB* (http://www.oxforddnb.com/view/article/14546, accessed 16 May 2005).

27. Jasper Mauduit (c.1696-1771), a London draper and woolen merchant, and Massachusetts province agent, 1762-65.

28. The American secretary was commonly regarded as being inferior to the two "ancient" secretaries of the Southern and Northern Departments, and it was not until the appointment of Lord George Germain in 1775 that confusion over the office's status was resolved. Margaret Spector, *The American Department of the British Government, Studies in History, Economics, and Public Law* ([New York], [1940]); Arthur Herbert Basye, "The Secretary of State for the Colonies, 1768-82," *American Historical Review* 28 (1922): 13-23.

29. Original in-letters from the Board of Trade and secretary of state are in BP, vols. 9-12. FB's original out-letters to the Board are in CO 5/7, CO 5/19, and CO 5/891, and to the secretary of state mainly in CO 5/754-758.

30. Labaree, *Royal Instructions*, 2: 748-750.

31. Thomas Pelham-Holles (1693-1768), the duke of Newcastle, was a long-serving British statesman who had been prime minister between 1754 and 1756. He was first lord of the Treasury in a coalition led by Pitt. William Pitt (1708-78) was secretary of state for Southern Department from 1756 until his resignation on 5 Oct. 1761; he was created earl of Chatham in 1766 and led the Chatham-Grafton administration of Jul. 1766-Oct. 1768.

32. John Stuart (1713-92), the earl of Bute, had been George III's tutor and secretary for the Northern Department under Pitt and Newcastle, 25 Mar. 1761-26 May 1762.

33. George Grenville (1712-70), a former friend and ally of Pitt, was briefly secretary for the Northern Department under Bute. He seemed destined for the political wilderness until George III offered to appoint him both first lord of the Treasury and chancellor of the exchequer.

34. Sir Charles Wyndam (1710-63), second earl of Egremont and secretary of state for the Southern Department, from 9 Oct. 1761 (under Bute and Grenville, his brother-in-law) until his death on 21 Aug. 1763.

35. George Montague-Dunk (1716-71), the earl of Halifax, was an energetic first lord commissioner or president of the Board of Trade, 1748-61; secretary of state for the Southern Department, 1762; and secretary of state for the Northern Department, 1763-65.

36. Sir Matthew Lamb, Bart. (1705?-1768), politician and lawyer. He was MP for Peterborough, from 1747, and king's counsel to the Board of Trade, from 1754 until his death.

37. "Privy Council" has been used throughout when referring to the institution, but it has been necessary to maintain the distinction between the full council and the council's plantation affairs committee. In the first instance, matters pertaining to the American Colonies were usually considered by a committee dignified by the cumbersome title "Lords of the Committee of the Council on Plantation Affairs," which has been shortened to "plantation affairs committee" or a variant thereof. The committee's recommendations were invariably rubber-stamped by the full council—"His Majesty in Council"— which designation has been retained when referring to this body.

38. See Nicolson, *The 'Infamas Govener'*, 63-64.

39. R. C. Simmons, *The American Colonies From Settlement to Independence,* (London, 1976), 292; Nicolson, *The 'Infamas Govener'*, 56-57.

40. See John Clarence Webster, ed., *The Recapture of St John's, Newfoundland in 1762 As Described in the Journal of Lieut-Colonel William Amherst, Commander of the British Expeditionary Force* (1928).

41. *APC*, 4: 576-579. After surveying the Passamaquoddy Bay area in 1764, Massachusetts assumed that, to use Native-derived names, the Magaguadavic River was the St. Croix, whereas Nova Scotia located the boundary twenty-five miles further west at the Cobscook River; in subsequent disputes with the United States, the British government favored the Schoodic River. Archeological evidence pointed to the Schoodic, whose Vanceboro branch was finally accepted as the main St. Croix. The St. Croix River was designated an international boundary between British North America and the United States by the peace treaty of 1783, thus ceding Sagadahoc to the latter. However, the physical border between Massachusetts and New Brunswick (created out of Nova Scotia in 1794) was not determined until 1798, by a British-US commission. David Demeritt, "Representing the 'True' St Croix: Knowledge and Power in the Partition of the Northeast," *WMQ* 54 (1997): 515-548, esp. 532, 535-538, 544; N. E. S. Griffiths, *The Contexts of Acadian History, 1686-1784* (Montreal and Buffalo, 1992), 62-94, 103-114; Richard G. Lowe, "Massachusetts and the Acadians," *WMQ* 25 (1968): 212-229.

42. *Acts and Resolves,* 17: 246.

43. *A Brief State of the Title of the Province of Massachusetts-Bay to the Country between the Rivers Kennebeck and St. Croix* (Boston, 1763).

44. The administrative history can be followed in William O. Sawtelle, "Sir Francis Bernard and His Grant of Mount Desert," *Publications of the Colonial Society of Massachusetts* 24 (19201922): 197-254.

45. FB's first three years as governor are discussed in Nicolson, *The 'Infamas Govener'*, 11-13, 49-50. Earlier detailed accounts of Massachusetts politics during this period are Leslie J. Thomas, "Partisan Politics in Massachusetts During Governor Bernard's Administration, 1760-1770," Unpublished Ph.D. Diss., Univ. of Wisconsin, 1960, 2 vols., 1: 1-169; Stephen E. Patterson, *Political Parties in Revolutionary Massachusetts* (Madison, Wisc., 1973), 52-65; William Pencak, *War, Politics & Revolution in Provincial Massachusetts,* (Boston, 1981), 150-184.

46. Clerk no. 3 may have been a Bostonian, judging by the phonetic rendition of "Havard" in **No. 187**.

47. Chirographical analysis followed procedures recommended by the Scientific Working Group for Forensic Document Examination. "Guidelines for Forensic Document Examination, Part 1," *Forensic Science Communications* 2 (2000), posted on the web sites of the American Society of Questioned Document Examiners and the National Forensic Science Technology Center (http://www.fbi.gov/hq/lab/fsc/backissu/april2000/swgdoc1.htm#Introduction, accessed 4 Jul. 2005).

48. Bollan's role in the publication in 1769 of Bernard's incriminating correspondence is discussed in Nicolson, *The 'Infamas Govener'*, 198-199.

49. Standard biographical directories include: *American National Biography Online* (New York, 2005-, http://www.anb.org); *Dictionary of Canadian Biography Online* (Toronto, 2003-, http://www.biographi.ca); Mark Mayo Boatner, ed., *Encyclopedia of the American Revolution* (New York, 1966); Sir Lewis Namier and John Brooke, eds., *The House of Commons, 1754-1790*, 3 vols. (London, 1964); Edward. A. Jones, *The Loyalists of Massachusetts: Their Memorials, Petitions and Claims* (London, 1930); David E. Maas, ed. and comp., *Divided Hearts: Massachusetts Loyalists, 1765-1790: A Biographical Directory* (Boston, 1980); *ODNB-e* (London, 2004-2006, http://www.oxforddnb.com); John A. Schutz, ed., *Legislators of the Massachusetts General Court* (Boston, 1997); Search & ReSearch Publishing Corp, *Early Vital Records of the Commonwealth of Massachusetts to About 1850* (Wheat Ridge, Conn., 2002); John L. Sibley and Clifford K. Shipton, eds., *Biographical Sketches of Graduates of Harvard University*, 17 vols. (Cambridge, Mass., 1873-1975); James H. Stark, *The Loyalists of Massachusetts and the Other Side of the American Revolution* (Boston, 1910); Nancy S. Voye, ed. and comp., *Massachusetts Officers in the French and Indian Wars, 1748-1763* (microfiche; Boston, 1975).

The Papers of
Governor Francis Bernard

❧❧❧ ❦❦❦

13 November 1759 — 29 December 1763

1 | From the Earl of Halifax

Downing Street Nov^r: ye 13th 1759

Sir

The Government of the Massachusets becoming vacant by Mr Pownall's being appointed to that of South Carolina,[1] and my Friend Lord Barrington[2] having informed me of your Desire, in Case of a Vacancy, of being removed there, I have accordingly recommended You to his Majesty as Successor to Mr Pownall; and have the Pleasure of informing you that the King yesterday approved the Recommendation. I heartily wish you Joy of your Promotion, and make no Doubt but you will make the People as happy in your new Government as you woud have done ^in new Jersey,^ had you continued there. Mr Thomas Boone is appointed to Succeed you in the Government of New Jersey,[3] where you will remain till his arrival. upon Mr Pownall's leaving Boston the Government will devolve upon Mr Hutchinson, Lieutenant Governor,[4] who will hold it, till you shall be replaced by Mr Boone. Your Commission and Instructions shall in due Time be sent you.

Before Mr Pownall Embarks for England I earnestly desire you woud pass a few Days with him at any Place you shall agree upon, in order that you may receive from him full Information of all Matters relative to the Province you are to preside over. It is impossible to pursue a better Plan of Government than what he directed himself by.

I am Sir Your Most Obedient Humble Servant

Dunk Halifax[5]

ALS, RC   BP, 9: 71-72.

Endorsed by FB: Lord Halifax d. 13 Novr r. Feb. 15 1760 a Feb. 18. This letter was probably enclosed in **No. 3**.

Here Halifax indicates that he had discussed the rotation of the governors with King George II on 12 Nov., two days before the Privy Council approved the Board of Trade's recommendation to appoint FB governor of Massachusetts. *JBT,* 11: 59-60. FB's appointment, together with those of governors Lyttleton, Boone, and Pownall, was announced in the *London Gazette* on 27 Nov. FB first learned of his promotion "in the beginning of January," several weeks before Halifax's official notification. BP, 1: 217. He may have read the news in the *London Gazette* for it was not announced in the court circulars reported in *The New-York Gazette*. FB replied to Halifax not on 18 Feb., but two days earlier, **No. 5**.

1. Thomas Pownall (1722-1805) was appointed governor of South Carolina in Nov. 1759, but had already requested a recall in a letter to Secretary of State William Pitt of 27 Oct. He returned to England in Jun. 1760, and subsequently resigned his commission. Charles A. Pownall, *Thomas Pownall, MP, F. R. S., Governor of Massachusetts Bay* (London, 1908), 153.

2. William Wildman Barrington (1717-93), second Viscount Barrington, MP for Plymouth, and secretary at war, 1755-61. He was a cousin to Amelia Bernard.

3. Thomas Boone (1730/31-1812), governor of New Jersey, Jan. 1760-Oct. 1761.

4. Thomas Hutchinson (1711-80) was one of Massachusetts's wealthiest inhabitants and most knowledgeable and able public servants; having retired from commerce, he devoted his time to government and the study of history. He served as the province's lieutenant governor, 1758-71; acting governor, Jun.-Aug. 1760, and again (after FB's recall) Aug. 1769-Jan. 1771; and governor, 1771-74.

5. George Montague-Dunk (1716-71), the earl of Halifax and first lord commissioner or president of the Board of Trade, 1748-61.

2 | *From the Board of Trade*

Sir,[1]

His Majesty having been graciously pleased to approve of your being appointed Governor of the Massachusets Bay, in the room of Mr Pownall preferred to the Government of South Carolina, We take this Opportunity of congratulating you upon this Mark of His Majesty's Favour; and of acquainting you, that His Majesty has also been pleased to approve of Thomas Boone Esqr$_{//}$ to succeed you in the Government of New Jersey. M$^r_{//}$ Boone is now resident in South Carolina, but will have Orders forthwith to repair to New Jersey; and therefore his Patent and Instructions together with your own for the Government of the Massachusets Bay will be transmitted to you as soon as they are passed. We are,

Sir, Your most obedient, humble Servants.

Dunk Halifax.

Soame Jenyns.[2]

W. G. Hamilton.[3]

W. Sloper.[4]

James Oswald.[5]

Ex[ecute]^d.

Whitehall Nov$^r_{//}$ 14. 1759

L, LbC   CO 5/998, pp. 141-142.

Entrybook title: To Francis Bernard Esq$^r_{//}$ Governor of New Jersey.

FB replied to the Board of Trade on 25 Feb. 1760, BP, 1: 135-137. For FB's General instructions and Trade Instructions, 18 Mar. 1760, see **Appendices 1** and **2**.

1. Left marginal note: "Letter from the Board to Francis Bernard Esqr// Govr// of New Jersey, acquainting him that His Majesty has been graciously pleased to approve of his being appointed Govr. of the Massachusets Bay."

2. Soame Jenyns (1704-87), author and politician, MP for Cambridge, 1758-80, and a lord commissioner of the Board of Trade, 1755-80.

3. William Gerard Hamilton (1729-96), MP for Petersfield, 1754-96, and a lord commissioner, 1756-61.

4. William Sloper (1709-89), MP for Great Bedwyn, 1747-56, and a lord commissioner, 1756-61.

5. James Oswald (1715-69), MP for Kirkcaldy, 1741-68, and a lord commissioner, 1751 to Dec. 1759.

3 | From John Pownall

Dear Sir,

The Letter from Lord Halifax & that from the Board which accompany this will I hope contain a better answer to your last kind letter to me & better reasons for my not answering sev^l former ones I had received from you, than I am able to give, let me however add with respect to the last, that, I think the points touched upon in sev^l. of your Letters to me, would in the prosecution of them have been attended with so many obstacles, & difficultys & so much expence & perplexity, that admitting All the Success you could have wish'd, which is admitting a great deal more than was likely to happen, they would in the end have been Objects in no degree worth the pursuit.__ and I really think a patent for the Gov^t. of Massachusets Bay, which I hope soon to send you, a better thing than a Grant of the Delawar Islands[1] or L^d. Melforts Estate, entangled as both are with such variety of Claims.

I have desired your ffriend Blackbourne[2] to write to M^rs. Beresford[3] & whom else he thinks proper concerning the prefering your Commiss^n. & Instructions, so that no difficulty or delay may arise as to that matter,— from Blackbourns state of matters I think there can be none:— nay I am determined there shall be none for I will be myself answerable for whatever may be necessary on that Score. I am

Dear Sir Your most Aff^t. Freind

J Pownall.[4]

[*London*] Novr. 14. 1759.

ALS, RC   BP, 9: 76 c-d.

Endorsed by FB: Sec^y Pownall r. Feb. 15. 1760. a Feb. 19. Enclosed **No. 1** and **No. 2**.

FB's interests in the Delaware Islands and the Melfort estates are not raised in any of his extant correspondence with John Pownall. (His reply to the letter printed here has not been found.) "L^d. Melfort" is likely Lord John Drummond (1682-1754), an unsuccessful claimant to the titles of his father John Drummond (1649-1714), the first earl and viscount Melfort. John and his brother James (1648-1716), the fourth earl (and first titular duke) of Perth, were among the original proprietors of East Jersey. The Drummonds were Roman Catholics and ardent Jacobites, and were attainted after the rebellions of 1715 and 1745, losing both their Scottish and American estates. Their lands in New Jersey were among some one-half million acres of land whose ownership was contested after 1745. See *DNB*, 4: 35-36; Ned C. Landsman, *Scotland and Its First American Colony, 1683-1765* (Princeton, N.J, 1985), 175, 275-78; Thomas L. Purvis, "Origins and Patterns of Agrarian Unrest in New Jersey, 1735 to 1754," *WMQ* 39 (1982): 600-27, at 610.

---

1. This may refer to one or more of the following islands in the Delaware River (using their modern names) that were within New Jersey's provincial boundaries: Petty, Treasure, and Burlington.

2. Leverett Blackbourne, a lawyer and FB's business agent. He resided in Great Marlborough Street, London, and subsequently at a "good-house" in Margaret Street, Cavendish Square, near to Lord Barrington. According to Thomas Hutchinson, he had "a large fortune" and exuded "great learning . . . as well as natural good sense." *The Diary and Letters of His Excellency Thomas Hutchinson*, 2 vols., ed. Peter Orlando Hutchinson, (London, 1883-1886), 1: 447.

3. Jane Beresford (c.1702-Nov. 1771), a cousin and close friend of FB. She was the daughter of FB's maternal aunt Mary Winlowe and John Tyringham, and had married William Beresford in 1722. She resided at Long Leadenheam, Lincs., c.1722-31, and, after her husband's decease, at Lincoln and Nether Winchendon House, Bucks., her husband's family home. Her only son died in 1740 and she bequeathed Nether Winchendon to FB in 1762. FB was her executor and he inherited Nether Winchendon. Napier Higgins, *The Bernards*, 1: 208; Nicolson, *The 'Infamas Govener'*, 18, 22-23.

4. John Pownall (1724/5-95), secretary to the Board of Trade, 1745-68.

4 | *From Lord Barrington*

Cavendish Square 14. Novr. 1759.

Dear Sir,

I have to my shame I confess it, several Letters of your's which I have not yet acknowledged. Some of them relate to forfeited Lands concerning which M^r. Pownal[1] and I have had several conversations. I need not explain the difficulties we should have found in a pursuit of that nature, as a fortunate circumstance has offer'd which will carry you from new Jersey to Boston. The Death of Colonel Haldane Governour of Jamaica[2] has occasion'd a general promotion of Governours in America: M^r. Lyttelton goes to Jamaica,[3] M^r. Pownall to Carolina, you go to Boston & M^r. Boon succeeds you. I found Lord Halifax in the best disposition to shew his regard for you and approbation of your conduct, & I am to wish you Joy of the thing you desired, given in the manner that must please you the most. I will endeavour that your Instructions shall be as little inconvenient to you as possible, and shall be happy in every opportunity of shewing my sincere regard & affection for you and your family. I hope this change will not be less agreable to my Cousin than it is to you; & I beg you will convey to her my sincere Compliments & congratulations.

I have not time to give you an Account of our Successes in Europe & in Asia as well as in America. They are great, and I hope they will produce us a good Peace; but hitherto no Overtures of that sort have been made.

All M^{rs}. Bernard's Relations in my family are well, except M. Genl. Barrington[4] who got an unlucky Accident ashooting in Norfolk: a friend of his firing at a Partridge one of the shots touchd the white of his Eye. He has been blind of that Eye ever since, & has sufferd great pain in different parts of his head; but he is now much easyer, the Eye is coming to itself, and there is the greatest Reason to think he will recover the Use of it. The other Eye never was in the least affected. All of us join in sincere Compliments & wishes to you and M^{rs}. Bernard. I am with the greatest truth & regard

Dear Sir Your Excellency's most faithful & most obedient Servt.

Barrington

It is expected that in a few days your Appointment will go thro' the forms of the Council.[5]

ALS, RC   BP, 9: 73-76.

Endorsed by FB: Lord Barrington r. Feb. 15 1760 a Feb. 18. The reply is **No. 6**.

1. See **No. 3**.

2. George Haldane (1722-59), governor of Jamaica, 1756-59.

3. William Henry Lyttleton (1724-1808), governor of Jamaica, 1761-66. Sir Henry Moore, Bart. (1713-69) was acting governor until Lyttelton arrived.

4. John Barrington (1719-64), a British army officer and the younger brother of Lord Barrington. He was appointed the first colonel of the 64th Regiment of Foot on 21 Apr. 1758, and held a brevet rank of major general in the West Indies.

5. See the source note to **No. 1**.

5 | To the Earl of Halifax

Perth Amboy Feb 16. 1760

My Lord

I had the honour of receiving your Lordships letter of the 13 of Nov[r]. yesterday[1] & beg leave to return your Lordship my most humble thanks for the favor you have shown me in recommending me to his Majesty for the Government of Massachusets bay. I am Very unacquainted with the Circumstances of that Government, but have the Pleasure of being Assured, that the Goverment is put into very good order by M[r]. Pownall, & that I shall have nothing to do but to keep it so; in which, as I dont apprehend that I shall be charged with any matter that will be subject to Contest, I promise myself success I shall give up to M[r]. Boone a People as well disposed to Government as any in America, There is at present an harmony ~~betwixt~~ between the Several branches of the legislature that never was known before; & I have rec[d]. so many Expressions of the peoples approbation of my Conduct & their intention of doing every thing in their power to make this Government Easy & agreeable to me, that I shall leave this place with regret, Tho' advanced & honoured according to my desire & beyond my Merits. And it is posible, that, after some years service at Boston, If I shall be intitled to ask further favors of your Lordship, I shall request to retire to Amboy.

I Congratulate your Lordship upon the Events of this Glorious Year, which is scarce equalled by any one in the Annals of the English history. As we have as yet no orders for preparing for the next Campaign, We apprehend that the business will be done without one, or at least without drawing out the provincial troops; which will be agreeable to the provinces; for I reckon that the raising & marching our Regiment to the Rendezvous at Albany (tho' they stir not a step further) will Cost 20,000 pounds.[2] I shall hold myself in readiness to Execute the orders I Shall receive for the next Campaign with all Possible Expedition as they will come,[3] if at all before M[r]. Boone can arrive here, to whom I shall write immediately.[4] I have wrote to M[r]. Pownall proposing a place for our meeting, in case he should not as I think it is Possible he may, take New York in his way to England.[5]

I have the honour to be with great gratitude & respect My Lord your Lordships most obedient & most humble servant

F. B.

Lord Halifax[6]

L, LbC   BP, 1: 192-194.

In the handwriting of clerk no. 1, except as noted. The postscript to this letter on pp. 196-197, which is in FB's hand, has been omitted, for it discusses in some detail affairs of state pertaining exclusively to New Jersey.

---

1. **No. 1**.

2. Likely meaning £sterling.

3. Gen. Amherst received his orders on the night of 20 Feb., about which he informed FB in a letter dated the following day (BP, 9: 89-92), in which he enclosed a copy of William Pitt's circular to the colonial governors relating to the coming campaign (Whitehall, 7 Jan. 1760, CO 5/214, ff 130-135).

4. FB to Boone, Perth Amboy, 18 Feb. 1760, BP, 1: 216-218.

5. FB discussed arrangements for the meeting in a letter to Pownall of 4 Mar. BP, 1: 221-223. The two governors met at New London, Conn., in Apr. 1760, and Pownall left Boston for England on 3 Jun.

6. This line in FB's hand.

6 | To Lord Barrington

Perth Amboy feb 18th 1760

My Lord

I received Your Lordships ~~lett~~ favor of Nov 14th last fryday[1] & want words to express my thankfullness to your Lordship for you[r] kind & Earnest Care of us. I need not repeat to your Lordship, that it is upon my Childrens account only that I have solicited this advancement, in regard to ourselves, we shall quit this place with regret, as the People have joined with the Country & Climate to engage our Affection for it. & therefore Your Lordship must not be suprised if some years hence when I can better afford to perfer ease & pleasure to profit, I shall trouble your Lordship to get me sent back to Amboy: which I suppose will allways be an easier task than the present has been; as competitors for governments are, in General, more attentive to the income than the Situation.

I have not been able at [as] Yet to form any Certain Judgment of the Value of that Government: It is generally said to be worth £1500 Sterling p[r]. an If so, as it is undoubtedly a cheaper market than NYork, I think we shall live for half that Money; especially as M[r]. Pownall has established a life of reserve[2] which tho' I could not so well begin it myself I can follow, & shall, as far as it is Convenient with the honours of the Place. As I am order'd to stay here 'till M[r]. Boone comes, I reckon I shall not set out for Boston till some time in May next; as soon as I get a little settled there, I will acquaint your Lordship with the particular situation &

the Circumstances of the Governm^t. It is one good one, that, as I am assured, M^r. Pownall has brought it into very good order; & I doubt not but I shall keep it so, as I have no reason to fear that any impracticable instructions will interfere.

I this day recd. a letter from Genl. Amherst,[3] desiring that I would set my Assembly about providing for the Campaign, But I must have a letter from M^r. Pitt[4] before they will mind me. It seems to me inevitable that the Provincial troops must take the field this Year, tho' there is little more to do than to take possession. But I hope the amazing Series of Success, that has attended his Majesty's arms, will authorise him to retain Canada: and I can Assure your Lordship that that Acquisition only will be worth all the Expences of the War.

We are extreamly concerned for Genl. Barrington's misfortune, but flatter ourselves that a Cure with a recovery of the Sight has been brought about; especially as we see in the papers, that he is going with a Command to Germany. We beg your Lordship will present our Congratulations to him on the Great honours he has deserved of & recd. from his Country.[5]

Our Compliments wait on Ladies & all our Friends. I am with the greatest Gratitude

      my Lord your Lordships most obedient & most humble Servant

Lord Barrington[6]

L, LbC   BP, 1: 194-196.

In the handwriting of clerk no. 1, except as noted.

---

1. **No. 4**.

2. Thomas Pownall's optimistic accounts of his own career progression indubitably encouraged FB to think that he might live in some comfort on his governor's salary and fees. Nicolson, '*Infamas Govener*,' 40-41. While FB thought Pownall prudent, some Bostonians considered him to be profligate because of his "lavish parties." Eliga H. Gould, "Pownall, Thomas (1722-1805)," in *ODNB-e*, (http://www.oxforddnb.com/view/article/22676, accessed 8 Dec. 2004).

3. Amherst to FB, New York, 13 Dec. 1759, BP, 9: 81-84.

4. William Pitt (1708-78), secretary of state for the Southern Department. He was leader of the coalition administration he formed with the duke of Newcastle, 29 Jun. 1757-5 Oct. 1761, that led Britain to victory in the Seven Years War.

5. On returning to England in the summer of 1759, John Barrington transferred to the 40th Regiment of Foot and later to the 8th (the King's) Regiment of Foot. He was rewarded with confirmation of his major-general's rank in recognition of his notable contribution to the capture of Guadeloupe the previous Apr. He was not posted to Germany but appointed deputy governor of Berwick-upon-Tweed, the English port and garrison town within the Scottish military district and the former parliamentary constituency of his brother Lord Barrington. Jonathan Spain, "Barrington, John (bap.1719, d.1764)," *ODNB-e* (http://www.oxforddnb.com/view/article/65499, accessed 12 Nov. 2004).

6. This line in FB's hand.

7 | *Instructions as Governor of Massachusetts,*

18 March 1760

See **Appendices 1** and **2**.

8 | *From Lord Barrington*

Cavendish Square 3ᵈ June 1760.

Dear Sir

I am favour'd by two Letters of your's One dated the 18ᵗʰ of February the other the 19ᵗʰ of April,[1] and I am happy to find that you are pleas'd with the Exchange of Governments. The paper you enclose shews plainly how well the people of Jersey are pleas'd with your administration; I make no doubt of your being as much lik'd at Boston. Your conduct in both governments will make it a pleasing and an easy task to sollicit one better than either, when ever ^any^ such shall be vacant, and agreable to You. I am also very happy to find that Mʳˢ Bernard likes America so well; I beg you will present my best Compliments to her together with my assurances of regard, and desire of contributing to whatever may be useful and agreable to her & her family. You have heard before this time that the Estate in Derbyshire is sold. Mʳˢ Porter's share I have put into the four per Cent Annuities of this Year with her approbation.[2] Her income will be a little increas'd by the Exchange.

All your friends here are well, and extremly happy to find that you are settled so much to your satisfaction. They all send the most affectionate Compliments to you and Mʳˢ Bernard. Major Genˡ Barrington's Eye mends apace, but his Constitution has not recover'd the shock of a West Indian Climate, so as to serve abroad this Campaign. He is going to Scotland, where he is to serve under Lord George Beauclerck,[3] who commands in Chief in that Country.

I assure you, without flattery that my Godson is a very fine Boy:[4] I have it from good hands that he is one of the best Scholars in Westminster School. I have never heard you say to what profession he is destin'd. If your Inclinations and his are for the Army I will endeavour to procure him a Commission before the War is over. I am with the greatest truth & regard

Dear Sir Your most faithful & most obedient Servant

Barrington

His Excellency Francis Bernard Esqr Governor of New England.

ALS, RC   BP, 9: 107-110.

Endorsed by FB: Lord Barrington r. Aug 7. 1760 a same day. The reply to this letter is **No. 9**.

---

1. **No. 6**; FB to Barrington, New York, 19 Apr. 1760, BP, 1: 201-203.

2. Barrington is alluding to the sale of some of the Offley family's property, for which see the **Introduction** n12. Mrs. Porter is not named as a beneficiary in Joseph Offley's will but evidently had some claim on his estate.

3. Lord George Beauclerk (1704-68), commander-in-chief of the British Army in Scotland. He was the son of Charles Beauclerk (1670-1726), the first duke of St. Albans and illegitimate son of Charles II.

4. Francis Bernard Jr. (27 Sept. 1743-20 Nov. 1770), FB's eldest son, known as "Frank."

9 | *To Lord Barrington*

Boston Aug^st. 7th 1760

My Lord

I was preparing to inform Your Lordship of Our Safe arrival at This Town when I rec^d your Lordship['s] favor of the 3rd of June which was brought by the Leicester Packet which arrived here this Morning,[1] As the Packet was drove in here by southerly winds, I ordered Genl. Amherst's dispatches to be sent from hence to albany under the Care of a Lieut of Highlanders & an Express rider by which means he will receive them a week sooner than he would by way of New York.

We made our Entry here last Saturday[2] in a very Magnificient Manner. It seems there had been no Instance of a Govr entring by land since Govr. Burnetts[3] time so the Ceremonial was in a Manner new. For this I shall refer your Lordship to the new[s][4] of the day, which I shall add to the triffles which your Lordships kindness for us has encouraged me from time to time to trouble you with. I have the Pleasure to inform your Lordship that I have a very fair Prospect of an easy Administration from the Assurances of All persons concerned in it that I have yet seen; as also from the favourable impressions, which I am told have been rec^d of me as well from London as from New Jersey.

I am very Glad that the money is laid out with M^rs. Porters approbation & for her Advantage. whatever your Lordship shall do therein will certainly have our approbation. Perhaps when the war is over if stock should Rise, & private intrest (as it Generally is) be higher than public, It may be more for her Advantage to Vest the Money upon land Security

We are Extreamly Glad that Genl. Barrington is in the Way of Recovery from all his shocks; we are much obliged to our friends for their kind remembrance of us & beg your Lordship will again present our Compliments

Your Lordship may imagine that I receive great Pleasure from your Accounts of my son; and I must do him Justice to say that it agrees with Accounts I receive from every one Else, I am very much obliged to your Lordship for your kind intention toward him: but I have not as yet formed nor do I intend ^for some time^ to form any resolution Concerning his profession. I intend at present to indulge his uncommon tast for literature; & for that purpose would have him to pursue his studies at Oxford for 3 or 4 Years. At Next Westminster Election (which is the Monday before Ascension day)[5] I hope to have him elected to Christ Church to secure this point with the dean of Ch. Ch.[6] I fear I must trouble your Lordship to add a little weight: a word from the duke of New-Castle (who I understand to be the Deans' patron) will make all safe. M^r. Stone[7] will I doubt not, save your Lordship any trouble you please in this business.

As this extention of his Education will superannuate him for the Army, I shan[t][8] be able to avail my self of your Lordships kind offer on that Account. But If the Placeing him out depended on me alone, I should not doubt to express my desire to see him (when his Education is Compleated) in some public office, if Possible, under your Lordship Eye

M^rs. Bernard begs leave to join with me in our best respects to your Lordships

I am my Lord Your Lordships most obedi^t. & most humble servant[9]

Lord Barrington

L, LbC   BP, 1: 272-274.

In the handwriting of clerk no. 1, except as noted, and with a minor emendation by FB. Enclosed a Boston newspaper, possibly the *Boston Newsletter*, 7 Aug. 1760, which reported FB's arrival in some detail.

---

1. **No. 8.**

2. 2 Aug.

3. William Burnet (1688-1729), governor of Massachusetts, 1728-29.

4. Manuscript torn.

5. 27 Apr. 1761, for Ascension Day was 30 Apr.

6. FB was hoping to obtain for Francis Jr. a Westminster School Studentship at Christ Church College, Oxford. These coveted studentships were originally intended for impecunious students, but had long since become a currency of patronage. Students were elected by the college dean, as FB was in 1729. The incumbent dean was David Gregory (1696-1767), who held the office from 1756 until his death. He was the son of the noted David Gregory (1661-1708), Savilian professor of astronomy at Oxford, 1691-1708. Nicolson, *The 'Infamas Govener'*, 24.

7. Andrew Stone (1703-73) was a Westminster scholar and graduate of Christ Church like FB, and an influential but not particularly well-known politician. He was a London banker, and, on being appointed private secretary to the duke of Newcastle in 1732, became the duke's "indefatigable aide and constant companion." He was undersecretary of state, 1734-51, and MP for Hastings, 1741-60; tutor and secretary to the Prince of Wales, the future George III; and prominent among Lord Bute's circle of "King's Friends." A. F. Pollard, "Stone, Andrew (1703-1773)." rev. M. J. Mercer, in ODNB-e, (http://www.oxforddnb.com/view/article/26565, accessed 12 Nov. 2004).

8. Letter obscured by binding.

9. This line in FB's hand.

10 | *To Lord Barrington*

Boston August 23. 1760

My Lord

In the Cover with this I inclose a duplicate of a letter I sent, soon after the time of its date, by the Ship Brittannia Cap[t]. Dashwood[1] bound from this port to London:[2] since which business has gone on extreamly well. What passed between the Assembly & me will appear from the following papers, which I take the liberty to enclose. To these I have only to add that the Assembly made the usual Grants viz £975 Sterling for the Salary of the current Year (of which near a quarter was spent) & £225 sterling for the Charges of Removal. This was done with a uncommon unanimity; and this bill passed both houses & received the Assent in one day.[3]

On the 14th Cap[t]. Stott of the Scarbrough brought to me Dispatches from England that came in the Vengeance Man of War: among these was a letter from your Lordship to Gen[l]. Amherst[4] & another to Col. Amherst[5] they were immediately dispatched for Albany: the Messenger that carried them is returned & brings advice[6] that on the 7th. inst Col. Amherst went from Oswego with the Vanguard; on the 10th Gen[l]. Amherst with the main body; & on y[e] 11th Brig Gage[7] with the rear: The Numbers were not ascertained. Also that on the 11th Col. Haviland[8] went down lake Champlan with 3000 Regulars & 2500 provincials. It is apprehended they will meet with Opposition at the Isle des Noix

This day a Sloop arrived from Quebeck, which she left on the 26th of July: the Master[9] brings advice that on the 13th Gen[l]. Murray[10] sailed up the River with 2500 regulars & left 1000 ~~in Garison~~ more in Quebec that about the 23rd a Schooner arrived with an Account that two forts had fired up on his fleet & killed an Officer & 5 or 6 men: and that the forts were afterwards abandoned: that he had met with no other opposition, the People in general submitting & giving up their Arms. He adds that he met the two Regiments from Louisburg at the Iles de Coudre:[11] they had been at sea 3 Weeks.

From all these we expect very intresting advises Soon: and I hope I shall have occasion to congratulate your Lordship before I seal this letter. We wish we could with as great probality[12] flatter our selves with seeing Capt. Barrington,[13] who we understand is arrived at Louisburg.

I am my Lord your Lordships &c

Rt. honble L Visct. Barrington

L, LbC   BP, 1: 275-276.

In the handwriting of clerk no. 1. May have enclosed a duplicate of a letter addressed either to John Pownall or the earl of Halifax, together with copies of the *Boston Gazette,* 18 Aug. 1760, or the *Boston Newsletter,* 14 and 21 Aug. 1760; both newspapers published the proceedings of the General Court of 13-15 Aug. (see *JHRM,* 37, pt.1: 84-85, 89-92).

---

1. Samuel Dashwood, a Boston sea captain and part-time importer of dry goods, who became, in 1769 and 1770, a prominent member of the merchants' committees that enforced the non-importation agreements. John W. Tyler, *Smugglers & Patriots: Boston Merchants and the Advent of the Revolution* (Boston, 1986), 125, 135, 151, 304n11.

2. The *Britannia* was a ship of 110 tons built in New England in 1757 and owned by the London merchant Thomas Lane. Captained by George Spender and crewed by just eight men, the *Britannia* regularly sailed between Boston and London before she was captured in the English Channel; this would account for the loss of the RC of this letter and its enclosures. Clearances from Boston, 1757, in Shipping Returns, 1756-1762, CO 5/851; John Pownall to FB, 18 Oct. 1760, BP, 9: 149-152.

3. In provincial currency the grant of salary was £1,300 and the removal expenses £300.

4. Jeffery Amherst (1717-97), general and commander-in-chief of the British Army in North America, 1758-63.

5. William Amherst (c.1732-81), the brother of Jeffery Amherst, was a lieutenant colonel of the First Regiment of Foot guards and deputy adjutant-general in America.

6. FB proceeds to describe the three main British assaults on Montréal, involving some twelve thousand men under Gen. Amherst's overall command.

7. Thomas Gage (1721-87) was an experienced career soldier in the British Army; he was a brigadier general, 1759-61, before succeeding Amherst as commander-in-chief and later serving, concurrently, as Massachusetts governor, 1774-75.

8. William Haviland (1718-84), a colonel in the 27th Regiment of Foot. The force of Regulars and Provincials he led actually totaled 3,500. Île-aux-Noix was captured on 28 Aug. Fred Anderson, *Crucible of War: The Seven Years War and the Fate of Empire in British North America, 1754-1766* (New York, 2000), 388.

9. Capt. [*Andrew?*] Gardner's news was reported in the *Boston Gazette,* 25 Aug. 1760.

10. James Murray (1722-94), the British general who led the assault force up the St. Lawrence, was governor of Quebec, 1763-66.

11. The 22nd and 42nd Regiments of Foot. Île-aux-Coudre is c.76 miles down the St. Lawrence River from Quebec.

12. From the adjective "probal" meaning "such as approves itself to reason or acceptance." *OED.*

13. Samuel Barrington (1729-1800), British naval officer and a younger brother of Lord Barrington. Capt. Barrington was in active service in Europe and America for much of the Seven Years War. In 1760, he commanded the Royal Navy war ship *Achilles,* which joined a squadron under Admiral John Byron sent to destroy the fortifications of Louisbourg captured by Amherst two years previously. He rose to the rank of admiral in the Revolutionary War.

11 | *Circular from William Pitt*

Duplicate

Whitehall 23^d. August 1760.

Sir,

The Commanders of His Majesty's Forces, & Fleets, in North America, & the West Indies, having transmitted repeated & certain Intelligence of an illegal & most pernicious Trade, carried on by The King's Subjects, in North America, and the West Indies, as well as to the French Islands, as [*and*] to the French Settlements on the Continent of America, and particularly to the Rivers Mobile, & Mississippi, by which the Enemy is, to the greatest Reproach & Detriment of Government, supplied with Provisions, & other Necessaries, whereby They are principally, if not alone, enabled to sustain & protract this long & expensive War; and it further appearing, that large Sums, in Bullion, are also sent, by The King's Subjects, to the above Places, in return whereof, Commodities are taken, which interfere with the Produce of the British Colonies Themselves, in open Contempt of the Authority of the Mother Country, as well as to the most manifest Prejudice of the Manufactures, & Trade of Great Britain; In order, therefore, to put the most speedy, & effectual Stop to such flagitious Practices, so utterly Subversive of all Law, and so highly repugnant to the Honor and Wellbeing of this Kingdom, It is His Majesty's express Will & Pleasure, that you do forthwith make the strictest, and most diligent, Enquiry, into the State of this dangerous & ignominious Trade, & that you do use every Means in your Power, to detect & discover Persons, concerned, either as Principals, or Accessories, therein; And that you do take every Step, authorized by Law, to bring all such heinous Offenders to the most exemplary, and condign Punishment; and you will, as soon as may be, & from Time to Time, transmit to me, for The King's Information, full & particular Accounts of the Progress you shall have made, in the Execution of these His Majesty's Commands, to which The King expects that you do pay the most exact Obedience: And you are farther to use your utmost Endeavours, to trace out, and investigate, the various Artifices & Evasions, by which the dealers in this iniquitous Intercourse find Means to cover their criminal Proceedings, and to elude the Law, in order that, from such Lights, due & timely Consideration may be had, what farther Provisions shall be necessary to restrain an Evil of such extensive & pernicious Consequences.

I am, Sir, your most obedient humble Servant.

W Pitt

Gov.r of Massachusets Bay.

dupLS, RC   BP, 9: 121-124.

In the handwriting of Robert Wood.[1] Endorsed by FB: M.r Pitt 23 Aug. 1760 Duplicate. r Jan 17. 1761. Variant text in Prov. Sec. Letterbooks, 2: 287-288 (L, Copy).
   In **No. 18**, FB replied to Pitt's principal letter (not found), which he received two months prior to the duplicate printed here. He continued to report on the trade with the French colonies (**No. 49**).

---

1. Wood was undersecretary of state, 1756-63 and 1768-70. He was probably based in the Northern Department in 1760, but during his second period in office he also served in the Southern Department.

12 | To the Board of Trade

Boston Sep 17. 1760

My Lords

   I have at length the honor to congratulate your Lordships on the Reduction of all Canada, Montreal with the all the french forces in it to the amount of 13,000 having surrenderd the 8.th instant:[1] I have just received advice of this great event by express in 8 days from the Isle aux Noix. I enclose a copy of one Letter & an extract of another, both from Men of credit & discretion. The March of three Armies by different routs thro' an enemies Country not unfortified has been performed with the loss of scarce more than 100 men in the whole: and We dont apprehend there has been much loss at Montreal. It is reported that the surrender was made before the two Generals had actually joined, but after the Enemy had found themselves between two fires, and that Col Haviland was advanced near enough to support Genl Murray.[2]

As I consider how necessary it is at this time that his Majestys Ministers should have the earliest advice of the success of his arms in this country, I am endeavouring to get a Vessel to sail from hence immediately; tho' I think it most probable that the Advice will come sooner from the river St Lawrence. I have the honour to be with great respect, My Lords

Your Lordships most obedient & most humble Servant

Fra. Bernard

The R^t Honble Lords Commrs &c

ALS, RC   CO 5/891, ff 11-12.

Endorsed by John Pownall: *Massachusetts* Letter from Fra^s. Bernard Esq. Gov. of the Massachusets Bay dated Septem^r. 17. 1760 congratulating the Board on the Success of His Majestys Arms in America & inclosing Reced Novr 26 Read__ 28. 1760. Ll.6.

The enclosures to which FB refers may have been two letters printed in the *Boston Gazette*, 29 Sept. 1760, p. 2: "Proceedings of the Army under General Amherst, from the Time they embarked at Oswego (on the 10th of August) to the happy Reduction of Montreal the 8th of September following" and "Authentick account of the Surrender of Canada . . . Published by Authority."

This letter was read by the Board of Trade on 28 Nov. 1760. *JBT*, 11: 146.

---

1. Actually, probably fewer than five thousand French regulars were among the besieged population, and no more than half of them were fit for battle; most of the Canadian militiamen had deserted. Anderson, *Crucible of War*, 407.

2. Amherst had reached Montréal first, and opened negotiations with the governor-general, the marquis de Vaudreuil on Sunday Sept. 7, whilst Murray and Haviland arrived and took up their positions; the articles of surrender were signed the following day. Anderson, *Crucible of War*, 388-409.

13 | To Jeffery Amherst

Boston Sep. 27. 1760

S^r.

I have this day received your letters of the 9th & 13th inst; & I do most sincerely & heartily congratulate you upon the accomplishment of your great work; & more especially upon the extraordinary manner, in which it has been conducted, whereby so great a conquest has been perfected with so little bloodshed. I have, pursuant to your desire, publickly invited the Traders to furnish Quebec & Montreal with goods: but as it was the opinion of some Merchants, that it was not now too late to freight for Quebec, in that particular I Varied from your Terms.[1]

I have been addressed by the Assembly[2] & received many private solicitations, to Procure the dismission of the Massachuset's Provincials whose time of Service had expired; who in their turns have deserted in large bodies carrying away with them Sloops &c to the great detriment of the public. I could not think of troubling you with business of this kind till the great Event was over; but now you will permit me to hope that with your next dispatches to Louisburgh & Halifax You will order the Massachusets Provincials to be discharged.

I am with great regard Sr Your most obedient and most humble Servant

Fra: Bernard.

ALS, RC   WO 34/26, f 79.

The reply to this letter is **No. 15**. FB's proclamation was the beginning of attempts to bring provisions into French Canada. For two years, it had been cut off from European trade, and, as Amherst commented in the letter of 13 Sept., while the country "is, initself, fruitfull" the British were anxious as to whether or not they would be able to provision their forces over winter. There is no mention as to how the inhabitants of Montréal and Quebec were faring.

---

1. The first letter recounted the capture of Montréal. Amherst to FB, Camp at Montréal, 9 Sept. 1760, BP, 9: 137-140. In the second, Amherst urges FB to persuade the Massachusetts merchants "to bring Quantitys of Molasses, Salt, Wines, Teas, Sugars, & all kinds of Grocery, as likewise Sheep, and every thing else, that may Occurr to them to be usefull; for all which they may depend upon finding good markets." Amherst to FB, Camp at Montréal, 13 Sept. 1760, BP, 9: 141-142. FB's proclamation is By Order of His Excellency the Governor, Whereas the Country of Canada, now entirely yielded to his Majesty's Dominion . . . the Traders and Adventurers within this Province are hereby invited to transport to Montreal & Quebec . . ., *Boston Gazette,* 29 Sept. 1760, p. 2.

2. 15 Aug. 1760, *JHRM*, 37, pt.1: 95-96.

14 | To the Earl of Halifax

Boston Sep 29 1760

My Lord

I beg leave to Congratulate your Lordship on the happy end of the North American war. The People here are filled with the most Excessive joy; which would be unalloyed if they were free from apprehensions of it's being hereafter restored, They have however the greatest dependence on his Majestys Councils & doubt not but that his ministers are fully acquainted with the Importance it is to Great Britain, & will therefore endeavour to retain it. In my Opinion It is the greatest prize that has ever been taken by Englishmen since the Conquest of France & much more benificial to the nation than that, as it was an acquisition not to be maintained. May his Majesty's Arms be every where, be as well conducted & as successful as in North America. I am with great Esteem

My Lord, your Lordships &c &c

Lord Halifax

L, LbC   BP, 1: 282.

In the handwriting of clerk no. 1 with minor emendations by FB.

15 | From Jeffery Amherst

Lake Champlain 14th. October 1760.

Sir,

I am to Return You thanks for the Publick Invitation You have given, at my request, to the Traders of Your Province, to provide Quebec & Montreal with goods; and I am hopefull, that the opinion which has prevailed, among the Merchants of Boston, that it was not too late to freight for the former of those two places will prove practicable; if it should not, the same Encouragement, that I offered them thro' You, shall be given them, whenever they shall think it more adviseable to follow the other Route.__

Immediately after the Reduction of Canada in the Disposition I made of the Troops, I provided for the Garrison of Nova Scotia, by ordering a Competent Number of Regulars thither, and upon their arrival at Halifax, such of the Forces of the Province of the Massachusetts Bay as may be there, will be immediately sent home; as will doubtless likewise those from Louisbourg after the Reduction of that place; but from what You mention,[1] and the Corroborating Accompts I have had from those two Provinces, of the shamefull Desertion of those Forces, It is more than probable, that but few are remaining of them: and now I am on that Topick, I cannot help repeating what I have Several times mentioned to Governor Pownall & L[t]. Gov[r]. Hutchinson, that these Deserters on their Return, ought not only to be discountenanced by the Province, but, at least ought to be Mulct[2] the Pay that may be due to them, as, without some such mark of disapprobation, it will be an Encouragement to all Others in future times; and as You must be Sensible how highly detrimental such behavior must be to the King's Service, You will agree with me of the absolute Necessity there is, to put the most Effectual stop to it possible: I leave it therefore to Your better Judgement to devise Such means as You shall think proper, more fully to answer these Ends, and, I am, with the greatest Regard,

Sir, Your most Obedient Humble Servant

Jeff Amherst

His Excellency Governor Bernard

LS, RC   BP, 9: 143-144.

Endorsed by FB: Gen[l] Amherst Oct 14 1760. Variant text in WO 34/27, f 207 (L, LbC).
    There were at least fourteen "troop disorders"—acts of "wilful disobedience including mutiny and desertion"—among the New England regiments between 1755 and 1759, including those stationed at Louisbourg and Halifax, which were sparked by inadequate provisioning, discontent over low pay, and fear of being sent to the West Indies. Fred W. Anderson, "Why did Colonial New Englanders Make Bad Soldiers? Contractual Principles and Military Conduct during the Seven Year's War," *WMQ* 38 (1981): 395-417, at 406-408.

---

1. **No. 13**.

2. That is to say, fined.

16 | From Lord Barrington

Cavendish Square 15th October 1760.

Dear Sir

I am favour'd by your Letter dated Boston August the 7th,[1] and am extremly happy to find by it that New England is so agreable to you & M[rs] Barnard. The prospect of an easy administration is by your account extremly fair. I most sincerely hope it will equal not only your expectations, but your wishes: I am sure you will do your part, I hope the people over whom you preside will do their's.

I most sincerely congratulate you on the happy reduction of Canada which has set the hands of Government at liberty in that quarter of the World. I think our affairs in other parts wear a favorable aspect; particularly in the East Indies, where we are strong and the French are become weak. Even in Germany, Superiority of numbers has not given the Enemy superiority of Success; which I hope will be evident and declared on our side before the Troops go into Winter Quarters. I wish the result of our good fortune may be a speedy and honourable peace; but I rather wish than expect it soon.

Some time before I receiv'd your Letter, my Brother Shute[2] put me in a way of serving my Cousin & Godson. The Duke of Newcastle at my desire, wrote to the Dean of Christ Church, whose answer to His Grace leaves me no room to doubt of your Son's success next Election.[3]

I am also to return you many thanks for your Letter of the 23d of August, and the papers enclosed therewith.[4]

All your friends here are extremly well, and send you their best compliments; General Barrington particularly, who serves at present on the Staff in Scotland, has entirely recover'd the use of his Eye. We all join in compliments to M[rs] Barnard. I am with the greatest truth & regard,

Dear Sir Your Excellency's most faithful & most obedient Servant

Barrington

His Excellency Francis Barnard Esq[r]

ALS, RC   BP, 9: 145-148.

Endorsed by FB: Lord Barrington r. Jan 17. 1761 a Jan 17. The reply to this letter is **No. 24**.

---

1. **No. 9**.

2. Shute Barrington (1734-1826), the youngest of Lord Barrington's five brothers and later his biographer, was appointed chaplain-in-ordinary to George III in 1760 and canon of Christ Church, Oxford, in 1761.

3. Frank Bernard was indeed elected to a Westminster Studentship in 1761.

4. **No. 10**.

17 | Circular from the Board of Trade

Duplicate/

Whitehall Oct[r]. 31 1760.

Sir,

Inclosed you will receive an Order from the Lords of his Majesty's most Hon[ble]. Privy Council, notifying to you the Death of Our late gracious Sovereign Lord King George of ever-blessed Memory, and directing you to proclaim the High and Mighty Prince George Prince of Wales, King of Great Britain, France and Ireland, and of all the Dominions thereunto belonging, &c. Defender of the Faith &c. We do therefore earnestly recommend to you, that you do proceed without loss of time to the Execution of these Orders, and that His Majesty be accordingly proclaimed in the most Solemn manner and most proper parts of Your Government, and you are to return to Us a speedy Account of your Proceedings herein.

Inclosed you will also find His Majesty's Warrant authorizing you to make use of the Old Seal of the Province until a new one can be prepared, together with four printed Copies of His Majesty's Proclamation, continuing all Officers in the Plantations, civil and Military, in their respective Employments, till His Majesty's Pleasure shall be further signified; which Proclamation you will take care to make publick in such manner, that All His Majesty's Subjects may be fully apprized of His Majesty's Pleasure in this respect.

Under the same Cover We likewise transmit to you an Instruction, signed by His Majesty containing His Majesty's Directions for an Alteration in the Prayers for the Royal Family, to which you will not fail to pay a due Obedience.

We are, Sir, Your most Obedient and most humble Servants,

Dunk Halifax
Andrew Stone.
WG Hamilton
W[m]. Sloper

Francis Bernard Esquire Gov[r]. of Massachusets Bay.

dupLS, RC   BP, 9: 153-156.

In the handwriting of John Pownall. Endorsed by FB: Lords of Trade d. Oct 30. 1760 r Jan 16. 1761. There are contemporaneous virgules in the left-hand margins to the first and second paragraphs marking off each of the enclosures. This circular to the North American colonial governors enclosed orders-in-council dated between 27 and 30 Oct. 1760, for which see *APC*, 4: 461-463; *JBT*, 11: 131-133. FB's reply is **No. 21**.

18 | To William Pitt

Duplicate

Boston Nov 8. 1760

S[r]

I have had the honour to receive your letter bearing date the 23[d] day of August last,[1] & immediately set about obeying the commands signified therein.

When I first arrived at this government, in the beginning of August last, having been previously informed of a trade Very detrimental to the British Empire being carried on between some parts of New England and the french settlements in Louisiana, I made it my business to enquire, whether this province was concerned in such trade; & was fully satisfied that it was not.

Nevertheless I thought it my duty to pay a greater deference to your letter than only giving my own opinion on the subject of it; and therefore I communicated it to the Council[2] & proposed that it should be referred to the consideration[3] of a committee. This has been done; & I now transmit to you the report of that committee approved by the Council.

If I apprehended that there was the least danger that this trade would be carried on from this province, I would immediately communicate your orders by circular letters to the sevral officers of the ports within my Government: But I apprehend that as things are such public notifications would answer no other purpose than to imply a charge against the province, of what I believe it quite free from.

I do not mean to answer for any other part of New England than the province of Massachusets bay: but I am informed that in those parts, where this trade has been practised, it has now entirely ceased.

I have the honour to be, with great respect, S[r] Your most obedient & most humble servant

Fra. Bernard.

The Right Honourable William Pitt Esq[r]

dupALS, RC   CO 5/19, pt.2, f 298.

Endorsed: Boston. Nov.[r] 8th: 1760. Gov.[r] Bernard. R Jan.[y] 14th. Enclosed a minute of the Massachusetts Council of 7 Nov. 1760, Council Chamber, Boston, CO 5/19, pt.2, ff 300-301. Variant text in BP, 1: 284 (AL, LbC).

1. **No. 11**.

2. On 31 Oct. 1760, in Council Executive Records, 1760-1766, CO 5/823, f 21.

3. LbC: "examination".

19 | To The Earl Of Halifax

Boston Nov. 17. 1760

My Lord

I have just heard from undoubted Authority that Gov.[r] Wentworth[1] is ^most^ dangerously ill; & thought it my duty to send your Lordship the earliest notice of it, that if his death should happen, you may not be surprised. I send this to NYork to be ready for the packet which is Very Sudden & uncertain in its ~~Motions~~ Movements.[2]

As I have no particular Occasion to call the Assembly sooner I have prorogued it to Dec 17[3] a time that will be more convenient & agreable to the Country than an earlier day would have been. No public business of consequence has been moved of late, except I may reckon the filling up the place of Chief Justice: This office became Vacant on the 10th of Sept.[r] & last thursday I appointed the Lieut Gov.[r] to it.[4]

I propose to explain my motives, to your Lordship for this proceding;[5] but must wait for another opportunity, as this letter must soon go to the Post office.

I am

Lord Halifax

AL, LbC   BP, 1: 283.

1. Benning Wentworth (1696-1770), governor of New Hampshire, 1741-66.

2. This authorial correction invites a scatological allusion to irregularities of the bowel.

3. FB had continued the General Court from 15 Aug. by successive prorogations.

4. The vacancy was created by the death of Chief Justice Stephen Sewall. FB appointed Thomas Hutchinson on 13 Nov. 1760 subject to Crown approval, which was forthcoming.

5. FB defaulted on this promise, and his motives for appointing Hutchinson have been a matter of speculation. Hutchinson later reported that "the governor declared that, if the lieutenant-governor should finally refuse the place, the other person [*James Otis Sr.*] would not be nominated. Thereupon, the lieutenant-governor was appointed. The expected opposition ensued. " *History of Massachusetts*, 3: 64. See John J. Waters and John A. Schutz, "Patterns of Colonial Politics: The Writs of Assistance Case and the Rivalry between the Otis and Hutchinson Families," *WMQ* 24 (1967): 543-567, at 558-561; Nicolson, *The 'Infamas Govener'*, 62-63.

20 | *Circular from William Pitt*

Duplicate/

Whitehall Decr. 17th. 1760

Sir,

His Majesty having nothing so much at heart, as, by the most vigorous Prosecution of the War, to reduce the Enemy to the Necessity of accepting a Peace on Terms of Glory & Advantage to His Majesty's Crown, and beneficial, in particular, to His Subjects in America; And as nothing can so effectually contribute to that Great and essential Object, as the King's being enabled to employ, as immediately as may be, such Part of the Regular Forces in North America, as may be adequate to some Great and Important Enterprize against the Enemy; I am commanded to signify to you the King's Pleasure, that, in order the better to provide for the full and entire Security of His Majesty's Dominions in North America, & particularly of the Possession of His Majesty's Conquests there, during the Absence of such Part of the regular Forces, you do forthwith use your utmost Endeavours & Influence, with the Council and Assembly of your Province, to induce them to raise, with all possible Dispatch, within your Government, Two Thirds of the Number of Men they raised for the last Campaign, & forming the same into Regiments as far as shall be found convenient, That you do direct Them to hold themselves in Readiness, and particularly as much earlier, than former Years, as may be, to march to such Place, or Places in North America, as His Majesty's Commander in Chief there shall appoint, in order to be employed there, under the Supreme Command of His Majesty's said Commander in Chief in America, in such Manner as he shall judge most conducive for the King's Service: And the better to facilitate this important Service, the King is pleased to leave it to you to issue Commissions to such Gentlemen of your Province, as you shall judge, from their Weight & Credit with the People, and their Zeal for the Publick Service, may be best disposed, and able to quicken & effectuate the speedy Levying of the greatest Number of Men, in the Disposition of which Commissions, I am persuaded you will have Nothing in View, but the Good of the King's Service, and a due Subordination of the Whole to His

Majesty's Commander in Chief: And all Officers of the Provincial Forces, as high as Colonels inclusive, are to have Rank, according to their several respective Commissions, agreeable to the Regulations, contained in his late Majesty's Warrant of the 30th. December 1757, which is renewed by His present Majesty.

The King is further pleased to furnish all the Men, so raised as above, with Arms, Ammunition, and Tents, as well as to order Provisions to be issued to the same by His Majesty's Commissaries, in the same Proportion and Manner as is done to the Rest of the King's Forces: The Whole therefore, that His Majesty expects and requires from the several Provinces is, the Levying, Cloathing, and Pay of the Men; And on these Heads also, that no Encouragement may be wanting to this great and salutary Service, the King is further most graciously pleased to permit me to acquaint you, that strong Recommendations will be made to Parliament, in their Session next Year, to grant a proper Compensation for such Expences as above, according as the active Vigour & strenuous Efforts of the respective Provinces shall justly appear to merit.

It is His Majesty's Pleasure, that you do, with particular Diligence, immediately collect, and put into the best Condition, all the Arms, issued last Campaign, which can be, anyways, rendered serviceable, or that can be found within your Government, in order that the same may be again employed for His Majesty's Service.

I am further to inform you, that similar Orders are sent, by this Conveyance, to New Hampshire, Connecticut, Rhode Island, New York, and New Jersey; The Southern Governments are also directed to raise Men in the same Manner, to be employed in such offensive Operations, as the Circumstances and Situation of the Enemy's Posts, and the State & Disposition of the Indian Nations, on that Side, may point out, and require.

It is unnecessary to add any Thing to animate your Zeal, in the Execution of His Majesty's Orders, in this important Conjuncture, which is finally to fix the future Safety & Welfare of America, and of your own Province in particular; And the King doubts not, from your known Fidelity and Attachment, that you will employ yourself with the utmost Application and Dispatch in this promising & decisive Crisis.

I am with great Truth and Regard Sir, Your most obedient humble Servant

W. Pitt

Governor of Massachusets Bay

dupLS, RC   BP, 9: 157-162.

In the handwriting of Robert Wood. Endorsed by FB: r Sec[ry] Pitt Dec 17 1760. According to **No. 35**, this letter was enclosed in Cadwallader Colden to FB, 15 Mar. 1761 (not found). FB received the triplicate first, on 21 Mar. (**No. 37**). Variant text in CO 5/214, pp. 183-186 (L, LbC).

An order-in-council of 1754 had subordinated provincial officers commissioned by the royal governors to those in the regular army holding the king's commission. Two years later, all general and field officers in the provincial forces were ranked no higher than "eldest captains" in the regular army. The 1757 warrant Pitt mentions gave provincial officers above and including the rank of colonel the same status in rank as British officers in the Regulars, although they were deemed "junior" to regular officers of the same rank. Anderson, *Crucible of War,* 214.

21 | To John Pownall

Boston Jan 11. 1761

Dear S[r].

Last night I rec[d]. a box containing dispatches for all the Governors on the Continent on the Occasion of his Majestys accession ~~to the~~ & as I am dispatching an Express to New York, I write a line to take the Chance of the Packet boat to inform you of my receipt & care thereof. We received certain advice of the death of his late Majesty & the Proclamation of his present Majesty on Saturday Dec[r]. 27th. I immediately called the Council to Consider whether I should proclaim his Majesty on this private, but undoubted intelligence (consisting of Many News papers between the death of the King & his funeral) or wait for public orders.[1] Upon this the books were searched & it appeard that every one of the three former proclamations in this Century were made in pursuance of private accounts and without waiting for public orders, and in the instance of the death of Queen Ann the Public orders, did not arrive 'till near 8 Months after her decease, the Ship that was first sent with them being lost. Also consideration was had that, tho' the Assembly was sitting, it would be necessary to suspend all business till the king was proclaimed: for it wo[d]. be absurd to use the Stile of the late King, when we knew he was dead, & improper to use that of his present Majesty before he was proclaimed. It was therefore judged proper & necessary to proceed to the proclamation. We therefore proclaimed the King on Tuesday the 30th of Dec[r]. & celebrated the obsequies of the late King according to the Custom of this Country, on thursday the first of Janry. The form of the proclamation we took from what had been used here before, and is, almost word for word the same as is ordered by the privy Council. For the rest of the Ceremonial, I refer you to printed papers, from whence you will observe that the General Court accompanied me to the Kings Chapel, an honour that the Kings Chappel never had before, & which was meant as a Compliment to the Gov[r]., & was agreed to in both houses unanimously.

I have a great deal to Write to you, & hope at the end of the Week to dispatch great part of it in a safe Vessel: this I dont much depend upon, as it is probable the packet may be sailed when this Gets to new York.

I am S[r]. &c

The Gov[r].[2] shall also hear from me by the next packet if possible. I have much to say to him.

John Pownall Esq[r].

L, LbC   BP, 1: 285-286.

In the handwriting of clerk no. 1. Enclosures not found. This letter is a reply to **No. 17**.

---

1. On the afternoon of Saturday 27 Dec., the *Race Horse*, master Samuel Partridge, arrived from London bringing news of the king's death on 25 Oct. 1760 and the accession of his grandson. The Governor's Council agreed to proclaim George III on 30 Dec., without waiting for official notification, which did not arrive until 16 Jan. 1761 (**No. 17**). Council Executive Records & Council in Assembly, Massachusetts, 1766-1769, CO 5/827, ff 29-30.

2. Thomas Pownall.

22 | *To William Bollan*

Boston Jan. 12. 1761

S[r].

I received your letters of the 25th. of Sept[r]. the first of Nov[r]. & the 3rd of Nov[r]. on the two days immediately preceding this.[1]

I am much obliged to you for your congratulation on my Arrival at this Government: the trouble which ordinarily belongs to business I Chearfully encounter; that which arises from unnecessary dissention I regret, but still submit to it; of the latter I flatter myself I shall know very little as I hope, I myself shall afford no cause for it. I am much obliged to M[r]. Wilbraham[2] for his kind remembrance of me: I set a high Value on his friendship in England, & should be sorry to be thought forgetful of it in America. I have always had it in my intentions to write to him; but, he knows, as well as any may how much the most urgent business is preferred to that mostre agreeable, but less pressing.

I return you my thanks for so readily engaging for the Expence of my patent; The Gentleman who gives me leave to trouble him with my Affairs in England is Levet Blackborne Esq[r]. in Great Marlborough street. He has lately vested some money of mine in the consolidated Annuities;[3] part of which will be readily drawn out for this purpose: M[r]. Child & C[o].[4] were concerned in it. I shall write to M[r]. Blackborne, but I cant do it before the Vessel, that is to Carry this, sails. In the mean time the business itself, or at least this letter will be a sufficient introduction to him.

My Case in regard to fees, is singularly hard: my former Government was worth about £800 a year and this seems to be not above £1100: & I shall have paid treble fees within 3 Years, to the amount of upwards of £1200.[5] I suppose there is no redress for this; if there is I should be glad to know how to obtain it.

I apprehend there may be some things unsettled in regard to my former Commission, relating to the dues from the wardrobe & Jewell Office, M[r]. Secretary Pownal, who was so kind as to take care of those Affairs can let you know whether there is anything of that kind left undone; if there is, one Solicitation will do for both. Gov[r]. Boone informed me, that his friends, upon his succeeding me, compounded with the wardrobe & Jewell Office for £130. I should be glad to have this done for me; for as these Expences come on so fast, I shall want Money more than plate or Damask. If I can get money Also for these dues on my former commission, they both will go far toward the present Expence. If any difficulty should attend this Composition, M[r]. Pownall can easily engage Lord Barrington to intervene in my favor, as there is so fresh a precedent for my request,

The Present Kings Picture I have promised to the Council Chamber, where I have already hung up his grandfather & great grandfather, [6] But I would not recommend hast in this business; for the more time is given to the Painter, the better we may expect the Picture will be,

I shall write to M[r]. Pownal by this Vessel what shall be further necessary to be added to this Subject & must desire you to consult him.[7] I have taken care of the dispatches to the other Governments & sent them all away except three which must wait here for shipping.

I am S[r]. Your most &c

W. Bollan Esq[r].[8]

L, LbC   BP, 1: 286-288.

In the handwriting of clerk no. 1 with minor emendations by FB.

On taking up the governorship of New Jersey, FB was obliged to pay the Jewel Office and Wardrobe £212 for communion vestments, table, plate and altar cloth, and bibles and common prayer books with their silk and gold trimmings, and decoration for the chapel furniture; on moving to Massachusetts he spent a further £138 on these items. (The Jewel Office and Wardrobe were originally of the lower part of the royal household, and by the eighteenth century were administered by the Lord Chamberlain.) Lord Chamberlain's Department: Accounts and Miscellanea, 1483-1901, LC 9, PRO: Bill Books for the Great

Wardrobe, 10 October 1756-10 October 1759, Comptroller of the Accounts of the Treasurer of the Chamber Bill Books, 1729-1782, LC 9/17; Quarterly Accounts, Michaelmas 1755-25 October 1760, Great Wardrobe Records, Series I and II, 1483-1800, LC 9/19; Accounts and Receipt Book, October 1728-March 1767, Jewell Office Delivery Books, Accounts Etc., 1660-1796, LC 9/48.

---

1. Not found.

2. Randle or Randall Wilbraham (1694-1770), of Rode Hall, Cheshire, was a friend of FB, a counsel to Oxford University and a bencher of Lincoln's Inn. He had been a MP since 1740, and represented Newton, 1754-64, in the process acquiring a reputation as an independent-minded Tory. Namier and Brooke, *The House of Commons, 1754-1790*, 3: 637.

3. The securities of the British government, deriving from various funds and annuities including the national debt, had been combined into a single stock in 1751. Investors like FB received interest at 3 percent. D. C. Coleman, *The Economy of England, 1450-1750* (London etc., 1977), 194.

4. A private bank of London, the archives of which are held by the Royal Bank of Scotland; there is no documentation pertaining to FB.

5. Sterling.

6. On 7 Nov. 1760, FB received a formal vote of thanks from the Council for presenting a portrait of King George II "in a rich Gilt Frame." It was to be hung in the Council Chamber alongside a portrait of the late king, George I. Council Executive Records, 1760-1766, CO 5/823, f 24. The provenance of these portraits is unknown, and they are not listed in the Smithsonian American Art Museum, Inventory of American Paintings Executed before 1914 (http://siris-artinventories.si.edu/).

7. **No. 23**.

8. William Bollan (1705-82), Massachusetts province agent, 1743-62.

23 | To John Pownall

Boston Jan 13. 1761

Dr. S.

Having just finished a letter to you on public business, I set about another on subjects relating to myself.

Soon after I got here I rec.d a letter from you inclosing a letter to Lord Chamberlain for me to sign:[1] I accordingly returned it signed & inclosed it in a packet directed to your Office & sent it by the brig Bristol Packet which sailed from hence for Bristol at the end of August last & of whose safe arrival we have now advice. Comparing the time of this with the late great Event, I am sensible that if you waited for the return of this letter you could not have settled the business at the Jewell Office & Wardrobe before the death of the King. if this Event should lay any difficulties in compleating this, I shall be sorry that this business could not be done in the first instance; as this repetition of fees will require every article of advantage to be preserved. But I cant suppose any difficulties will be created by this delay. In a former letter wrote from Amboy,[2] I desired to have my Plate in particular pieces & to have a suit of Velvet from the Wardrobe; but since I have been acquainted with M[r] Boones composition, I find it more adviseable to get £130 for both, especially at this time, when by these fresh expences I am more in want of money than fine things

By the same ship that brought the orders I rec[d]. a letter from M[r]. Bollan[3] informing me that he had rec[d]. full & proper Assurances that my Commission would be renewed, & that not knowing who my agent was he had engaged for the expence thereof. I therefore suppose he has proceeded in solisciting this business & have therefore wrote to him & referred him to Levet Blackborne for Money, who is better prepared for this time than he was the last, having lately Vested some money in the funds on my account, from which he can draw out what will be wanted. I desired M[r]. Bollan to advise with you concerning what remained undone upon my last Commission, & take off your hands, which I suppose will be fully Employed for some time, any trouble that you should choose to transfer to him. I also acquainted him with the late Composition, which M[r]. Boones friends made for him of £130 for Plate & furniture & desired him to make the same for me adding that if the same was made on my former Commission, both together would go a great way to pay the Charge of this, I concluded, that if any difficulties should attend this Composition, you would easily engage Lord Barrington to intervene in my favor as there was so fresh a precedent for my request. As to the Kings picture due upon my former commission, I dont intend to relinquish it, as, tho it is too large for a private house, it makes a very acceptable present for a public room. I had rather exchange it for another picture of the present King: but if any difficulty attends it I will waive them both & content myself with one picture only for both Commissions.

And now give me leave to state to you how particularly hard my case has been Circumstanced in regard to fees. I have now by me a list of the fees of my first Commission amounting to £400 within a trifle. This will have been paid by me three times within 3 years within which time all the income of my Govern[mts]. will have been from New Jersey 2 years at £800 a year from this the Current Year at about £1100. I beg you would take this into your Consideration & advise me whether upon account of the particular circumstances of the Case, (which perhaps never happened before) I could not by application, to the Lords of the treasurey, or whom else obtain a grant of some sum, by way of Alleviation, I intend to write to Lord Barrington on this subject but cannot do it by this ship: I could wish you would find an opertunity to mention this to him; and if it should be thought proper to make an Application, I must desire you would engage Lord Halifax's favor therein. I have mentioned this in my letter to M[r]. Bollan but am desirous not to trouble him in this business, if you can undertake it yourself; but if you should Chuse to have him for an Assistant, you will engage him accordingly.

As I have many things to write to you, I shall keep the different Subjects confined to different letters & must here end this.

I am S[r]. Your most &c &c

Secrety Pownall

A P.S[4] containing thanks to Lord H, L[d] Chamberlains letter
Fire at Faneuill hall.[5]
To the duplicate a P.S. informing that I had wrote to L[d] B & proposed making use of My Services at Easton in solicitation[6]

L, LbC   BP, 1: 289-291.

In the handwriting of clerk no. 1, with minor scribal emendations. Enclosure not found.

1. Dated 13 Jun. 1760, BP, 9: 111-114. The correspondence with the lord chamberlain has not been found.
2. Not found.
3. Not found.
4. The addressee and postscript are in FB's hand.
5. The original building was erected in 1742 with a bequest from merchant Peter Faneuil, but the interior was badly damaged by fire on 13 Jan. 1761. Faneuil Hall was quickly rebuilt with provincial funds and lottery monies, and reopened in Mar. 1763. See **No. 109**.
6. **No. 24**.

24 | *To Lord Barrington*

Boston January 17. 1761

My Lord

I am favoured with yours of the 15th of Oct.[1] which like every other adds much to my Obligations to Your Lordship. I beg through your hands to return my thanks to M[r]. Shute Barrington for his concern for my son. I have had that business so much at heart, especially as I had rec[d]. advice that there would be great intrest made on that Occasion, that I have been unnecessarily troublesome to your Lordship, having then rec[d]. Advice that a Ship which Carried a letter to your Lordship, was taken & not knowing then that my second Venture had escaped.[2]

I have received advice from M[r]. Bollan the Agent for this Province that he has had full & proper Assurance that my Commission will be renewed.[3] As I am undoubtedly indebted to your Lordship for this repeated favor I must beg leave to return your Lordship my Particular thanks for my being continued in His Majestys service. And at the same time I must beg leave to state my present case, as it is very singular, without any imputation to the gratefull sense I have of the unmerited honour that has been conferred upon me.

It is no uncommon thing for a man's purse to be impaired by perferment coming too fast upon him. I remember to have read of a Bishop's being undone by too frequent translations.— My case is as uncommon as I suppose that of Any one whatsoever: I shall have had three Commissions within the space of 3 years; the two latter will I suppose be within the space of one year. The fees of a Commission are not less than £400: I have now before me an account of the fees of my first Commission to the amount of £390, tho it does not include all. So that by this time I suppose I shall have P^d. £1200 in fees, & I shall have received from New Jersey 2 years at £800, £1600 & 1 year from Boston including the whole of the Current Year to the End of May next £1100, total £2700, dèd £1200 remains 1500 Thus my public account would stand, according to which I should have £500 a year for my 3 years service But when I apply my private Account to this I find it more against me. I expended in fitting myself out at least £1600, including my fees which may be thus divided: fees £400, Expences of Voyage £300 Expences of Journeys, carriage & living in London & Portsmouth £300 Cloaths Equipage & other trapings of Government £600 So that adding the three last articles to the former one of fees I have Expended in the whole £2400 in qualifying myself for these Governments. There are two articles that may be added to my receipt; the Gratuities received at my accession which were at New Jersey £300 at Boston £225.[4] These are give[n] towards the Expence of removing & settling; & considering that against this be sett the extraordinary expence of two settlings & one removal, they will go far to Answer both, But supposing the least of the sums will Answer these Extraordinary expences, my Account will stand thus

Cr.	The Expences of fitting out &c.	1200	Dr.	the 3 years income	2700
	The fees of 3 Commissions	1200		The Jersey Gratuity_	3[00]
		1400			3000
		[2400]			

After this I need not say that after 3 years service I have not got a step forward towards retrieving my first Expence: & this is not owing to any miscalculation mismanagement or disappointment but only to the uncommon accident of having so many Commissions to sue out in so short a time.

Pardon me my Good Lord for being so explicit on this subject: It is only to apologise for a request (as I have too often occasion to do) which I have to make that your Lordship would be so good to advise M^r. Pownal to whom I have wrote on this Subject[5] whether it may not be proper to petition the Lords of the treasury for a grant on this uncommon occasion to what may be urged in my favor on this Subject, may be added my Service at the Indian treaty at Easton, which produced immediately the surrender of Pittsburg & soon after the entire reconcilation of the 6 Nations, I have learnt to set a value upon this service, from the great Compliments I have rec^d. on the Occasion; but never expected a particular reward nor should have mentioned it in that light otherwise than a make weight to another request.[6] If their Lordships of the treasury will be pleased to grant me £800 (being the fees of two Commissions) they will amply reward me if they will grant me £500 or 400 I shall be quite satisfied & thankfull. If this Applicasion should be approved of I have desired M^r. Pownall to communicate this request to my Lord Halifax; but I did not care to write to him my self, till I was better satisfied about the reasonableness & practability of my request.

I am

Lord Barrington

L, LbC   BP, 1: 292-295.

In the handwriting of clerk no. 1 with minor scribal emendations.

Nothing came of FB's request for reimbursement, as Barrington reported in a letter of 6 Jun. 1761. "I have made enquiries whether any allowance could be made by the Government here in consideration of the expence you have been at, and particularly of the enormous fees paid on the passing of your Patents. I have talk'd to the duke of Newcastle on this Subject, but I find nothing can be obtain'd; whatever is paid on such occasions, must come out of the Civil List, a fund considerably lessened by the King's moderation when it was settled, and his bounty since: besides great apprehensions of the danger of making a precedent. I should think your best way would be, to get your case properly represented to the Assembly." BP, 9: 209-212.

---

1. **No. 16**.

2. For the first letter see **No. 10**. The second is FB to Barrington, Boston, 29 Sept. 1760, BP, 1: 282-283.

3. William Bollan to FB, 1 or 3 Nov. 1760, not found.

4. Sterling.

5. **No. 23**.

6. When governor of New Jersey, FB participated in a conference at Easton, Pa., 8 to 26 Oct. 1758, arranged ostensibly to solemnize existing treaty agreements between the colonists of Pennsylvania and New Jersey and the Iroquois Confederacy, the Delawares, and other Native Americans. From a New Jersey perspective, the Easton conference succeeded in pacifying frontier tribes, thus enabling the colony to devote more resources to the British offensives against French Canada in 1759. Nicolson, *The 'Infamas Govener'*, 44.

25 | To [John Pownall]

Boston Jan. 19. 1761

D^r. S^r.

I steal a minute in sealing up my letters to let you know, I shall have a Voluminous business to write to you upon as soon as I can find time. M^r. Barrons[1] has plaid the Devil in this town, He has put himself at the head of a combination of Merchants all raised by him with the Assistance of two or three others to demolish the Court of Admiralty & the other Customhouse officers, especially one who has been active in making Seizures.[2] I was not all naturally concerned in this business; but because I endeavoured to prevent M^r. Barrons raising this flame & afterwards expressed my Disapprobation of his proceedings, he & his emissaries have turned the fury of his party against me. They are now endeavouring to make a Breach between the Assembly & me, by setting them to demand of me to Assent to very unwarrantable proceedings. But I shall adhere to my duty & act steadily. I will acquaint L. H.[3] either to him or you or both with a state of this Afair before it comes to the public offices in form.[4] I hear the Surveyor[5] will send M^r. Barrons over to Answer for himself but am not certain of such his intention. there never existed such mischeivous folly in all my acquaintance of mankind as in this Gentleman. Y^{rs}.

L, LbC   BP, 1: 296.

In the handwriting of clerk no. 1.

---

1. Benjamin Barons had been a London merchant in the Portuguese fruit trade and secretary to Admiral Sir Charles Hardy (1717-80), governor of New York, 1755-57. He was appointed collector of Customs at Boston in 1759 and was twice suspended from office on corruption charges before being dismissed from the service in Dec. 1761. In 1765, Barons was appointed postmaster-general of the southern district of North America, and kept the general post office at Charlestown, South Carolina. Tyler, *Smugglers & Patriots*, 25-63.

2. Charles Paxton (1704-88), surveyor and searcher of customs at Boston, 1760-67.

3. Lord Halifax.

4. See letters to Pownall **Nos. 29** and **38**.

5. Thomas Lechmere (d.1766), the scion of a distinguished English family of judges, was surveyor general of Customs for the Northern District, until he was replaced by John Temple c.Jun. 1761. FB to Lechmere, Province House, 2 Jun. 1761, BP, 2: 113.

26 | To Thomas Boone

Boston Feb. 2. 1761

S^r.

I was favoured with yours of Decr. 27th which I communicated to the Council[1] who have desired me to give you their thanks for your endeavours to Serve the Sufferers at Boston. I Also Communicated it to the Select men &c. who also desire me to make their thanks Acceptable to you. I am also to signify, that they suppose that the Negative did not arise from a want of Charitable sentiments, but from a doubt of the power of Representatives to appropriate the public money to works of Charity. This was the Case in Connecticut, who therefore did the business very handsomely by way of breif or Church Collection. The Collections in Maryland & Virginia were also made in the same manner,[2] they therefore hope, that as soon as the recess of Winter will Afford a proper oppertunity, you will be so good as to recommend the Collection to be made thro't the Country in such manner as you shall think best.

My regard for the Province of NJersey makes me very desirous that it should not be singular on such an Occasion. The loss fell Cheifly on those that were least able to bear it; & all the Collections that have been returned, which are near all that are Expected, amount but to 5 in the Pound.

I am S^r. &c &c

Govr Boone[3]

L, LbC   BP, 2: 97-98.

In the handwriting of clerk no. 1, except as noted.

A fire on 20 Mar. 1760 ravaged the centre of Boston: the four hundred buildings that were destroyed affected one-fifth of householders. Thomas Hutchinson reported that FB estimated property damage to be £100,000 sterling, twice as much as some observers were suggesting, but less than one-third of what the town's newspapers were claiming. Gary B. Nash, *The Urban Crucible: Social Change, Political Consciousness, and the Origins of the American Revolution* (Cambridge, Mass., 1979), 251; Hutchinson, *History of Massachusetts*, 3: 58.

---

1. The letter has not been found and there is no mention of it in the Council's Executive Records, CO 5/823.

2. See FB to Horatio Sharpe, Boston, 22 Sept. 1760, William H. Brown, ed., *Correspondence of Governor Horatio Sharpe, 1753-1771,* 4 vols.; *Maryland Archives,* 9 (Baltimore, 1888-1911), 3: 574; FB to Francis Fauquier, Boston, 7 Feb. 1761, BP, 2: 98; FB to Fauquier, Boston, [*Mar.*] 1761, BP, 2: 100-101.

3. This line in FB's hand.

27 | To Jeffery Amherst

Boston Feb 7 1761

Sʳ

I am favoured with yours of the seventeenth of January & am glad that the advices I sent you were so opportune:[1] I can assure you that the pleasure I had in sending them could not be Very short of yours upon the receipt of them.

I made the Assembly acquainted with what you communicated to me by your former letter[2] that the assistance of these Colonies in the prosecution of the War would be expected for next year. As no Destination is as yet proposed, I could not ask for a previous provision: but I have made a short prorogation, which, if I hear of nothing to the contrary before Monday next, I shall continue to the 4ᵗʰ day of March, by which time I may hope to be fully instructed concerning the King's commands

I have been earnestly solicited by one Simon Butler,[3] to use my intrest with you in behalf of his Son Simon Butler, who being in the provincial Service last year was inlisted, on his return to Albany, by a Serjeant in Capt Crookshanks independant company.[4] The Father, who is a considerable ~~farmer~~ ^landholder^ in this province, is Very uneasy on this occasion, & begs that he may [be] released, he paying all charges & as much more as shall be wanted: he is ready to pay 10 guineas & would go to 20, if required or further. I suppose this Money will procure the King a better man, & therefore am desirous that, if it does not too much break thro' rules, he may be released. If you'll please to order the officer to Signify to me what sum will be required, it will be sent to NYork directly.

I am desired by the Assembly to make application to you for the fourpences billeting money allowed to the provincials on thier return home:[5] these were not paid to them on their leaving the camp, by reason of the officer charged therewith declaring his intention, to set off the hospital account, which could not be settled by those who were to receive the billeting money; and therefore they received nothing. I have ordered the account of the billeting money to be made out; if you will order that of the hospital to be ready & appoint some person here to join with a Commis[sioner] of mine to settle them, It will easily be done.[6]

We have here 10 prisoners of War that were sent here from Quebec last fall: they cost us more than the groats, which I suppose, is all you can allow for them. They will wait your orders, & an Account of the time they will have been here will be ready when wanted.

The Detachment of Royalls[7] which put in here & have behaved Very well during their stay here, sailed for Halifax last Tuesday. They have had in general a fair Wind; at present it is Very fair for them but blows rather to hard.

I am, with great Truth & Regard, Sʳ Your most obedient & most humble Servant

Fra. Bernard

His Excellency Mʳ General Amherst

P.S.

Having recommended to the Assembly to establish Truck-houses for the Indians, they have enabled me to set up two in the North East parts of the province.[8] In regard to the Westerly parts We could not determine, on any thing, not knowing what may be depended upon, out of our own province. I am therefore to desire you to let me know whether I may be at liberty to establish a provincial Truck-house at Crown point with leave to have subordinate stores at Montreal or any other places within reach especially at the times of Fairs or other public meetings. It is proposed to carry on this trade by Truck-masters on the account of the province, who will be put under all possible regulations that may oblige them to deal honestly & fairly. If I have proper encouragement, I will endeavour to settle such a Trading House, as shall be of great public use, whether We keep Canada or not.

ALS, RC   WO 34/26, ff 80-81.

Contains minor emendations. Endorsed: Governor Bernard 7ᵗʰ Febʳʸ. Rᵈ 10ᵗʰ. Dᵗᵒ __ Ansᵈ. 22ᵈ. d. Enclosed a copy of the address of the Massachusetts Council to FB, 22 Dec. 1760, WO 34/26, ff 82-83. The reply to this letter is **No. 31**.

1. Amherst to FB, New York, 17 Jan. 1761, BP, 9: 163-166.

2. Amherst to FB, New York, 1 Jan. 1761, not found. This was brought down from the Council on 20 Jan. *JHRM*, 37, pt.2: 198.

3. Possibly Simon Butler (d.1795), of Leominster, Mass., a deacon.

4. Charles Cruikshanks, a British army officer, who, from 16 Apr. 1757, was a captain in one of four independent companies of foot stationed at New York.

5. 24 Dec. 1760, *JHRM*, 37 pt.1: 121-124.

6. A total of 1,320 Massachusetts men were mustered at Fort No. 4 after the campaign of 1760, and were due £132 sterling for billeting. Amherst to FB, New York, 16 Nov. 1761, WO 34/27, p. 233.

7. 60th (Royal American) Regiment of Foot.

8. FB first approached the House on 13 Jan. 1761 with a proposal to establish truck-houses at Fort Pownall, on the Penobscot River, and at Fort Halifax, at the confluence of the Kennebec and Sebasticook Rivers; the House agreed and the Council concurred on 26 Jan. *JHRM*, 37, pt.2: 178-179, 214.

28 | *Account of the Coast of Labrador*

La Terre de Labrador, or the land for cultivation, if settled and improved by civilizing the natives, would afford a great fund for trade, especially that part of it called the Eskimeaux shore, between Cape Charles in the straits of Belle Isle, in lat. 51: and Cape Chudley, in lat. 60 North, bounding East on the Atlantic ocean. There is but one noted writer of the French nation who mentions the Eskimeaux Indians: The derivation of Eskimeaux must depend entirely on him, as it is a French termination.[1] What nation of Indians he intends by his descriptions of a pale red complexion, or where situated, it is not easy to conceive; he surely don't mean those on the east main of Labrador, as it evidently will appear by the following observations that no foreigner had ever been among them, till Anno 1729; at least since Capt. Gibbons, in Anno 1614, who, had he seen any of the natives, it is probable, would have mentioned it;[2] and therefore I suppose the French writer must mean those who live on or between the lakes Atchoua, and Atchikou, who have been known to trade with the French in Canada, and perhaps at St. James' Bay factory.[3]

The Eskimeaux coast is very easy of access early in the year, and not liable to the many difficulties, either on the coast of Newfoundland or Cape Breton.

This coast is very full of islands, many of them very large, capable of great improvements, as they have more or less fine harbours, abounding in fish and seals, water and land fowl, good land, covered with woods, in which are great numbers of fur beasts of the best kind. Along the coast are many excellent harbours, very safe from storms; in some are islands with sufficient depths of water for the largest ships to ride between, full of cod fish, and rivers with plenty of salmon, trout, and other fish. The climate and air is extremely wholesome; being often refreshed with thunder and lightning, though not so frequently as to the southward of Belle Isle straits: fresh water is found every where on the coast and islands in great plenty.

What follows shall be a plain narration of facts, as I received them from several persons who have been on the Eskimeaux coast, with now and then a digression, which I hope may be pertinent.

Captain Henry Atkins sailed from Boston in the ship called the Whale, on a voyage to Davis's straits, in 1729.[4] On his return to Boston, he went on shore in several places southward of Davis's inlet, in lat. 56; but could not discover any where the least sign of any persons but the natives, having been there before him. In lat 53: 40: or thereabouts, being hazy weather, he could not be very exact, he descried twelve canoes with as many Indians, who had come from the main, bound to an island not far from his ship. The Indians came near and viewed his ship, and then paddled ashore to the island as fast as possible. Capt. Atkins followed them, and came to anchor that night, where he lay till the next day in the afternoon. He went on shore with several of his men, with small arms, cutlasses, and some small articles, to trade with the Indians, who made signs to him to come round a point of land, but he chose to go ashore on a point of land that made one side of a fine harbour. The Indians stood a little distance from the point, and by their actions shewed signs of fear and amazement. He being resolved to speak with them, advanced toward them without any thing in his hands, the Indians took courage and suffered him to come near them, he shewed them a file, knife, and sundry other little articles, to exchange for fur, whalebone, &c.: they did not apprehend his design, which obliged him to send on board his ship for a slab of whalebone, on sight of which they made a strange noise; it being near sunset, they pointed to the sun going down, and then lay down with their faces to the ground, covering their eyes with their hands: In a few minutes they arose again, pointing to the sun, and then turned themselves to the east, by which Capt. Atkins understood they would come to him again the next morning. The Captain then went ashore, and carried with him some trifles he thought most agreeable to the Indians, who returned to the same place, and brought a quantity of whalebone, at least fourteen feet long, and gave him in exchange for about 10s. sterling value, as much bone as produced him £120 sterling at Boston.

The Indians were chiefly dressed in beaver clothing of the finest fur, and some in seal skins. He could not distinguish their sex by their dress, but one of his seamen, being desirous to know, approached one of them, who, opening her beaver, discovered her sex, which pleased the Indians greatly. Capt. Atkins ordered one of his men to strip himself, which caused the Indians to hollow as loud as possible; while they were thus engaged one of the Indians snatched up a cutlass, upon which they all run off; Capt. Atkins resolved not to lose it and followed them, and making signs, they halted. He applied to one of them, whom the others payed most respect to, and got it returned; he then fired one of his guns pointed to the ground, which terrified them extremely, which their hollowing plainly discovered I am the more particular in this account from his own mouth, as I think it plainly indicates that the Indians on this coast and islands had never any trade or commerce with any civilized people from Europe or America of course not with the French from Canada, or the Hudson's bay factories.[5] The Indians signified to Capt. Atkins, that if he would go over to the main, he should have more whalebone, but he did not choose to trust them. He observed their beaver coats were made of many pieces sewed together, being the best patches in the skin, which shews plainly they set light by their beaver skins, and this undoubtedly for want of trade.

Capt. Atkins observed they were dexterous, and active in the management of their canoes or boats, which were made of bark and whalebone, strongly sewed together, covered with seal skin, payed over with a dark sort of gum. These Indians

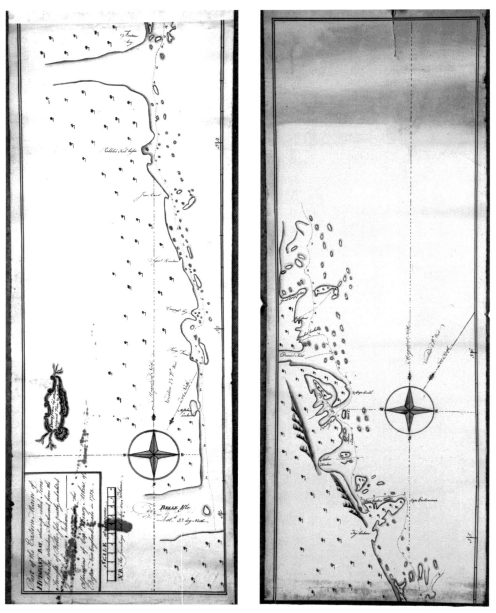

Map of the Coast of Labrador. Drawn by J. Leach from an original plan by Capt. Henry Atkins, 1764, in D/SB MP/8. The dotted line shows Atkins's journey along the coast. Courtesy of the Centre for Buckinghamshire Studies. Photograph by Peter Hoare.

were well made, and strong, very fat and full of blood, owing to their living on raw whale fat, and drinking the blubber or oil. Their limbs well proportioned, their complexion a dark red, their hair black, short, and straight, having no beard nor any hair but on their heads. Their behaviour very lively and cheerful; their language guttural and dissonant; their arms were bows and arrows, some of bone and some of wood; their arrows feathered and barbed; they sling their darts through a piece of ivory, made square and fastened to the palms of their hands. Capt. Atkins conceives them to be a very cunning, subtile people, who could easily apprehend his meaning, when he made signs to them, but took no notice of his speaking to them. As Capt. Atkins coasted that main, he found the country full of woods, alder, yew, birch, and witch-hazel, a light fine wood for shipbuilding; also fine large pines for ship masts, of a much finer grain than in New England, and of course, tougher and more durable, though of a slower growth; and no question but naval stores may be produced here. The two inlets called Fitch and Davis, it is not known how far they run up the country; Fitch's is a fair inlet, bold shore, and deep water, and great improvement might be made upon it, there being many low grounds, and good grass land: Capt. Atkins sailed up Davis's inlet, about 25 leagues. This coast is early very clear of ice, though at sea a good distance off there are vast islands of ice that come from Hudson's and Davis's straits, which are frequently carried as far as the banks of Newfoundland, by the strong current that sets out from those straits southward.

Capt. Atkins made his last voyage on this coast. Sailed the beginning of June, 1758, arrived at Mistaken Harbour, which he called so, having put in there July 1st, following, in a foggy day, and went northward, (with fine weather, very hot, with some thunder and lightning) to lat. 57, searching for the Indians to trade with. Saw two large canoes which run from him: Despairing of meeting any more there, he returned southward, and went on shore in lat. 56: 40: at the Grand Camp place, which he called so from great signs of Indian tents that had been fixed there; here he also saw two Indian men, one woman, and three children, who run from him; he pursued and took them and carried them on board his vessel, treated them kindly, and gave them some small presents, and then let them go. They were well pleased with Capt. Atkins: they called whalebone Shou-coe, a woman Aboc-chu, oil, Out-chot. When he sent his seamen to fetch one of their canoes that had drifted from the vessel's side, they said Touch-ma-noc.

I shall once for all take notice that the several harbours and places named by him, was from any thing remarkable he found in them, as Gull Sound and Harbour, from the prodigious number of gulls he saw there, also after the name of some of his particular friends.

The entrance of Hancock's inlet, in lat. 55: 50: a very fair inlet; very little tide sets in or out; from fifteen to twenty fathom water going in; five hundred sail of ships may ride conveniently in this harbour, secure from any weather. On the east side, the harbour is a natural quay or wharf, composed of large square stones, some of them of prodigious bulk. This quay is near three miles long; runs out into the harbour in some places sixty, in others two hundred feet broad; eight fathom water at the head at high water; so that ships might lay at the quay afloat, and save their cables. The harbour abounds in cod fish very large, that a considerable number of ships might load there, without going outside, which may be cured on the shore and at the quay, except in very high tides; while some are employed in the cod fishery, others might be catching salmon, seals, &c. in the harbours so called. Capt. Atkins and his people waded in Salmon river in two feet water, and catched some salmon in their hands, as many as they had salt to cure, one of which measured four feet ten inches long. How far up this river reached, he could not tell, but believes a good way in land, (though shallow in some places), to be capable of breeding such vast shoals of salmon, salmon trout, and other small fish that passed by them while fishing there; also several acres of flats in Salmon river, filled with clams, muscles, and other shell fish, among many other conveniences necessary to a good harbour, and some falls of water suitable to erect saw mills, grist mills, &c.; all kinds of sea fowl are very plenty and easily taken; a good settlement might be made on Fort island in this harbour, easily secured from any attacks of Indians.

On Cape Cod there is a vast plenty of wood; some pines he saw there sufficient to make masts for ships of six or seven hundred tons, and he doubts not but a little way in land they are much larger, and witch hazel, and other woods fit for ship building; the soil in this harbour is capable of great improvements, there being rich low grounds. The woods abound in partridges, pheasants, and other game, as well as bears, deer, beavers, otters, black foxes, hares, minks, martins, sables, and other beasts of rich fur. The beavers are of the black kind, of the finest fur in this country; he took particular notice of some small birds of passage, among them some robins, well known to love a pleasant climate; and on the shore side great plenty of geese, ducks, teal, brants, curlews, plovers, and sand birds; and from all Capt. Atkins and his people could observe, they are all well persuaded that the winters at this harbour, (he now called Pownal harbour in Hancock's inlet[6]), are not so uncomfortable as at Newfoundland and Louisbourgh, though so much further northward. In September 29th, 1758, he left this delightful inlet in fine weather, bound home to Boston, searching the coast and trading, put into Fortune bay, and left it October 16th; some sleet and rain and a little cold; had five days passage to St. Peter's bay in Newfoundland, where the weather had been so cold and tempestuous for fourteen days before, they could not catch fish, which Capt. Atkins might have done at Fortune bay the whole time.

I can hear of no vessel having wintered on that coast, except a snow which Capt. Prebble[7] found at Fortune bay, when sent on that coast by Capt. Atkins in

1753. Capt. Prebble traded with the natives, about seventy men, women and children; got from them about 3000 lb. of bone for a trifling value. Capt. Prebble carried with him a young Frenchman, in hopes that some Indians might be found who understood the French language, but they could not find one who took more notice of it than of English; a plain proof these people had never left their own country to trade with the French; for it is very observable that the Indians who have been used to trade with the French, speak that tongue well. Capts. Atkins, Prebble and others agree, that the current sets southward; in the several harbours they went into they found the tides flowed about seven feet.

The river St. Lawrence being now opened to us, a passage from Boston may be made early to the Eskimeaux coast, through the straits of Belle Isle. I might here add sundry observations made by Capt. Atkins and others, respecting the advantages that might accrue to the whalemen and others, on this coast; and of their conjectures of the richness of this country in mines and minerals; but I, at present, content myself with a bare relation of facts, sincerely wishing the foregoing observations might be of any advantage to future navigators.

Boston, Feb. 16th, 1761.

PC   Collections of the Massachusetts Historical Society, 1st ser., 1 (1792), 233-237.

When this document was first published no information was provided about its location other than in the preface: "The following account of the Coast of Labrador was found among some papers of the late Sir Francis Bernard, Governour of the Province of Massachusetts Bay, at the time it was written." The original text has not been found in any of Massachusetts's repositories or in the PRO.

Capt. Atkins's voyages are not discussed in the classic Lewis Amadeus Anspach, *A History of the Island of Newfoundland* (London, 1819) or any recent study, as far as can be ascertained, but are mentioned in W. Gillies Ross, "The Annual Catch of Greenland (Bowhead) Whales in Waters North of Canada, 1719-1915: A Preliminary Compilation," *Arctic* 32 (1979): 91-121. This "Account" provides a glimpse of Labrador before it became a British possession in 1763, whereupon an influx of colonial American and British vessels sparked conflict with the Inuit. FB composed the "Account" after speaking with "several persons" who had visited the Labrador coast: Atkins himself (FB notes that one anecdote came "from his own mouth"), Jedidiah Preble, and others who had accompanied Atkins, and probably Atkins's business partner Thomas Goldthwait (1718-79), FB's secretary at war. Nothing is known about Atkins's voyages other than what can be deduced from this document. He was certainly an interpid mariner and able navigator who headed for the Davis Straits in search of baleen, as many Massachusetts fishermen did in this period. He landed on the Labrador coast in 1729, probably when he was just a sailor, and returned as captain of his own vessels in 1753 and 1758; he likely made other voyages there also. The names of the bays and inlets, if chosen by Atkins, might indicate patronage by Thomas Hancock or Thomas Pownall. His journey along the coast in 1758 can be followed in a map that FB had prepared to accompany the "Account": Map of the Coast of Labrador, drawn by the Massachusetts cartographer John Leach from an original plan by Capt. Henry Atkins, 1764, in Spencer Bernard Papers MP/8 (see illustration p. 78). FB may have intended to write a scholarly paper, but, after sending Barrington a précis of the "Account" (**No. 83**) he did not persevere with the project.

---

1. Augustin Le Gardeur de Courtemanche (1663-1717), French-Canadian soldier and commandant of the coast of Labrador. The journal of his exploration of Labrador in 1705 was published, although a copy has not been found.

2. William Gibbons, arctic explorer and leader of a voyage of 1614 sponsored by the Company of the Merchants Discoverers of the North-West Passage. Sailing in the *Discovery*, a vessel once owned by the explorer Henry Hudson, Gibbons was forced to turn back from an ice-bound Hudson's Bay and spend ten weeks on the Labrador coast at c.58 ½° latitude, probably in Saglek Bay. *Dictionary of Canadian Biography Online* (http://www.biographi.ca, accessed 28 Feb. 2007).

3. FB is likely referring to Ashuanipi Lake, to the south of Labrador City, and Lake Nichicun to the east of the city.

4. This is the earliest recorded date for a colonial American whaling fishing vessel in the Davis Strait, although the Europeans had been regular visitors since 1719. Ross, "Annual Catch of Greenland (Bowhead) Whales." Henry Atkins's dates are unknown, though he would have been a young man on the 1729 voyage. Vital records record one Henry Atkins marrying Mary Snelling in Boston in 1745. Atkins joined Thomas Goldthwait and other proprietors of Point Shirley in leasing from the town Deer Island in Boston Harbor, between 1753 and 1758, for the purposes of establishing a fishing station. The lease was conditional on the partners being able to "send out and employ" twenty fishing vessels per year. Perhaps Atkins was aiming to harvest whaling grounds in Hudson's Bay, but the disruption to commercial fishing occasioned by the war undermined the project. Finally, Henry Atkins was assessed in the Boston tax list of 1771, for £13 6. 8d, which places him in the bottom third of taxpayers. *Early Vital Records of Suffolk Co., MA*, CD-ROM (Wheat Ridge, Conn., 1996-2002): *Boston, Suffolk County*, vol. 28, city document no. 150: 236 and *History of Chelsea, Suffolk County*, vol. 1: 606; Record Commissioners of the City of Boston, *Reports of the Record Commissioners of the City of Boston*, 38 vols. (Boston, 1886), 16: 15-16; Bettye Hobbs Pruitt, ed., *The Massachusetts Tax Evaluation List of 1771* (Boston, 1978), 6.

5. If this is true, then the Inuit whom Atkins encountered in this part of southern Labrador may have traded with the French through Inuit middlemen. Inuit-French trade was well established by 1750, and often involved the Inuit making seasonal visits to French posts. Historical ethnologists, however, have begun to doubt that the Inuit presence in this area was impermanent. See Marian P. Stopp, "Reconsidering Inuit presence in southern Labrador," *Études Inuit Studies* 26 (2002), (http://www.erudit.org/revue/edudinuit/2002/v26/n2/007646ar.html, accessed 28 Feb. 2007).

6. Thus in document.

7. Jedidiah Preble (1707-84), a resident of and representative for Falmouth, 1753-54 and 1766-71; he was brigadier general of provincial forces during the French and Indian War.

29 | To [John Pownall]

Boston feb. 21 1761

Dear S[r].

I wrote to you a Short letter dated January 19.[1] by the Tavistock mastship from New hampshire, wherein I acquainted you that M[r]. Barrons was playing the Devil in this Town, having formed a Confederacy to demolish the Admiralty Customhouse & all Authority immediately proceeding from the King. I was in hope before this time to have sent particular accounts of these tran[s]actions: but the extraordinary business M[r]. Barrons had cut for me has employed all time that was not Engaged by my ordinary employments. As I imagine an explanation of this Extraordinary Affair will be impatiently wanted, & I suppose M[r]. Barrons has already sent partial Accounts of it. I shall endeavour to get this in time for the Packet at New York, (for there is no Ship going from this Port that I choose to trust to) to inform you how this Affair stands. The Embarrasm[t]. His Confederates brought me under with the Assembly, I got rid of with credit & honour: The Votes of the house Sufficiently explain that matter: Since which the tumult has quite subsided in regard to me. Soon after the prorogation of the Assembly which was the last day of January, M[r]. Paxton the Surveyor of the Customs delivered unto the Surveyor General a Charge against M[r]. Barrons consisting of 20 Articles. the surveyor General by letter[2] desired that I & the Judge of the Admiralty[3] would assist him in making an enquiry into M[r]. Barrons Conduct therein. To this I agreed on condition the judge of the Admiralty would accede thereto: & the Judge of the Admiralty accorded thereto

We have opened our Conferences & have had two Meetings & are to continue the same untill the whole enquiry is gone thro' which will take up a good deal of time. this cannot be avoided if we would, as we are desirous to do, render the proceedings unexceptionable. Nor ought we to grudge the trouble (tho for my Part I can very ill spare the time) for it is not a Question of dispute between the two Officers, but of a contention between the Kings Authority & Law and the Subjects & Objects of them; Either this confederacy of M[r]. Barrons must be broke or the whole body of the Laws of trade must be given up, I would not anticipate particulars of this enquiry until, the whole is finished; therefore I will only repeat my Assurance that I will give Lord Halifax a full account of this business, before it comes in form before your board or any other.

I have a Great deal to write to L[d]. Halifax upon this & other subjects; & therefore greatly regret my time being taken up by a business that I ought not to have been troubled with. All that I have to say for my self is, that I work as hard as I can & have but one head & one P[r]. of hands. As fast as they will serve I will get thro' all the business I have before me

I long desired to write fully to the Govr.; but waited for a safe Conveyance to which I might trust my thoughts. But as your last letter[4] & some letters from him to others, quite ascertain his departure to Carolina, I must now wait till I hear of his Arrival there, I wrote to you by the Packet Boat sailed from NYork Jan 19th. by the Lucretia Snow Folgier[5] Master Sailed from Boston Jan 16. by the Tavistock mast-ship sailed from Portsmouth Jan 22.__ I am obliged to conclude this Letter that it may be ready when called for: & desiring that our Compliments may be made acceptable to your self & Lady[6] I am S^r. &c &c

You will present my respects to L^d. Halifax & inform him of such part of the foregoing as you shall think necessary.

L, LbC   BP, 1: 296-298.

In the handwriting of clerk no. 1.

---

1. **No. 25**.

2. Not found.

3. Chambers Russell (1713-66) was a vice admiralty judge from 1746 until his death, a justice of the Superior Court from 1752, and a county judge. He was an experienced legislator: he represented several towns (Charlestown, 1744-46; Concord, 1740, 1750-52; and Lincoln, intermittently between 1754 and 1765) and was a member of the Governor's Council, 1759-60.

4. 18 Oct. 1760, BP, 9: 149-152.

5. Timothy Folger (1732-1814), a sea captain and whaler of Nantucket, and cousin to Benjamin Franklin for whom he charted the Gulf Stream.

6. Mary Pownall (d.1807).

30 | *From Randle Wilbraham*

D^r S^r/

You see I commence in a Style of ffreedom & not with, a May it please Y^r Excellency__ however I heartily wish you Joy of Y^r Removal to Boston__ & wish that you may have Health to enjoy Y^r Promotion__ ^I hope it will be more agreable to you as Boston sounds like Lincolnshire.^ This is to be forward^d. to you by the hands of Mr Bollan I rejoice at his being replaced[1] in his Nest[2] & Agency for y^t part of New Engld over wch you preside. I beleive him to be a very honest—very Able & very Diligent Man__ I hope you have Comfort in Y^r Correspondence with him__.

A Great Change in Governm^t has lately happened by the Change of our Prince__ So far as we yet see of him his Heart seems to be incorrupt__ And ^he^

aims Well__ God grant he may use his own Judgm[t]__ Curse on him that perverts it to wrong Views & Designs__. What Alterations are to be made Heaven knows, I know not__ A new parliam[t] w[ch] will be chose in Ap[l]. will pduce something new__ God Grant it may be for the best__ Our war in Germany lyes heavy on us but I hope we may still Extricate our forces with Honor__

Nothing has happened of late in our Sphere of y[e] Law very Extraordinary youl see by y[e] public papers that L[d] Henley[3] is made L[d] Chan[r] your ffriend M[r] Justice Noel[4] I think declines much__ Serj[t] Hewett[5] Stands Candidate for Coventry__ & is likely to Succeed__ Old Viner[6] is to be deserted in Y[r] Co. & therefore he declines__ All the Lds ^have^ joyned agst him__. I beleive I shall come in again__ My son[7] stands for Chester if S[r] R[d] Grosvenor[8] is ennobled__ & I beleive will have no opposition__.

To show that I have not quite forgot my old friend I have (tho: you are a prore[9] & in New Engld) ventured to send you a bitt of Old English Old Cheese May it not fall into the hands of a french Privateer but may you datermine many a Meal with a Relish of it is the most Sincere Wish of

D[r] S[r] Y[rs] most sincerely

R Wilbraham
Lincolns Inn Feb. 21 1761.

My Compl[ts]. I send Y[r] Lady.

ALS, RC   BP, 9: 167-168.

Endorsed by FB: M[r] Wilbraham r June 7. 1761 a July 28 1761.
    Wilbraham is briefing FB on the some of the candidates who were to contest the general election of Apr. 1761.

---

1. Meaning restored.

2. Meaning niche.

3. Robert Henley (c.1708-72), first earl of Northington and lord chancellor, 16 Jan. 1761-66.

4. William Noel (1695-1762), lawyer, MP for Stamford, 1722-47, and judge of Common Pleas 1757-62.

5. James Hewitt (1709-1789), lawyer, magistrate, mayor, MP for Coventry, 1761-66; a noted advocate of the repeal of the Stamp Act; later created Baron then Viscount Lifford.

6. Robert Vyner (c.1685-1777), MP for Lincolnshire, 1724-61. He represented Tory interests but withdrew in Jan. from the upcoming election.

7. George Wilbraham (1741-1813) was not elected to Parliament until 1789 as the member for Bodmin, and was succeeded by his brother in the 1790 general election.

8. Sir Richard Grosvenor (1731-1802), MP for Chester, 1755-61; created Baron Grosvenor in 1761, and later first earl.

9. Meaning poet. *OED*. This is probably an allusion to [Francis Bernard], *Antonii Alsopi Ódarum Libri Duo* (London, 1752).

31 | From Jeffery Amherst

New York 22ᵈ. February 1761.__

Sir,

I have before me Your two favors of the 7ᵗʰ. & 8ᵗʰ. Insᵗ. the latter Accompanying a Copy of the Council's address to You at the opening of the late Sessions; the not sending of which sooner, give me leave to Assure You, requires not the least apology; as I am very Confident that business of much greater moment, must have been the occasion of it:[1] however as the honorable mention made of me in that address Deserves the most warm Return on my part, I beg, that, if You do not think it too late, You will be my kind Interpreter, and permit me to make Use of Your Channel, to Convey to them my most gratefull Acknowledgements, with Assurances that I shall ever Esteem myself happy in the opportunities of Contributing to the well being & prosperity of His Majesty's faithfull American Subjects, and that it Shall be my Constant Study never to neglect any.__

I Come now, Sir, to Your first Letter, Acquainting me with Your having Communicated to the Assembly the notification I had given You, that the Assistance of the Colonies in the prosecution of the War would be Expected for this Year; but that, as no Destination was as yet proposed, You could not ask for a previous provision and that therefore You had made a short prorogation; for which I am much obliged to You; And as I am in daily Expectation of the King's orders, for the Ensueing operations, and hope to receive them soon enough to be able to Impart them to You before the 4ᵗʰ. of march, I need not at present Say anything more on that subject than, if You should not receive any Application from me in Consequence thereof before, or by that time, that You will be so good as to Continue those Short prorogations, untill You do, in order that this business may be sett about & settled without delay, which the then advanced Season will not admit of.

Altho' I do not permit any men to be Discharged at this time, Yet as You seem to Interest Yourself so strongly in behalf of Mʳ. Butler, I will order Capᵗ. Cruikshanks to Enlist, a good able bodied man in the room of Mʳ. Butler's Son, and to let me know what that Recruit Stands him in, that I may Inform You thereof, and You Enquire of the father, whether he Chuses to be at the Expence, in which Case his Son shall be immediately Discharged without any other reward.__

As I have not Yet heard from Lieut. Small,[2] who was the officer appointed to pay the Provincial Troops their fourpences in lieu of Provisions, I must Deferr Settling that Accompt untill I do; and as I Expect that will be eare long, I shall say nothing further on the subject at present.__

I was ignorant of Any Prisoners of War, having been sent to Your Province from Quebec; if they are belonging to the Regular Troops, I shall Desire they may be sent here in order to go to France, & their Acco.ᵗ Shall be settled; but if they are Canadians, or Sailors they Should be released & permitted to seek their own livelyhood as no Charge can be brought in Accompt for them: there are Numbers in the like Case here, & the Provinces adjoining, the Inhabitants of whom are glad to have them, nay even secret them, to prevent their returning home.__

I am glad to hear the Detachment of the Royal behaved so well during their stay among You; am glad they are sailed; And hope they have reached their Destination in Safety.__

I Cannot Sufficiently Commend Your, and the Assembly's wise Views for the Establishing a free and open Trade with the Indians, and approve much of the two Truck Houses they have Enabled You to set up in the North East parts of Your Province; As to that You propose Establishing at Crown point, I must postpone advising You thereto, untill I receive my Dispatches from England, when I shall best know whether it will be advisable or not.__

I am, with great Regard, Sir, Your most Obedient Humble Servant.

Jeff: Amherst

His Excellency Governor Bernard

LS, RC   BP, 9: 169-172.
Endorsed by FB: Genl Amherst Feb 22 1761. Variant text in WO 34/27, pp. 210-211 (L, LbC).

---

1. **No. 27**; FB to Amherst, Boston, 8 Feb. 1761, WO 34/26, f 84, in which he apologized for "a failure in a Ceremonial" after neglecting to enclose the Council's address of 28 January 1761 (for which see CO 5/822, ff 159-160).

2. John Small (1726-96), a British army officer, was a lieutenant in the 42nd Highlanders (the Black Watch) and promoted to captain in 1762 during the Martinique expedition.

32 | To John Pownall

Boston Mar 2. 1761

D.ʳ S.ʳ

I am obliged to break into the business that I am engaged in for your board[1] to represent to you an affair, that is thought to require immediate dispatch & will take up but little of my time.

You know with what reluctance my predecessors have bore with the Naval Office having been in the last instance granted from England, which had ever before been in the Governors gift.[2] This is not much to be wondered at, when it is considered, that this Office was the principal part of the Governors ^little^ patronage & worth all the rest. For my own part I with my 10 children want as much of these little helps as any of my predecessors have ever done: but I had determined when there should be an occasion to make a decent remonstrance on the Subject, & after that, acquiesce in what should be orderd, in good humour.

But the death of the late King has brought forward this business sooner than was expected. M[r] Pemberton[3] thinking it necessary to renew his commission, has been desirous to have the Governors good will in his future proceedings. This produced a mutual explanation, which ended in M[r] Pembertons making the proposals mentioned in the enclosed Memorial, which I readily accepted: and We are now to endeavour to get our scheme put in execution. I hope it will appear to be a fair one; M[r] Pemberton proposing to get a colleague to assist him when he shall begin to want one; & I only desiring that my son may be provided with an employment for which he is have a payment. If any thing should happen to prevent my Son entering upon this business at the time proposed he shall give up the office: but in such case I must own that I shall hope to be allowed to substitute my second son John who is but 16 months younger in the place of the elder. M[r] Pemberton is a hearty hale man between 60 & 70, that may well ~~expect~~ promise himself above 10 years more & may reasonably expect 20.

The kind & disintrested regard which you have allways exprest of me & the good effects of it which I now feel, induce me readily to trouble you upon this occasion to lay the enclosed Memorial before my Lord Halifax, & enforce it with such Arguments as your judgement & your friendship together shall dictate. I have made it as short as I can consistently with its being explicit. I shall give my Lord Halifax no further trouble upon this occasion than to inform him, that I have transmitted to you this Memorial to be laid before him at a proper time & apologise for it. I write also to Lord Barrington upon this subject.[4] M[r] Pemberton writes to M[r] Stone, whom he has allways had leave to trouble since he received his last appointment. M[r] Pemberton declares appointing a Sollicitor for this business, being encouraged by me to hope you will undertake that trouble; of which he depends upon your giving him leave to express his gratitude

I hope by next week to finish my dispatches relating to the troublesome affair M[r] Barrons has engaged me in. If it was all ready now, I should not care to put it on board the Vessel that is to carry this. I have not yet heard of the arrival of the packet boat &c. I am

P.S.

To obviate any apparent inconsistency in the sevral accounts of our agreement, It may be proper to add that the proposal to join my Son in the commission came from me; that the terms on which he should be admitted came from Mr Pemberton: That both proposals being readily agreed to, there were Very few words used.

J Pownall Esq~r~

AL, LbC   BP, 1: 299-301.

The enclosed memorial to the earl of Halifax has not been found.

1. The inquiry into Benjamin Barons's conduct at the Boston Customhouse, for which see **No. 29**.

2. Naval officers were appointed by governors in the first instance. However, since 1697, appointees were required to give security to the Board of Customs Commissioners in London or the surveyor general of the Customs for the Northern District, thus in the process traducing the governor's influence over them. Labaree, *Royal Instructions*, 2: 760-761.

3. Benjamin Pemberton (1697-1782) had been naval officer since 1734 and had no thoughts of retiring. Walter Kendall Watkins, "The Pemberton Family," *New England Historical and Genealogical Register* 44 (1890), 396.

4. **No. 34**.

33 | To The Earl Of Halifax

Boston Mar 3. 1761

My Lord

Mr Pemberton the Naval officer here, intending to solicit a renewal of his commission, applied to me for my advice & assistance. This produced a conversation which ended in his proposing that my eldest son (now about going from Westminster College to Christ Church in Oxford) should be joined with him in the commission & in about 4 or 5 years hence be admitted to a share of the business & profits. This I readily agreed to but it wholly depends upon your Lordship to put it in execution. For this purpose I have sent to Mr Pownall a memorial to be laid before your Lordship at the most suitable time.[1] I would be understood not to pretend to any right but thro' your Lordships favor which, as it has been allready so far extended toward me I make my whole dependance. I am

Earl of Halifax

AL, LbC   BP, 1: 301.

1. See **No. 32**.

34 | To Lord Barrington

Boston Mar 3. 1761

My Lord

As I am well assured that all my honest endeavours to provide for my children will have your Lordships approbation, & assistance too, when it shall be advisable, I need make no Apology for the enclosed. It is the Copy of a memorial which I have sent to Mr Pownall to be laid before my Lord Halifax: at the same time I wrote to my Lord to desire his favorable acceptance of it. And I now am to desire your Lordships kind interposition on behalf of my request, which is sufficiently explained in the memorial.

I think, I have before informed your Lordship, that I considered the opportunities I should have of placing out my Sons among the chief advantages arising from my removal to Boston. This Government the worst supported, considering its importance & trouble, of any in the Kings gift, in its certain income does not exceed New Jersey by more than £300,[1] which is not much more than the difference of the expence of living at one & the other. The opportunities of placing out my Sons now I survey them, I find but few: the Naval Office is much the best & is an handsome provision for a person that executes it himself.

Your Lordship will recollect that I've before intimated my desire to have my eldest son settled in business in England: and I do not now mean to determine against it. But it must be observed that this appointment is to be partly reversionary: and We may have 5 years before We shall be obliged to determine. If in that time, He should have an opportunity of engaging in better business, he may quit this office to my second son, who will then be of full age & well qualified for the office. The latter I am now going to put to a Merchant in this town, having given him as much school learning as the Way of live [*life*] he is designed for will require[2]

As my two eldest Sons are so much further advanced in life than the rest of my children, It is much my desire to see them well settled in life. For then I shall have provided natural guardians for the rest of my children, in case I should be called away. For this reason I shall in general, prefer such means for their advancement as are capable of the quickest Maturity. The subject of my present request will fully answer that purpose for one of them. I am

Lord Barrington.

AL, LbC   BP, 1: 302-303.

Enclosures not found.

---

1. Sterling.

2. John Bernard (26 Jan. 1745-25 Aug. 1809) was educated at Lincoln Grammar School but did not attend university, and came to Boston in 1761 or 1762.

35 | *From Jeffery Amherst*

New York. 15th. March 1761.__

Sir,

On the 1st. of January last I signified to You[1] that by the Dispatches I had received the preceding day from His Majesty's Principal Secretary of State, it was the King's firm Resolution, steadily to Support his Allies, and to prosecute the War with the utmost Vigor, and that in Consequence of this Resolution, I made no doubt but You should soon receive His Majesty's Requisition for such a number of men from Your Province, as should be thought requisite to answer the proposed End of procuring a good & lasting peace.

This Requisition was, in fact, Dispatched from the Secretary of State's Office on the 17th. of December last,[2] and I Conclude, sent on board the Leicester packet, which sailed from Falmouth on the 29th. of said month, but being unfortunately taken in her passage the Triplicates of those Dispatches are but this moment arrived in His Majesty's Sloop Tamer, and M^r. Presid^t. Colden to whom they have been delivered, is to forward them without delay.__

It remains therefore with me, after this unexpected and unlucky Detainder,[3] most Earnestly to Entreat You to make up for this loss of time in immediately upon receipt thereof Convening Your Assembly, & laying before them the aforesaid Letter of the Secretary of State, and that You will forthwith Use Your Utmost Endeavors, & Influence with the Council & Assembly to induce them to raise with all possible Dispatch within Your Government Two Thirds of the Number of men they raised for the last Campaign.

The King's Reasons for His Majesty's Requisition of this further aid from His faithfull American subjects, are too obvious & too Clearly pointed out by the aforesaid Circular Letter of His Secretary of state, to need any additional Enforcement and Yet I cannot refrain from repeating a Recommendation which ought, & I doubt not, will have with it all the weight and Impression, which from its prudence & sagacity it has a Just right to Expect, since it proceeds from that Spirited View of Reducing the Enemy to the necessity of accepting a peace, on terms of Glory & Advantage to His Majesty's Crown, & beneficial in particular to His subjects in America, to which great, & Essential Object, nothing can certainly so Effectually

Contribute, as the King's being Enabled to Employ, as immediately as may be, such part of the Regular Forces in N°. America as may be adequate to some great, and Important Enterprize against the Enemy.__

And as such are the King's Resolutions, and that His Majesty the better to provide for the full and Entire security of his Dominions in N°. America and particularly of the possession of his Conquests there during the absence of such part of the Regular Forces to be Employed on the aforesaid Enterprize has Desired that the several Provinces and Colonies of this Continent should forthwith raise two thirds of the number of men they raised the last Campaign. I cannot, from the past Zeal I have Experienced upon all former occasions on the part of Your Province but firmly rely and trust that it will upon this Exert itself to its Utmost, and that I shall have the satisfaction to report to His Majesty how Chearfully it has Acquiesced with his Recommendation.__

Nothing therefore now remains for me to add than that You will Observe by the aforesaid Circular Letter of the secretary of state; that as a further Encouragement to such Exertion on the part of the Provinces His Majesty has Ordered, as heretofore that the Provincial Forces should be Victualled in the Same manner, and in the same proportions as the Regulars, & that they should be supplied with Arms & Tents at the Expence of the Crown; moreover that Strong Recommendations will be made to Parliam^t in their session next Year, to grant a Compensation to the Provinces, for the Expences they may be at on this occasion, according as their respective Vigor and strenous Efforts shall Justly appear to merit.— I must therefore, as this aid of Troops will be immediately wanted, most seriously recommend it to You, to obtain them from the Assembly without loss of time, and to hold them in readiness to march wheresoever I may have Occasion for them, upon the first notice You shall receive from me for that purpose.—

I have it also in Command from His Majesty to Enjoin You to Collect, And Cause to be put into proper Condition, all the Serviceable Arms that can be found within Your Province; for every one of which that shall be brought to the field, & shall not return by reason of being spoiled, or, lost in actual Service, I shall pay the Usual allowance of Twenty five shillings per firelock.—

As it is very Essential to the Services I have in Command from the King, that I should be as Early as possible Informed of the Resolves of Your Assembly on this head, and of the time that the Troops will be ready, I beg that as soon as You are acquainted therewith, You will signify the same to me by Express, that I may regulate myself accordingly.__ I am, with great regard,

Sir, Your most Obedient Humble Servant.

Jeff: Amherst

His Excellency Governor Bernard.

LS, RC   BP, 9: 175-178.

Endorsed by FB: Genl Amherst r Mar 21. 1761 a Mar 23. The reply to this letter is WO 34/26, f 86.

On Pitt's requisition see **No. 38**.

---

1. Not found.

2. **No. 20**.

3. A variant of "detainer," a legal term (*n.* & *a.*) meaning holding a person in custody or a writ to that effect. *OED*.

36 | From Jeffery Amherst

New York, 29th. March 1761.__

Sir,

It is with the utmost satisfaction that I learn from Your favor of the 23ᵈ. Instant, that You flatter Yourself there will be no great Difficulty in obtaining *4000* men and that You will use Your best Endeavors to get them well fitted out;[1] from Your known Zeal, & that of the Assembly for promoting the good of His Majesty's service, I am Confident I shall soon have the pleasure to hear that You have Succeeded in the first, & that the latter will meet no obstacles; meanwhile I must offer You my most sincere acknowledgements for Your Intended proposal that these men may be raised for one Year to be Computed from the 1ˢᵗ. of may; this is a most Convincing proof how much You have the good of the service at heart; Experience has shewn what Inconveniences attend a more confined limitation and I have frequently Endeavored to get this Evil removed but without success; I leave You therefore to Judge, how agreable this proposal is to me; & how much I wish that You may Carry it: As a greater Encouragement thereto You may Assure the Assembly from me, that altho' their men are raised for such a Certain time, Yet if their Services can be dispensed with, prior to its Expiration they shall not on that accompt be detained one day longer than needs must; this I should hope will Ensure Your Success of so wise & Commendable a measure, which I cannot sufficiently thank You for.__

I am, with great Regard.__ Sir, Your most Obedient Humble Servant

Jeff: Amherst.

His Excellency Governor Bernard.

LS, RC   BP, 9: 179-180.

Endorsed by clerk no. 1: Genl Amherst March 29 1761. Variant text in WO 34/27, p. 214
(L, LbC).

---

1. FB: "I flatter myself that there will be no great difficulty in obtaining 4000 Men; & I shall use my
   best endeavours to get them well fitted out." Boston, 23 Mar. 1761, WO 34/26, f 86. FB's misplaced
   optimism can partly account for Amherst's anger on receiving news about conditions attached by the
   House (**Nos. 38** and **41**).

37 | *To John Pownall*

Boston March 30th. 1761

Dear S[r].

I am just going to send to New York a set of Papers[1] relating to a Commotion
M[r]. Barrons has made in this Town & Province, for the perusal of the Lords of your
Board; if my Lord Halifax shall think it proper, before a set of the same, which the
Surveyor General will send to the Comonrs of the Customs, shall Arrive. These are
not Quite complete but want little more than the form of conclusion: but I was not
willing to lose the benefit of the Tamar Man of war, which is to sail from NYork
next week. you must excuse me ^not^ writing to their Lordships by this conveyance, but I will endeavour not to fail the next. I have wrote a long letter to my Lord
Halifax[2] on the subject of these papers: which together with the papers, will be
Sufficient to give a full account of this Affair. These papers are too Voluminous,
but I could not help it; tho' I prevented their being more so. I had intended to have
methodised & abbridged them, that they might be more easily perused & readily
referr'd to; but I have not had time to do it.

From the experience I have had of the Violence of M[r]. Barrons resentment
here, I must expect that he will ^endeavour to^ misrepresent me in England. And
yet I cannot Charge my memory with any one thing that can afford an oppertunity
for so doing. As to what has passed between him & me I can truly say with Lear,

> I am a Man
> More sinn'd against, than sinning,[3]

If any such thing should be offered, I will depend upon you to give me an oppertunity to refute it.

there is due to your office an answer to the Complaint of the Mashbe'a Indians:
This was reported to the great council last sessions, but was not certified in form
proper to be sent to you. This will be done this week: It may be sufficient to say
there is no ground for the complaint.[4] There are also due to you Books of the laws:

they are but just new printed: a set will be sent by a ship which sails from hence next week.

The taking of Leicester packet boat & the delay of the Harriot packet boat, which is but just arrived in great distress, has very much kept back the public business. I received M[r]. Pitts letter[5] (the triplicate first) not till the 21st. ins[t].: I got the Assembly together in a few days; they have voted 3000 men for 15 Months & tho they have not heretofore been used to cloath their troops, they have agreed to do it now.[6] The number is about 600 less than M[r]. Pitt required which was two thirds of the former Year's Number But the expence of the province will be greater in providing these men than that of any other year. And if Gen[l]. Amherst should want a few more, I believe I can get them upon proper Assurance.

I am Dear S[r]. Your most faithful &

John Pownall Esq[r]

L, LbC BP, 1: 305-306.

In the handwriting of clerk no. 1 with scribal emendations.

---

1. These "papers" have not been found, and may not have been forwarded to Alexander Colden (1716-74), postmaster at New York, until 11 May. FB to Pownall, Castle William, 12 May 1761, BP, 1: 316-317.

2. Not found.

3. William Shakespeare, Lear, in *King Lear*, 3.2.59-60.

4. On 8 Jan., the House and Council established a joint committee to consider the petition of the Mashpee Indians that protested encroachments on their land in Barnstable County and infringements of their fishing rights on the Mashpee River. The complaints were not upheld. *JHRM*, 37, pt.2: 165, 225-226, 322-323. See **No. 45**.

5. **No. 20**.

6. See **No. 38**.

38 | To Jeffery Amherst

Boston Ap 4. 1761

S[r],

I wrote to you last Monday, to inform you that the Assembly had voted 3,000 Men; but as It was subject to further consideration, I could not depend upon the effects of that Vote, till I had seen the further proceedings upon it.[1] And it is but this day that the Resolutions for raising the Men have passed both the Houses. There was a party formed for lowering the Number as much as possible, which, tho' too insignificant to carry their point by open reasoning or voting, yet could not be prevented interposing difficulties tending to delay & intended to embarras. These were chiefly created by infusing groundless suspicions & fears, concerning the destination of the Men, & their being detained beyond the time for which they have been voted. To quiet these, my friends, at my instance proposed that a Message should be sent to me concerning those points; my answer to which quieted the scruples of those that meant well.[2] I enclose a copy of it to you, & hope I have not promist any thing but what will be quite agreable to you. And I hope you will ~~allow~~ ^authorize^ me to use your name in a more positive manner, not only for confirmation of what I have promist, but also for facilitating the raising the levies, which I fear will not be carried on successfully, without some public assurances concerning the limitation of the Service both as to place & time.

I believe I could have got more men, if I had made a point of it: but It was by no means advisable to press it. For as the utmost Number I could have required as the proportion mentioned in Mr Pitts letter[3] would have been but 600 more, (& even that has been disputed) It would not have been proper for that addition, to have run the risk of occasioning a dimunition:[4] especially as the raising the Number now granted will employ the whole time between this & the meeting of the new Assembly at the End of May. And then, as the Nature of the Service will be better known, perhaps It will not be difficult to get an additional Corps, if the public exigency should appear to require it.

In point of time they have exceeded my utmost demands: I proposed the 1st of May 1762 as the least time but recommended the 1st of June; and they have Voted the first of July 1762. I promised that the Men should not be sent south-west of the River Delaware; they have stipulated that they shall not be employed South of Albany; which are bounds Very convenient to the Service, as it includes all Canada up to the Lake Ontario & even that Lake itself if necessary. These two points are made a proviso in the Resolution, in this form "to be put under the Command of Genl Amherst, upon his giving assurance that they shall not be employed Southward of Albany & be discharged on the 1st day of July 1762, or, if a peace takes place, immediately after such peace".[5] A compleat Uniform is made part of the Bounty, which is the same as usual, being in the whole £6 15s. sterling. And at my desire, the Cloaths are not to be delivered, till they arrive at their station, in order that they may be obliged to carry another suit with them. The other Articles relate to the provincial Œconomy. Upon the whole, I must needs say, that I think that the Business is well concluded; and I doubt not but you will think so too, especially when It is considered that this appointment, if carried to its length of time, will be as expensive a one as Any that has been made in former years.

You will be pleased, in your own time, to acquaint me with the destinations that I may order the rendezvous accordingly. If Any are to be sent away in transports, the Castle Barracks will hold 1000 or upon occasion 1500 at a time. Whilst I have been writing this letter your favour of the 29th of March came to hand.[6] I hope tho' I have not come up to the Numbers I first proposed, my whole proceeding will have your approbation. I am, with great regard,

S[r] Your most obedient humble Servant,

Fra. Bernard

His Excellency Maj[r] General Amherst

P.S.

I must add that the Resolution passed the Council unanimously upon the first reading

ALS, RC   WO 34/26, ff 88-89.

Contains minor emendations. Enclosed a copy of FB's message to the House of Representatives, 2 Apr. 1762, in *JHRM*, 37, pt.2: 284-285.

---

1. FB to Amherst, Boston, 30 Mar. 1761, WO 34/26, f 87.

2. *Acts and Resolves*, 16: 721-723.

3. FB presented Pitt's requisition (**No. 20**), together with a letter from Amherst dated 21 Mar. 1761 (not found), to the Council and the House of Representatives on 25 Mar. *JHRM,* 37, pt.2: 250-252.

4. Thus in manuscript.

5. The proviso was to prevent Amherst sending the Provincials to the West Indies where troop mortality rates were inordinately high.

6. **No. 36**.

39 | *To William Pitt*

Boston Ap. 6. 1761

S[r]

I had the honor to receive your letter of the 17th of Dec[r] (the triplicate) on the 21st of March.[1] I had, in expectation of his Majesty's Commands, continued the Assembly by short prorogations, so that I got them together on the 25th of March. I enforced his Majesty's orders in general by a Speech, & for particulars by a Message. In the latter I argued, that the Nature of the Service & the delay of it by the

Kings orders arriving so late made it impossible for them to expect that the Men they should raise could be discharged before Winter; & therefore it would be necessary to enlist them for at least a year. This was a new point never before gained in any of the provinces, at least not in this; but it seemed to me so necessary to the Service that I gave more attention to the time than the Numbers. However I succeeded well in both: The Assembly voted 3,000 Men (very few hundreds short of the largest Number that could be reckoned as their proportion) for *fifteen* months & fully cloathed & accoutred.[2]

It is generally supposed that this province gives the lead to its neighbours: if so there could not be a better precedent than that of carrying the Service of the Men into the next summer, which I hope, with the blessing of God, will be extensive enough for the present War. General Amherst, to whom I communicated my intention, of urging this point, expresses his great satisfaction at my proposal to engage the Men to the first of May 1762: that I have gained two Months more, namely, to the 1st of July[3]

It is with great pleasure that I am able to assure you that the distinguished Loyalty & public spirit of this people have received no abatement: of which it will be sufficient proof to observe that the appointments now made for the Kings Service, notwithstanding the Danger is so happily removed from their neighbourhood, is in itself as expensive, as that of any other year whatsoever; since tho' the Numbers are less, the time of the Service is more than doubled.

I have the honor to be, with great respect, Sr Your most obedient & most humble Servant

Fra Bernard.

Right Honble William Pitt Esqr

ALS, RC   CO 5/20, ff 109-110.

Endorsed: Boston. April 6th: 1761. Govr. Bernard. R May 16th.

---

1. **No. 20**.

2. For these proceedings see *JHRM*, 37, pt.2: 253-254, 293-295; **No. 38**.

3. Amherst to FB, New York, 5 Apr. 1761, BP, 9: 181-182.

40 | To John Pownall

Boston Ap. 6. 1761

D[r] S[r]

The Ship Benjamin & Samuel, Hills Comm[r] being just now sailing from hence to London,[1] I will take hold of this opportunity to inform you what letters I have sent for you since the beginning of this year

(Account of letters)[2]

Having given you an Account of letters I have sent you (for the safe arrival of which I have reason to fear, having already since I came to Boston lost 3 packets of letters by different ships) I shall add a short account of the public proceedings.

On the 21st. of March I rec[d]. the triplicate of M[r]. Pitts letter[3] & I got the Assembly together on the 25th, and made a requisition of men. As the occasion of raising the men was new & the service they were destined to not clearly known, it gave room for 2 or 3 discontented People to raise difficulties; which had no worse effect than to create a delay of a few days & to give me some trouble in removing the prejudices they had inculcated; on the other hand it has served to show the stability of the Government, the friends of which had a Majority of 2 to 1 on the most trying Question.[4] They have granted 3,000 men to be full cloathed & to serve for 15 Months, if the war lasts so long. Considering the time for which these men are to serve, It is as expensive an appointm[t]. as that of any former Years & fully answers the Credit this province has before obtained: it will also in the great extention of the time, be of great service as a precedent to the other provinces.

I shall send by this ship a set of Laws, as also the Acts passed last sessions:[5] Every ship from hence to London shall carry a set, till you have your number. I also send you some sermons on the Kings Death: one of them is the most extraordinary one that ever appeared here, having been preached before the General Court in a Church of England by a minister of that Church.[6] This is an uncommon instance of the moderation of the present principles of this province, & the more so, as there is but one member of the Church of England in the Council[7] & not above 3 in the House of Representatives. It was meant as a Compliment to me, but was what I could never have expected: I shall also, enclose a Copy of the memorial concerning the Navil Office, which, if the Ships in which the letters &c concerning that business are sent should fail, may enable you to guess at the meaning & intent of those letters.

I am D[r]. S[r]. Your most faithful &c

I much want to hear of the Governor that I may know how to write to him: I can't expect that this will find him in England

The cover to Lord Halifax contains only the two sermons[8]

Secry Pownall[9]

L, LbC   BP, 1: 306-307.

In the handwriting of clerk no. 1, except as noted. Enclosed copies of two sermons on the death of King George II, one of which was Henry Caner, *Joyfulness and consideration; or The duties of prosperity and adversity A sermon preached at King's-Chapel, in Boston, before His Excellency Francis Bernard, Esq; captain-general and governor in chief, the Honourable His Majesty's Council and House of Representatives, of the province of the Massachusetts-Bay, in New-England, January 1, 1761. Upon occasion of the death of our late most gracious Sovereign King George the Second* (Boston, 1761). The other is likely to have been Samuel Cooper, *A sermon upon occasion of the death of our late Sovereign, George the Second Preach'd before His Excellency Francis Bernard, Esq; captain-general and governor in chief, the Honourable His Majesty's Council, and House of Representatives, of the province of the Massachusetts-Bay in New-England, January 1. 1761. At the appointment of the governor and Council* (Boston, 1761).

---

1. The *Benjamin and Samuel*, master Stephen Hills, was owned by Benjamin Hallowell and left Boston on 6 Apr. CO 5/851, f 69.

2. This line and the preceding paragraph are in FB's hand. The "Account" is missing.

3. **No. 20**.

4. For these proceedings see *JHRM*, 37, pt.2: 253-254, 293-295.

5. See *Acts and Resolves*, 4: 436.

6. The Rev. Henry Caner (1700-93), rector of King's Chapel.

7. John Erving Sr. (1693-1786).

8. Not found.

9. This line in FB's hand.

41 | From Jeffery Amherst

New York, 9th. April 1761.

Sir,

I am this day favored with Your Letter of the 4th. Inst^t.;[1] I had flattered myself it would bring me a Confirmation of my most Sanguine hopes that the Assembly of the Massachusetts Bay would have been no ways deficient in His Majesty's Requisition, but on the contrary would have prided themselves in Setting a worthy precedent of the most strict Compliance with the King's Expectations; Instead thereof, I find they have not only Voted short of their Numbers, but that there were even Parties formed to diminish those that had been proposed; The difficulties these Endeavored to raise, sufficiently Evince that they were actuated by no other principles than those of mere opposition, for they could not have the least foundation for their Insinuations; and I cannot help Expressing my Concern, that notwithstanding such frivolous pretences, which ought to have fallen to the ground of themselves, You have been obliged, in order to quiet those restless Spirits, to give them assurances to which they were not Entitled, and that from Circumstances & Events, unforeseen at present, may prove prejudicial to the General Good; for tho' I never proposed the New England Forces should be Employed South of Albany, nor that I do not foresee it will be necessary to Continue them in the service beyond, or even to, the time for which they are to be Raised, yet You will own, that by being tied down to these Conditions, I may be debarred from making Use of that Force, where, when the Regular Troops are Employed in their Intended Operations, they may be most necessary, the result of which may be a failure in part of His Majesty's Instructions, which must then lay at the door of the Provinces, who, when too late, will repent being the occasion of it.

However, since You could not Obtain the *3000* men, without these Assurances, I must Yield to the disagreable necessity that Compelled You thereto; and that You may not forfeit Your word with the Assembly, I must Corroborate the same, and You may Assure them that their Forces shall not be sent South West of the River DeLawarr, and that they will, in all human probability, be discharged long before the First day of July 1762.__ But I will not promise that they shall return immediately after a peace; for as their Assistance is demanded to secure His Majesty's Conquests in North America, and that this End cannot be Answered but by finishing the Forts that have been begun for that purpose, suppose I was to receive tidings of a peace by the next packett, is it to be Expected that they should immediately withdraw their aid? I am hopefull they have a better sense of what they owe to the King and to themselves, and that they would not harbour any such wild thought.

The Rendezvous will be at Albany and Crown Point, of which more hereafter; at the same time, I must just hint to You, for Your own private Information, that if I should find it necessary to Call away any more of the Regular Forces from Nova Scotia, the protection of that Valuable Province may require some of the Massachusetts Troops to put it into a perfect State of Security; and, in that case, I shall give You timely Notice thereof, but in the present uncertainty, it is needless to Add any thing further on that Subject.

I am, with great Regard, Sir, Your most Obedient Humble Servant

Jeff Amherst.

His Excellency Govr: Bernard.

LS, RC   BP, 9: 183-185.

Endorsed by clerk no. 1: Genl Amherst April 9 1761. Variant text in WO 34/27, p. 216 (L, LbC).

---

1. **No. 38**.

42 | To Jeffery Amherst

Boston Ap. 18. 1761.

S^r.

I am favoured with yours of the 9th inst & can not but be concerned, at your being dissatisfied at what has been done here, especially as I had flattered myself that upon the whole the public business here was brought to a good Conclusion.[1] I am sensible that I have myself contributed to your disappointment, by the intimation I gave of my hopes of getting 4,000 men: but tho' I had the best authority for that expectation that could be at the time I wrote, yet at the same time I considered, that if I[2] succeeded in getting them for an unusual length of time, it might probably be at some expence of their Number. As to the doubts & difficulties with which this business was embarrased, you are sensible that it is in the power of a very few persons to start objections which tho' they wont defeat will serve to delay any business; since the most groundless insinuations will allways be so much attended to, as to occasion some delay. But it would be hard to charge the whole body, with what 2 or 3 designing men & 20 or 30 misled are only answerable for; especially in this Case, where two thirds of the Assembly, among which were allmost evry one of the principal

Gentlemen of the province, were on the right side. As for the stipulation which was required of me, It must have been given some time or other. I will own to you, that I believe, I could have prevented the Question being put to me, if I had thought it advisable: nay I will own that I previously consented, that it should be put to me. If I had prevented this, I am satisfied I should not be able to raise the Men: for after It had been insinuated that these Men were to be sent to the Southward, if a satisfactory answer had been refused concerning their destination, these suspicions would have gained such credit throughout the Country, that perhaps, it would have been impracticable to have removed the prejudices arising from them. And as It would be necessary on account of the levies to give some assurances concerning the destination It seemed to me to be much the best to give them before the Apprehension of their being sent to the south had been circulated & gained credit, than after: as I find it much easier to prevent prejudices than to remove them. I must add that I had not the least apprehension that this stipulation would probably (I wont say possibly) hurt the Kings Service: And tho' the Assembly were not entitled to these Assurances, yet the Men, who are all to be Volunteers, are.

Before the Number was fixed, I endeavoured to get as large a one as I could: Now it is fixed, it will equally become me to Vindicate the honor of the province by showing that what they have done is fully equal to, if not exceeding, their proportion. I must premise that from the idea of the Service which I had formed from Mr Pitts letter,[3] I thought it quite necessary that the Men should be raised to serve thro' the Winter: and therefore I made that a material point & of such consequence, as to make it worth while to abate in Number to gain in time. I find the other provinces are not of the same opinion, but yet I cant find fault with my own apprehension. Now I find that the same money that will raise & maintain 3,000 men for 14 months would raise & maintain 4,700 men for 7 months, the time that Connecticut &, I suppose, other provinces have raised their Men for. Upon the best enquiry I can make, I find this province raised 5,500 men last year & therefore their proportion this year would be 3,666: but suppose, for the sake of square Numbers, We should reckon their proportion at 4,000, still they must be considered as exceeding their proportion by 700 men. If the truth of this reasoning should be suspected, it may be put out of doubt; for I dare say the Assembly would readily (as it would be plainly for their advantage) add 1000 men in consideration of a release of the time, from the 1st of Decr next, of the whole Number. If I was to agree upon a comparison from the other provinces & instance Connecticut (as it is more immediately relative to this province); The Advantage would be more on the side of this province: for as the proportion between Connecticut & Massachusets is settled as 5 to 7, if Connecticut grants 2300 Massachusets should grant 3220. The proportional Difference is Very small in regard to Number; & yet the time of the one is double of that of the other.

I assure myself, that you will excuse my giving you the trouble of this recapitulation, when you consider, that it cannot be a matter of indifference to me that this province should be seen in a worse light than it has hitherto appeared in; and especially when I think I can still promise, that if upon an advisement of the Wants of the Service to be provided for, it should appear that this province has been deficient in the proportion of its appointments, this shall be fully made good.

I have taken particular Care in my appointment of officers, which has been made in a manner different from what has been usual here. I have not one Captain but what has served as such before & has undergone a through[4] scrutiny concerning his Military merit.[5] The field officers I will mention in a separate paper, together with the formation of the Regiments & the parts where they are to be raised, that you may judge of their sevral appointments. In short, whatever the Number is, I will endeavour that the Corps shall be compleat & formed to the best advantage that may be.

I am with great regard, S[r], Your most obedient humble Servant

Fra. Bernard.

P.S

I enclose a Copy of my message to the House,[6] which was immediately agreed to, by which the Terms are settled, as you have proposed.

ALS, RC   WO 34/26, ff 91-92.

Endorsed: Governor Bernard 18th April 1761 R _[d] 25th D[to] Ans[d]__ 26th. D[o]. Variant text in BP, 2: 106-108 (L, LbC). Enclosed [FB], "Massachusetts Forces for 1761," [*Apr. 1761*], WO 34/26, f 94 (AMs). Other enclosures not found. The reply to this letter is **No. 44**.

According to the extant enclosure, the first regiment was to be placed under the command of Col. Nathaniel Thwing (1703-68) of Boston, who had been a captain at the siege of Louisbourg in 1745; the second under Col. Jonathan Hoar (c.1720-71) of Concord, Middlesex Co., a veteran of both expeditions against Louisbourg (1745 and 1758); and the third under Col. Richard Saltonstall (1732-85) of Haverhill, Essex Co., a future Loyalist. FB relayed the soldiers' preferences concerning their prospective deployment: the first and second regiments wanted to be sent "to the North East" of the province—to Nova Scotia and Canada—while the men of the third preferred to be sent "Westward"—to upper New York.

---

1. **No. 41**.

2. LbC: the phrase "considered, that if I" is missing.

3. **No. 20**.

4. Meaning "thorough."

5. In this, FB sought the advice of Timothy Ruggles (1711-95). FB to Ruggles, Boston, 6 Apr. 1761, BP, 2: 105. Ruggles, a lawyer by profession and representative for Hardwick, was one of Massachusetts's most experienced officers. He served in the expeditions to Crown Point in 1755 and 1756, Fort William Henry in 1757, and Canada in 1759. He held the provincial rank of colonel when he was promoted to brigadier-general by Gen. Amherst in Feb. 1760, and left the service in Dec.

6. FB, message to the Council and the House of Representatives, Province House, 15 Apr. 1761, for which see *JHRM*, 37, pt.2: 337.

43 | *From The Board Of Trade*

(Duplicate)

Whitehall April 21st. 1761.

Sir

We have had under Our Consideration, the Laws passed in the Province of Massachusets Bay, between February and April 1760, amongst which, there are several providing for temporary and inconsiderable Services of Ferries, Roads &c. by Lotteries, which is a mode of raising money, that in Our Opinion ought never[1] to be countenanced, and hardly to be admitted into practice upon the most pressing Exigency of the State, more especially in the Colonies, where the forms of Government may not admit of those regulations and Checks, which are necessary to prevent fraud and abuse, in a matter so peculiarly liable to them.

We cannot therefore but disapprove these Laws upon this general principle,[2] but when We consider the very unguarded and loose manner in which they are in general framed, the Objections are so many and so strong that We should certainly have thought it Our Duty to have laid them before His Majesty for His Majesty's Disapprobation, were We not restrained by the consideration, that the purpose for which they were passed, having been carried into full execution and the Acts had their full Operation and Effect, some Inconveniences might attend the disannulling them; but it is Our Duty to desire, that you will not for the future give your Assent to any Laws of the like Nature

We are, Sir, Your most obedient humble Servants

Sandys

E. Bacon

Geo: Rice

John Roberts[3]

Francis Bernard Esqr. Govr: of Massachusets Bay

dupLS, RC   BP, 9: 186-189.

In the handwriting of John Pownall. Endorsed by FB: Duplicate Lords of Trade 21 Ap. 1761 r. Feb. 20. 1762 Orig[l] receivd before. Variant text in CO 5/920, pp. 44-46 (L, LbC).

This letter could not have been sent until after the appointment of commissioner John Roberts, which was after the letter's given date. The date of Roberts's appointment is uncertain: Oct. 1761, according to his biographer, or 3 Dec. according to official records. However, Roberts's name is not appended to the entry-book copy, which instead has those of his predecessor Andrew Stone and his colleague Soame Jenyns. The dates of receipt suggest that both the duplicate and the original were dispatched late in 1761.

On 17 Apr. 1761, the Board of Trade considered twenty-six acts passed by the General Court between Jan. and Apr. 1760, together with a report of Sir Matthew Lamb, K.C., dated 12 Apr. No objections were raised "in point of law" regarding the legislation, but it was agreed to prepare a draft letter to the governor of Massachusetts outlining the Board's "dissatisfaction" with the practice of "raising money for temporary and inconsiderable services by lottery." Lotteries had been a commonplace in Britain and the colonies since the seventeenth century, and the first licensed colonial lottery was in Massachusetts in 1745. Subsequently, British opposition, according to one historian, "probably arose" from apprehensions that lotteries "interfered with the development of trade and commerce," and on 30 Jun. 1769, the secretary of state issued a circular requiring governors to obtain the royal sanction before assenting to any public or private lottery bills. *JBT*, 11: 189-190; John Ezell, "The Lottery in Colonial America," *WMQ* 5 (1948): 185-200.

---

1. LbC: "not".

2. LbC: "their general Principles,".

3. John Roberts (1711/12-72), British politician. A loyal supporter of the duke of Newcastle, Roberts held a number of minor offices and sinecures; he was MP for Harwich, 1761-72, and a lord commissioner of the Board of Trade, 1761- Nov. 1762. Martyn J. Powell, "Roberts, John (1711/12-1772)," in *ODNB-e* (http://www.oxforddnb.com/view/article/23760, accessed 2 Mar. 2005); J. C. Sainty, *Officials of the Boards of Trade,* 1660-1870 (London, 1974), 31.

44 | *From Jeffery Amherst*

New York, 26th. April 1761.___

Sir,

I have Yesterday received the favor of Your Letter of the 18th. Instant,[1] Enclosing a Copy of Your message to the Gentlemen of the Council, & the House of Representatives as likewise the Formation of the Corps of *3000* men into Three Regiments, by which I see it will be most agreable that Colonel Twing's Regiment, or Colonel Hore's should be sent to Halifax, as I must send one of the three Reg[ts]. to that Place; I shall therefore leave it to You to appoint either of those Regiments

You think proper for that Service, and I intend the other two Regiments should proceed to Crown Point in the same manner as the Troops did last Year.__

I greatly fear the Levies will be more backward this Year in several of the Provinces, than what they have been heretofore; but as it is very necessary, that Troops should go to the different posts where they are allotted, I must beg of You to hasten the Compleating of the Regiments as fast as possible.__

I acquainted You in my Letter of the 9th.,[2] that in all probability a part of the Massachusetts Troops would be required for the service in Nova Scotia; whichever of the two Regiments I have mentioned You fix on for this service, I should think can't be Assembled at any place so well as at the Castle Barracks, from whence they may Embark to proceed immediately to Halifax.__

I shall write to Mr. Hancock[3] that the necessary Quantity of Tonnage may be ready for Conveying this Regiment to Halifax; and to Capt. Moncrieffe,[4] who is at Boston, that he shall muster them, and pay them the four pences from the time of their Enlistment to the time they are put on board, at which period they will be Supplied with the King's Provisions; and as there can be no Occasion for a Convoy at present there need not be the least delay in their proceeding to Halifax, so soon as they are ready.__

I Come now to Inform You of my Intentions, in regard to the other two Regiments, which are, that I would have them march in the same manner as Your Troops did last Year to Worcester & Springfield where there shall be Sufficient magazines formed for Victualling these Regiments in their march to Albany, where I propose they should Rendezvous.

I shall also send an Officer, or two, to pay the men the four pences from their time of Enlistment to that of their receiving the King's Provisions, and I trust to Your Zeal for the good of His Majesty's Service that You will hasten as much as You can the march of these two Regiments, as well as the Embarkation of the one Destined for Halifax.__

I am, with great Regard, Sir, Your most Obedient Humble Servant.

Jeff: Amherst

His Excellency Governor Bernard.

P:S: Colonel Jarvis[5] of Boston has already orders from the Contractors Agents for supplying the Troops with Provisions in their march to Albany.__

JA

LS, RC   BP, 9: 190-193.

Endorsed by clerk no. 1: Genl Amherst April 26 1761. Variant text in WO 34/27, p. 217 (L, LbC).

1. **No. 42**.

2. **No. 41**.

3. Thomas Hancock (1703-64), whose position as Boston's richest merchant owed much to his success in negotiating supply contracts with British forces.

4. Possibly Thomas Moncrieffe of the 55th Regiment of Foot, commissioned as a captain on 14 Feb. 1760.

5. Possibly Leonard Jarvis (1716-70), a Boston merchant.

45 | *To the Board of Trade*

Boston Ap. 28. 1761

My Lords

I take this opportunity to lay before your Lordships the Answer of the General Court to the petition of the Mashbee Indians; from which it will appear that there is no ground for the complaints they have troubled your Lordships with. Reuben Cognehew has been with me & seems to me to be a Very self-important fellow. I shall nevertheless give Ear to him; & if He can point out to me any thing that really wants redress, He shall have it. From the enquiries I have made, the Matters that want redress among them are what they will not complain of. They are suffered to run in debt beyond their abilities & then are allowed to sell their children to pay their debts; They are suffered to harrass one another at Law for trivial disputes, which sometimes end in the ruin of both parties; When they are condemned in criminal prosecutions, they are subjected to Fines instead of corporal punishment, so that where the Criminal only ought to be corrected, his family is ruined; In civil actions, they are charged with exorbitant costs, when it is known they have nothing to pay with. All these arise from the abuse of the Law, which in some hands will not spare a naked Indian. I have allready recommended these Matters to the consideration of the two Houses & will endeavour to get them redressed in the next Session.

I have dissolved the General Court[1] & issued writs for a New one. Before the next meeting, I shall, transmit to your Lordships the Acts that have been passed with observations upon such as require them.[2] I shall also give your Lordships an account of such other transactions as shall deserve your notice. In laying Mr Pitts Letter before them, I made it a particular point, to engage them to provide for the Men for 12 months or more, instead of 7 or 8, as usual; thinking the Nature of the present service required it: This I succeeded in so that they Voted the Men for 14 months. I was in hopes that other provinces would have followed this precedent: but I dont learn that any other has provided for more than the summer. The extension of time could not but cause some diminution of Numbers; but the latter is by no means in proportion. The full Number, according to Mr Pitts letter, would have been 3666: and they have granted 3000. But 3000 for 14 months is equal (according to a calculation which makes an allowance for the expence of inlisting) to 4700, for 7 months. And if the other provinces had raised their full Number for 12 months or more, I am satisfied that this province would have added 1,000 more.[3] So that It has, & at all events would have, kept up its distinction of contributing more than its share to the public Service.

I am, with great respect, My Lords, Your Lordships obedient & most humble Servant

Fra. Bernard.

The Right Honble the Lords of Trade

ALS, RC   CO 5/891, ff 27-28.

Endorsed by John Pownall: *Massachusetts Bay.* Letter from Francis Bernard Esqr. Govr of the Massachusets Bay, to the B. dated April. 28. 1761. transmitting the report of the Genl. Court upon the Complaint of the Mashbee Indians and acquainting their Lordships with what has been done in that province in consequence of his Maj's. Order for raising men for the levies of the Year 1761. Reced. July. 10. 1761. Read Sepr. 1. Ll.14. Variant text in BP, 2: 39-40 (L, LbC). Enclosed a copy of the Report of the General Court of Massachusetts Bay, in answer to the complaints of the Mashpee Indians, [*10 Apr. 1761*], CO 5/891, ff 29-30.

Reuben Cognehew was a Mashpee Indian and schoolteacher who, in Jul. 1760, embarked on a remarkable journey to England to deliver personally a petition to the king on behalf of his tribe. Setting sail from Rhode Island, Cognehew was "inhumanly carried" to the West Indies, whence he somehow managed to get to London (CO 5/890, ff 31-32). The petition complained of the General Court-appointed guardians having infringed his fishing rights in the Mashpee River and of land encroachments by the colonists. On his return from England, Cognehew met with FB sometime between Dec. 1760 and Apr. 1761, probably to discuss Britain's extraordinary response. Following a report by the Board of Trade, an order-in-council dated 12 Aug. 1760 obliged FB to lay the Mashpee's petition before the General Court, which he did on 19 Dec. FB urged the assembly to conduct an enquiry into the guardians' conduct; however, he also took the opportunity to suggest that the province go beyond the Mashpee's particular complaints by revising the "Laws concerning Indians." (*APC*, 4: 460-461; Order of His Majesty in Council, 12 Aug. 1760, Mass. Archs., 303: 102.) A joint committee reported on Cognehew's petition on 29 Jan., dismissing his claims, and both houses formally responded to the governor in a message of 10 Apr., the content of which is the same as the General Court's "Report" enclosed with the present letter. *JHRM*, 37 pt.1: 105; 37 pt.2: 225-226, 322-323.

The Board of Trade delivered a representation to His Majesty in Council on 10 Sept. 1761, enclosing a copy of the General Court's report and an extract of FB's letter. These were noted by the Privy Council's plantation affairs committee on 12 Oct. There the matter rested until 1763 when the General Court resolved to incorporate the Mashpee tribe as a self-governing community (**No. 225**). *JBT*, 11: 210-211; *APC*, 4: 461.

1. On 21 Apr.
2. **No. 59**.
3. See **No. 42**.

46 | *Circular from the Board of Trade*

Whitehall April 28th. 1761.

Sir,

His Majesty having been graciously pleased by Commission under the Great Seal of Great Britain to constitute and appoint Us His Commissioners for promoting the Trade of this Kingdom, and for inspecting and improving His Majesty's foreign Colonies & Plantations, It is Our Duty to acquaint you therewith, and to desire, that you will, from time to time, give us frequent and very full Information of the State and Condition of the Province under your Government, as well in respect to the Administration of Government and Justice, as to the Trade and Commerce thereof; and that you will also will regularly and punctually send Us the several Papers required by His Majesty's Instructions to you to be transmitted. And to the end that We may be the better enabled to form a true Judgement of the present state of the Province under your Government, We must desire your speedy Answer to the several heads of Enquiry herewith transmitted to you, and that you will every six Months make a return thereto, that We may be from time to time apprized of any Alterations which may happen in the Circumstances of the Province.

We are, Sir, Your most obedient humble Servants,

Sandys[1]

Soame Jenyns

E. Bacon[2]

Edmond Thomas[3]

Geo: Rice[4]

Francis Bernard Esq[r] Gov[r]: of Massachuset's Bay

LS, RC   BP, 9: 194-197.

In the handwriting of John Pownall. Endorsed by FB: From Lords of Trade inclosing Queries 28 Ap. 1761 r Aug 15. 1761. A contemporaneous virgule in the left margin marks the enclosure.

This letter was the first communication to the colonial governors from a new Board of Trade appointed by royal commission on 21 Mar., on the direction of the earl of Bute as incoming secretary for the Northern Department, and meeting for the first time on 1 Apr. *JBT*, 11: 181. The enclosed heads of enquiry have not been found, but the endnotes to FB's "Answer" contain reconstructions, based on contemporary documentation, of the questions that would have been asked (**No. 234**).

---

1. Samuel Sandys (1695-1770), the first Baron Sandys of Ombersley and noted critic of Robert Walpole and his ministry, was president of the Board of Trade, 21 Mar. 1761-Feb. 1763. FB acknowledged Sandys's appointment in **No. 63**.

2. Edward Bacon (1712?-86), MP for Norwich, 1756-84, and a lord commissioner, 1759-Jul. 1765.

3. Sir Edmund Thomas (1712-67), MP for Glamorgan, 1761-67, and a lord commissioner, 1761-63.

4. George Rice (1724?-79), MP for Carmarthenshire from 1754 until his death and a lord commissioner Mar. 1761-1770. He was a friend of and election agent for the duke of Newcastle, and a political ally of Lord Bute. He was a "hardliner" critic of the colonists who opposed repealing the Stamp Act. Peter D. G. Thomas, "Rice, George (1724?-79)," in *ODNB*-e (http://www.oxforddnb.com/view/article/23477, accessed 7 Jun. 2006).

47 | To Jeffery Amherst

Boston May 4. 1761

S[r]

A few days ago I made a discovery of a Vessel trading to the Missisippi: She had sent her cargo up to Town & lay 2 miles below the Castle amongst the Islands. I sent the Sheriff[1] with a party from the Castle, who seized her with two Men on board, whom I have kept in Custody at the Castle.[2] I have examined them sevral times, & have made full discovery of the iniquitous trade, which is carried on from Jamaica to New Orleans, whereby the Cherokees are enabled to maintain their War against Carolina. As I have not yet finished the examination or pursuit of these offenders, I cant acquaint you with particulars now: but such as relate to the state of the Enemy I would by no means postpone.

The most intelligent of these prisoners informs me that he was taken at Fort Loudon[3] together with the other of these two Men & carried by the Indians to New Orleans & there delivered to the French & by them kept prisoners, till they were put on board this sloop which sailed the same day. From Fort Loudon He went to Fort Cherokee[4] 500 miles by water in about 4 weeks: This is a log Fort pretty well gunned & garrisoned. For thence by water in 5 days to Mississippi Town: here he saw a large Log fort but could not see any guns in it or in the Town. This stage would take 30 days by land being round about.[5] From thence to Illinois 18 miles where is a stone fort mounted with 16 or 20 guns, among which are some 9 pounders & garrisoned by about 200 regulars.[6] From thence they passed by a little fort called Natchee' fort with about 150 men but no great guns that he saw,[7] & from thence to New Orleans. From fort Cherokee to New Orleans is called 500 leagues, & yet they went it in 20 days proceeding by water day & night.

New Orleans has no fort & is only defended by palisades about 6 inches thick: there are many guns, but they all lie upon the ground unmounted, not one being Mounted that he could see. They have no regular forces but the whole Country is armed & do duty by turns. Altho' they are furnished by the English, yet they want Ammunition, the Indians carrying it off as fast as it comes in. A Flag of truce from Jamaica[8] brought in a 1000 weight of powder at a time; & yet soon after they were obliged to mount guard without one round. He sayes He sees nothing to hinder a frigate of War from coming close to the Town: A french frigate of 50 guns, which was designed for Canada, was lying there, when he came away. They say that they expect the English & named Sr William Johnson:[9] that they shall fire a few guns for their credit, & then surrender; for they know the English will leave them in possession of their habitations.

This Account I had from him this Morning: I had before set people to talk with him on this Subject; & I had one of them by, when I examined him & he was quite consistent. The other spoke to the same purpose to some of my people but not so fully: I did not examine him myself. As soon as I have done with this Man I will send him to you: he sayes he'll go Any where ~~you~~ that he shall be orderd & should be glad to settle there when it is subdued.

I am with great regard Sr Your most obedient humble Servant

Fra. Bernard

His Exlency Genl Amherst

ALS, RC   WO 34/26, ff 96-97.

Endorsed: Governor Bernard. Boston, 4th. May 1761. Recd.__ 10th. Ditto.__ Ansd.__ 11th. Ditto.__ Variant text in BP, 2: 110-111 (L, LbC).

1. Stephen Greenleaf (1704-95), a resident of Boston, sheriff of Suffolk County from 1757 to the Revolution, and a future Loyalist.

2. Benedict Thoms and Francis Layton.

3. Fort Loudon, near present-day Vonore in eastern Tennessee, was constructed by the Virginia militia in 1756. The Cherokees captured the fort in Aug. 1760 and massacred the garrison.

4. Fort Cherokee, at the confluence of the Tennessee and Ohio Rivers, was originally called Fort Ascension when it was constructed by the French in 1757; it was renamed Fort Massac in 1759, by which name it is best known.

5. Probably Fort Kaskaskia, the second permanent French settlement on the Mississippi River in what was to become Illinois; if that was so, then the party would have traveled along the Ohio River to the Mississippi River, and proceeded up river to Kaskaskia.

6. Probably Fort Chartres, up river from Fort Kaskaskia; it was constructed from logs in 1720, but by the 1760s was an impressive, strongly-defended stone fortification. From here it was over 490 miles south to Natchez.

7. The French Fort les Natchez, on the Mississippi River, was an earthen construction from 1716, but had been in a ruinous state since its capture by the Natchez Indians in 1729.

8. The "flag of truce trade" was the term given to the generally illegal commerce between British and French settlements during wartime, on which see **Nos. 11** and **234**; Tyler, *Smugglers & Patriots*, 34; Thomas C. Barrow, *Trade and Empire: The British Customs Service in Colonial America, 1660-1775* (Cambridge, Mass., 1967), 163.

9. Sir William Johnson (1715-74), the widely respected superintendent of Indian Affairs for the Northern Department and prominent landowner in upper New York.

48 | To Jeffery Amherst

Boston May 5. 1761

S[r].

I am obliged to trouble you again on the affair of Simon Butler: I have received this day a letter from the father, that He carried a Man to Fort Edward, who was judged unfit; he thereupon went to Albany got another man, presented him & he was judged unfit: Upon which He gave over all thoughts of redeeming him, finding that there was no end of this method, especially if Cap Cruikshanks should not be disposed to part with him[1]

I must therefore recollect my first proposal; which was to give 10 guineas for his release, or if that was not enough (I meant for the expence he had been to the Corps, for I did not imagine any profit from him would be expected) as much more as should be required. Cap Cruikshanks changed these terms into those of producing a man that he approved of. The Father brings one man; he is not liked: he brings another; he is not liked. Can any end be prescribed to this method of proceeding? He has allready expended as much money, as would, I suppose, in my method have redeemed his Son: but in the present He may expend ten times as much & not redeem him after all.

The chief motive for my engaging in this business was to releive a family distressed by the unwaringness of the Son: I could have added some circumstances concerning his inlistment, that would have given some kind of title to a discharge upon the terms of reimbursement. But as I have not been able to succeed, I am sorry, that this Man has over rated my importance so much to his cost. I must however, at all events return my thanks to you for the trouble you have given yourself on this subject. I am, with great regard, S^r

Your most obedient humble Servant

Fra. Bernard

His Excelly Genl Amherst

ALS, RC WO 34/26, f 98.

Contains minor emendations. Variant text in BP, 2: 112 (L, LbC).

Amherst's solution was for Butler's father to take a substitute recruit to Capt. Moncrieff, who was to advise on his suitability pending an examination by the army surgeon. Amherst to FB, New York, 17 May 1761, WO 34/27, p. 219.

1. According to Cruikshanks, "Simon Butler is a very likely Young Man 5 feet 10 Inches high, presently at Fort George, and shall be Discharged as soon as Your Excellency pleases, tho' Instead of money, of Which I refused £20, for him Offered by the Enclosed Letter from M^r. Sanders, I would much rather Wish Governor Bernard would send a trusty Young man in his Stead." Quoted in Amherst to FB, New York, 2 Mar. 1761, WO 34/27, p. 212.

49 | To William Pitt

Boston May 5. 1761

S^r.

In obedience to your letter of Aug 23^l I made enquiry concerning the french trade carried on from this province & made a report in the favor of the province by my letter of Nov. 8. Nevertheless I meant not to aver that there was no one instance of such practise, but that it was generally not known to be carried on to such pernicious purposes. But I have, at length, caught a Missisippi trader, & the discoveries I have made thereby are the occasion of my troubling you with this letter.

When I was informed of this sloop, she had landed her cargo & lay behind an Island about 5 miles from Boston. I sent the Sheriff with a party of soldiers from the Castle, who seized her with two Men on board who were orderd into the Custody of the Castle. The next day I went to the Castle & took their examinations, which I hereby transmit to you. At the time that the sloop was seized, a Custom house officer[2] seized some part of the cargo consisting of skins & some Indigo. I had also at the same time orderd another party to take into custody two french passengers: but this part miscarried for want of being timely & properly conducted; and I have since found reason to decline proceeding therein for the present.

From the Accounts I have got, which I take to be quite authentic, This is the History of this sloop. She sailed from hence to Monte Christo,[3] there loaded with Sugar & was in going thence taken by an English Man of War & carried to Jamaica. There the Master[4] of her teized the Captain of the Man of War to give him the sloop again; for indeed She is worth but little. He then in conjunction with one Thomas an English Renegade, (who by living a good deal at St Thomas's passed for a Dane[5]) fitted her out with Naval stores & from thence went to New Orleans. There they freighted her with what they brought here & took in another partner one Anneau a frenchman who has been Very much versed in trade with the English & is, I am told, familiarly known in Rhode Island. Their Cargo is supposed to have been worth £5,000 sterling & they brought an Iron chest with them, which is believed to have contained some specie. Their purpose is to buy shipping & freight it with provisions, naval stores & ammunition.

Upon my return from the Castle on yesterday, I had determined to take them all into custody & publish the business: but I found it necessary to alter my resolution for these reasons; I had then received ~~another~~ information of another Vessel expected from the same place to this or some other port of this province: and, if a public prosecution of these people had been begun, it would ~~have~~ prevent the expected Vessel from coming in here; By an immediate proceeding I could make no further discovery than I have at present; whereas by lulling them into the state of security, which a stop of proceedings must necessarily produce, I shall be able to come at the secrets of their exportation. This I am, at present, about, & will spare no pains to discover & punish this abominable intercourse.

In the mean time I transmit to you this account together with the copies of the depositions. The information concerning New Orleans, I have sent to Genl Amherst;[6] the two Men, whose Examinations I send, I shall keep at the Castle, till I have fully considered what use they may be of, especially to Genl Amherst. I cannot conclude this with^t informing you that I owe all this discovery & shall be indebted for what shall be hereafter made to the Care & Diligence of Mr Paxton,

Surveyor of the Customs of this port, who is a most excellent officer being both indefatigable & incorruptible. I am also much obliged to Mr Temple Surveyor of the Customs of this port,[7] who has had the cheif charge of the execution of these seizures.

I have the honour to be, with great respect, Sr Your most obedient & most humble Servant

Fra Bernard.

The Rt Honble Wm Pitt Esq_r

ALS, RC   CO 5/20, ff 123-124.

Contains minor emendations. Endorsed: Boston. May 5th: 1761. Govr. Bernard R June 29th: Variant text in BP, 1: 309-311 (L, LbC). Enclosed signed copies of the depositions of Benedict Thoms and Francis Layton, taken at Castle William on 2 May 1761, CO 5/20, ff 125-128, together with an "Account" by Thoms of having been "taken prisoner at Fort Loudon & carried from thence to New Orleans," Castle William, 4 May 1761, CO 5/20, f 129 (MsS).

1. **No. 11**.

2. Robert Temple, the brother of the surveyor general John Temple, and comptroller of Customs at Boston in 1761.

3. Monte Cristo, Hispaniola; modern-day San Fernando de Monte Cristi in the Dominican Republic.

4. Capt. Daniel Martin according to the deponents.

5. St. Thomas had been a royal Danish colony since 1754, and today is one of three islands comprising the US Virgin Islands. Inward clearances for the port of Boston 5 Apr.-5 Jul. 1761 show only one vessel from St. Thomas's, the *John*, master John Miles, a thirty-ton schooner with a crew of four and owned by John Baker, a Boston merchant: there is an entry of two hogsheads of molasses and six of sugar, but the date has been torn from the manuscript. CO 5/851, n.p.

6. **No. 47**.

7. John Temple (1732-98), lieutenant governor of New Hampshire and surveyor general of Customs for the Northern District, which office he held from c.Jun. 1761 until its abolition in 1766.

50 | From William Warburton

Dear Sir

I some time ago had the honour of a very obliging Letter from You,[1] dated from your old Governm^t: but understanding that your Excellency was about to remove to a new one I deferred my acknowledgments till I could get information of your address. which the favour of the two Sermons, you was so kind to send to me, has very opportunely afforded.

I heartily rejoice with you in this instance of the true Christian moderation that seems now begining to prevail in your long-bigotted Province. a temper less inexcusable in that part of Puritanism: for when men were driven by persecution into a new World, it was no wonder they should arrive in an ill humour, and like a Comet set on fire by the bad neighbourhood of the Sun, should be some Centurys in cooling, tho' removed to the greatest distance from it's Hierarchical heat.

I know of none properer than your Excellency to improve these good dispositions. The justice & gentleness of your Nature will best teach them that the bearing with religious contradiction is not only a politeness but a duty, and that liberty of Conscience is not only an indulgence but a right.

I have the honour to be, your Excellency's most Affectionate & faithfull humble Servt

W. Gloucester[2]

Prior Park [*Bath*], June 3^d 1761

ALS, RC   BP, 9: 202-204.

Endorsed by FB: Bp of Gloucester r. Aug. 15. 1761. No reply has been found.

---

1. Not found.

2. William Warburton (1698-1779), Church of England cleric and noted theologian. He was a practising lawyer before entering the church, where he held a number of benefices prior to becoming bishop of Gloucester in 1760. Warburton thought highly of FB, with whom he probably became acquainted while rector at Brant-Broughton, Lincs., 1728-30. Warburton was a signatory to the House of Lords' protest against the repeal of the Stamp Act in Mar. 1766. Nicolson, *The 'Infamas Govener'*, 33.

51 | To Jeffery Amherst

Castle William June 14. 1761

S^r

I have got upwards of 420 men embarked for Halifax & expect they will sail to morrow: I hope in a week or 10 days to send 300 more all of Thwings Regiment. The Enlistments in general go on Very poorly: the Assembly have made some alteration in paying the bounty from which they expect good effects. But I beleive the true Cause of the Want of Men, is the lateness of making the levies; by which means the people in general had engaged for the Summer, before It was known that Troops were to be raised.

If the Service would have admitted of sending two Regiments to Nova Scotia, It would have been Very agreable to Col Hoar's Regiment & would, I beleive greatly assisted the completion of it. For that Regiment (as well as Col Thwings) being raised in the Maritime Counties, they are Very desirous of going Eastward. On the other hand Col Saltonstall's Regiment being raised in the inland parts are as earnest for going Westward. I intend, as soon as the Assembly rises, which may be a week hence, to order a Muster of Col Saltonstalls Regiment at Springfield, being desirous that the Gentlemen should return into the Country to assist the enlistments before a general Muster. About the same time I shall put the Regiment of Col Hoar into motion for the same rendezvous: unless you should direct the contrary. I am with great regards,

Sr Your most obedient humble Servant

Fra Bernard

His Excellency Major General Amherst.

ALS, RC   WO 34/26, f 99.

Variant text in BP, 2: 117-118 (L, LbC). The reply to this letter is Amherst to FB, Albany, 25 Jun. 1761, BP, 9: 213-215.

52 | To John Pownall

Boston June 15th. 1761

Dear S[r].

I find my self obliged to transmit to you the following Narrative as a supplement to what I have before sent concerning M[r]. Barrons proceedings in his office here.[1]

You are acquainted with M[r]. Pitts circular letter to the Gov[rs]: of America concerning the french trade & especially that to the Missisippi & the strong terms in which they are required to discover & censure that trade.[2] To this I returned an answer, wherein I showed that this province was generally esteemed to be unconcerned in that trade; but that I should nevertheless keep a good Look out.[3]

At the end of April last I rec[d]. advice that a Sloop supposed to be from the Missisippi lay behind an Island at 9 miles distance from Boston. The mate of the sloop had been up in Town & enterd her with M[r]. Barrons as from S[t]. Thomas's with 5 hhds of sugar & 2 of Molasses, tho' she really had neither one nor the other on board. M[r]. Paxton who made this discovery was ill in bed: he therefore engaged M[r]. Temple the Comptroller to prosecute it They had discovered where part of the Cargo was lodged; & it was thought advisable that the sloop & Cargo (then at 9 miles distance from one another) should be siezed at the same time. I therefore directed M[r]. Temple to engage the deputy sherriff for the former business, whilst the principal Sherriff assisted at the latter. And I gave the Deputy sheriff a written order on the Captain of the Castle to assist him with armed men; & I gave verbal orders to the sheriff to secure the sloop. & commit all the men he found on board to the Custody of the Captain of the Castle. The Sheriff executed his orders and having found two men on board committed them to the Castle. The next day I went down & took a justice with me, who assisted in Examining them. A Copy of these examinations I sent to you & another to M[r]. Pitt,[4] they were material in discovering the constant communication between Jamaica & New Orleans, by which among other things the Cherokees have been constantly supplyed with Gunpowder. These I sent by the packet that left New York the 15th of May.

I must now return to the sheriff After he had seized the Sloop & before he could bring her to the castle, a boat came alongside with a man in it, who said he came from M[r]. Barrons with an order to seize that Vessel & demanded the possession of her. The sheriff said, he had already seized by a power from M[r]. Temple & by the immediate orders of the Governor and he should not let any one come on board. However M[r]. Barrons men attempted to force an entrance & persisted in it, Untill one of them got a slight prick with a Bayonet: They then desisted & went of with Many threats of M[r]. Barrons resentment. in the Afternoon M[r]. Barrons came to an house where I dined, & with great heat told me, that there was an end of the

Customhouse, if the Governor was at liberty to employ the Soldiers of the Castle in preventing the Custom house officers seizing contraband ~~goods~~ Vessels, & that he should send home a complaint of it.

I told him that If he wrote on this subject he should learn the truth of it; which was that I had ordered the Vessel to be seized in pursuance of the special injunctions of the Secretary of state & that after the men or [*on*] board had been committed, I should deliver her to M^r. Temple to be prosecuted in the Court of Admiralty, where if he had any Claim upon her he might make it.

But this did not satisfy him for soon after on the same day, meeting with the Sheriff on the great Wharf of the Town, he abused him with very gross words among which were the Words following "damn you, you are a pack of Rascalls your Governor & all, and you may go and tell him so". It may be asked, what could induce him to use such violent & indecent Expressions against a Commander in Chief in the most public part of the Town: I can only answer that I have before set forth all the provocation I gave him; nor can I learn that he has ever pretended to Assign any other cause or indeed any cause at all for so public an outrage against my office. The Sheriff was taken Ill soon after his return & confined for a fortnight. As soon as he got out he made his complaint to M^r. Dana a justice of the peace;[5] who thinking the subject matter of too public a nature to be determined by him, sent him to advise with the Attorney Genl: but the Attorney preferring a proceeding before a justice to a more public prosecution, The Justice heard the complaint & M^r. Barrons defence & adjudged the Charge against him to be proved. The particulars will appear from a Copy of the whole proceeding as drawn up by the justice, wch. is herewith enclosed.

As I have before transmitted to you all I have had occasion to send concerning M^r. Barrons I continue the same method, hoping that when these papers shall be laid before their Lordships, they will be accepted as well thro your hands, as if they had been immediately addressed to their Lordships. the reason I took this method, in my first transmission of this kind, arose from the desire & some hopes I had of these disorders being composed before any Complaints of M^r. Barrons were made too notorious. But these hopes are at an End & it now becomes an inexcusable Duty to represent the proceedings of M^r. Barrons, not so much as injurious to my person, as destructive of Government itself.

I am &c

Mr Secretary Pownall

L, LbC   BP, 1: 317-320.

In the handwriting of clerk no. 1 with minor scribal emendations.

---

1. **No. 37**.

2. **No. 11**.

3. **No. 18**.

4. FB to Pownall, Boston, 9 May 1761, CO 5/891, ff 31-32; **No. 49**.

5. Richard Dana (1700-72), justice of the peace for Suffolk County and a future member of the Sons of Liberty.

53 | To Jeffery Amherst

Castle William July 5. 1761

S[r].

I am favoured with yours of the 25th of June & 1st July:[1] and having given orders for Col Hoars Regiment to proceed immediately for Springfield, I shall return to Boston tomorrow to make further dispositions both for hastening the march of the present levies, & for completing the intended Corps

I find here more than 70 privates since the last embarkation; & as some more are expected, I hope to morrow to make an embarkation of near 100 more including officers. And I think upon the whole, that Thwings Regiment will be soon compleated.[2]

I wish I could say the same of the other Regiments: the returns made to me dont make them quite half full. But the musters must turn out better, as many of the returns are of an old date. I am satisfied that the principal Cause of the deficiency of the levies arises from the delay of beating up, by which the people in general were engaged for the summer before it was known that troops would be wanting. There maybe some that lie by for an encrease of bounty, in which, I beleive, they will succeed, the Assembly being generally disposed to do something more, to encourage the inlistment; and the Scheme proposed for that purpose I think will be sufficient. This will be determined as soon as a Business of great consequence now before the House is finished.[3]

I am Very sorry that this Business has been so prolonged; but hope We shall still fullfill our engagements.

I am, with great regard, S[r] Your most obedient humble Servant

Fra. Bernard

His Excellency Maj[r] Gen[l]. Amherst

ALS, RC   WO 34/26, f 101.

Variant text in BP, 2: 115 (L, LbC). Amherst acknowledged receipt of this letter on 16 Jul. 1761, WO 34/27, p. 222.

1. Amherst would have preferred the embarkations to have proceeded earlier and to have been permitted "to have Sent more Troops to Nova Scotia," by which he likely meant either Hoar's or Saltonstall's regiments, or both. Amherst to FB, Albany, 25 Jun. 1761, BP, 9: 213-215. As it was, Amherst instructed Hoar to proceed to Albany as quickly as possible. Amherst to FB, Albany, 1 Jul. 1761, BP, 9: 217-220.

2. Some 630 men of Thwing's regiment embarked for Halifax on 26 Jun., though FB evidently still hoped to reach a regimental total of seven hundred. He reported that enlistments were slower than expected ever since Amherst's desire to send more Provincials to Halifax had become common knowledge. FB to Amherst, Boston, 27 Jun. 1761, WO 34/26, f 100.

3. FB is referring to the new evaluation of estates for tax-raising purposes that were settled by the House on 9 Jul., after which the House discussed incentives to encourage enlistment. *JHRM*, 38 pt.1: 103-105.

54 | To John Pownall

Boston July 6. 1761

D^r. Sir

the letters inclosed with this were wrote to convey further information of the proceedings of Mr Barrons which you will be pleased to lay before their Lordships at such time & in Such manner as you shall think fit, I cannot now offer a Suppresion of the Complaint against him with such propriety as I did before; because every thing of the Complaints & proofs, which I send now & have sent, except such as meerly relate to myself will be transmitted to the Commrs of the Customs by the time you receive this: the Surveyor Genl. (Mr Lechmere) being now engaged to collect the necessary pappers & send 'em away.

The Assembly keeps in very good temper; all necessary business is properly done notwithstanding an opposition is kept up (seldom raising the minority to one third) by Mr Otis Junr.[1] who has been Mr Barrons faithfull Councellour from the first beginning of these commotions to the hour of this present writing. the Assembly has gone thro' a very great & intresting work, the Valuation of the Estates of the whole province with uncommon temper & moderation:[2] there wants nothing but to bring this into form; so I suppose I shall dismiss them by the end of this week, after which I Shall keep working, till I get rid of My Epistolar Debts public & private; among which I reckon a letter to your Brother one of the principal.[3]

I should be glad to pay my Compliments to my Lord Sands; but think I must wait till I have a notification from the board, If I am wrong, get me excused till I can get right

I am S[r].

L, LbC   BP, 1: 322-323.

In the handwriting of clerk no. 1. Enclosed a copy of **No. 37** and other enclosures not found.

---

1. James Otis Jr. (1725-83), the lawyer and prominent Patriot, who, as representative for Boston, 1761-69 and 1771, and moderator of the town meeting, was one of FB's foremost critics.

2. See *JHRM*, 38 pt.1: 103-105.

3. **No. 67**.

55 | *To Jeffery Amherst*

Boston 11 July 1761—

Sir

M[r]: Bollan, the Province's Agent in England has wrote to the General Court[1] that he is of opinion, the Lords of the Treasury in their next Apportionment of the monies granted to the Colonies will govern themselves wholly by the number of Troops raised by each Colony and their time of Service taking the General's Certificate or account of that matter as the proper conclusive evidence without entring into any other points or proofs: and he earnestly recommends a proper application to General Amherst to certify the number and time of Service of the Province Forces which kept Garrison at Louisbourgh & Nova Scotia in the Year 1760, as well as of the other Forces of the Province. And a Committee of the two Houses have been with me to desire me to write to You and to ask such a Certificate from You; and for the greater security I would pray the favour of You to send duplicates at least of the same.

If any consideration has been had of the Expence this Province was at for the Men detained in Nova Scotia & Louisbourgh, it is certain, it was to the 1 of January 1760 only, and the Service of the last Year it is expected will be computed from that time.

I have sent this Express principally to desire such certificate from You, and have given him orders to wait until he shall receive your Answer.

I am, with great regard, Sr Your most obedient humble Servant.[2]

Fra Bernard

His Excellency General Amherst

LS, RC   WO 34/26, f 102.

In the handwriting of clerk no. 3, except as noted.

Bollan's letters were "communicated" to the House by the Speaker on 28 May, and a committee reported on the letters on 13 Jun. As a result, the province secretary was direct-ed to collect and forward a number of papers to Bollan in support of the province's claim for reimbursement. (The assembly ordered Bollan to apply the parliamentary subsidy of 1759 to the payment of bills of exchange totaling £60,000 sterling.) Also, on 11 Jul. the House requested that FB obtain the service-record certificates from Amherst. *JHRM*, 38 pt.1: 9, 55, 108. *Acts and Resolves*, 17: 46-47. Amherst refused to furnish the certificates in the absence of Treasury instructions, protesting that it would impose an unnecessary burden on his staff, but he relented after FB made a second request. Amherst to FB, Albany, 16 Jul. 1761, WO 34/27, p. 222, and 2 Oct., WO 34/26, f 109. The certificate for 1759-60 was enclosed in Amherst to FB, New York, 6 Dec. 1761, for which see WO 34/27, pp. 234-235. Hereafter, Amherst received directions from the Treasury (**No. 170**).

---

1. Bollan to Andrew Oliver, Leicester Square, 12 Feb. 1761, Prov. Sec. Letterbooks, 2: 300-302; Bollan to Oliver, Leicester Square, 14 Feb. 1761, Prov. Sec. Letterbooks, 1: 329-330.

2. This line in FB's hand.

56 | To Jeffery Amherst

Boston July 12. 1761

S[r].

Last fryday another Sloop sailed for Halifax with about 90 men including Officers, which makes about 720 in the whole: I expect more in, & hope that Regiment[1] will soon be completed. The Musters at Springfield I hope will turn out better than has been expected: There has been a delay in that business by Capt Campbells[2] requiring the inlistments, which the Militia Colonels who paid the bounties kept in their hands: but I hope that is set right, & the Musters go on. The inlistments will be collected & delivered to the Colonels of the 3 Regiments & may be resorted to in case of Any doubt.

I hope soon to complete all the Regiments, as the Assembly have granted a further Encouragement. The Objection to encreasing the Bounty, was that it would have a retrospect to those that were allready inlisted. To obviate this, I proposed that they should allow to evry person, that shall hereafter inlist 6 weeks wages extraordinary to be reckoned before the day of inlistment; which has been agreed to.[3] This is in effect a bounty, tho' it goes under the Name of Wages, & thereby avoids the inconveniency before mentioned. I expect that this Resolution & the Assembly's having risen & thereby put an end to all further expectations will have a full effect.

I beg leave to congratulate you on the late Honour His Majesty has conferred upon you[4] & am, with great regard,

S[r] Your most obedient humble Servant

Fra. Bernard

We have advice here that Dominico is surrendered.[5]

ALS, RC   WO 34/26, f 103.

---

1. Col. Thwing's regiment (see **No. 51**) was brought by the *Seaflower*, Jonathan Davies, master, which was owned by Elijah Davies, and cleared Boston on 9 Jul. 1761. CO 5/850, f 71.

2. A British army officer.

3. On 9 Jul., the House considered FB's message of 1 Jul., and the following day passed a resolution offering new volunteers six weeks' pay in addition to the bounty. *JHRM*, 38 pt.1: 91, 101; *Acts and Resolves*, 17: 43.

4. Amherst had been made a knight bachelor, an ancient reward for public service.

5. The British occupied Dominica in Jun. 1761 after attacking the French town of Roseau with an expeditionary force led by Commodore Sir James Douglas (1703-87) and Andrew Rollo (1703-65), the fifth Lord Rollo.

57 | To [Thomas Pownall]

Duplicate

Boston July 12. 1761

D.ʳ S.ʳ

I shall make apologies to you for not writing, untill they amount to the size of a long letter. The truth is I have no oppertunity of a conveyance safe enough for me to trust an intresting letter to. Even now I write for a private ship & must accordingly prescribe to me a reserve, particularly in regard to the politicks of this place. A month hence I shall have a Man of War to convey my letters & then may venture to be a little more explicit.

A little while ago, I wrote to your Brother two letters on the Subject of M.ʳ Barrons, whom M.ʳ Lechmere has suspended for better & more forcible reasons than he did before.[1] M.ʳ Lechmere, has sent his letters & papers to NYork, I dispatched my letters & papers thither also; & they all wait for the Packet. I thought it proper that the same ship that carried M.ʳ Lechmere's complaints should also convey to your brother all necessary information concerning M.ʳ Barrons further proceedings unto the time of his suspension.

My Acquaintance with Mankind has not been very extensive nor very confined: but I can say that in all my Knowledge of Men I never met with one like that Gentleman; so wonderfully wrongheaded & so wantonly mischevious. In direct opposition to Common sense & reason, to his Obligations his Duty & his intrest, did he make a formal attack upon the Government & the two public Offices more immediately Subject to the Kings Ministers. When any one attempted to set him right, He treated it as an opposition to his will & let him know that he must expect to feel the Effects of his resentment. And this without distinction of persons: I did not wonder at his telling Paxton that he would not hold his office 6 months longer; but I was surprised at my hearing that he fixed a time for my being removed & named for my successor in this government a Gentleman who is already such in another.[2]

These things I could laugh at, if he had not created me a deal of plague by serious Mischief. I can truly say that all the trouble I have had in this Government is owing to him & his Confederacy. And tho the good disposition of the Assembly has in a great measure put me out of their reach, yet there is still remaining enough of his party to teize tho' not to hurt.

But this is not all: Self defence has made it necessary for me to accuse him. And tho' I have acted therein with a due regard to truth & a proper temper of mind, & with as little resentment as can be expected from such extraordinary provocations; yet I may appear to those who don't know me, or are not acquainted with the Case to act upon Vi[n]dictive Motives. I say to those that dont know me; for they that do I flatter myself, know well that my natural & habitual disposition is the Very contrary to a vindictive temper.

For this purpose I can appeal to no ones Testimony better than to yours: you know me well & also know enough of my opponent. If therefore any doubts arise that shall make it necessary to refer to our general Characters, speak fairly what you know or think of Either; tho' I cannot but think that the facts will be found so positive & conclusive, as to make such a reference unnecessary.

I have felt most sensibly you[r] disappointment, of which you wrote in your last.[3] but even to this hour I flatter myself, that it was a little misunderstanding that has been since set right & impatient wait to hear of it. I must have a better opinion of a Lady that you have singled out, than to think she will persever in refusing you, after you have made so great a sacrifice of your own intrest to recommend yourself to her.

I imagine your attention to the Affairs of this province is not quite dead; and tho' it is well entertained by your other friends here, yet I conclude you will expect some account from me. The Political History is all that I think worth my writing or your reading: of that you have before a good reason for my silence, as well as a promise that I will be explicit when & as far as I can safely. In the mean time it will be enough to say that I find myself upon a good bottom: for tho' M'. B's confederacy has given me a good deal of trouble in the Town I don't perceive that they have any influence out of it that is worth notice.

I am S'. your &c &c &c

dupL, LbC BP, 2: 6-8.

In the handwriting of clerk no. 1 with scribal emendations.

Thomas Pownall likely discussed his career aspirations with FB in previous (nonextant) correspondence, as well as the personal matters referred to herein. He may have been determined to secure a position in England after resigning his governor's commission sometime in 1760. However, on 29 Jun. 1760 he was appointed commissary for the British forces in Germany, and did not return to England until 1763. His future wife, the wealthy widow Harriet Churchill (1726–77), whom he married on 25 Aug. 1765, is not the "Lady" alluded to above.

1. **Nos. 52** and **54**.

2. FB provided more details in **No. 85**.

3. Not found.

58 | From John Pownall

London. July 22. 1761.

Dear Sir,

Although I confess myself a bad correspondent & take shame for it, yet I hope I do not stand accused of want of attention to the solid & real Interests of my ffriends, amongst whom none can claim or hold a higher place in my regards than yourself.

I have endeavourd to the utmost of my poor ability to support & promote your Interest in evry case which you have entrusted to my ffriendly care, and I should have been very happy if my endeavrin had been more successfull in that which seemed to me the most important; but Unfortunately Pembertons Commision, which had been delayed a long time, was rinewed[1] before I reced your letters upon that Subject, and tho' Lord Halifax's real regard for you & your interests would have prevaild over some difficultys yet he thought it not consistent with the delicacy with which he managed matters of this nature in the Closet, to make such a proposition, where he was upon the point of being promoted to a higher station __ and the resumption of the nomination to all offices with the hands of the Secrt[y] of State, puts it absolutely out of my power to move a jot further; M[r]. Stone who is at ^least as^ much your ffriend as M[r]. pembertons, would have assisted me in evry thing that might have attain the Object you desired but told me from the beginning that in this Situation things were (with respect to M[r]. pembertons renewal, having taken place) nothing could be done.

It has been determined that Governors have in no case claim to the Allowances of Chappell plate &c upon a renewal in consequence of the demise of the Crown; all therefore I could do was to endeavour to obtain what was due to you upon your first appointment to the Gov[t]. of Massachusets Bay, in the way you desired it, and even in this the Absurdity of Office put 'me to much difficulty & trouble & renderd the produce less than it ought to have been; as you will see from the inclosed Acc[t]. the balance of which shall be paid to your order by Draft or in any other way you please to direct.

The Indiscretion of Barons has been amazing,__ his ffriends all condemn him, tho' I have seen some symptoms of an inclination in those who are most nearly connected with him to mix in this disapprobation of his conduct some charge of blame in yours ~~conduct~~, be not however uneasy on this score, for it neither has had nor will have any Effect, to your prejudice.

I am very happy to find by your last letter,[2] that the embarrasments & difficultys arising from this disagreable affair were dissipated; & that tho attempts of your Enemy had only the Effect to establish your interest still stronger, — The Attempts of Malevolence & malice opposed with resolution supported by Integrity will always have that Effect. One thing I will mention to you upon this occasion is an observation & hint occurring from the particulars of this dispute, which is that the Fees & charges of proceedings in Admiralty Courts in the plan[t]. in Gen[l]. are become so shamefully exorbitant, as to be matter of notice of Gov[t]. & have been in one or two cases, pretty severely censurd by the Council.

M[r]. Hancock who left London yesterday to embark for Boston will fully inform you of evry thing which regards our ffriend the Governors Situation, since you last heard of him: It became absolutely necessary that he should be taken out of that miserable state of Mind which his disappointm[t] had involved him in, & tho[h] the office he is employed in is not in inay circumstances the most Eligible, yet it keeps him in the line of publick Service & diverts his thoughts from disagreable reflection:[3]

The publick papers & the many Govt[s]. that I understand are upon the point of contracting for councill will better inform you of the State of publick Affairs in gen[l]. than I can do.__ a fortnight ago evry body thought we were at the Eve of a peace, the Gen[l]. opinion now is just the reverse.__ with respect to my own opinion it is not quite so sanguine; I see many untoward circumstances, but do not yet despair of a peace this Year.

M[rs]. pownall desires to be joined with me in our sincere respects to yourself & M[rs]. Bernard, and I have only to add that I am with the most sincere regards

Dear Sir Your most faithfull & Aff[t]. humble Servant

J Pownall

ALS, RC   BP, 9: 221-224.

Endorsed by FB: M[r] J Pownall r Oct 29. 1761 a Feb. 13 1762. Enclosure not found. The reply to this letter has not been found.

---

1. On 11 Mar. 1761. *JBT*, 11: 178.

2. FB to Pownall, Castle William, 12 May 1761, BP, 1: 316-317.

3. See **No. 57**.

59 | To The Board Of Trade

Boston Aug 3 1761

My Lords

Your Lordships will observe among the Acts of Assembly passed here in April last one for erecting part of the County of Hampshire into a New County called Berkshire.; & another for erecting a Plantation called Pontoosuck into a Town by the name of Pitsfield.[1] Together with the bill for the new County were sent up for my consent five other bills constituting New Townships, 4 whereof are within the County of Berkshire. As these bills were wholly silent about these Towns sending Members, I by a message informed the House of my instruction on that subject & desired they would alter the bills so that I might be able to pass them. (See Votes 354)[2] This produced some popular harangues which ended in an Answer to my Message, as in the Votes 360.[3] The Towns themselves were willing to waive their right of sending representatives; but some Gentlemen in the house opposed the allowing them to waive their priviledge: the result of which was I rejected four of the bills;[4] but in regard to Pontoosuck The Circumstances were so distinguishing, that I could not so easily get rid of that. This Town was appointed immediately one of the two County towns, & from its situation & other advantages will probably be the only County Town. In favor of this Town's sending a representative It was averred that it was not intended by that instruction to prevent New settled Counties being represented but only to put a stop to multiplying representatives in the Old Counties; And that this has been understood in regard to Pownalborough the cheif Town in the new County of Lincoln,[5] which it was expected would soon be allowed to send a Member. I could not either admit or contradict this; & therefore I took a middle way: I passed the bill upon their adding a clause suspending the right of sending a representative untill the Election in 1763. By these Means If your Lordships should disapprove its sending a Representative there will be time enough for the condemning the Bill before the Right takes place. But I flatter myself that your Lordships will not disapprove of this Town's sending a representative: With this one included The County will have but 3 representatives, And as It promises to fill Very fast, will probably soon have occasion to petition for more. I hope however, if I should be wrong, The Caution with which I have proceeded will in part excuse me

It seems plain to me, that the prohibiting instruction,[6] had its rise from a practice which had prevailed of dividing towns & thereby increasing the Members in the Old Counties & was cheifly intended against that. It is also Obvious that the New settled Counties have a right to be represented. But yet there is such danger to be apprehended from the house of Representatives continually increasing, that it is time to put a stop to it by some means: tho' it were to be wished that It could be done without denying New settlers the natural & constitutional right of being represented. The encrease of the Number of Representatives seems to endanger the Constitution itself: By the Charter the Council & by usage many other officers are elected by the Council & Representatives voting promiscuously. In the year 1718 there were but 91 writs issued, in 1692 when the Charter was opened probably not above 84, Now there is near 170. And yet the Council keeps its old Number of 28. So that the Assembly were to the Council at the time of their first meeting as 3 to 1 now they are as 6 to 1; & consequently the Councils share in elections is diminished by half. It is also known by experience, that a large Number of People do not dispatch the public business so well as a more confined Number would do. And yet I fear It will be found Very difficult to persuade the Assembly to reduce their Number to purpose, altho' it would be very agreable to many towns to be discharged from the expence of sending a Member; or, what would be more proper, sevral Towns might be united into one Borough, as in Scotland.[7] Something of this kind should be done, before Any considerable Addition of Members should be made from the New Counties.

The Assembly has since got over the difficulty of suspending the Right of sending Representatives in the bills for erecting Townships. In the bills of the last Session may be seen sevral instances of that Clause being inserted, but they are not in a New County, excepting one which is taken out of an Old Town.

I am, with great respect, My Lords Your Lordship's most obedient & most humble Servant

Fra. Bernard

The R[t] Honble The Lords Commissioners for Trade & Plantations.

ALS, RC   CO 5/891, ff 53-55.

Contains minor emendations. Endorsed by John Pownall: *Massachusetts Bay* Letter from Francis Bernard Esq[r]. Gov[r]. of Massachusets Bay dated. August. 3. 1761 containing his Sentiments upon the Inconveniencys likely to follow from the continual increase of the number of Representatives. Reced. Oct. 26. 1761. Read Nov[r]. 19. L.l. 26. Variant text in BP, 2: 41-43 (L, LbC).

On 19 Nov. 1761, the Board of Trade "spent some time" deliberating FB's letter, the relevant parts of the Province Charter of 1691, and a clause in the provincial act of 1692 (4 Will. 3 & Mary, c. 38) concerning the election and apportionment of representatives, and replied to FB on 25 Nov. (**No. 79**). The Board's reconsideration of the matter on 9 Jun. 1762 is discussed in a letter of 11 Jun. (**No. 124**). *JBT*, 11: 226, 286. FB later enclosed a triplicate of **No. 59** in **No. 205**.

1. An act for dividing the county of Hampshire, and for establishing a new county of Berkshire, 1 Geo. 3 c. 33 (passed 21 Apr. 1761); an act for erecting the new plantation called Pontoosuck, in the county of Hampshire, into a town by the name of Pittsfield, 1 Geo. 3 c. 34 (passed 21 Apr. 1761). *Acts and Resolves*, 4: 432-435.

2. Journals of the House of Representatives, 27 May 1761 to 11 Jul. 1761, CO 5/842, pp. 3-112 (Prt, RC). The page numbers cited by FB are consistent with *JHRM*, 37 pt.2.

3. FB's message to the Council and the House of Representatives is dated Province House, 17 Apr.; the House of Representatives answered the following day. *JHRM*, 37 pt.2: 354, 360.

4. Bills to incorporate Plantations Number One, Three, and Four, and Colrain. *JHRM*, 37 pt.2: 343, 338, 350.

5. Incorporated in 1760.

6. See Article 40, General Instructions as governor of Massachusetts, **Appendix 1**.

7. The Treaty of Union (1706-07) between England and Scotland limited Scottish representation in the House of Commons to forty-five members: thirty for the shires and fifteen for the burghs. This entailed the sixty-five Scottish burghs, excluding Edinburgh, forming nine groups of five burghs and five groups of four to return fifteen members. J. D. Mackie, *A History of Scotland* (Harmondsworth, Eng. and New York, 1978), 260-261.

60 | To The Board Of Trade

Boston Aug 6, 1761

My Lords

Since my arrival here, about this time twelvemonth, I have been much employed in defending the Court of Admiralty & the Custom House against the attacks of a party formed & supported by Mr Barons Collector of this port. I was Very unwilling that Your Lordships should be troubled with this business hoping that Mr Barons would return to a sense of his duty; or at least that the Board to whom he was immediately subordinate would have time to interfere with proper effect. Nevertheless I informed Mr Pownall of these proceedings, & transmitted to him duplicates of such papers as I found would be laid before the Commissioners of the Customs, that they might be ready for your Lordships perusal if it should be thought necessary.[1] But the Mischeifs that have been foreseen & foretold to be arising from this combination become so serious, that I find myself obliged to address Your Lordships immediately upon this Subject.

The Means which seem now most likely to be pursued to destroy the Court of Admiralty & with it the Activity of the Laws of trade are to bring frequent Actions at Common Law concerning the Business determined in the ~~Customhouse~~ ^Court of^ Admiralty or proceeded upon in the Custom house; & by overhawling the Decrees of that Court before a Jury, & bringing Actions of the Case upon the Acts both judicial & extrajudicial of the Custom house officers, to render it certain Ruin for such officers to do their Duty. How probable it is that this Scheme will succeed without the extraordinary intervention of the Kings Authority at home will appear from what follows.

There are now depending in the Common Law Courts here 5 Actions of this kind; 3 of which are in Mr Barons's own Name; all which I will state to your Lordships in order, with observations on the ^probable^ consequences of them.

I Gray[2] agst Paxton.[3] This is an Action brought by the Treasurer of the Province against Mr Paxton a diligent Custom officer, of which I have allready given full information,[4] it being one of the first fruits of Mr Barons's confederacy, in which I had a principal share of trouble, it being particularly designed by some of Mr Barons's friends to involve me in a dispute with the General Court which however I prevented. For this I must refer Your Lordships to the Votes of the House of Assembly & other papers allready transmitted.[5] This Cause is determined against Mr Paxton in the inferior Court & he has appealed against that determination to the Superior Court.[6] If Judgement should be given against Mr Paxton in this Court also, these two points will be settled: 1, that Money paid in pursuance of a decree of the Court of Admiralty having jurisdiction in the Case & unappealed from, may be recovered ^in a Court of Common Law^ by other persons & for other uses, notwithstanding such decree. 2 That Money given by Act of parliament to His Majesty for the use of the province can be recovered by the provincial Treasurer ex officio, without the intervention of the Kings Attorney or Any person acting by immediate Authority under his Majesty.

II Erwing ag Cradock. This is an Action brought by the honble John Erwing Esq$_r$ one of the Council against Mr Cradock heretofore & now temporary Collector of this port.[7] This Case is this: Mr Cradock about 16 months ago, as collector, seized a Vessel of Mr Erwings charged with contraband trade & libelled her in the Court of Admiralty. Mr Erwing appeared personally in Court & prayed leave to compound, which, being agreed to by the Governor & Collector as well as the Kings Advocate,[8] was allowed by the Court at one half of the Value, which upon appraisement was ascertained at above £500 sterling. This Sum Mr Erwing paid into Court; & it was equally divided between the King the Governor & the Collector. Mr Cradock remitted the Kings Share to the Commissioners of the Customs; The Governor received his third, & Mr Cradock his own. And now Mr Erwing has brought his Action against Mr Cradock for damages accrued to him by means of this seizure; & in the inferior Court has got a Verdict for the sum of near £600. This is also appealed to the Superior Court;[9] & if it should be so determined there, it will be concluded that whatever sum a Man pays into the Court of Admiralty, tho' decreed in pursuance of his own petition, may be recoverd again at common Law with damages. The Consequences of this in regard to the Execution of the Laws of Trade are obvious.

III Barons ag Lechmere. This Action is brought against Mr Lechmere Surveyor general of the Northern district &c by Mr Barons for the former's suspending him. The day upon which Mr Barons received his suspension, He arrested Mr Lechmere in an action for 7,500 sterling damages, &, to the shame of the Laws of this Country, held him to bail. I have before transmitted the Papers relating to this Affair:[10] No Judicial Determination has yet been had. The Consequence of this Action must be, that No Superior residing here can hereafter Venture to censure an inferior Custom house officer in any Case whatsoever.

IV Barons ag Cradock. This Action is brought against the Gentleman whom Mr Lechmere appointed to execute the office during Mr Barons's suspension & untill the pleasure of the Commissioners should be known. And He is accordingly charged with being an adviser & abetter of such suspension No one hereafter must dare to meddle with the Office of a Suspended Officer.

V Barons ag Paxton. Mr Paxton exhibited a complaint against Mr Barons before Mr Lechmere as his Superior; Upon the examination of which & in pursuance whereof (amongst other causes) Mr Barons was suspended. So that No body from henceforth must presume to complain of a Custom house officer let him do what he pleases.

I state to your Lordships only the Actions that are now brought. But it is generally understood that Mr Erwings is only a leading Action to a great many others; And that, if he meets with Success, Evry One that has had goods condemned or been allowed to compound for them at their own request, will bring Actions against the Officer who seized them.

Your Lordships will perceive that these Actions have an immediate tendency to destroy the Court of Admiralty & with it the Custom house which cannot subsist without that Court. Indeed the Intention is made no Secret of: In the two Cases abovementioned, that were tried in the inferior Court, the cheif Subject of the haranges of the Council for the plaintiff (and some of the Judges too) were on the expediency of discouraging a Court immediately subject to the King & independant of the province & which determined property without a jury; & on a necessity of putting a stop to the practices of the Custom house officers, for that the people would no longer bear having their trade kept under restrictions, which thier Neighbours (meaning Rhode Island) were entirely free from. And One Gentleman,[11] who has had a considerable hand in promoting these disturbances, has been so candid as to own to me, that it was their intention to work them up to such a pitch as should make it necessary for the Ministry to interpose & procure them justice (as they call it) in repealing ^or qualifying^ the Molasses Act, & in obliging the Neighbouring Provinces to observe the same restraints which this is to be kept under. In regard to both these points, if they were sollicited in another Manner, there would be much to be said on their behalf.

I must add that this Commotion has hitherto been wholly confined to Boston: but It must be expected that if it succeeds here it will soon extend to the other ports. It cannot be said to be a provincial Concern: for tho' by means of sevral other concurrent Circumstances, it was made a subject of contention in the former Assembly; yet that is subsided, & most of the principal Members of the present Assembly (among which may be reckoned the representatives of most of the Neighbouring ports) disapprove of these proceedings & are by no means disposed to give their sanction to the schemes of unfair traders. For my own part I have steadily followed my resolution to support the Offices with all my power: It has given me a great deal of trouble & subjected me to some abuse, but no other inconvenience.

I would not pretend to dictate to your Lordships what remedies to apply to these disorders: One however I will take the liberty of mentioning; That your Lordships would recommend to the Lords of the treasury to order their sollicitor to take upon him the conduct & maintenance of these Suits. They are all of them (not excepting Gray ag Paxton) Actions against the King; whose Authority in evry one (& in one the Very money now in the royal Treasury) is at stake. As for the Expence, The Money brought into the Treasury by ^the seizures of^ Mr Paxton only (from whence This persecution of him & the other office[r]s takes his rise) will more than defray it. But what more induces me to propose this to your Lordships is, that I am persuaded that as soon as it is known that the Defence of these causes is put into the hands of the solicitor of the treasury, it probably will put an immediate stop to the present proceedings & prevent any future of the same kind. As to Mr Barons's 3 Actions, He himself is, to my knowledge, subject to such large penalties in strictness of law, that the Very showing him his own danger must make him glad to drop his Actions & to submit his cause, as He should have done at first, to the judgement of his superiors in England, who have power enough to do him justice, if he has suffered wrong.

I am, with great respect, My Lords, Your Lordships most obedient & most humble Servant

Fra, Bernard.

To The Rt Honble The Lords Commissioners of Trade & Plantations

ALS, RC   CO 5/891, ff 41-45.

Endorsed by John Pownall: *Massachusets Bay* Letter from Francis Bernard Esq[r]. Gov[r]. of Massachusets Bay. dated August. 6. 1761. containing an Account of sev[l]. Actions brought in the Courts of common Law these tend [only?][12] to set aside the Jurisdiction of the Admiralty Court, & the Officers of the Crown. Reced. Oct. 26. 1761. Read Novr: 18, L.l. 21. Variant text in BP, 2: 45-50 (L, LbC). Enclosed copies of *Barons v. Lechmere, Barons v. Craddock, Barons v. Paxton*, all dated Boston, 23 Jun. 1761, CO 5/891, ff 46-50.

A delay in posting meant that this letter was enclosed in **No. 64**. After a reading at the Board of Trade on 18 Nov. 1761, FB's letter and enclosures were copied and referred to the Lords Commissioners of the Treasury. *JBT*, 11: 225. For the Board's reply see **No. 79**.

1. FB to John Pownall, Boston, 13 Jul. 1761, BP, 1: 323-324.

2. Harrison Gray (1711-94), province treasurer, 1753-74, and member of the Governor's Council, 1761-72, was a moderate Whig and a Loyalist during the Revolution.

3. See Josiah Quincy, Samuel M. Quincy, and Horace Gray, *Reports of Cases Argued and Adjudged in the Superior Court of Judicature of the Province of Massachusetts Bay, Between 1761 and 1772* (Boston, 1865), 541-547.

4. FB to Pownall, 13 Jul. 1761.

5. A House of Representatives' resolve of 13 Jan. "impowered and directed" Treasurer Gray to recover over £475 sterling from the vice-admiralty court in respect of deductions, including fees and payments to informers, made from the province's share of customs seizures. FB reluctantly consented to the resolve: his stated objection was not the first point he raises in this letter, concerning the challenge to the vice-admiralty court, but the second—the procedural irregularity of having the treasurer instead of the attorney general initiate the suit. A resolution of 27 Jan. named Paxton as the defendant. See *JHRM*, 37, pt.2: 181, 231-248; Tyler, *Smugglers & Patriots*, 41-42.

6. Superior Court of Judicature, Record Books, 1760-62, p. 235, Massachusetts Archives.

7. John Erving (c.1692-1786) was a wealthy merchant and a member of the Governor's Council, 1754-74, whose brig *Sarah* was seized by customs officers led by George Craddock on 26 Apr. 1760. George Craddock (d.1771) of Charlestown, was deputy judge of the court of Vice Admiralty, 1742-?, and collector at Boston for the duration of Barons's suspension. For the case see Quincy, et al.., *Reports of Cases Argued and Adjudged in the Superior Court*, 553-555.

8. James Otis Jr. was deputy advocate-general of Vice Admiralty, 1757-62.

9. Superior Court of Judicature, Record Books, 1760-62, p. 230.

10. Not found.

11. Possibly James Otis Jr.

12. Smudged.

61 | To Jeffery Amherst

Castle William Aug 9 1761

S[r]

Some time ago the Chesterfield Man of War Cap Scaife[1] came in here & brought with him an Ordinance Store-Ship, which was order'd to stay here till She could get a Convoy to New York. Capt Scaife left with me a Copy of an order from Admiralty for Any Man of War that should come in here to convoy that Ship: And I undertook that if the King George, who is now out on a cruise, should come in I would employ her for that purpose.[2] But neither of these contingencies having happened, the Store ship is still here: and I yesterday received a Letter from Lord Colville expressing his inability to send a Ship for this business & his Concern least these stores should be Wanted by you. I therefore write this, that if you would have this Ship proceed without Convoy, you may give orders for it. We have no advice of french privateers being near this Coast. And to the Southward It is pretty well guarded; the Penzance of 44 guns, the Greyhound of 20 & the King George of 20 being now cruising between Rhode Island & Virginia.

To morrow We are to have the last Muster of Col Thwings Regiment which is more than full. I expect there will be 1000 privates besides Officers; altho' I have transferred one officer with 40 men to the other Regiments. I could not well re-move Any More: so must desire to have credit for the supernumeraries of this in the musters of the other Regiments, which I expect are or soon will be completed.

I congratulate you on the Surrender of the Citadell of Bellisle, the Capitulation of which I received from a Master of a Brig that arrived here yesterday from Bristol in 7 weeks. I read the paper in such hurry & parted with it so soon that I have forgot the date of the Capitulation.[3]

I am, with great regard, S[r] Your most obedient most humble Servant

Fra, Bernard.

ALS, RC   WO 34/26, f 104.

1. John Scaife (d.1773), a British naval officer, raised to captain on 22 Feb. 1759.

2. The *King George* came into port c.22 Aug., and FB reported that she would be ready within five days to escort the storeship to Sandy Hook, New Jersey. FB to Amherst, Castle William, 22 Aug. 1761, WO 34/26, f 105.

3. Admiral Augustus Keppel (1725-86) forced the surrender of the fortified Belle Isle in Quiberon Bay, off the French coast, on 7 Jun. 1761 after a two-month siege.

62 | *To Lord Barrington*

Boston Aug.ˢᵗ. 10. 1761

My Lord

When I first arrived at This Town I received from your Lordship a recommendation of Mʳ. Barrons Collector of this Port: upon which I assured him that I should take a pleasure in obeying your Lordships commands by serving him. I soon found that the best service I could do him would be to advise him concerning his public conduct; & the duty of my Office making it quite necessary, I was soon given to understand that I had so far incurred his displeasure, as to be thought deserving a formal opposition to me & my Government. The injuries and insults I have received from him & his party make a part of a long story which has been already communicated to Lord Halifax & Secretary Pownall; & must now if it has not Already, be made public.

I should not have troubled your Lordship on this Subject if It could have been avoided. But Mʳ Lechmere the Surveyor General having Suspended Mʳ. Barrons from his Office, & having sent away the articles exhibited against him together [*with*] the proofs taken in support of them, as also some fresh charges to the commisioners of the Customs; & having prepared another set for the Lords of the Treasury I find this business must come before your Lordship in your public character; & therefore beg leave to use the access your Lordships has allowed me to have to your private station

I have wrote so much upon this subject that I am quite tired of it; but if I was ever so much disposed to write on, I could not give your Lordship a better information of the part I have acted, than by the copies inclosed. The I is a Copy of my declaration by way of Evidence, which is among the proofs. The II is a Copy of a letter I wrote to Lord H. As this contains little more than plain Narrative, I presume I am not wrong in sending this Copy to your Lordship. If there is any danger of my being blamed for it, your Lordship will keep it to your self. The III is a copy of a letter I now write to the Lords of trade. The subject matter would have made it more properly addressed to the Lords of the treasury, if the regulation of My Correspondence had not directed me to apply myself to the Lords of Trade. your Lordship will consider this as designed only for your own private information, untill It shall be formally transmitted from the board of trade. Among the papers sent by Mʳ. Lechmere (Copies of which I have sent to the board of trade) you will find a good deal more matter than what I now trouble your Lordship with.

Ever since the commencement of these disturbances which is now near 12 months I have been ready & desirous to take hold of every oppertunity that offered to compose these troubles but have not been able to do any thing towards it The

defence of my self & my Authority as well as of the Court of Admiralty & the Customhouse has found me full employment.

A few weeks ago some Gentlemen applied to me in behalf of Mr Barrons, desiring I would intervene in his favor. I told them that the actions he had brought
against M^r. Lechmere Mr Craddock & M^r. Paxton were such open acts of his setting at defiance the King['s] Authority under which he was placed by his office, that
I could do him no service, whilst he persisted in maintaining them, but If he would
withdraw them, I would waive all resentment of my own, (altho' some injuries I
then mentioned them were Very fresh) & immediately treat with them about what
could be done for M^r. Barrons. They used their endeavours to persuade him to
comply with this preliminary, but could not prevail.

It has been no small part of my Concern at being thus embrangled in this dispute, that It may tend to impeach a Character which I have borne thro all my life &
which I own I am proud of, that of a good natured Man. I very much regret that the
unreasonable Man has made the censuring him necessary to my defence & part
of my duty. Without these considerations I could wish him all the good he desires:
I heartily wish he had a place of twice the Value any where else: and I have often
wished that I could consistently with my duty recommend his being restored to &
continued in this. But I dare not make my self answerable for such a representation: the same prejudices passions & connexions that I have had so much reason to
complain of, still seem to prevail.

I shall take the first oppertunity to lay before your Lordship a state of the Customhouse in this and the Neighbouring Governments; from whence will plainly appear the Causes which have induced the Merchants of this port to be less disposed
to Obey the Laws of Trade than they have hitherto been. The Remedies for these
inconveniences will be very obvious & I hope as practicable; & like to be attended
with very good consequences. But this I must defer to a further time.

I am with great respect, My Lord your Lordship's &c &c &c

The R^t. Honble The Lord Visc^t. Barrington

L, LbC   BP, 2: 2-4.

In the handwriting of clerk no. 1. The enclosures FB mentions were copies of **No. 60** and
Papers concerning charges of corruption brought against Benjamin Barons, 18 Feb. - 16 Apr.
1761, T 1/408, ff 177-178; the letter to Halifax has not been found.

63 | To Lord Sandys

Boston Aug^st. 17. 1761

My Lord

I have just received the orders of your Lordship & the othe[r] Commissioners for trade &c. requiring my Answers to the Queries therewith enclosed.[1] I shall use due diligence to answer the same as fully & expeditiously as the importance of the Subject will admit. In the mean time I beg leave to congratulate your Lordship upon your being placed at the head of the board of trade, & to Assure your Lordship that I shall always think myself honored by your favorable acceptance of my Service. I am, with great respect,

My Lord, your Lordships &c &c

The R^t. Honble the Lord Sandys

L, LbC   BP, 2: 1.

In the handwriting of clerk no. 1.

---

1. **No. 46**.

64 | To the Board of Trade

Boston Aug 27 1761

My Lords

The inclosed letter has laid by me so long that I am enabled to give your Lordships a short Account of the Success of the two appeals before mentioned; the Causes having been heard before the Superior Court.

Gray ag^st Paxton. This Cause was determined without a Jury, by a plea of abatement to the Writ,[1] which the Court determined in favor of the defendant. The Point upon which it turned was that the Treasurer could not sue for this Money ex officio: And there was no order of the General Court to enable him. There has been an order made since the bringing this Writ; And it is expected that a New Writ will be brought in pursuance of that order, And then will arise another Question whether an Order of the general Court can enable a person not authorised by ~~Act of Parliament~~ his Office to sue for Money given to the King by Act of Parliament.

My Reasons for the Negative Your Lordships will see in the Votes of Jan 1761 pa 246.[2]

Erwing ag. Cradock. This Action came before a jury in the Superior Court. Upon the summing up the Evidence the Judges were all of opinion that tho' Mr Cradock might by means of some irregularity in the seizing the Ship have been guilty of a trespass (which however was neither proved nor admitted) yet it was wholly purged by the composition confirmed by the Court of Admiralty, the decrees of which were of equal force with a Judgement at Common Law. It was urged by the Cheif Justice that the Court of Admiralty was part of the Constitution of the Province, it being expressly provided for by the Charter. The whole ~~Judges~~ Bench directed the Jury, as strongly as they could, to find for the Def^t. Nevertheless they found for the Plaintiff & gave upwards of £550 sterling in damages, being all that he said he was out of pocket. This was no Surprise to those that were acquainted with the Violence with which these proceedings are carried on. It was remarkable that Mr Erwing according to the usage of these Courts, spoke a great deal for himself, when he admitted Evry thing Necessary to prove that he had incurred a forfeiture & declared he had acquiesced only in expectation that a time would come when He should have his revenge: a word he used sevral times to express the purpose of his conduct. He declared ^after the Verdict^ that he should be Supported by the principal Merchants of London against Any representations the Governor could make.

Mr Cradock will take care to enter An Appeal to the King in due time: as he will Nevertheless be subject to Execution, Care will be taken to prevent his being sent to Goal before Orders come from England. They now begin to talk of bringing more Actions against Custom house officers who have made seizures & have had them Condemned or compounded in Court for them. A Custom house officer has no chance with a Jury, let his Cause be what it will. And It will depend upon the Vigorous Measures that shall be taken at home for the defence of the Officers, whether there be Any Custom house here at all.

I am, with great respect, My Lords, Your Lordships most obedient & most humble Servant

Fra Bernard

To the R^t Honble The Lords Commissioners for Trade &c.

ALS, RC   CO 5/891, ff 51-52.

Endorsed by John Pownall: *Massachusets Bay* Letter from Francis Bernard Esqr. Govr. of the Massachusets Bay dated Aug. 27. 1761. containing an Acc^t. of the issue of two Actions brought in the Superior Court, upon an appeal from the Judgements of the Superior Courts mentioned in a former Letter. Reced. Octr. 26. 1761. Read Nov^r: 18. L.l.25. Variant text in

BP, 2: 51-52 (L, LbC). Enclosed **No. 60** and Journals of the House of Representatives, 27 May 1761 to 11 Jul. 1761, CO 5/842, pp. 3-112 (Prt).

This letter was considered by the Board of Trade on 18 Nov. 1761 and referred to the Lords Commissioners of the Treasury. *JBT*, 11: 225.

---

1. This procedure entails defendants contesting a writ or other legal instrument on the basis that it contains extrinsic errors.

2. FB had warned the House of Representatives in Jan. that only the province attorney general could initiate Crown actions. *JHRM*, 37 pt.2: 246-247.

65 | To Lord Barrington

Boston August 28. 1761

My Lord

I am extreamly obliged to your Lordship for you[r] kind letter of the 6th of June[1]: whilst I return my thanks I must again apologise for the trouble I gave your Lordship on account of the fees. I was very diffident of the propriety of the application & trusted more to your Lordships Benignity than I depended on the singularity of the Case; which perhaps may still have some weight, when your Lordship's kind attention to us shall favor some other request. I mentioned to your Lordship before how Very inequal the Income of this Government was to its business & importance, with a View to excuse my self for being so Solicitous for providing for my Sons by places.[2] To come to particulars, the Salary is 1,000 the fees at most 100, to which if the Annual Value of the Governor's house is reckoned (which would be highly estimated at 100) the Government is worth at the most 1200 a year.[3] As for the share of seizures which, if the Authority of the Customhouse is maintained, would be worth reckoning, in the present state of the Customhouse, It is a profit neither to be expected nor wished for. Nevertheless I can Assure your Lordship that I am quite pleased with my being placed here, as the advantages I may hope to gain for my Children will make good the deficiency of the income.

For these reasons I hope your Lordship will excuse me, if I still wait in expectation of a favourable Event to my request concerning the Naval Office. I wrote to your Lordship[4] on this Subject the very day of the date of your Lordships letter now before me, wherein I informed, that M[r]. Pemberton had received a sign Manual, yet he was very willing to let it lye by to give me an opportunity to procure another in the manner I have proposed, being still desirous that our Agreement should be carried into Execution. I added that as this business seemed to be an affair of consent of parties, I hoped it would meet with no difficulty. That there may be no doubt in M^r. Pemberton's behalf, he proposes to write to M^r. Pitt to acquaint him that he has not put in execution the former Sign Manual & is very willing that another should be issued in the Manner I have desired. I shall write a short letter to M^r. Pitt my self, which I beg leave to inclose to your Lordship to be delivered to him or not as your Lordship shall ~~think fit~~ Judge fit. My pretentions to this favor will be more effectually represented by your Lordship than they can by me. I hope the expectation of the place after M^r. Pemberton's death will not be thought of any great Value as to be opposed to my request; for I can Assure your Lordship that his health & Vigour promises many more years.

M^r. Pemberton has brought me a letter from him to M^r. Pitt, as also one to your Lordship.[5] He has acted with great Candor in this Affair; And I think my self obliged to him what ever the Event is.

I am with great gratitude & respect, My Lord Your Lordships &c

R^t. Honble the Lord Viscount Barrington

L, LbC   BP, 2: 4-5.

In the handwriting of clerk no. 1 with scribal emendations. The enclosure FB mentions was likely **No. 66**, composed after this letterbook entry. Other enclosures have not been found, but are mentioned in **No. 74**.

---

1. Barrington to FB, Cavendish Square, 6 Jun. 1761, BP, 9: 205-208.

2. **Nos. 24** and **34**.

3. In £sterling.

4. FB to Barrington, Boston, 6 Jun. 1761, BP, 1: 313-314.

5. Letters not found.

66 | To William Pitt

Boston Aug[st]. 28. 1761

S[r]

Sometime after his late Majesty's Decease, I sent a memorial for the Earl of Halifax praying that he would recommend that my son Francis Bernard might be joined with M[r]. Pemberton in the Naval Office of this Province, M[r]. Pemberton having agreed thereto. But before this Memorial could be presented, A Sign Manual passed for the grant of this Office to M[r]. Pemberton alone & My Lord Halifax quitted the board of trade. M[r]. Pemberton having received the sign Manual[1] acquainted me with it, but said he did not desire that it should be carried into Execution, if the like order in favor of him & my son could be procured. I must therefore beg leave to lay my case before you & desire your favourable consideration of it. My Lord Barrington who honours me so far, as to regard me & mine with the kindest concern, will be so good as to state my pretentions to your favor in a better manner than I can my self; I can add that I shall always endeavour to be deserving of it.

I am, with great respect &c &c

R[t]. Honble W. Pitt Esq[r]

L, LbC   BP, 2: 6.

In the handwriting of clerk no. 1. This letter was probably enclosed in **No. 65**. Its own enclosure(s) has not been found.

---

1. On 6 Jun. 1761.

67 | To Thomas Pownall

Castle William Aug 28. 1761

D^r S^r.

I intended you a long letter by this Conveyance, but must confine my self to one subject which has employed so much of my writing, that I am obliged to postpone all letters that will bear it.

You may learn from your Brother the proceedings of M^r. Barrons & his confederates against the Government & all the Royal Offices. M^r. Otis Junr. is at the head of the Confederacy: If you are acquainted with the natural Violence of his temper, suppose it to be augmented beyond all bounds of Common decency inflamed by & inflaming the general Clamour of Ilicit traders, who think they now have the Custom house at their Mercy, & seem determined to show none. Under such a conductor you may imagine the law is like to thrive & accordingly there are now 5 Actions depending against Customhouse officers, not one of which could be advised by a Lawyer that had any regard for his credit. I shall refer you to the Secretary for the particulars of these,[1] but as you have a considerable intrest in one of them I shall give you a short account of that

It is an Action of trespass brought by Cap Erwing against M^r. Cradock (at the instagation of M^r. Barrons as appears from two depositions) for seizing a brig of his in April 1760. This you may remember was compounded in the Court of Admiralty, at the desire of M^r. Erwing for £500 sterling M^r. Cradock remitted the King[']s] share to the Custom house, paid yours to M^r. Hancock, & out of his own gave $^{1}/_{3}$ or ¼ to M^r. Sheafe his Clerk;[2] so that he had to him self not above £100. the pretence for this action is, that the Seizure was illegal & a trespass, & that the payment of M^r. Erwing was not Voluntary but extorted by Violence & *duress*. Upon this shadow of reason, two of the Judges of the inferior Court, M^r. Watts & M^r. Wells[3] directed the jury to find a Verdict for the Plaintiff & give him for damages every farthing he was out of pocket; & ~~M^r. Wells~~ said they, must put a stop to these proceedings of the Custom house officers; if they did not there would be tumults & bloodshed; for the people would bear with them no longer, The Jury accordingly gave the Pl^{tf}. near £600 sterling damages. This being appealed from came to a hearing before the superior Court; where the Judges were unanimously of opinion that there were no grounds for the Action; for without entering into the merits of the seizure, if there was any tresspass in it, it was cured by the composition, which was a deliberate Act done by advice of Council & confirmed by the Court of Admiralty, whose Decrees were equal to the Judgements of the common law Courts. In fine they all directed the Jury to find for the Defendant nevertheless they found for the Plaintiff & gave him upwards of 550 sterling.

If this Verdict can be maintained It is plain there is an End of the Custom house & the Court of Admiralty too. I therefore recommend in the strongest terms that these Actions may be publickly defended by the Kings sollicitor, which will soon put a stop to them. When the Cause I have mentioned comes before the Privy Council The Defence of the Verdict wont bear the Shadow of an argument. But this appeal must be Carried on at the Expence of the King, as should all the others. The Treasury will never suffer their Officers to be ruined for doing their duty. If this Judgement shou[ld] be carried into execution M^r. Hancock must refuse the third that he received for you; but I think there is [no] danger of that.

I have heard that some of M^r. Paxton's Enemies have given out that he has treated your name disrespectfully. I have never been able to learn any foundation for this Charge that they have & believe, it only a scheme to prevent your favouring his cause. I know of one thing that may possibly be made use of against him tho' Unjustly. M^r. Barrons was informed (not by M^r. Paxton) that, upon his last going home to England, you wrote to advise that his friends should provide for him there & not send him back again, for he was so very silly, that he would certainly disgrace his recommenders if he returned here. This M^r. Barrons charged M^r. Paxton with knowing & not acquainting him with it which he urged to be very unfriendly. And now possibly M^r. Barrons may turn the tables & charge M^r. Paxton with discovering this. But if it was true that M^r. Paxton did first acquaint him with it (which I dont believe) It only gives an instance of your penatation[4] & shows that a knowledge of mankind may sometimes take the appearance of prophecy, at least M^r. Barrons has been indefatigable in making your words good.

I am D^r. S^r. &

Thos. Pownall Esq_r

L, LbC   BP, 2: 9-11.

In the handwriting of clerk no. 1. Conjectured readings in roman type are for letters obscured by tight binding.

---

1. **Nos. 60** and **64**.

2. William Sheaffe (1705/06-71), deputy collector of Customs at Boston.

3. Samuel Watts (1697-1770), a merchant and extensive property holder, had been a justice of the inferior court of Common Pleas of Suffolk County since 1748 and a member of the Governor's Council since 1742. Samuel Welles (1689-1770) had represented Boston in the House on several occasions and had been appointed a judge in 1755.

4. Thus in manuscript. Probably meaning penetration, although pensitation is also a possibility.

68 | To Jeffery Amherst

Castle William Aug^st. 30th. 1761

S^r.

I have just rec^d yours of the 20th instant.[1] The King George is under orders to convoy the Ordinance ship, & will, if the weather permits, sail tomorrow.[2] The last of Thwings Regim^t. sailed to day.[3] By the end of this week the Musters of the other Regiments will be finished, which I hope will not be much short of their Compliments. I am Sorry they have been so delayed; but there have been no pains spared to complete them sooner. The want of Men is felt in all kind of business, especially in shipping, where the wages are become exorbitant.

I am with great regard, S^r. your most obedient &c &c

His Excy Maj^r. Genl. S^r. Jeffery Amherst.

L, LbC   BP, 2: 119-120.

In the handwriting of clerk no. 1.

---

1. Amherst to FB, Albany, 20 Aug. 1761, WO 34/27, p. 223.

2. Amherst was in camp at Staaten Island, preparing for the march to Albany, and awaiting the storeship's arrival.

3. On 22 Aug., when FB reported that the regiment was at full strength of one thousand men, excluding officers and deserters, he noted that twenty-six soldiers were waiting on a vessel to take them to Halifax. These were the "last" of Thwing's men. The other two regiments were "Very near" full strength. FB to Amherst, Castle William, 22 Aug. 1761, WO 34/26, f 105.

69 | To Jeffery Amherst

Boston Sep 4. 1761

S^r.

I am favoured with yours of the 28th. August.[1] It is Very agreeable to me to have your approbation, ^even^ in minute things: but the Civilities I showed to Capt Moncrief were due evry way, to his personal behaviour, to his rank, & most especially, to the Commission He bore under you.[2]

Your proposal concerning providing our troops with spruce beer was so striking, that I lost no time in laying it before the Council, who have this day advised, that I order the sevral Colonels to provide immediately Spruce beer for their Men at the rate of 2 quarts per. man a day or more if desired; & that they immediately enter into contracts for that purpose, being directed to draw upon the Commissary-general for the sums that shall be due upon such contracts, which will be duely paid. I am also advised to desire that you would give orders to the sevral commanding officers to assist this purpose with their power; and that, where our troops shall be detached in so small parties as to render a special provision of spruce beer impracticable, they may have credit for spruce beer from those that supply the regulars, on the same terms, which shall be duely acknowledged here.

I must add for myself, that It would be very agreable to me, if, whilst We are providing spruce beer for them, some method may be hit upon to prevent their being supplied with Rum; & for that purpose, I should be glad, if such orders for this, as you shall subject the regulars to, may be extended to our provincials.[3] I have allready wrote to our Colonels,[4] that I expect, that, if such orders should be issued, they take care to see them punctually obeyed. If these two purposes shall be well pursued, (as I have allready prevailed in another of no less consequence, their being well cloathed) I flatter myself, that the returns at the end of this Service will be Very different from what they have usually been.

I am, with great regard, S[r], Your most obedient humble Servant

Fra. Bernard.

His Excellency Maj[r] Gen[l] S[r] Jeffry Amherst.

ALS, RC   WO 34/26, f 107.

Contains minor emendations. Several non-authorial (and probably non-contemporaneous) annotations have been ignored. There are two copies in BP, 2: 121 and 123-124. The reply to this letter is Amherst to FB, Staaten Island, 17 Sept. 1761, WO 34/27, p. 228 (L, LbC).

---

1. Not found.

2. Amherst reported that Moncreiffe "Expresses the remarkable politeness, and Civilities he has met with from You, in the Execution of the Service he was Sent upon," which was to supervise the mustering and embarkation of the provincial soldiers for Halifax. Amherst to FB, Staaten Island, 28 Aug. 1761, BP, 9: 225-228.

3. Amherst had proposed supplying spruce beer to the Massachusetts troops working on the fortifications at Halifax, as had already been done for the British Regulars there. At a cost of less than three farthings per gallon, he supposed it an inexpensive and, according to his officers' reports, a highly effective means of combating the "Dissenteries & mortal Disorder" induced by contaminated water and the drunkenness attendant to the overconsumption of rum. By Jun. 1762, if not earlier, FB had appointed Messrs Taylor and Blodget to undertake the brewing at Crown Point. Amherst to FB, 28 Aug. 1761; Council Executive Records, 1760-1766, CO 5/823, f 99; FB to Amherst, Boston, 17 Jun. 1762, WO 34/26, f 165.

4. FB to Cols. Thwing, Saltonstall, Hoar, Boston, 4 Sept. 1761, Prov. Sec. Letterbooks, 2: 321-323 .

70 | To [Nathaniel Thwing]

Castle William Sep 16. 1761

S[r].

whereas I have by my letter bearing date the 15th inst ordered you to call a Regimental Court Martial to enquire whether Capt. Edward Blake hath supplied any private Men of his Company with Sutlers stores, after he was informed that David Wyer was appointed by me & assigned by you to be sutler of his Company, It is now my order that if the Court shall find him guilty of the Charge, you suspend him untill you shall receive further orders from me.

I am &c.

L, LbC   BP, 2: 125-126.

In the handwriting of clerk no. 1.

   Blake's profiteering at Crown Point reflected badly on his commanding officer, Col. Na-thaniel Thwing. In a draft of his letter to Thwing of 15 Sept. FB upbraided the colonel, whom he thought "ought to have exercised more Authority over Capt Blake on this occasion" (BP, 2: 120). This was omitted from the letter he dispatched, however, perhaps because Thwing's assistance was essential if the suttling issue were to be resolved satisfactorily, in the interests of the soldiers (BP, 2: 124-125). The court-martial found Blake guilty but he continued in the service until 1763. Blake admitted to ordering provisions worth over £90 for his men and en-gaging in "irregular and illegal" accounting, sometimes placing orders to the value of a soldier's entire wages. CO 5/823: 222.

71 | To Colonels Nathaniel Thwing, Richard Saltonstall, and Jonathan Hoar

Castle William Sep 16. 1761

S[r].

For regulating the abuses in regard to the furnishing the provincial troops with necessary stores, I thought proper to appoint certain Sutlers to every Company of the provincial regiments who might be subject to orders & answerable for misbe-haviour; & I thought that such an appointment contained in it sufficient restriction of the scandalous practise of Officers Suttling to their own men. Nevertheless as the want of written orders upon this occasion is made an excuse for Officers per-sisting in this unwarra[n]table & disgraceful practise, I think proper to issue these orders.

1 That you give public Notice that no officer or other person belonging to the Regiment presume to stuttle[1] to the private men, except such as shall be appointed by me or under my authority.

2 That if any officers shall be charged with a breach of this order you immedi-ately call a regimental Court Martial to enquire upon their Oaths into the fact & if such court shall find that such Officer has suttled to the men, you shall immedi-ately suspend him, untill I give order thereon, transmitting to me true copies of the charge defence, Depositions & sentence.

3 That you give orders to each suttler, that he keep a day Book wherein he shall enter every article delivered to the men & a ledger book wherein these Articles shall be brought to the account of each man And that a Company roll of the Sutlers Account be settled at the end of every month containing the sum total due from every man & signed by him which roll being compared with the ledger & day book shall be signed by the Capt of the Company, & also by the Colonel or commanding Officer.

4 That you settle with the sutlers a list of the prices of the several goods sold by them at a fair & reasonable rate; and that Copies of such list be delivered to every Captain & be fixed up at the stores, at the Guard room & at other propper places. And that the sutlers may not be induced to make an higher charge upon account of the Credit that they are obliged to give, you may assure them that if their charge of the goods shall be at the rate of what is called a ready money price, they shall re-ceive intrest at one half p[r]. cent for every month that the payment shall be delayed after two months from the settlement of Each monthly Roll.[2]

5 You shall transmit to me a copy of the list of Prices so settled by you, & also an account of the prices which the Sutlers of the regulars charge to their men, with you[r] opinion concerning the comparison of the two rates, if they shall differ materialy: this to be repeated as often as there shall be occasion.

6 The Sutlers are to give credit to the Men for no more than half their pay: and no other deductions will be suffered to be put upon the rolls except the Sutlers credit not exceeding half their pay

I am &c &c &c

To Col. Thwing Col. Saltonstall Col. Hoar

L, LbC   BP, 2: 126-127.

In the handwriting of clerk no. 1 with minor scribal emendations.

These regulations were issued as a result of Capt. Edward Blake's indiscretions (**No. 70**).

---

1. Thus in manuscript.

2. In addition, FB had requested that the sutlers at Halifax be exempt from any provincial duties on goods supplied to the regiments, and be placed under the protection of Maj. Gen. John Henry Bastide (c.1700-c.1770), a British military engineer. Bastide had supervised the demolition of Louisbourg in 1760, before taking charge of the construction of the fortifications at Halifax. FB to Bastide, Boston, 29 Jul. 1761, BP, 2: 119; FB to Jonathan Belcher, Boston, 29 Jul. 1761, BP, 2: 118.

72 | To Jeffery Amherst

Boston Sep. 20. 1761

S[r]

By a return of Col Thwings Regiment, I find there are now there 1063, and there are 2 or 3 more to join. I have not as yet got returns of the other two regiments, but understand that there are above 1700 marched to Albany. The deserters I suppose are above 100 in the whole; so that I expect our deficiency will not exceed 100. It is not worth while at this time, to endeavour to make good this deficiency for this year: and I presume there are a great many more than will be wanted beyond it. I thought proper to communicate to you this state of our forces, as it now appears to me.

I am, with great regard, S[r] Your most obed[t] humble Servant

Fra Bernard

His Excellency S[r] Jeffry Amherst

ALS, RC   WO 34/26, f 108.

Variant text in BP, 2: 123 (L, LbC). The reply to this letter is Amherst to FB, Staaten Island, 4 Oct. 1761, WO 34/27, p. 229.

73 | To the Rev. Edward Bass

Boston Sep^{br}. 21st. 1761

S^r.

    M^r. Caner has communicated to me your letters concerning an intrusion on your church.[1] If that intrusion has been made with a View to disposses you & the Church wardens of your right to the Church I should advise & assist you in defending your right But as it seems to be only a Violent enforcing a request of being permitted to use the Church, at such times when it shall not be wanted for the service of the Church of England, & untill they can build a Meeting house for them selves I must recommend to you & the Church wardens to grant such requests, they disclaiming all right to the Church & disavowing the force that has been used by them.[2] Such accommodations are Very common in many parts of Europe between communions of different religious persuasions, And I hope the Church of England will not be out done by any Church whatsoever in Christian Moderation towards it's dissenting Brethern.

    It may be proper to have an acknowledgem^t. in writing that they claim no right to the Church, to prevent any unfair conclusions being hereafter drawn from the use of it,

I am S^r your humble servant

The Rev^d. M^r. Bass[3]

L, LbC   BP, 2: 123.

In the handwriting of clerk no. 1.

---

1. Not found.

2. The governor was obliged to help maintain the bishop of London's ecclesiastical jurisdiction in America. Labaree, *Royal Instructions*, 2: 490. The Congregationalists assumed that he would promote the interests of the province's Anglican clergy and churches to the deteriment of their own.

3. The Rev. Edward Bass D.D. (1726-1803), the rector of St. Paul's Church, Newbury (later Newburyport), who in 1796 was consecrated the first Episcopal bishop of Massachusetts. Newbury's sectarian rivalries are discussed in Benjamin Woods Labaree, *Patriots and Partisans: the Merchants of Newburyport, 1764-1815* (New York, 1975), 2-3, 8.

74 | To Lord Barrington

Castle William Sep 27. 1761

My Lord

Last night I rec[d]. your Lordships ~~letter~~ favor of the 11th of July[1] as also the duplicate of that of the 6th of June,[2] the original of which I have received some time ago. Upon the receipt of the former of the 6th of June, I had a conversation with M[r]. Pemberton; when (observing to him, that tho' he had signified his consent to a joint patent by many letters wrote before he knew that a sign manual was issued to him alone, yet since that, He had only signified such consent by a letter to M[r]. Alderman Baker,[3] & that probally M[r]. Pitt would Expect a letter to himself) He wrote a letter to M[r]. Pitt to that ~~subject~~ purpose; which together with another from M[r]. Pemberton to your Lordship,[4] one of mine to your Lordship,[5] another to M[r]. Pitt[6] & a Copy of the memorial which I before sent to your Lordship,[7] I enclosed in one cover[8] & sent it enclosed again in a large packet to the Lords of Trade[9] by the Chesterfield Man of War Cap Scaife. The Captain himself took it in charge & sailed for England sep'. 3. This contains all the papers required by your Lordship in your last, & as they go by a 50 Gun ship, I hope no inconvenience will arise from my not having provided duplicates.

I was very sorry to find myself obliged to trouble your Lordship with the papers contained in another cover sent by the same conveyance, relating to the conte[st][10] between the Merchants & the Custom house, But as this business must inavoidably come before your board, I thought it would be agreeable to your Lordship to have some previous knowledge of the Affair I propose soon to write to your Lordship on the subject of the present state of the trade of this Country, possibly to more purpose than giving details of Custom house Squabbles.

I have not the honor of being personally known to M[r]. Pitt: and it was my misfortune to be prevented paying my duty to him in person, before I left England, by his indisposition, I should think a great honour, if your Lordship would recommend my service to him. My previous Studies in England & my attention to the Kings Service in N America, ^*have* ~~given me great opportunities~~ *induced me to turn my thoughts upon the political state of this province,*^[11] to which my different stations have not a little assisted. If after a peace a general disquisition of the constitutions of the several Governments here, should take place as it is much expected, I should be very proud to be of the least use in such a work.

I have received a letter from my son wherein he acknowledges his negligence in not waiting on your Lordship before he went to Oxford.[12] I hope your Lordship will excuse the inadvertency of youth: I persuade myself that he has not ingratitude in his nature however his carelessness may make him appear so.

I beg your Lordship will make our Compliments to the ladies & all our friends acceptable. I am with the utmost gratitude & respect. My Lord your Lordships most obedient &c

R^t. Honble Lord Visct Barrington

PS If a sign Manual should be prepared, I must desire your Lordship will give notice to W^m. *Bollan Esq in Liecester Square* to sue it out, pay the fees & transmit it. I shall write to him on the occasion[13]

L, LbC   BP, 2: 11-13.

In the handwriting of clerk no. 1 with scribal emendations. Enclosed in **No. 77.**

---

1. Not found.

2. Barrington to FB, Cavendish Square, 6 Jun. 1761, BP, 9: 205-208.

3. William Baker (1743-1824), a merchant and Alderman of the City of London, he was MP for Plympton Erle, 1768-74, and Aldborough, 1777-80. He was a noted friend of America.

4. These letters have not been found.

5. **No. 62**.

6. **No. 66**.

7. FB, memorial to the earl of Halifax, c.Mar. 1761, not found.

8. **No. 65**.

9. Not found.

10. Letters are obscured by binding.

11. Three words are written vertically in the right margin: "province" follows two cancellations which are difficult to decipher because of tight binding. Left marginal note, opposite the interlineation: "2 the Orig^l Duplicate this" in FB's hand.

12. Not found.

13. Bollan was to seek reimbursement for his expenses from Leverett Blackbourne. FB to Bollan, Boston, 28 Sept. 1761, BP, 2: 13.

75 | To William Pitt

Boston Oct. 5. 1761

S^r.

I had the honor, by a letter dated the 5th day of May[1] last to inform you of the taking a Missisippi Trader in this port & in the close of my letter I gave some expectations that I should make a further discovery concerning their exportations. For this purpose I kept a dilligent watch over them: but if they had any intention since the seizure, to fit out a Vessel for New Orleans, they soon laid it aside; and the two french men after hiding themselves here for some time, escaped to New York. After this It would have Answered no purpose to prosecute the Master, who was drawn into this trade by the (perhaps unlawfull) capture of his Vessel, & was not suspected to be engaged in it in any other instance; I therefore found myself obliged to let this matter drop.

In one of the depositions I transmitted upon this occasion, there was an account of a Vessell belonging to one tucker from Rhode Island lying at New Orleans in March last. I have very lately rec^d. advice that Cap. Tucker[2] is just arrived at Newport in Rhode Island publickly & professedly from the Missisippi. I suppose by the name that he is the same person that was lying there in March last & that this is another Voyage made since that. However it is the common talk, what a good Voyage he has made & what a large fortune he has acquired in the Missisippi trade.

It is no secret that this trade is carried on at Rhode Island in a notorious manner: and It is the same with the trade called the dutch trade. About two months ago the custom house Officers here received advice from the secretary of the Customs of some particular Vessels & especially one called the Venus being sailed from Europe laden with Dutch Teas & supposed to be designd for this Coast. The officers here kept a dilligent look out & published a promise of a very large reward for a discovery: 'till they learnt that the Venus arrived at Newport, landed a small part of her cargo, which was all Dutch Teas, there, & sailed from thence (with a Clearance for the rest) as is supposed for New York.[3]

I should not think it my business to animadvert on other Governments, if their proceeding did not tend to discompose that over which I am placed. This port has been distinguished by its observance of the laws of trade & is still, I doubt not, the most commendable in that respect of Any in NAmerica. But the open & barefaced disregard of the Laws of trade which is now carried on by the most dangerous practices, in Rhode Island, has render'd the Merchants here disposed no longer to submit to the usual restraints. This has occasioned a great commotion in this Town, in which I have steadily supported the Kings Offices at the expence of my ease, but without any other damage. Particular accounts of these transactions have been transmitted to the Lords of the Treasury, the Lords of Trade, & the Commissioners of the Customs;

The whole of the Merchants complaints may be reduced to this "That it is very hard that the Merchants of this Province, who deserve at least as much favor as any other of the continent, should be restrained in their trade, while their neighbours are allowed to carry on an unbounded trade with any parts of the world they please; & acquire large fortunes by means, which, tho' not legal, are as publickly permitted to them, as they are disallowed here. That it is but a reasonable requisition That these distinctions be removed, either by letting the ports of this province be as open as those are, or by laying the latter under the the same restraints that these are."

To this I can only say "that the request is reasonable: and I dare say, that as soon as the Cessation of War shall afford an opportunity for Civil regulations, they will receive redress, not by suspending the laws in this port, but by putting them in execution in others. In the mean time they will discredit themselves & their cause if an opposition to the Laws & an attack upon the Kings Courts & Offices are used for redressing themselves."

I have extended this letter further than I proposed: but it may not be amiss; as it affords a contracted View of the uneasiness of the Merchants of this Town & the avowed cause of it. It now begins to subside, as, I believe, they see that they have not taken the proper means to redress themselves. Much is due to the steadiness & Unanimity of all the Kings Officers both of the Admiralty & of the custom house (except one) The Judges of the Superior Court have also assisted in the support of the Laws of trade, which still maintain their Activity in this province

I am with great respect S^r your most obe^t & most humble servt

R^t Honble William Pitt Esq$_r$

L, LbC   BP, 2: 14-16

In the handwriting of FB clerk no. 1. Annotations by FB at the beginning and end of the letter: "This letter was not sent." Variant text in BP, 9: 229-232 (ADftS, AC).

FB may not have sent the letter because he was embarrased by the escape of the two Frenchmen mentioned in the first paragraph and whom, in **No. 49**, he had referred to as "passengers." Alternatively, he may have thought that ministers would have been puzzled by his advocacy of the concerns of the Boston merchants in the latter part of this letter, given his previous forthright condemnation of their connections with Benjamin Barons.

---

1. **No. 49**.

2. Possibly Richard Tucker of Glocester, Rhode Island.

3. Opening parenthesis supplied. The advertisement is in the *Boston Gazette*, 14 Sept. 1761, p. 1/3.

76 | To Jeffery Amherst

Boston Oct 12. 1761

S.

Last Saturday[1] I had advice of a Sloop with a Flag of Truce from the Governor of Martinico[2] being in her way to this port: and that Evning M.r Stevens a Master of a Ship from this port lately taken & carried into Martinico, arrived here having landed at Plymouth together with a french Gentleman the owner of the Sloop. From M.r Stevens I learnt that at the desire of him & some other Masters of Ships belonging to New England prisoners at Martineco, This Gentleman bought & fitted out this Sloop. They put on board of her 12 prisoners 5 of which were Masters of New England 5 common sailers & 2 boys. Soon after they left the port, they were brought to by a Kings Brigantine who rummaged them throughly, but finding nothing but some Madeira Wine claimed by M.r Stevens, dismissed them, first taking out the 5 common sailers. After this the Small pox broke out among them, which carried off 2 of the English Masters: afterwards, they putting in at Martha's Vineyard, 2 other of the Masters went on shore against the remonstrance of the rest. From thence they came to Plymouth where M.r Stevens & the french Gentleman went on shore, without doubt, improperly.[3]

I cant find that Any purposes of trade are designed by this Voyage, at least, at present. If they want to gain intelligence concerning the expedition supposed to be designed against them, they will be disappointed, for I shan't permit the Sloop to return till I have your approbation of it. Her present condition will make three weeks at least necessary for fitting her for Sea: and in that time I shall have your directions. She is not come in yet & I have not seen her papers: as soon as She arrives, She will be stopt at the Castle & from thence caried to the Hospital Island[4] to perform a short Quarantine. M.r Stevens imputes the motives of fitting out this Vessel to the benevolence & humanity of the Owner, of which he gives an extraordinary account, as well as of his fortune & figure in the Island. This Gentleman expresses a desire of leave to stay here this Winter: but I shan't give it upon the present terms that the two Nations are upon in regard to one another: If I should be advised of an alteration in this respect, I shall reconsider the request.

All the intelligence I can learn is, that there are at Martineco about 1400 regulars; the Militia are numerous, but more desirous of a good Capitulation than carrying things to extremities. Port Royal is a strong well fortified place, & on that is their chief dependance. S.t Pierre is a weak place, defended only by detached Batteries. They are in full expectation of being attacked, unless a peace prevents it. They depend upon a favorable Capitulation & say, "if our properties are secured what signifies whether it is under a white or red flag?"

I am obliged to conclude this that it may not delay the post: I am with great regard S^r

Your most obedient humble Servant

Fra, Bernard.

His Excellcy Sr Jeffry Amherst &c.

ALS, RC   WO 34/26, ff 111-112.

Variant text in BP, 2: 128-129 (L, LbC).

It is conceivable, as FB suggests, that Acquart was gathering intelligence about British plans to invest Martinique. (The expedition was launched from New York in Nov. 1761 and the island captured in Feb. 1762.) If he was a spy, however, it is more likely that he had come to inspect Boston's defences and ascertain British naval strength in the North Atlantic station in advance of French counter-operations in Newfoundland. Amherst was decidely wary of Acquart, but also like FB thought it more valuable to engage in counter-intelligence than to confine him. "The French man, I don't doubt will try to see Every thing he can: he can be Come with no good Design for Us; I have always my suspicions of them; and I Don't doubt but You will take the proper precautions that he may not receive any Intelligence, that may be useful to him." Amherst to FB, Staaten Island, 18 Oct. 1761, WO 34/27, p. 230. There is no other documentary evidence in British or American repositories to confirm that Acquart was a spy, other than the items printed here, although French archives may contain further leads on this matter. In the event, FB praised Acquart for his philanthropy in returning the POWs and later recommended him to the new British commander of Martinique (**No. 101**)—which suggests that his suspicions had been dispelled.

1. 10 Oct.

2. Louis Le Vassor de La Touche de Tréville (1710-81), governor of Martinique, c.Feb. 1761-1 Mar. 1762.

3. There were two legal issues of concern. First, the "the french Gentleman," Mons. Benjamin Acquart, ought to have obtained a certificate of safe passage from FB prior to sailing, such as were occasionally supplied to transports coming from Martinique. (For example, Andrew Oliver to de La Touche de Tréville, 20 January 1762, Prov. Sec. Letterbooks, 2: 331-332.) Second, Acquart's ship and all aboard her ought to have been quarantined and examined before being allowed into port, given that in Boston smallpox was responsible for more "concentrated mortality" than any other disease. John Stevens, however, was given immunity from arrest by a resolve of the General Court. John B. Blake, "Smallpox Inoculation in Colonial Boston," *Journal of the History of Medicine and Allied Services* 8 (1953): 284-300, a 285-286; *Acts and Resolves*, 16: 674.

4. Rainsford Island.

77 | To Lord Barrington

Boston Oct 20th. 1761

My Lord

The Cover of this encloses the duplicate of a Letter I wrote to your Lordship on the 27th of Sepbr. the day after I recd. your favor of the 11th of July:[1] the Original is on board the General Wall packet boat, which sailed from NYork

The time between my receiveing your Lordships Letter & dispatching my Answer to it would not afford an oppertunity of seeing Mr. Pemberton But upon my talking with him soon after & observing to him that possibly Mr. Pitt may expect a more formal signification of his consent, than what his letter contained, it was agreed to transmit to your Lordship a duplicate of the agreement with an addition thereto signifying Mr. Pembertons still adhering thereto This I now enclose & must now conclude this, uncertain whether I shall be able to write to your Lordship on other Subjects by the same ship which waites only for wind. I am with great respect

My Lord your Lordships

Rt honble Lord Vist. Barrington

L, LbC   BP, 2: 16.

In the handwriting of clerk no. 1. Enclosed **No. 74** and other enclosures not found.

---

1. Not found.

78 | To William Bollan

Boston Nov. 16. 1761

Sr

I have long intended to write fully to you on the Subject of the Court of Admiralty, which the late Commotions have obliged me to give a particular attention to. But hitherto I have not had leisure to enter upon that Subject with the Consideration it wants: nor are matters ripe enough for the proposals I may have to make. As New Commissions for the offices there are now made out, this business may wait a little longer: only I must desire your Care in the following particular; that you will not resign your office of Advocate General; or if you have signified your intention of not resuming it that you will prevent that office being disposed of, untill I can represent the present state of the Court & what I think requisite to put it in a good condition.[1] I have allready sacrificed a great deal of my time & ease to the Support of the Court; and it is My intent to place it on the firmest bottom. The Very attacks that have been lately made upon it will be renderd conducive to its better establishment. But this purpose may be defeated, if I am not consulted in the future appointment of the Officers. What I shall have to propose will pass thro' your hands: in the mean time I must desire you to guard against Any Appointments without proper recommendation I am &c

Wm Bollan Esq$_r$

AL, LbC   BP, 2: 17.

---

1. There is no record of Bollan's resignation as advocate general of the Vice Admiralty Court, which position he had occupied since Dec. 1742. In Bollan's absence, the duties were carried out by a deputy, which office was held by James Otis Jr. between 1757 and 1761. Sometime in 1762, Bollan was replaced by Robert Auchmuty (1724-88), a Massachusetts lawyer whose father had tutored Bollan in the law. Auchmuty was made a judge of the court in 1767.

79 | *From the Board of Trade*

Sir,[1]

We have received your Letters to Us dated the 3^d. 6.th & 27.th of August last, and the Papers transmitted with them.[2]

The Subject matter of the first of these Letters is, of so great Importance, and so many Doubts and Questions have occurred to Us upon a Consideration of those parts of the Charter, and of the Act of 1692,[3] which relate to the Constitution of the House of Representatives, that We do not care hastily to pass a Judgement upon it; We are convinced however, that the Directions contained in the 40th. Article of His late Majesty's Instructions to you, were by no means a proper Remedy to the Evil complained of, and have therefore omitted it in the Draught approved and signed by his present Majesty,[4] intending when the Act for establishing the Township of Pittsfield, shall come before Us,[5] to take that Opportunity of laying before His Majesty Our Sentiments at large upon this matter; in the mean time We cannot but be of Opinion, that those Acts for erecting Townships which are totally silent as to the

Right of choosing a Representative, are most consistent with the Constitution as settled by the Act of 1692. by which the Circumstances under which each Township shall elect, one or more Representative are fixed and ascertained.

It is not necessary for Us to say any thing further upon your Letters of the 6[th]. & 27. of August, than, that We are much concern'd that the Facts therein stated should have occasioned so much Trouble & Per[p]lexity to you in the administration of your Government; Our Sentiments upon the Facts themselves, and the measures necessary to be pursued, for bringing the matter in question, before His Majesty in Council, are fully contained in the inclosed Copy of Our Secretary's Letter to M[r] West,[6] Secretary to the Lords Commisioners of the Treasury.

We are, Sir, Your most Obedient humble Servants,

Sandys

Soame Jenyns

E[d]. Bacon

E[d]. Thomas

Ex[d].

Whitehall Nov[r]. 25. 1761

L, LbC   CO 5/920, pp. 130-133.

In the handwriting of John Pownall. Entrybook title: To Francis Bernard Esq[r]. Governor of Massachusets Bay. Enclosed a copy of John Pownall to James West, 20 Nov. 1761, for which see CO 5/920, pp. 125-129.

In his letter to West, Pownall notes having forwarded to the treasury secretary copies of FB's letters of 6 and 27 Aug. 1761, and their enclosures, in which FB discusses at length the court cases arising from the Barons affair. Surveyor General Lechmere had suspended Barons from office a second time, on 20 Jun., but Pownall purported to avoid commenting on Barons, who, as a customs officer, was subject to the jurisdiction of the Treasury rather than the Board of Trade. None the less, Pownall suggested that "his Conduct both in respect to personal Insult to the Governor, and the embarrassment and Obstructions which have arisen to His Majesty's Service from it, cannot escape censure and Animadversion." The Treasury upheld Barons's dismissal.

1. Annotation in left margin: "1761. Nov[r]. 25[th.] Letter to Fra[s]. Bernard Esq[r]. Gov[r]. of the Massachusets Bay, in Answer to three from him, of the 3[d]. 6. & 27.th of Aug. last."

2. **Nos. 59**, **60**, and **64**.

3. The Charter of the Province of the Massachusetts Bay in New England, 7 Oct. 1691, in *Acts and Resolves*, 1: 1-20; an act for ascertaining the number and regulating the House of Representatives, 4 Will. 3 & Mary, c. 38 (30 Nov. 1692), ibid., 88-90.

4. General Instructions as governor of Massachusetts, Court at St. James's, 27 May 1761, Nether Winchendon House, Bucks. Eng. For Article 40 see **Appendix 1**.

5. On 9 Jun. 1762. *JBT*, 11: 286-287. The Board raised these matters in **No. 124**.

6. James West (1703-72), lawyer, politician, and antiquary. He was MP for St. Albans, 1741-68, and Boroughbridge, 1768-72; treasurer (1736-68) and president (1768-72) of the Royal Society; and joint secretary to the Treasury, 1746-56, and Jul. 1757-May 1762.

80 | To Jeffery Amherst

Boston Nov 28 1761

S[r].

I am favoured with yours of the 16 inst,[1] & have informed the Assembly of the intended reduction of their troops, which is Very agreable to them, as the Want of hands is evry where Very sensibly felt.[2]

I am sorry that there has been Any cause for complaining of our Men at Halifax: I have taken pains to make them orderly & particularly gave strict orders against the scandalous practise of officers suttling to their Men. In this I was not supported by Col Forster; & therefore less wonder at other irregularities. But I don't mention this by way of complaint as I suppose my orders were misrepresented or misunderstood.[3]

In my former letter I informed you[4] that last year the Camp of our forces broke up so irregularly occasioned by the diseases with which the Men were inflicted as well as by other Causes, that it would be Very hard to make the returns of the Muster master the rule for allowing the billeting money, since I suppose it does contain half the Number that returned at that time. I therefore proposed that the provincial muster rolls, by which the Province has Paid the billeting, & in which it is hoped No deserters have been made up, should be made the Rule of that settlement. I shall therefore send a Gentleman to NYork with these rolls & other proper Vouchers to settle all the accounts[5] now outstanding.

I am, with great regard, S[r] Your most obedient humble Servant

Fra. Bernard

His Excellency S[r] Jeffry Amherst

ALS, RC   WO 34/26, f 113.

Contains minor emendations. Variant text in BP, 2: 130-131 (L, LbC).

---

1. Amherst to FB, New York, 16 Nov. 1761, WO 34/27, p. 233.

2. On 23 Nov., FB reported that Amherst had discharged the regiments but had retained 238 provincial troops at Halifax and 320 at Crown Point for winter service. *JHRM*, 38, pt.1: 145.

3. Col. William Foster, the British commanding officer at Halifax, had complained to Amherst "of some very Irregular practises Committed by the Officers of the massachusetts Troops, by hiring the men to the Towns, people &c." Amherst scolded him for not calling a general court-martial immediately. Amherst to FB, New York, 16 Nov. 1761. FB subsequently appointed Maj. Jotham Gay (1733-1802) of Hingham, Mass., to command the Provincials at Halifax, where he was already stationed, no doubt expecting that he would root out the "Irregular practises" Foster had brought to light. FB to Nathaniel Thwing, Boston, 9 Dec. 1761, BP, 2: 132.

4. Not found.

5. Amherst warned that the contribution of the Massachusetts troops to the hospital account had not been paid for 1759, and urged FB to send an agent to the upcoming muster at Fort No. 4 for troops returning from Crown Point. Amherst to FB, New York, 16 Nov. 1761. FB dispatched Thomas Goldthwait, province secretary at war, to New York in early Dec. FB to Amherst, Boston, 9 Dec. 1761, WO 34/26, f 114.

81 | *Circular from the Earl of Egremont*

Duplicate:

Separate.

Whitehall 12th. Dec[r]. 1761.

Sir,

The King having taken into his most serious Consideration, how highly essential it is to the Interests & Security of his Subjects in North America, that the regular Regiments, serving in that Country, be recruited, with all convenient Expedition, to their full Complement of Effectives, &, at the same time, seeing the Impracticability of compleating them from Great Britain, considering how this Country is drained by the great number of Men, furnished for the various Services in all Parts of the World, I am therefore to signify to You the King's Pleasure, that You do, immediately on the Receipt of this Letter, exert your utmost Influence, to induce your Province, to carry into the most speedy & Effectual execution this very important Object, by immediate Compliance with any Requisition, which Sir Jefferey Amherst shall, in Consequence of His Majesty's Orders, make, for furnishing on certain Conditions, which he will explain to you, such a number of Recruits from your Province as he shall demand, as their Quota, towards compleating the regular Regiments, which have been sent to America, for the Defence & Protection of the Possessions of His Majesty's Subjects there; And the King cannot doubt, but that the Provinces will, chearfully & and readily, comply with this reasonable Demand, so obviously calculated for their own Security & Advantage, at the same time, that your Zeal for His Majesty's Service will naturally excite you to use all your Influence, & Power, in bringing effectually to bear a Measure, which His Majesty has so much at Heart, & with regard to which, any Failure or Disappointment would be extremely disagreeable.

I have at also in Command from the King to acquaint You, that, though the present Situation of Affairs would have fully justified the having required of the Provinces as large a number of Men, as they ever have raised for any of the former Campaigns, instead of the Quota which was demanded the last Year, yet, His Majesty, considering the high Importance of the Service, which makes the Subject of this Letter, and being desirous to ease the Burthens of his faithfull Subjects, as far as shall be consistent with their own Safety, has been pleased to require only the same number of men as for the last Year, in order thereby to facilitate a Measure, so essential as the compleating the regular Regiments, by Recruits, to be furnished from the Provinces in North America; & the King is persuaded, that the said Provinces, duly sensible of His Majesty's tender & paternal Care for their Welfare, will, in return, readily & chearfully comply with the Orders now sent you.

I am, with great Truth & Regard, Sir, Your most obedient humble Servant

Egremont

Gov.: of Massachuset's Bay.

dupLS, RC   BP, 9: 241-244.

Endorsed by FB: Lord Egremont dat Dec 12. 1761. Variant texts are in CO 5/214, pp. 247-251 (L, RLbC); CO 5/214, pp. 252-254 (Dft, LbC); Prov. Sec. Letterbooks, 1: 348-349 (L, Copy). The reply to this letter is **No. 102**.

82 | *To Lord Barrington*

Boston Dec.ʳ. 14. 1761.

My Lord

I am favoured with your Lordships of the 28th of August.[1] The trouble I have given your Lordship about the Naval Office has been greatly increased by the difficulties wᶜʰ. attend explanations at a distance: for it has more than once happened that your Lordships letters & mine on the same subject have crossed the sea about the same time & possibly before I recᵈ. this last your Lordship may have found in my Letters matter sufficient to remove the difficulties which this affair has laboured under.

I wrote to your Lordship by the Chesterfield man of War inclosing all necessary papers with Letters from M^r. Pemberton for your Lordship & M^r. Pitt.[2] I wrote again by the packet Boat which Sailed in Octr. last; & I sent a duplicate of the last letter (together with a duplicate of the agreement with M^r. Pemberton & a supplement to it signifying his consent to the new grant as proposed)[3] by the Lucretia Snow I also sent another part of the agreement by the Adventure Snow So I apprehend that your Lordship has all necessary pappers now by you.

As for Objections against an appointment in joint Names, I was always aware of them & endeavoured to obviate them in my memorial, which I suppose M^r. Pitt not seen when he made the objections. My arguments in favor of a joint appointment arise from the office having usually been granted so, for which I alledged the appointment immediately preceeding M^r. Pembertons which was to two. And I understand that in all public offices in London where there has been an usuage of granting to two, an office may be granted to one or two at pleasure. For this there are frequent precedents in the Custom house Exchequer Chancery &c.

I believe I have not mentioned the reason of my being so desirous of having this Affair settled in a public way. I know very well that reversionary promises of Offices in America are now very much solicited. I have particular advice that there are some people in pursuit of this very office and I can form to my self no adequate Security against a surprize but an Actual Grant. A Promise of the Secretary of State extends only to himself; and if it is not to be executed till M^r. Pembertons death, the Office probably will be in anothers disposal, at that time: to guard against which it will be necessary to make a fresh application whenever there is a Change in the Secretarys Office.

As my Son is to have no intrest in the Office till sep 1764 I could have no objection to letting the Office, continue, as it is, to that time if my life & Continuance in this Government were certain & if this delay would remove the difficulties now started, But in regard to the first, the number of my Children makes me desirous of leaving as little to the hazard of my life as ~~possible~~ I can. And as to the latter, the same difficulties will remain, if they can not be obviated now If a Joint appointment should be thought exceptionable then I shall not be able to contrive an appointment to one that will answer my purpose. For If M^r. Pemberton is to be the Grante'e it will give me no power over nor much dependance upon the reversion. And if I should ask M^r. Pemberton to let my Son be the Grante'e I know not what Security I could give him to indemnify him if my son should die before him. Besides, I have thought it advisable to press the dispatch of this business now, because as M^r. Pemberton's Age & health are now, The Reversion of his Office is of little or no Value to the present Secretary of state, But as his Age increases & his health impairs, the Reversion will become [an] object of much more Value than it is at present, & therefore more hard to obtain.

I have another reason to desire that the grant may be made in the Manner requested which is that it will put an end to your Lordships trouble, which has already been more extended than I flattered my self it would be when I first made the Application, which I considered to amount only to this, for leave to make such a grant of the Office as [my] predecessors have been used to make, with the consent of the present possessor of the Office M^r. Pemberton has been so good as to allow me to defer the issuing his patent as long as I shall see occasion. I shall therefore wait untill the paper[s] I sent by the Chesterfield &c shall have had their Effect.

I have the highest sense of your Lordships continued favor & Am with great respect My Lord your Lordship most obedient &c

Viscount Barrington

L, LbC   BP, 2: 18-20.

In the handwriting of clerk no. 1 with scribal emendations. Conjectured readings are for letters obscured by tight binding.

---

1. Not found.
2. See **No. 65**.
3. **No. 77**.

83 | To Lord Barrington

Dec 15. 1761.

My Lord

In a letter dated yesterday[1] I acknowledged the receipt of your Lordships of Aug 28 & have therein submitted to your Lordship all that occurs to me to be wanting for the determination of that affair: to which I need only add that any resolution on the subject will be agreable to me, as it must, at all events, afford a fresh instance of your Lordships ^kind^ concern for me & mine. I can truly assure your Lordship that your friendship is the cordial of my life & contributes more than any thing else (except my own conscience) to support that Spirit & Resolution, which the due exertion of the powers that are here committed to me, requires. My friends in this Country find another advantage from my connexion with your Lordship: they say that your Lordships family has been allways the patrons of this Country;[2] (for at the present the Memory of Gov' Shute is truly honoured), and there it is happy for it[3] that it has now the means of an easy access to your Lordship.

In a former letter of the 27th of Sept last[4] I desired your Lordships general recommendation of me to M[r] Pitt: I must now request the like introduction of me to Lord Egremont. I presumed to think that when a Revisal & settlement of the political state of N America should have a place in the British Councils, I might possibly be of some service. This self-flattery has not had its rise from any extraordinary opinion I have of my own ability, but upon a reflexion upon the particular circumstances of literature & professional studies[5] that have directed & enabled me to make a more critical survey of the politicks of N America, than can be expected from the generality of those that are sent here with a public Character.

But the time of peace, which must preceed the regulation of the North American governments, seems now at a greater distance than ever. Nevertheless, as they may happen in the course of this Winter a change in the present intractability of our Enemies which may bring about a peace, when it is least expected, I will add a few more lines to what I have before wrote on this Subject

There is in my opinion no System of Government in N America that is fit to be made a module of. The royal Governments are faulty in their constitution as well as their popular; of late they have given more instances of it than the latter. If therefore there should be a new establishment of the governments in N America upon a true English-constitutional bottom, it must be upon a new plan: and upon the formation of it will depend all the Ease or Difficulty of the Work.

It will be readily apprehended that the greatest difficulty will be with the New England charter Governments. I am willing to admit this for the sake of the conclusion that follows from it. But I do not think there will be much difficulty in the New England Governments; and yet will readily ~~admit~~ conclude that upon ^such^ a supposition it will be best to begin with those Governments. In Rhode Island the sensible people neither expect nor desire that their charter should be continued. In Connecticut I have heard it frequently mentioned without contradiction that it would be better for the people & most agreable to the thinking part of them to have a royal Governor rather than the present elective one.[6] And for this Province; its constitution by charter & its strict observance of the stipulations contained therein on behalf of the royal prerogative makes it, in my opinion, better disposed to a more perfect establishment than Any Government I am acquainted with, either Royal or other. I therefore conclude that when ever a New establishment of Government in N America shall be thought advisable, New England is the proper place to begin it.

Whenever this subject shall be brought on the tapis[7] I must again repeat I shall be proud to offer my Service. If It should be accepted, I shall readily obey an order to attend in person. In such case that there may be as little loss of my emoluments here as possible, It would be advisable that the order might be so timed, as not to be known here, till after time of settling the support of Government which is in the beginning of June in each year. In a letter, which I hope to send to your Lordship on the subject of the trade & Customs of this Country,[8] I shall have occasion to mention some particulars that may be of great service to the regulation of the American Governments whenever it shall be undertaken tho' according to our last advices from Europe, these considerations seem to be ill timed.

a paragraph on Gen[l] Whitmore's death & funeral[9]

A paragraph on the Voyage to Newfoundland.[10]

I am &c

Lord Barrington

AL, LbC   BP, 2: 21-23.

---

1. **No. 82**.

2. Samuel Shute (1662-1742), governor of Massachusetts, 1716-28. His sister Ann Shute was Lord Barrington's aunt. Perhaps Hutchinson was trying to avoid offending FB and Barrington when he later published a tactful assessment of Gov. Shute's administration in his *History of Massachusetts*, 2: 218. Hutchinson suggested it was unfortunate that Shute arrived at a time of intense partisanship, whereas modern historians emphasise that Shute's growing hostility to the New Englanders was fueled by accusations of disloyalty and contests to manage the House of Representatives and establish a permanent salary for the governor. Richard L. Bushman, *King and People in Provincial Massachusetts* (Chapel Hill, N.C., 1985), 31, 95.

3. Thus in manuscript.

4. **No. 74**.

5. *Barrington-Bernard*, 43: "standing."

6. There is no documentary record of FB having visited Connecticut since his meeting with Thomas Pownall at New London in Apr. 1760.

7. Meaning under discussion or consideration. *OED*.

8. **No. 85**.

9. Edward Whitmore (c.1694-1761), a British army officer. After participating in the capture of Louisbourg in 1758, Maj. Gen. Whitmore was appointed governor of the fort and also of Cape Breton and St. John's. He died on 11 Dec. while travelling to Boston on leave, and was buried at King's Chapel.

10. See **No. 28**.

84 | To Jeffery Amherst

Boston Dec 28. 1761

S^r.

I received the favor of yours of the 6th inst[1] with a certificate, which I hope will answer all that is wanted. I now inclose an account of a debt due to Castle William by artillery & stores taken from thence for his Majesty's Service, which I suppose may be now restored without any inconvenience. I particularly desire We may have the 2 24pounders now at New York, as they belong to a particular train & are now wanted to mount (with 4 others of the same) a new battery finished last summer to defend an approach to the Castle, not before well provided against. If there is any doubt of their being our guns, I will give further proof of it. As for the others I dont expect the same pieces but a compensation as near in kind as may be. As for stores I have no particular account of them, but that they were all sent away well furnished with shot shells &c; & shall therefore desire a return in the same manner as may be convenient. I must also become a beggar for a further stock out of the spare artillery; & have added a short list of what I think so much wanted that I shall find it necessary to send to England for them if they are not to be had out of the trains here. Of this I have made a small list which will bear adding to in evry article without overstocking us.

I beg your favor for an order for the delivery of the two 24 pounders & a recommendation to Col Williamson,[2] or whomever else it shall belong to, for the other things whether they be of right or of grace[3]

I am, with great regard, Sr Your most obedient & humble Servt

Fra Bernard

His Excellency M Genl Sr Jeffry Amherst.

I beg leave to trouble with the inclosed to go with your next packet, as it is now difficult to get a good conveyance from hence

ALS, RC   WO 34/26, f 115.

Variant text in BP, 2: 133 (L, LbC). Enclosed copies of [FB], "A List of the Artillery taken from Castle William for the service of his Majesty in the present War," [*1761*], WO 34/26, f 116; [FB], "Artillery wanted at Castle William . . . for the further improvement of the defence of the place," [*1761*], WO 34/26, f 117. Other enclosures not found.

1. Amherst to FB, New York, 6 Dec. 1761, WO 34/27, p. 234.

2. George Williamson (d.1794), a British army officer and lieutenant colonel in command of the Royal Artillery in North America.

3. The province had expended considerable money and effort in fortifying Castle Island in Boston harbor, but the artillery had evidently not been returned when FB reported on the building programme in Sept. 1763 (**No. 234**).

85 | To Lord Barrington

Boston Jan 12. 1762

My Lord

The packet which is to enclose this having been detained beyond expectation, I find my self obliged to add another letter upon a subject with which I hoped I should not have had occasion to trouble y^r Ldshp again. I mean Mr Barons.

In my letter of Aug 10[1] sent by the Chesterfield Man of War, I acquainted your Lordship that some Gentlemen had applied to me in behalf of Mr Barons desiring I would intervene in his favour. I told them that if the Actions he had brought against the Surveyor general &c were such open acts of his setting at defiance the Kings Authority that I could do him no service whilst he persisted in them: but if he would with draw them I would immediately enter into a consideration of what could be done for him. They urged their endeavours to persuade him to comply with this preliminary, but could not prevail & thereupon gave over their Negotiation. I can only add that it was then my intention, if he would have given Any proof of his disposition to return to his duty to have assisted him to have retrieved his credit & recovered his office.

When Mr Temple the Surveyor general came here (about 6 weeks ago) he brought with him the most favorable intentions towards Mr Barons & had I believe, predetermined (as much as he could without knowing the Case) to restore him. But when He came to be acquainted with the nature of his offences and the proofs of them, & understood that the whole process had been laid before the Lords of the treasury as well as the Commissioners of the Customs I suppose he found the affair was gone too far to be accommodated here. Nevertheless, as I saw Mr Temple was desirous to favour Mr Barons, I told him that, if he could persuade himself that Mr Barons might be restored with safety to the Government & Security to the Kings offices I would concur with him in proper means for it. I know not now what Mr Temples Sentiments are; but understand he will wait for orders from home, he having just now appointed a new temporary Collector

As I have hitherto acted chiefly on the defensive I have preserved great moderation toward Mr Barons, of which the two forementioned are not the only instances.

And yet this Man is now forming a plan to engage me again ~~with~~ in dispute with the Assembly & to libell me in the public papers.[2] His former attempts of this kind, which by Vigilance & discretion I have heretofore defeated I have endeavoured to forget, hoping that his late Censure would bring him to his Senses. But I am just now informed of these new attempts by a Gentleman of undoubted Credit, to whom M[r] Barons of his own accord communicated the particulars of the Scheme to inflame the Assembly, & read over the whole of the libell against me (being a bundle of personal invective & improbable lies) which he had prepared for the press. He added that he had engaged the best writer in Town[3] to write against me & assured him that I should not be Governor of this province one year longer: and that M[r] Hardy would be Governor here.[4]

As this is the Case I can not keep myself from declaring, that I have no longer any hopes of the Government of this province being maintained in dignity & peace whilst M[r] Barons has an office in it. At present The Governor L[t] Gov[r] All the Judges of the Superior Court the Judge of the Admiralty & his officers, all the Officers of the Customs ~~house~~ the Kings Authority in general & the Court of Admiralty & Custom house more particularly are the Defendants & M[r] Barons & C[o] Assailants. If M[r] Barons has any merit there is room enough for rewarding it without fixing him here. But I can not think He is of consequence enough to expect to have the peace ~~of~~ & wellfare of this province sacrificed to his Caprice and Malevolence. I am &c

R[t] Honble Lord Barrington

AL, LbC   BP, 2: 24-26.

---

1. **No. 62**.

2. The printers refused to publish the letters. See **No. 89**.

3. James Otis Jr.

4. Josiah Hardy (1716-90), governor of New Jersey, 1761-62. His father had been a commissioner of the Admiralty and an MP, while his brother Charles had been governor of New York, 1755–57. Despite his family's connections, Hardy was obliged to relinquish office by 1 Sept. 1762 after being dismissed for approving judicial commissions on terms contrary to his instructions.

86 | From Lord Barrington

Cavendish Square 14th. January 1762__

Dear Sir

I was in hopes by this Packet to have given you an account that the affair between you and M[r] Pemberton, had been settled in the manner desired; and I know that Lord Egremont both from his willingness to oblige, and his long uninterrupted friendship for me, was very much disposed to do it. I now find he has scruples which cannot be removed; they regard two points: One is the making a joint Grant; The other, your Son's being under age. He has promised me, that when time has remov'd the last objection, he will, in case he then holds the Seals, give the Employment to your Son, the moment it becomes vacant, either by death, resignation or otherwise. I am sorry the thing has not Succeeded, but I cannot think Lord Egremont in the wrong, tho' perhaps there may be precedents the other way. His Lordship has promised to write me a Letter on this Subject, which may be of use hereafter with his Successor in case he should not hold the Seals three years hence. In a former Letter,[1] I acquainted you with the removal of M[r] Barones, but I think I did not add that he was removed entirely in consequence of representations from the Boards of Trade & Customs. I never said one word upon the Subject, which I thought would be unfair on account of my relation to you.

I am to return you a thousand thanks for the Fish you so obligingly sent me, and to M[rs] Bernard for the instructions I have received from her, as to the manner of dressing it: I beg you will present my best compliments to her. I intended to have wrote an answer to her most obliging Letter,[2] but as I write to you, it would be an unnecessary trouble to her.

I hope in the course of this Summer, I shall be able to prevail on your Son to come sometimes to Beckett.[3] My Brother Shute has had the good fortune to get a Cannoncy of Christ Church, which I hope will not be a disadvantage to Our Cousin. All your friends are well & present their comp[s]. to you & M[rs] Bernard. I am with the greatest truth & regard.

Dear Sir Your Excellencys Most faithful humble Servant

Barrington

His Excellency Governor Bernard

ALS, RC   BP, 9: 245-248.

Endorsed: Lord Barrington r May 16. 1762 a. May 24. The reply to this letter is in BP, 2: 190-192.

1. Barrington to FB, Cavendish Square, 12 Dec. 1761, BP, 9: 233-236.

2. Not found.

3. Becket House at Shrivenham, Berkshire, is the Barrington family estate.

87 | From the Board of Trade

Whitehall Feby 4th . 1762.

Sir

We have had under our Consideration Nine Acts passed by you in December 1760, and January 1761, The Titles of which are set down in the inclosed note, and as no material Objection has occurr'd to any of them they will of Course be confirmed.[1]

It is necessary however We should observe to you, that, as the Act for the better observation of the Lord's day,[2] does repeal other Acts passed for the same purpose in 1692, 1716 and 1727,[3] all of which appear'd to have been confirm'd by the Crown, it was your Duty, in obedience to His Majesty's Instructions,[4] not to have assented to an Act for rescinding the former Laws, without having first transmitted a Draught of it for His Majesty's Approbation, or without a Clause being inserted therein suspending it's execution until His Majesty's pleasure could have been known.

We are not without Apprehension, that the very few Instances there are in the Administration of your Predecessors of a due observance of that Instruction, to which this Case referrs, may have produced the like inattention in you: But as it appears to us that this Instruction is founded upon just constitutional principles of Government, it ought never to be departed from, but in cases of real exigency, not admitting of the loss of so much time as would necessarily intervene between the passing of the Act and the notification of the Crown's Assent to it.

This Act however does not come within that description, and therefore you ought not to have assented to it, under the Circumstances We have stated, before the Crown's Assent could have been known.

Upon consideration of the Act for granting to His Majesty certain duties of Impost and Tonnage,[5] it appears to us, that it would be more correct if in that part of it, where it states the duties payable upon Importation of goods in general, There were some words which should restrain the Importation of such Goods to those Ships only which by Law may trade thither.

If an Amendment of this nature can be obtained, it will, in Our Opinion render the Act more consonant to the Acts of Parliament for regulating the Plantation

Trade, and therefore it is Our Duty to recommend it to your consideration when another Act shall be offered for your Assent.

The examination of this Act naturally led us to enquire what was the annual Amount of the Duties imposed by it; which We found charged in general in the Treasurer's Accounts; but as it does not appear, from those Accounts, what has been the Amount of the Duties upon each Article, We should be glad you would transmit to us an Account thereof for seven Years last past, distinguishing particularly the Amount of the Duties upon Rum, Sugar and Melasses and what part thereof has been paid upon these Articles imported from foreign Colonies.

We are Sir Your most obedient humble Servants

Sandys

E. Bacon

Edmond Thomas

John Roberts

Francis Bernard Esqr. Govr: of Massachusets Bay

LS, RC   BP, 9: 249-253.

In the handwriting of John Pownall with a minor addition. Endorsed: Lords of Trade 4 Feb. 1762 r. May 16 1762. Variant text in CO 5/920, pp. 134-138 (L, LbC). Enclosed [John Pownall], "Titles of Acts passed in the Province of Massachusets Bay [24 Dec. 1760-31 Jan. 1761]," 4 Feb. 1762, BP, 9: 253-258 (AMs).

The Board had considered nine acts passed in Massachusetts in Dec. 1760 and Jan. 1761, along with the report of Sir Matthew Lamb, and ordered the acts to "lye by probationary until the further effect and operation of them should be known." *JBT*, 11: 246-248. FB replied to a duplicate of the Board's letter a month before receiving the letter printed here, in **No. 203**.

---

1. A contemporaneous virgule in the left margin marks off the enclosure.

2. An act for repealing the several laws now in force relating to the observation of the Lord's Day, 1 Geo. 3, c. 20 (passed 31 Jan. 1761). *Acts and Resolves*, 4: 415-419.

3. An act for the better observation and keeping the Lord's day . . . 4 Will. & Mary, c. 22 (22 Oct. 1692), *Acts and Resolves*, 1: 58-59; An act in addition to the act entitled an act for the better observation and keeping the Lord's day, . . . 3 Geo. 1, c. 13 (26 Nov. 1716), ibid., 2: 58-59; An act in further addition to the act entitled an act for the better observation and keeping the Lord's day, . . . 13 Geo. 1, c. 5 (12 Jan. 1727), ibid., 2: 456-457.

4. See Article 7, General Instructions as governor of Massachusetts, **Appendix 1**.

5. An act for granting unto His Majesty several rates and duties of impost and tonnage of shipping (passed 31 Jan. 1761). *Acts and Resolves*, 4: 407-413.

88 | *To [John Pownall]*

Boston Feb. 13. 1762

Dear S^r.

I expect that this will arrive in London about the time of your return from Ireland; for which purpose I have hitherto postponed my Acknowledging the receipt of your kind letter of the 22^d. of July

I am much obliged to you for your close Attention to my interest: as for M^r. Pembertons affair I am Satisfied that as things stood My Lord H could not, consistently with his own rules, assist me, I have since pursued it in the Secretarys office: It meets with difficulties; but I have not yet given it over.

The money arising from the Chapple furniture I intended to be applied toward paying ffees; and if not Already, may be paid to Blackborne. The Jewell office is fair enough: but at the wardrobe they plunder me too much. The 100 y[ards]^1 of damask which were given to your Brother & to me would sell for £80; and Govr. Boone could not have less allowed him to make up his money: but they Allow me but £40 15s. I have Already given you too much trouble to Attempt a redress of this, if it was practicable.

The Flame that Barons & his People lighted this time twelve month Still continues having taken Several different turns in the course of which I have got clear of the disputes in the General Court & am now only a Spectator of & Sometimes a moderator in them. But there is such a violent Spirit of disunion Still prevails that unless I can Appease it, which I am Sometimes flattered with the hopes of, It will require nice conduct as well as good luck to keep my self quite clear of Contention. At present I stand entirely upon my own bottom, & have some real friends & a great many profest ones on both sides: and I have the Strongest Assurances from the most Active, that care should be taken not to embarrass me: but I trust to nothing but my own discretion & Integrity.

Out of Doors, Barons's party among the merchants are very Angry Against me at this time, upon some Advices they have received of my representations against Barons and are now preparing to send home a packet of papers upon his Subject: in which there are at present some personalties against me but whether they will remain or not at the final Settlement of them is a question As for Barons himself, He contents himself with traducing me in conversation & endeavouring to libell me in the publick papers.^{2} I have seen some of his libells in the known hand of his Amanuensis; & have been informed of the contents of others from some to whom he communicated them: but hitherto he has not been able to get them printed. When he is asked how he can Attempt to propagate improbable lies, he justifies himself by the right a man has to revenge in what way he can.

I have condoled with your Brother on his disappointment long agoe, it greatly chagrined & provoked me: but I hope it is entirely over & not a trace of it left in his mind I shall write to him[3] by the Ship which is to carry to this I have also more to write to you which I shall keep for one or more other Letters, this being designed only as an Answer to yours__

I am dear S[r]. Your most faithfull & Affectionate Servant

F B

P.S. Mar. 1

This has waited so long for the Ship that was to carry it that I have an oppertunity to acknowledge the receipt of their Lordships letter of Nov[r]. 25.[4] & my obligations for their Support of me in their representations to the Lords of the treasury as soon as the Assembly is up I shall write to their Lordships: in the mean time I would desire you to inform them if necessary that I have hopes that none of the suits Against the Custom house officers will give any trouble to the Council board. Barons has withdrawn two of his Actions & been nonsuited[5] in the third: the Cause of M[r] Gray Ag[st]. Paxton has been heard in the Superior Court when pursuant to the direction of all the Judges the Jury found a Verdict for the defendant.[6] There remains only Erving v[s] Cradock which is appealed home but I expect every day that M[r] Erving will withdraw his Judgment to prevent his answering in Appeal

The proceedings in the Assembly do not go on so Smoothly as I could wish: but they have given a Strong proof of their having no personal disregard to me by unanimously granting to me the Island of Mount desart near Penobscot bay *in consideration of my extraordinary Services* as they say[7] This is worth regarding as a thing of value, being a very fine Island contain[g] near 50,000 Acres; but I set a greater value on it as it affords the Strongest proof that the Annimosities that have prevailed here do not arise in any way from me, my Conduct or estimation. However tho[h] the Kings Service labours hard as to the new requisition of men I have carried a vote that I think will facilitate the whole business in good time.

L, LbC   BP, 2: 29-31.

The handwriting is similar to that of Amelia Bernard.

---

1. Letters are obscured by tight binding.

2. See **No. 89**n4.

3. FB to Thomas Pownall, 13 Feb. 1762, BP, 2: 31 (noted). See mention of the "Governors Situation" in **No. 58**.

4. **No. 79**.

5. Judges were empowered to order the discontinuance of a suit in instances where the plaintiff was unable to make a legal case or submit enough evidence. *OED*.

6. *Province of Massachusetts Bay v. Paxton*, 1762. in Quincy, et al., *Reports of Cases Argued and Adjudged in the Superior Court*, 548-552.

7. *Acts and Resolves*, 17: 168.

89 | To Lord Barrington

Boston Febry~ 20. 1762

My Lord

I have just now received your Lordships favor of Dec.r 11[1] which much increases the great sum of our Obligations to you it has given me great concern that I have been obliged to trouble your Lordship with such quantitys of paper: And I could have been glad to have Stopt a letter which I sent to NYork about a month agoe,[2] which was wrote before I had any advice of the resolutions taken in regard to Mr. Barons It contained an Acco.t of his intention to embarras me with the House & to libell me in the papers. But both those purposes were soon defeated: His petition was rejected by the House[3] & his libell was refused by the Printers So I hope I shall never again after this letter, have occasion to name his name to your Lordship.

The ferment in this place begins to subside: Mr Barons has withdrawn two of his own Actions & been nonsuited in the third and I hope means may be used to prevent the other two from troubling the privy Council. The contests in the General Assembly begin to abate: I have been no party to them since the meeting of the present Assembly in May last; Since that time I have been Chiefly a Spectator of disputes which I could not prevent: but if I have the general credit, which some of both partys flatter me with I shall hope to be an effectual mediator between them. When I consider what a deal of trouble I have had in this government, it sounds very odd to me to be told that there is not one member of either house that is not friendly to me. But I am not on so good terms with the merchants: some of them have been above this fortnight preparing papers to be sent home which, I believe will Answer no other purpose than to keep up the remembrance of things which they should desire should be forgotten. Some few of them labour hard to get some clauses reflecting upon me included: but I can't blame them; for if it had not been for me, there would have been now neither Court of Admiralty nor Custom house here[4]

Not but that the merchants here want redress in regard to several of the Laws of trade: but they don't use proper means nor take the proper time. I tell 'em again & again that they must wait for the conclusion of peace before they can ask the Ministry to set about civil regulations: and Assure them that at such time I will Assist them to the Utmost of my power. It is with this view that I have so long intended to lay before your Lordship a State of the Laws of trade in America & the necessity of Altering some of them &c: which I still hope to do before it is wanted__

We find this Country to agree very well with us & in general enjoy good health I have Seven of my Children now with me my Second son is to be put under a merchant here next month.[5] I expect my eldest son (upon a visit in order to Settle the further plan of his Education) this next Summer. He writes me word,[6] he has been at your Lordships door Several times. He shall take care to Signify to your Lordship the time proposed for his departure by a line. He returned to school at the coronation & became a Kings Scholar again. We are pleased here with the Appearance of Spring: I long to get to the castle, notwithstanding the narrow escape I had last Year,[7] with the Additions & improvements I have made, It is the prettiest summer residence I know: and it is the only place where I can read & write to any purpose but business__

I herewith enclose the printed Account of a publick Audience I gave to an Indian an Orator, a Councellor & a warrier; & my friend.[8] He was a principal Manager at the Treaty at Easton in 1758 & from thence joined Gen¹ Forbes[9] & was the first that entred Fort du Quesne after the French abandoned it. He commanded the English Indians at the Battle of Niagara, afterwards[10] Attended Gen¹ Amherst to Montreal & now having nothing to do, He travelled 400 Miles to visit me I took hold of the oppertunity to pay a Compliment to the 6 Nations & therefore gave him a publick Audience to Authenticate his dispatches. This I did more out of regard to the King's Service in general than any want that this province has of those Indians. And they on the other hand will distinguish between a Compliment unattended with any requisitions or expectations of a return & those they are most used to, which are visibly founded upon self Interest & therefore, as they wisely discern no instances of real friendship.

Mʳˢ. Bernard desires I will express her most gratefull Acknowledgments for your kind care of her & hers. If the political estimate of the value of a Family be reckoned by a combined proportion of the number & usefulness of the persons produced by it, I hope, my children will hereafter be reckoned in the estimate of the family of your Lordships Grand father[11]

I am with due Compliments to the Ladies & all other our friends with great respect.

My Lord, Your Lordships Most Obedient & Most humble Servant

My Lord Barrington

P. S. Febry⁻ 27. 1762
Since my writing this letter the 4ᵗʰ: suit Against mʳ Paxton a Custom house officer is ended by the Jury pursuant to strong recommendation from the Judges find-

ing for the defend[t]. the 5th Cause I apprehend will be soon ended by the plant[*iff*]. discharging the Judgment to prevent his Answering in Appeal[12] So that the King's Authority is now triumphant in every instance: but in the Assembly things are not so quiet as I could wish

However I have the pleasure to Acquaint your Lordship that the Assembly has given an evident proof that a personal Opposition to me has no part in their dissentions. For this day a vote passed both Houses in the following words

> Resolved that in consideration of the extraordinary Services of his Excellency Governor Bernard there be granted to him his heirs & assignes the Island of Mount desart lying northeastward of penobscot bay and that a grant thereof to be laid before his Majesty for his Approbation be signed by the Secretary & Speaker on behalf of the two Houses.

This Island is distinguished in most maps & is about 15 Miles long & 5 or 6 wide at a medium: it contains between 40 and 50,000 Acres Among which is some very rich land. I shall visit it this Summer & will then give your Lordship an Account of it at present unknown as it is to me I would not take £1000 Sterling for it.

L, LbC   BP, 2: 27-29.

The handwriting is similar to that of Amelia Bernard. The "printed Account" to which FB refers was a minute of the Massachusetts Council of 31 Dec. 1761, for which see CO 5/823, f 122.

---

1. Barrington's letter of 12 Dec. (incorrectly dated above) brought news that Barons had been dismissed "with the entire approbation" of the Treasury and the Board of Customs. BP, 9: 233-236.

2. **No. 85**.

3. On 2 Feb. *JHRM*: 38, pt. 2: 220.

4. The papers in preparation included a memorial of the Boston Merchants, 18 Feb. 1762, T 1/415, ff 157-162. The merchants felt "obliged to vindicate" themselves from "unjust Aspersions" cast by FB in his official correspondence— in short, that that they were lawbreakers and smugglers. The rumor of FB's indiscretion was propagated in Boston by Barons himself, having been raised in correspondence between Theodore Atkinson of New Hampshire and a London contact. See Tyler, *Smugglers & Patriots*, 55-57. In his official correspondence, FB made no secret of his view that the merchants were to the fore in a "party formed & supported by M[r] Barons," but he did not actually disparage particular persons as smugglers (**No. 59**). He was less circumspect in his correspondence with Barrington, however, wherein he pinpointed the weakness of the Customhouse as one of the "Causes which have induced the Merchants of this port to be less disposed to Obey the Laws of Trade than they have hitherto been." (**No. 62**). Barrington may have passed this letter to Secretary of State Lord Egremont, but there is no evidence that it was considered formally by the Treasury or the Board of Trade. Elsewhere, FB wrote that "disregard of the Laws of trade which is now carried on by the most dangerous practices, in Rhode Island, has render'd the Merchants here disposed no longer to submit to the usual restraints" (**No. 75**); but this letter was never sent.

5.   The identity of this merchant is unknown, but may have been John Timmons, an Anglican and general merchant, into whose care John Bernard placed his stock when he left Boston in 1776. John Bernard was established as a merchant in Boston by 1765, and entered into partnership with William Gale. He was among the handful of importers determined to defy the non-importation movement of 1768-70.

6   Not found.

7.   Perhaps this was a swimming-related accident.

8.   Hougougsaniyonde (or Segughsonyut) a.k.a. Thomas King, a sachem of the Oneida tribe. FB was grateful for King's advice and his interpreter's skills at the Easton conference. BP, 1: 177.

9.   John Forbes (1707–1759), a Scots-born British army officer, was appointed brigadier-general in 1757 and built the famous Forbes Road over the Alleghenies. He led the force that captured Fort Duquesne in Dec. 1758, a strategic victory for the British in the war, and died 11 Mar.

10. The British force that successfully besieged Fort Niagara, 10-25 Jul. 1759, was commanded by Brig. Gen. John Prideaux (bap.1720?-1759).

11. Benjamin Shute, a London merchant, of whom little is known.

12. FB described *Barons v. Paxton* as the fifth case in **No. 60**. Here he is referring to *Erving v. Craddock*. Craddock had appealed to His Majesty in Council, but the process ceased when Erving, as FB suspected he might, discharged Craddock from the Superior Court's judgment on account of the expense of mounting a defence in England. Tyler, *Smugglers & Patriots*, 49; Carl Ubbelohde, *The Vice-Admiralty Courts and the American Revolution* (Chapel Hill, N.C., 1960), 35.

90 | *To The Earl Of Egremont*

Boston NE, March 4th. 1762

My Lord

I beg Leave to Submit to your Lordships Consideration a grant made to me by the assembly of this province of the Island of Mount desert, which Lying within the Territory of Sagadehock according to the Charter requires His Majestys approbation before it has its full force, M[r]. Bollan the Province Agent will attend your Lordship with Documents necessary to explain the right of the Province to make this grant in the manner they have done: but perhaps a Copy of the Charter & a Map showing the Situation of this Island may be sufficient

Altho the Assembly is pleased in their resolve to mention My Extraordi[n]ary Services, as the Consideration, of their making this grant, yet I believe they had also in mind the extraordinary expences I have been at in entring upon this Government having been obliged to sue out two Commissions within one year; for which this Island in its present state is little more than an Equivalent.

The Country adjacent as well as this Island is at present a Desart; but if Canada should be annexed to the Brittish Empire This Country will soon wear a New face; as the obstacles to the settling it will be then removed, which hitherto have prevented this province from doing anything more than erecting forts & thereby maintaining such settlements as can be secured within their Range. But as this Mode of settling will never produce an extensive population, their dependance now is upon the removal of the french Enemy which must be immediately followed by the reconciliation of the Indians: This has indeed already taken place by means of our truckhouse at Fort Pownall on the River Penobscot; but will not be durable if the french power should be again restored.

As this is the first fruits of homage to his Majesty from the Territory of Sagadahock, I humbly hope it will be favourably received.

I am with great respect My Lord &c &c

The Earl of Egremont

L, LbC   BP, 2: 34-35.

In the handwriting of clerk no. 1 with minor scribal additions. Enclosed a copy of **No. 91**.

91 | *Mount Desert Island Grant*

L. S.[1]

By the Gov[r]. Council and House of Representatives of the Province of Massachusets Bay in New England in the Great and General Court Assembled.

Whereas their late Majestys King William and Queen Mary by their Letters Patent bearing date the seventh day of October in the third Year of their Reign did give and Grant unto the Inhabitants of the Province of the Massachusets Bay (among other things) all those Lands and Hereditaments lying between the Territory of Nova Scotia and the River Sagadehock then and ever since known and distinguished by the name of the Territory of Sagadehock together with all Islands lying within ten Leagues of the Main Land within the said Bounds to have and to hold the same unto the said Inhabitants and their Successors to their own proper use and behoof forevermore Provided always that no Grant of Lands within the said Territory of Sagadehock made by the Gov[r]. and General Assembly of the said Province should be of any force or effect until their Majesties their Heirs or Successors should signify their approbation of the same. The Gov[r]., Council and House of Representatives of the said Province of the Massachusets Bay in the Great and General Court Assembled, have given and Granted and hereby do give and Grant unto Francis Bernard Esq[r]: All that Island lying North Eastward of Penobscot Bay within the bounds of the Territory of Sagadehock aforesaid, commonly called and known by the name of the Island of Mount Desert. To have and to Hold the said Island with all and every its appurtenances unto the said Francis Bernard and his Heirs, to the only use and behoofe of the said Francis Bernard his Heirs and Assigns forever Yielding and paying therefore Yearly unto His Majesty his Heirs and Successors one fifth part of all Gold and Silver Oar and precious Stones which shall happen to be found and gotten in the Land of the said Island, Provided always that the present Grant shall be of no force or effect until His Majesty his Heirs or Successors shall signify His or their approbation thereof. Given in the Great and General Court and Sealed with the public Seal of the Province at Boston this twenty seventh day of February in the Second Year of the Reign of His Majesty George the Third by the Grace of God of Great Britain France and Ireland King, Defender of the Faith &c[a]. And in the Year of Our Lord 1762.[2]

By the Gov[r].——   Fra. Bernard

For the Council by Order—   A Oliver Sec[y].

For the House of Representatives by Ord[r]:   James Otis Speaker

A true Copy as of Record

Attest A. Oliver Sec[y].

Ms, Copy   CO 5/891, f 193.

Docket by FB: Copy of the Grant of Mount desart Feb 27. 1762. Enclosed in **No. 90**. A copy was also enclosed in FB to Pownall, Boston, 4 Mar. 1762, BP, 2: 33-34 and later in **No. 248**. Variant text in PC 1/60/7 (Ms, Copy).

The province granted Mount Desert Island to FB ostensibly in respect of his "extraordinary services." *Acts and Resolves*, 17: 168. FB requested Pownall to seek confirmation of the grant from the Board of Trade. The Board considered the matter on 3 Mar. 1763, but without having received an actual copy of the grant (for which see the source note to **No. 193**).

---

1. Encircled.

2. *Acts and Resolves*, 17: 168.

92 | To Jeffery Amherst

Boston Mar 6. 1762

S^r

I this day fortnight received My Lord Egremonts letter[1] signifying his Majesty's commands that I should engage this province to raise the same number of men as it did last year,[2] & also yours upon the Same subject.[3] I laid them both before the Assembly, then sitting, with the most forcible recommendation of the requisition contained therein. Their Deliberations on this occasion took different turns, till I got the best resolution I could procure, which was to raise two thousand men immediately (over & above the 600 men allready in the service) & to postpone the further considerations of this business till the next Session, I was offered 1500 fresh men & a reenlistment of the 600 men in the Service for the end of the campaign, with an assurance that the House would provide for 900 more to compleat their number, if peace did not intervene before the middle of April: but I chose rather to get 2000 fresh men raised immediately & trust to general assurances that the 600 should be reenlisted & compleated ^to 1000^ by fresh levies, if they should be wanted. For I desired to avail myself of this time of the Year which is more favorable to recruiting than the more kindly Months: and I am enclined to think that the Bounty (which is £7 lawful= £5 5s. sterling) will much easierly raise men now than it will two months hence. I was thereby desirous to leave as little of the business of raising new men undone as possible; not doubting but that the 600 will readily reenlist upon the bounty intended which has been mentioned at £4; & is allowed to be enough.[4]

I will not trouble you with ^all^ the particulars of the resolution, but am obliged to mention one of them "upon the General giving assurance that they shall not be employed Southward of Albany, & be discharged on the last day of October next: and if a peace takes place between England & France before that time, that they be immediately discharged after such peace."[5] This I beleive is the same stipulation as was last year, & I suppose will be perfectly agreable to the intended[6] Service.

Altho these 2000 are mentioned to be formed into two Regiments yet I shall not think myself confined therein any otherwise than in not exceeding the establishment of the pay of the field officers. I shall therefore form them in so many battalions as shall be suitable to the Service for which they are destined: this will be determined by the Number of men you shall order to Halifax. This I should be glad to know as soon as it is resolved upon, that I may order the rendezvous accordingly. To prevent desertion, I shall give orders that the Officers inlist no one but such as are known in the Country & have a place of residence, hoping I shall be able to raise the whole Number out of such only.

When I have mention'd that I could not at this Session get this business compleated, you will conclude that I have not moved the other concerning the recruiting the regulars. I shall make use of the liberty you give me of postponing this business no longer than I think absolutely necessary in order to obtain it. At ^present^ The raising these two thousand men will find us full employment untill the next Session, which I propose about the middle of April.

I am, with great regard Sr Your most obedient & most humble Servant

Fra Bernard.

His Excellency Sr Jeffry Amherst.

P.S

I beg leave to trouble you with a letter to the Lords of Trade to be sent with your next packet

ALS, RC   WO 34/26, ff 119-120.

Endorsed: Governor Bernard. Boston, 6th. March 1762. Rec^d. & Answ^d: 14th. Ditto.___.
Variant text in BP, 2: 134-135 (L, LbC). The reply to this letter is **No. 94**.

---

1. **No. 81**.

2. The province voted 3,000 men in 1761.

3. Amherst to FB, 9 Feb. 1762, not found; Amherst to FB, New York, 21 Feb. 1762, Prov. Sec. Letterbooks, 1: 352-353.

4. FB had presented the letters on 20 Feb. and the resolutions were passed on 3 Mar. *JHRM*, 38 pt.2: 273-276, 287-288. The bounty for the Provincials had been raised to artificially high levels in 1759—£14 provincial currency or c.£10 sterling for new volunteers—when wages generally were high and it was proving difficult to attract recruits. Anderson, *Crucible of War*, 319.

5. *Acts and Resolves*, 17: 177-178.

6. LbC: "present."

93 | *To John Pownall*

Boston March 10th 1762

Dear S^r.

By the Ship Wolfe Cap Diamond[1] which put to sea this morning & by the next packet boat I have sent duplicates of a Grant from the General Court to me of the

Island of Mount desart.[2] When I wrote my Letters upon this Subject I was so fully satisfied that this grant in no ways contradicted my 12[*th*] instruction concerning gifts & presents, that I took no notice of it But as I have since thought that it is better to anticipate an objection than to answer it after it is made, I have thought proper to add some observations concerning the instruction which forbids the Gov[r]. to Assent to or receive any *Gift or present* from the Assembly.[3]

1 The words *Gift or present* have always been understood to signify pecuniary only: and even in that sense it has never been thought contrary to that instruction to pay the Gov[r]. for extraordinary expences, such as a journey to a congress, treaty or building a fort; and particularly the expences of the Commission & other Charges of coming into the Government So that I apprehend that I might on Account of the extraordinary expences of my second Commission have accepted a Sum of Money without disobeying my instruction.

2 A Grant of unsettled Lands cannot be reckoned a Gift or present but is a contract for the clearing & settling the lands; which may or may not be beneficial to the grantee as the ballance between the expences of Clearing & settling & the Value of the lands shall hereafter prove.[4]

3 if this grant could be considered as a gift or present, yet it would not be contrary to the instruction, as it is not to be in force untill his Majesty shall signify his approbation of it: which approbation being made a condition precedent must amount to a relaxation of the instruction before there is any act of disobedience.

Perhaps you'll think that I have taken unnecessary pains on this subject: but abundant caution seldom does hurt. on that Account you will excuse this trouble.

I am S[r]. your most &c

John Pownall Esq[r]

L, LbC   BP, 2: 36.

In the handwriting of clerk no. 1, with minor scribal emendations.

---

1. George Dymond was the master of the *Wolf*, owned by Nathaniel Wheelwright. CO5/850, f 13.

2. Enclosed in FB to Pownall, Boston, 4 Mar. 1762, BP, 2: 33-34, and possibly FB to Pownall, 13 Feb. 1762, not found.

3. The correct instruction was Article 13, General Instructions as governor of Massachusetts, **Appendix 1**; it had been in force since 1730. Labaree, *Royal Instructions*, 1: 258.

4. The actual grant made no mention of any timescale for clearing and settling the land, although these conditions were normally written into land grants, such as the six years allowed the grantees of the Penobscot townships, in addition to a clause requiring confirmation by the Crown.

94 | *From Jeffery Amherst*

New York, <u>14</u>th: March 1762.

Sir,

I Have Just now the favor of Your Letter of the <u>6</u>th. March; and, at the Same-time that I beg leave to Return You My thanks for the Early notice You have Sent me of the proceedings of Your Assembly, on the King's Requisition, and I cannot forbear Expressing my Disapprobation of the whole of their Conduct, since they have, not only Come far short of His Majesty's Demands, but Seem Determined to make Such Stipulations, as can only Serve to Clog the Service, and which I can by no means approve of; I am very Sensible You have left nothing undone in Your power to Induce them to a full Compliance with His Majesty's Requisition; And I am very Sorry Your Endeavors had not the Desired Effect. For my own part, I am astonished they Should be so blind to their own Interests, as well as wanting in Duty to the King, to be so backward in Contributing to a measure which tends so much to the future Security and happiness.__

Your Intention of giving Orders to Inlist None but Such as are known in the Country, if they can be procured, will be Attended with very good Effects; And, I am apt to think, those men when they Return from the Campaign, will be of much more Service to the Country than before.__

As to the Destination of the Troops I can Say Nothing thereon, untill I am honored with His Majesty's Commands, which I Expect daily; And You shall have Immediate Notice thereof: In the meantime all Diligence should be Used to have them ready, as the Season Advances fast, when their Service will be necessary.__

I Need not Repeat to You the necessity of Influencing the Assembly to Comply with the King's Orders, in relation to the Recruiting the Regular Corps. The Earl of Egremont's Letter,[1] with mine on the Same Subject,[2] are so full, that I can add nothing more, than to Request that a due Obedience may be paid to the King's Commands in Every particular, as it certainly is the indispensable Duty of His Subjects to Exert themselves in promoting Such measures as His Majesty may be graciously pleased to Direct, for the Honor of His Crown, and the good of His Kingdoms in General.__

I am, with great Regard, Sir, Your most Obedient, Humble Servant.

Jeff: Amherst.

His Excellency Governor Bernard.

LS, RC   BP, 9: 259-262.

Endorsed: Gen[l]. Amherst r. Mar 20.1762. Variant text in WO 34/27, f 238 (ALS, RC). This letter is a reply to **No. 92** and elicited a rejoinder: FB to Amherst, Boston, 20 Mar. 1762, WO 34/26, ff 121-122.

---

1. **No. 81**.

2. See correspondence listed in **No. 92**n3.

95 | *To Israel Williams*

Boston March 16th 1762

S[r].

before you left Boston you knew that the ministers of Boston had been with me to desire that I would call a meeting of the overseers of Cambridge College to consider whether the charter proposed to you would not be determental to that College; & I accordingly appointed Monday fore noon for such meeting.

On Saturday[1] while I was ~~at the Council board~~ in the Chair in Council, M[r]. Otis Junior came up to the board with a resolve that a joint Comittee should wait on the Gov[r]. to desire "that If he had not delivered the Charter for Hampshire College it may not be delivered till next Session": which I promised it should not.

On Monday[2] at the Meeting of the overseers of Cambridge College It was resolved "that notwithstanding his Excellency's apprehension which he has pleased to express to the board of the force & effect of the charter for the Hampshire College, they were of opinion that the establishment of another College, tho' only as a Collegiate School within this Province will be greatly prejudicial to Harvard College & Voted that the Governor be desired not to grant the said Charter"

You will see that by these resolutions the issuing this Charter must be postponed; you will also consider, that as I have no intrest in this business but what arises from my duty & inclination to promote literature, It will not become me to make myself a party in this business, whatever my sentiments have been or are concerning it.

I am S[r]. &c

The Honble Col. Williams[3]

L, LbC   BP, 2: 136.

In the handwriting of clerk no. 1.

    Williams was a leading proponent of the unsuccessful scheme to found Queens College in Hampshire County. Both his and Bernard's role are discussed in detail in Henry Lefavour, "The Proposed College in Hampshire County in 1762," *Proceedings of the Massachusetts Historical Society,* 3d ser., 66 (1936-1941): 53-79; William L. Welch, "Israel Williams and the Hampshire College Project of 1761-1764," *Historical Journal of Massachusetts* 13 (1985): 53-62.

1. 13 Mar.

2. 15 Mar.

3. Israel Williams (1709-88) of Hatfield, Hampshire Co., Mass., was one of the most influential political leaders in western Massachusetts. His family had extensive landholdings and dominated local and county offices. Williams deservedly acquired a reputation for distinguished public service as an officer in the provincial regiments, a town representative, 1733-58, and member of the Governor's Council, 1760-66.

96 | From Jeffery Amherst

New York, <u>28</u>th. March 1762.__

Sir,

    I am to own the favor of Your Letter of the <u>20</u>th. Instant,[1] and I flatter myself that Your Assembly, on their next meeting will fully Comply with the King's Requisitions, which I shall be Extremely glad to Learn.__

    I Cannot see any Reason for altering the Words in my proposal for the time the men to be Raised by the Regular Corps are to Serve; Since, they will, of Course, be Discharged at the End of the War, or when the Reg^{ts}. Return to Europe: This, in my opinion, can admit of no Quibble, and as the Demand has been worded in the same manner to the Other Provinces, I can't agree to any alterations to that of the massachusetts bay.

    I Can say Nothing of the Destination of Your Provincials untill I receive the King's Orders, which I am in hourly Expectation of, and then You shall be acquainted with the Number that are for Halifax: In the mean time the Levies cannot go on too fast; and I would not have them fix their minds on any particular Destination, if they propose that the King should reap any Advantage from their Services.__

    You may be Assured that I shall take Care to order the men to be supplied with spruce Beer, as usual, as well as to take Every method in my power to prevent their getting any Rum, being thoroughly Satisfied of the great advantage the former is to the mens healths, & the pernicious Effects of the Latter.__

I am, with great Regard, Sir, Your most Obedient Humble Servant.

Jeff: Amherst.

His Excellency Governor Bernard.__

LS, RC   BP, 9: 263-266.

Endorsed by FB: Genl Amherst r. Ap. 3. 1762. Variant text in WO 34/27, f 239 (L, AC).

---

1. FB to Amherst, Boston, 20 Mar. 1762, WO 34/26, ff 121-122.

97 | To the Board of Overseers
of Harvard College

To The Honble & Revd Board of Overseers of Harvard College in Cambridge.

Gentlemen,

I find that my Intention of granting a Charter for incorporating a Collegiate School in Hampshire has been subject to two Objections: 1. That being the first Instance in this Province for granting a Charter of Incorporation, it may be suspected of being an Infringement of the rights of the people; 2. That the incorporating of this Society will in it's consequences be prejudicial to the College at Cambridge.

The first of these propositions you very properly decline arguing upon, Nevertheless I will take this opportunity to declare that, as it has never been my intention, either in this or any other instance, to exercise the royal prerogative to the prejudice of the rights of the people, so, I shall always avoid the unnecessary exercise of such royal rights as I shall find to be disagreable to the people.

As to the second proposition, you do me Justice in declaring your belief that it was far from my intention to do a real prejudice to Harvard College: My repeated declarations & some proceedings in consequence thereof ought to exempt me from even a suspicion of such a charge. But I can go further, my intention was not only just to the rights of the College, but, as far as public duty would permit, partial to it's Int'rests.

But whatever my Sentiments on this Subject have been, whatever they are, I think I may now be permitted to withdraw myself from a business, in which I trusted to my disint'restedness & uprightness as sufficient to secure my conduct from all exception. I therefore shall suspend the issuing of the Charter and I shall not assist any applications for a like Charter elsewhere.

Fra. Bernard

Province House Mar: 31. 1762.

L, RbC   Records of the Board of Overseers, II,

1744-1768, Harvard Archives, UAII 5.5.2, pp. 119-120.

98 | To the Board of Trade

Boston Ap. 12. 1762.

My Lords

I have before me the Acts of the general Court of this Province which passed the last Session[1] & shall trouble your Lordships with my observations on such as seem to require particular Notice.

Act to incorporate the Society for propagating Christian Knowledge among the Indians of North America.[2]

The Profest Design of this Act would have made it Very difficult for me to have refused my consent to it if it had been more exceptionable than it really is. But I had no other exception than that it afforded a Caution that if all Incorporations were done by Acts of Assembly, it would tend, in time, to a prescription against the Kings right to Grant Charters of incorporation. The Danger is not at hand at present; as this is the second Act of the kind ever known; An Act for incorporating the Marine Society being the first.[3] I don't reckon within this Rule of the Acts for enabling parishes to put out Trust Money for their Church &c (which are frequent) because they are private, for a particular purpose, & contain no greater powers than parishes have by general Law. But It seems to me that before another Act of this kind is tender'd, It would be proper to provide for the support of the Kings right to incorporate by Charter: especially as this right has been denied, by some people both in the agitation of this business & upon another occasion: which was as follows.

Some Gentlemen at the Western Extremity of this Province projected a scheme for founding a College; and brought in a Bill for that purpose which passed the

House & was rejected by the Council.[4] The reasons given by the Council for rejecting it were that the College was to be vested with University powers: that the province could not support two Universities; they would interfere with one another. The Gentlemen then applied to me for a Charter under the Province Seal: & they agreing to drop the powers excepted to, I ordered a Charter to be made out; which giving no other powers but to hold lands & Money & sue & be sued, I thought must be unexceptionable. Nevertheless this would not do: a great Cry was made against this Charter upon two points; that it would be detrimental to the old College; that it would be injurious to the rights of the people. I had given so many proofs of my regard for the old College, that there was no pretence to suspect me of the design to hurt it; and there was as little room to presume an injury to the rights of the people: for As the granting Charters is a right belonging to the Kings Seal, & the Charter of the province is entirely silent about it, it is certainly belongs to the Kings Seal within this province in the Same Manner as it does in other royal Provinces.

Nevertheless as the prosecution of this affair was no ways an intrest of my office & it might have impeded affairs of greater consequence, I put a stop to the Charter, still insisting on the Kings right of granting Charters, tho' I did not think proper to persist in perfecting this particular one: Upon which the whole Dispute immediately subsided. It however persuaded me, that it would be necessary to guard against the Kings right being impeached by an usage of granting incorporations by Act only: which I humbly submit to your Lordships consideration.

An Act in addition to an Act &c for ascertaining the rates of coined gold & silver &c.[5]

This Act may seem unnecessary, as the former Act by ascertaining the rates of particular pieces of gold & silver Coin must be supposed by implication to make them a tender. But this was very necessary to quiet the disputes in the Province arising from the carrying away dollars to be transmitted to England, being the best specie for that purpose. If, as some contended, Dollars only was the standard of lawful money, gold would have depreciated: but if the standard of lawful Money was founded only on a proportion to sterling as 4:3, as seems evident to me both from Queen Ann's Act[6] & the above recited Act, then the demand for silver would not depreciate gold. This Act has had all the good effects expected from it. It has quieted all the disputes about particular coins, & has fixed the standard of lawfull money by a proportion with sterling, & is, in my opinion not a New Law but only declaratory of an old one, whose meaning seemed to be plain enough before, tho' it might not be free from the doubts of legal interpreters.

An Act for securing the possessions of the Province treasurers Notes &c.[7]

This Act was occasioned by a discovery of divers forgeries of the Treasurers Notes, which were indeed too little guarded against such frauds. By this Act there are so many Checks contrived for the New Notes, as render the counterfeiting them almost impracticable. Another Advantage from this Act will be that the out-standing Notes of the treasury will be quite ascertained & the whole of the forger-ies discovered within a certain time. But this is not all: the former treasurers Notes were payable only in dollars or silver at 6s. 8d. an ounce (near 3[d]. less than dollar silver). As Dollars were leaving the province & silver, allready undervalued ^in comparison with dollars^, advancing in real Value greatly above the rate of dollars, the province would have suffered Very much if it had been obliged to make its pay-ments in the tenor of its bills. It was therefore a Very timely prudence to change the tenor of the bills & make them payable in gold & silver indiscriminately. The Credit of the Treasurers Notes (which is above par) made this Very practicable; and now there is no distinction between Silver notes & Gold & silver Notes; no more than there is between gold & silver money.

The following Acts[8] for supplying the Treasury differ only from others pre-ceding them in the regulations before-mentioned. But I must not omitt observing to your Lordship the extraordinary Credit & good State of the Finances of this province. Besides the advantage of a gold & silver currency, in which it is allmost singular on this Continent & in which the treasurers Notes, the only government Securities, bear little or no part, All the Debts of the province are provided to be sunk in June 1765: tho' indeed it will be necessary, to alleviate the burthens of the years ^immediately^ ensuing, by ~~postpone~~ ^providing for^ some part of the payments by allocations at a year or two further distant: even supposing that the extraordinary expences of the war should end with this Year.

As the next Session will be Very short, The Acts of it will probably accompany this;[9] as no proper Vessel for the conveyance of this at present offers.

I am, with great respect,

My Lords, Your Lordships Most obedient & most humble Servant

Fra Bernard

To the Right Honble The Lords of Trade &c

ALS, RC   CO 5/891, ff 70-72.

This letter may not have been sent until after 24 Apr. Variant text in BP, 2: 53-56 (L, LbC). Laid before the Board of Trade on 19 Nov. 1762. *JBT*, 11: 297-298.

The forgeries to which FB refers may concern the activities of Joshua Howe and "Dr." Seth Hudson, who were jailed in Oct. 1761 having counterfeited £800 worth of Trea-surer's notes. Their trial before the Superior Court on 1 Mar. attracted a large crowd and much public interest; sentenced for a number of offences, their punishments were the pillory, whipping, fines, and a year's imprisonment. Kenneth Scott, *Counterfeiting in Co-lonial America* (New York, 1957), 222-223. A counterfeiter of Connecticut bills—"one of a Confederacy"—was jailed in Boston in Jun. 1762. FB to Thomas Fitch, Boston, 23 Jun. 1762, BP, 2: 161.

1. For a complete list of the sessional acts to which FB gave his consent on 6 Mar. see *JHRM*, 38 pt.2: 297-298.

2. An act to incorporate the Society for Propagating Christian Knowledge among the Indians of North America (passed 11 Feb. 1762). *Acts and Resolves*, 4: 520-523.

3. The Boston Marine Society was established in 1742 and incorporated by the General Court in 1754.

4. An act for incorporating a society for the founding and regulating an academy in the western parts of the province was sent up to the Council for concurrence on 24 Feb. 1762 and rejected the same day. Welch, "Israel Williams and the Hampshire College Project of 1761-1764," 55.

5. An act in addition to an act made and passed in the twenty-third year of King George the Second, entitled, an act for ascertaining the rates at which coined silver and gold may pass in this government, 2 Geo. 3, c. 28 (passed 6 Mar. 1762). *Acts and Resolves*, 4: 515-516. The act referred to herein was passed on 3 Jan. 1749. Ibid., 3: 430-444.

6. An act for ascertaining the rates of foreign coins in Her Majesty's plantations in America, 6 Anne, c. 57.

7. An act for the better securing the possessors of the province treasurer's notes, 2 Geo. 3, c. 29 (passed 10 Feb. 1762). *Acts and Resolves*, 4: 516-518.

8. An act to supply the treasury with the sum of twenty-five thousand pounds, 2 Geo. 3, c. 23 (passed 29 Jan. 1762). *Acts and Resolves*, 4: 491-493; an act to supply the treasury with the sum of twenty thousand pounds, 2 Geo. 3, c. 40 (passed 6 Mar. 1762). Ibid., 4: 528-529; an act in addition to an act entitled an act for supplying the treasury with the sum of forty-nine thousand one hundred pounds, to be thence issued for the discharging the public debts, and drawing the same into the treasury again, and to one other act to supply the treasury with the sum of thirty-nine thousand pounds, 2 Geo. 3, c. 22 (passed 31 Jan. 1762). Ibid., 4: 490-491. With regard to 2 Geo. 3, c. 22, above, the first act referred to herein is 1 Geo. 3, c. 4 (passed 22 Jun. 1761), ibid., 4: 460-462, and the second, 1 Geo. 3, c. 15 (passed 11 Jul. 1761), ibid., 4: 469-471.

9. The legislation from this session is discussed in **No. 109**.

99 | *To the Board of Trade*

Boston Ap 13. 1762.

My Lords

I have in a letter dated yesterday troubled your Lordships with my observations on such Acts of last Session as seem to require them.[1] I shall in this acquaint your Lordships with my rejecting a Bill of a very popular construction & my reasons for & manner of doing it.

The Bill, of which I here inclose a Copy, was the last effort of the confederacy against the Custom house & Laws of Trade. The intention of it was to take away from the Officers the Writ of Assistance granted in pursuance of the Act of Will 3;

& substitute in the room of it another Writt which would have been wholly ineffi-cacious. This was cover'd with all the Art which the thing was capable of: but I was too well acquainted with the Subject to be deceived in it. I had not the least doubt, upon the first reading of it, of rejecting the bill. Nevertheless as it was Very popular; & I knew that the negativing of it would occasion a clamour, I gave it a more solemn condemnation than it deserved; the manner of which will appear from the enclosed copy of the Act of Council.[2]

This anticipated all objections & reduced the popular cry to a murmur only, which soon ceased: & I beleive there is now a total End to this troublesome alterca-tion about the Custom house officers[3]

I am, with great respect, My Lords, Your Lordships most obedient & most humble Servant

Fra Bernard

The Right Honble The Lords of Trade &c.

ALS, RC   CO 5/891, ff 75-76.

Endorsed: *Massachusets Bay* Letter from Francis Barnard Esqr. Govr. of the Massachusets Bay, to the Board, dated Boston Apr. 13. 1762. giving his Reasons for having refused a Bill relative to the Officers of the Customs & inclosing Receiv'd Sepr. 6 Read Novr. 19. 1762. L.l.34. 2 Papers. Variant text in BP, 2: 58 (L, LbC). Enclosed a copy of the General Court's Act for the better enabling the Officers of His Majesty's Customs to carry the Acts of Trade into execution, CO 5/891, f 77, and an extract of a minute of the Massachusetts Council of 6 Mar. 1762, CO 5/891, f 79.

This letter was read by the Board of Trade on 19 Nov. 1762. *JBT*, 11: 298.

---

1. **No. 98**.

2. FB refused to consent to the bill on the grounds that, as he told the assembly on 6 Mar., it was "plainly repugnant and contrary to the Laws of *England*," especially an act for preventing frauds and regulating abuses in the plantation trade, 7 & 8 Will. 3 c. 22 (1696). *JHRM*, 38 pt.2: 299.

3. Colonial resentment of and opposition to sheriffs enforcing trade laws with writs of assistance surfaced again in 1766. See Maurice Henry Smith, *The Writs of Assistance Case* (Berkeley, 1978); George G. Wolkins, "Daniel Malcom and the Writs of Assistance," *Proceedings of the Massachusetts Historical Society*, 3d ser., 58 (1924-1925): 5-88.

100 | *From Jeffery Amherst*

New York, 15th: April 1762.__

Sir,

As from Several Papers that have fallen into my hands, I have undoubted proofs of the Enemy being Supplied with Provisions from almost Every port on the Continent of North America; I must Represent to You the Necessity of putting an Effectual Stop to Such Infamous practices; particularly at a time when there is the greatest Demand for Provisions to Supply the King's Troops; And as I am well Assured that there are large Quantitys in Store in the Several Provinces, kept up by merchants on purpose for Exportation; and that very large Supplies will be wanted for the Troops that are to Assemble on this Continent for Immediate Service, I should Desire an Embargo on the Shipping, were I not averse to Such a measure, which might be attended with Several Inconveniences; and as I think the preventing any Provisions from being Exported may Answer the Same End; I must therefore Request You will be pleased to take Such Steps as You think best for Effectually prohibiting any kind of Provisions from being shipped at any of the Ports within Your Province, Except for the above mentioned Services; & for obliging the merchants to Deliver what they have in their Stores to Persons that shall be Appointed to purchase the same for the Crown, (the Contractors or any other Agents having no Concern therewith) that the King's Service may be Carried on, & may not Suffer for want of that most Essential Article.__

I am, with great Regard, Sir, Your most Obedient Humble Servant.

Jeff: Amherst.

His Excellency Governor Bernard.

PS: I Have Employed M^r. Hancock to purchase the Provisions for the Crown in Your Province.

J: A:_

LS, RC   BP, 9: 267-268.

Endorsed by clerk no. 1: Genl Amherst April 15 1762.

101 | *To Robert Monckton*

Boston April 16. 1762

S^r.

Mr Benedict Aquart a Gentleman of Martineco arrived at this Province in October last in a Vessell of his own, commissioned by the Governor of Martineco for transporting prisoners of War to this Port & brought with him, among others several masters of Ships belonging to this & the neighbouring provinces.[1] But the Investing that Island being then expected & soon after taking place He was neither permitted to nor could he return till the fate of Martineco was determined. which happily ending in the subjection of that Island to the English Government, He hath required & hath obtained of me a passport to render himself there to take the benefit of the favourable Terms granted to the peaseable Inhabitants of that Island. And in regard that the said M^r. Aquart hath as well by his contributing to the return of several useful subjects of this Country as by Assisting others who have been taken by the Enemy by letters of credit & by other acts of benevolence given proofs of his humane disposition & particular regards to the English Nation I cannot excuse myself recommending him to your considertation as a Gentleman well intitled to the first favours which the Governor of Martineco shall have occasion to confer on his Majesty's New Subjects now made such by this important Acquisition; on which I beg leave most heartily to Congratulate you. I am

S^r. Your &c

His Excy Genl. Monckton[2] or the Govr. or Com^r. in chief of Martineco.

L, LbC   BP, 2: 141-142.

In the handwriting of clerk no. 1.

---

1. The clerk has overwritten "colonies."

2. Robert Monckton (1726-82), a British army officer and colonial administrator who commanded the expeditionary force that captured Martinique in Feb. 1762.

102 | To The Earl Of Egremont

Duplicate

Boston Ap. 16. 1762

My Lord

I had the honor by letter of March the 5th to acknowledge the receipt of your Lordship's commands dated Dec 12th, and to inform you that I immediately laid them before the Assembly then sitting, who thereupon empower'd me to raise 2000 fresh men to add to what they had then in their pay.[1] But as it was at the end of a long Session & the House very thin, they deferred compleating their forces till the next Session.

I called the Assembly together on the 14th of April & desired they would again take into consideration your former letter & proceed in compleating their forces in the proportion desired. I also communicated to them your Lordships second letter concerning the recruiting the regulars, together with a letter from S[r] Jeffry Amherst containing a requisition that they would give the same bounty they gave to their own troops, that is 5 guineas each, for raising 893 recruits for the regular service. They very readily complied with evry thing I could ask of them: they compleated their forces to 3220 men (besides 150 men on board the frigate King George a Ship of 20 guns supported by the province for his Majesty's Service) & have rather exceeded their proportion in comparison with other provinces. They also granted a sum of Money for recruiting the regular forces to the full of the Generals requisition both as to Numbers & Bounty.[2]

I cannot excuse myself doing justice to the Assembly by assuring your Lordship that their resolutions were the result of a free deliberation uninfluenced by any motives but a sense of their duty to his Majesty arising from the present state of Affairs, in which they consider themselves as much intrested, as they were, when the War was carried on in their Neighbourhood.

I have the honor to be, with great respect, My Lord, Your Lordships most obedient & most humble Servant

Fra Bernard.

The Right Honble The Earl of Egremont.

dupALS, RC   CO 5/755, ff 5-7.

Endorsed: Boston April 16th: 1762. Gov[r]. Bernard. R June 14th: Variant text in BP, 2: 180-181 (L, LbC).

---

1. FB to Egremont, Boston, 5 Mar. 1762, BP, 2: 179.

2. Egremont's first letter is **No. 81**. His second letter and Amherst's letters of 9 Feb. and 21 Feb. 1762 have not been found. The House voted to raise six hundred recruits on 15 Apr. in addition to the two thousand voted in Mar. and the six hundred soldiers already in service. *JHRM*, 38 pt.2: 287-288, 308-309.

103 | To Jeffery Amherst

Boston Ap. 17. 1762

S[r].

I have thought proper to send an express to advise you that the Assembly has complied with evry thing that I had to ask of them. They have voted to compleat their Forces to 3220 men: this is precisely their proportion in regard to the Numbers voted by Connecticut & exceeds that of Any other province. And as this province has a right to reckon into their Number the 150 men on board his Majesty's Ship the King George, they exceed by that number Connecticut. The additional Number of 220 men are all privates which may be equally divided among all the Regiments or unequally, as there shall be occasion. There is a Regiment now forming at the Castle which will be ready to march by the middle of next week: out of which it is proposed to draw what Men shall be wanted for Halifax. The other Regiment is ready to rendezvous at the Westward whenever they shall be order'd. As We depend upon reenlisting the 600 men now in the service, I have but 620 more men to raise; & I beleive they are all ready.[1]

As for the requisition for recruiting the regulars, The Assembly has exactly complied with your Terms: they have granted a bounty of £7 (5 guineas) for raising 893 men. And now It will rest on the execution, which will not be without it's difficulties. I will immediately consider of a set of a proper officers for this business. I suppose I may make use of provincial officers in the present Service: for without that liberty, I shant be able to provide for this service effectually. I suppose it will be agreable to you to take such as shall be willing to inlist into the regular service out of the provincial ranks, having assurance of supplying such Vacancies by fresh recruits. I apprehend this method will considerably assist the regular recruiting. I am also desirous of not paying the bounty untill they are approved by the regular officer: and therefore it may be proper to make the Castle the general rendezvous where they are to receive the bounty. I own I am apprehensive that this will lay the recruiting in the Country under some difficulties, as they may expect to touch the Money before they march from home: but this may be obviated by allowing the recruiting officers to advance a small part of the bounty. And the inconvenience that remains will be fully recompensed by the saving the loss of whole bounties. I should also for the same purpose of preventing desertion think that it would be better that the recruits should be taken from the Castle in transports than marched cross the Country

I write in great hurry & with continued interruption: the Vote is not yet come up to me, being detained on account of some literal amendments. But as the Substance has passed both Houses, It may be depended upon.[2]

I am, with great regard, S[r] Your most obedient & most humble Servant

Fra Bernard.

His Excellency S[r] Jeffry Amherst.

AL, RC   WO 34/26, ff 123-124.

Contains minor emendations. Endorsed: Governor Bernard. Boston. <u>17</u>[th]. April 1762. Rec[d]. & Ans[d]. <u>21</u>[st] Ditto.___. Variant text in BP, 2: 181-182 (L, LbC).

Amherst was agreeable to all of FB's proposals concerning recruitment to the regular regiments. The general requested that 732 provincials, the same quota as in 1761, be assembled at the Castle barracks for embarkation to Halifax in transports to be organised by Thomas Hancock. The rest of the provincials were to proceed to Albany as quickly as possible. Lt. or Capt. Lt. Elliot(t), (possibly John Elliot of the 42nd Regiment of Foot) was to muster the new recruits, issue crown supplies, and pay the bounty. Amherst to FB, New York, 18 Apr. 1762, BP, 9: 269-272; Amherst to FB, New York, 21 Apr. 1762, BP, 9: 273-276.

---

1. For these proceedings see **No. 120**.

2. The resolves were voted on 16 Apr. and passed 21 Apr. *JHRM*, 38 pt.2: 308-309; *Acts and Resolves*, 17: 200-202.

104 | To John Pownall

Boston April 25th. 1762

D[r]. S[r].

Yesterday ended the last session of the Assembly which lasted but 10 days, in which time the Kings business was done in the most chearfull & ample manner & every thing was transacted in the best good humour between me & the Assembly: as will appear in some degree from the inclosed speeches. But in regard to one business which I was neither advised with nor Concerned in, it was carried on with greater heat & impetuosity than I should have chose, if it had been in my power to have interfered to any good purpose: I mean the dismission of M[r]. Bollan from the Agency. This was passed last Monday Evening[1] in a thin house where the Majority of 42 was near two thirds of the house. This was conducted with such secrecy that it was wholly unexpected: and the next day contrary to Expectation, it was concurred by the Council by a Majority of one only of 21. As it was sent up to me I could not with common prudence refuse my consent to it; especially as I had for very good reasons profest a neutrality in regard to this Question, which but a little while before my coming into the Governm[t]. had twice divided a full house into almost equal parties.[2] I went as far as I could; and having, without entring into the merits of the question, expressed my dissatisfaction at the hasty & indeliberate Manner in which this business was determined, I endeavoured by all means, except interposing my Authority & thereby making my self a party, to prevail that the election of a New Agent might be postponed till the meeting of the New Assembly. But it was impossible to stop the impetuosity of the movers of this business: nor would it have been of any service to M[r]. Bollan if I had succeeded in the last mentioned proposal. I give you these particulars in as full a manner as my time will permit, that if it should be insinuated that I have assisted in this dismission, you may contradict it & may, as far as my word will go, Assure M[r]. Bollan & his friends (if there should be occasion) that I have acted with all possible Candour in regard to him; & if I had attempted to do more, I should only have embarrast myself without doing M[r]. Bollan any Service. I have allways given him the credit of my good opinion of his Abilities & integrity & further I could not go.

I confine this business to a separate letter,[3] that if you should have occasion to communicate it, you may do it with more Ease.

I am S[r] &c

To John Pownall Esq[r]

L, LbC   BP, 2: 183-184.

In the handwriting of clerk no. 1 with minor scribal emendations. Enclosed a copy of FB's speech to the Council and the House of Representatives, Council Chamber, 14 Apr. 1762, for which see *JHRM*, 38 pt.2: 302-303.

---

1. 19 Apr.

2. Bollan had been dismissed from the province agency on 12 Feb. 1760 but was reinstated four months later.

3. **No. 105**.

105 | To John Pownall

Boston April 25th 1762

D[r]. S[r].

I proceed in my narrative of M[r]. Bollans dismission. As soon as the vote had passed the Council & I found they were determined to proceed immediately to an Election, I set about endeavouring to get M[r]. Jackson appointed Agent. M[r]. Mauduit[1] had been prejudged to the Office, & the prepossessions in his favor were strengthened by an Intrest which you know had introduced him as a Candidate for this Office some years ago. Nevertheless I had such promises of success in the favor of M[r]. Jackson that I had great expectations of his carrying it. But on the morning of the Election The L[t]. Governor being set up by the whole strength of his friends, the other side were so alarmed that they determined to reduce the Candidates to two. & there being no time to over come the prejudices in favor of the one & to explain the superior qualities of the other, who was a stranger to the generality of the Court & only known to some of the leading members who remembered & gave testimony of the strong recommendations which Gov[r]. Pownall had made of him: the friends of M[r]. Jackson having in vain endeavoured to bring M[r]. Mauduits friends over to them were obliged to join to secure M[r]. Mauduits election[2] & he was accordingly elected by a considerable Majority.

Nevertheless, as M[r]. Jacksons Character in the course of this short Canvas, which lasted but 3 days, had appeared in the most respectable light: immediately after the Election, a bill was brought in & passed to substitute M[r]. Jackson in the receipt of the public Money in case of the death or other incapacity of M[r]. Mauduits[3] And The Committee appointed to prepare the letters on this occasion have in that to M[r]. Mauduit directed that in all matters of Law concerning the province He shall advise with M[r]. Jackson.[4] I also expect that M[r]. Mauduits friends will recommend to him to consult Mr Jackson & make use of his Assistance in all matters of Importance. This Distinction of Mr Jackson is professedly meant to introduce Mr Jackson into the Office when Mr Mauduit shall decline it, which It is expected his Age &c will make it agreeable to him to do at some time or other. I have therefore wrote to Mr Jackson to desire he will accept of this Appointment as it now stands, & hope you will use your influence to engage him so to do. I shall write more fully on this subject by the next ship;[5] & shall point out some business which I shall depend upon him to Assist; & shall have the same signified to Mr Mauduit.

All the disputes concerning the Admiralty & Custom house are ended & in evry instance are determined on the Side of the Kings Authority. The last & finishing stroke was my negativing a Bill for the substituting another kind of writ in lieu of the writ of assistance granted by the Act of the 7 & 8 of Will 3. This I did in So conclusive a Manner that, tho' it was much grumbled at, it could not be impeached[6] Of this I shall give a particular Account when I come to report the proceedings of the two last Sessions which I shall do as soon as I can get the necessary papers.[7] I hope to get out of debt to your board before the next Assembly meets: but I have Such a deal of Military business in my hands that I cant promise it. Things at present wear a Very good face: I fight hard for my own independency & am obliged to preach up that of the Assembly. I am assured that evry thing shall be settled to my own Mind: but till the passions of contending parties are more quieted than they are at present, I must expect my share of trouble. I am

J. Pownall Esq.~~r~~

L, LbC   BP, 2: 184-186.

In the handwriting of clerk no. 1, except the last paragraph, the closure, and the addressee's name, which are in FB's hand.

---

1. Jasper Mauduit (1696-1771), Massachusetts province agent, 1762-65.

2. On 23 Apr.

3. An act for empowering Jasper Mauduit, Esq; and in case he is prevented by sickness, death, or any other way, Richard Jackson, Jun., Esq; to receive any sum or sums of money that are or may be due or payable in Great-Britain, to the Province of the Massachusetts Bay, 2 Geo. 3, c. 48 (passed 24 Apr. 1762). *Acts and Resolves,* 4: 536-537.

4. General Court to Jasper Mauduit, 15 Jun. 1762, Mass. Archs., 56: 386-402.

5. Letters not found.

6. An act for the better enabling the officers of his Majesty's Customs, to carry the Acts of Trade into execution. See **No. 99**.

7. FB neglected to to do this in the next letter to Pownall that enclosed copies of provincial legislation, **No. 123**.

106 | To Randle Wilbraham

Boston April 25. 1762

Dear S^r.

 I am sorry to acquaint you that M^r. Bollan is dismissed from his agency: this affair was brought into the Assembly with such secrecy, & pushed forward with such preciptancy, that it was impossible for his friends to prevent it. I don't doubt but that they will inform ^him^ that I acted a fair part in this business: but least they should not I take this Oppertunity to Assure you, that the same testimony which I have given ^to you of my good opinion of^ ~~you of~~ M^r. Bollans Abilities & Integrity I have made a public declaration of upon all proper occasions. Before I came into this Government M^r. Bollans Appointment had been the subject of a contention so nicely ballanced, that I found myself obliged to profess a Neutrality in regard to it: and if I had departed from it in this late business, I should only have embarrest myself without doing M^r. Bollan any service

 I have wrote to Secretary Pownall on this subject a little more fully,[1] which I have desired him to Communicate to M^r. Bollan, if He should find my candour impeached

 M^rs. Bernard joins with me in compliments to yourself your Lady & family.

I am S^r. Your most obedient &c

Randal Wilbraham Esq_r

L, LbC

BP, 2: 186-187.

In the handwriting of clerk no. 1.

---

1. **Nos. 104** and **105**.

107 | To Jeffery Amherst

Boston Ap. 29. 1762

S[r]

In pursuance of your Letter of the 15th of April[1] I have laid an Embargo on provisions, & have for the present refused permits for sending them to our own Colonies.[2] Nevertheless some Difficulties are like to arise in regard to which I should be glad to know your Sentiments as soon as may be on these Articles

1 Halifax Newfoundland & Quebec depend a good deal upon us for some sorts of provisions: shall We stop them going there?

2 We, in time of plenty, depend upon Pensylvania for flour, upon Connecticut for Pork &c. In this present time of Scarcity, It is apprehended that this province, which has suffered prodigiously by the last unfruitful Summer, will be greatly distrest, if the transporting provisions from Pensylvania Connecticut &c to this province ~~may not~~ ^should be^ be stopt. I am therefore desired by the Council to interpose a request, that you would signify your approbation (to the sevral Governors) of coasting provisions between Philadelphia & this province, as We are willing that the same liberty shall extend to the Colonies Northward of us.

3 Is it your Desire that Fish shall be included? For tho' We have this day refused a permit for fish, yet I think it will be impossible to persevere in it, without occasioning great discontent & probably much inconvenience in the West India Islands.

I will endeavour to keep things quiet under the present restrictions untill I hear from you. I have carefully avoided intimating a great want of provisions for the Kings use, as M[r] Hancock apprehended it would contribute to raise the price, which allready begins to rise a pace. But I apprehend that no considerations of price should hinder the Neighbouring Colonies from being permitted to supply one another: as such a restriction would probably tend to encrease the rise of the prices

I yesterday reviewed at the Castle 1000 good men & gave particular orders that the Surgeons should examine them carefully as to bodily infirmities. I gave orders that 738 private men besides commissioned cfficers should be ready to embark on Saturday next, when I expect to have transports ready for 500 of them. This Number (738) will, according to my calculation, compleat the Regiment at Halifax to 1000 men besides Commissioned Officers, which was the Number of the Regiment last year at Halifax. The rest of the Men at the Castle I shall join to the second Regiment which will be put in motion next Week; as the third Regiment, whose inlistments are now compleat, shall be the week after.

I must suspend writing on the subject of the regular inlistment till I have made a further progress in the establishment for that purpose; only assuring that nothing shall be left undone. I heartily congratulate you on Genl Monckton's Success & am, with great regards, S^r

Your most obedient & most humble Servant

Fra Bernard

His Excellency Sr Jeffry Amherst

ALS, RC   WO 34/26, ff 126-127.

Contains minor emendations. Endorsed: Governor Bernard. Boston, 29th. April 1762. Rec^d.__ 5th. May__. Variant text in BP, 2: 139-141 (L, LbC).

1. **No. 100**.

2. On 26 Apr., the Governor-in-Council issued orders prohibiting the shipment of all provisions out of Massachusetts without special permission. Council Executive Records, 1760-1766, CO 5/823, f 155.

108 | To Cadwallader Colden

Boston 1 May 1762__

Sir!

I have receivd an account from Stockbridge of a notorious murder that has been lately perpetrated at Kenderhook by one Abraham Hunkamug of Stockbridge upon Chineagun another Indian of the same Tribe, and that the Murderer is taken and committed to Goal in this Province. And Although it has been the antient and constant usage of the Indian Nations in such cases for the Relations of the persons slain to avenge themselves on the Murderer, yet in this Instance they have applyed to the Civil Magistrate for Justice to be done agreeable to the English Laws; and as the Murder was committed in the County of Albany, the Trial must of course be had within your Government. It seems to be a matter of importance that strict Justice should be done in this case, that the Indians may be brought to acquiesce in the legal execution of Justice for the future, and be thereby brought off from seeking their customary private Revenge, so contrary to the Laws of the Land.

I must therefore desire that you would be pleased to give orders to the Sherriff of the County of Albany to receive the supposed Murderer upon the Borders of the two Governments in order to take his Trial and that You would recommend it to the Judges and the Attorney General to be very exact in inquiring into the Fact. When I am informed of the time you shall set for receiving the Indian in custody I will give orders for his delivery. If the Sherriff was to apply to Joseph Dwight Esq[r]. of Sheffield, or to Timothy Woodbridge Esq[r]. of Stockbridge, they will either of them take proper care to forward him on to your Government.

I am, with great regard, S[r] Your most obedient humble Servant[1]

Fra. Bernard.

Hon[ble]. C. Colden Esq[r][2]

LS, RC   Colden Papers.

In a handwriting style similar to that of Andrew Oliver, except as noted. Contains a minor addition. Endorsed: *1st May 1762* Letter from Gov[r]. Bernard desiring that the shf of Albany may be directed to receive the Body of one Hunkamey, confind for Murder in Massachusets Bay. 12 May 1762 Read in Council__ The Prisoner is to be delivered to the sherif of Albany on the 1st. of June.

Abraham Unkamug was a Stockbridge Indian who had recently returned to the community after being held captive by "Canadian Indians." His victim may have been a relative. He was tried at Albany in June and subsequently released (the verdict is unknown). Patrick Frazier, *The Mohicans of Stockbridge* (Lincoln, 1992), 172-173.

---

1. This line in FB's hand.

2. Cadwallader Colden (1688-1776), the Scots-born lieutenant governor and acting governor of New York, 1761-75, and a celebrated botanist and historian.

109 | To the Board of Trade

Boston May 3. 1762

My Lords

I now proceed to consider the Acts of the Session just now past.[1]

An Act to explain &c an Act for raising a sum of Money by lottery for repairing Fanueil Hall.[2] I take notice of this Act only to declare that I am not unmindful of your Lordships orders concerning Lottery Acts,[3] from which, I hope, this Act will not be considered as a departure,[4] altho' it does make some addition to the Sum originally granted. Faneuil Hall (the noblest public Room in North America) was burnt down about a year & a half ago. It belonged to the Town & should have been rebuilt by a general Tax: but the great losses by fire which the Inhabitants have suffered made that method to raise the Money impracticable. The Assembly passed the Original Act to raise 2000 pounds. The Trustees immediately set about the Work, in assurance that they should have leave to raise such further sum as should be wanted to compleat the Work. It was evident that the Original sum would not do: if an addition should not be made to it, the former grant must be renderd useless by the incompletion of the purpose for which it was granted. This Act was therefore necessary for carrying the original into Execution.

An Act to enable Mary Hunt to convey her Lands &c.

The Occasion & Reasonableness of this Act appears in the preamble. I take notice of it only to inform your Lordships that this bill was tender'd to me in the former Session: but I refused to pass it because they had not given public notice of the intention to bring it in. But such Notice having been given by advertisements in the public papers for 3 weeks together, which advertisements were produced at the Council board & filed there I then passed the bill.

I am, with great respect, My Lords Your Lordships most obedient & most humble Servant

Fra. Bernard

ALS, RC   CO 5/891, ff 73-74.

Contains minor emendations. Endorsed by John Pownall: *Massachusets Bay.* Letters from Francis Barnard Esq[r]. Gov[r]. of the Massachusets Bay, to the Board, dated the 12 April & 3 May 1762. containing his Observations on certain Acts lately passd there Reced. Sep[r]. 16. Read. Nov. 19 1762. L.l. 55. Variant text in BP, 2: 56-57 (L, LbC).

The most contentious piece of legislation was the act for enabling Mary Hunt of Boston to dispose of and convey her lands and interest in Holden. On 14 Feb. 1761, the Governor-in-Council, which body authorized divorces and marriage settlements, granted her a separation of "bed and board" from her husband, Richard, on the grounds of his "cruel usage," along with alimony and the rents and profits deriving from that share of the estate that she had held before marriage. She petitioned the Governor-in-Council on 26 Nov. for leave to sell inherited property in Holden in order to support her three children, lest they become public charges, and was allowed to bring in a bill at the next sitting. The bill was engrossed on 22 Jan. 1762 and received FB's consent on 24 Apr. Council in Assembly, Massachusetts, 1761-1762, CO 5/824, ff 72-73; *JHRM*, 38 pt.1: 152; pt.2: 187, 333.

When the Board reviewed the act, Sir Matthew Lamb suggested that it appeared contrary to law, and on 31 Jan. the Board referred the act to His Majesty in Council. CO 5/891, ff 100-103; CO 5/920, pp. 149-151. The act was consequently disallowed on 16 Mar. in accordance with a report by the plantation affairs committee, on the grounds that it was "contrary to Law that a Femme Couverte should sell her real Estate for her own use" and did not contain a suspending clause. *JBT*, 11: 329-330; *APC*, 4: 558-559. Mary Hunt's petition for separation is in itself unremarkable, for it was one several which came before the Governor's Council in the early 1760s; what is significant is the intervention of the Board of Trade in this and a handful of other cases. By 1773 the Board succeeded in preventing royal governors consenting to provincial divorce laws. Nancy F. Cott, "Divorce and the Changing Status of Women in Eighteenth-Century Massachusetts," *WMQ* 33 (1976): 586-614.

---

1. Five acts were passed at the end of the session held from 14 to 24 Apr. *JHRM*, 38 pt.2: 332-333.

2. An act to explain, amend, and carry into execution an act made in the first year of the reign of His present Majesty, entitled, an act for raising a sum of money by lottery for repairing Faneuil Hall in Boston, 2 Geo.3, c. 49 (passed 24 Apr. 1762). *Acts and Resolves*, 4: 537. The act referred to herein is 1 Geo. 3, c. 26 (passed 18 Apr. 1761), which limited lottery funding for the building project to £2,000, excluding expenses; the 1762 act raised the limit to £3,000 sterling. Ibid., 4: 425-426.

3. **No. 43**.

4. The act was noted on 18 Nov. 1762, and there are no recorded objections by the Board of Trade. *JBT*, 11: 297-298.

110 | *To Jeffery Amherst*

Boston May 5. 1762

S[r]

Last Monday sailed for Halifax 4 Vessels having on board 460 men besides officers: this day another Vessel falls down to take 70 more men on board. M[r] Hancock expects to have Vessels for the rest, which will be 208, before the end of the Week. This will compleat the Regiment to 1000 men besides com[d]. Officers. This day I shall give orders for the rendezvous of the other Regiments at Worcester, except such recruits as lie westward of that Town, who will be allowed to rendezvous at Springfield; thro' which Town the whole will march. The Men are in general better chosen than they have been in Any year before; and the officers are pickt men, I having disregarded all recommendations in opposition to merit & the right of rank.

I am affraid the recruiting the regulars will go on Very heavily; as Captn Elliots orders obliges him to reject men that seem to me capable of doing the King good service. I regret the loss of an healthy sturdy lad for want of half an inch in his height or a few months in his age. I see no prospect of raising the men under much restriction[1] if it can be done at all. I therefore submit it [to] you whether it would not be best that such sound & strong lads who cannot be placed in the regular ranks at present should be formed in separate corps,[2] rather than be entirely lost to the service without any probability of replacing them by other men.

I wrote to you last thursday[3] on the subject of the embargo. I have since talked with Mr Hancock & some other Merchants: and it is the general Opinion that if the coasting from Pennsylvania inclusive to the Northward is not permitted, it will cause great distress & tend very much to the rise of the price of provisions, which has risen greatly within a few days. If We cant be permitted to draw provisions from Pennsylvania & Connecticut, We must for self-preservation stop them going from hence *any where*; and that will be greatly inconvenient to the Northern garrison Towns and the Newfoundland fishery, which are usually supplied from hence. I shall therefore be glad to know that the Southern ports will be open to bring provisions to us, that We may open our ports to supply Nova Scotia Newfoundland Quebec &c. The sooner I have this assurance the better, as there are sevral Vessels laden for the Northward that are stopt on this account.

Since I have wrote this I have receiv'd a copy of part of a letter from Lisbon[4] advising the arrival of Lord Tyrawley[5] his Secretary & Aid de camp there, by whom & by the post they have advice that the King of Prussia has concluded a peace with the Czar, who has accepted a subsidy from England &, it is said, is to keep up 35,000 men in Germany for the service of England & prussia. It is also said that the King of Prussia was about concluding a separate peace with the King of Poland. I congratulate you on this important & timely revolution. I am, with great regard,

S^r your most obedient & most humble Servant

Fra Bernard.

His Excellency Sr Jeffry Amherst.

P.S.

In regard to the Number of our forces 3220 & 150 on board the King George make 3370, which is 36 above the complement you set us at.

ALS, RC   WO 34/26, ff 128-129.

Contains minor emendations. Endorsed: Governor Bernard. Boston, 5th. May 1762. Rec^d. & Ans^d. 10th Ditto.__. Variant text in BP, 2: 142-144 (L, LbC). The reply to this letter is in BP, 9: 281-284.

1. LbC: "that may be spared" added here.

2. LbC: "as rangers or for Garrisons" added here.

3. **No. 107.**

4. Not found.

5. James O'Hara (c.1682-1773), earl of Tyrawley and former governor of Gibraltar, 1757-58.

111 | To Jeffery Amherst

Boston May 6. 1762

S^r.

This day there were laid before the Council divers petitions for liberty to transport provisions to the Northward: when it appearing that this Country is like to be very much distressed if the Southern ports should not be allowed to send provisions to this Province, the people being now obliged to come from a distance to purchase provisions from the stores here for the support of their families, They therefore advise that I immediately send an express to represent this to you & desire that You will permit provisions to be coasted on giving bond, & have postponed the consideration of these petitions untill the return of the express. The Answer to a Memorial of Mr Hancocks I herewith send you a Copy of. All possible care will be taken that the liberty of coasting provisions shall not be abused from the ports of this province.

I am, with great regard, Sr Your most obedient & most humble Servant.

Fra. Bernard

His Excellency Sr Jeffry Amherst.

ALS, RC   WO 34/26, f 130.

Contains minor emendations. Enclosed a minute of the Massachusetts Council of 6 May 1762, WO 34/26, f 131; other enclosures have not been found.

Thomas Hancock was already permitted to transport provisions to British and provincial soldiers at Halifax, but consideration of his and other petitions regarding the coastal trade in and out of Boston was delayed pending the receipt of Amherst's views. Amherst, however, continued the embargo (citing the recent discovery of Mons. Comte's smuggling operations as justification) with only one non-military exception—the resourcing of settlers in Nova Scotia. Council Executive Records, 1760-1766, CO 5/823, f 156; Amherst to FB, New York, 10 May 1762, BP, 9: 281-284.

112 | From Jeffery Amherst

New York, <u>6</u>th. May 1762.__

Sir,

I Had last Night the favor of Your Letter of the <u>29</u>th. Ultimo;[1] Acquainting me of Your having Laid an Embargo on Provisions, but mentioning Some Difficultys that were likely to arise from that measure, and Desiring my opinion thereon.__

I must first Return You my Sincere thanks for the orders You had given for Expediting the Embarkation of the Troops Intended for Halifax, as well as hastening the march of the Remainder to the westward.__

The Readiness with which You have Complied with my Request for prohibiting the Exportation of Provisions, likewise Demands my Acknowledgements, as at the time when I wrote You last on that Subject,[2] I had great Reason to Suspect that Schemes were forming by Sundry merchants on this Continent, to Supply the Enemy with all sorts of Provisions, by means of False Clearances & other Frauds, Countenanced, I am afraid, by the Officers of some of the Ports; but, within these few Days, I have made full Discoveries of the whole Plan, the Lieut. Governor having granted his Warrant to Seize the Persons & Effects of the French King's Subjects at present Residing in this place; among whom is a monsr. *Comte*, who is now in Custody, who appears to have been sent on purpose to Establish such a Commerce with the Enemy, that not only their Settlements in the west Indies; but their Fleets & Troops, were to be Supplied with Provisions from this Continent: As his Papers mention some People at Boston concerned with him, I think proper to send You the originals (having kept Copies thereof) that You may take such steps as You Judge best for bringing the Guilty to Condign Punishment; and I likewise transmit You a List of Some Names and memorandums, which were found among his Papers as some of those mentioned therein may also belong to Your Government. Monsr. *Comte* was furnished with Circular Letters to almost all the Governors on the Continent as well as to the Governors of Some of the west India Islands both English & Dutch, Couched in such terms as plainly Discover his Design, altho' he is Recommended to the King's Governors, as a Person coming to their respective Governments, on account of his Health (of which no mention is made to the Dutch); and to settle some Affair of his own: I do not find a Letter for You, but perhaps he may have Delivered it.__

From what I have told You, and a perusal of the Enclosed Papers, I am persuaded You will Joyn with me in thinking it highly Necessary to put a Total stop to this Iniquitous Trade, which is not only Infamous in itself, by Supporting the Avowed Enemies of the King; but occasions great Difficulty in procuring the necessary Supplies for Carrying on His Majesty's Service: I have felt the good Effects already at this Port, by the merchants making offer of the Provisions, which I am well Convinced were Intended to have been sent to the Enemy; but finding from the orders given that they could not Effect it, they are now willing to Dispose of them to the Crown. This however would do but little towards preventing the Enemy's being Supplied, if an Effectual Stop is not put to the Exportation of Provisions from all the other Ports; and I must therefore Request, notwithstanding the Inconveniences mentioned by You that will arise, by prohibiting Fish to be Carried to the West India Islands & other Provisions to Halifax, Newfoundland, & Quebec, You will Continue a General Embargo for the present, for without that I Do not see any possibility of hindering those whose Sole views seem to be to get money, without the least Regard for the good of their Country, from Accomplishing their Designs.__

I Have wrote fully on this head to the Governor of Connecticutt,[3] having received Certain Intelligence that sundry vessels have sailed from the Port of New London, Loaded with Provisions, Since the orders given to Stop all Such; and that some of those vessels have even ventured out without any Clearances at all.__

I am, with great Regard, Sir, Your most Obedient Humble Servant.

Jeff: Amherst.

His Excellency Governor Bernard.

P:S: To Save You the trouble of having the Papers translated, I have Caused a Translation to be made, which I herewith Enclose You.__

Notwithstanding what I have said in the foregoing Letter, I would not prevent the New Settlers in Nova Scotia from Receiving the Necessary Supplies; and therefore Such vessells as take in provisions for that Province, and that give Bond, to Your satisfaction, that they Deliver their Cargo there, may be permitted to go thither.__

J.A.__

LS, RC   BP, 9: 277-280.

Endorsed: Genl Amherst dat May 6. 1762. Variant text in WO 34/27, pp. 242-243 (L, LbC). Enclosures not found. The reply to this letter is **No. 113**.

---

1. **No. 107**.

2. Amherst to FB, New York, 18 Apr. 1762, BP, 9: 269-272.

3. Amherst to Thomas Fitch, New York, 5 May 1762. Correspondence between the Governor of Connecticut and the Commander-in-Chief, Sept. 1756-Nov. 1763, War Office Records: WO 34/28, f 83, PRO.

113 | To Jeffery Amherst

Boston May 17. 1762

S^r.

I received yours of May 6 & 10[1] on Saturday Evning & this morning I laid them before the Council.[2] They had sat on fryday & Saturday in expectation of Lowders return. But he not coming in the forenoon of the last of those days, they took into consideration many petitions for leave to send Fish to the West Indian Islands, & unanimously advised me to exempt fish from the Embargo as it usually, if not always, had been. This Morning I desired them to take the subject of fish again into consideration, as you seemed desirous that the Embargo should extend to that commodity. When it appearing that at this time of the Year the detaining of fish would be so Very ruinous to Numbers of People, for whom they had no prospect of any satisfaction from the Crown or otherwise, that they continued their advise that fish should be exported to the Principal Islands only on bond given to return a certificate, & oath made that they will not carry any other provisions. The Council also advised to the permitting Mr Hancock to send 3 months Provisions for Annapolis & Fort Cumberland;[3] & also for sending some livestock & fresh Victuals to Halifax for the use of the Garrison & Fleet there. In all things ^else^ the Embargo on provisions is kept up.

The Council could not conceal their disappointment at not receiving any assurances from you that this Province would be at liberty to import provisions from the Southern Provinces particularly Pensylvania & Connecticut. The impending Danger of Want & distress which threatens this Country is far from being imaginary: Another summer such as the last will produce a famine here. It is therefore hoped that you will remove from them the Apprehension ^of want,^ whilst their Neighbours abound in superfluities. I have been able this day to get over this apprehension in favor of the Garrisons of Nova Scotia: But I am satisfied that the Discontent & Disorder which will arise from having the ports, from whence they have been used to draw their provisions, shut against them, in an uncommon time of scarcity, will be Very great unless I am ^soon^ enabled to remove their fears. I enclose a Copy of the resolution of Council upon this subject.

As to the Correspondence of M^r Le Comte my time will not permit me to write on that subject now, but shall not fail to do it in my next dispatches.

I am, with great regard, Sr Your most obedient humble Servant

Fra Bernard.

His Excellency Sr Jeffry Amherst

ALS, RC   WO 34/26, ff 132-133.

Contains minor emendations. Endorsed: Governor Bernard Boston, 17th. May 1762. Recd.__ 22d.__ Ditto. Ansd.__ 23d. Ditto.__ Enclosed a copy of a minute of the Massachusetts Council of 17 May 1762, WO 34/26, f 134.

Amherst replied that the "Reasons" for continuing a general embargo were "greatly strengthened from the certain Intelligence" he had received about the plans of some Pennsylvania merchants to run contraband to Havana, via the Bahama Islands. However, Amherst asked FB to supply him with the names of the masters and vessels to be employed in shipping supplies to Boston from Connecticut and Pennsylvania in order that they be given special dispensation to deliver their cargoes. Amherst to FB, New York, 23 May 1762, BP, 9: 285-286. FB continued to press Amherst to lift the embargo, assuring him that there was no "danger of provisions being sent to the Enemy" from Massachusetts. FB to Amherst, Boston, 10 Jun. 1762, WO 34/26, f 167.

---

1. **No. 112**; Amherst to FB, New York, 10 May 1762, BP, 9: 281-284.

2. These proceedings are in Council Executive Records, 1760-1766, CO 5/823, ff 157-158.

3. Annapolis Royal, N.S., and Fort Cumberland at Wills Creek on the Potomac River, Md.

114 | To the Board of Trade

Boston May 17. 1762.

My Lords

I have just received your Lordships letter dated Febry 4th: and in regard to your Lordships observations on the act for the better observation of the Lords day, would lose no time in informing your Lordships of what occurred to me in passing that act.[1]

I did not consider it [to] be a repealing Act, but rather a consolidating One: tho', when many acts are reduced into one it is expedient to repeal the others, yet if the substance of them is preserved in the new Act, the old ones are not virtually tho' formally repealed. If I had thought it to be within the Spirit of the instruction & therefore to have required a suspending clause, I must have negatived the Act; for such is the present prejudice against suspending clauses, that they would give up an useful act, which I take this to be, rather than agree to a suspending clause and perhaps this may have been the reason why my predecessors have not strictly observed that instruction.

But tho' I think this an useful Act, as it appears to me to be a quieting one, I am not so well satisfied with the act additional to it which passed the next Session. And yet I could not negative it, because I could not avow the reasons of my disapprobation of it; which were founded on a suspicion that the power thereby granted to the Wardens was too great to be committed to officious & injudicious people into whose hands it must sometimes fall, especially as an extraordinary show of Zeal would often direct the Choice

I will order the proper officer to make out an Account of the duties of tonnage & impost specifying the duties upon Rum Sugar & Molasses as well as he can. But I much doubt whether he makes any distinction between Foreign Sugars &c and those of our own Islands.[2]

I am, with great respect, My Lords, Your Lordship's most obedient & most humble Servant

Fra. Bernard

To The Right Honble The Lords of Trade &c

ALS, RC   CO 5/891, ff 81-82.

Endorsed: *Massachusetts Bay,* Letter from Francis Barnard Esq[r]. Gov. of the Massachusets Bay, to the Board, dated 17. May 1762. in answer to their Lordship's Letter of 4 Febry. concerning The Act for the better Observation of the Lord's Day. Receiv Sep[r]. 6 Read Nov 19. 1762. L.l.37. Variant text in BP, 2: 58-59 (L, LbC).

Read and considered by the Board of Trade on 19 Nov. 1762. *JBT,* 11: 297-298.

---

1. **No. 87**.

2. [James Russell], An account of impost and tonnage [*on West Indies goods imported into the Province of Massachusetts Bay*], received between May 1755 and May 1762, c.May 1762, CO 5/891, ff 83-89.

115 | To Jeffery Amherst

Boston May 18. 1762

S[r].

I yesterday wrote to you[1] on the subject of the embargo, a letter which you must perceive to be dictated in an hurry; as indeed it was, being wrote before I left the Council chamber that it might be ready for the post. I then acquainted you that I would write to you on the subject of the illegal trade carried on by the traders of some of the North American provinces as soon as I could take into consideration the full purport of the papers you favoured me with and recollect my own ideas of the matters contained therein. Before I could set about this I have the pleasure to acquaint you of an affair relative thereto that I believe will be very agreable to you.

When I sent out the province Ship King George upon its cruise, I instructed the Captain to consider the Victuallers of Hispaniola & Missisippi as the Kings Enemies. He has accordingly sent into this port, as a Prize, the sloop Sally John Shoals Master laden with Sugar & Indigo from Hispaniola. From the depositions which have been taken this day, (being the same the prize arrived) It appears that She left New York laded with flour without any clearance or any public papers except her Register. That She went to the port aux Cayes near Port Louis in Hispaniola, where she disposed of her cargo, & took in a lading cheifly of Sugar & some Indigo. The Master of her has behaved in so candid a Manner that I could not use any greater Severity against him than obliging him to stipulate in the Admiralty for his appearance there. His owner is M[r] Lawrence Kortright of New York.[2] I must add that when this Sloop left port aux Cayes there came out in company the sloop Rover [*blank*] master bound to Rhode Island. From a Dutch Gentleman who was a passenger in this Sloop I learn that Vessels from Jamaica are not uncommon in French Hispaniola. I have also this intelligence; that between 6 & 7 weeks ago 14 ships of the line Supposed to be the English Fleet from Martinico to Jamaica passed by Hispaniola; and that it was expected at Cape Francois that 21 Spanish ships of the line would join the french to attack Jamaica.

I write this without the papers referr'd to before me, that it may be ready for the first opportunity of sending it away. If I have time I shall rectify & authenticate it; being now setting out for Castle William in order to give some necessary orders both for the provincial & regular service. In regard to the latter M[r] Hancock has a brig ready, which We shall load with recruits, as full as may be, on Monday next.[3] I shall referr what I have to say on that business to that conveyance.

I am, with great regard, S[r] Your most obedient humble Servant

Fra Bernard

His Excellency Sr Jeffry Amherst.

P.S. Council chamber May 20.

I inclose a resolve of the Council this morning & earnestly recommend the contents to your consideration that I may have your consent to permitt flour to be shipt for the ports Northward of this port. I have been very much pressed to permit it immediately but am desirous to have your previous Approbation. I will send Copies of the Examinations of Shoals &c by the next post.

I enclose you an extract of a S Carolina Gazette which is just come to hand, tho I suppose it has come to you before. I send this by an express that as little loss may be made by the damage of the flour (part of which is supposed to be spoiling evry day) as possible.

ALS, RC   WO 34/26, ff 135-136.

Contains a minor addition. Endorsed: Governor Bernard. <u>18th</u>. ^& 20th^ May 1762, Rec^d. & Ans^d: 24th. Ditto.__. Variant text in BP, 2: 144-145 (L, LbC). Enclosed a copy of a minute of the Massachusetts Council of 19 May 1762, WO 34/26, f 137; other enclosures not found.

1. **No. 113**.

2. Lawrence Kortright (1728-94), a New York merchant, was a Crown-authorized privateer during the French and Indian War. Much of Kortright's extensive landholdings in New York were confiscated during the War of Independence on account of his Loyalism; his daughter married future U.S. President James Monroe. The seizure of his sloop *Sally* is also discussed in **No. 119**.

3. 24 May.

116 | To William Shirley

Boston May 21st. 1762

S^r.

I have been much concerned at my letting last summer slip without acknowledging the favors I received from you at the begining of it:[1] the Hurry of business that I was then in, & the little previous advice I have had of Vessells sailing to your Government was the occasion of it. This is the first oppertunity that I have been acquainted with of a conveyance to New providence,[2] since last winter. I have hoped however that my Compliments to you thro' the hands of M^r. Erving[3] did not fail to arrive in due time.

I was flattered last Summer with the expectation of seeing you here; but that is now gone off: and it is very agreeable to me to understand that this disappointment has been occasioned by the establishm^t. of your health where you are; and your being engaged in business more intresting to you than anything that could have engaged your attention here.

Your Excellency's Knowledge of this province will readily induce you to give me credit for my plea of hurry of business: My Resolution, when I arrived at this Government, of not making my self a party in the divisions I found here, has not exempted me from trouble more than was necessary, nor from sometimes seeing public Affairs conducted otherwise than I could have wished: but I hope it will lay a foundation for maintaining my own independency,

I am with great regard S^r. Your Most &c &c

His Excellency Genl. Shirley.[4]

L, LbC   BP, 2: 147.

In the handwriting of clerk no. 1.

---

1. Not found.

2. In the Bahama Islands.

3. Probably George Erving (1738-1806), merchant of Boston and son of John Erving Sr.

4. William Shirley (1694-1771), former governor of Massachusetts, 1741-56, and governor of the Bahama Islands, 1759-68.

117 | To Jeffery Amherst

Castle William May 22. 1762

S^r

I have had no time to set down to give you my sentiments upon the papers you sent me[1] concerning Mr Comte's negotiation before now, altho the Ideas I formed upon the first reading them are just the same as I have now. But the Multiplicity of business prevented me giving them a through consideration: which I thought might be postponed, as it seemed clear to me that it would answer no purpose to make a public animadversion of them.

Mr Aquart is the person I mentioned to you above 6 months[2] to have arrived here from Martineco in a flag of Truce. As He had actually brought from that Island

13 or 14 English Prisoners half of which were Masters of Ships of this Country, I could not treat him with incivility. However I consulted the Council in evry thing I did in relation to him.[3] As the Armament was then ready to embark from Staten Island I thought it Very necessary to detain him here. After some time He petitioned for leave to sell his Vessel, which being English-built he had leave to do. From that time He staid here, professedly till the fate of Martinico was determined, neither with my leave nor contrary to it. I could not act otherwise than I did: for having refused leave for him to return to his Country whilst he could have reached it, I could not drive him from hence whilst it was invested: and therefore there was nothing left but a tacit permission for him to tarry here till the Affair at Martinico was over.

His accomplishments both natural and acquired introduced him with effect to most of the fashionable tables in Town. And no Umbrage could be taken at this; as there was no reason to apprehend that his purposes extended any further than to Martinico: and as it was supposed that either a Peace or the Cession of Martinico must take place, neither of those alternatives afforded any occasion to apprehend any hurtful consequences from his Commercial connexions. And indeed it appears plain that his intensions reach'd no further than his own Island, untill his accidental intercourse with M[r] Comte.

As for the latter, I suppose he is the same who was introduced to me about the time mentioned in the letters. He produced a letter from the Governor of Port Louis, desiring a protection for him whilst he stayed in this Country for the recovery of his health. I asked him what port He arrived at? "Newport:" in what Colony he intended to reside? "Rhode Island:" how long he intended to stay in Boston? "2 or 3 days." I then told him that I could do him no other service than to let him return to the place he had fixed upon for the purpose of recovering his health. After which I never saw nor heard of him, except that I understood that he was returned to Rhode Island soon after I saw him.

For the Gentlemen of this Town who are mentioned in these letters I dont see that I can, from this Evidence, proceed any further than a reprimand; and even in regard to that I have a doubt whether that should be public. But I will think upon what is best to do: at present I have communicate[d] these papers to no one; as I find myself utterly incapable at present to proceed upon any business that can be postponed; next Wednesday being the day of the meeting of the New Assembly. In the mean time I hope the Capture of Capt[n] Hallowell,[4] of which I advised you by a letter sent by express last thursday[5] will vindicate this province from the charge of these practises; which are so far from being familiar here, that they seem ^in no instance^ to have gone further than intention. And I can assure you that Capt Hallowells sending in the Hispaniola Victualler meets with the general Approbation of the ^best^ people here, whilst those who blame him are forced to whisper their resentments.

I am with great regard Sr Your most obedient humble Servant

Fra. Bernard

His Excellency Sr Jeffry Amherst

ALS, RC   WO 34/26, ff 138-139.

Contains minor emendations. Endorsed: Governor Bernard. Castle William Boston, 22^d. May 1762. Rec^d.__ 29th. Ditto.__ Ans^d.__ 30th. Ditto. Variant text in BP, 2: 148-149 (L, LbC).

Amherst did not share FB's leniency toward the Boston merchants named in Mons. Comte's papers (and whose identities are unknown). "I should be very glad to see some Examples made of those who have been Concerned in this Infamous Commerce, which I am persuaded would have a good Effect by Deterring others from being Guilty of the like practices." Amherst to FB, New York, 30 May 1762, BP, 9: 291-294.

---

1. **No. 112**.

2. **No. 76**.

3. There is no formal record of FB bringing this matter to the Council's attention.

4. Benjamin Hallowell, captain of the province sloop the *King George* and a member of the Boston Marine Society (admitted 1748/49). William A. Baker, *A History of the Boston Marine Society, 1742-1981* (Boston, 1982), 331.

5. **No. 115**.

118 | To Jeffery Amherst

Castle William May 23. 1762.

S^r

There is now lying here a Brig which will sail from hence on Tuesday next with what regular recruits can be got together, to what number I can't now say. Five have gone off from hence after they were past: four of them are lurking in the Neighbourhood & are so well known that there is no doubt of their being taken. The other, who is a stranger, I fear is got out of reach. The remaining have been put on board the Brig; as all others shall be as fast as they are brought here.

There is among the recruits the Son of a Minister, who has been to demand him, producing a certificate of his age, from which it appears that he was not 17 when he inlisted. As the Age of 18 is made one of the Terms of the grant of the Assembly, I can by no means disregard the claim of a young man under that age made by his parent. And if it was not a matter of right, yet it would be necessary to comply with it as a matter of favor: for to carry away a Minister's Son in spight of his prayers and tears would do the Service more harm than 50 such lads would do it good.[1]

There was another recruit that came to the Castle & offered himself: his appearance gained the attention of evry one; and upon enquiry he proved to be a Merchant of London; & some of this town have been acquainted with his former affluence, tho' he is now so reduced. I therefore desired of Capt Elliot that I might place him in the provincial service; & finding him Very able with his pen & at accounts, I recommended him to Gen¹ Bastide to oversee the stables at Halifax, & have orderd him an Ensigns commission. But All this is to have your approbation, which I doubt not of: for if you had seen him & heard his story, your humanity would have been moved in the same manner as mine has been.[2]

Notwithstanding these two instances you may assure yourself that I neither do nor shall Spare any pains to encrease the Number of recruits. But as I succeeded, beyond all expectation, in obtaining the grant for this purpose, I must take care that it be executed in a manner agreable to the people; as I, only shall be answerable for it. I foresee many little occasions for popular clamours which may arise in the course of this service, which it will be my business to obviate. I should therefore desire that Capt Elliot may be instructed not to interpose any Authority of his own against the discretionary measures I may be obliged to take with particulars, before they are out of my hands.

Cap Elliot informs me that you have orderd him to reject Indians: as this will cause the loss of many a good Man, you should be apprised that All our Indians are baptised & civilised & are in all respects as orderly as the rest of the people. There is now on board the Brig an Indian, that, if I mistake not, is the best Man in the whole embarkation.[3]

The Party reserved for recruiting is thus formed: L¹ Col Gay of Ingersol's Regiment is commanding officer at the Castle to whom all recruiting officers are to make their returns. He has under him as Quartermaster Lieut Miller[4] of Hoars Regiment. The Officers engaged in recruiting are picked out so as to leave three officers to evry company. As soon as the Country has been throughly tried, I shall order them to their head Quarters, unless there should be, which I dont expect, an encouragement to continue the recruiting beyond the first Essay.

I am, with great regard, Sʳ Your most obedient and most humble Servant

Fra Bernard

His Excellency Sʳ Jeffry Amherst.

ALS, RC   WO 34/26, ff 140-141.

Contains a minor addition. Endorsed: Governor Bernard. Castle W^m. Boston, 23^d. May
1762. Rec^d.__ 29th. Ditto. Ans^d.__ 30th. Ditto. Variant text in BP, 2: 150-151 (L, LbC). The
reply to this letter is in BP, 9: 291-294.

---

1. Amherst thought it "reasonable" that the father furnish a substitute for his son, noting that he did not
   "think it absolutely necessary" to reject seventeen-year-old recruits who were "abler & fitter" than many
   twenty-year olds. Amherst to FB, New York, 30 May 1762, BP, 9: 291-294.

2. When Capt. Elliot informed Amherst of this destitute merchant, the general commended FB "in
   providing for One, Whose misfortunes Seem to Claim Compassion." Ibid.

3. Amherst reversed the exclusion order and instructed Elliot to accept Native American volunteers. Ibid.

4. FB thought highly of Francis Miller, who was appointed an ensign in the 45th Regiment of Foot on 14
   Dec. 1762. See **source note** to **No. 171**.

119 | *From Jeffery Amherst*

New York, <u>24</u>^th. May 1762.

Sir,

Lowder arrived here this moment, and Delivered me Your Letter of the <u>18</u>^th.
with a Postscript of the 20th.[1] Enclosing a Resolve of the Council regarding the
Exportation of Flour, which is so Contradictory to the one You transmitted me
in Your Last, that I cannot Reconcile them: In the first they Represent "the great
Distresses of the Inhabitants for Want of *Flour* &ca.; and Desiring those Commodities might be allowed to be Exported from Pensylvania & Connecticutt, upon
Bond being given to Land them at Boston"; This You will find by mine of Yesterday
I agreed to, on certain Conditions;[2] but by the last Resolve the Council seem ap-
prehensive from no Embargo being Laid at Philadelphia (as they supposed) that
the merchants of Boston already overstocked with Flour would be Considerable
Sufferers unless they were permitted to Export Flour (the very article which they
were before afraid of being in want of) & therefore Requesting a Relaxation of the
Embargo at Boston, might be obtained with respect to the Article of Flour, & that
they might be permitted to send it to Quebec, Newfoundland, or other English
Ports to the Northward.__

You will have seen by my last, that I had certain Intelligence of the Enemy's
having Entered into a very Extensive Scheme for being Supplied with Provisions
for their Fleets & Armies at the Havannah, from this Continent, by the way of
Providence:[3] The Discoverys You have made by the seizure of the Sloop *Sally* like-

wise Confirm their Designs; And as this is a matter of the most serious Consequence, and that nothing but a General Embargo can prevent the Merchants from supplying the Enemy, as they seem Determined to try Every means to Carry on a Trade, however Destructive to the Country in General, that promises a Considerable profit to themselves; I must once more, Request that the Embargo may be Continued in the Strictest Sense on all vessels, but Such as I have already Excepted.__

I Shall acquaint L^t. Govr. Colden of the Seizure of the Sloop Sally: Altho' the master has Seemingly behaved in a candid manner, I must observe, that he has either Sunk, or Secreted his Papers, for it appears by a List of vessels now in my Custody, that were Suspected to *be* out on this Clandestine Trade, that the Sloop Sally, John Shoals, master, & Lawrence Kortwright owner, was Cleared out for Jamaica the 26th. Jan^{ry}. 1762, Loaded with Provisions, Deal Boards, &ca.; but I am very glad she has fallen into the hands of the Province Ship, and You will take such measures with the master as You judge best.__

I Thank You for the Extracts from the south Carolina Paper, which I had not seen before; and I am particularly obliged to You for the orders You were giving for forwarding the Recruits: I wish to see Some of them here, as they are greatly wanted to fill up the Corps that are going on Service.__

I am, with great Regard, Sir, Your Most Obedient, Humble Servant.

Jeff: Amherst.

His Excellency Governor Bernard.

LS, RC   BP, 9: 287-290.

Variant text in WO 34/27, p. 247 (L, LbC).

---

1. **No. 115**.

2. Amherst to FB, New York, 23 May 1762, BP, 9: 285-286.

3. In the Bahama Islands.

120 | *To Jeffery Amherst*

Boston May 25. 1762

S^r.

Mr Goldthwait is returned from Springfield where he has been to muster the Men & pay them the bounty of the province allowance towards there billeting: he has made me a return of 1695 non com & private men musterd there, who are all marched on to Albany. From whence It appears that, as our Number was actually levied to a man, so there is a great probability that it will be found very little deficient in the Camp: at present there does not appear to be wanting 20 men of the whole.

The Men were very uneasy that they were not paid the Kings billeting at Springfield, but were quieted by being assured that will certainly be paid at Albany. I must strongly recommend that Care be taken that they may be paid there ^or soon after^: for disappointments of this kind not only create a present uneasiness, but hurt the Service by the complaints they make when they return home.

I am, with great regard, Sr Your most obedient & most humble Servant

Fra Bernard.

On the other side is my estimate of the Musters.

P.S. I have just received advice that the last party of Hoars Regiment is got safe to Halifax. I have a return of exactly 1000 men besides commissioned Officers.

ALS, RC   WO 34/26, f 142.

Enclosed a copy of FB, "Estimate of the Musters," 25 May 1762, WO 34/26, f 143. Variant text in BP, 2: 152-153 (L, LbC).

121 | *To Jeffery Amherst*

Boston May 30. 1762.

S^r.

Last Night I received your letters of the 23^d & 24th instant.[1] In regard to the first I can add a further confirmation of the provision trade to Hispaniola, having advice that the Sloop which I mentioned in my last to have sailed from *Aux Cayes* in company with the Sally is arrived safe at Newport as are also two or 3 other Vessels from Hispaniola, whose names I have not yet learned. As to the offer you have made of permitting particular Merchants whose Names shall be certified to you, to bring provisions from Pensylvania & Connecticut to this province, it will be Very acceptable; And they will most readily give any security that shall be required to land the provisions here. As for pork there is now so great a Want of it that there will be a general obstruction of the trade & fishery of this province for want of Ships provisions & Victualling the fishing boats upon our own coasts unless there is a speedy importation of pork. The Very Garrisons of Castle William & our two Forts at the Eastward will soon be in want, not to repeat what I have mentioned before of the Want of Victuals in the inward parts of the province. Also the Launceston Man of War & the Mast ships which are just come in & are to return to England with all possible Expedition depend upon being Victualled here which can't be done without importing pork. I shall therefore send to you with all expedition the Names of such Merchants here as want provisions with the quantities & qualities wanted: but it will be impossible to send the names of the Vessels & Masters who are to carry such provisions, as it is not usual to send the Vessels from hence but to employ their Agents to freight the goods at the ports in Vessels used in coasting only & not fitted for Sea Voyages.

The seeming contradiction which you observe upon in your letter of the 24th, of the Council's first desiring leave to import flour & afterwards asking to export it, is easily obviated by a consideration of the distance of time between the two requests & what happened in the interval. When I first wrote to you No flour had arrived from Philadelphia; & the Merchants finding that the Pork they had contracted for in Connecticut was stopt expected that their Flour from Philadelphia would meet with the same obstruction. But since that, many Vessels with flour have arrived from Philadelphia, which bring advice that a good deal more may be expected. If therefore they should require their whole orders from thence & not be permitted to Supply the Northern ports with what was designed for them, there must certainly be a superabundance: but this was so far from being the Case when I wrote my letter, that I question whether it does not now exist in expectation more than possession.

There is another consideration in favor of the Northward Coasting of flour: in support of which I must premise my hopes that the People of this province is intitled ^to favor^ equally at least with any other. This is, that as they have hitherto supplied the Northward provinces with provision of this kind; if any great & durable interruption should be made in it, the Trade would probably get into another channel: and this public spirited Province can ill afford at this time to lose any branch of the little trade remaining to it.

As for fish, It never was apprehended that there could be a want of that. Unhappily for this Country, the Breach with Spain will leave too much of that Commodity in the hands of the owners after all legal & reasonable exportation of it is allowed. This is now the cheif staple of this Country, & this only: and if it should be stopt going to the English Islands, now it is excluded from the European markets, it must bring great distress upon this province; ^which has been^ allmost, if not quite, unconcerned in the pernicious trade which has occasioned these restrictions: and it would be Very hard if the Delinquency of other Colonies should fall most hardly upon an innocent one.

While I write this I mean to assure you that the utmost Care & the most certain means are intended to prevent any abuse in the two Articles of fish & flour &c. to the Northward. Evry thing that has been allowed to go hence to the Garrisons to the fleet to the Settlers &c is bonded. If Any Caution can be added to those allready devised, it shall be done. I know but of one; and that is obliging Vessels carrying Fish to the West Indies to sail with convoy: and that I will enforce [*it*] if it can be made practicable. I am assured you do not doubt my activity in evry necessary duty that belongs to me & comes within my power: and I will say for myself that I keep myself Superior to any necessity of conniving at any mercantile practices detrimental to great Britain. Nothing is better known here than that the perpetrators of such will not be spared if discovered.

As I shall not be able to lay your letters before the Council time enough to write by tomorrow's post, I have given you, in this hasty manner, my thoughts on this subject, which will, most probably, prove conformable to the Sentiments of the Council upon a further consultation. Upon the whole I do not apprehend that our being allowed a discretionary power of letting fish go to the West Indies & flour to the Northern ports upon Security given both by bond & Oath, can be attended with Any danger of supplying the Enemy.

I am, with great regard, Sr Your most obedient humble Servant

Fra Bernard

His Excellency Sr Jeffry Amherst.

ALS, RC   WO 34/26, ff 145-147.

Contains minor emendations. Variant text in BP, 2: 153-156 (L, LbC).

---

1. Amherst to FB, New York, 23 May 1762, BP, 9: 285-286; **No. 119**.

122 | To the Earl of Egremont

Duplicate

Boston June 7. 1762.

My Lord

I had the honor by my letter of Ap. 16[1] to inform your Lordship that the Assembly of this province have obeyed his Majesty's commands, as signified by your Lordship, in the fullest manner. I have now to add that the powers granted to me for raising the provincial troops were executed with a spirit not known before; the regiments having been complete & ready to march before the end of April.

It will be agreable to your Lordship to know that there is the most perfect Harmony in the Government of this Province: as a proof of which I beg leave to enclose the address of the House of Representatives, the professions of which do not exceed their real disposition. I must at the same time do them the justice to declare that this disposition does not arise from Management, but from a conviction that the Support of his Majesty's Government is their true intrest

I am, with great respect, My Lord, Your Lordship's most obedient and most humble Servant

Fra. Bernard

The Right Honble The Earl of Egremont.

dupALS, RC   CO 5/755, f 9.

Endorsed: Boston. June 7th: 1762. Gov[r]. Bernard R Sep[r]. 6th. Variant text in BP, 2: 192 (L, LbC). Enclosed a copy of the House of Representatives's address to FB, 1 Jun. 1762, CO 5/755, f 13 (Prt).

---

1. **No. 102**.

123 | To John Pownall

Boston June 7. 1762

D^r. S^r.

The Acts of the General Assembly for the two last Sessions now lie before me & shall be transmitted by the first Vessell that Goes from hence to London: there has been no oppertunity hitherto

In the mean time I transmit to you my speech at the opening the New Assembly & the Adress of the Representatives; and that the same time Assure that the professions in it do not at all exceed the real disposition of the House as there is now a perfect Harmony in the Government.

The men required this year were granted in the fullest manner; they were raised with an Expedition unknown before, the Regiments being all complete before the end of April: & they have been sent to the places of their destination without any loss by sickness or desertion which has been considerable in other Years.[1] If you should think proper to lay the subject of this before their Lordships you will present my Compliments.

I am with great regard S^r. &c & & &

John Pownall Esqr.

PS let my predecessor know that I consider the election of his friend Brig^r. Ruggles to be speaker as a great point in favor of Government.

L, LbC   BP, 2: 193.

In the handwriting of clerk no. 1 with a minor scribal emendation. Enclosed a copy of FB's speech to the Council and the House of Representatives, Council Chamber, 27 May 1762, for which see *JHRM*, 39: 10-11.

---

1. For a discussion of recruiting problems pertaining to the provincial regiments see **No. 102**, and for the regular regiments **No. 103**.

124 | From the Board of Trade

Whitehall June 11th: 1762

Sir

His Majesty's Counsel at Law appointed for the Service of this Board, having made his Report to Us upon the Acts of the Province of the Massachusets Bay passed in April June & July 1761. We have had them under our Consideration, and as they do for the most part relate to the internal Police and more private œconomical Concerns of the province, nothing material has occurred to Us upon any of them except the Acts which are for incorporating and establishing new Counties & Towns, more particularly those for incorporating the County of Berks and Town of Pitsfield mention'd in your Letter to Us of the 3^d. August 1761.[1]

We entirely agree with you in Opinion that the great Increase of the House of Representatives, whilst the number of the Council remains fix'd and unalterable, must from the Nature & Form of the Constitution as established by the Charter have very pernicious Consequences and destroy that Ballance which We presume was originally intended to be kept up between the Upper and lower House of Assembly.

It appears however to Us to be an Evil resulting from the original frame of the Constitution in what regards the Right of the People to choose Representatives laid down in the Charter itself and in the Act of the 4. of W^m. & Mary Cap: 19[2] which was founded upon the Charter and has been confirmed by the Crown, and therefore We much doubt the Propriety of any Measures on the part of Government which might have the Effect to restrain the Operation of those fundamental Principles of the Constitution.

In this View and Consideration of the Question, it seems to Us that the Remedy to the Evil must lye in the Discretion of the constituent Parts of the Government and which We observe with Pleasure have in many Cases where Townships have been divided in the old Settlements given the part set off all the Priviledges of Incorporation, except that of choosing a Representative, all therefore that We can do upon this Occasion is to recommend to you to take Care that in every future Division of a Township by Act of Legislature you do use your best Endeavours, either that the Part set off be so formed as that it will have all the Benefit of Incorporation without being entitled under the Charter or the Act of 1692 to choose a Representative or that if it's Circumstances be such as that it is absolutely necessary to be incorporated as a Township, that there be the like Clauses of Exception as those We have just mentioned, or that the Inhabitants be directed to join in the Choice of a Representative with those of the Township from which they have been set off.

As to those Settlements in the Eastern Parts of the Province which from an Increase of Inhabitants[3] are become entitled to Incorporation, they have in our

Opinion a clear indisputable Right to be represented in Assembly, not only in virtue of the Charter and the Act of 1692 but of those Principles of Reason and Justice which require that they should have some Share in the formation of those Laws by which they are to be bound and governed, and therefore We cannot disapprove of the Act for erecting the Town of Pittsfield, commending however the Caution and Prudence with which you acted in taking Care that the Rights of choosing a Representative should not take Place till His Majesty's Pleasure might be known upon the Act. We are

Sir, Your most Obedient humble Servants

Sandys

E. Bacon

Edmond Thomas

Geo: Rice.

John Roberts.

Francis Bernard Esqr Govr: of the Massachusets Bay

LS, RC BP, 9: 307-314.

In the handwriting of John Pownall. Endorsed by clerk no. 1: Lords of Trade June 11 1762. Variant text in CO 5/920, pp. 139-143 (L, LbC). Enclosed a copy of Sir Matthew Lamb's Opinion for the Board of Trade, Lincoln's Inn, 22 May 1762, for which see CO 5/891, ff 65-67.

---

1. **No. 59**.

2. An act for ascertaining the number and regulating the House of Representatives, 4 Will. 3 & Mary, c. 38 (30 Nov. 1692). NB: the legislative chapter given in this footnote is consistent with modern notation.

3. In the 1764 census, the counties of Lincoln, York, and Cumberland accounted for 8.9 per cent (or 21,867) of Massachusetts's total population. Robert V. Wells, *The Population of the British Colonies in America Before 1776, A Survey of Census Data* (Princeton, N.J., 1975), 79.

125 | *From Jeffery Amherst*

New York, <u>13</u>th: June 1762__

Sir,

As I have Received advice of a Quantity of Provisions coming out from England, which I hope will arrive safe, and that I have nearly Compleated the Tonnage of vessells, which I want for the Transport Service, I take the Earliest opportunity of Acquainting You that I Intend, for the Convenience of the merchants on this Continent, to free the several Ports from the Restrictions that have been Laid in Consequence of my Request, to prevent the Exportation of Provisions, and I trust that no more attempts will be made to Supply the Enemy, or Carry on the Illicit Trade that has been so lately Detected.__

You will therefore be pleased to give the necessary Directions for taking off the Embargo that has been Laid in Your Province; and I flatter myself I shall have no further Reason to apply to You on the subject which occasioned me to Desire that measure to be put in Execution.

I am, with great Regard, Sir, Your most Obedient Humble Servant.

Jeff: Amherst.

His Excellency Governor Bernard.

[PS][1] I am obliged to You for Your Care in forwarding the Letter Enclosed in Yours of the 7th.[2] I send You a Copy of it as I know nothing of the author.__

JA

LS, RC   BP, 9: 315-318.

Endorsed by clerk no. 1: Genl Amherst June 13 1762

---

1. Letters obscured by the binding.
2. FB to Amherst, Boston, 7 Jun. 1762, WO 34/26, f 162. The enclosure has not been found.

126 | To Jeffery Amherst

Boston June 14. 1762

Sr.

I have received yours of the 6th of June[1] informing of the arrival of the 1st party of recruits;[2] I hope the second party is arrived by this time. We are preparing for a third embarkation, of what Number I cant now say. I shall be sorry that Any of them should prove diseased; for they are examined by the Surjeon of the Castle before they set out: but possibly some may have escaped his inspection.

Particular care is taken concerning the exportation of fish & such provisions as are allowed. The permissions are granted in Council & Bond is taken for the performance of the conditions. The Notice that has been given of your intention to allow provisions from Connecticut to certified persons has lowerd the price of pork, (which was got to an exorbitant highth) 25 p[r] cent: and there is still room for it to fall allmost as much more. The Cover of this will inclose some more memorials for provisions. I have been much harrased about the stopping the fish: but have got a little Ease by promising a 20 gun ship letter of marque to take such Vessels as were loaded with that commodity, under convoy. I have sevral petitions lying by for leave to carry provisions (cheifly flour & bread) to Quebec Halifax &c. I suppose I may now let them go taking Security that they shall deliver the goods there & certify &c.

I am, with great regard, S[r] Your most obedient & most humble Servant

Fra. Bernard

His Excellency S[r] Jeffry Amherst.

ALS, RC WO 34/26, f 164.

Contains minor emendations. Enclosures not found.

1. Amherst to FB, New York, 6 Jun. 1762, WO 34/27, p. 250.

2. Lt. Francis Miller brought the first contingent of regular recruits to New York; Lt. [Philip?] Richardson of Col. Hoar's regiment brought the second, some twenty recruits. FB to Amherst, Castle William, 25 May 1762, WO 34/26, f 144; FB to Amherst, Boston, 4 Jun. 1762, WO 34/26, f 161.

127 | To Jonathan Belcher

Boston June 17: 1762

S[r]:

I wrote to you on the 3[d]: of April last[1] inclosing a resolve of the General Court to which I have had no Answer I now inclose another Resolve of the same kind, I have only to add that from what appears to me, the sole doubt concerning the Line dividing the two Provinces will arise from this Question; *which of the Rivers which fall into the Bay of S[t]: Croix is the River S[t]: Croix?* And this will depend upon the comparison of those Rivers with the accounts given of them by the first Voyagers particularly Champlain.

I am with regard &c.

(Signed) Fra Bernard

Hon[ble]: Jon[a]. Belcher Esq[r].[2]

L, Copy   CO 5/891, f 153.

In the handwriting of Andrew Oliver. Attestation: Copy as of Record. Compared.
Variant text in Prov. Sec. Letterbooks, 2: 343 (L, Copy). The RC of this letter enclosed
an extract of the record of the election of Massachusetts's boundary commissioners (CO
5/891, f 153). Both were enclosed in **No. 202**.

The provincial governments of Nova Scotia and Massachusetts were confused as to
which particular river it was that in 1604 French explorers named the "St. Croix" and that
Samuel de Champlain (1567-1635) recorded in a map of the region. The different topo-
nomic practices of the emigrants settled in the area and the Native peoples they displaced
added to the uncertainty. Demeritt, "Representing the 'True' St Croix." See also **No. 154**.

---

1. FB to Belcher, Boston, 3 Apr. 1762, Prov. Sec. Letterbooks, 2: 336.

2. Jonathan Belcher (1710-76) was the son of Jonathan Belcher (1681/2-1757), the former governor of
   Massachusetts and New Hampshire. He practised law in England and Ireland before being appointed
   chief justice of Nova Scotia in 1754 (which he held until his death) and was lieutenant governor of the
   province, Nov. 1761-26 Sept. 1763.

128 | To Jeffery Amherst

Castle William June 19. 1762

S[r].

Lieut Miller will wait on you with this having the command of a third parcell
of recruits[1] which I suppose will not be less than 25. When these are gone I have
no great expectation of sending many more for the present, especially as the Hay
Harvest is begun. All I can say is that I beleive the Country is throughly beat up;
and all that were to be got have been.

I have had occasion to observe that other Men might have been got upon other
terms: but I did not care to make a new proposal[2] whilst there was any probability
of raising the Men upon your terms. I was well assured that at the time of rendez-
vousing our Provincials It would have been easy to have raised 2 or 3 companies
out of the Regiments who would have engaged in the Kings pay & Service during
the War, if they had been inlisted for separate ^entire^ corps & under officers of
their own Country. And even now (tho' it is the Very worst Season in the year for
inlisting) I beleive it would be practicable to raise a company or two of rangers
under officers of my nomination, either as independant companies or to be added
to Gorhams Corps.[3] In such case I could pick out 6 or 8 very good officers, among
which L[t] Miller would be one. But there is a great shyness in inlisting, where the
Men are to be separated one from another & put under Officers they dont know.

Lieut Miller has been asked by Maj^r Gorham to go on the expedition with him, & has asked my leave for it. I have answer'd that If He can get an appointment suitable to his rank under your orders, I shall have no objection to his continuing in the province pay, untill he can obtain the Kings pay. He is a spirited & steady Young Man.

I am, with great regard, Sr Your most obedient & most humble Servant

Fra Bernard.

His Excellency Sr Jeffry Amherst.

ALS, RC   WO 34/26, f 168.

Contains minor emendations. Variant text in BP, 2: 160 (L, LbC).

---

1. **No. 126**.

2. Amherst rejected FB's suggestion of raising separate provincial companies for regular regiments, on which see FB to Amherst, Castle William, 5 Jul. 1762, WO 34/26, f 169.

3. LbC: "of Rangers" added here. Maj. Joseph Gorham (1725-90) was commanding officer of the Corps of Rangers in North America. The regiment had been renamed the Corps of Rangers in 1761, having been called Gorham's Rangers when they were placed on the British establishment in 1760. The rangers were originally formed in Massachusetts in 1744 by John Gorham (1709-51) of Barnstable Co., Mass., and after his death were commanded by Joseph, his younger brother.

129 | *From Jonathan Belcher*

Halifax 30th: June 1762[1]

Sir,

Altho' I have not been enabled fully to Answer Your Excellency's Letters 3^d: of April and 17th: instant[2] for want of perfect informations in some of the essential points for the Consideration of this Government, yet I did not delay to propose to the general Assembly, what respected the western limits of this Province, as Your Excellency will find by the date in the Copy of the Votes of both Houses inclosed, in result of their deliberations, upon the resolutions of your Government, for Settling these Boundaries, laid before them by the inclosed Message from me.

The difficulty does not seem to rest, upon settling the denomination of the River S^t: Croix, so much as upon the Authority of this Government, to settle any Boundaries of this Province, more especially as the Limits of Acadia must remain for the express determination of his Majesty, nor can this Government with propriety proceed to the decision of any territories so immediately belonging to his Majesty.

I would offer it to Your Excellency's consideration whether the Proviso in the 11th: Page of the printed Charter of the Massachusetts Government, relating to the Granting away Lands in Sagadohoc territory, does not seem to interfere with, and throw difficulties in the way of settling those Lands, and of adjusting the Limits between the two Provinces.[3]

M[r]. Secretary Oliver having signified to me,[4] his desire of some Explanation of the Grant by this Government of the Island of Great Menan, I am to apprise Your Excellency, that it was judged to be within the Limits of this Province, and was accordingly granted by the late Governor of this Province,[5] to certain persons who afterwards forfeited their Rights, by failure in performance of the Conditions. A promise has since been made to others on Condition of their Arrival and Settling in a certain time, but they have likewise failed, and I shall now desist from any further prosecution of that design, until his Majesty's Pleasure relating to the limits of the two Provinces shall be known. I submit it to Your Excellency, Whether it may not be advisable, for both Governments to forbear making any Grants upon the Borders that maybe disputable, til the bounds shall be legally adjudged. Upon receipt of your Excellency's Letter, by and in favor of M[r]: Freeman, owner of the Schooner Peggy a Transport in his Majesty's Service, I sent to the Collector of the Customs, who assured me, that measures would be taken agreeable to your Excellency's intentions, that he might not incurr any disadvantage, for want of a Clearance upon those special Circumstances of his Case stated in Your Excellency's Letter. I have the honor to be with great respect, Sir, Your Excellency's most humble and most Obedient Servant__

Jonath[n]: Belcher

L, Copy   Prov. Sec. Letterbooks, 1: 359-360.

Enclosed Jonathan Belcher, message to the Council and the House of Representatives of Nova Scotia, Halifax, 3 May 1762, for which see Prov. Sec. Letterbooks, 1: 360 (L, Copy); other enclosures not found.

---

1. Left marginal note: "Gov[r]. Belchers Letter to the Gov[r]: with respect to the bounds of this Province & Nova Scotia."

2. 3 Apr. 1762 in Prov. Sec. Letterbooks, 2: 336 and **No. 127**.

3. This may refer to *The Charter Granted by Their Majesties King William and Queen Mary, to the Inhabitants of the Province of Massachusets-Bay in New England* (Boston, 1692).

4. Not found.

5. Charles Lawrence (c.1709-60), governor of Nova Scotia, 1756-60.

6. Not found.

130 | To the Earl of Egremont

Boston NE. July 1ˢᵗ 1762.

My Lord

The President and Fellows of Harvard-College in Cambridge in this Province having prepared a small Collection of Verses[1] on the subjects of his Majesty's Accession & Marriage, have desired me to introduce them to your Lordship & beg your favor to present their small oblation to his Majesty, humbly hoping that the indulgence his Majesty has shown to the two great Universities in England in accepting their offerings will in some measure excuse the presumption of this little Seminary.

I have upon this occasion to apologise for the dilatoriness of this address, which is best done by stating the facts. This Undertaking was not begun till the beginning of last summer: when it was near completed the Advice of the Kings Marriage arrived,[2] when it was thought desirable to enlarge the small collection by adding a few pieces on that happy occasion. This carried the Work into the Winter; since which It has waited for a safe Conveyance.

If the distance of place would have permitted it, it would have been very agreable to the President & Fellows to have submitted their Copy to perusal, before it was printed off. But as that was impracticable, they hope that if Any improprieties shall occurr, they will be excused by the good intention of the writers, & the unfeigned Zeal of the whole Society for the happiness & Welfare of their most gracious King. I am, with great respect, My Lord, Your Lordships most obedient

& most humble Servant

Fra. Bernard

Rᵗ Honble the Earl of Egremont

ALS, RC   CO 5/755, ff 15-18.

Endorsed: Boston July 1ˢᵗ: 1762. Govʳ. Bernard. R Septʳ. 15ᵗʰ: from Mʳ. Jackson NB. Mʳ. Jackson presented the Letter Himself. Variant text in BP, 2: 201-202 (L, LbC). Enclosures not found. The letter itself was enclosed in **No. 133**.

---

1. *Pietas Et Gratulatio Collegii Cantabrigiensis Apud Novanglos Bostoni, Massachuttensium* (Boston, 1761 [1762]).

2. King George III married Princess Charlotte of Mecklenburg-Strelitz on 8 Sept. 1761.

131 | *To Richard Jackson*

Castle William July 6th. [1762][1]

D^r. S^r.

I wrote to you at the beginning of march last a letter, which send by the Packet,[2] containing an Acct. of the province of Sagadehock & the methods the Government was taking to settle it, also some particulars concerning a part of it. as these went by the packet inclosed in a Cover to the Lords of trade I sent no duplicates of them. in the latter end of April I wrote to you informing that M^r. Bollan was suddenly discharged from being Agent, that M^r. Mauduit was chosen in his room, & you was appointed an Second, in case of his disability or refusal, & he was directed to consult you in all Law matters &c. This letter went from Boston ^ap 26^ in the Brig Bristol Packet Bartlet for Bristol; and the duplicate of it in the Brig New Swallow Gardner for Bristol which Sailed May 5th[3] The displacing M^r. Bollan (which was quite unforeseen by me) & the relation to this province which I hope you will be content to bear in its present imperfect manner in which you are called, will oblige me to be very troublesome & especially in some businesses which more immediately belong to me at present than the General province. And first of the first.

In February last the General Court made a grant to me of the Island of Mount desart on the North East side of Penobscot Bay. As this is part of the territory of Sagadehock, this grant by the terms of the charter of William & Mary, must have the Kings Confirmation before it can be effectual. For this purpose. I sent the Grant under the province seal & signed by my self the secretary for the Council & the speaker for the House to M^r. Bollan desiring that he would solicit the Kings confirmation, ~~before it can be effectual~~ with all convenient speed, I wrote Also to the Secretary of State & M^r. Pownall for the Board of trade,[4] As these letters did not go from hence 'till March 6th I cant expect now to hear to any purpose from M^r. Bollan, having but just learnt that the ship which carried the first set of these papers arrived safe at London. Nevertheless as it may be apprehended that M^r. Bollan upon hearing of his dismission may resolve to leave England this Summer, I thought it necessary to engage some one to take this business of his hands, if he has not already taken or shall not find it convenient to take Effectual Measures to finish it: & I could not propose any person more fit to undertake this business than you being Confident that your inclination to assist me will equal your Ability Upon that Assurance I must desire you would with all convenient Expedition, look into this Affair, & either as an Assistant or a Principal, as you shall see expedient, bring it to a good Conclusion as soon as may be

If you should take this into your hands you will consider it as a Provincial Affair: for tho' this particular grant is only intresting to me; yet the Right underw^{ch} it's claimed & the precedent it will make in regard to the townships which the Genl. Court has agreed to grant as soon as the Surveys which are now making can be returned, make the event of this sollicitation of great Consequence to the province in general It would therefore be proper to desire M^r. Mauduits Assistance as provincial agent; at the same time you may let him know that as soon as a survey of the River S^t. Croix shall be taken, which is to be done next month, & some certain Enquires made a full state of the provinces right to the continent & Islands thereto belonging up to the River S^t. Croix will be prepared & sent to him, who will according to his instructions advise with you about it. As for Lord sterlings claim (the only one I know of ~~at present~~) that it is under a grant from the Plymouth Company to the first Earl of Stirling (whose Heir the present Earl does not pretend to be)[5] made 140 years ago without any possession ever taken, or any claim made within these last 100 years & more untill within these 4 or 5 years last past.

Tomorrow 4 weeks I set out for the Eastward with the Committe appointed to survey the Bay of S^t. Croix. whilst they are about that I shall reconnoitre Mount desart, erect an house there, which I have now framing on this Island; lay out a Town for which I suppose ~~there~~ a 100 families now waiting;[6] contract for erecting 2 or 3 saw mills, look for brick clay & Limestone &c I should not precipitate in this manner, if I was not hurried by the importunity of the people, whom I should entirely lose, if I was to put them of till I heard of the confirmation of my grant. Nevertheless my entring into expence will make me Very desirous to get the Confirmation as soon as possible; and for that purpose I Should not grudge a little Money for Expedition. I will suspend my acc^t. of the Island till I have seen it; in the mean time will assure you that it is a thing of much greater value than was apprehended at the time of the Grant; and therefore I would not spare money to obtain the Confirmation.

As this Affair finishes the sheet, I will conclude it by assuring you that I am

D^r. S^r. &c &

R Jackson Esqr.

L, LbC   BP, 2: 194-197.

In the handwriting of clerk no. 1 with scribal emendations.

---

1. Written as "1761²".

2. Thus in manuscript, meaning that he had already sent the documents.

3. These letters have not been found.

4. FB to Bollan, Boston, 2 Mar. 1762, BP, 2: 32-33; **No. 90**; FB to Pownall, Boston, 4 Mar. 1762, BP, 2: 33-34.

5. William Alexander (1576-1640), baronet and first earl of Stirling, Scottish statesman, and poet. King James I granted Alexander proprietary rights to New Scotland in 1621; while he sent out several expeditions, none was able to establish a permanent settlement. William Alexander (1726-83) of New Jersey, the future Patriot general, revived claims to his forbear's lordship of Stirling in Scotland and the lands in Sagadahoc.

6. Thus in manuscript. This is an ambiguous clause, for FB had not yet contracted with any body of settlers. The cancelled text suggests that originally FB was estimating the population of the planned town, but the correction could imply that FB was trying to impress Jackson (perhaps to attract his financial backing) by disingenuously suggesting that he already interested potential settlers. However, in subsequent letters to Jackson, notably **No. 220**, he did not claim to have engaged any settlers though he continued to proffer generous population projections.

132 | To William Bollan

Castle William July 7th. 1762

Sr.

I am favoured with yours of feb 13th1 & am much obliged to you for the trouble you gave yourself in the business therein mentioned. I am advised by Lord Barrington that the Affair is postponed for the present, the objection of my sons minority not being to be got over2

In the beginning of march last I sent to you a Grant of the Island of Mount desart made to me by the General Court, desiring you to get the Kings confirmation of the grant according to Charter.3 I could not expect to hear from you on this subject having but just received advice that the ship wolfe Cap Diamond which carried the first set of these papers arrived safe at London Nevertheless upon account of some transactions here I think it necessary to add a few lines upon that subject

I mean the proceedings in the General Court concerning the Agency; which have given me a good deal of Concern. As I knew you would receive many Letters upon this subject, I did not write to you upon it. But as I was unwilling to appear to a friend of ours to act a part contradictory to my professions in regard to you, I did write to Mr. Wilbraham a short letter accounting for my ~~professions~~ conduct in that affair which I suppose he has shown to you: I also wrote to Secretary Pownal4 to the same purpose. the Resolve in the house was certainly very exceptionable, & I mad5 no doubt but that the Council would, as they ought to have non concurred it. But as they left it to me to stem the whole torrent, I found myself obliged to consent to what I professedly disapproved of.

I made no doubt but that the part I acted in this transaction would appear to you in such a light, that your disposition to do me good offices would receive no abatement: and therefore I made no further provision for procuring the confirmation of my grant than, what I had before made. But having since considered that it is probable that you will leave London before my business is finished, I find it necessary to engage a Gentleman to take so much of this trouble of your hands, as you shall want to part with. I have therefore wrote to M^r. Jackson (Rich^d. Esqr. Paper building Inner temple last staircase) to concert with you what remains to be done, & to take such a part therein as shall be most agreeable & convenient to you both.[6] I should be glad to have it concluded before the grants of the 12 New Townships shall be sent up, which wont be 'till next winter: especially as I am obliged to act under the Grant unconfirmed as it is, otherwise I shall lose a set of settlers that now offer & wont be delayed.

I shall be very glad of an oppertunity of acknowledging my obligations to you by such services as are in my power & am

S^r. your & &

W^m. Bollan Esqr.

L, LbC   BP, 2: 197-198.

In the handwriting of clerk no. 1 with minor scribal emendations.

This is FB's first letter to Bollan after his dismissal from the province agency in Apr. FB's concern that Bollan would do nothing to assist the confirmation of the Mount Desert grant overrode his embarrassment at having acquiesced in his removal. While Bollan passed the paperwork to Jasper Mauduit (**No. 172**), FB continued to write Bollan about the problems arising from the administrative inertia of the British government, with which Bollan was certainly familiar; his response was probably less than sympathetic .

---

1. Not found.

2. **No. 86**.

3. FB to Bollan, Boston, 2 Mar. 1762, BP, 2: 32-33.

4. **Nos. 104** and **105**; FB to John Pownall, Boston, 4 Mar. 1762, BP, 2: 33-34.

5. Thus in manuscript.

6. **No. 131**.

133 | To Richard Jackson

Castle William July 10th 1762

D^r. S^r.

The College at Cambridge in this Province have at my incitement prepared a Book of Versese[1] to be presented to the King on the Subjects of his Accession & Marriage; and have put it into my hands to get it presented to the King. As the Conducting this Matter will require some management, I do not to know whom to trouble upon this occasion but you, to whom I flatter myself, it will not be wholly disagreeable, as you bear a kind of Affection to this Society.

The first trouble you will have will be to get a Sufficient Number of these books properly bound for the King Queen & royal family &c. you will then have to wait on the Secretary of state to desire that he would present the books; or if it should be thought more proper, to introduce you to present the Books; or, if it should be thought more proper, to introduce you to present them. in Either Case It may be proper to ask M^r. Mauduit to attend with you; for tho' this is not properly a provincial business, & therefore I was not at liberty to trouble M^r. Mauduit with it, as I am not personally acquainted with him; yet it has such a relation to the province, that I think it would be very proper for him to join in it.

My greatest Concern is that this will arrive in London whilst you are in the Country; and there is such a necessity for losing no time that I must importune you to come to Town immediately that the books may be presented as soon as possible. A little delay may occasion them to be publick, before they get into the Kings hands, which would be very improper. And the Delay allready may be thought unacountable: some of these verses were made above a year ago; before they were collected the Kings Marriage intervened, and it was thought proper to add some verses upon that Subject. This carryed the business into the winter & ever since the time has been spent in printing & waiting for a Safe conveyance.

I suppose it will be necessary to present Books to several Ministers of State & others besides the Royal family. I will therefore make a list of such as occur to me wch you will add to me[2] as you shall see occasion. I will also inclose a letter to the secretary of state to introduce this subject to him. There is a fund provided for payment of expences, by selling of Books. a Box of which will be sent to London for that purpose. I send you old Copies 30 off which are upon Superfine Paper, in a Box directed to you to be left at Richards Coffee house[3] It goes by the Launceston Man of war which convoys the Mastships.

I have no more to add but with great earnestness to recommend this business to your care, as I have it very much at heart & am answerable for the Conduct of it

I am S[r].

Rich[d] Jackson Esq[r]

L, LbC   BP, 2: 198-200.

In the handwriting of clerk no. 1. Enclosed the RC of **No. 130.**

---

1. See **No. 130**n1.

2. Thus in manuscript.

3. In Temple Bar.

134 | To Jeffery Amherst

Boston July 11. 1762.

S[r].

I have this day received advice of a Spanish Fleet being at Newfoundland, that I think proper to send the particulars of to you by express; as it seems to me improbable but that it has some foundation, however the Circumstances may be exaggerated. Garrason Meirs,[1] who came by land from Cape Ann to bring this Account, tells me the Winds have been so contrary, that I must not expect to hear from Halifax of the arrival of the advice of the Account he has brought for some days yet. If Any thing comes to morrow before the post goes out I will send it. The Launceston Man of War ^40 guns^ is here & the province Ship. If Lord Colville[2] sends orders they will both join him. He has only the Northumberland 70 guns & the Sirene 20, & may be join'd by the Antelope 50 guns from Newfoundland This is the total of the Maritime Force north of Virginia. I am unwilling to delay the Express by waiting for Copies of the enclosed papers to send to Gen[l] Monckton & therefore must beg you will communicate these to him & excuse my not writing to him.

I am, with great regard, S[r] Your most obed[t] humble Servant

Fra. Bernard

His Excellency S[r] Jeffry Amherst.

ALS, RC   WO 34/26, f 171.

Enclosed copies of the declarations of Samuel Doggett, a Boston mariner, and Garretson Meers taken at Boston and Castle William, respectively, on 11 Jul. 1762, WO 34/26, ff 172-173. Variant text in BP, 2: 162 (L, LbC).

---

1. Garretson Meers was a master of a fishing vessel, and his declaration was the first to be publicly acknowledged, in the *Boston Gazette*, 12 Jul. 1762, p. 3/1.

2. Alexander Colvill (1717-70), seventh Lord Colvill of Culross and commodore RN. When Colvill arrived in England on 26 Oct., he was promoted to rear-admiral of the white, and subsequently given command of the North Atlantic station, 1763-66. His name is often misspelled "Colville."

135 | To Sir George Pocock

Boston July 16. 1762

S[r].

We have had for some days past Reports of an Enemys Fleet having attacked Newfoundland: and this day a Vessel arrived which brought certain account of such Attack and some information of the force of the Enemy This become very alarming to this Coast as there is not a Man of War North of Virginia except the Northumberland at Halifax & the Syren frigate which is supposed to have escaped from Newfoundland. It is said that there was a 20 gunship at S[t]. Johns when it was invested, supposed to be the grammont. I have thought proper to send these Advices to you by a Vessel Express and have sent the same by land to Gen[l]. Amherst at New York[1]

I am with great Regard &c &c

His Excy S[r]. George Pococke[2] KB or the Commander in chief of his Majestys fleet in the West Indies

PS Since the above I wrote two other Vessels are come in the information of whose masters I herewith enclose.

July 25 P.S. to the Duplicate of the former dated July 16. Since the Original of the forewritten was dispatched by the Schooner Good Intent Witty Master who saild from hence on Monday last,[3] Divers Persons are come in from Newfoundland & which bring further advices Copies of the informations I have taken I have to add to the duplicates of what I formerly sent. It is now generally allowed that this fleet came directly from France; and It is hoped that the 4 Ships, which came into the Bay of Bulls are all of it: tho' it is ^still^ Contended that there are more of them. This morning the Master of a Vessel just come in averred to me that North of Cape Bonavista He saw 5 or 6 large Vessels, some of which He could distinguish to be

Ships &, seemingly large: and that No English Ships or Any Vessels of that Size had any business so far Northward,[4]

dupL, LbC   BP, 2: 164, 168-169.

In the handwriting of clerk no. 1, except where noted, with scribal emendations. Enclosures not found.

---

1. Not found.

2. Sir George Pocock (1706–92), a successful naval officer and vice-admiral of the fleet that led the assault on Havana in 1762.

3. 19 Jul.

4. This paragraph in FB's hand.

136 | To Jeffery Amherst

Boston July 16. 1762

S[r].

This day We have certain advice of S[t] Johns being attacked by a french fleet.[1] All the particulars that the Master of the Vessel now come in ^brings^ are contained in the enclosed Declaration. I am endeavouring to get a Vessel to sail immediately to carry these advices to S[r] George Pococke.[2] But as I dont know at present whom I can get, I would ^not^ thereby prevent your sending the like express. I am, with great regard,

S[r] Your most obedient humble Servant

Fra. Bernard.

His Excellency S[r] Jeffry Amherst.

ALS, RC   WO 34/26, f 175.

Variant text in BP, 2: 164 (L, LbC). Enclosed a copy of the declaration of Silas Akins, Castle William, 16 Jul. 1762, WO 34/26, f 176.

---

1. This corrected the intelligence provided in **No. 134**.

2. **No. 135**.

137 | To William Shirley

Castle William July 19th 1762

S^r.

I am Just now dispatching the Schooner good intent William Witty master express to Admiral ~~Pocke~~ ^Pococke^ with advice that a French Fleet has taken S^t. Johns in Newfoundland. As I can't get a Pilot to carry her thro' the Bahama Islands, I have orderd him to go directly to New Providence there to get a Pilot for the Havanah or wherever Adm^l. ~~Pocke~~ ^Pococke^ or the commander in chief is And I must beg of your Excell[e]ncy to order him to be forwarded with all possible expedition.

The French fleet is supposed to be the same that attempted the relief of Martineco. It's said to consist of about 8 ships 5 of which are of the line: but only 4 Ships Attacked s^t. Johns, the other four it is said took Placentia at the same time. The land forces are from 1500 to 3000 They use the people that remain very well & seem determined to keep Possession. The fishery is entirely broke up & all the Settlers South of S^t. Johns except what have been prevented, have left the Country. The whole Coast is very much alarmed.

I am with great regard S^r.

His Excy Lieut Genl. Shirley.

L, LbC

BP, 2: 163.

In the handwriting of clerk no. 1.

138 | From Jeffery Amherst

New York, 20th July 1762.

Sir,

Wier Arrived here this morning with your Favor of the 16th.[1] and the Intelligence Enclosed therewith puts it out of all Doubt that Some Vessells seen on the Newfoundland Coast belong to the Enemy: Altho' I cannot think but their Numbers are greatly Exaggerated, for it appears Incomprehensible to me, that they should Send so many Men of War to Attack Newfoundland, at a time that the most Interesting parts of their own Dominions are at Stake: Your Express came very luckily before the *Lyon* armed ship that I had Ordered for Martinique was Sailed; And I have Sent Copys of this Intelligence by her to Admiral Rodney,[2] Enclosing the Same to Sir Geo: Pococke, to be forwarded to him by the Admiral.[3] The Lyon is by this time, I hope, under way, so that they will be made Acquainted with this News in the West Indies, as soon as We could well Expect.

If any thing further should come to your knowledge, I must beg the favor you will Acquaint me, and I am particularly Obliged to you for the Dispatch you have Used in forwarding what you have already Sent me.

I am, with the greatest Regard, Sir, Your most Obedient Humble Servant,

Jeff: Amherst.

His Excellency Govr. Bernard.

LS, RC   BP, 10: 1-2.

Endorsed by clerk no. 1: Genl. Amherst July 20 1762. Variant text in WO 34/27, p. 261 (L, LbC).

---

1. **No. 136**.

2. George Bridges Rodney (1718-1792), British naval officer, commodore-governor of Newfoundland, 1749; MP for Okehampton (1759-61), Penryn (1761-68), and Northampton (1768-84); rear-admiral of the blue in command of the Leeward Islands station; naval commander of the British expeditionary force against Martinique in 1762 and subordinate to Sir George Pocock in the campaign against Havana later that year. Created first Baron Rodney in 1764 and later won distinction in the American War of Independence for his victory over the French fleet at the Battle of the Saintes in 1782.

3. **No. 135**.

139 | To Jeffery Amherst

Castle William July 25. 1762.

Sr

I am favoured with yours of the 20th inst by Wyer.[1] I hope you have received the further Accounts I sent you by the Post on Monday[2] & that a letter of mine & a packet from Halifax which were dispatched on Thursday last by the Hartford River to be forwarded with the best expedition ^will arrive in a day or two^.[3] All these contain evry declaration I have taken, except one of Evan Pitts of not much consequence, the substance of which was in our last Thursday paper.[4] I have also seen a Merchant from London who has been drove off Newfoundland, who sayes that before he left London, they had advice that a fleet of 7 Ships which had escaped from Brest was seen bearing for America. And it seems to me that that is the probable Number of the Enemies Ships at Newfoundland, tho' there is not positive proof of more than the 4 ships in the Bay of Bulls of 74, 64, 40 & the Bomb.[5]

I dispatched a clean Schooner on Monday last for Admiral Pococke with Copies of all the Advices I had then received, which included all sent to you. I orderd her to New Providence there to take a good pilot for the Havannah or wherever Sr George Pococke was. I wrote to Genl Shirley[6] to desire him to forward her with all expedition: If She has good luck, she may get to the Havannah in 10 or 12 days; the passage from Providence thro' the Bahama Islands being Very short with a skilfull Pilot.

I have just now received a ~~second~~ letter from Lt Govr Belcher dated 11 July wherein he desires that I would send him any additional troops that I can.[7] I can make up about 50 provincials that have been employed in the recruiting Service, (without any hurt to that Service) & perhaps may get together near 20 regular recruits. I shall send these away probably by the middle of the Week: but I dont see how I shall be able to raise Any fresh forces, unless it is by Way of replacing those that have refused to reenlist or have enlisted in the regular Service: and of these I have not received a regular return ^& believe that at Halifax the Deficiency is supplied by fresh recruits^. However I shall lay this request before the Council tomorrow morning. If it produces any thing material, I will add it in a postscript.[8]

I am, with great regard, Sr Your most obedient & most humble Servant

Fra Bernard.

His Excellency Sr Jeffry Amherst.

P.S.

Since I have wrote the preceding Sevral Vessels are come in from Halifax, from a passenger in one of which I have got a deposition a copy of which I inclose. I find it Very difficult to do any thing material to reinforce Halifax but have not quite given it up.

ALS, RC   WO 34/26, ff 184-185.

Endorsed: Governor Bernard. Boston, 25th. July 1762, Rec^d.__ 31st. Ditto.__ Ans^d. 1st.__ August. Variant text in BP, 2: 165-166 (L, LbC). Enclosed a copy of the declaration of William Dobel, 26 Jul. 1762, WO 34/26, f 186. The reply to this letter is in BP, 10: 3-4.

---

1. **No. 138**.

2. FB to Amherst, Castle William, 19 Jul. 1762, WO 34/26, f 178.

3. FB to Amherst, Cambridge, 22 Jul. 1762, WO 34/26, f 181.

4. *Boston Newsletter,* 22 July 1762.

5. Usually bomb-ship or bomb-ketch, a small mortar-carrying vessel. *OED.*

6. **Nos. 135** and **137**.

7. Belcher to FB, Halifax, 11 Jul. 1762, Mass. Archs., 5: 473.

8. The Council took no action other than to send an express rider to Crown Point to ascertain how many of the Provincials there had re-enlisted. CO 5/823, f 167. FB may have thought of sending deserters to Belcher (**No. 141**) before he replied to him (**No. 144**).

140 | To Sir George Pocock

Castle William near Boston July 26. 1762.

S[r]

This day sev'night I dispatched the Schooner good intent Witty Master with orders to sail directly for New Providence & there take in a Pilot for the Havanna or where else he might expect to find you.[1] The contents of my dispatches were that a French fleet consisting of 2 Ships of the line, one 40 Gun ship & one bomb, had entred the Bay of Bulls in Newfdld & destroyed the settlement there & landed 1500 men (at least) & Marched by land to S[t]. Johns which surrendered to them without firing a gun. Since which several other Vessels have arrived here confirming these Accounts.

Having just rec[d] Advice that a schooner will sail tomorrow from this Port for New Providence, I have thought to add this letter to my former to guard against a Miscarriage. And as I have not by me the depositions of which I sent you copies, you will excuse me if instead of other copies of them I enclose some printed Articles in our New Papers, which are conformable in substance to the Depositions themselves. Never the less one that I have taken to day I shall enclose a Copy of.

Our Port begins to fill with Vessells which have escaped the General Wreck. This day I have rec[d]. a letter from the Lieut. Gov[r]. at Halifax[2] desiring such reinforcements as we can spare. I shall do the Best I can. But I think Halifax will not be in danger, if the French force Amounts to no more than what I have before stated: and there is no possitive proof of any More at present. But if they should Maintain their lodgment till they are reinforced, no body knows where it will end. I need not tell your Excellency that the Maritime force on this Coast is uncommonly ~~low~~ ^small^. They profest to Maintain their ground, & immediately upon the Surrender of S[t]. Johns Sent a frigate to France. But it now seems that a General Devastation along the Coasts is more intended than securing particular ports. However at present all is in confusion & uncertainty & the Earliest Relief must be from your Fleet. Gen[l]. Amherst to whom I have communicated the earliest Accounts of this Affair,[3] informs me, that he has dispatched the Lyon Armed ship to Martineco,[4] with these advices: it is therefore convenient that I have directed mine by another course

I am with great regard S[r] Your most &c &

His Excellency S[r]. George Pococke

L, LbC   BP, 2: 167-168.

In the handwriting of clerk no. 1 with scribal emendations. Enclosed a copy of Dobel's declaration from **No. 139**, and a copy of the *Boston Gazette*, 26 Jul. 1762.

---

1. **No. 135**.

2. Belcher to FB, Halifax, 11 Jul. 1762.

3. **Nos. 134**, **136**, and **139**.

4. **No. 138**.

141 | To Benning Wentworth

Boston July 29. 1762

S^r

Having orderd a general Search to be made for deserters from the provincial troops of this province in his Majesty's Service, I learn that there are many Such residing in your province, & sheltring themselves under the distinction of jurisdiction. Altho' I don't doubt but that the Magistrates of New Hampshire will act with a due sense of their duty upon this occasion yet as there is at present a particular demand of Men I've persuaded myself that it would be agreable to you to interpose your Authority to bring these people to justice, that they may make good their former deficiency by a present Service. For which purpose I have orderd the officers employed in this business to wait on you. I am

His Excellency Govr. Wentworth.

AL, LbC   BP, 2: 169.

142 | To Jeffery Amherst

Castle William Aug 1 1762.

S^r.

The Brig Neptune Cockran Master[1] is just arrived; who informs that He left Halifax last Monday:[2] that they were strengthening themselves there but did not expect a Visit from the french; as there was certain advice that the latter were fortifying themselves at St Johns with additional Works both to the Sea & the land. That the french fleet came from Brest consisted of a 70 gun a 64 a 44 a 24 & another frigate, which latter was dispatched for France. There are, on the best reckoning,

1600 french regulars. There was on board this Brig, a Man who was at St Johns 6 days after it was taken. I have orderd his information to be taken & shall inclose it with this. There is an officer coming express to you in a Sloop, which is not yet arrived; but may be expected to morrow.

I am, with great regard, Sr Your most obedient & most humble Servant

Fra. Bernard

His Excellency Sr Jeffry Amherst.

P.S

Since I have wrote this another Ship is come in the information of whose Master I inclose.

ALS, RC   WO 34/26, f 187.

Variant text in BP, 2: 170-171 (L, LbC). Enclosed copies of the declarations of George Maddicks and Thomas Lamb taken on 1 Aug. 1762, at Castle William and Boston, respectively, WO 34/26, f 188-190.

---

1. The *Neptune* had left Boston for Newfoundland in June and was owned by Boston merchant George Bethune. CO5/ 850, f 14. Its master, William Cochran (d.1821), was admitted to the Boston Marine Society 7 Jun. 1763. Baker, *History of the Boston Marine Society,* 323.

2. 26 Jul.

143 | To Sir George Pocock

Castle W^m. Near Boston Aug^st. 1st. 1762.

S^r,

A Ship is just arrived here which Sailed from England on May 22, under Convoy of the Antelope; I thought proper to send the Masters declaration, that you may judge of the probability of the Antilope's falling into the Enemys hands. The Sirene Man of War & another Vessel hired for that purpose were cruising on the Banks of Newfoundland to meet the Antilope; but it is probable She has missed them, as this Ship arrived on the Coast 2 days after she lost the Antilope Another Vessel which arrived to day brings advice that the french were repairing & adding to the fortifications of S^t. Johns both to the land & sea. This is to be put on board the schooner Shirley packet now lying off this Castle bound for New Providence; which has allready on board a packet containing duplicates of & additions to the

Advices of the french having taken S^t. Johns, which I sent to you Express by the schooner Good intent Witty Master, which Sailed from hence on Mondy July 19th which I hope will arrive Safe[1]

It is now generally allowed that this french fleet came from Brest & is the Same which was seen off the Western Islands[2] by the Superbe, the Danae & the Gosport It consists of the Robuste of 74 or 70 one of 64 one of 44 or 40 one of 24 & another frigate which was dispatched to France on the Surrender of S^t. Johns. The land forces are 15 or 1600 Regulars.[3] It is said the Grammont is sent to England as a Cartel with the Garrison.

I am with great regard,

His Excellency S^r. George Pococke &c &c

P.S.[4] ~~Since I wrote this another Ship is come in the information of whose master I inclose~~. I add another Declaration which I have received since I wrote the former

L, LbC   BP, 2: 170.

In the handwriting of clerk no. 1 with minor scribal emendations. Probably enclosed copies of the declarations mentioned in **No. 142**.

1. **No. 135**.

2. The Azores.

3. The French ships were commanded by Charles-Henri-Louis d' Arsac de Ternay (1723-80) and the military force by Louis-Bernard de Cléron, the comte D' Haussonville and colonel of the Royal de Roussillon Regiment, 1759-61.

4. The postscript is written in the left margin.

144 | To Jonathan Belcher

Boston August 5th 1762

S^r_

I have sent Capt. Hallowell in the provincial Ship with all the regular recruits that could be got together since the last party went to NYork.[1] It is not in my power to raise Men for this purpose, unless the Danger was more urgent, untill the Assembly meets; which cant be till the End of this Month. I sent Admiral Pococke advise of the Invasion of Newfoundland by an Advise Boat express which probably is arrived there by this time; as She Sailed on Monday 19th of July. I shall keep the King George cruising between Halifax & Boston & probably add another armed Vessell to her, The Captain will have orders to communicate to you any Intresting advices that shall occur.

I am with great regard

The Honble. Lt. Govr Belcher

L, LbC   BP, 2: 172.

In the handwriting of clerk no. 2.

---

1. See **No. 139**n8.

145 | To Jeffery Amherst

Boston Aug 9. 1762.

S^r.

I am favoured with yours of the 1st of Aug.[1] In regard to those of our Provincials who had refused to reinlist in the provincial Service, or had inlisted into the regular Service, I had authorised Col Hoar to supply their places by recruits at Halifax & therefore I could not raise them here. I had thereupon no other to send ~~him~~ ^to Halifax^ but regular recruits: and accordingly despatched 18 of them by the King George 2 days before, I received your letter.[2] Tho this is not agreable to your intention, yet as they have been sent there without any expence to the King & will there join a Corps of the same recruits I presume it cant occasion much inconvenience.

We are alarmed here with an account of a French privateer, cruising in the Gut of Canso, within which We have a large intrest in fishing Vessels. I am just now ordering the Province Sloop to be armed in a respectable manner & despatched there.

I am with great regard Sr Your most obedient & most humble Servant

Fra. Bernard

His Excellency Sr Jeffry Amherst

I beg you will excuse me enclosing a letter to Mr Stevens[3] & desiring you would order it to be deliverd to *Him*

ALS, RC   WO 34/26, f 191.

Variant text in BP, 2: 171-172 (L, LbC). Enclosure not found.

---

1. Amherst to FB, New York, 1 Aug. 1762, BP, 10: 3-4.

2. Amherst had asked FB to send new regular recruits to New York rather than Halifax. Ibid.

3. John Stevens (1715-92), merchant and shipowner of Perth Amboy, N.J., a member of the provincial assembly, and a future New York Patriot. Stevens was one of several Anglican assemblymen close to FB when he was governor of New Jersey. See FB to Halifax, Perth Amboy, 18 Jul., 1760, BP, 1: 270-271.

146 | To Jeffery Amherst

Boston Aug 18. 1762.

S[r].

I have just received yours of the 12th inst. I sent ^Capt[n] Hallowell with^ the King George to Halifax on thursday the 5th inst by way of short cruise.[1] His Instructions were to land the 18 regular recruits, to wait on the Governor & Lord Colville, & to return immediately. But I privately directed him to consult with Lord Colville, as far as the latter would give him opportunity, about the expedition to dislodge the French; & to let him know that I should readily order the King George to join in such expedition if She should be wanted. As We know that Lord Colville, was advised of the state of the french fleet & of the Antelope & Sirene being at Placentia, ^probably,^ before Capt Hallowell got to Halifax; I make no doubt but Lord Colville has detained him: especially as the Capt[n] proposed to be at home by Saturday last: and the Wind has been ^good^ enough.

Last Sunday The Province Sloop with 8 carriage guns 12 swivells & 50 men sailed to the Gut of Canseau to protect the fishery there, from the small armed Vessels which the french may have sent into those seas: tho' I doubt whether there is a true cause for the alarm; as I can learn nothing more than that a fishing Vessels[2] was fired at in those Seas. Nevertheless, as this Armament has been with very little expence, I shall not repent my caution, whether there was occasion for it or no; especially as it has greatly eased the Minds of those concerned in that fishery.[3]

If, notwithstanding my conjectures, the King George should come into this port, I shall order her to join Lord Colville. I dont apprehend the least danger to the transports, no Enemy's Vessel having as yet appeared between this port & Halifax.

I am, with great regard, Sr Your most obedient & most humble Servant

Fra. Bernard.

His Excellency Sr Jeffry Amherst.

ALS, RC   WO 34/26, f 195.

Variant text in BP, 2: 174-175 (L, LbC).

<hr>

1. Amherst had asked that the *King George* escort the six transports of soldiers bound for Halifax, under the command of Lord Colvill, that comprised the force gathered to retake St. John's, Nfld. Amherst to FB, New York, 12 Aug. 1762, BP, 10: 5-6.

2. Thus in manuscript.

3. Amherst later reported intelligence from Quebec suggesting that a vessel that fired on the fishing boats was a pirate ship. Amherst to FB, New York, 25 Aug. 1762, BP, 10: 9-10.

147 | To Sir George Pocock

Boston Augst. 19th 1762

S^r.

On the 19th of July I despatched a schooner express to you with advice that a french fleet had taken S^t. Johns in Newfoundland on the 27th June and broke up the whole fishery there.[1] On the first of August I sent to you Duplicates of the former & some further Accounts of the french proceedings in Newfoundland by the Brig tartar a privateer bound to New Providence, inclosed in a Cover to Genl. Shirley.[2] Having now a Master of a Sloop ready to sail to the Havannah I take this oppertunity to inform you of the present state of Newfoundland.

The french force consists of the Robuste 74 guns Eveille 64 Licorne 26 Garonne a transport of 30:[3] but they are so extreamly ill manned as to Sailors, that they can scarce work their ships. Their land forces are 1300 pickt troops. They have fortyfied S^t. Johns all around as well as they can & have laid a Boom across the mouth of the harbour. They have unbent their sails & struck their Yards, & declare that they will stay there 'till September & then leave a Garrison behind them however they will find their quarters beat up before that time

Lord Colville has now under his Command the Northumberland, Antelope, Gosport, Sirene & our provincial Ship the King George a Complete 20 gun Frigate; & is, I believe, now preparing to Sail to S^t. Johns with a body of troops that are collecting at Halifax. This force will be Sufficient to block up the Port for the Present, if not to take the Port. All the danger we apprehend at present is from the French being reinforced, which by their remaining in such security, they seem to Expect. On the other hand there is as good reason for us to expect Succours from England or from your fleet

I thought Proper to give you this short detail & am, with great regard S^r. your most obed^t. &c & &

His Excellency S^r. George Pococke

L, LbC   BP, 2: 175-176.

In the handwriting of clerk no. 1.

1. **No. 135**.
2. **No. 137**.
3. The numbers of guns carried by the *Licorne* and the *Garonne* are wrongly reported. Corrections were made in **No. 153** and **No. 162**.

148 | To Jeffery Amherst

Boston Aug 20. 1762.
5 p.m.

S^r.

I have just received a letter from Lord Colville informing me that He should sail on the 10th of August with the Northumberland Gosport & King George for New-foundland.[1] I have also a letter from Capt Hallowell inclosing a Copy of Lord Colvilles orders to him; which are quite agreable to me & were necessary for Capt Hallowell, as my written orders would not have been sufficient for that length of Voyage.

I understand that your dispatches for supplying Lord Colville with Troops were not ^then^ arrived. As I presume they are now expedited, I have immediately given you this Account, that you may ^have the earliest time to^ send such further orders as this Movement of Lord Colville's may make necessary. I dont apprehend there is, at present, any danger on this Coast. And as Lord Colville will call at Placentia for the Antelope & Sirene, I dont apprehend that the French Ships will choose to face him.

I am, with great regard, S^r. Your most obedient & most humble Servant

Fra. Bernard

His Excellency Sr Jeffry Amherst.

P.S. I wrote to you by yesterday's post in answer to yours of the 12th inst

ALS, RC   WO 34/26, f 196.

Variant text in BP, 2: 176 (L, LbC).

---

1. Not found.

---

149 | To Jeffery Amherst

Boston Aug 23. 1762

S[r]

I wrote to you last fryday[1] advising that Lord Colville with the Northumberland Gosport & King George sailed from Halifax on the 10th inst to join the Antelope & Sirene at Placentia & thence proceed to S[t] Johns. And as It seemed Very necessary that you should know this as soon as possible, I engaged M[r] Hancock to dispatch it by express. Since this I received your last letter.[2]

I have nothing now left, but to desire your order for releasing Ichabod Wright an Indian Mulatto enlisted at the Castle & sent to Quebec. I think there is a proof of his being born a Slave which would satisfy a Jury, in case an Action was brought against the Officer who inlisted him, as is threaten'd.[3] The order should go by the Vessel which is to bring him away: for if he has notice of it he will go off. Another Man is to be put in his stead for the same bounty &c. Col Robinson[4] may transact this business with M[r] Goldthwait.

I am, with great regard, S[r] Your most obedient & most humble Servant

Fra. Bernard

His Excellency S[r] Jeffry Amherst.

ALS, RC   WO 34/26, f 197.

---

1. **No. 146**.

2. Possibly Amherst to FB, New York, 12 Aug. 1762, BP, 10: 5-6.

3. See **No. 207**.

4. Andrew Robinson, a British army officer, was appointed colonel of the 45th Regiment of Foot on 24 Sept. 1761, having been a major general since 1759.

150 | To Jeffery Amherst

Castle William Aug 29. 1762

S^r.

Thursday last[1] in the Evning arrived here The Dorothy Brig a french Parlementaire from St Johns orderd with 120 English including 19 Women & Children for England; but so poorly Victualled, that tho' they arrived here in 3 weeks they had nothing for the last 4 days but bread & bad Water. The English were landed the next day: they consist of 30 Souldiers (11 of which are of the train[2] & 19 of the 40th Regiment no Officer higher than a Corporal) 42 Sailors from different Vessels 28 Inhabitants of Newfoundland & about 19 or 20 Women & Children. The French Crew consists of but 6.

I have orderd the Souldiers into the Barracks, at Mr Hancocks desire, who has engaged Col Jarvis to Victual them. They want some money in part of pay: but Mr Hancock declining to advance it, no body else will. They have sent me two papers by Way of pay rolls, which I shall inclose with this. By the french Roll, which I shall inclose, they are charged with the being prisoners during the War: but they in general know nothing of their being under such an engagement; tho' One of them said he did hear such a thing mentioned by an indifferent person.

The French Master desires that I would fit him & Victual him for Old France & that I would give him so many french sailors in return as will enable him to carry his Vessel to Europe. This is Very necessary, if he is to go there; for his present Crew is quite incapable of such a business. But I have no french prisoners under my charge that I know of. I am told there may be some french sailors prisoners of War pick't out from among the french now brought to Halifax, & must desire to know if I have your leave to apply any such, if this Man urges being returned to Old France. His Brig is an English Prize but is now protected by his Flag. It is not improbable but that protection will be bought off in favor of the former owner.[3]

In my former examinations of people from St Johns, I have declined entring into their resentments at the surrender of the fort,[4] being unwilling to add to the load which is like to fall on the commanding Officer. But at present there is something due to your information, & for that purpose I send you the Account which some of these men give of this affair, confining it to facts only as much as might be. I have not mentioned the Names of the declarants nor sworn them to it, being desirous that no other use should be made of the inclosed paper but for your private information. The whole was wrote in their presence & read to them: the enclosed is a copy.

I am, with great regard, Sr Your most obedient humble Servant

Fra. Bernard

His Excellency Sr Jeffry Amherst

ALS, RC   WO 34/26, f 198.

Contains minor emendations. Variant text in BP, 2: 177-178 (L, LbC). Enclosed copies of "Role des noms at surnoms des prisoniers embarqués, sur le Parlementaire Le Dorothée et des Batimens dont ils proviennent" [trans.: *roll of the names and surnames of the prisoners embarked on the parlementaire Le Dorothée and of the ships they come from*], WO 34/26, ff 199-200; [FB], A Return of Arrears of Pay and Cloathing [due to British prisoners of war of the 40th Regiment of Foot, taken at St. John's, Newfoundland], Castle William, 29 Aug. 1762, WO 34/26, f 201; **No. 151**.

The French cartel *Le Dorothée* was carrying some 140 prisoners to England, having set out from St. John's on 18 Aug., putting in at Louisbourg for water and provisions. It was from this vessel that Lord Colvill learned about the size of the French naval squadron and expeditionary force that the British were to face at St. John's. C. H. Little RCN (Ret'd), "The Recapture of Saint John's, Newfoundland: Dispatches of Rear-Admiral, Lord Colville, 1761-1762," *Maritime Museum of Canada Occasional Papers* 6 (http://ngb.chebucto.org/Articles/colville-1762.shtml, accessed 20 Apr. 2006). Another cartel vessel carrying sixty-two inhabitants of Newfoundland arrived at Newbury, Mass., c.2 Sept. with letters from the French commander Charles de Ternay stating that "the inhabitants in general are Prisoners for the whole War according to the Terms of the Surrender and certified as such and will be treated with rigor if they shall be taken in Arms." FB to Amherst, Boston, 2 Sept. 1762, WO 34/26, f 204. Plans were laid, shortly after the recapture of Newfoundland, to return the refugees to St. John's (CO 5/823, f 175). While Amherst was ignorant of the terms of capitulation at St. John's, he nevertheless deplored any "scandalous Terms" that would designate British soldiers as "prisoners" for the duration of the war. Amherst to FB, New York, 5 Sept. 1762. FB transferred responsibility for the disposition of the British soldiers to Capt. Elliot, who was to engage Thomas Hancock to transport them to New York or wherever the general ordered. FB to Elliot, Castle William, 26 Sept. 1762, BP, 2: 281.

---

1. 26 Aug.

2. Artillery train.

3. Amherst advised FB to provision the vessel for a voyage to England rather than France, since the former was *Le Dorothée*'s original destination. Amherst to FB, New York, 5 Sept. 1762, WO 34/27, p. 276.

4. Fort William.

151 | *Account of the Surrender of St. John's, Newfoundland*

[*c.*29 *August* 1762]

When the French came before S[t]. Johns the Garrison consisted of 3 officers & 23 privates of the Train of Artillery & of 2 officers & 50 or 51 privates of the 40. Regiment Cap[t]. Ross commanding the Garrison & regulars & Cap[t]. L[t]. Rogers commanding the Train.[1] There were 36 guns in the fort & Battery adjoining (besides six in the South Battery,) of which 20 were 24 Pounders 8 18 pounders & 8 6 pounders (including 2 field pieces one of which had its carriage broke) 10 of which guns pointed towards the Ground, where the Enemy advanced; And there was ammunition sufficient. The Cap[t] of the Gramont brought 100 Sailors & Marines.[2] The People of the Country that came in to the defence of the fort were 370 according to the Armourers Account who delivered out so many Arms & Cartouch boxes. This was when the french were above a mile off the fort. The French that attackt the fort were about 500, according to the best account, when they marcht from the Bay of Bulls; & some were left by the Way: they had no Cannon with them or nearer than the Bay of Bulls. At first, preparations were made for defending the fort: When the french were within half a mile One Cannon 24 Pounder was fired at them —twice once with round shot & once with grape. The French advanced to gain the Shelter of a hill about 300 Yards off, & then they sent a flag of truce which was met by Cap[t]. Rogers & blindfolded & conducted to the fort. Soon after the French Officer (a Major) was carried into the Room of Cap[t] Ross, where a Council was held, the Cap[t] of the Grammont came out of Cap[t] Ross's Room, to the platform of the Curtain opposite the french & wringing his hands Said "My Lads you are all sold: I have ruined my Character for ever by coming into this damned place"; & cryed very heartily. The French Officer returned blindfolded & came again in the same manner and returnd the second time with his Eyes open; upon which Some of the Men cried out it was all over. Soon after A Serjeant came out with orders for the Men to ground their arms & the French presently after Marcht in. When the French officer went out the Second time The Cap[t]. of the Grammont Sent A Man out & gave him orders publickly, that when he hoisted a flag which lay before him they should Spike the Guns & scuttle the Ship & soon after he hoisted the flag, & the Ship soon after that drove on Shore.___[3]

When the french first advanced Cap[t]. Rogers had pointed one Cannon & sent 3 or 4 Messengers after Cap[t] Ross to come & give orders. At lenght he came & Cap[t] Rogers asked him if he should fire; twice or thrice he made no answer, at lenght he said "you may if you please". The Men of the train were never Stationed nor received any other orders than as before. The Batteries were en barbet,[4] but were sufficiently covered with Sand bags the day before the French approached, The inner row of pickets were not good, the outer row was Very good: but if there had been no pickets, the ramparts could not have been taken without cannon by that force. Some of the People of the Country came in from Portugal Cove the day before the french arrived to offer their Service but were answered by Capt Ross & Justice Gill[5] that when they wanted thier Service they would send for them. this they declared publickly on the platform & went away disgusted.

Ms, RC   WO 34/26, ff 202-203.

In handwriting of clerk no. 2. Endorsed: Acco^t. of the Surrender of S^t. John's on Newfoundland. Enclosed in Govr. Bernard's of the <u>29</u>^th. August 1762.__

The cover letter is **No. 150**. This document provides a soldier's view of the British surrender of St. John's, as FB explains in the cover, and reveals Capt. Ross's failure to stage a show of resistance. There is no record of Ross having been court-martialed, in General Courts Martial, Apr. 1762–May 1764, WO 71/25, PRO.

---

1. Walter Ross, a captain in the 40th Regiment of Foot since 19 Mar. 1758, and possibly George Rogers, a lieutenant in the 46th Regiment since 22 Jul. 1758.

2. Capt. Patrick Mouat (1712-90) put the *Gramont* into St. John's on 26 Jun., the day before its capture, intending "to stay in the Place for its Defence." Most of the convoy that Mouat had escorted from Ireland managed to escape capture by the French. Lord Colvill to John Clevland, HMS *Northumberland*, at Mauger's Beach, near Halifax, 24 Jul., 1762, ADM 1/482, f 210. Mouat subsequently captained the *Tamar* on Commodore John Byron's circumnavigation of the globe, 1764-66.

3. The *Gramont* was a prize ship taken in 1757, and was brought back to France by Capt. de Ternay.

4. A raised platform enabling artillery to fire over a parapet. *OED*.

5. Michael Gill, justice of the peace for the district of St. John's, Nfld.

152 | From Jeffery Amherst

New York, <u>30</u>^th: August 1762.

Sir,

By a Letter I received last Night from L^t. Governor Belcher,[1] he Acquaints me of his having, in Consequence of the Opinion of His Majesty's Council of Nova Scotia, and the Address of the House of Assembly, thought it Expedient for the Safety of that Province, to Transport a Number of Accadians, who, from their late Behavior to the New Settlers, had become not only Troublesome, but very Dangerous: And M^r. Hancock Acquaints me, that Five Transports, with these People, were Arrived at Boston.

I make no doubt but L^t. Governor Belcher has Wrote to You concerning them;[2] but as he Writes me, "that he had given Orders to the Transports to proceed to Boston, & there Remain, with the People on Board, untill they Receive my Directions for the Disposal of them; and that they were to Lye, untill that time, under the Command of the Castle," I am, to Acquaint you, that, as Circumstances now are, my Opinion is, that those People should be Disposed of in the Province of the Massachusetts Bay, for the present; and must Desire you will Do it in such a manner as you shall Judge best, by Separating them as much as possible, that they may have no opportunitys of Doing mischief, or Returning to their Old Habitations; and I am persuaded the Country must Reap an advantage from their Labour: The Removing of them from Nova Scotia Appears to be Necessary at this time, as the greatest part of the Troops are Ordered from thence; but I must Confess had that not been the Case, I should have rather Advised the keeping them where they were; for Notwithstanding the Natural Aversion all New Settlers have to any Neighbors who have been Suspected of Disaffection, yet such a Number of Hands in a New Country could not fail of being of great Service for its Cultivation & Improvement.__

I Think it necessary to Acquaint you, that I have received Intelligence of the Enemy's having Sent a Double Deck'd Schooner from Newfoundland, to some part of the Continent, for a Cargo of Flour: The Master's Name is not known, but he is an Irish man, and there is likewise One *Casey* of the same Country on Board, who has a Bill of Sale of the Vessel, and is Employed by the French to get the Flour, &ca. I Need not, I am Certain, Desire you to give the Necessary Directions for Stopping the said Vessel & Crew, if She comes into any of the Ports in your Government.__

I am, with great Regard, Sir, Your most Obedient Humble Servant

Jeff: Amherst

His Excellency Governor Bernard.

LS, RC   BP, 10: 11-14.

Endorsed by FB: Genl Amherst. dat Aug. 30. 1762. Variant text in WO 34/27, p. 275 (L, LbC). The reply to this letter is **No. 155.**

Those Acadians who had not been evicted from Nova Scotia were considered a potential military threat by Belcher's administration, though not by Amherst, particularly after the French raid on St. John's. In Aug. 1762, Belcher deported the Acadian "prisoners" to Massachusetts on the erroneous assumption that Amherst, who acquiesced in their removal, would make provision for their detention or subsequent resettlement. Thomas Hancock brought six hundred Acadians into Boston harbor, fully expecting that the refugees would become the responsibility of the provincial government. Thomas B. Akins, ed., *Selections From the Public Documents of the Province of Nova Scotia* (Halifax, N.S., 1869), 323-338.

1. Belcher to Amherst, 12 Aug. 1762, in *Selections From the Public Documents of Nova Scotia*, 331.

2. Belcher to FB, Halifax, 13 Aug. 1762, Prov. Sec. Letterbooks, 1: 364-365.

153 | To [Lord Barrington]

Castle William Aug.st. 30.th. 1762

My Lord

As I have given your Lordship a false Acc.t. of the french force at Newfoundland, as it was reported at the begining of the Alarm,[1] I must endeavour to make you amends by a more true Account now. The french fleet Consists of the Robuste 74 guns Eveille 64 guns Licorne 36[2] & a transport with 26 or 30 guns (no matter which) called the Garrone. The ships are extreamly ill maned with Sailors, but the land forces are very good consisting of 900 Granadiers & 300 Marines. They have fortifyed St Johns & propose to keep it this winter depending, no doubt, upon the seasons not permitting a relief from England or the West Indies. But they will find themselves mistaken. Upon the Antelope arriving at Placentia & joining the Sirene there, & the Gosport arriving at New York & being ordered to Halifax I sent our Province Ship the King George (a complete 20 gun Frigate) to Halifax. And my Lord Colville immediately After, on the 10th of August, sailed from Halifax with the Northumberland Gosport & King George to join the Antelope & Sirene & proceed to St John's to block up the french fleet there. In the mean time Genl. Amherst has fitted out a land Armament under the Command of Col Amherst of Sufficient force to Attack St. Johns by land: and I expect every day to hear that they are sailed from Halifax to Join Lord Colville so that we hope to have a good Account of the French fleet & Army before Winter sets in. It happened that Lord Colville left Halifax before he received Advice of the land Armament being forming: but such measures have been taken, that this is not like to create any disappointment or delay in the execution of the scheme. I mean not to make myself Answerable for Consequences, but think that this expedition has a very promising Appearance: & therefore take the oppertunity of a Snow sailing for Bristol to inform your Lordship of it.

I am with great respect My Lord Your Lordships most &c &c

By the Snow Bristol packet saild Sep. 4[3]

PS. Sep 14th

I take this oppertunity of a Brigs sailing from this port for Bristol to transmit to your Lordship this duplicate & at the same time to inform you that Col. Amherst with the landforces saild from Halifax on the 26th for Newfoundland: as it is now 5 Weeks since Lord Colville sailed for S[t]. Johns & I have heard nothing from the Captain of our ship I Conclude that they arrived at S[t]. Johns time enough to block up the french there: & if the Sufficiency of their strength was doubtfull before I hope it will be put out of all doubt by the junction of the Enterprize lately arrived from the Havana & with the Addition of some troops just returned to New York.

I beg leave most sincerely & heartily to Congratulate your Lordship upon the Reduction of the Havanna a Conquest more great & Important than living memory or British History can Afford.[4]

Duplicate & P. S By the Brig Rainbow potberry for Bristol sailed[5]

L, LbC   BP, 2: 207-208.

In the handwriting of clerk no. 1, except as noted. A postscript dated 14 Sept. was added to the duplicate of the RC, according to **No. 163**.

---

1. FB to Barrington, Castle William, 17 Jul. 1762, BP, 2: 203-204.

2. Over-written "26."

3. This line in FB's hand.

4. The British besieged Havana, Cuba, from 8 Jun. until 13 Aug. 1762.

5. This line in FB's hand. Thomas Potberry was the master of the *Rainbow*.

154 | From Jonathan Belcher

Halifax Nova Scotia 4th September 1762.

Sir,

I have paid all possible Attention to Your Excellency's Letter 13th July last[1] respecting the Boundaries, between Your Government and this Province, and from the best Information I can collect, I am to remark, that the King's Commission and Instructions for the Government of this Province, extends it indiscriminately to all the Country known either by the Name of Nova Scotia or Acadie, & seems to comprehend all those Countryes, which were ceded to the British Crown in the Treaty of Utrecht by the French King.

The Commissaries appointed to settle the line and determine the Bounds of that Cession have proved that from former Treaties, Demands & Rescripts, Acadie extended towards the Province of Main, in the smallest Limits as far Westward as Pentagoet[2] or the River of Penobscot.__ They were very particular in distinguishing the Boundaries of the Country known by the Name of Acadia that being the point of their Commission, as this Country under that Name was formerly held by the French and was so ceded to the British Crown but their Attention was not equally necessary, to ascertain the English Claim of Nova Scotia, since that Name depended on Several Grants of the British Crown, which could not so absolutely affect the Matter in Dispute.__

That Nova Scotia by the several Grants from the Crown of England, was the same Country as Acadie, if not of greater extent, will appear, from the Grant made to Sir William Alexander 1621 which as Your Excellency observes, extended no further than the River S^t. Croix Westward, but Sir William after he was created Earl of Sterling, obtained another Grant, which comprehended all those Lands lying to the Westward of S^t. Croix, as far as Kenebec River, which Country was also called by him Nova Scotia, and this was obtained in 1635 three Years after King Charles the first had Ceded the other Grant to France, So that of the Name of Nova Scotia became of equal Extent with the Country of Acadie, according to the most enlarged Bounds, ever claimed by the French.

The Grant of the Government of Nova Scotia or Acadie as mentioned in Your Charter, was rather a Claim or Memorial of a Right, which the Crown formerly had or might have, to that Country, for upon Searching the Records of Your Province, You will find, that the French at that Time, were in [full?] Possession of the whole Country as far West as Penobscot River and the appointment of the Jurisdiction by the Crown over a Country then in the immediate possession of the Enemy, must be invalid, and could have no Effect, and therefore King William notwithstanding such delegation did upon the Subsequent Peace, cede & give up to the French the Country called Acadie or Nova Scotia, and it remained in the Hands of the French till the Year 1710, when it was reconquered by the English and by the Treaty of Utrecht in 1713,[3] it was fully confirmed to Great Britain, and soon after it was erected into a District and Seperate Government, from that of the Massachusetts.__

The Crown has ever since esteemed this Country and all the Territories thereto belonging, the Right of the Crown excluded from your Charter, & in consequence of which the several Governors of this Province, have been impowered indiscriminately to grant any Lands upon certain Conditions, within the Province of Nova Scotia or Acadie, and in 1730 an Express Order and Royal Instruction was sent to Governor Phillips,[4] to take Possession of the Lands between the Rivers St Croix and Kenebec and a Detachment of Soldiers was sent accordingly, & a Garrison kept at Pemaquid and tho this restriction was afterwards revoked and the Inhabitants suffered to remain under the Protection of the Massachusetts Bay, no Determination was made by the Crown, as to the Right of Government.

Upon the whole therefore it should seem, that the Government and Property, of Right belong to the Crown, and that Application ought to be made there, for the ascertaining such Boundaries, as His Majesty may think will best answer his most gracious intentions of settling these Countries, the better to secure them to his Crown and Dominions.__

This Representation is by no means intended, to controvert the Title, to any Lands or Claim of Right as belonging to the Massachusetts Bay by Charter, much less to hinder the Settlement of these Desert Lands for which good purpose I shall at all times most chearfully exert my utmost endeavours, but from the station I am honoured with, from the Duty and obligation I owe the Crown, it is incumbent on me to endeavour to set this Matter in a Clear point of light in behalf of the Crown, and I hope no groundless Suspicions nor unnecessary Trouble will arise or the least occasion of any; for whatever Measures His Majesty shall be pleased to injoin or direct, this Government will undoubtedly carry into immediate execution.—

I shall avoid making any Grants of the Island of Grand Menan, or any other Lands you mention, till this Matter is determined by the Crown, agreeable to your request, altho' that Island will be included even in S^r: Willam Alexander's first Grant, which comprehends all Islands lying within Six Leagues of its Western boundaries, much less, Sir, shall I have any Objection to Your Excellency's taking and presenting any Depositions or Testimonies, you may think essentially necessary for Supporting your Claim, or for better ascertaining such Lands and Rivers, as you may think will fall within the Limits or Claims made by Your Government.

I have the Honor to be with very great respect,
Sir Your Excellency's Most Obedient and Most Humble Servant

Jonath$^.$ Belcher

His Excellency Governor Bernard.__

ALS, RC   Mass. Archs., 5: 474-478.

Conjectured material replaces faint script. Endorsed: Govr. Belcher of Nova Scotia [his?] Letter__ 4 Sept 1762__.

---

1. Not found.

2. Fort Pentagoet, established by France in 1613 and recaptured from the English in 1635, was the capital of the French colony of Acadia.

3. The Treaty of Utrecht (1713) ended Queen Anne's War in North America and the War of the Spanish Succession in Europe, 1702-13.

4. Richard Philips (161-175), governor of Nova Scotia, 1719-49.

155 | To Jeffery Amherst

Castle William Sep 5. 1762

S^r.

Yesterday morning I received yours of Aug. 30th.[1] I am fully convinced of the necessity of sending the French out of Nova Scotia, &, as there was ^no^ time to make a formal disposition of them, am satisfied with their being sent to this province. I am willing to charge myself with any trouble which this Measure shall occasion: but as to the expence, I conclude that it is not intended to make this province chargeable with it any otherwise than as Creditors. I form this conclusion not only from Governor Belcher's assurance that all expences should be reimbursed, but from the reasonableness of the thing. In this confidence I shall lay this Matter before the Council to morrow: but as the Assembly meets on Wednesday, I know they will refer it to the general Court. I shall be for removing them from the Sea, & placing them in the Counties of Worcester Hampshire & Berkshire, from whence if they do escape, it must be towards New York province or Crown point &c.

I wrote to you that I should want 3 or 4 old France Sailors to man the French parlementaire for France.[2] There are about that number of such among the french: there are also 8 or 10 old france Prisoners of War, who have petitioned me to send them home in the french Ship. I should have no doubt of making this return, if they were at my disposal: but, as it is, I could wish to have your Authority for it; & expect that the french Vessel may not be ready to sail 'till I can have an Answer to this. The Master of the Vessel will not part with her, but insists upon the priviledge of his Flag to carry him to France: and the 3 or 4 Sailors will be necessary for that Voyage.

I shall be Very busy all tomorrow morning, & therefore must conclude this, leaving what shall occur to morrow, if any thing, to a postscript. I am, with great regard, S^r

Your most obedient & most humble Servant.

Fra. Bernard

His Excellency Sr Jeffry Amherst.

We have got near 20 recruits now here: there have been near 50 listed at Halifax besides the 18 I sent there.

P.S.

Since I wrote the foregoing, the affair has been fully talked of in Council, the result of which I transmit to you in the Copy of a short Minute thereof. Upon looking over Lt Govr Belcher's letter I find he is silent about the expence of maintaining them, it being in two other letters from Halifax, which were read in Our Council at the same time with Lt Govr Belcher's, in which it is said that they were supported by the Crown & would be of no expence to this Government.[3] Without being assured of this I shall not know what to do with them: as it will be in Vain to expect that the Assembly will undertake the supporting them throughout this Winter at the Province Expence: in the former transportations of Acadians, It is said the whole burthen lay upon this province & Connecticut. As the Assembly will be for rising before the post can return & probably will do nothing in this till I can receive your orders, I am obliged to send this by express. I have allowed some sick Women & children to go on shore on Shirley point;[4] where the whole might be accommodated, if the expence was settled: & there might be a guard of the 40th regiment (if they had cloaths) set over them. They brought 2 months provisions with them.

ALS, RC   WO 34/26, ff 206-207.

Contains minor emendations. Endorsed: Governor Bernard. Boston, 5th Septem^r. 1762, Rec^d. & Ans^d: 10th Ditto.__. Variant text in BP, 2: 269-270 (L, LbC). Enclosed a copy of a minute of the Massachusetts Council of 6 Sept. 1762, for which see CO 5/823: 171.

On 17 Sept., the House and the Council unanimously refused FB's request to make an appropriation to facilitate the refugees' temporary settlement in the province, claiming that such a matter was the responsibility of the Crown. The Acadians were duly returned to Halifax, prompting Belcher to accuse Hancock and Amherst of incompetence. *JHRM*, 39: 107-110. Amherst refused to contribute Crown funds to resettle the Acadians, and in his reply to FB dismissed concerns that the expense of resettling the Acadians would fall on the province "Since they may be obliged to work for their Livelyhood." And once dispersed throughout the province they were unlikely to "contrive Mischeif." Amherst to FB, 10 Sept. 1762, WO 34/27, p. 277. FB acquiesced in Amherst's refusal, intimating to the assembly that he "did not expect any other Answer than what I have." FB to Amherst, Boston, 17 Sept. 1762, WO 34/26, f 217.

---

1. **No. 152**.

2. **No. 150**.

3. Belcher to FB, Halifax, 13 Aug. 1762, Prov. Sec. Letterbooks, 1: 364-365. Other letters not found.

4. Council Executive Records, 1760-1766, CO 5/823, f 171.

156 | To Jeffery Amherst

Boston Sep. 11. 1762

S^r.

I think I have discovered the occasion of the alarm at Canso; it appearing to be wholly owing to the indiscretion of the Commander of an armed Frigate sent into those Seas from Quebec. This Person drove before him many of the fishing Vessels, firing shot after them & thereby fully persuading them that he was a frenchman; & in the sight of other Vessels took two, put Men on board & sent them away.[1] The owner of one of these Vessels has been with me to desire my interposition to recover his Vessel sent to Quebec: and I have transmitted his Memorial to Genl Murray, desiring he would order satisfaction to be made to the Man.[2]

His case is Very hard: The only pretence for seizing his Vessel (besides resentment at his not bringing to) was that the Vessel had not a Register. The Poor Man in vain pleaded that Fishing Vessels, that did not trade, were not required by Law to take Registers & did not usually carry any. The Captains Anger at the Master's taking him for an Enemy & endeavouring to escape never subsided 'till he had sent the Fishing Vessel away. Thus an industrious Man has lost the best part of a years income of a fishing Vessel by the misunderstanding of an angry Officer.

I inclose a Copy of a memorial of this transaction divested of several circumstances of oppression with which the Story was related. I hope Genl Murray will have no difficulty in procuring justice for this man: if any should occurr, I should be obliged to you for your interposition. If the Captain had been right in his law, he might as well have sent in 50 Vessels as two.

Our Sloop is returned from Canso: She heard of a french Pirate being in those Seas & went to the Island of St Johns to look after her, but could see nothing. However She was of some service by encouraging some Vessels that were there to stay & compleat their lading.

I am, with great regard, Sr Your most obedient & most humble Servant

Fra. Bernard

His Excellency Sr Jeffry Amherst

ALS, RC   WO 34/26, ff 210-211.

Contains a minor emendation. Endorsed: Governor Bernard. Boston, 11th. Septem^r: 1762. Rec^d.__ 18th. Ditto.__ Ans^d__ 19th. Ditto__. Variant text in BP, 2: 270-271 (L, LbC). Enclosed a copy of the declaration of Richard Durfey, c.Sept. 1762, WO 34/26, f 212, and a minute of the Massachusetts Council of 6 Sept. 1762, for which see CO 5/823: 171. Amherst's reply has not been found.

---

1. Including the *Swift*, Samuel Doty, master.
2. FB to James Murray, Boston, 8 Sept. 1762, BP, 2: 270.

157 | To Jeffery Amherst

Boston Sep. 13. 1762.

Sᵣ.

I am favoured with yours of Sep. 5 & Septʳ 6.[1] In regards to the latter I beg leave most sincerely to congratulate you upon the great & important conquest of the Havanna, which reflects the greatest honour on the British Nation & must most effectually secure her intrests.

In regard to the Soldiers from Sᵗ Johns I make no doubt of their being prisoners during the War, altho' they know nothing of it themselves. If it is so, as this is the Act of the Officers, without their in any ways acceding to it before or after the surrender, nothing can be imputed to them, altho' they must abide with what has been done for them.

I have given orders for the Cartel Vessel to be ready; & am told She may be fit to sail in a Weeks time. The French Captain disputes going to England: but I shall cut the Matter short. I dont imagine it is common to send Prize Vessels as Cartels: but as in this case there was no other to be had, I doubt not but She is protected by her Flag.

The Men in general are very glad that they are going to England; but there is a Man in the train, that listed in America & has a family here that takes it much at heart. He sayes that he has allways depended upon not being sent from America. I think I remember such a promise in the Advertisement for recruiting the Train. The Man is Very willing to serve on, if he may be allowed to do it: if his hands are tied as a soldier, he desires to remain here subject to orders when he shall be at liberty.

As I have not time to write to Col Williamson my self I have given the Mans Memorial to Cap Elliot to transmit to the Colonel

I am, with great regard, SʳYour most obedient & most humble Servant

Fra. Bernard

His Excellency Sʳ Jeffry Amherst.

ALS, RC   WO 34/26, ff 213-214.

Endorsed: Governor Bernard. Boston, 13ᵗʰ. Septemʳ 1762. Recᵈ.__ 18ᵗʰ. Ditto.__ Ansᵈ.__ 19ᵗʰ.__ Ditto.—. Variant text in BP, 2: 273-274 (L, LbC). Amherst's reply has not been found.

---

1. Amherst to FB, New York, 5 Sept. 1762, WO 34/27, p. 276; 6 Sept. not found.

158 | To Jeffery Amherst

Boston Sep. 16. 1762

Sʳ.

Yesterday The Assembly past a Vote to enlist the Number of Men you have desired to serve thro' the Winter, allowing them a bounty of four pounds which is sufficient.[1] I shall immediately sent orders both to Crown Point & Halifax for reenlisting these Men, which I hope will meet with no difficulty.

As to the sending home the Cartel Ship with the Soldiers, It is well known to you how ready I allways am to undertake any trouble for the furtherance of the Kings Service, without considering whether it belongs to me or not. But when such business is attended with difficulties unsurmountable by me alone & I am refused assistance by those to whom only I know to apply; I must decline giving myself trouble that is not like to produce any effect.

The Difficulties which attend this business are these. The French Captain having landed his prisoners here refuses to take any of them on board again & absolutely refuses to go to England unless in custody & under command.__ If He was willing to go, his Vessel is not fit for such a Voyage, neither has he sailors on board capable of undertaking it.__ His Ignorance & Obstinacy is such that He will not put his Ship in order for such Voyage, altho' two Masters of Ships who have surveyed her, have reported that it would take up four riggers the best part of a Week to fit her for Sea.__ If the French Captain would take the command of her to England he must have an addition of more & abler Seamen; and as you object to french Sailors being put on board they must be English.__ If the French Captain persists in refusing to take the command of her to England, there must be an English master provided & an entire English Crew.__ Either of these methods will require expence: but Mʳ Hancock refuses to disburse any thing upon this account; I have no one else to apply to, & I dont think it proper, after he has declined it, to advance money myself.

Finding it impracticable for me to dispatch this Vessel to England, I proposed to M[r] Hancock to send the Vessel to NYork with the Soldiers on board, to be immediately under your command: but this also he declines. I must therefore beg to be excused proceding any further in this business. I propose to give the french Captain a receipt for such prisoners as have landed here except the Soldiers, in regard to whom I shall refer him to you & your orders: and I shall desire Capt Elliot to take charge of the Vessel 'till your Orders arrive;[2] in the execution of which I shall interpose my Authority if it shall be wanted.

As to the Acadians I am quite at a loss what to propose. I have therefore laid before the Assembly a full state of the Case, & having urged such reasons as have occurred to me for their providing a temporary settlement for them, I have left to them to devise the means & manner.[3]

I am, with great regard, S[r] Your most obedient & humble Servant

Fra Bernard

His Excellency S[r] Jeffry Amherst.

ALS, RC   WO 34/26, ff 215-216.

Endorsed: Governor Bernard, Boston, 16th. Sep[r]: 1762, Rec[d] & Ans[d]: 21st. Ditto.___. Variant text in BP, 2: 274-276 (L, LbC). Amherst's reply is **No. 159**.

1. *Acts and Resolves*, 17: 270. Amherst had requested "At Halifax, Three Captains, Seven Subalterns, Eighteen Non Commissioned Officers, & Two Hundred & Forty Privates; And to the Westward, Three Hundred & Twenty Three Men, Including Three Captains, & Six Subalterns." Amherst to FB, 4 Aug. 1762 New York, Mass. Archs., 4: 190-191.
2. FB to [John?] Elliot, Castle William, 26 Sept. 1762, BP, 2: 281.
3. See **No. 155**.

159 | *From Jeffery Amherst*

New York, 21st. Septem[r]: 1762.

Sir,

Wier is just now Arrived with both your Letters of the 16th. & 17th. Instant;[1] and I am very glad to Find the Assembly have past a Vote for Continuing the Number of men required for the Winter Service, and much Obliged to You for your promise of Sending Immediate Orders for ReEnlisting the men.

I am Sorry you should have had so much Trouble about the Cartel Vessell, but as I know Nothing Either of the Terms of Capitulation, or of the Orders the French master may have Received, all that could be done by me, was to Order a Sufficiency of provisions to be Laid in for our own People, which Indeed the French ought to have Supplied them with, that they might pursue their first Course: If the French master Refuses to proceed to England I Acquaint M^r. Hancock that on the Men's coming round to this place, I shall take Care of them, & Send them to England, in One of the Transports, when they Return, but the Shortest & least Expensive way, I still think, is that they should go directly from Boston to England, as was first Intended.__

The Assembly's message to You, in regard to the Acadians gives me great Concern, as this is a particular Exigency, when I would hope they would not Start Objections which can only Serve to Encrease the Expence without Answering any End; for as these Acadians are sent from Nova Scotia, & that it would certainly be Imprudent to Order them back thither at this time, & that the Sending them to any other Province would be Attended with the Same, & perhaps more Difficulties than can Arise by Dispersing them in the manner already proposed in the Back parts of the Massachusetts, I must Request you will Use your utmost Influence with the Assembly that they may Reconsider the matter, & Empower You to give Directions for Landing the People, & for Disposing of them, untill His Majesty's Pleasure is known concerning them, for which purpose I have already Acquainted you, I shall Transmit an Account thereof to the King's Ministers & Doubt not but the Province will be hereafter Reimbursed for any Extraordinary Expence it may be put to, on Account of these Acadians.__

I am, with great Regard, Sir, Your most Obedient Humble Servant.

Jeff: Amherst.

His Excellency Governor Bernard.

LS, RC   BP, 10: 19-20.

Variant text in WO 34/27, p. 280 (L, LbC).

---

1. **No. 158**; FB to Amherst, Boston, 17 Sept. 1762, WO 34/26, f 217.

160 | To Jeffery Amherst

Castle William Sep. 26 1762

S[r].

I this morning received yours of the 19th inst & soon after that of the 21st.[1]

I am much obliged to you for your order for Louisburg coal which I shall transmit to the commanding officer there & hope it will not come too late. I shall make use of the liberty you give of permitting the Man of the Artillery company to remain here: it will be a great help to him & his family; and he will remain answerable to Col Williamson.[2]

I have given orders for reenlisting the Men for the Winter service; which I persuade myself will succeed fully at the places of their stations. As I shall not be able to attend to the french Cartel ship, I have recommended to M[r] Hancock to send her with the Soldiers to NYork, from whence He may take his departure as shall be there determined. I have given him a certificate for all the Men except the soldiers, for which I have referred him to you.

I am sorry I could not prevail upon the Assembly to let the Acadians land here. As it is, I cannot act contrary to their resolution, especially as the Council afterwards joined in it. I cannot apply for a reconsideration, as I prorogued them the morning after I received this Message. The cheif Apology I have to make for them is, that this province has allready spent near £10,000 in maintaining Acadians & tho' they have often sollicited a reimbursement, they have never been able to attain it

I set out tomorrow on a short Voyage to the Eastern parts of the province in the province Sloop: from whence I hope in a fortnight to return. Your orders in the mean time will be received by the Secretary & taken proper care of.[3]

I am, with great regard, S[r] Your most obedient & most humble Servant

Fra Bernard

His Excellency S[r] Jeffry Amherst.

ALS, RC   WO 34/26, f 221.

Variant text in BP, 2: 279-280 (L, LbC).

After refusing Capt. Brookes's request to dock the transports, FB referred him to Thomas Hancock and Lt. Gov. Belcher for further orders. Brookes duly returned the refugees to Halifax. FB to Brookes, Castle William, 26 Sept. 1762, BP, 2: 279; *Selections From the Public Documents of Nova Scotia*, 323-338; see also the source note to **No. 155**. Six French soldiers, who were among the Acadian refugees, petitioned FB to be allowed to join the *Le Dorothée* when she put in to Boston; permission was granted shortly before the ship left for New York. FB to Brookes, Castle William, 27 Sept. 1762, BP, 2: 282.

1. Letter of 19 Sept. not found; **No. 159**.

2. See **No. 157**.

3. On his return, FB learned of the recapture of St. John's and sent his congratulations to Amherst forthwith. FB to Amherst, Castle William, 25 Oct. 1762, WO 34/26, f 225.

161 | Journal of a Voyage to the Island of Mount Desert

1762

Sep 28   I went on board the Sloop Massachusets lying off Castle William in Boston Bay at 5 p.m. weighed Anchor at 10[1] Wind SE passed Deer Island on the left.

29   Morning hazy, passed Cape Ann by reckoning at 5 am, stood for Portsmouth, lookt for the Isles of shoals: a thick fog arose; bore out to Sea, keeping a good offing to avoid a rock called Boon Island Ledge; saw it at 2 miles distance at 2 p.m. weather cleared up; a fresh gale arose from S by E; bore for cape Porpoise at N by W with all the sail we could set; passed into the harbour in a narrow channel between frightful rocks, and came to anchor at 4 o' clock. found sevral fishermen there who had put in for shelter; who supplied us with excellent fish for our dinner.

Night Windy & rainy; lay Very quiet, tho' there was a great storm at Sea.

30   Morning hazy; cleared up. at 9 a.m. went out with a small breeze at NW, which failing in the narrow passage We were in danger of being flung upon the rocks: but the breeze freshning carried us out. Very little Wind & great rowl of Sea: put out lines & caught some cod and haddock. at noon a fresh breeze arose from W. Course E N E. passed Wood Island, Cape Elisabeth, Segwin Island. Wind fair but a great swell of Sea: at 6 alter'd our course to E by N, stood for Menhiggon Island Breeze freshend about Midnight

Oct 1   At day break enterd Penobscot Bay, passed the Muscle ridges & the Owls head on the left & the Fox Islands on the right. Between the Fox Islands saw Mount desert hills at near 30 miles distance. passed by long Island on the left; at the end thereof saw Fort Pownall at 6 miles distance. a fresh Gale from the NW. Went above the fort & anchored at 11. The Fort saluted us with 11 guns; We returned 7 guns. Went on shore dined at the fort; spent the afternoon in reconnoitring the Country. Went on board in the Evning.

2   Weighed anchor at 7 a.m. fresh gale from NW. passed by many Islands on the right which with the continent on the left formed many pleasant sounds & bays. Came to Neskeag point, 30 miles from Fort Pownall, at 11. Found sevral Vessels there, among which was a Schooner with My Surveyors on board, who left Boston 5 days before me: took them on board & with a pilot proceeded for Mount desart: arrived there at 3 o'clock; but the Wind being against us, We were 2 hours turning into the harbour. At first We came into a spacious bay formed by land of the great Island on the left & one of the Cranberry Islands on the right. Towards the End of this Bay which is called the Great Harbour, We turned into a smaller bay called the South West Harbour. This last is about a Mile long & ¾ of a mile wide. On the North Side of it is a narrow opening to a River or sound which runs into the Island 8 miles & is Visible in a streight line with uneven shores for near the whole length. In the View of this river We anchored about the middle of the South West Harbour about 5 p.m.

3   After breakfast went on shore at the head of the bay & went into the woods by a compass line for above half a mile; found a path which led us back to the harbour: This proved to be a passage to the Saltmarshes. In the afternoon some people came on board, who informed that four families were settled upon one of the Cranberry Islands, And two families at the head of the river 8 miles from Our Station[2]

4   We formed two sets of Surveyors: I & Lieut Miller took charge of the one & M[r] Jones My Surveyor had the care of the other.

4   We begun at a point at the head of the S West Harbour, proceeded in different courses & surveyed that whole harbour except some part on the South side.

5   It rained all morning &c: We compared our observations & protracted the Surveys: in the afternoon surveyed a Cove in the North River

6   I & L[t] Miller surveyed the remainder of the S.W. harbour & a considerable part of the great harbour. M[r] Jones traced & measured the ^path to the^ Bass Bay ^creek^ & found there many haycocks In the afternoon We made some general observations & corrected our former surveys. The Gunners had good Luck; plenty of Duck Teal Partridge &c.

7   Took an observation of the Sun rising: Went up the river, a fine channel having sevral openings & Bays of different breadths, making from a mile to a quarter of a mile breadth. We passed thro' sevral hills covered with woods of different sorts; in some places the rocks were allmost perpendicular to a great highth. The general Course of this river is N 5° E; & it is not less than 8 miles long ^in a streight line^. At the end of it We turned into a bay & there saw a settlement in a ^lesser^ bay. We went on shore & into Solmes's log-house; found it neat & convenient, tho' not quite finished; ~~found~~ & in it a notable Woman with 4 pretty girls clean & orderly.[3] Near it were many fish flakes with a great quantity of fish drying there. From thence We went to a Bever pond, where We had an opportunity to observe the artificialness of their dams & their manner of Cutting down trees to make them. We returned to our Sloop about 4 o'clock: it must be 8 miles distance. The Gunners brought in plenty of Ducks & partridge.

8   We observed Sun rising; but could not take his amplitude by reason of clouds near the horison. Mr Miller surveyed the Island on the East side of the river. Mr Jones ran the base line of the intended Township. I went thro' the Woods a mile & a half to the Creek of Bass Bay. We went above a mile on the Salt meadow, found it fine, the hay remaining there good, & the Creek a pretty rivulet capable of receiving considerable Vessels, the meadow on each side being a furlong or two wide & the upland having a gentle declivity to it. We returned to dinner after two. In the afternoon Mr Jones finished his line, & We gathered curious plants in the Woods. In the Evning I receivd sevral persons on board proposing to be settlers; & it was resolved to sail the next morning if the wind would permit.

9   At half after 8 we weighed Anchor; stood for the Sea in a course S S W, thro sevral Islands; thence by a course W by S to Holt Island 10 leagues from Mount desart Harbour. At half past one Wind fell to a faint breeze; passed Martinicus Island at 5, Metennick Island at 9 ^& Mohiggan Island at 12^. Night fine & calm.

10   Sloop rolled very much 'till 5, when passing Segwin Island a fresh breeze came from NE. arrived at Falmouth Channel half after 8, just 24 hours ^from Mount desart^. It rained hard; we came to an Anchor at Falmouth half after 10. I went on shore, dined at Col Waldo's[4] & lay there.

11   We went about the Town; a Very growing place: some fine houses then building, many Vessels, among which Were some Ships, upon the Stocks: Were saluted by the Fort with 5 guns & by a Ship in the harbour with 7:

Our sloop returned 5 guns. We dined at Col Waldo's, supt at Cap Rosses[5] & went on board at half past 10.

12   We weighed anchor at half past 8: saluted the Town with 5 guns. kept within sight of the shore all the way; & anchored near the fort Island in Piscataway about 3 miles from Portsmouth at 5 o'clock. The Fort hailed us to know if I was on board: at 6 Gov[r]. Wentworths barge came along side to carry me to his house about 3 miles from the Sloop & 2 from Portsmouth.

13   I went to Portsmouth in my own boat the Boats crew being in their uniforms, of red faced with blew: was received at the wharf by sevral Gentlemen & conducted to M[r] Wentworths house. At 3 M[rs] Bernard arrived in the Charriot.

14   We passed an agreable day at Portsmouth

15   & on the 15th set out in the Charriot for Boston.

AMs, AC   BP, 10: 21-28.

Docket by FB: Journal of Voyage to Mount desart Oct 1762. FB probably wrote the journal serially, and as far as be can be ascertained he did not maintain any other journal or diary during his life.

The voyage was undertaken not only for the purpose of surveying the island, but to exert some control over the few settlers there. "I find myself obliged to enter into Conditional contracts with proposed Settlers, to put a stop to the depredation of others, & to engage in several Articles of Expence in the same manner as if my title was absolute. In short I am obliged to enter into possession of the Island as the positive owner thereof, or also must see it overrun by Numberless people without any title at all but possession." FB to Bollan, Castle William, 11 Aug. 1762, BP, 2: 205-206. The meeting with the settlers on 8 Oct., which FB mentions, was arranged in order to stop their "wast of the timber," but for his plea to carry any weight he evidently felt obliged to promise them land lots in the intended township (**No. 177**).

---

1. Fathoms.

2. One of the families was that of James Richardson, who had left Gloucester, Mass., earlier in the year. George E. Street, *Mount Desert: A History* (Boston and New York, 1905), 115.

3. Abraham Soames had relocated his family from Gloucester, Mass., to the island in 1762, having first visited a year earlier. Street, *Mount Desert: A History,* 115.

4. Samuel Waldo Jr. (1723-70) of Falmouth and proprietor of his father's vast patent in Maine. He had represented Falmouth in the General Court and was a probate judge.

5. Thomas Ross (d.1804 or 1808), mariner of Falmouth and future Loyalist.

162 | To John Pownall

Castle William Octr 20th. 1762

Dear Sir

In a former I acquainted you[1] with the preparations that were making on this part of the Continent to dispossess the french of Newfoundland. Happily they have succeeded, as you will be advised long before this comes to hand. But possibly you may not be fully acquainted with the particulars of this expedition so far as to know how nicely the scale was turned. I mentioned to you that Lord Colville had only the Northumberland at Halifax: soon after the Antelope & Syren got to Placentia; & the Gosport from England to NYork repaired from thence to Halifax.[2] I kept the King George ready in order to start upon the first warning, & upon receiveing advice that the Gosport had sailed for Halifax, I ordered the King George there, & upon her arrival Lord Colville immediately sailed for Placentia & from thence to face the enemy. The Naval forces stood thus.[3]

F[rench].			E[nglish].		
Robuste	74			Northumberland	64
Eveille	64			Antelope	50
Licorne	36			Gosport	40
Garonne	26			Sirene	20
Grammont	16			King George	20
	216				194

With this force Lord Colville offered the french fleet battle whenever the wind blew out of the harbour. The land forces under Col. Amherst Afford another ballance of force

F.			E		
Granadiers	900			Regulars	900
Marines	300			Provincials Massach.	500
	1200				1400[4]

With this force Col. Amherst took about 780 prisoners besides the killed & dispersed, He Allowed the french no time to reconnoitre his force: and it is said they fully believed when they surrendered that he had 5000 men. The whole work, untill he came to bombarding, was done by 3 Companies of Light Infantry, one of which of the provincials of the Massachusetts, which behaved equally well with the rest. for my part I do not regret the escaping of the french ships[5] for if they had stayed & the strength of the English had been known, they could not have been such poltroons as to have given up the place. Next to the Conduct of the execution may be reckoned the Secrecy of the preparation, which was such, that neither the destination of the Naval or the land force which sailed at different times was in the least suspected, untill after they had sailed. In my little department the junction of the King George with Lord Collville appeared to be an accidental meeting instead of a Concerted Measure.

I have thought proper to give you this private Acc^t. of an Expedition, whose uncommon success I hope has given great pleasure in England. I must add that I rec^d. from L^d. Colville such an high testimony of Capt. Hollowel Comm of the king george, that If I knew to ask for some honorable distinction for him, I would do it. your brother knows him well, and if some mark of honor could be devised for him, it would be well bestowed.

I am S^r. Your most faithful serv^t.

John Pownal Esqr.

L, LbC   BP, 2: 209-211.

In the handwriting of clerk no. 1.

1. Not found.
2. Lord Colvill led the *Northumberland* out of Halifax on 10 Aug., and, on arriving off St. John's on 11 Sept., he blockaded the French vessels in the harbor.
3. The figures record the number of guns per vessel.
4. Col. Amherst estimated a total of 1,559 men including 520 "Massachusetts Provincials." Clarence Webster, ed., *The Journal of Jeffrey Amherst from 1758 to 1763* (Chicago, 1931), 2.
5. Capt. de Ternay was able to lead the French ships out of the harbor on the night of the 15th, evading Colvill's blockade under cover of fog, and reach France on 28 Jan.

163 | To Lord Barrington

Castle William Oct. 20th 1762

My Lord

By a Letter dated Aug[st]. 30[1] & a postscript added to the duplicate thereof I informed your Lordship of the measures which were taking for the recovery of S[t]. Johns by an immediate armament from the continent: and happily it has the success which I then flattered myself with. When the French arrived here, this Coast was Very defenceless: & yet it could not be regretted, Since it was occasioned by the Assistance which North America gave to the Expedition against the Havannah without which it could not have succeded. & therefore if the taking S[t] Johns had been more detrimental than it was; it would be but fair to ballance it with the Havannah. The French Commander, upon his arrival at Newfoundland, declared that he knew there was no Man of War upon the Coast but the Northumberland: in which, if he meant to confine himself to Halifax, he was not mistaken. He therefore thought himself safe in determining to hold the place thro' the winter concluding that no Armament could arrive from England or the West Indies time enought before the Winter was set in; and that North America was unable to fit out one: but in the latter he was disappointed. The Sirene of 20 guns arrived upon the coast of Newfoundland about the same time with the french fleet, & soon after the Antelope of ^50 guns^ arrived & escaped the Enemy. These rendevoused at Placentia. Soon after, The Gosport arrived at NYork with a Convoy & immediately after, sailed for Halifax. I had kept our Province Ship the King George (a complete 20 gun frigate & then in Very good order)[2] in readiness to join Lord Colville, & upon hearing the Gosport was Sail'd from NYork I ordered the King George to Halifax; which arriving a few days after the Gosport Lord Colville immediately sail'd to join the Antelope & Sirene & face the Enemy The Naval Force stood thus

		guns			guns
French	Robuste.	74	English.	Northumberland	64
	Eveille.	64		Antelope.	50
	Licorne	36		Gosport.	40
	Garonne	26		Sirenne.	20
	Grammont	<u>16</u>		King George.	<u>20</u>
		216			194

In the mean time a land Armament was preparing, tho' with so much secrecy that Lord Colville was not acquainted with it when he sail'd. This was under the command of Col. Amherst, & formes another ballance of Land Forces

French.	Grenadiers of France	900	English.	Regulars	900
	Marines.	<u>300</u>		Provincials	<u>500</u>
				of Massachusetts Bay.	
		1200			1400

Irish recruits uncertain

Artillery not reckoned:

chiefly on board the Ships

With this force, in which the besiegers very little exceeded in number the beseiged, has this place strong by nature, made stronger than ever by additional fortifications, & defended by, what the Enemy called, the best troops of France, been taken. The sum of the french prisoners with that of the killed added thereto is very near equal to the whole Number of the English Regulars. But We must make due allowance for the provincials; one company of which being light Infantry & joined to the same corps of regulars was no ways inferior to them in driving the french from the severall out posts which they endeavoured to maintain. Two days after the Place was taken arrived 4 Men of War from England: So that this Expedition was favoured to the last by the whole honor of it being preserved entire to the first adventurers.

As I had before informed your Lordship of this Expedition, I have thought proper to conclude the History of it.

I am &c

The Right Honble The Lord Viscount Barrington

L, LbC   BP, 2: 219-221.

In the handwriting of clerk no. 2.

---

1. **No. 153**.

2. The sloop *King George* was armed with fourteen nine-pounders and six six-pounders on the main deck, and twelve swivel cohorns (grenade-throwing mortars) on the quarterdeck, and was crewed by 150 men. FB to Amherst, Boston, 10 Jun. 1762, WO 34/26, f 167.

164 | To The Board Of Trade

Triplicate[1]

Boston October 21: 1762

My Lords

At the last Session of the general Assembly A Bill was prepared to be brought into the House to raise by Lottery a sum of money in addition to the sum of £4250[2] before granted by the general Assembly to erect a new building for the use of the College at Cambridge in this Province.[3] The Case was this. By the increase of the Students of the College there have been of late near 80 more than can be lodged &c in the College: in consequence of which some disorders have arisen which have been irremediable, whilst a considerable part of the collegians have been for the greatest part of their time not subject to the inspection of their Governors. The obvious remedy for this was the bringing them all within the Walls of the College: for which purpose upon an application from the College, the Assembly granted the sum of £4250. being the precise estimate of a building to contain lodgings for 64 Students.

Upon a further consideration of this Scheme, it was found that something more than mere lodgings were wanting; particularly an addition to the Dining Hall, which was not capable of receiving an additional number. It has therefore been thought expedient to add the library (which at present adjoins) to the Hall and build a new library in the New building. It was impossible to ask the Assembly (after the former ample beneficence) to contribute a further sum for this new Expence; and therefore the Expedient of a lottery was the only one that could be resorted to.

This being the Case, I should have made no doubt of consenting upon general principles: nor does it seem to fall within the rules which your Lordships have laid down in your exceptions to the former lottery Bills. But as in consequence thereof your Lordships laid a general injunction upon me not to pass any more lottery Bills, I prevailed on the Gentlemen concerned not to bring in this Bill, untill I had time to lay the case before your Lordships and obtain from you a relaxation of that injunction in this Case, or rather a declaration that the rule of reasoning, upon which your Lordships disapproved of the raising the money by Lotteries for making bridges, mend roads &c, matters due from the Community either of the County or Township,[4] does not extend to this Case. If there is any case wherein a Lottery may be said to be lawful and advisable, The providing for the education of Youth in the higher path of learning, for which the generality of the People are no ways obliged to contribute, is one. Upon this principle, The Academy at Philadelphia has received great part of it's support from an annual lottery. And lately when A Scheme was formed for cutting off that resource by a general Act against lotteries, it was thought more advisable to allow a general licence for lotteries of all kinds, (abused as it was sure to be) than to suffer a learned seminary to be defeated of a considerable part of its usual income. For these reasons it is much more to be hoped that your Lordships will allow me (who am under no other injunction than a signification of your Lordships Sentiments upon lottery bills of another kind) to consent to this Bill for the benefit of a Society well deserving your Lordships favor, which is neither like to be abused or to be repeated.

I beg leave to take this oppertunity to congratulate your Lordships upon the reduction of the Havanna and the Recovery of Newfoundland; in the latter of which this Province had so considerable a share as to turn the ballance of its practicability.

I am with great respect My Lords, your Lordships most obedient and most humble Servant

Fra Bernard.

The Right Honble The Lords of Trade and Plantations

tripLS, RC   CO 5/891, f 94.

In the handwriting of Andrew Oliver, except as noted. Endorsed: *Massachusets.* Letter from Francis Bernard Esqr. Govr. of Massachusets Bay, dated 21 Oct. 1762, inclosing Sketch of a Bill for raising money by a Lottery for the use of Harvard College, Cambridge, & desiring the Board's Permission to assent to such a Bill. Reced Read Decr. 20 1762. L.L.41. Variant text in BP, 2: 60-62 (L, LbC). Enclosed an abstract of an act for raising a sum of money by lottery to complete an "additional Hall" for the use of Harvard College in Cambridge, [c.*Oct. 1762*], CO 5/891, ff 95-97. The Board of Trade's response is **No. 182**.

---

1. This line in FB's hand.

2. Sterling.

3. A resolve of 12 Jun. 1762 appropriated £2,000 for that purpose. *JHRM*, 39: 68; *Acts and Resolves*, 17: 250.

4. **No. 43**.

165 | To John Pownall

Boston Octr. 21st. 1762

D^r. S^r.

M^r. Pemberton Naval Officer here is a little Alarmed at a certain Gentleman's going from hence to England professedly to get a place & fears he has a design to get the Naval Office in Salem separated from M^r. Pembertons Office: He therefore desires that I would enter a caveat against it. I am unwilling to trouble the secretarys office with a suspition of this kind, so soon after M[r]. Pembertons reappointm[t]. & my receiving favorable Assurances concerning the Same office. Nevertheless as it is possible that some misrepresentations may be made & misapprehensions of the Office may be conceived I should be glad if you would remind M[r]. Wood[1] that the Naval Office to which M[r]. Pemberton has been lately admitted by order of sign manual comprehends all the ports in the province.

I am S[r]., Your most faithfull

John Pownall Esq[r].

L, LbC   BP, 2: 211.

In the handwriting of clerk no. 1 with minor scribal emendations.

---

1. Robert Wood, undersecretary of state.

166 | To Lord Barrington

Castle William Oct. 21. 1762

My Lord

At the desire of M[r] Pemberton, Naval Officer throughout this Province, I am to inform your Lordship that he is apprehensive that A Gentleman lately gone from hence professedly to get A Place in this Country by appointment from England, has a design upon that part of the Naval Office which lies in the Port of Salem:[1] & therefore He begs the favor of your Lordship under whose Patronage he considers his Office to be, to bespeak my Lord Egremont's attention, that such an application, if it should be made, may be duly considerd. I dont apprehend that there is any probability of such an attempt succeding, but by the means of misrepresentation or misapprehension: & therefore I Should think that it would be quite sufficient to Enter a Caveat with M[r] Wood. Indeed I Should not have troubled Your Lordship with this, but that I could not refuse M[r] Pemberton in assisting him in Such acts of Caution, which he Shall think proper to take

I am &c

The Right Hon[ble] The Lord. Viscount Barrington

L, LbC

In the handwriting of clerk no. 1.

BP, 2: 223-224.

---

1. The identity of FB's rival is unknown. FB had warned Barrington earlier of a "design" afoot to establish two naval offices in the province, and requested his "patronage" to defeat it. Castle William, 24 May 1762, BP, 2: 190-192.

167 | To Richard Jackson

Castle W^m. Octr 29. 1762

Dear S^r.

I have rec^d upon my son's Arrival 3 letters from you, one dated Augs^t. 11th another without a date & the third dated Aug. 16 in that without date you mention the Grant of Mount desart with the difficulties attending the Motion for the Confirmation of it.[1] If it is already determined that the Right of our province shall not extend beyond Penobscot, it wont become me to argue about it, on my own account. But the province I am persuaded will contest for their right to the last drop of Ink & the last word of Council. All I have to do is to keep my self out of the dispute as well as I can: for if I should be half so warm for my Island as this people are like to be for the lands which they apprehend to be granted to them by their Charter I fear I should not fail giving Offence. To avoid which it is my earnest desire to give my Affair such a turn as may bring it out of this dispute; I mean by solliciting a simple Grant from the King that may not conclude the Question, but may be left to operate either as a Confirmation of the grant of the Province, or as an original Grant, according as the Question shall be determined. Besides the withdrawing myself from this disquisition, which as it will be considered by the people here as a partial impeachment of the Charter, will probably grow very warm, I have reason to desire to avoid the delay which this dispute will occasion, which will ill suit with my time of life & much less with the oppertunities I have of improving this Island, which will be wholly lost if not speedily used. Before I enter upon the new proposal for confirming to me this Island, it may be proper to state my pretentions to this favor

I need not mention to you the extraordinary expences that have particularly attended My frequent Commissions: you could not Avoid taking notice of it your self. It may be said that the Commission for Massachusets Bay at first was my own seeking; & the second is common to all Governors that were in Commission at the demise of the late King. But is not my case singular in having 3 of these Commissions to sue out in 3 Years (at the Expence of near £400 a piece, I may say fully so to me) for 2 Governments the least not exceeding £900 p an. the greater fully reckoned at £1200 contingencies Allowed for? I thought it so extraordinary a case that I submitted it (in a private manner) to the Lords of the treasury; & received for answer that such an Allowance would make a bad precedent &c: and that I had a right to apply to the province, who ought & would undoubtedly make an Allowance for my extraordinary expences upon the entry of My Goverm^t. I then talked with some chiefs of the people who advised me rather to take my Compensation in lands than Money as the latter came harder than the former. Besides the fees of an extraordinary Commision I had expended near 200 Pound sterling in Additions & Alterations at the Province House & the Gov^{rs}. apartm^{ts}. at the Castle over & above what the province Allowed, which amounted to so considerable a sum that I could not ask for all that I wanted. So that the Pecuniary consideration of this Grant amounted to near £600 Sterling As for the consideration of extraordinary services It has arose both from the state of the Country being engaged in a War at home & abroad & from my way of doing the public business wholly by my own hands using my Secretaries in nothing but Copying. But the ordinary business of this Government requires an extraordinary compensation. There is no one so ill paid in All America the whole certain income of it being scarce £1100 pr. an; to which may be added £100 more for contingent profits such as seizures &c The people are very sensible of it & therefore the Assembly, tho' it will not increase the salary beyond the instruction, frequently takes an oppertunity of making the Govr. a compensation for particular services to make amends for the deficiency of his general income It was not upon account of the meer profits of the Government that I changed my situation: it was to put myself in a more public way to lay hold of an oppertunity to make a provision for my Children. Such Oppertunities can happen but seldom; and if I am defeated of this, I know not when & how to expect another. The little savings to be made out of my income (such as it has been & is) have hitherto been exhausted by extraordinary expences & never can amount to much; without some such favor as this, My service is like to be paid with little more than subsistance

I have said thus much to state to you my pretentions to favor in this business: the means to prosecute it independently from the Claim of the province of Massachusetts Bay & yet so as not to preclude that Claim are thus founded. Whether this Island belongs to the Province or not, the King has now a right to grant it to me. if it belongs to the province It will amount to a Confirmation of the Assembly's Grant: if it does not belong to the Province it will operate as an original Grant. I would therefore now solicit the Kings Grant without reciting the Assembly's Grant or naming the Province it lies in, in which I would desire no other words to be used than *Grant & Confirm* to be under the signet Privy seal or great seal as shall be thought most advisable. They may then settle the provinces Right at leisure: and I can wait the Event with out the inconvenience which the particular Circumstances of this Affair, will occasion now. There will be one thing wanting to give this new turn to the Affair; which is a new memorial to the Secretary of State. This I will prepare to go by the next Vessell: for this I can't get it ready. I will draw it in such a manner that it may bear any alteration that may be thought advisable to make after you receive it. Nevertheless if this Business could be put in this Channel under my former letter, without delivering in a new memorial, I should be well pleased. In this you must consult M^r. Pownall: the only way of doing this that I can see is to obtain a report from the Board of Trade, recommending me to favor expressing their doubts of this Island being within the province & therefore proposeing such a Grant as I mention. The Practicability of this I must submit to M^r. Pownall, whom I've desired to suspend the report, if as things now stand, it cannot be made in my favor.

In one of your letters you seem ~~desirous~~ very Anxious about the recovery of S^t. Johns: you have therefore been agreeably surprised with the retaking of it. It has been a most Singular expedition much to the honor of those engaged in it: This province has had a considerable share of the Credit both by sea & Land. Upon the surrender of that place I foresaw that it would not be retaken by winter unless it was by expedition from this Continent, of which there was no prospect then, all our forces having been sent to the Havanna without whose assistance that place could not have been taken. Nevertheless in hopes of Men of War droping in I kept our Man of War King George which you know is a very fine frigate & was then in Complete order, to join Lord Colville at a proper time. As soon as he had got 4 ships, I added the King George to his fleet & he sailed immediately to face the Enemy The Naval forces stood thus

E.			Fr.		
	Northumberland	64		Robuste	74
	Antelope__	50		Eveille__	64
	Gosport__	40		Licorne	36
	Sirene__	20		Garonne__	26
	King George	20		Grammont	16
		194			216

The french suffered themselves to be blocked up untill the land forces under Col. Amherst in several transports joined the fleet The Land Forces stood thus

E			Fr.		
	Regulars	900		Granadiers of France	900
	Provincials of of Mass: Bay	500		Marines	300
		1400			1200

The Col. landed, drove them from place to place, bombarded them into a surrender, took 785 prisoners beside killed &c The Ships escaped in a dark night. Two days after the surrender arrived 4 Men of War from England. This is a short estimate of this extraordinary Event.

I am D[r]. S[r]. Your most faithfull &c

R Jackson Esq[r].

L, LbC   BP, 2: 214-219.

In the handwriting of clerk no. 1 with scribal emendations.

---

1. Letters not found.

168 | *To Lord Barrington*

Castle William Oct 30th 1762

My Lord

I have the pleasure to inform your Lordship that my eldest Son arrived here safe on Tuesday last. He received your Lordships favor with a letter to M[r] Clevland[1] to procure him a passage in a Man of War: but a Ship ready to sail for NYork offering, he thought it best to save time by going on board her. On this side the Madeira he shifted himself on board a Ship bound for this port & came directly hither. I fear I am blamed by my friends in England for engaging him in such a Voyage merely for a Visit as they may call it: But I see it in a stronger light. It has seemed to me absolutely necessary at this most critical time of his life to explore his genius, so as to direct his studies & farther pursuits to proper objects. Parts He by no means wants, & he has hitherto not being deficient in acquiring such learning as has belonged to him: but judgement in choosing his Walk of life & steadiness in keeping in it he has Still to gain. To settle this & to initiate him in Mathematicks ~~he has still to gain. To settle~~ & Natural Philosophy, so as to make those studies pleasing to him, will be our business for the 9 or 10 Months in which I propose he shall stay here.__

In some of my former letters[2] I mentioned to your Lordship the grant of the Island of Mount desart made by the Assembly to me in consideration of extraordinary expences & Services. I find the confirmation of it is like to labour, from the Lords of Trade not being at present inclined to allow the lands on the East side of Penobscot Bay to belong to the province of Massachusets Bay, altho' thier Right to it has heretofore been formally admitted in pursuance of the Opinion of the Atty & Soll' general, Be that as it will, I perceive that the litigation of this Question, if it is carried to its full lenght, will be very tedious & very warm. And therefore I am Very desirous of getting my business exempted from it, which I think may be done by giving it a new Turn by making a little change in the terms of my Application for the Kings confirmation. I must not conceal from Your Lordship, that this Island is a great object to one who has such a Number of young children as have fallen to our lot; & therefore must not be lost for want of any pains of mine or any assistance I can procure from my friends, I shall endeavour to avoid giving your Lordship un-necessary trouble: when it cannot be spared I know you'l excuse it

I am &c

The Right Honble The Lord Viscount Barrington

L, LbC   BP, 2: 221-223.

In the handwriting of clerk no. 2.

---

1. John Clevland (1706-63), a long-serving naval administrator who became first secretary of the Admiralty, 1759-63.

2. FB to Barrington, 22 Feb. 1762, not found, and Castle William, 17 Jul. 1762, BP, 2: 203-204.

169 | To John Pownall

Castle William Octr 31st. 1762

Dear S^r.

I have wrote to you several letters about the Grant of Mount Desart,[1] express-ing in some the great disappointment & discouragement I shall receive from being defeated of the Compensation intended me by the province for the extraordinary expences which attended my entering upon this Government: extraordinary ser-vices it won't become me to mention any further than that my application to the Kings service has at all times engaged my utmost attention, at some times rather exceeded my strength. When this grant was made to me, it was not apprehended by any one (I am sure not by me) that the provinces right to the lands eastward of Penobscot would be disputed. It was apprehended that it might be made a ques-tion wch. was the River S^t. Croix by which they were to be bounded: & accordingly measures were taken by the General Court for ascertaining that River but it was not doubted but that they would be allowed to extend to that River which ever it should be adjudged to be. I have now the mortification to find that this Grant to me (which I must own is so peculiarly circumstanced to my young family, as to deserve my utmost endeavours to Avail my self of it) is like, apparently to give birth to a disquisition that promises to be Volumnious tedious & expensive & possibly may be attended with more than necessary trouble.[2] And by my intrest therein I shall lose the little Credit I should otherwise have of interposing my sentiments concerning this Question. You will not therefore wonder that I should earnestly desire to withdraw my self from this dispute by finding out some method whereby I might have this Island confirmed to me without determining the Question concerning the right of the province's lands to the eastward of Penobscot one way or another. If this Could be done I should be at liberty to give my thoughts upon the subject from time to time as they shall occur, without being under the imputation of being bi[nded?][3] by an intrest of my own.

I have been induced to think of this expedient from an observation of M[r]. Bollans & my own confidence, that if this Request of mine was to be determined by personal considerations, it would be readily concluded in my favor. I therefore want to have it reduced to that Crisis; and therefore would propose that the terms of my application for the Kings grace should be so far Altered as to make it a ~~grant~~ ^petition^ for an Original grant of this Island from the King without reciting the Grant of the General Assembly of Massachusetts bay or using any Addition of the province to which the Island belongs. By these means nothing will be concluded concerning the Question in dispute; but if hereafter this Island shall be Allowed to Massachusetts bay this will Amount to A Confirmation of the provincial grant; otherwise it will operate as an original, I am apprehensive that if this business is to take this turn, it will be necessary on my behalf to deliver a new memorial to the Secty of State.[4] This I will prepare & send by the next ship; for I cant get it ready to go with this, I shall send it to M[r]. Jackson who will immediately communicate it to you, & will be desired by me to make such Alterations in it as shall be most advisable. In the meantime if my affair should be brought before your board, & you don't see a clear way for reporting it in my favor, be so good as to suspend the report (if it can be done consistently with the rules of business) untill this new proposal can be considered. Nevertheless if you think it practicable, under my former Application to make report in my favor by the way of this or any other expedient that will obviate the Difficulty arising from the Right of the province to the lands between Penobscot & S[t]. Croix being thereby concluded, I should be very glad to have the most early determination in my favor, that may be.

I am S[r]. your most faithfull most obedient Servant

John Pownall Esq[r].

L, LbC   BP, 2: 211-214.

Letter in the handwriting of clerk no. 1 with minor emendations by FB.

---

1. 4 Mar. 1762, BP, 2: 33-34; 17 Jul. 1762, not found; **No. 93**.

2. See **No. 154**.

3. Letters are obscured by binding.

4. Instead, he addressed the memorial to the Board of Trade (**No. 177**) where it was considered on 2 Mar. 1763, and informed the secretary of state of what he had done. FB did not send a memorial to the secretary of state until Jan. 1767. FB, memorial to the earl of Shelburne, [*Jan. 1767*], CO 5/756, ff 33-37.

170 | *From Jeffery Amherst*

New York, 31st: October <u>1762</u>

Sir

Colonel Amherst Joyns with me in Returning our Compliments for Your very polite Letter of the 25th. Instant, which I had the favor of Receiving last Night.[1]

I had likewise a Letter from Mr. Goldthwait,[2] In Regard to the Employment of the Provincials that Remain at the Castle: I am Still of the Same Opinion that it would by no means Answer to forward them Either to Halifax, or to the Westward: If they were Deserters, their Serving as Provincials is not punishment Sufficient, And I Should be glad they were Obliged to Enlist into the Regular Service, provided they are proper Subjects, of Which Lieut Elliott may Judge.

As Your Letter of the 23d. Septem:[3] came to hand About the time of Your Setting out for Penobscott, I Deferred Acknowleging it untill your Return; I am now to Acquaint You that having Received Directions from the Lords of the Treasury[4] to Transmit to them Certificates of the Number of Troops Levied, Cloathed &c. by Each of the Provinces for the Service of the Year 1760, and to Continue to Return the Like certificate for Every Year, I am preparing those for 1760, 1761, and 1762. In which the Massachusetts Government will of Course be Included, and So Soon as they are ready I shall Transmit the whole to the Lords Commissioners of His Majesty's Treasury, Agreable to their Lordships Directions.

I am with great Regard Sir &c.

Governor Bernard, Boston.

L, LbC   WO 34/27, p. 283.

---

1. FB to Amherst, Castle William, 25 Oct. 1762, WO 34/26, f 225.

2. Not found.

3. FB to Amherst, Boston, 23 Sept. 1762, WO 34/26, f 220.

4. Not found.

171 | To Jeffery Amherst

Castle William Nov 6. 1762.

S^r.

As the recruiting for the regulars is proposed to be continued thro' the Winter by such officers as will be willing to engage in it without pay, it will be necessary to establish a place of head quarters at the barracks here, to which the recruits may be returned; and to have an officer with a small party of about 12 men to keep guard. For this purpose, If you should approve of this, I would submit to you an easy method of doing it. By the returns from Crown point I learn that the recruits reenlisted for the Winter service there fall short of the Number by 27 men. I am desirous of making this deficiency good, but should be glad to avoid sending them across the Country, now the Winter is begun. I would therefore out of the 27 men to be raised here retain a Serjeant & 12 men ^as a guard^ for the recruits; and as Lt Miller is engaged for the Winter Service at Halifax, I would with your leave retain him here as Commanding Officer of the recruiting party. Without some such appointment as this, I know not how the Recruits can be taken care of: for the Garrison of the Fort is so small, that I cannot detach a Guard for the Barracks from thence. The rest of the 27 I would send to Halifax, if you approve of it upon account of the greater Ease of transporting them. I have had no returns as yet from Halifax; so can only hope that the Winter party there is fully recruited. I shall wait your directions concerning this; & before I receive them depend upon having a return from Halifax. There are now 22 recruits lying here, for which Mr Hancock cannot at present get a passage: And I have no other guard for them but insolvent deserters ^of former years^, who will not stay here much longer without being guarded themselves; as they have ^allready^ worked out what they owed to the Province by their Service ^here^ & on board the Province Sloop.

I am, with great regard, Sr Your most obedient & most humble Servant

Fra Bernard.

His Excellency Sr Jeffry Amherst.

ALS, RC WO 34/26, f 228.

Variant text in BP, 2: 284-285 (L, LbC).

After writing this letter, FB learned that Miller had "engaged for an Ensigncy" in the 45th Regiment pending Amherst's "approbation." FB to Amherst, Boston, 23 Nov. 1762, WO 34/26, f 230. Miller arrived at New York on 14 Dec. with twenty-five recruits, two of whom Amherst deemed unsuitable (one being "Quite Crazy, and the Other a Frenchman.") Amherst granted FB's request that Miller be allowed to remain at Boston, insisting that he fully intended to sign a commission as soon as there was a position. Amherst to FB, New York, 20 Dec. 1762, WO 34/27, p. 286. The provincials at Castle William under Miller's command were discharged by FB on 1 May 1763, **No. 209**.

172 | To Jasper Mauduit

Castle William Novr 6 1762

Sir

I am favoured with your Letter of the 2^d of August.[1] I did not consider Mr Bollans Sollicitation of the confirmation of the grant of Mount Desert as a meer provincial Business, altho' it is certain that the Province is much interested in the Event of it; and for that reason I did not think it necessary immediately upon Mr Bollans quitting the Agency to engage you or any other person to transact that Affair. But as Mr Bollan thought proper to Consign the grant made to me to you to your care with the other provincial business, you have taken the most proper steps you could, in acting in Concert with Mr Jackson; As you by my Letters wrote to Mr Jackson in July last.[2] In these I desired him to take upon him the management of this business when Mr Bollan should quit it, & as it was of great consequence to the province, I recommended to him to desire your Assistance as Provincial Agent. Your Conception of the part you Should take in this Affair has theretofore exactly tallied with mine.__

It is not my intention to take upon myself alone the defence of the provinces right to that Country: There is a Committee appointed to prepare instructions for that Purpose. and therefore, if the confirmation cannot be Obtained, you should take care that the determination of the question be suspended untill the Province can intervene for themselves. In this you will advise with Mr Jackson.

I shall be glad to contribute anything in my power for making your Agency easy & comfortable to you, consistently with my Sentiments of the Exigencys of the province, which are Such, that I cannot be indifferent about the Interests of the province being properly supported, & its rights effectually defended

I am &c

Jasper Mauduit Esq

L, LbC   BP, 2: 224-225.

In the handwriting of clerk no. 2 with minor scribal emendations.

---

1. Not found.
2. Thus in manuscript. See **No. 131**.

173 | To John Stevens

Castle William. Nov: 8 1762

S[r]

By a letter I sent you by M[r] Pratt,[1] I inform'd you of the arrival of my Son at Boston, whom I had before expected by way of New York. There has been such extraordinary treatment of him by Captn Chambers[2] with whom he embarked that I cannot pass it by. The Case is this. A Gentleman in London engaged a bed in the Cabbin for my Son, & paid Capt: Chambers on his own demand £25 Sterling for it. When my Son came on board, He was put in the Steerage, under pretence there was no room in the Cabbin altho when the place was taken he engaged for the Cabbin. Whilst he lay in the Steerage, he had Shirts & other goods to the Value of 3 or 4 pounds stolen from him. This was told to Capt: Chambers: but nothing was done for recovering them. When the Fleet stopt at Madeira, some Gentlemen bound to Boston, being informed how my Son was used on board his Ship, invited him to theirs, in which he arrived at Boston. Capt: Chambers let him go on board, without offering to return any part of the money he recieved for his passage, or to make any satisfaction for his loss.

I must therefore desire you would speak with Capt: Chambers, & ask him whether this ^is or^ is not a true state of the Case, & whether he does or does not intend to make any satisfaction for this treatment of my Son. Upon his Answer will depend my further Proceeding. I am &c

J Stevens Esq[r]:

PS. I must defer writing to you on another subject to a further time.[3]

L, LbC   BP, 2: 285-286.

In handwriting of clerk no. 2 with scribal emendations.

---

1. Letter not found. Benjamin Pratt (1711-63), lawyer, former Boston representative, and chief justice of New York, 1761-63.

2. Possibly William Chambers, admitted to the Boston Marine Society on 7 Aug. 1759. One Capt. Chambers was master of the *Pembroke*, which sailed between Newcastle, Eng., and Boston. *Boston Gazette*, 18 Jul. and 12 Sept. 1763.

3. **No. 183**.

174 | To Jeffery Amherst

Boston Nov 11. 1762.

Sʳ.

I have received your favour of the 31ˢᵗ of Octʳ.[1] As for the deserters, I have done as much as I could to engage them in the regular Service: & sevral of them have been accordingly recruited. As for those who remain at the Castle most of them have such pretensions to mitigation that I must be content with such satisfaction as can be got, I mean, in regard to myself: at least, I could by no means take upon me to force them into the Service. The Recruiting has hitherto been carried on with the good will of the Country: And I should be glad to have it conducted so to the end.

I this day communicated the clause ^of yours^ relating to the certificates of the number of the provincial troops in each Year to the Council, & I am desired by them to acquaint you that the rolls for the service of the troops of this Province for the Winter 1759–60 (at which time none of the other Provinces had any troops in the service) have been made out separately, in order to obtain a compensation for this service; and desire to know if you would please to have copies of these rolls sent you in order to be authenticated: or to desire you to certify this service in some other method. The rolls are all given in upon the Oaths of the sevral Officers: and therefore I suppose are not willfully ^or knowingly^ false. The Desertion you mentioned in a former letter,[2] I am told, did not begin until after the first of May when the Engagement for the Winter Service expired: and therefore the Certificates for that Service need not be uncertain upon that account. The Lords of the Treasury in the allotment of the grant for 1760 have reserved 10,000 to answer this claim of the Province, &, by agreement of the Agents, have apportioned the rest.

If you should choose to have these or any other papers, I shall send Mr Goldthwait with them, who will then be ready to assist in settling Any other Matters in doubt, particularly the billeting Account which, by reason of the recruiting, will be different this Year from that of Any other.[3]

I am, with great regard, Sr Your most obedient & most humble Servant

Fra. Bernard

His Excellency Sr Jeffry Amherst.

ALS, RC   WO 34/26, f 229.

Contains minor emendations. Variant text in BP, 2: 287-288 (L, LbC).

---

1. **No. 170**.

2. Not found.

3. The total cost on the billeting rolls was £341 18s 4d. FB to Amherst, Boston, 13 Dec. 1762, WO 34/26, f 231.

175 | To Thomas Boone

Boston ~~Octo^r~~ ^Nov^r^ 16 1762

Sir

Your letter dated Sepr 6th[1] arrived here whilst I was absent on a Voyage to the Eastern parts of this province: and since my return I have been unavoidably prevented answering it untill now. In this province, (which is a mixture of the royal & Charter ~~Government~~ Constitutions) there does not lie an appeal from the Supreme Court to the Governor & Council: The Appeal is immediately to the King in Council. I therefore can give you no information from hence but what arises from my own notions of such appeals in the royal Governments, of which I had not one instance whilst I was Governor of New Jersey__

I have always understood that Appeals to the Governors & Councils in the Royal Provinces from the Supreme common law Courts are entirely of the nature of writs of Error from the King's bench to the House of Lords: and I know of no difference between them but, what arises from the exigencies of the Country, a greater allowance for non observance of the strict forms of Law. For instance: in writs of error in England the Error assigned must appear upon the face of the record & no other Error can be assignd. But in America where Special pleading and the preciseness of recording is not much practised or even understood, it will be necessary to consider the Error of the Court appealed from more liberally than is allowed in England; & sometimes it may [*be*] proper to examine the matters of fact upon which a Verdict & a Judgement in Consequence thereof are founded. I own I think it a nice business to set proper bounds to this kind of disquisition, as the Common Law considers the Verdict of a Jury to be conclusive: But it is the Common Practise of the privy Council to overhawl matters of fact as well as matters of Law; & therefore I dont see how a Governor & Council, from whom an Appeal to the Privy Council lies, can avoid determining by the same rules & methods as the privy Council will use in the farther Appeal.

I wonder to hear that such appeals have never been used in your Government; because I look upon the Governor & Council to be a necessary medium (in meer Royal Governments) from the Common Law Courts to the King in Council. Appeals from the Superior Court here to the King in Council have been Very frequent: but I don't imagine any Copies of them can be of the least use to you

I am Sir &c

His Excell^{cy} Govr Boone[2]

L, LbC   BP, 2: 289-290.

In the handwriting of clerk no. 2.

---

1. Not found.

2. Boone had been appointed governor of South Carolina on 14 Apr. 1761; he assumed office on 11 Nov. and served until 1766.

176 | To John Pownall

Duplicate

Boston Dec: 1 1762

S^r

Since I wrote to you in March[1] last desiring you would introduce to their Lordships the subject of a grant of the General Court of this Province to me of the Island of Mount desart, I have been informed[2] that[3] there is like to be difficulties occur as to the recommending it for his Majesty's approbation. The Objection apprehended is that the Charter of King William is not valid as to the lands between the Rivers Penobscot & St Croix because He was not possessed of those lands at the time of making the Grant.

It is unlucky for me that this Objection has not been started before: if it had, I am inclined to think that this Difficulty would not now have stood in my way. As it is, If their Lordships should think there is Weight enough in it to require a public Disquisition, I must be content to wait till it can be brought on in other instances than my own. I can neither dispute with the Crown nor take upon me the defence of the Province for which reasons I could wish that some means could be devised to extricate my business from this difficulty.

For this purpose I enclose a Memorial, with a desire, that you would lay it before their Lordships at such time & in such manner as you shall think most proper. I also send with it short reasons to obviate the Objection before mentioned, by application of historical facts to it, together with the proofs of such facts, as are therein alleged. If these reasons should be sufficient to induce their Lordships to waive this objection, at least in my instance, I shall have no further request to make. But if their Lordships shall not think these reasons conclusive, I must then intreat their further favor to recommend me for a grant of this Island in such other manner as they shall think proper.

In the memorial I suggest no other pretensions previous to the grant, than what were the considerations upon which the Assembly acted: but if I could with propriety enter into other particulars of Œconomy, their Lordships would be convinced that without some such beneficialty as this, there is little more to be expected from this Government than a bare subsistance.

I mention in the memorial my intention by examining the lands & making experiments thereon to make them most beneficial to the Mother Country. Least these should be taken for words of course, I will mention two things, both greatly wanted in this Country, which I propose to set forward: the one is raising hemp; the other making pot ash. For the first there are lands upon this Island very similar to the hemp lands in Lincolnshire which I have had opportunities to make particular observation of: and it will be no difficult matter by proper encouragement to induce some Lincolnshire hemp raisers to settle here. For the other, the lands affording all the materials, Iron excepted, necessary to make Potash according to a plain & practicable Method lately publish'd by the Society of Arts,[4] I make no doubt but that I can engage proper people to undertake it. And in both Cases, when the Novelty is over & the Advantage apparent, It will soon be followed.

I mention this to show that my own interest is not the only Motive that makes me desire a confirmation of this Island; & that your personal regard for me may not be your only inducement to promote my sollicitation: I know well that your private freindship never is more active than when it Cooperates with your public Spirit.

I am Sr Your most faithful & most obedient Servant

Fra Bernard

John Pownall Esq$_r$[5]

dupLS, RC   CO 5/891, ff 104-105.

In handwriting of clerk no. 3 with minor scribal emendations. Endorsed by John Pownall: *Massachusets Bay*. Letter from Governor Bernard to the secry, dated Boston Decr 1. 1762, relating to a Grant made to him by the Genl. Court of the Island of Mount Desart & enclosing, Read March 2^d 1763 L.L. 11. Variant text in BP, 10: 45-48 (ADftS, AC) and BP, 2: 226-228 (L, LbC). The LbC incorporated the emendations made to the draft, and there is no variation of substance between it and the authoritiative text.

Enclosed **No. 177**; "Consideration of an Objection to the right of the Province of Massachusetts Bay to certain Lands between Penobscot and St. Croix," with marginal annotations by FB, c.December 1762, CO 5/891, ff 111-114; and "Extracts from the General Court's books of the Province of Massachusetts Bay, relating to the Lands between Penobscot and St. Croix," c.December, CO 5/891, ff 115-119. This letter and its enclosures were subsequently enclosed in **No. 180**. On 2 Mar. 1763 the Board of Trade ordered that the letter and enclosures lie for further consideration when the grant of the island of Mount Desert should come before the Board, and replied to FB with **No. 193**. *JBT*, 11: 338.

FB's hope that potash production could make the settlement of Mount Desert viable was probably not misplaced. One contemporary estimated that by 1775 New England was exporting £35,000 worth of potash annually, over seventy percent of the total value of colonial exports of this staple. John Mitchell or Arthur Young, *American Husbandry* (New York, 1939), ed. Harry James Carman, 493-494.

---

1. FB to Pownall, Boston, 4 Mar. 1762, BP, 2: 33-34.

2. By Richard Jackson. See **No. 167**.

3. Dft: the remainder of the paragraph is enclosed in quotation marks.

4. Possibly [John Mascarene], *The Manufacture of Pot-Ash in the British North American Plantations Recommended* (Boston, 1757). FB's encouragement of American potash manufacturer Levi Willard is discussed in **No. 232**.

5. This line in FB's hand.

177 | Memorial To The Board Of Trade

To The Right Honorable The Lords Commissioners for Trade & Plantations

The humble Memorial of Francis Bernard Esq: Governor of the Province of Massachusets Bay showeth

That the Memorialist was in the year 1760 appointed Governor of the Province aforesaid & entered upon the Government on the 2ᵈ day of August in the same year.

That on the 25 day of Octʳ: following his late Majesty died, & his present Majesty having been graciously pleased to reappoint the Memorialist to the said Government he sued out new Commissions for the same at the same expence as the former, but without the usual allowances of Chappel furniture plate &c

That the Memorialist's family being, by means of the Number of his children, considerably larger than that of his predecessor, upon his accession to the Government, He found himself obliged, (besides the assistance he had from the Province which was very liberal) to expend considerable sums of his own Money in improvements & additions to the Governor's house at Boston & his apartment at Castle William.

That the extraordinary expences the Memˢᵗ: had been at as well in the charges of his second commission as in the improvements & additions to the Governor's House & apartments as aforesaid being taken into consideration by the House of Representatives, They of their own accord proposed to make the Memˢᵗ: a compensation for the expences aforesaid by a Grant of lands, being more suitable to the state of the Provincial Finances during an expensive War & to the particular Circumstances of the Memˢᵗˢ family, than a pecuniary Retribution would be.

The Governor of Massachusets Bay, considering the importance of the Province & the variety & extensiveness of its publick business, is allowed to be the worst supported of all the Royal Governors, the whole income consisting of 1000 pounds a year salary, (according to the Royal instructions) & casual fees of less than 100 pounds a year more. The House of Representatives have been so sensible of this, that, tho they would not increase the state salary beyond what has been required of them, yet they frequently have been known to make the extraordinary Services of the Governors motives for occasional additions to the Salary & by that means have in some degree made up the general deficiency of the appointment.

For these considerations the General Court of the said Province in their Session in febry 1762 did grant unto the Memorˢᵗ: & his heirs the Island of Mount desart lying North Eastward of Penobscot Bay, subject to his Majesty's Approbation. And tho in the said Grant the only Consideration mention'd is of the extraordinary Services of the Memˢᵗ:, (in regard to which He only pretends to a close attention & steady application to the public business in arduous & interesting times) yet he begs leave to assure Your Lordships that a Compensation for the Expences aforemention'd, then estimated at above 600 pounds, was intended by the said Grant as well as a consideration for extraordinary services.

Under these Circumstances the Mem[st]: received this grant, at the same time flattering himself, that if the value of it should hereafter appear to be greater than the Considerations for which it was made, He might, in some part, make up the difference, by encouraging a speedy settlement there & rendring it subservient to the general purposes of extending & improving his Majesty's dominions. For this Reason He immediately declared his intention, that (as soon as the grant had recieved his Majestys Approbation) he would settle a Township there by grants of land to the settlers thereof wholly gratuitous & free from any charge whatsoever. And he according recieved proposals from upwards of 60 families to settle there upon free grants of ~~lands~~ a certain quantity ^of land^ being made to each family, which have been accepted by him & are ready to be carried into Execution.

Soon after this, the Mem[st]: was informed that there were several persons settled upon the Island without pretending to any right thereto & were making great Havock among the Timber & particularly such part thereof as is by law reserved for the use of his Majesty. The Mem[st]:, thereupon, found it necessary to visit the Island in person; which he did in Oct: 1762. When, having call'd the persons settled there before him, he prevailed upon them to engage to stop their wast of the timber, by assuring them that he would grant unto them sufficient lots of land for their families in the New intended Township, which he promis'd them should be mark'd out without delay.

The Mem[st]: begs leave to assure your Lordships, that He should not, under his present grant unconfirmed by his Majesty, have thought of entring into possession of the Island or acting as the proprietor thereof, if the Circumstances of the times & the urgency of the people he has had to deal with, had not made it necessary. It would not, in point of prudence, have been advisable for him, with so imperfect a title, to have entered into the Expence he has already incurred in making a Voyage thither & employing Surveyors to lay out a Plan for a Township there, if it could have been well avoided. But He was fully convinced that, if he did not interfere immediately, irregular settlements not hereafter to be easily reduced into order, & a general devastation of the Timber there would have presently ensued. He thought it therefore better for him to enter upon the Island under an imperfect Title than to suffer it to be possessed & wasted by Persons who can pretend to no title at all.

Whilst in this state of uncertainty and diffidence, The Mem[st]: has been inform'd, that upon a reference to Your Lordships, it is to be apprehended that Your Lordships may not recommend the confirmation of this Grant, upon a doubt concerning the legal effect of the Charter of K William & Qu Mary,[1] under which this Grant is made; which arises from this Objection; "that in regard to the Lands between the Rivers Penobscot & St Croix (among which this Island may be accounted) King William was not in possession of them at the time of making the Charter, & therefore could not legally grant the same." The Mem^st. begs leave to assure Your Lordships that at the time of the Genl Court's making the Grant to him It was not apprehended by him, nor, as he believes, by any ^one^ of the Genl Court that this Objection or Any other of Consequence lay against the Right of the Province to originate a Grant of this Island under the Charter of King William & subject to the restrictions thereof; The Records of the Province seeming to afford full Proof that King William, at the time of making the Charter, was in possession of the Country in question.

But the Mem^st: desires to be understood that he does not mean to enter upon a controversial examination of this question: it is sufficient for him, that he is satisfied that Your Lordships will give it a full Consideration, before you form your judgement of it. In his present situation it would ill become him to make himself a principal in a dispute concerning the rights of the Crown; nor could he think it prudent to take upon himself the defence of the province in so important a Claim as the present. All He can do is to wait untill the Province shall have an opportunity to interpose on their own behalf; a full Consideration of their Claim to the benefit of the letter of their Charter, if it should be thought necessary, can be had; & a determination thereof shall be made.

But as a disquisition of this importance must necessarily take up a good deal of time; as the Circumstances of the Mem^st's case both in regard to the Considerations of the Original Grant & the necessity he is under to enter upon & defend the lands at further expence will but ill suit with much delay; as the avowed purport of the Mem^st: is to establish a new Town in a Wilderness, before he begins to percieve any profit to himself; as it is his firm intention, as soon after the confirmation of his Grant as may be, by examination of the Lands, & by experiments thereon to elucidate the best means to make them most beneficial to the Mother Country; & as he has reason from the testimonies he has recieved, to flatter himself that his publick Services have hitherto been favourably accepted by your Lordships: He is bold to hope that if upon account of the Objection before mentioned or any other which shall bring the Province's right to make this grant in question, your Lordships should not think it proper at present to advise the confirmation of this Grant, under the Title of the Province of Massachusets Bay, You will be so favorable to him as to recommend him to his Majesty's Grace, for a grant of the Island in such a form & Manner as shall neither confirm nor conclude against the Right of the Province of Massachusets Bay; but be equally available whether the Question concerning the same shall be determined on the one side or the other.

And your Lordships may be assured, that the Mem^st. will use his best endeavours so to improve the said lands, as not only to perform the Condition of a speedy population, which is inherent to grants of this kind; but also by all other means to make them as conducive to the general utility as the Nature & Extent of the Island will admit of

Fra. Bernard

Boston Dec 1. 1762

MsS, RC   CO 5/891, ff 106-109.

In handwriting of clerk no. 3 with scribal emendations. Docket by FB: Memorial of Francis Bernard Esq, Dec 1. 1762. Endorsed by John Pownall: *Massachusets* Reced Read March 2. 1763. L.l. 45. Enclosed in **Nos. 176** and **179**, and possibly **No. 178**.

The manuscript printed here is a fair version of draft in BP, 10: 49-56 (ADft, AC), on which the only previously published version (a clear text transcript) was based. Sawtelle, "Sir Francis Bernard and His Grant of Mount Desert," 212-215. The fair copy incorporates most of the additions and corrections that FB made to the draft, and does not differ in substance.

The memorial was read by the Board of Trade on 2 Mar. 1763, for which proceedings see source note to **No. 193**.

---

1. The Charter of the Province of the Massachusetts Bay in New England, 1692.

178 | To The Earl Of Egremont

Boston Dec: 1 1762.

My Lord

By a letter dated the fourth of March last,[1] I intreated your Lordship's favor to recommend me to his Majesty for a confirmation of a Grant of the Island of Mount desart made to me by the General Court of the Province of Massachuset's bay, in consideration of extraordinary Services & also extraordinary expences.

I have since been informed that upon a reference to the board of Trade there is like to be a difficulty concerning the confirmation of this Grant, upon an objection newly started concerning the validity of King William's Grant to the Province of the lands between Penobscot & St Croix of which this Island must be allowed to be part.

This is a very interesting Question to the Province & will be supported on their behalf with great earnestness, both as it is a part of their Charter, & as they can show special & very honorable Considerations for these lands being included by King William in the united Province of Massachusets. In such a dispute I shall be very desirous to avoid being a party myself, otherwise than as an intercessor: in my present situation it would ill become me to dispute the rights of the Crown, & it will be no less improper for me to undertake the defence of those of the Province. All that I have now to desire is to get out of the dispute without the loss of the compensation designed for me if it may be so.

For this purpose I have prepared a Memorial to be laid before the Lords of Trade, (to whom, I am told, my subject in the Course of business will be referred) praying that, in Consideration of my Case, therein more fully stated, If their Lordships should, upon account of any doubt concerning the Province's title, not think it proper at present to advise the confirmation of this grant as a provincial act, they would recommend me to his Majesty's favor, for a grant of this Island, in such a manner as may neither confirm nor impeach the title of the Province. In this Case I must beg leave to alter the terms of my petition to your Lordship & instead of only praying his Majesty's approbation of the Provincial Grant, intreat your Lordship's favor to recommend me for his Majesty's Grant & confirmation of the Island to me in such a manner & form as shall be most advisable.

If I thought myself at liberty to lay before your Lordship the particulars of My Services in North America & the unexpected & unavoidable expences & draw backs which I have been subject to, I am satisfied that your Lordship's Generosity & Justice would interest you in confirming to me the compensation now proposed to my utmost hopes. I have the honor to be with &c Your L &c

The Right honble The Earl of Egremont.

L, LbC   BP, 2: 228-230.

In handwriting of clerk no. 3 with scribal emendations. May have enclosed a copy of **No. 177**.

---

1. **No. 90**.

179 | To John Pownall

private

Boston Dec: 5. 1762.

Dear S^r

I wrote to you 3 letters dated Oct: 20, 21, 31:[1] The Originals went by the Snow Bristol Merchant Kerr for Bristol; the duplicates by the Ship Jenny & Nelly Lyall for Glascow. In the conclusion of the last of the last of these[2] I desired you would procure the report concerning my grant of Mount desart to be suspended (unless it was to be in my favor) untill I could transmitt a new memorial. This Memorial I now send, with this difference from what I proposed, that I address it to the Lords of Trade, & not to the Secretary of State; to whom I content myself with writing a letter informing him that I have preferred such a memorial. I have also drawn up a short enquiry of the Fact of the possession of the lands in question, which together with the proofs, I send to be laid before their Lordships, if you shall think proper. From these it plainly appears to me that King William at the time of granting the Charter was in actual possession of the Lands between Penobscot & St Croix, & acquired & held such possession by the Means of the Province of Massachusets Bay. If this should have the effect desired to remove the objection to the Confirmation of the Province Grant, or if they should be inclined to recommend me for a Royal Grant in such a manner as shall not determine the Question of the Province's right, I shall be happily withdrawn out of this dispute, which I foresee will cause a good deal of trouble. If their Lordships shall not think proper to favor me in the one way or the other, I must then desire that no determination may be made against me, but that my business may rest untill the Province shall intervene for their own interest, which I expect they very soon will do. For my part I foresee that my being disappointed in this grant will create in me such a despondency, that I shall not be inclined to give it up, whilst any means, except my personal contention, are left untried.

I should have mention'd before, that with these papers I enclose a letter to you to introduce them, which is intended, if you think fit proper, to be read to their Lordships with the other papers. As to my intention therein mention'd of raising hemp & making potash ^upon the Island if y^t should be like^ to promote my grant, you may add that I will engage to set up one or the other, if not both, within 3 years after I recieve an absolute grant.

As this Letter is intended only for your own perusal, I shall communicate to you freely some general reflections which have occurred to me on the subject of this Objection to the Province's right, trusting that they will be reciev'd with your usual Candour, & whether agreeable or not to your sentiments, will be understood to be well intended.

If the speedy Population of the Country between the rivers Penobscot & S[t] Croix was the chief object it would by all means be advisable to continue it within the Province of Massachusets Bay: as there are numberless People, therein, who are so attach'd to their own Government, that they would not go out of it's jurisdiction, & yet would readily settle on these lands if allowed to be part of the Province.

If these lands are intended to be added to Nova Scotia it will not be worth the while. Nova Scotia wants no such addition; it would be unwise to desire it; it is allready too large to be soon well peopled. Besides the Peninsula & the Isthmus, The Great River of S[t] Johns alone would swallow up a vast number of People. So that there is no Province [that][3] wants to be endowed with lands at the expence of their Neighbours ^less^ than Nova Scotia.

If they are intended to be erected in a separate Government, they are not sufficient for that purpose. There will be wanted other part of the Territories of Massachsets Bay, against which the Objection before mentioned does not lie, to compleat such a Territory, as will be sufficient for this purpose.

It will not be worth while, for either of these purposes, to encounter the petitions complaints Remonstrances &c &c which will be sure to ensue upon the attempting to dismember the Constitutional Territories of the Province, which have been allowed for upwards of 70 Years & confirmed by the Crown above 30 by the means of a point of law now first started. The lopping of a considerable Branch of their Territorial Tree may perhaps be little less alarming than laying the Ax to the root of it.

If it should be thought adviseable to erect a new Government between the Massachusets & Nova Scotia (which may be very practicable if pursued by proper means) it should be done by a Convention with the Massachusets; & not by legal Exceptions to their Charter; which being to be determin'd by legal judgement, will probably produce nothing but fruitless trouble.

Such a scheme may be both advisable & practicable: for instance: If it should be proposed to the Massachusets to add to their jurisdiction New Hampshire & Rhode Island (unless it should be thought proper to continue the Government of the latter which no good Man among them either expects or desires) with such other lands to the Westward as will contribute to the arrondisement of the Province, upon their quitting claim to the lands Eastward of Piscataqua, most probably they would accept of the Offer: & the Consent of parties being had, legal titles would not be in the Way.

If such an Agreement could be brought about The Lands between the Rivers Newichewanock & S[t] Croix, with Casco Bay for the Metropolis would make one of the finest Provinces in America & would by it's vicinity greatly contribute to peopling the Parts of Nova Scotia, which lie in the Bay of Fundy.

I must not conclude this Subject without assuring you that I have not the least Authority for making this Proposal: & that the only Reason I have to think it would be acceptable is my Opinion that it would be very beneficial to the Province by bringing its territory more into a circle without diminishing it. I am S[r]

John Pownal Esq:

L, LbC   BP, 2: 230-234.

In handwriting of clerk no. 3. Enclosed copies of **No. 176** and its enclosures (inc. **No. 177**) and a triplicate of **No. 91**.

---

1. **Nos. 162**, **165** and **169**.

2. Thus in manuscript. This is not a dittograph.

3. Faint.

180 | To Richard Jackson

Boston Dec[r] 6th 1762

Dear Sir

I wrote to you Octo. 29 a full letter concerning Mount desart: The Original went by the Snow Bristol Merchant, Keer, for Bristol, the duplicate[1] by the Ship Jenny & Nelly, Lyall, for Glascow, both inclosed in A Cover to the Lords of trade.[2] At the end of this I promise a Memorial for the Secretary of State to be sent by the next ship. Upon second [thought] I think it more proper to address this Memorial to the Lords of Trade & a letter to the Secretary of State informing him that such a Memorial has been given in. Both these you'll receive with this under flying Seals for your Perusal. you may consult M[r] Pownal before they go out of your hands, that if there is anything, improper it may be altered, or the whole new drawn if thought best. With this you will also receive a refutation of the Objection concerning King William's Possession drawn from Historical Facts with the Vouchers thereunto annexed. These with the Memorial & a letter to M[r] Pownal in officio will be in one Cover under a flying Seal for your perusal. I shall send another Set of them by the next Ship:[3] in the mean time you may make use of these either before or after you give them to M[r] Pownal. you will also receive a state of the Provinces right to the lands in Question: This has been drawn up by the Lieu[t]. Gov[r] who is chairman of a Committee of both houses, appointed to prepare instructions to the Agent for the defence of the Provinces right to these lands. It is to be reported to the Gen[l] Court at thier sitting in Janry & then will probably come to you in form. At present you must consider it as put into your hands only for private information, and as a direction for your own researchers.[4]

If the difficulty concerning the confirming my grant arises only from the Objection of King William's not being in possession of these lands, I think it must be removed by what I offer, which seems to me to be conclusive for the possession of the English: Especially when it is considered that Casteen whose settlement was the only one left remaining after S[r] William's Phipps's expedition, Submitted to the English & swore allegiance to King William & corresponded at Boston as a Subject of England for severall years after the grant of the Charter.[5] If therefore He is to be considered as an European, His Settlement from S[r] W[m] Phipps's conquest was under the English; if as an Indian, his Submission to the English is an argument of their Possession. There seems to be no other French left upon these lands after S[r] Will[m] Phipps's expedition but this one. If the Settlement upon the Island of Pasimaquody was restored, (which if not probable considering the Massachusets kept possession of Port royal) that is Part of Nova Scotia being within 6 leagues of the Continent as granted to S[r] W[m] Alexander. But supposing it is not conclusive as to this Question, Surely it renders it so doubtful as not to make it worth while to attempt to take this land from the Province by means of a legal exception to the Validity of the Charter (70 years after the grant of it & thirty years after it's confirmation by order of Council) the determination of which must be doubtful, but the ill humour, Animosity & litigation which this attack will produce certain.

For my part I cannot percieve any purpose that this measure can serve that is in the least adequate to the trouble & uneasiness it is like to occasion. If it is intended to add this Tract to Nova Scotia, it is a most unnecessary Work: Nova Scotia as bounded by S[r] W[m] Alexanders patent, has an extent of Territory that the next 100 years will not Settle. Massachusets Bay wants this Tract immediately for the use of thier Superabundant people: shall it be taken away from them to be added to the boundless Wastes of Nova Scotia.__

Is it intended to make this a seperated territory from either of the present Provinces? As a Government it will not be sufficient unless other parts of the Massachusets Grant, against which this Objection dont lie, be also taken in. Is it wanted for a grant to private Adventurers for this, there is no occasion to cut off a portion of the Massachusets grant, the North Side of the Bay & River of S[t] Croix, the Sea-Coast between that & S[t] Johns the great River of S[t]. Johns (which has lately been accurately surveyed) will afford a field large enough for adventurers, without impeaching the Title of the Massachusets.__

I own I think it might be adviseable to erect the Province of Main & Territory of Sagadehock into a new Government, & that it is practicable without injuring the

THE PAPERS OF GOVERNOR FRANCIS BERNARD

rights of the Massachusets, that is, by gaining thier consent. The Seperation of the Western from the Eastern Territory by the intervention of New Hampshire & the distance of the extreme eastern parts from the Capital are obvious inconveniences and will be felt as such when that Country is when peopled.[6] The bounding the Old province of Massachusets by the New Hampshire line of latitude has been much regretted. If therefore the Crown would give the Province of New Hampshire (with the addition of Rhode Island, whose Mobboccracy must be determined one way or other) to the Massachusets in exchange for Main & Sagadehock, I should think it would be accepted, because I think it would be for the benefit of the province to make such exchange. If such an exchange could be made with the good will of the people, The province of main & sagadehock with Falmouth in Casco Bay (a Very fast growing Town) for the Capital would make as fine a Province as any in America. And, as the whole Coast from Piscataqua to St Croix would soon be settled, it would help to strenghten Nova Scotia, This would be a Scheme worth pursuing & probably would not meet with much difficulty: tho' one cant always determine what will be agreable to a people by Judging what will be beneficial to them: And therefore I would not have it known that such a hint came from me.

I recieved a letter Yesterday from Lord Barrington,[7] wherein he writes "I shall also, if necessary, give any assistance in my power to the Agents you employ about the grants made to you by the Province." It is impossible for me to know wherein it will be necessary to trouble; and therefore I can only renew my request, that you will apply to him when you see occasion: you cant have a better Mediator with Lord Egremont. If you are not allready known to him, it would be best for you to be introduced to him before you have occasion to trouble him with business, unless it should allready offer

I am &c

R. Jackson Esq

L, LbC BP, 2: 234-240.

In the handwriting of clerk no. 2 with minor scribal emendations. Enclosed a duplicate of **No. 176** and its enclosures, and other enclosures not found.

---

1. **No. 167**.

2. Not found.

3. **No. 179**.

4. General Court, A brief State of the Title of the Province of Massachusetts-Bay to the Country between the Rivers Kennebeck and St. Croix, 1 Feb. 1763. *JHRM*, 39: 289-307. This was subsequently published: *A Brief State of the Title of the Province of Massachusetts-Bay to the Country between the Rivers Kennebeck and St. Croix* (Boston, 1763).

5. Sir William Phips (1651-95), governor of Massachusetts, 1691-94, led the 1690 expedition against Port Royal, Acadia, which, though successful, provoked French and Native American reprisals in Sagadahoc.

6. Thus in manuscript.

7. Barrington to FB, Cavendish Square, 11 Sept. 1762, BP, 10: 15-18.

181 | From The Board Of Trade

Whitehall Decem[r] 24th. 1762

Sir

The inclosed copy of the Minutes of our proceedings upon some papers which we have lately received from the Lieutenant Governor of Nova Scotia, will mark out to you the Sense we have of your conduct, in entring upon a negotiation with the Government of Nova Scotia for ascertaining the Boundary Line between that Province and the Massachusets Bay, without having communicated the affair to Us as it was your Duty to have done.

You cannot be ignorant that the River Penobscot has always been deem'd and declared to be the western boundary of Accadia or Nova Scotia, as possessed by France under the Treatys of Breda and Ryswick, and as ceded to Great Britain by the Treaty of Utrecht, and tho~ we do not take upon us to declare that the Province of Massachusets Bay is, under this circumstance, absolutely precluded from any claim of property to the Eastward of that River, yet it was so far a matter of question, that, We cannot but think, that it was improper in you to assent to any Grants of Lands between Penobscot and S[t] Croix, untill the question was determined; and that the Countenancing a proposition for ascertaining a Boundary which implys a restriction of the limits of Acadia to the River S[t] Croix, without the participation of the Crown, was such an aggravation of your misconduct as our Duty to His Majesty will not permit us to pass over without animadversion.

We are Sir Your most Obedient humble Servants

Soame Jenyns

Ed Bacon

John Yorke[1]

Edmond Thomas

Francis Bernard Esq[r] Governor of Massachusets Bay

LS, RC   BP, 10: 41-44.

In the handwriting of John Pownall. Virgule in the left margin marking the first paragraph may have been added by FB. Endorsed by clerk no. 1: Lords of Trade 24 Dec. 1762 r Ap. 15 1763. Variant text in CO 5/920, pp. 146-147 (L, LbC). Enclosures not found. This letter is a reply to **No. 164**. FB responded with **No. 197**. (For the governors' correspondence on the boundary dispute see **Nos. 127** and **129**.)

On 10 Dec. the Board of Trade, considered a memorial from Richard Jackson on behalf of the province's land grants in Sadagahoc and for the moment upheld Belcher's argument. *JBT*, 11: 312-313.

---

1. John Yorke (1728-1801), MP for High Ferrers, 1753-68, and Reigate, 1768-84; a lord commissioner for Trade and Plantations, 1761-63; and a lord of the Admiralty, 1765-66.

182 | *From The Board Of Trade*

Sir[1]

We have received your Letter to Us of the 12th. of October[2] inclosing heads of a Bill for raising a Sum of money by Lottery to compleat an additional Hall, for the use of Harvard College in Cambridge, and tho' We are still of Opinion that Lotteries in the American Colonies ought to be countenanced, and are fully convinced that the too frequent practice of such a mode of raising money will be introductive of great Mischief, Yet in consideration of the General propriety and Utility of the Service to be provided for by this Bill, We have no Objection to your passing it into a Law, desiring at the same time, that it may be understood, that such a permission shall not be drawn into precedent in any other Case whatever.

We are, Sir, Your most Obed[t]. humble Servants

Whitehall Dec[r]. 24. 1762

Sandys

Soame Jenyns

John Yorke

Ex[d].

L, LbC   CO 5/920, p. 148.

In the handwriting of John Pownall with minor emendations. Entrybook title: To Francis Bernard Esq[r].

The Board of Trade considered **No. 164** on 20 Dec. 1762 and permitted an exception to made in Harvard's case. *JBT*, 11: 317. However, the final cost of the new building, £4,821 7s. 2d., was met by the General Court without recourse to a lottery bill. Hollis Hall was completed in Dec. 1763 and dedicated by FB on 13 Jan. 1764. *Acts and Resolves,* 17: 442-443; FB, Warrant to Harrison Gray, Boston, 4 Jan. 1764, Mass. Archs., 58: 487.

---

1. Left marginal note: "Letter to Frans. Bernard Esq. Govr. of the Massachusets Bay in answer to One from him of 12th Oct."

2. Should be 21 Oct., **No. 164**.

183 | To John Stevens

Boston Decr. 27th. 1762

Sr.

I should have acknowledged your favor ~~of Apr~~.[1] concerning Capt. Chambers sooner if I had not been engaged in writing of much more importance. In Answer to Capt. Chambers Assertions I now send you my son's Narrative, on the truth of Which you may depend, as my Son's Veracity, to those who know him, is unquestionable to those who know him; and as he could appeal to several persons, that he complained of his being put in the Stearage & being denied a birth in the Cabbin. What therefore Major Gates[2] sayes of his lodging in the steerage by choice & that he might have lodged in the Cabbin if he thought proper, must be from report only; for he was certainly much dissatisfied with his birth, Altho his good nature & Easiness of Temper might make him appear satissfied to Majr. Gates. As to Civilities in other things, especially from his fellow passengers, he has given all due credit for them. As for those of Capt. Chambers, they have a great counter-ballance by excluding him from the Cabbin in so rude & imperious a Manner. As I cannot reconcile myself to this, I must once more desire you to communicate the Enclosed paper & such part of this letter as you shall think fit to Capt. Chambers & take his further answer. I am sorry to give you so much trouble: but really this treatment of my Son has much offended me

I am Sr. your most faithfull & obedient &c &c

Mr J Stevens[3]

L, LbC   BP, 2: 291-292.

In the handwriting of clerk no. 1, except as noted. Enclosures not found.

---

1. No such letter has been found.

2. Horatio Gates (1727/28?–1806), the future Revolutionary general. Gates had been resident in London since Mar. 1762, and the following month was appointed a major in the 45th Regiment of Foot. He returned to New York in Aug.—probably on the vessel that Frank Bernard abandoned at Madiera— where he was an aide to Gen. Robert Monckton, governor of New York, 1761-65.

3. This line is in FB's hand.

184 | To Richard Jackson

Boston Jan: 6 1762[3][1]

Dear S^r

My Writings to you have been pretty voluminous of late, & yet I am inclined to add another letter to a large packet, which will set out, I hope in 2 days time.

Since I made up my last letters[2] We have advice that Lord Halifax is made Secretary of State. As the appointment to that office don't necessarily determine the department, It is generally expected here that he will soon if not immediately enter upon that branch to Which N America belongs.[3] Every one that wishes well to this country must desire to have it under the care of Lord Halifax: There is not only an intimate acquaintance, but also, what is the consequence of it a mutual affection between them; & there cannot be a finer field (Ireland not excepted) for him to exercise his abilities & virtues upon than this Continent is like to afford. If this appointment is like to take this turn, I should be glad to have the earliest advice of it.

My obligations to Lord Halifax are such that I have thought it my duty to pay my compliments to him, upon the several promotions he has been honoured with, since he has left the Board of Trade. I shall certainly not neglect this; but propose to stay till the packett comes in, in hopes that I may have an opportunity of con- gratulating America as well as his Lordship. I say this with a due regard to Lord Egremonts merit by whom I have been personally favour'd, but I suppose such an exchange of departments cannot be unpleasing to him.

I dont expect that what I urge in behalf of the province's right to the lands between Penobscot & St Croix will have weight enough to overcome opinions of so long standing as those against the Province seem to be: but this I think, that it may serve to evince that the Objections to the Province's right are founded upon such refin'd reasoning, that if the Province should be precluded from these lands without a convention or a compensation, it will most probably be thought hard treatment by the Provincials

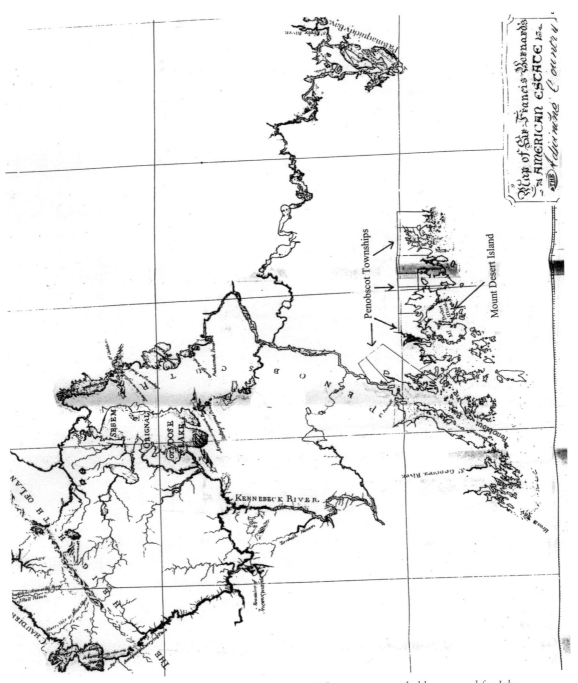

Map of Sir Francis Bernard's American estate, c.1786. This map was probably prepared for John Bernard who in 1785 recovered title to half Mount Desert Island after its confiscation by the Commonwealth of Massachusetts. He later sold the island to speculators. By permission of Robert Spencer Bernard.

Upon revolving in my mind, what I have mention'd both to you & Mr Pownall of a Scheme for erecting a New Province, the Expediency & practicability of it seem ^to me^ more & more evident. If it should be seriously thought of, give me an early hint of it. I am D S Y m fa & Aff Ser

R. Jackson Esq.

L, LbC   BP, 2: 244-246.

In handwriting of clerk no. 3.

---

1. The clerk erred in overwriting "1763" with "1762."

2. FB to Jackson, Boston, 10 Dec. 1762, BP, 2: 240-243; **No. 180**.

3. FB welcomed Halifax's appointment, partly because he was politically close to Barrington, but also because of the earl's reformist outlook where imperial administration was concerned. Nicolson, *The 'Infamas Govener'*, 41-42, 87, 90. Halifax had been appointed secretary of state for the Northern Department on 14 Oct. 1762, which department did not normally administer American affairs, but he moved to the Southern Department one year later.

185 | To Richard Jackson

Boston. Jan: 23 1763

Dear S^r

I have sent you a great quantity of paper of late by different Vessels:[1] my present will be confined to a ~~different~~ separate subject, which I should rather have chose to defer, If I was not persuaded that other letters might go by This Vessel which might require some explanation from me as well as caution on my behalf.

I informed you before that the displacing Mr Bollan & electing Mr Mauduit was carried on with great heat & hurry.[2] I did not chuse to appear to be too great a respecter of Persons: but I could not be indifferent that the interest of the Province in the difficult & intricate disputes of it[s] territorial rights which are now opening should be well supported. After giving Mr Mauduit full credit for all his good Qualities, I saw it to be most improbabable that he should be able of himself to conduct so arduous a business as was to be put into his hands. As for his craving assistance from Lawyers (the only set of men he could resort to not being one himself) there was so little probability ~~of his~~ that he would meet with one who was previously acquainted with ye state of the Province & its rights, or, if not well acquainted therewith, would have ability industry & leisure enough to make himself master of the Subject, y^t I had not great hopes from a resort of this kind. under this difficulty I turned my Eyes toward you & considered that if I could engage you to assist Mr Mauduit in the difficultest part of his Business, I could reconcile it to myself to consent to his election, without which Consideration, I must at least have suspended the consideration of his appointment to a further day. This being accepted by those, who Proposed Mr Mauduit; (who could not of themselves answer for his Ability to undertake or his disposition to accept of this Office) at the time he was appointed Agent, you was provisionally substituted to him by the Act for the receipt of the money &c;[3] & in regard to other affairs, he was ordered by his instructions to advise with you in all matters of law. This I thought must be so agreeable to him, but I did not wonder that hearing he declared that your offering him your Assistance, in every thing he should want it, cheifly induced him to resolve to act.

Thus I thought this affair was put in a good way of settlement for the Present: till about 3 or 4 Months ago a Public Letter from Mr Mauduit came to the Secretary,[4] wherin he desired that his Brother Mr Israel Mauduit[5] might be substituted to him in case of his disability &c. This was accompanied with a private letter declaring that he did not thereby intend to make any encroachment upon your appointment. It is probable he did not: but if He had lookt into the Act of Assembly enabling him to recieve the money, he would have seen that this proposal is directly contrary to that Act, which latter must have been repealed in order to have carried the former into execution. Could this be done without putting a slight upon you? I wont suppose that Mr Mauduit intended to make you decline the Service of the Province: but I wont so readily conclude that this intention rested no where else: at least I will say that it must have this effect, whether it was intended or no.

I therefore immediately declared against this proposal in terms so positive, that it produced some conferences between me & Mr Mauduit['s] friends, in all which I persisted in my resolution of dissenting to a substitution unless you was included in it. But I thought it much better to let this Matter rest, till you & Mr Mauduit could be made acquainted with the difficulties I was under: & possibly you & He might settle this Affair in such a manner as might be agreeable & satisfactory to me; the whole of my purpose being to secure to the Province your Services in these difficult times, & to avoid giving any umbrage that might deprive it of them. Notwithstanding all I could say Mr Mauduits friend[6] persisted in bringing this matter before the Assembly in the manner I had excepted to, imagining I suppose that if He could have sent up a vote of the two Houses to me, my resolution of negativing it would have been shaken: but in regard to that he would have found himself mistaken. Accordingly on the afternoon of Monday last (a time when the House is always thin & it is not usual to bring on business of consequence) He moved that Mr Israel

Mauduit might be associated to the Agent as a substitute.[7] There were but 48 in the House including the Speaker; 24 of which being for the motion, the Speaker having no voice it was carried in the Affirmative. In the Council it was twice debated & flung out by 11 to 5. After this it was again brought into the House, & an Hour appointed for it: when after a debate of 5 hours length it was thrown out by 40 against 32. And here at present the matter rests.[8]—I am not willing to impute to Mr Mauduit the trouble which this affair has occasioned. I have given him all possible assurances of my desire to make his business easy to him; I therefore cannot think that he intends to create any uneasiness in my Government: You have given particular proofs of your disinterested regard for him; I cannot concieve that he would endeavour to break y^t connection which for the Provinces sake & not for yours, I have endeavour'd to create between it & you. I shall therefore suspend my judgement on this affair & leave myself as open as ever to the establishing a good understanding between me & him, untill I percieve it not to be desired by him. His old friend Secretary Oliver is an honest sincere man, & will allways be glad to assist Mr Mauduit in a friendly Correspondence with me, if he desires it. As for Mr Israel Mauduit, I never heard of his name till within these four months: I know nothing of his estimation, so as to form any certain idea of him; & therefore can have no personal exception to him.

Before I conclude this Subject, I must mention that there have been some endeavours to make this altercation a religious Concern: & tho this distinction has been sufficiently exploded in both houses, yet I am not sure that it may not operate without doors. But this I think I may depend upon: that if such insinuations to my disadvantage are transmitted to Mr Mauduit, he will be cautious how he propagates them;[9] because they will be contradicted by the general tenor of my professions & conduct which will plainly prove that I am a friend to religious liberty upon the best of principles that of it's being a natural right: nor can I concieve the most distant probability of the rights of the New England Churches being in danger. Your m Faithful &c

R Jackson Esq.

L, LbC   BP, 2: 248-252.

In handwriting of clerk no. 3 with scribal emendations.

---

1. Including **No. 184**.

2. **No. 131**.

3. An Act for empowering Jasper Mauduit (passed 24 Apr. 1762). *Acts and Resolves*, 4: 536-537.

4. Jasper Mauduit to Andrew Oliver, 29 Jun. 1763, which Oliver brought down from the Council to the House on 14 Sept. 1762. *JHRM*, 39: 102.

5. Israel Mauduit (1708-87), brother of province agent Jasper and a Dissenting minister by training, ran the family's draper business trading with the colonies and wrote several notable tracts on colonial affairs while acting as a lobbyist for the colonists.

6. James Otis Jr.

7. On 17 Jan., the House voted that Israel Mauduit be "impowered to act as Agent," but without pay, in "all Cases" where his elderly brother was "necessarily prevented" from attending to business. *JHRM*, 39: 138. On 20 Jan., James Otis Jr. delivered a message to the Council enquiring as to whether or not they had passed the House vote. As FB notes, the Council did not concur. *JHRM*, 39: 155, 160.

8. For subsequent developments see **No. 186**.

9. This suggests that FB may have been aware of the contents of letters from James Otis Jr. and the Rev. Charles Chauncy to Jasper Mauduit in which FB's Anglican credentials were disparaged. Worthington C. Ford, ed., *Jasper Mauduit, Agent in London, 1762-1765, Collections of the Massachusetts Historical Society*, vol. 74 (Boston, 1918), 71-80. FB may have been privy to Mauduit's private correspondence. **No. 206**n5.

186 | To Richard Jackson

Boston. Jan: 25. 1763.

Dear S^r.

The Letter inclosed with this is intended to be communicated to Mr Mauduit, if you shall think fit. The Secretary writes to him by this Vessel, & I believe, greatly condemns his bringing on this affair in so hasty a Manner, without considering how injurious this proposal was to you, & how disagreeable it must be to me. However I shall at present leave a door open for this Matter being set right: but if after my sentiments are known, Mr Israel Mauduit shall determine to push his fortunes here in opposition to me, He may be sure that whoever is Agent, he will not be. If on the other hand, He can propose to you a compromise, which will leave to you the conduct of those affairs which belong to your Profession & save you the trouble of lesser Matters, if you approve of it, I doubt not but that I shall. I know but of two ways of doing this: the one is by appointing you joint Agents without any distinction in the commission, but with separate departments to be settled by instructions or by private Agreement. The other is to appoint You Council & him Agent by separate & independant Commissions. The former is the best method & has a very Authoritative Precedent for it: In 1693 immediately after the opening the Charter, Sr Henry Ashurst (I suppose a Citizen of London) & Constantine Phipps (a noted Councellor) were appointed joint Agents without any distinction of Professions or of departments.[1] All this is supposed upon a supposition that Mr Israel Mauduit is a suitable Person to be connected with you in this ~~Affair~~ Manner; if that should not be so what relates to him must have a further consideration.

For this purpose I could wish that you would at all events look out from among the dissenters a sensible discreet Man, & such an one as you should like to be connected with & whom you could depend upon: if he had a public Character it would be better but it is not necessary. There is a great hankering after a dissenter for an Agent: & tho this distinction was treated in the two houses with more indifference than I could expect; yet it is got among the Clergy & may be revived again with more power. I should therefore be glad to be provided with a proper Person of that Sort, in case such an one should be wanted by the affair's taking a religious Turn, which I know some People will labour to give it.

When first your Name was mentioned, an obvious objection against you arose, that you was agent of Connecticut, which Colony has intrests opposite to those of this province. I have gained great ground upon this & in general have turned it to your advantage, but still it has it's difficulties. It is certain that the interests of the Province & Colony are so united by a similarity of priviledges manners & religion, that an Union of the Agencies would be advantageous to both, as it would give them more weight. And tho' there may be questions of interest, arising between the two, yet they must be very trifling in Comparison of those great Points in which they are jointly interested. And yet if they had one Agent, it should be previously settled what part he should act in Cases of dispute between them. To answer this in your own Case, it is certain that you cannot be desired by this Province to relinquish the defence of the right of Connecticut to the Townships which you have already undertaken: on the ~~contrary~~ other hand Connecticut could not take exception if this Province should expect, as the Superior, to have your assistance in such other Matters of controversy as shall hereafter arise: especially as it is not easy to foresee that any such will arise. What you say in Your Letter of the dispute concerning the Townships seems to amount to this: but I should be glad to be allowed to make such a stipulation in positive terms if it should be expedient.

Febry 1st.[2]

Since I wrote the foregoing, Mr Mauduits friend Mr Otis (A Gentleman of ~~much~~ ^great^ warmth of Temper & much indiscretion) has workt himself into such a passion by his dissappointment, that none but the most violent measures are pursued by him & his friends. On Saturday last (on the Mornings of which, as on Monday Evenings, the House is always Very thin) there being but 45 in the House, he introduced a Letter in the Name of the House to Mr Mauduit, apologising for thier not having complied with his request, & assigning for reason thier not being able to bear any additional expence in thier Agency. This was notoriously false, because in the Vote there was an express proviso that the province should be put to no further expence by the appointment of a substitute; and the Arguments against it turned almost wholly upon other reasons.[3] Nevertheless the House being very thin, one Side prepared & the other Surprised, it was suffered to pass. It being a new thing for the House to write to the Agent without the concurrence of the Government^nor^ & Council, The Council on Monday (yesterday) afternoon, appointed a Committee to join with a Committee of the House to answer Mr Mauduit Letter, & sent the Vote down to the House. The House being thin, as before nonconcurred it, alledging they had already answerd the Letter But this Morning the House being filled, as before, with 72 persons members, The Vote of the Council was reconsidered & concurred by the same Majority as the Vote for substituting M^r Is, Mauduit had been rejected: and A Committee was appointed to join the Committee of the Council After which the Speaker demanded of the Clerk the former letter, who answered he had delivered it to Mr Otis, who said he had sent it away.[4] As It was known that no Vessell could stir out of this port during this time, He was asked by whom he sent it: he refused to declare. upon which Violent debates insued; in the Course of which it was proposed to oblige him by Censures of the House to answer what he had done with the Letter; but moderate Men prevented the Question being put.

I believe Mr Mauduit has no idea of the confusion which the use of his & his Brothers Name is creating in the Councils of this Province; which must occasion great trouble to himself & cannot fail to defeat his purposes of introducing his Brother into the Agency; for which the Means at present used are directly opposite to propriety. The only way to retrieve this business is for Mr Mauduit to advise more with his old friends & trust less to his new ones; and then he will learn that the Governor Council & Assembly of this province are not to be drove in this Violent Way.

I expect this letter will go tomorrow the harbour being now clear; so shall conclude with assuring you that[5]

I am Sr Your &c

R. Jackson Esq_r

P.S. A Packet is arrived at NYork last fryday was sevnight Jan 21,[6] which we are told has brought account of a Cessation of arms; yet such is the Management of the post office here that I have not received my dispatches nor do I expect to have them till next Saturday 15 days after their coming to NYork

L, LbC   BP, 2: 252-257.

In handwriting of clerk no. 3, except where noted, with scribal emendations. May have enclosed a copy of Andrew Oliver to Jasper Mauduit, 7 Feb. 1763, Ford, *Jasper Mauduit*, at 92-94. A first draft of the enclosure was likely revised and re-dated in the light of the delays explained in the postscript to this letter.

1. Thomas Hutchinson was the source of this information, which was first published in 1767. Hutchinson, *History of Massachusetts*, 2: 85.

2. The following two paragraphs are in the hand of clerk no. 2.

3. The House's letter, adopted on 29 Jan., protested reasons of "publick Oeconomy" for not appointing Israel Mauduit as a joint agent or a deputy to his brother. The Speaker of the House of Representatives (Timothy Ruggles) to Jasper Mauduit, Boston, *JHRM*, 39: 189.

4. For these proceedings see *JHRM*, 39: 189, 193, 195.

5. This paragraph, the closure, and the postscript are in FB's hand.

6. Thus is manuscript: meaning that the package had arrived at New York on Friday 14 Jan.

187 | To Richard Jackson

Boston. Feb: 7. 1763.

Dear S^r

I have at length recieved my letters from N York & with them yours of Nov: 10,[1] informing me that you presented the book of Verses to the King.[2] As soon as the Assembly which is now sitting is up I shall communicate the contents of it to the Members of the College & have some care taken for the payment of the charges &c.

I had some difficulty to persuade them to undertake this work, they being diffident (& with great reason) of the Ha^r^vard[3] Muses, of whom I made a trial by giving premiums for different compositions on the Kings death, of which there were not many that deserved a place in the book. I was obliged to engage my assistance to get this business thorough & accordingly at different times flung in the first & the last Odes the Sapphic Epithalamium & all the Epigrams (excepting those two pretty Poems on the junction of Sol & Venus, which are too long to be called Epigrams) which specie[s][4] of Poetry they have but little idea of at Ha^r^vard College. I also undertook with another Gentleman to prepare the dedication, which was thought ~~to be~~ more proper to be in English Prose, as the College had never presented an Address. This I wrote wholly myself & it was recieved by them with great approbation. I hope the whole will have a good effect & not only set the College in a favorable light in England, but also help to enlarge the internal Discipline of it, which is at present too much narrowed by the old prejudices of the country, which still keep a considerable footing here tho they seem to wear off a pace every where else.

You give me great comfort (the first I have had) in saying that Pownall thinks there will be no difficulty in getting my grant confirm'd: tho the Island is not to answer expectation in regard to it's size: & the Value of it will greatly depend on the settling the adjacent Continent by the Grants of the 12 Townships: 6 of which extending from Penobscot river to mount desart which is not above 18 miles longitude, will be ready to send up in about a fortnights time. I shall also send a triplicate of my Grant the duplicate intended for the board of Trade being lost in its passage.[5] I have said so much on this subject in my former letters, that I need add no more. This being intended as an Answer to yours I here conclude & am

Dear S^rY^r M Affect &c.

R Jackson Esq

PS. I inclose with this an Address from the two Houses to me upon my informing them of the Cessation of Arms &c. If this Testimonial of this Provinces approbation of the Terms of peace is like to do it any Credit or Service among you, It may be put into some London Paper: which if you think Proper, you shall recieve in a Boston News Paper; & then it will become only an Article of News. The republishing at London is left to your discretion. I send the Secretary of State & the Board of Trade a Copy each. ^Since I wrote this, The News papers are come in, & I find in one of them my message & the Address[6] to me are printed, (not by my order or leave) & on the other side a whole page of Mr Otis's libelling;[7] which I should not have troubled you with if the address had been printed in any other paper If you think it fit to be reprinted cut it out &c^[8]

L, LbC   BP, 2: 260-262.

In handwriting of clerk no. 3, except where noted. Enclosed three copies of the *Boston Gazette*, 17 Jan. 1763.

FB authored or co-authored nine of the thirty-one contributions. He was the sole author of five (No. 6: "Adhortatio Præsidis"; No. 18: "Proximus A. Primo"; No. 19: "   Á   ;" No. 20: "Epitaphium"; and No. 31: "Epitaph") and the possible author of two (No. 8: "Cum Britonum Regem" and No. 9: "Cum Rex sciret Avum"). FB claimed authorship of another ode (No. 24: "In Regis Inaugurationem") plus the Epithalamium. He also co-wrote with Thomas Hutchinson the dedication piece, No. 1: "To the King." Justin Winsor, "Pietas et Gratulatio: An Inquiry into the Authorship of the Several Pieces," *Harvard University Library Bulletin* 1 (1879): 305-308.

---

1. Not found.

2. *Pietas Et Gratulatio Collegii Cantabrigiensis.*

3. The first written form of Harvard College was probably a phonetic rendition.

4. Letters are obscured by binding.

5. **No. 91** enclosed in **No. 191**.

6. Address of the Council and the House of Representatives to FB, 15 Feb. 1763, *JHRM*, 39: 245.

7. [James Otis Jr.], Letter to the Printers, *Boston Gazette*, 17 Jan. 1763, p. 3.

8. This insertion in FB's hand.

188 | From the Board of Trade

Sir,

Having had under Our Consideration the Acts passed in Massachusets Bay in 1761. & 1762, We have found amongst them no less than seven[1] (a List of the Titles of which is inclosed) for erecting New Towns, and giving such Towns all the Privileges of Other establishd Towns in the Province.

As it does not appear to Us, whether these New Towns will by this form of Constitution, be entituled to Representatives in the General Court; We shall suspend any determination upon them, untill We shall have received from You full Information upon this Point, to which end, and that We may know, with certainty & precision what is the Constitution and Practice of the Province in this case; We must desire that you will lose no time in transmitting to Us, an Exact List of the several Towns and Places, which send Representatives, distinguishing the Number, which each Place sends, when and by what Authority the right of Representation was first Establish'd and in what way this Right takes Place, whether by Petition to the General Court, or by direct application to the Governor.[2]

As the Knowledge of these matters is essential to His Majesty's Service, We desire you will be punctual in your Obedience to Our directions; of the want of which in Other Cases, We have but too much reason to complain, not having yet received from you any Answer to Our General heads of Enquiry, transmitted to You so long ago as the 28th. of April 1761,[3] and which Answers are in the present State of Affairs very materially necessary for Our Information.

We are, Sir, Your most Obedient humble Servants

Sandys.

Soame Jenyns.

Ed. Bacon.

Edmond Thomas

Geo. Rice.

Orwell[4]

Ex^d.

Whitehall Febry. 8th. 1763.

L, LbC CO 5/920, pp 151-153.

In the handwriting of John Pownall. Entrybook title: To Francis Bernard Esq'. Enclosed a copy of a List of the Titles of Acts Passed in Massachusets Bay in 1761 and 1762, for which see CO 5/920, pp. 151-153.

The Board's letter was issued following consideration on 27 and 28 Jan. of forty-eight acts passed in Massachusetts between Nov. 1761 and Jun. 1762, along with a report by Sir Matthew Lamb. The Board decided that those acts constituting new towns with the privileges of existing towns required further consideration. *JBT*, 11: 330-335.

---

1. Left marginal note: "five pass'd 6 March, & Two 11. & 12. Jun. 1762."

2. See **No. 205**.

3. **No. 46**.

4. Francis Vernon (c.1715-83), first Baron Orwell and created first earl of Shipbrook in 1777; first lord commissioner, 5 Jan.1763-12 Aug. 1765.

189 | To The Earl Of Egremont

Boston Feb 16. 1763

My Lord

I received the honor of your Lordship's Letter Signifying his Majesty's commands for my publishing his Royal Proclamations for a Cessation of arms.[1] As the general Assembly of the Province was then sitting, I immediately communicated these good tidings to the Council & the House of Representatives, who Very cordially joined with me in the solemnities used upon this occasion & have since presented to me an address expressing their sentiments upon this happy Event.

A Copy of this Address I beg leave to lay before your Lordship, as a public Testimonial of the unanimous Voice of the people of this Province in their grateful presentment of his Majestys paternal Care of the intrest of his American Subjects.

I am, with the greatest respect, My Lord, Your Lordship's most obedient & most humble Servant

Fra Bernard.

The Right Honorable The Earl of Egremont.

ALS, RC   CO 5/755, ff 19-22.

Enclosed a copy of the address of the Council and the House of Representatives to FB, 15 Feb. 1763, CO 5/755, ff 23-25.

---

1. Letter not found. The preliminary articles of the Treaty of Paris were signed on 3 Nov. 1762.

190 | To The Board Of Trade

Boston Feb 19. 1763.

My Lords

On the 20th of last Month M[r] Robert Temple Brother of the Surveyor general came to me & produced a Deputation from the Surv[r] gen[l] & praied that I would administer the Oaths of Allegiance & the Oath of Office of Depty Surv[r] gen[l] to him. I told him that I had heard that Gov[r] Shirley had refused to admit a Deputy to the late Surveyor general on account of the Gov[rs] 25th inst[n] (as it stands in my set) by which the Power of the Surv[r] gen[l], in some Cases, upon his absence devolves on the Gov[r].[1] This Instruction I read to him & observed to him it did by no means favour the Surveyor gen[l]'s deputising. But if his appointment contained such a power in express words, upon sight of that I might possibly be able to remove the Objection. Without that I could not think it proper to admit a person into an office not belonging to me, without any warrant or authority for so doing, at least without consulting your Lordships. Upon the whole I said, I would enquire into what Gov[r] Shirley did upon the like occasion & inform him further. In the mean time if He had a mind to take the Oaths of Allegiance, he might do it before two Councellors, as well as before me.

On the 26th of the same month M[r] Rob[t] Temple was with me again by appointment to meet M[r] Paxton, who was present at the transaction with Gov[r] Shirley, which he related as follows. "M[r] Lechmere (the late Surveyor gen[l]) attended Gov[r] Shirley with a letter from the Commissioners of the Customs giving him leave to go to England & directing him to appoint a Deputy; & presented M[r] Brinley[2] as his Deputy & desired he might be sworn. Gov[r] Shirley said he was orderd by the Kings instruction to fill up vacancies in the Custom house during the absence of the Surv[r] gen[l]; and that the Commissioners of the Customs could not supersede that instruction or authorise him to depart from it. Nevertheless if they would stipulate that the Deputation should be confined to matters not contained in the instruction & not set up in opposition to it, he would admit the Deputy: which being agreed to was accordingly done." Upon this I observed to Mr Temple that his Case differed from the former, in that he brought no letter from the Commissioners of the Customs to desire me to swear him in, as is usually done in appointments in the Custom house: nevertheless, if he would previously agree, that a express reservation of the powers of the instruction should be inserted in the Memorandum of the Oath to be indorsed on the Deputation, I would administer the oaths to him. This He refused, altho' for more certainty I repeated the offer more than once.

I have been since informed that Mr Temple has qualified himself before the Govr of New hampshire; & must therefore expect that some time or other this Deputation will be set up against the instruction; I must therefore desire your Lordships directions how to act upon the occasion. It seems to me at present that it was never intended that this instruction should be avoided by the Surveyor general's appointing Deputies, who not being known to or personally answerable to his Majesty's Ministers cannot be supposed to be so fit to be intrusted with the filling up Offices in the absence of the Surv^r gen^l, as the Governors of the sevral Provinces are: and if this Power is Vested in the Governors so as not to be avoided by a Deputation, the instruction which gives it can be superseded or relaxed no otherwise than by the same means by which it was at first made. All which I humbly submit to your Lordships, and am, with great respect,

My Lords Your Lordship's most obedient and most humble Servant

Fra. Bernard

To The Right Honble The Lords Commrs for Trade & Plantations

ALS, RC   CO 5/891, ff 132-133.

Endorsed: *Masssachusets*. Letter from Fra Bernard Esqr. Govr. of the Massachusets Bay, dated 19 Febry 1763, desiring the Boards directions upon a Claim of the Surveyor Genl. of the Customs to appoint Deputies, which he conceives will effect the intention of the 25th Article of his Instructions concerning the filling up Vacancies in the Offices of the Customs Reced Read April 27 1763. L.l. 49. Variant text in BP, 2: 62-64 (L, LbC).

The Board of Trade upheld FB's decision to refuse John Temple, in **No. 211**.

---

1. General Instructions as governor of Massachusetts, 30 Jun. 1761, CO 5/920, pp. 85-88. In the previous set, printed in **Appendix 1**, this was article 31.

2. Thomas Brinley (1726-84), merchant, distiller, Anglican, and future Loyalist. In 1749 he had married Elizabeth Craddock, daughter of George Craddock.

191 | To Richard Jackson

Boston. Feb: 21. 1763

Dear S^r

I have postponed continuing my letter from Feb: 1,[1] in hopes of the Sessions ending before I should be called upon for my letters. But the affair of Mr Mauduit has created such a deal of unnecessary squabbling that the Session is at least lengthen'd by a fo^u^rtnight more than it would otherwise have been.

I left the subject with the appointment of a joint Committee to answer Mr Mauduit's letter. The Chairman of that Committee reported a draught very much to the purpose of Mr Otis's letter, but so artfully disguised as to pass the Committee. But this would not stand the Test of the Council, who accordingly rejected all that tended to encourage Mr Mauduit to renew his application; & reduced that paragraph to terms of general civility only.

This being sent to the House they non concurred the amendment & concurred the original draught. Upon this the board adhered to the amendment & sent it down again. The second time the House concurred the amendment allmost unanimously, 6 out of 9 of the Committee voting against their own Report, & many who voted against it declared that they had misunderstood the question.[2] M^r O himself gave it up for which he afterwards gave his reasons for in these Words, as I am informed, "Damn the letter & D— M^r M[auduit][3]: I dont care a farthing for either but I hate the L— G— should prevail in any thing."[4]

Since this affair has been stirred, The press has swarmed with libels of the most scurrilous & most ~~abusive~~ vio^ru^lent kind: which have no other effect than to raise the abhorrence of all good Men, & all others who would be thought such. It's given out by O & his party, that M^r M is with the help of the dissenting interest, to get ^me^ removed. In short, his Name & Cause, is used to such infamous purposes, that he would be heartily ashamed of his Partisan; if he knew how he used ~~only~~ him as a tool ^only^ of his faction & turbulency

I before gave you a Caution about my being misrepresented to the Dissenters in London. I must now add that I should be glad if you would secure to yourself an early information of any thing of that kind that shall come to hand. And if it should seem to require preventing a prejudgement, untill the falsehood (for such it must be founded on) can be detected. I believe Lord Barrington will be a very proper & a ready Mediator. I am D^r S^r &c

R Jackson Esq$_r$.

P.S. I desire you would give me the earliest advice of an alteration in the administration of the plantations either in persons or offices. I have enclosed a triplicate of my Grant in the Cover to Mr Pownall[5]

L, LbC   BP, 2: 262-263.

In handwriting of clerk no. 3, except where noted. Enclosed a triplicate of **No. 91**.

---

1. **No. 186**.

2. These proceedings are noted in *JHRM*, 39: 201, 214, 268.

3. The first letter of Mauduit's surname is distinct but the rest of the letters have been erased.

4. Closing quotation marks supplied. Otis is referring to Lt. Gov. Thomas Hutchinson.

5. Postscript in FB's hand.

192 | To John Pownall

Boston. Feb: 22. 1763

D^r S^r

I hereby transmitt to you a Copy of an Address from the Council & House of Representatives in answer to my Message, informing them of the cessation of Arms, which if you think it proper, you will lay before their Lordships. I have sent a copy of the same to the Secretary of State.[1]

I was in hopes to have sent you the Acts of this Session by this conveyance: but the public business has been very much retarded by the animosities which have been introduced into the general Assembly by a violent prosecution of a request of Mr Mauduits to have his Brother Israel Mauduit associated with him in the Agency This purpose having failed in the Assembly is now become the Subject of Virulent libells against all concerned in the Administration or the support of the Government. If Mr Mauduit knew what a wicked use was made of his name & cause, & that they are now in the hands of a person, as his tools for the declared purpose of raising a flame in the government, I should think he would withdraw himself from those connexions as fast as he can.[2]

I find that the Miscarriage of the duplicates of my grant[3] which I sent for the use of your board has occasion'd some inconvenience: I therefore now send a triplicate. It is not on paper fit to go thro' public offices; but it is the only one I have: & I hope it will be tenderly handled.

I expect the Assembly will rise the End of this week, & then I shall write to you with more liesure than at present.[4]

I am S[r] &c

J Pownall Esq.

L, LbC   BP, 2: 264-265.

In handwriting of clerk no. 3. Enclosed copies of FB, message to the Council and the House of Representatives, Council Chamber, 7 Feb. 1763, for which see *JHRM*, 39: 218; address of the Council and the House of Representatives to FB, 15 Feb. 1763, ibid. 245; and **No. 91**.

---

1. FB to the earl of Egremont, Boston, 16 Feb. 1763, CO 5/755, f 19.
2. See **Nos. 185** and **191**.
3. **No. 91**. See **No. 193**.
4. **No. 198**.

193 | From the Board of Trade

Whitehall, March 11th. 1763

Sir

We have taken into Our Consideration your letter to Our Secretary, dated the first of December,[1] and the several Papers which you have addressed to the Board, relative to the Grant of the Island of Mount Desart, which the General Court of Massachusets Bay is represented to have made to you in July 1762.[2]

We can have no objection to your acceptance of this Grant as a Testimony of the approbation and favour of that Province, in whose Service, and in the Conduct of whose Affairs, you have manifested so much zeal and capacity, nor should We have delayed Our Representation upon it to the Crown, if the deed itself had been before Us. You are sensible there are some Circumstances peculiar to the situation of this Tract of Country which make it necessary to consider both the Case itself, and the manner of carrying such a Grant into Execution: When We shall be actually in Possession of the Grant We will bring the Matter to issue with all possible Dispatch, and endeavour to decide whatever questions arise upon it, in a manner which shall be agreable, and upon grounds which shall be just to all Parties concerned.

It may be proper to observe to you, that the doubt conceived upon the Claim of the Province of Massachusets is not founded upon the Allegation, that the lands to the East of Penobscot were not in the Possession of the Crown at the time of Granting the Charter, but upon the Operation which the Treatys of Riswick and Breda (by which Treaties this Tract of Country was ceded to France) should be admitted to have had upon the Charter itself.

We cannot take upon Us at present to say how far all future Consideration of this Question is precluded by the Order of Council grounded upon the Opinion of the Attorney and Solicitor General in 1731, this is a delicate point, which should be reserved till the deed shall come regularly before Us, and in the mean time We cannot think it expedient to advise any conditional Grant whatever of this Island. We are

Sir Your most Obedient humble Servants

C Townshend

Soame Jenyns

E^d: Bacon

Orwell

Francis Bernard Esqr. Govr. of the Massachusets Bay

LS, RC   BP, 10: 63-66.

In the handwriting of John Pownall. Endorsed by FB: Lords of Trade r May 14. 1763. Variant text in Prov. Sec. Letterbooks, 1: 379 (L, Copy); CO 5/920, pp. 154-156 (L, LbC).

A new Board had been constituted on 2 Mar. 1763, and at its first meeting considered FB's request for confirmation of the provincial grant of Mount Desert. *JBT*, 11: 338-339. When confirmation was refused, FB tried to break the deadlock on the question of provincial jurisdiction over Sagadagoc with a petition to the Privy Council delivered in Dec. (**No. 248**).

---

1. **No. 176**.

2. The correct date is February 1762.

194 | To Benning Wentworth

Boston March 14th. 1763

Sr.

I am desired by the Genl. Court of this Province to acquaint you, that they find it necessary to provide against the wast committed upon their lands at the Head of Nychiwannock river adjoining to your province. They have therefore appointed three Gentlemen to join with such as may appointed by your province to perambulate the line between the Province ^of New hampshire & the Province^ of Main so called, and to Ascertain the same by proper boundary marks: And I hereby request your concurrence with this proposal on the behalf of your Province. It will be necessary to provide a good practical Mathematician that may be depended upon for taking the Variation of the Compass: if you can furnish such a one we will look no further; if not, I will endeavour to procure a proper person

I am with great regard Sr. your most obet. and most

His Excellency Govr. Wentworth

L, LbC   BP, 2: 294-295.

In the handwriting of clerk no. 1 with scribal emendations.
     The Massachusetts-New Hampshire boundary dispute can be followed in Hutchinson, *History of Massachusetts*, 2: 290-297.

195 | To James Murray

Boston. Ap: 7. 1763

Sr

Last summer among the recruits which this Province raised for the Regulars there was a Mulatto, who was sent to Quebec. Before he left the Castle here, which was the head Quarters for recruiting, A Man of this Province claimed him as his Slave: but bringing no proof of his Title to him & the recruit appearing to ~~have~~ ^be^ more of the Indian than ~~Mulatto in him~~ ^negro^ cast, his claim was disallowed & the Recruit was forwarded with others to Quebec. Afterwards the Mans Title as his Slave being in some degree cleared up & the Officers concerned in the recruiting him being threatned with actions at law, I wrote to Genl Amherst[1] to desire he might be return^d^. In answer to this he wrote me word by a letter dated 29 Aug; that he would write to you to exchange the man for another, which I proposed to send to replace him.[2] But before this could be put in execution The Communication by Sea between this Town & Quebec was stopt. In this interval the Claimer of the Slave has brought an action against the commanding officer at the Castle (who was no ways concerned in recruiting him) for detaining him there, & has got a Verdict against him.[3] It is therefore become more necessary that this man should be returned. And as these kind of recruits are to be discharged upon the conclusion of peace, so that we have now, agreeably to the General, put a stop to this Service it will be to no purpose to send you another man in his Room, as was first proposed. The cheif concern will be to prevent this Man's escaping, as he will certainly endeavour to avoid returning to his Master if he can. The Master of the Vessel that carries this will take the charge of him: but I am afraid it will necessary to give orders that he be kept in custody till the master is ready to take charge of him. ^for^ if [he] has any notice of the intention, he will probably get out of the way.

About a year & a half ago Lt Peach came here from his surveying the River St Johns, & brought with him a letter of credit from you to me; upon which at his desire I gave him an order upon the Treasurer of the Province for 60 pounds Sterling, which he recieved. This still remains unpaid: the reason, why I have not troubled you with this before, was that I expected that an order for the repayment of this would come from New York: but I find myself referred to you for it.

Sometime after this, a Tradesman of this Town, Mr Gay,[4] had some Furrs, which he imported from Quebec, siezed for want of a certificate of their being ~~im~~ ^ex^ ported from thence. He applied to me to remitt the Governor's share of the forfeiture being £9 3s. 3d. Sterling, alledging in his favor that there was at that time no regular office at Quebec for the issuing such certificates. I told him that I apprehended (& the Judge of the Admiralty had been of the same opinion) that the fact of forfeiture being at Quebec, the Governors share would belong to you & not to me: And therefore I could do him no other Service that to report to you his Plea who was the proper judge of it:[5] I must add that it appeared that he had no interest to induce a fraudulent intention, as the acquiring a certificate would have cost nothing but the office fee. This money, to the amount above mentioned is in my hands & will not wait your order.

With the Greet &c

His Excell: G Murray.

L, LbC   BP, 2: 296-299.

In handwriting of clerk no. 3.

1. **No. 149**.

2. Amherst to FB, 29 Aug. 1762, New York, WO 34/27, p. 274.

3. For details see **No. 207**.

4. Martin Gay (1726-1809), a coppersmith and merchant of Boston, whose brass foundry brought him considerable wealth and status. He held several minor municipal offices and became a prominent Loyalist.

5. Thus in manuscript.

196 | To Jonathan Belcher

Boston. Ap: 7 1763

S^r

I am favoured with your letter of Jan: 21st.,[1] Since I first wrote to you on the subject of ye Boundary between the two Provinces, the Question has been quite changed: instead of, which is the River St Croix? as I then apprehended it, it is now, "Whether the River St Croix shall be the Boundary?"[2] We find this is the Question at home & like to be controverted. Therefore the General Assembly here appointed a Committee to examine their Right to the lands between Penobscot & St Croix; their report has been printed: & I shall order Mr Oliver to send you a Copy of it.

I dont find that there is any probability that more grants of this kind, will be applied for. Only six of the 12 Townships voted for are as yet made out; & they are not as yet sent home; but will be by the first opportunity These lie between Penobscot River & a River called Mount Desart river, and are so compactly laid out that they dont extend to more than 15 miles longitude. Of the other 6 I am told only three will be taken up at all which will extend from the East side of Mount desart River about 18 miles of longitude more. These will reach beyond the Island of Mount Desart, about 6 miles more or less. The other three I understand, are given up, on account of the badness of land as they say; but I rather believe from the incapacity of the adventurers to bear the Expence. There has been some little application for some Islands, which lie opposite to these Townships, but I dont find that the Assembly is inclined to encourage them.

Upon the whole I apprehend that we have Nothing to do at present but to wait for orders from home. My grant has not been brought upon the Carpet that I have learnt. I am advised that it's success will not depend upon the determination of the boundary; but that it may be favored at all Events.

I am with greatest &c your m obedt

The Hon: Lt Govr. Belcher.

L, LbC   BP, 2: 299-300.

In handwriting of clerk no. 3 with minor scribal emendations.

1. Not found.

2. Closing quotation marks supplied.

197 | To the Board of Trade

Boston Ap. 8. 1763

My Lords

I write this to introduce to your Lordships the Grants of six townships laid out on the East side of the River Penobscot, made by the general Court of this Province[1] & submitted to his Majesty for his royal confirmation according to the terms of the Charter. And tho' the soliciting this confirmation is properly the Business of the Grantees only, yet the Event is so intresting, to the Province in supporting their Right to originating grants of lands in this Territory, & to the Nation in encouraging a speedy cultivation of the Wast lands of North America, that I think it my duty to lay before your Lordships my sentiments upon both these points.

In regard to the Province's originating these Grants, I shall not enter into any disquisition of their Right to do so: If that is made a Question, the support of it must not depend upon me. I have perhaps allready engaged too far in it, in what I have before wrote upon this Subject. At present I only mean to show in what manner they have exercised this power in these instances which are the first of the kind; and from thence to show that this power is in hands, which are not like to abuse it.

1 These Grants have been made without any other consideration than a Covenant to settle the lands; not a farthing has been paid or stipulated for on the behalf of the province. 2. The Grants are not only made strictly conformable to the restrictions of the Charter, but there is also a limitation of the time in which the King's Confirmation is to be obtained; after which the Grants, which are in strictness only recommendations, for want of confirmation cease & determine. 3. The general Court has been so intent upon their main purpose, peopling the Country, that they have not trusted to the forfeiture for not settling, which in other grants has been the only obligation hitherto used, but they have obliged the grantees to give Security to settle their lands within a certain time after the Grants shall be confirmed; which bonds were lodged in the Secretaries Office, before the Grants were made.

From this I would infer, That the general Court having had the strictest regard to the public good in making these grants has shown itself worthy to be intrusted with this power & therefore deserves to have its acts approved & confirmed, if weightier reasons not known here should prevail against it.

I need not urge to your Lordships the expediency of encouraging, by all proper means, the cultivation of the wasts of Nº America. The Sentiments of your Lordships have been fully shown by your unwearied endeavours to promote such purpose: And now the Motives to it have received much additional strength by the late great enlargement of his Majesty's N American Dominions. But perhaps It may be of use to endeavour to remove the obstructions which may lie in the Way of your Lordships approving this settlement, & arise from your doubts concerning the Province's right to originate Grants of land within this Territory: which Question, if it is to be discussed with that deliberation which it's importance will require, may not be determined within the time necessary to resolve upon allowing or putting a stop to the proposed settlement.

Undoubtedly This Settlement must be of general advantage to the public, whether it shall appear hereafter to be in this or that province or in neither of them: and the undertakers deserve all possible encouragement to induce them to pursue their Scheme, which is certainly planned with good judgement for the mutual support of one another. The whole 6 Townships are laid upon a Neck of land lying between Penobscot River & a River called Mount desert river the Mouth of it being near the West End of the Island of that name. The whole Plan of the 6 Townships (each of which is intended to contain the Area of 6 miles square) extends not above 15 miles of longitude. The Spot is at present a Wilderness, & lies at a great distance from the settled parts of the Massachusets Province & at a much greater distance from the nearest Settlements of Nova Scotia, & would, if duly promoted, be the means of connecting, in time, one with the other. On the other hand if this settlement should be now prevented, It will cast a great damp upon undertakings of this kind, & may contribute to keep this great length of coast in the desert state in which It has hitherto continued.

I must therefore submit to your Lordships whether, in case your doubts concerning the right of the Province should still remain, It might not be advisable to disengage this Settlement from the dispute concerning the Right of the Province, & let the settlement go on to wait the determination of the right. To whatever province the Land shall be allotted, it will not be the Worse for having 360 families upon it. I urge this not on behalf of the Province which will gain nothing by such a proceeding but for the sake of the settlers, many of whom are embarked so deep in this Adventure that the disappointment may be their ruin. And with great submission I conceive, that this Method of favouring them is Very practicable, as it seems to require nothing but that in the Kings confirmation there be a recital of the doubts concerning the Provinces Right to these lands and a proviso that this Grant & Confirmation shall not prejudge the same, but that It shall still remain to be considered & decided, this Grant & confirmation notwithstanding.

I have been the more particular and indeed the more earnest in this representation, as I think it would be a great pity that a Settlement so compact & so well calculated for the public Utility should be prevented. There was an Application made to the general Court for 6 other Townships; but they do not go on: 3 of them are drop't allready; one of the other 3 proceeds and I beleive the other two will, if they are encouraged. These 3 Townships adjoin to the other six, & will help to strengthen them. The whole, if they are allowed to proceed, will form a settlement of 540 families. The first settling of a wast Country is so hardy a work that a little Discouragement is apt to defeat it: I therefore hope that this undertaking will meet with your Lordships favour.

I am, with great respect, My Lords Your Lordships most obedient and most humble Servant

Fra Bernard.

The Right Honble The Lords Commissioners for Trade & Plantations.

ALS, RC   CO 5/891, ff 136-138.

Contains minor emendations. Endorsed: *Massachusets* Letter [of][2] Francis Bernard Esq. Govr of the Massachusets Bay dated April 8 1763 informing the Board that the General Court had made [Grants] of six Townships on the East side [of the river] Penobscot, & hope for His Majesty's Confirmation according to the terms of their Charters And give sev.^l Reasons for the great Advantages that accrue thereby, & also inclosing Reced Read August 4. 1763 L.l.51. 1 Paper.
Variant text in BP, 2: 64-68 (L, LbC). Enclosed a copy of the General Court, Grant of six Townships on the East Side of the River Penobscot, 24 Feb. 1763, CO 5/891, ff 140-144 (signed by FB as governor, by Andrew Oliver for the Council, and by Speaker Timothy Ruggles for the House of Representatives).
This letter was read by the Board of Trade on 4 Aug. 1763. *JBT*, 11: 377.

---

1. On 2 Mar. 1762.

2. Faint here and below.

198 | To John Pownall

Boston. Ap. 8. 1763.

D^r S^r

A Grant of 6 Townships on the East side of Penobscot, being part of the 12 heretofore mentioned having Past the General Court last Session,[1] I take the opportunity of a small Schooner sailing for Bristol to send you one part of it together with a Copy of a State of the Province's right to the lands in question, which was reported to the general Court last Session by a committee appointed for that purpose.[2] I shall send other Copies of the same together with all other Papers due to the board of Trade by a Ship which will sail in a fortnight or three ^or four^ weeks. The Present is intended to prepare this business for consideration that as little time may be lost as may be. I apprehend that this business will not be got thro' before next Vacation: if it could it would be better, as it would much encourage & forward the Settlement. You will observe that this grant had its commencement at the Same time with my grant, that is before the Province had any notice of their Right to the Territory being doubted.

I am sensible that my recommendation of this settlement will seem to be influenced by my own interest. But I do assure you that if that was out of the Question, I should be as earnest, as I am, in this representation. For I do really think that this Scheme is so well calculated for the public utility, that it would be a great pity that it should miscarry.

With the next parcell I shall send you a map of these Townships,[3] that you may see how compleat & close they are laid down Altho their extent in longitude is not above 15 miles, yet Every one of them has a frontage to the Sea or to one of the Rivers which they lie between. I have sailed round great Part of this Land & can bear witness of the convenience of its Situation.

The Grantees are to take upon them the charge of obtaining his majestys confirmation; but if the Right of the Province to make such Grants is question'd, then the Province Agent is to undertake its defence. It is to provide for that the enclosed state has been prepared; which is not now sent to you as a memorial to be laid before your board For the Province has not had any formal Notice that their Right is disputed, & they therefore cannot defend it in form. you will therefore consider this paper only as a part of the Votes of the Assembly. Mr Jackson will be appointed to sollicit the conformation, as soon as the Grantees can be called together to name a Committee: in the mean time I am desired by a Principal man among them,[4] who has hitherto been Agent for the Whole, to use my Interest with Mr Jackson, that no time may be lost in the Prosecution of their business. Of the other 6 Townships you are not like to be troubled with more than the three which lie next to these Six, & of them only one has yet given bond to perform the conditions of settling.

As my Letter to their Lordships is only meant to introduce these Grants, I suppose it need not be presented till Mr Jackson is ready to offer the Grants for confirmation. I dont think it necessary for me to write to the Secretary of State: if I should, I can only refer to my ~~former~~ letter to their Lordships to whom in course of business it must be referred.[5] As I detain an impatient Vessel for these dispatches I shall enter upon no other business, reserving many other things for the next packett.

D^r S^r your &c.

John Pownal Esq

P.S. I have got a small Map of the land made to accompany this, the other is on a larger scale[6] & will accompany the duplicates in the next dispatches.[7]

L, LbC   BP, 2: 265-267.

In handwriting of clerk no. 3, except where noted, with scribal emendations. Enclosed copy of enclosure to **No. 197**; [FB], The boundary lines of seven townships east of Mount Desert or Union River, Feb. 1763, see BP, 10: 109-110 (AMs, AC); *A Brief State of the Title of the Province of Massachusetts-Bay to the Country between the Rivers Kennebeck and St. Croix.*

FB's plans to submit supporting documentation on the province's claim to Sagadahoc were disrupted when he was obliged to respond to a censure from Board of Trade (**No. 181**), but he managed to finish a paper in late April or early May (**No. 216**). FB's schedule is explained in **No. 213**.

---

1. On 3 Mar. 1762.

2. FB consented to the *Brief State* on 1 Feb. 1763.

3. Enclosed in **No. 200**.

4. The agent may have been one of the leading grantees such as David Marsh or Enoch Bartlett.

5. **No. 197**.

6. Enclosed in **No. 200**.

7. Postscript in FB's hand.

199 | To Richard Jackson

Nº. 10

Castle William. Ap: 9th [1763]

Dr Sr

The Grants of the 6 Townships on the East side of Penobscot River are at length finished: they have waited for the returns of the Surveyors, the Grantees giving them the Security &c. & I have but just now got some of them executed. I was very desirous that this business, if it should be practicable, might be got thro' the Offices before the vacation: but that I now give over. Nevertheless I am not inclined to leave any thing undone on my part, as I have already forwarded it as far as I have been able.

The General Court has left it to the Grantees to procure the Kings Confce ssion ^firmation^ of these Grants at their own Expence: which is but reasonable, as they are wholly gratuitous. But if the Right of the Province to make these Grants is disputed then the Province Agent is directed to support such Right. This is reasonable too: For it can't be expected that the Grantees should defend such Charter, or that the Province should leave such defence to them. The first Motion therefore to be made must be by the Grantees tendring their Grants at the proper Offices for his Majesty's confirmation

This business has been hitherto transacted with me by one gentleman living in Boston who is considerably engaged in this undertaking & has a great weight with the other Adventurers. I have promised to him that I would endeavour to engage you to undertake the Conduct of solliciting the Confirmation, which he thankfully accepted. But as He had no formal appointment to act for the others He has advertised a meeting of the Grantees to appoint a joint Committee to direct the solliciting the Confirmation & to raise a sum of Money for the expence of it. And he desired that in the mean time I would prevail upon you to take all necessary steps to bring the business forward & save time.

In this State things were, w hen I was informed 3 days ago that a Schooner was ready to sail for Bristol. As I know of no other Vessel that is like to sail from hence to England this month Yet, I laid hold of this opportunity to send you some papers to be doing with. I have prepared one of the Grants (the whole 6 being in the ^one^ deed) with a letter to the Lords of Trade to recommend *it* & a letter to Mr Pownall. I also send a printed Copy of a state of the Province's right to these lands as reported to the Assembly by a Committee for Mr Pownall & another for you: this I before sent in MS as a private paper.[1] I must refer to my letter to the Lords & Mr Pownall to prevent repeating which I have no time for. Nevertheless I shall give you some more of my thoughts upon this Subject just in the manner as they shall occur.

If the Lords should not be inclined at present to admit the Right of the Massachusets to this tract of land, yet I think they must have great reluctance to prevent the Settlement which at all Events must be very advantageous to the generality of his Majesty's Dominions. Most certainly if it is suffered to proceed, it will be a nest egg of an extensive population: on the other hand if it is disappointed, it will probably very much discourage the like Attempts for the future. This spot is at least 50 Miles distance from the nearest settled parts of the Massachusets, & I suppose near a hundred miles from the nearest settlement in Nova Scotia: I say this without having here any map to refer to. What a fine beginning may this Afford to connect the two Provinces together? And what a pity will it be that this opportunity should be lost upon account of a refined distinction against the plain letter of the Charter? & how will it be regretted, if after all, the Right of the Massachusets should be supported? as I can't help thinking it will if it is to be determin'd by legal Arguments only. I am sensible there may be good reasons for postponing the determination of the right of the Massachusets, not only upon Account of deliberation (if the exceptions to it shall be thought to des[erve]² it) but also in expectation of a new arrangement of this Country under a Compromise. But then let the Settlements go on with a proviso that it shall not determine the jurisdictional right. Whether this land shall [be] adjudged to the Massachusets within whose bounds it is literally contained, or to Nova Scotia, within whose bounds it ~~is literally~~ certainly is not contained, or to a New Province, which would perhaps be most advisable, if it could be done without change of injustice, It will not be the worse for having 700 or 1000 families upon it. For these reasons I have wrote to the Lords to recommend to them, with as much truth & sincerity, as if I had no Expectation in this Country, that if they are at present ^not^ disposed to Allow the right of the Province, they would, in favor of population, recommend the confirming these Grants, tho' with a proviso that they shall not prejudge the Provincial Right.

The Original Resolve of the General Court was for 12 Townships of which these are the 6 nearest to Penobscot. The other 6 go but slowly on, chiefly I believe on Account of the difficulties this business meets with. 3 of them are absolutely given up; the other 3 which are next to these 6 I believe, will go on. These kind of undertakings require the utmost encouragement: a little damp presently knocks 'em up. I fear I shall lose the proposed Settlement at Mount Desert for want of ability to close absolutely with them.

R. Jackson Esq_r³

L, LbC   BP, 3: 45-49.

In handwriting of clerk no. 3, except where noted. Enclosed copies of **No. 197** and its enclosure, plus two copies of the published version of *A Brief State of the Title of the Province of Massachusetts-Bay to the Country between the Rivers Kennebeck and St. Croix*.

Grants for twelve townships along the Penobscot River were voted on 20 Feb. and passed 2 and 3 Mar. *JHRM*, 38 pt 2: 265-267; *Acts and Resolves*, 17: 171-173. In 1764, the Board of Trade and the Privy Council considered the grants along with FB's Mount Desert grant and delayed confirmation of both until 1771. *JBT*, 12: 58, 63, 100; *APC*, 4: 614; 6: 369-371.

1. Enclosed in **No. 197**.

2. Letters are obscured by tight binding.

3. This line in FB's hand.

200 | *To John Pownall*

Boston. Ap. 17. 1763

D^r S^r

Last Night I recieved a letter from their Lordships dated Dec: 24 referring to a resolution of the board dated Dec: 10[1] in both which I find myself severely censured for having negotiated with the Province of Nova Scotia for ascertaining the boundary line between that province & this, & for assenting to grants of lands between Penobscot & St Croix

Ever since I have been in America I have studied not only to obtain but to deserve the approbation of their Lordships; upon some occasions I have been favoured with honorable testimonials of this acceptance of my services; & I have never as yet that I can recollect, been charged with one instance of gross neglect. I cannot therefore help taking to heart my being condemned without having an opportunity to explain my principles or conduct, either of which I'm persuaded would have made this reprimand unnecessary.

I shall be quite uneasy, till I have vindication myself from this charge: & as to do this, in as full a manner as my present feeling seems to demand, will require a retrospect of this business for near two years past & a resort to many public papers, I have no other way to ease myself for the present, but to transmitt to you the heads of my proposed vindication drawn up hastily & without any address, that it may be used in such a manner, as you shall see Cause to apply it.

I should have wrote directly to their Lordships, if the time between the coming & return of the New York post, by which I send this, would have admitted of it. As it is I must desire you would not let this Apology, hasty as it is be wanting to my vindication: but will lay it before their Lordships whenever you shall see a fit & necessary occasion for it. I shall consider at more leisure, what will be necessary to add to it in my next dispatches.

I am S^r your most faithful

J Pownall Esq.

PS. Ap: 30 to the Preceding Letter

The foregoing Letter in the original was sent to New York last Monday sevnight & I hope is now at Sea on board the Harriot packet. In the hurry, both of Time & Mind, which I was in When I wrote it; I did not think proper to address their Lordships. I have since revised the memorial I sent to you of which I now send a duplicate, & find no[thing] ~~more~~ improper in it & little more wanting than the Proofs that are to support it. These I now send with a letter to their Lordships explaining them & referring them to the memo[rial]. The single Fact of Govr Pownalls taking a formal possession of the East side of Penobscot on the behalf of the Province of Massachusets Bay & having it recorded in the Secret[ary's] Office[2] is alone sufficient to justify me in what I have done.

L, LbC   BP, 3: 49-50; the postscript is on pp. 55-56.

In handwriting of clerk no. 3. The conjectured readings are for letters obscured by tight binding. This is a fair version of a heavily annotated rough draft in BP, 10: 67-73 (ADft, AC), that incorporates most of the substantive corrections. Enclosed **No. 201**; John Jones, Plan of Twelve Townships east of the Penobscot River [*Apr. 1763*], formerly stored in Spencer Bernard Papers, MP/14, but which has not been found.

---

1. **No. 181**; *JBT*, 11: 313.

2. On 23 May 1759.

201 | Apology to the Board of Trade

[16-17 Apr. 1763]

The Heads of an Apology for the Conduct of Governor Bernard in regard to the lands Eastward of Penobscot.

I was not a prime mover in any of the proceedings of the General Court of the Province of Massachusets Bay in regard to the lands Eastward of Penobscot, not even in the grant made to me. I was only the Executor of the general Court's resolutions, in which I have acted with a conscientious regard to my duty, as far as my judgement could point it out. It was in pursuance of such resolutions that Application was made to the Govern.: of Nova Scotia to join in a Survey of the River S.t Croix, which was supposed to be the undoubted boundary of the two Provinces: altho it might be doubted which was the River S.t Croix.

The Distinction of the River Penobscot bounding French Acadia & from thence being applicable to the limiting the Territory of Sagadehock was not then known to any of the members of the general Court, as far as I can learn. For my own part I can say that it was quite new to me, when I was first advised of it long after that time.

The apprehension that it might be a question which was the river S.t Croix was founded upon an observation, that there were at least two rivers that fall into the Bay of that name. As the determining this Question must depend upon comparing the apparance of the Country with the description of it as given by former Navigators, it became a Matter of surveying only; & therefore there was no doubt but that the two Provinces might ^take upon them to^ join in ascertaining such facts as should be necessary for the determination of the boundary.[1]

It was never in the least presumed that these observations should prejudge his Majesty: they were expressly designed to be submitted to him as informations subject to his judgement. And as soon as it was known that the Question of the boundary would not depend upon the identity of the River S.t Croix, but upon Arguments distinct from those of local Observation, the Purpose of the Survey of S.t Croix was laid aside.

The Grants of the 12 Townships Eastward of Penobscot were not resolved upon till after repeated sollicitations of the intended Settlers & at a time when there was no apprehension on either side that the right of the Province to these Lands would be disputed. It was above 6 months after the resolution of the general Court, which empowred the Grantees to survey the Lands, that I recieved an intimation from London that the Right of the Province to lands eastward of Penobscot was doubted. I had before that, wrote to the Lieutent Gov.r of Nova Scotia to let him know that I would consent to ^no^ others Grants on that side [of] Penobscot, till his Majesty's pleasure concerning these should be known.[2]

But I did not think, I coud with Propriety, stop the completion of these grants: for that 1 The Grantees upon the credit of a resolution of the General Court having put themselves to considerable expence in surveying etc it would ^scarce^ have been equitable to have refused them an opportunity of applying to his Majesty for a confirmation of their Grants: 2 the Province being desirous to settle these lands as soon as possible & earnest to support their right thereto, the question whereof could be brought on, by no means so proper as submitting a grant to his Majesty for his confirmation, I could not consistently with the good understanding which I have hitherto preserved in the Gene^l^: Court, have obstructed their proceedings, without having any instruction, or order for so doing. 3 I had a third reason for letting these Grants proceed; which was, that the settling this country must be advantageous to the King at all events, whether it should be adjudged to one Province or the other. And on this I have cheifly relied in my recommendation of these grants to their Lordships.

Nevertheless I took care that in the draught of the grants all proper Reservations & Provisos should be inserted; & that the whole tenor of them should be significant of the humility with which they are submitted to his Majesty. Not only the Terms of the Charter are observed, but there is a proviso for avoiding the Grants, if his Majesty's confirmation shall not be obtained in 18 Months time: a caution which exceeds that of a suspending clause; which last is generally allowed to be a sufficient Apology for a Governors consenting to an Act the expediency of which he doubts of.

In regard to the Grant made to me, It was meerly accidental that it was in this country.[3] It took its rise from an opinion, which prevailed in the general assembly, that the Province ought to make me a Compensation for the expences of my second Commission & for some Charges I had been at in making some additions & improvements at the Province-House & at ~~of both these~~ the Governor's apartment at the Castle: the whole of both these amounting to 600 pounds sterling. This Compensation w^d^ have been made in money if the expences of the War had not discouraged Pecuniary Grants. It was then proposed to do it by Grant of lands to the Westward; & one or two Spots were mentioned for that Purpose. Afterwards the Application of Settlers at Penobscot being agitated, the Assembly turned their Eyes to the Eastward for a grant for me: & ^it was^ not many days before the Grant was made, that I first heard of the Island of M^r^. Desart: I had all along left it to the Assembly to make this Compensation in what manner they Pleased: & to the last I was no otherwise active in it than barely signifying my acceptance of this proposal.

This affords a plain Proof, that I did not at that time Apprehend that the Right of the Province to these lands was like to be disputed. If I had, I should have certainly chose, as I might have done, a grant of lands to the Westrd, where the right was undoubted, preferable to these where it is controverted.

Ms, LbC   BP, vol. 3: 51-56.

In handwriting of clerk no. 3. The "Apology" was composed before FB finished the cover letter to John Pownall in which it was enclosed (**No. 200**). He likely drafted and emended the document during the night of 16 Apr. and the following day his clerk entered a fair copy in the letterbook. The draft is in BP, 10: 69-73 (ADft, AC). There is a clear text transcript of the draft in Sawtelle, "Sir Francis Bernard and His Grant of Mount Desert," at 225-228.

---

1. See **No. 169**.

2. **Nos. 181** and **196**.

3. This is most unlikely, since FB's ownership ultimately depended upon the province's claim of jurisdiction over Sagadahoc. The Mount Desert Island grant may also have been intended to soften FB's opposition to a provincial bill to supplant the writs of assistance, although in this Otis and his colleagues were disappointed. Nicolson, *The 'Infamas Govener'*, 73-74.

202 | *To the Board of Trade*

Boston Ap 25. 1763

My Lords

By a letter dated the 8th inst I informed your Lordships that the general Court had passed a Grant for 6 Townships on the East side of the river Penobscot to be submitted to his Majesty for his confirmation: and I humbly offer'd to your Lordships such observations & reasons as have induced me to recommend this settlement to your Lordships favour.[1]

About a week after this packet was sent away, I received your Lordships letter of Dec 24,[2] which has given me a most sensible mortification: for I had flatterd myself that I stood in such a degree of credit with your Lordships, that I should not easily have been suspected of acting, with intention, in opposition to your Lordships opinion or in prejudice of his Majesty's right. As I am persuaded that upon a full & true state of this affair, Your Lordships will readily acquit me of this imputation, I was desirous of being discharged from it as soon as possible. I therefore by the return of the Post to New York sent a short defence of my Conduct inclosed in a letter to M[r] Pownall,[3] desiring him to lay it before your Lordships at such time as he should think it fit and necessary. I should have addressed myself immediately to your Lordships, if the hurry I was in had not made me prefer the form of a memorial. And as upon a revisal I find it contains the cheif substance of my defence, I shall avoid repeating, as well as I can, &, in this, explain such proofs, as I shall think proper to introduce in support of my allegations

The Proofs I have to submit to your Lordships are these: a Copy of the order of the general Court for the settlement of the line between the Massachusets & Nova Scotia; a Copy of the report of the Committee appointed for that purpose; a Copy of my letter to The Lt Govr of Nova Scotia, in pursuance of the report of the Committee, wrote in Council & recorded there; A Copy of the record of the election of Commissioners to join those of Nova Scotia to repair to St Croix & ascertain the line &c; a Copy of my Letter to the Lieut Governor of Nova Scotia, in pursuance of the last mentioned act of the general Court, wrote in Council

From these will appear; 1 That I was not a mover of this intended Survey, and that, if I am blameable for any thing, it is only for consenting to the resolutions of the two houses: with what propriety I could refuse my consent thereto will be considered hereafter. 2 That the deliberation of the general Court turned solely upon these questions: which stream was the river St Croix? and from what part of that river the Northern Line was to be run? and that they were not aware of an objection to their title arising from any other consideration. 3 That in my consenting to these resolutions & consequentially communicating them to the Lt Govr of Nova Scotia, I judged for the best, if nothing then appeared to me to invalidate the report of the Committee, which I found to be agreable with the letter of the Charters of Nova Scotia & Massachusets Bay.

I cannot say whether at that time the boundary of Acadia as ceded by Charles the second to France was in my thoughts or not: but this I am sure of, that I had not the least apprehension that such boundary was applicable to the limitation of King William's Grant to Massachusets Bay. As a presumptive proof thereof (the only kind of proof which such an Asseveration is capable of) It appears that my immediate predecessor Govr Pownall, altho' he came to this Government directly from England, was not acquainted with this objection to the Provinces right. If He had, I am sure that He, who was never reckoned inattentive to his Duty would not have taken a formal & monumental possession of the East side of Penobscot on the behalf of the Province of Massachusets Bay;[4] as it appears, from the inclosed Copy of the record of that transaction, that he did. This Transaction alone, which I must suppose was communicated to your Lordships board & was never, that I have heard of, excepted to, must justify me in presuming that the East side of Penobscot was allowed to belong to Massachusets Bay.

In regard to my consenting to the grant of the 6 Townships, I beleive, I might, after what I have allready said, safely trust my justification to the grant itself, in which so much care has been taken to provide for the Kings rights & the public Emolument. But It may be necessary to state to your Lordships the times & manner in which it was made. The first Grant originated in the House of Representatives Feb 20. 1762; (see Votes pa 265) & having been concurred by the Council received my Consent. This Grant amounted to a positive assurance of 6 Townships, of the contents of 6 miles square each, to the 360 Grantees, altho' it was incomplete, untill, by an actual survey, the boundaries of The Townships could be ascertained. This Survey was not perfected till the end of the Summer following; and it was certified upon Oath to the general Court at the first Session after: when on Feb 24 1763 a positive Grant was order'd to be passed under the Province Seal to be laid before his Majesty for his approbation. (See the Votes pa 277)

Between the times of the originating the grant & the completing it by an Authentic instrument, I was advised that probably an Objection arising from the bounds of Charles the seconds cession might be urged against the Provinces right; and the general Court received the same intimation from the Province-Agent. But I was so far from thinking that that would authorise me, without an order from your Lordships, to put a stop to this business, that I was rather inclined to forward it as much as might be, thinking it the best & easiest Way of bringing this right into Question. And I still persuade myself, that, when your Lordships have perused this grant, you will think that the general Court has introduced their claim, in as respectful & proper a manner as they could well have done. Nevertheless upon the first notice of these doubts concerning the Provinces right, I resolved to consent to no more grants 'till the present shall be determined upon.

I am Very unwilling to extend the trouble I now give your Lordships unnecessarily: and therefore for the rest I shall only refer to my former letters upon this subject; from the whole tenor of which I flatter myself your Lordships will perceive that from the first time I had reason to think that this Question was like to be controverted, I have expressed an earnest desire that I might be engaged in it as little as my station would permit: and tho' I have thought it my duty to lay before your Lordships such arguments as I knew would be urged in favour of the Provinces right, yet your Lordships must have observed that the general Service of his Majesty in extending the population of his Dominions has been my cheif purpose.

> I am, with great respect My Lords, Your Lordships most obedient & most humble Servant

> Fra. Bernard.

To The Right Honble The Lords Commissioners for Trade & Plantations.

ALS, RC   CO 5/891, ff 146-149.

Contains minor emendations. Endorsed: *Massachusetts* Letter from Francis Bernard Esq[r]. Gov[r]. of the Massachusets Bay dated 25. April acknowledging the receipt of the Boards Letter of 24th. Decem[r] and is extreemly concerned by incurring their Lordships Displeasure in respect to the Settlement of the Line between that Province and Nova Scotia—gives some Reasons in his Justification—as well as to the Grant of the six new Townships & inclosing, Reced June 27. 1763. Read August 4.— L.l. 53. 1 Paper.

There is a heavily corrected first draft in BP, 10: 75-82 (ADft, AC) and a fair copy incorporating the revisions in BP, 2: 69-74 (L, LbC). The differences between the RC and the other variants are insubstantial, except where noted.

Enclosed **No. 127**; certificate of Gov. Thomas Pownall's taking possession of the east side of Penobscot for Massachusetts, 23 May 1759, CO 5/891, ff 150-151; an order of the General Court for the settlement of the Massachusetts-Nova Scotia boundary line, 26 Jan. 1762, CO 5/891, f 152; FB to Jonathan Belcher, Boston, 3 Apr. 1762, CO 5/891, f 152; an extract from the report of a committee of the Council and the House of Representatives on the boundary line and the Penobscot land grants, [*18 Feb. 1762*], CO 5/891, f 153; an extract of the record of the election of Massachusetts's boundary commissioners, CO 5/891, f 153.

The letter and enclosures were referred to the secretary of state on 13 Oct. 1763.

---

1. **No. 197**.

2. **No. 181**.

3. **No. 201** in **No. 200**.

4. LbC: clause ends with "East side of Penobscot Bay."

203 | *To the Board of Trade*

Boston Ap. 29. 1763

My Lords

The Secretary having prepared Copies of the Acts passed last Session to be transmitted to your Lordships, I have looked them over & do not find Any thing in them but what is in usual Course of business or what I have before observed upon.[1] The Act for continuing expiring Laws[2] is the same with many others which have been before approved: this Legislature deals so much in temporary Laws that it is become necessary to include many of them in one act of Continuation to avoid the immense multiplication of Paper & Parchment, which would otherwise follow. And as all these Acts have separately received his Majesty's approbation I apprehend that there can be no inconvenience arise [*arising*] from their being continued by one act. There's a Bill to continue a former lottery bill to raise the additional Sum of 225 pounds sterling for building a bridge:[3] The Commissioners advanced the Money out of their own pocket & the Sum is so trifling, that I presume it needs no Apology.

I am much concerned that your Lordships have wanted my Answer to your general heads of Enquiry transmitted to me in 1761:[4] The whole Reason of my delaying it has arose from my desire of making it as complete as possible. Many of the Queries, especially those, which are like to Vary from former reports of this kind, could not be answered so precisely, in time of War as upon the conclusion of peace. And, as from the time I received your Lordships commands, We have been continually led on from day to day with the hopes of that happy Event, I have in like manner been insensibly drawn in to postpone this business to a greater length of time that I was aware of. I think it was much above a year that I acquainted M[r] Pownall of my intention to make this my first business after the conclusion of peace; and I shall immediately, with as little loss of time as possible, bring this Matter to a speedy conclusion.[5] The cheif Article that will take up much time will be the Numbring the People under Proper heads of Age sex Town &c. This will take up great part of the Summer & cannot be set about till after the Assembly meets, as I shall want their assistance in it. I shall however finish my Answer to the other Articles & leave this to be sent after it.

As soon as I received your Lordships letter concerning the return from the impost office[6] I communicated it to that officer[7] & desired him to give your Lordships all the further information that is in his power, which he promised to do. I expect to receive this time enough to Send by this packet; when I shall acquaint your Lordships with the difficulties he is under in distinguishing between British & Foreign Sugar & Molasses, that your Lordships may judge how far the best account he can give is to be depended upon.

Since I have wrote the last paragraph I have received the Account of the Impost officer which I hereby inclose. From the Conversation I have had with him I write what follows, as from his own mouth.

When I first acquainted the impost Officer with your Lordships first order, He said He could not take upon him to distinguish between British & Foreign Sugars & Molasses; for the duties He was to receive being the same on both, it was no concern of his office whether they were the one or the other: and therefore he never intrested himself in an inquiry from what port the goods came.

Upon my communicating to him your Lordship's last letter[8] & requiring him to give all the information upon these Articles which he could, He has given me an Account of these goods with all the distinctions which are enter'd upon his books: but at the Same time he is obliged to give his reasons why the Authority of such distinctions is not to be depended upon 1: His Office not being intrested in the distinction of the port; whence the goods come & the Act not requiring any such distinction he has taken the Word of the Master for the entry of the Port from which, without any enquiry into the truth of such report. 2. As the Duty of Sugar & Molasses is the same, he has taken the report of the Master for the quality of those goods, without enquiry into the truth of it: and he has been occasionally informed some times, that Sugar has been enter'd as Molasses

Nevertheless He beleives that in general the Entries made from the West Indies are of foreign Sugars &c; as he knows of no reason that can induce those Masters who came from British Ports not to enter as from such; and that the entring sugars as Molasses is not Very frequent, & probably onely in the coasting trade. Upon the whole, He thinks that in regard to the West Indies, his Entries may afford a probable calculation of the proportion of the import of British & Foreign Sugar & Molasses. But then He conceives it is not Very applicable to times of peace, especially in regard to Sugars; which last will not be to be had in any quantity from French Settlements, tho' Molasses may possibly be procured from thence.

He observes that the Entries from Salem[9] in the Years 1755-6-7 & 8 must be supposed to be mostly included in the Entries from the West Indies, the greater part of which in those years were made at the Port of Salem. The Molasses enter'd from Barbados & Antigua are generally supposed not to be the Produce of those Islands but foreign Molasses brought into them in prizes or otherwise. The other British Islands, but most cheifly Jamaica, have of late sent Molasses of their own growth in some quantity to North America.

This Gentleman, who is of the Council, is a Very fair & candid Officer: but as his appointment is by an annual election, He is obliged, in point of prudence, not to carry the execution of his office any further than the Duties of it necessarily require.

I am, with great respect, My Lords Your Lordships most obedient & most humble Servant

Fra Bernard

To The Right Honble The Lords Commrs of Trade & Plantations

ALS, RC   CO 5/891, ff 154-157.

Endorsed: *Massachusets* Letter from Fra[s]. Bernard Esq[r]. Gov[r]. of the Massachusets Bay, to the Board, dated 29. April 1763, transmitting Acts &c with some Observation, and promising a particular answer to the B[ds]. Queries. Reced June 27. 1763. Read Aug[st]. 4.__ L.l.55. 1 Paper.
Variant text in BP, 2: 78-82 (L, LbC). Enclosed copies of [James Russell], an account of West Indies goods imported into the Province of Massachusetts Bay from 1755 to 1762, Apr. 1763, CO 5/891, ff 158-173; a survey for six townships on the east side of the River Penobscot, Feb. 1763, for which see BP, 10: 97-100. This letter was read by the Board of Trade on 4 Aug. 1763. *JBT,* 11: 377.

1. There is a full list of legislation that FB consented to on 25 Feb. 1763 in *JHRM,* 39: 286-287.

2. An act for reviving and continuing sundry laws that are expired and near expiring, 3 Geo. 3, c. 23 (passed 24 Feb. 1763). *Acts and Resolves,* 4: 617-618.

3. An act for the continuation of a lottery (granted and allowed by an act entitled, an act in addition to an act entitled an act for raising a sum of twelve hundred pounds by lottery, for building and maintaining a bridge over the River Parker, in the town of Newbury, at a place called old town-ferry) for raising a further sum for that purpose, 3 Geo. 3, c. 21 (passed 26 Feb. 1763). *Acts and Resolves*, 4: 615-616. The act herein referred to is 33 Geo. 2, c. 35 (passed 28 Apr. 1760). Ibid., 4: 326-327.

4. **No. 46**.

5. This is not mentioned in any of the extant letters to John Pownall.

6. **No. 87**.

7. James Russell (1715-98), brother of Chambers Russell and a merchant of Charlestown, Mass., was the representative for Charlestown, 1746-50 and 1753-60, a member of the Governor's Council, 1760-73, and annually elected commissioner of Impost, 1763-74.

8. **No. 87**.

9. In James Russell's report, Salem (as well as Connecticut, New York, and Halifax) is listed under the same heading as the West Indies as if it were a source of imports.

204 | *Circular from the Board of Trade*

Whitehall April 29th. 1763[1]

Sir

The King having judged it proper that a Publick Thanksgiving to Almighty God, should be observed throughout all his Majesty's Colonies in America, on the happy Conclusion of the Peace; We have received his Majesty's Commands to signify to you his Royal Pleasure that you do, upon receipt of this Letter, appoint a proper and early day of Thanksgiving[2] to be observed by all his Majesty's good Subjects under your Government, in such manner and with such Forms of Prayer as have been usual on like Occasions, We are Sir your Most Obed[t] humble Serv[ts]__

Shelburne

Orwell   Soame Jenyns

Bamber Gascoyne[3]   Edw[d]: Bacon

John York

Geo: Rice

Francis Bernard Esq[r]. Gov[r] of Massachusetts Bay

L, Copy   Prov. Sec. Letterbooks, 1: 418.

In the handwriting of John Cotton, deputy province secretary. Enclosure not found.

This letter is the first communication from a new Board established by the Grenville ministry in Apr. 1763. *JBT*, 11: 354-356.

---

1. Left marginal note: "Lords of Trade order for Thanksgiving."

2. 11 Aug. 1763, as advised by the Governor-in-Council on 27 Jul. Council Executive Records, 1760-1766, CO 5/823, f 224.

3. Bamber Gascoyne (1725-1791), politician, MP for Maldon, 1761-65, and Midhurst, 1765-68; a lord commissioner at the Board of Trade, 1763-65; returned to the Commons in 1770, as MP for Weobley, and to the Board, where he remained until 1779.

205 | To the Board of Trade

Boston. Ap 30. 1763

My Lords

I have received your Lordships letter of Feb 8th requiring a full information concerning the constitution of the House of Representatives of this Province.[1] This I shall state to your Lordships with all the precision I am able to do.

By the Charter Evry Town is impowered to elect two Persons to serve for & represent them in the general Assembly. But by an Act of the 4th of Will & Mary ca 19[2] No Town is allowed to send 2 members but what has 120 freeholders: Evry Town that has 40 freeholders is obliged to send one representative; A Town tha[t] has above 30 & under 40 freeholders may send a representative or not as they please; A Town under 30 freeholders may send a representative or join with the next in the choice of a Representative; Boston alone is allowed to send 4. By an Act of the 5th of Will & Mary ca 11 The Qualification of a Voter is declared to be his giving Oath that he is worth 40 pounds sterling or a freehold estate of 40 shillings per an.[3]

If according to this regulation Evry Town should avail itself of its utmost power to send representatives, The Number would be very large indeed. But as the sending a Member is a burthen upon a Town instead of being exerted, it is avoided as much as possible: so that it scarce ever happens that a Town, which has a right to be excused, sends a representative: and of those which are obliged by law to send one, a great many make default; that it is frequent for the House of Representatives to fine Towns for not sending Members. (see Votes pa 12). Your Lordships will see at the beginning of the Votes of each year a list of the Towns supposed to send Members distinguishing who have made returns & who not: These are not correct, but near so enough to form a calculation.[4] In the list in 1762, being the last return, there appear to be 168 Towns (reckoning joint Towns as one) which are supposed to be obliged to Send Members, of which 64 have made default & 104 have returned: of these last only 4 have sent more than one member, so that there appears to be 110 (including the supernumeraries of the 4 towns) Representatives returned. I will suppose that much the greater part of these Towns have a right, if they please, to send two representatives & that there are many other Towns not named in this list which have a right to send one representative: so that the House is capable of a great encrease even tho' there was no New Settled Country to contribute to it.

I wrote to your Lordships upon this Subject in a letter dated Aug 3 1761,[5] which I desire may be read, as if inserted here; for which purpose I shall inclose with this a triplicate of it. Upon account of my representations in that letter your Lordships sent me his Majesty's Relaxation of the instruction. Altho' this left me at liberty to consent to incorporating Townships without any restriction, yet I hav[e] observed ^the instruction^ in all instances of carving new Townsh[ips] out of old ones, in which Case, I have made it a rule that the New Town should join with the old one, from whence it was taken, in a representative. An instance of this the Town of Great Barrington lately constituted by Act[6] will afford.

Since I have received the relaxation of the instruction, The Bills for constituting Townships in the new settled Counties have been silent in regard to their being represented; of course they are left to the laws, which I have before stated. When one of these Towns has a sufficient Number of freeholders It is intitled to a precept as a matter of right. But it is generally expected that they will decline that priviledge as long as they can, to avoid the Expence of it. In short, My Lords, It were to be wished that some proper method could be devised to limit the general Number of Representatives: But It seems to me that it should be done rather by contracting those of the old Counties than by preventing a New County from being competently represented.

I dont apprehend that the difficulty of this reform will be so great in the planning the Work as in the reconciling the People to an alteration which tends to the contracting their representation. It might be done effectually by enlarging the Number of freeholders that shall give a Town a right to send one Member & as for Towns that have not such a Number, to join them together in chusing a Representative, as many allready are. The ascertaining this Number will depend upon the Whole Number of freeholders in the Province, which I shall endeavour to learn, this Summer; & from thence may be calculated what Number of freeholders should go to the constituting a Representative to keep the House within a proper Number of Representatives.

I am, My Lords, with great respect, Your most obedient & most humble Servt

Fra. Bernard

To The Right Honble the Lords Commrs⁵ for Trade & Plantations

ALS, RC   CO 5/891, ff 174-176.

Contains minor emendations. Conjectured readings are for letters lost where the manuscript is torn. Endorsed: *Massachusets* Letter from Francis Bernard Esqr Govr. of the Province of the Massachusets Bay dated April 30th 1763, acknowledging the receipt of the B^ds. Letter of the 8. Febry & giving a full Information concerning the Constitution of the House of Representatives. Reced Read August 4. 1763. L.l.57.
Variant text in BP, 2: 74-78 (L, LbC). The "triplicate" letter which FB mentions he enclosed was **No. 59**. This letter was read by the Board of Trade on 4 Aug. 1763. *JBT*, 11: 377.

---

1. **No. 188**.

2. An act for ascertaining the number and regulating the House of Representatives, 4 Will. 3 & Mary, c. 38 (30 Nov. 1692). NB: the legislative chapter given in this note and those that follow is consistent with modern notation.

3. An act to prevent default of appearance of representatives to serve in the General Assembly, 28 Nov. 1693, c. 14, sect. 8. An act of 1692-93, c. 36, setting a voting qualification of £40 of property was disallowed by the Privy Council (although subsequent acts containing that provision were not: 1693-94, c. 14; 1694-95, c. 28), while later acts (1696, c. 5; 1697, c. 7 and c. 15; 1698, c. 40) raised the bar to £50. *Acts and Resolves*, 1: 363n to c. 4.

4. LbC: "general Calculation."

5. **No. 59**.

6. An act for erecting the north parish or precinct, in the town of Sheffield, into a separate town by the name of Great Barrington, 2 Geo. 3 c. 9 (passed 30 Jun. 1762). *Acts and Resolves*, 4: 465-467.

206 | To Richard Jackson

Boston. May. 4. 1763

D^r S^r

    I have before now acknowledged the receipt of all your letters, except that Sent [me?]¹ by Govr. Franklin the cheif substance of which I had in other letters:² Your latest is dated Nov: 10.³ I could have wished to have heard either from you or Mr Pownall, by the last packet, by which I received a severe reprimand from the Lds of Trade⁴ for intermeddling with the affair of Nova Scotia. I am told that I could not be ignorant that the River Penobscot being the boundary ~~of Nova Scotia. I am told that I could not be ignorant that the River Penob~~ of Acadie as ceded to France made the Provinces Title to Lands East of that River so questionable that it was improper for me to assent to Grants East of that River & that the countenancing a proposition for ascertaining the boundary at St Croix was an aggravation of my misconduct.

I have given an answer to this in a hasty, but I hope in a decent & a full manner. The Substance of my defence is this: 1st I was ignorant of the objection to the Province's right to Lands Eastward of Penobscot arising from the Cession of Acadia to France & so was, as far as I know, Evry Member of the General Court: so was also my Predecessor Govr Pownall, as will appear from the record of his taking a formal possession of the East side of Penobscot in the behalf of Massachusets Bay: And I know not how we could be otherwise then ignorant of it: for we had no papers printed or written to learn it from: & it seems to me not to be so obvious as to occur of itself. 2 This is a sufficient Answer why I consented to the Grants: but if I had at first known of this objection it would not have induced me to refuse my consent to some Grants of this kind, since the Province has a right to have this matter put in a course of determinatn; & I know of no way so proper as tendring a Grant for confirmation: ~~And~~ 3dly We had no notion of there being any other question between the two Provinces, but which of the two Rivers that fall into the Bay of St Croix was the river St Croix: We imagin'd that the Government of Nova Scotia would insist upon the Westerly River called Passimaquoddy being the boundary & we were ready to prove from the relations of Voyagers & living Indians that the Easterly River was the true River St Croix: & this required an Actual Survey. 4 There was not the least intention of determining the boundary without the Participation of the Crown there was nothing more in my thoughts than to transmitt an exact account of this Survey, Whether it had been joint or ex parte to the Board of Trade immediately after it had been finished.

The Displeasure of their Ldships is no secret here: the Agent in a publick Letter gives an Account of the Province being threatned for making these grants, & in a Private letter he writes that Mr Pownall said "His friend Govr Bernard was got into an ugly Scrape".[5] People here are amazed that I should incur the displeasure of my superiors by appearing as an advocate for the Province in a ~~matter~~ ^question^ of right. The Govr of this Province will never fail having many occasional difficulties & some perverse Spirits to strive with; I have had a large share of both: & yet I have kept myself steady, have got all the publick business done in an ample manner & have secured to myself a competency of credit & respect. And I can account for this no better than my having persuaded the People to look upon me as their true & natural Freind, as I have thought that, with a proper regard to my duty, I might really be. And I will own that in the matter in question I have rather magnified my

Zeal than kept it under, as will easily appear to a nice observer of my Messages to the House, Letters to the Lᵗ Govʳ: of Nova Scotia, & some papers which I sent to the Board of Trade not without the privity of some leading men in both Houses. But if it should be understood here that I cannot engage in the service of the Province & the defence of their Constitutional Rights without endangering my own intrest at home, I shall be considered only as a Spy placed over them & my intrest will be accordingly

It is common with People, when they can't account readily for any thing to resort to occult causes. In the present case many refined arguers insist that the opposition to the Province's ^right^ arises from the private intrest of the Claimants under Ld Stirling. When I endeavour to show the Absurdity of this supposition, I am answer'd that they have good Authority for the conjecture. And indeed I have heard that a certain Gentlemen on this side of the Water, who tho certainnly not heir to the 1ˢᵗ Ld Stirling & in the opinion of many not related to him, first revived this obsolete claim, boasts much of the strong connections he has formed in support of that pretended right. But I can never think that the Lords of Trade have given any Countenance to this extravagant Pretension.

I have already carried this Letter to a Greater length than I intended: to prevent its further extension, I must confine myself to the Sheet.

I am Sʳ Yʳ most faithful & obedient Servt

F Bernard.

R Jackson Esq.

PS.

Govʳ Franklin writes me word[6] that you have got into Parliament accept my congratulation

L, LbC   BP, 3: 56-60.

In the handwriting of clerk no. 2 with scribal emendations. The enclosures FB mentions were copies of **Nos. 91** and **196**, and the enclosures to **No. 202**.

---

1. Letters are obscured by tight binding.

2. **No. 191**.

3. Not found.

4. **No. 181**.

5. Jasper Mauduit to Andrew Oliver, London, 23 Jun. 1762, Prov. Sec. Letterbooks, 1: 361. The "Private" letter has not been found.

6. William Franklin (1730/31-1813), eldest child of Benjamin Franklin and governor of New Jersey, 1762-76. The letter to FB, c.1763, has not been found.

207 | To Jeffery Amherst

Boston May 14. 1763

S[r]

L[t] Col Gay late in the Provincial Service will wait on you with this to lay before you an hardship arising from his Duty in the Kings Service, which He now lies under & I cannot redress. He was commanding Officer of the party placed at the Castle for supporting the Provincial recruiting for regulars last Year. Among the recruits that were returned thither & sent from thence was a mint breed Indian who was afterwards sent to Quebec. This Indian[1] was claimed as a Slave: but no proper proof being brought of his being such, He was sent off. Col Gay was no ways concerned in recruiting this Man nor in detaining or sending him off than by being Commanding officer there. And yet the Master has brought an Action against Col Gay: and tho', upon the trial the judges told the Jury that there was no Evidence against the Deft, nor the least pretence to charge him in such an Action, The Jury found a Verdict against him with 50 pounds sterling in damages. As He suffers this injury for doing his duty in the Kings Service, He hopes that He shall not be left loaded with this burthen, which is a great Matter to him, but some how or other releived from it.

As I have it not in my power to redress him myself, I must recommend him to your favor. If there is a difficulty in releiving him in a direct way, a compensation by giving him some employment would be Very acceptable. He has been in the service ever since 1755 when he was a subaltern at the taking Beausejour. In 1759 He was a Captain & Commanding officer at Pisgit; In 1760 He was commanding Officer at Liverpool in Nova Scotia; In 1761 He was Major in Thwings Regiment; In 1762 He was Lt Col in Ingersols.[2] He is a steady punctual honest Man: & fit for a Civil employ as well as a Military one: He will make a faithful & active Commissary; & will thankfully accept of any employment which you shall think suitable to him.

In the year 1760, with the assistance of the assembly, I employed a Surveyor supported by a party of Men to survey the River Kennebeck & the passage from thence to the River Chaudiere & another communication between the two rivers. The surveyor proceeded to the 13th day when he was unfortunately & by accident killed by one of his own men: and there the Survey stopt.[3] I employed L[t] Miller, who has lately much improved himself in drawing, to protract this Survey from the field book of the deceast; and, before he was engaged in the regular Service, had agreed with him to proceed in this Work this Summer, if the province would provide for the expence. I beleive it would still be agreable to him to undertake this business, if you should approve of it & excuse his absence from his duty. In such case I will apply to the Assembly to provide for the expence, at the next Session. I hereby desire your acceptance of the Plan: the River Kennebeck above Fort Halifax is laid down from the deceast's book which was full of small drawings upon the Spot; the rest of the plan is taken from other Surveys.[4]

I am, with great regard, Sʳ Your most obedient & most humble Servant

Fra Bernard.

His Excelly Sr Jeffry Amherst

ALS, RC   WO 34/26, ff 233-234.

Contains minor emendations. Endorsed: Governor Bernard. Boston, 14ᵗʰ. May 1763. Recᵈ.__ 21ˢᵗ. Ditto.__ Ansᵈ. ___ 26ᵗʰ. Ditto.___. Variant text in BP, 2: 304-306 (L, LbC).

1. See **No. 149**.

2. Major Gay served in Nova Scotia 4 Apr.-25 Dec. 1761, and held the rank of lieutenant colonel from 3 Apr. 1762 to 1 Jan. 1763, when he evidently left the provincial service. The reasons for Gay not pursuing a career in the regular army are sketched in **No. 218**.

3. John Small (1722-60), a British army officer, and resident of Scarborough, York Co., Mass. One local historian suggests that he may have been killed by John Howard, a soldier stationed at Fort Western. Old Fort Western (http://www.oldfortwestern.org accessed 16 Mar. 2007).

4. Amherst suggested that there were errors in Small's map, whereupon FB made several requests for the general to send him a copy of a "sketch" of the Kennebec River made by a British army engineer, inc. **No. 218**.

208 | To James Cockle

Boston May 16 1763

Sʳ

Having received orders to make some enquiries concerning the state of the trade of this Province I must desire that you will attend me at Castle William on fryday next to answer such questions as I have occasion to put to you concerning the Subject aforesaid

I am

Jam^s Cockle Esq Coll^r of Salem

AL, LbC   BP, 2: 306.

This letter is the first documentary evidence linking FB to the notorious customs officer
James Cockle, whose zeal to enforce the trade laws rebounded on both men. Cockle had
arrived in the colonies from Lincoln, Eng., in c.1760, leaving behind a large business debt.
FB knew Cockle's father, an alderman of Lincoln Common Council, and this prior associa-
tion may have prompted him to secure Cockle the vacant position at Salem. Cockle's assiduous pursuit of smugglers won him few friends—save FB, who, as governor, was entitled
to one-third of all seizures. In 1764, Surveyor General John Temple accused FB and Cockle
of colluding in a scheme to defraud the Treasury; Cockle was dismissed from the service,
but FB escaped censure. Nicolson, *The 'Infamas Govener'*, 88, 100-104; Jordan D. Fiore,
"The Temple-Bernard Affair," *Essex Institute Historical Collections* 90 (1954): 58-83.

209 | *To Jeffery Amherst*

Boston May 18. 1763.

S^r.

   I have received yours of the 8th inst, signifying that you had order'd the Provincials at Crown Point & Halifax to be dismissed on the *1st of July*.[1] These Men
were listed to serve only to the *1st of May*. If they can be prevailed upon to serve
2 months longer, I dont apprehend that the extraordinary expence will be much
grudged; as it must be supposed to be necessary to his Majesty's Service by your
ordering it. As for the small party at the Castle, It was impracticable to keep them
beyond their day.

   I am, with great regard, Sr Your most obedient humble Servant

Fra. Bernard

His Excell^y Sr Jeffry Amherst

ALS, RC   WO 34/26, f 235.

Variant text in BP, 2: 307 (L, LbC).

---

1. Amherst to FB, New York, 8 May 1763, WO 34/27, p. 289.

210 | To Charles Townshend

Boston. May 18th 1763

S[r]

I beg leave to take the earliest opportunity to congratulate you on your being placed at the head of the Commission for Trade & Plantations with Powers sufficiently ample for the great purposes for which you are designed.[1]

British America has wanted nothing more than to be well known to the Mother Country. it is not for many years that her importance has been rightly understood. At this time, when her rights have been effectually vindicated by a successful War & firmly secured by an honorable peace, it must be a great additional Pleasure to her Inhabitants that their interests are put into the hands of one so well acquainted with them, as you, S[r], are known to be.

In the course of five years residence in this Country, I have given particular attention to the Policy of the several Governments that have lain within my view, & particularly that of the Province over which I now preside: & I have of course formed conclusions, within my own breast, concerning the present state of the Colonies both in regard to their original Constitutions & the modern modes of their administration. This Province alone affords an ample field for such disquisitions: but they are too delicate for any but private letters.

I shall be very proud to be honourd with y[r] commands to deliver my sentiments upon such subjects as you may think I may contribute any useful information: I have now before me the queries[2] sent me from the Lords Commissioners some time ago. I have deferred answering them only upon account of my desire of being as exact as possible in regard to those subjects which are fluctuating; particularly the Number of the People: The ascertaining this will be the Work of a whole Summer; & could not properly be set about till after the conclusion of Peace

I have the Honour &c to[3] be, with great respect, S[r], Your most obedient & most humble Servant

The Right Honble Charles Townshend Esq

L, LbC   BP, 3: 60-62.

In the handwriting of clerk no. 2 with minor scribal emendations, except where noted.

---

1. Charles Townshend (1725-67), politician, MP for Great Yarmouth from 1748 until his death, chancellor of the exchequer, 1766-67, and president of the Board, 1 Mar.-16 Apr. 1763.

2. Enclosed in **No. 46**.

3. The remainder of the closure, but not the addresse's name, is in FB's hand.

211 | From the Board of Trade

Sir,[1]

The inclosed Copys of two Letters from the Secretary to the Commiss[rs]. of the Customs, to M[r] Pownall, will shew you the result of Our proceedings upon Your Letter to Us of the 19th of Febry last,[2] and as it appears, from these Letters, that the Surveyors General of the Customs in America, have no power by their Commissions to appoint deputys, nor any Authority for it, either from the Lords of the Treasury, or the Commissioners of the Customs, except in cases of Leave to come to England, We entirely approve of your having refused to Administer the Oaths to M[r]. Robert Temple, and think that the admitting him to qualify as Deputy Surveyor General under any Stipulation whatever would have been improper and irregular, and would have a manifest tendency to set aside the Effect and Intention of the 25th: Article of His Majesty's Instructions to You.

We have received An Authentick Copy of the Conditional Grant made to You by the General Court of the Island of Desart,[3] and tho' it would be very agreeable to Us, to Concurr with the Legislature of your Province in so proper a testimony & Approbation on their part of your Services to the Publick, yet We cannot think it advisable to bring the Questions which may arise upon this Case, into discussion, until the new Governments, which are proposed to be formed in consequence of the Cession in N[o]. America, made to His Majesty by the Treaty of Peace, shall be settled.

We are Sr. &c[a].

Whitehall May 18th 1763

Soame Jenyns[4]

E[d] Eliot[5]

E[d]. Bacon

Jn[o] York

Geo. Rice

Orwell

Bamber Gascoigne

L, LbC   CO 5/920, pp. 161-162.

In the handwriting of John Pownall. Contains minor emendations. Entrybook title: To Francis Bernard Esq[r]. Enclosures not found.

1. Left marginal note: "1763. May 18th. Letter to Francis Bernard Esqr. Governor of the Massachusets Bay in Answer to one from him of 19th. Febry last."

2. **No. 190**.

3. **No. 91**.

4. Right marginal note, opposite signatures: "Ex^d."

5. Edward Craggs-Eliot (1727-1804), first Baron Eliot and a lord commissioner, 1760-74.

212 | To Lord Barrington

Castle William May 21. 1763

My Lord

I am favoured with your Lordships letter of the 13th of Febry^{~1} informing of Lady Barrington's Death.² I should think an easy determination of a well spent Life rather a subject for congratulation than condolance, if it was not for the pain which the separation gives the relatives left behind.

I was loath to give your Lordship the last trouble concerning the Naval Office; but M^r. Pemberton is a cautious Man; and I could not avoid satisfying his fears. And now there is occasion for further trouble: by the new establishment of the board of Trade, This Office falls into the patronage of M^r_ Townshend, and I suppose it will be necessary to secure his Confirmation of Lord Egremonts Designation. Your Lordship will judge what will be the best method of procuring that: that nothing may be wanting, I inclose an abstract of the Memorial submitted to Lord Egremont; which, tho' contracted in words, is sufficiently explicit in matter.

I must also beg your Lordship to recommend me in general terms to M^r_ Townshend, I have wrote to him upon the Subject of his appointment & have made a ready offer of my Service in giving him information of what has occured to me in regard to such matters as are too delicate for public letters. I wrote to your Lordship (dated Decr. 15 1761)³ a short state of my pretensions to being of some use, in case a Revisal & new Settlement of the Political state of N. America should have a place in the British Councils: to that letter I would now refer; what addition to it shall be necessary, I shall consider & forward by the best oppartunity.

The Grant of Mount desert still remains in suspension, for want of the original grant, which having been delivered into the Secretary's Office is mislaid so that it cannot be found. A Duplicate of it sent to the Lords of Trade was taken; but a triplicate, I sent lately, was arrivd.⁴ At the beginning of last Winter My Conduct &

the Provinces was I believe misrepresented from Nova Scotia; and The Lords hearing that Side only judged us rather too hastily. Some time after, my papers arriv'd, which, I understand have shown my conduct & the Provinces right in a different light from what they were seen in before. I have upon this occasion received a kind letter from thier Lordships which makes amends for a ^un^pleasant one which the Nova Scotia Representation produced.[5] I am much obliged to your Lordship for the concern you have expressed in this affair. I hope your Lordship will not have much more trouble in it; as it seems to me that the right of the Province to those lands is too strong to be set aside: And M^r_ Jackson is full in this Opinion. There have certainly been great pains taken in the defence of the Province's right; and I have had my full share of them & I hope without giving offence, as appears from the following Clause in thier Lordships last letter to me "Wee can have no objection to your acceptance of this grant as a Testimony of the approbation & favour of that Province in whose service & in the conduct of whose affairs you have manifested such Zeal & Capacity"__

We have passed thro' a very Severe Winter in good health. I have now 8 of my 10 Children in family with me. Frank will soon take his departure for England; when I shall acquaint your Lordship with my thoughts concerning him. I am with our joint compliments to your Lordship, & our friends &c My Lord Your Lordships &c

The R^t_ Honble L^d. Barrington

L, LbC   BP, 3: 62-65.

In the handwriting of clerk no. 2. Enclosure not found.

---

1. Barrington to FB, Cavendish Square, 13 Feb. 1763, BP, 10: 57-58.

2. Anne Shute Barrington (née Daines, [d.1763]), the daughter of Sir William Daines of Bristol.

3. **Nos. 210** and **215**; **No. 83**.

4. **No. 91**.

5. **Nos. 193** and **181**.

213 | To Richard Jackson

Castle William. May. 21. 1763

D^r S^r

By the Schooner Hannah Doggett f^r Bristol. Ap 11, I sent to Mr Pownall, a grant of 6 Townships next to Penobscot with a Small Map of the Same, & a letter to their Lordships recommending the settlement to them,[1] that they would not disappoint it tho' the right of the Province should be disputed, as this settlement must in general be advantageous let the right of jurisdiction belong to one or the other Province: & by the Devonshire Capt Hunter for London May 9 I sent two more of parts (originals) of this Grant over to you with a large map of the Lands from an actual survey, & dupl^s: of the others Papers.[2] After the first of these dispatches viz on Ap: 15. I recieved a severe letter from the Lords reprimanding me for consenting to grants of Lands east of Penobscot &c without consulting them. I took this so much at heart that I immediately wrote to Mr Pownall (by the Packet) with much concern & I hope with all due respect: & I afterwards by the Devonshire wrote to thr Ldships on the same subject, referring to my letter to Mr Pownall. But I find that I might have saved their Lordships this trouble; for on the 14th instant I recieved a very kind letter from their Ldships, dated Mar. 11[3] on the subject of my grant; by which I must understand that the Papers I sent in Dec: last have suf[fici]ently vindicated my conduct from the Nova Scotia impeachment. From this Letter & from yours which I have recieved with it I percieve that both my grant & the Provinces right are seen in a more favorable light than they were some months ago.[4] I should be glad to learn the Particulars of the No. Sco. remonstrances & the prejudices Ld E[5] was influenced by & from whom the latter came: as to the former I can concieve it possible that deeper designs than the disputing this Country may be at the bottom of it.

I have wrote to Mr Townshend[6] to congratulate him upon his appointment, & have freely made him a tender of submitting to him my thoughts concerning such matters as are of too delicate a nature to be made subjects of public letters, nay some of them too nice to be committed to any letters but the most secret. I have a considerable collection of ideas concerning the Political state of America, & have committed very few of them to writing, having no correspondent of Authority to trouble with them since Ld Halifax left the Office. If I could be of use in making a report in Person I would not grudge the journey; but I could not well bear the expense, without some compensation direct or collateral. I spend ^here^ my whole income: indeed evry thing is very dear, as well on account of the war as of two unfruitfull Seasons following each other. But we may well hope that the times will mend: & in that hope I remain quite contented. I should be obliged to you, if you would recommend or get me recommended to Mr Townsend. I have asked the same favour of L B:[7] but know not what the Connection is between them; should be glad to hear.

In a former letter[8] I have mentiond to you the expediency & apparent possibility of forming a new Government on this side of N Scotia. The more I have since thought of it more practicable the Scheme appears, as it seems to me certain that a proposal of this sort might be made so agreeable to the Massachusets as by way of exchange to make 'em satisfied with an equivalent compensation for their Eastern lands which is all the difficulty attending this Scheme. When I have a little leisure I will reduce this into form: in the mean time I only mention it again that you may turn y^r thoughts upon it.

I informed the College of what you have done, they will direct the Payment of the money & the board of overseers (Governor Council & Ministers of Churches) have passed a Vote of thanks to you & Mr Mauduit. I find I sent you too few books for public & private use. I will send more by this Ship if I can get them. I wish L^d. Barrington had had one. I must leave you to make an Apology to him when you recieve the next parcell.

Mr Townsend is the first Commoner that has presided at the board of trade: & I had some doubt what address was due to him. But as my letter was to him alone & in some degree private, I thought I could not properly use the word Lordship. If I am wrong set me right. I am with &c

R Jackson Esq.

L, LbC   BP, 3: 65-68.

In the handwriting of clerk no. 2.

---

1. **Nos. 197, 198**.

2. See **No. 206**.

3. **Nos. 181, 193, 200** and **202**.

4. **No. 177**; Jackson's letter not found.

5. Lord Egremont.

6. **No. 210**.

7. Lord Barrington; **No. 212**.

8. **No. 180**.

214 | To John Pownall

Castle William. May 22. 1763

D^r S^r

On the 14th instant I recieved letters from the Lds of 9 & 11 of Mar.[1] I am extremly glad that y^r board is again vested with full Powers.[2] Let the abilities of a Secretary of State be ever so great, if his office is over charged with business the inconvenience will fall some where. In the former times, America has experienced this very feelingly. I have wrote to Mr Townsend[3] to congratulate him upon this occasion & to make a tender of my Service. As the Letter was addressed to him alone, I thought it not proper to use the term[4] Ldship: sure I am right.

If I had recieved the kind letter of their Ldships dated March 11. sooner I should have saved you the trouble of the Apology I sent you. Since I may now conclude that my conduct has appeared in a different light, that the NS remonstrance had set it in. Certainly my intentions were upright, & I informed my Judgement as well as I could.

I have sent you by the Hannah Brig Capt Jarvis, which is arrived in London about the end of March, with many Letters, a triplicate of the Grant of Mt Desart: it was my original draught;[5] but hapening to be fair wrote I had it authenticated with the other two, one of which was lost at Sea in a cover to their Ldships.[6] I have sent by the Devonshire Hunter for London, 4 letters to the Lords,[7] 2 to y^r self,[8] 1 to Mr Jackson, 2 original Grants of the 6 Townships in a Cover to M^r. Jackson, a large map of the 6 Townships from an actual Survey, & very neatly drawn all which I hope will come safe to hand.[9]

I am &c

John Pownall Esq.

L, LbC   BP, 3: 69-70.

In the handwriting of clerk no. 2 with minor scribal emendations, not shown, and one correction in FB's hand.

---

1. The letter of 9 Mar. has not been found; **No. 193**.

2. FB is likely referring to a limitation to an administrative reform introduced by the Privy Council on 15 May 1761. When the Privy Council repealed an order-in-council of 11 Mar. 1752, and thereby transferred from the Board to the secretary of state the sole authority to make recommendations on appointments to colonial offices, it retained the instruction that royal governors should continue to communicate directly with the Board in the first instance, and to contact the secretary of state only in matters requiring his "immediate Directions." *APC*, 4: 154-157; *JBT*, 11: 338; FB to Robert Wood,

Boston, 17 Aug. 1761, CO 5/20, ff 169-170.

3. **No. 210**.

4. FB substituted this for "word."

5. In **No. 176**.

6. Copies not found.

7. **Nos. 197, 202, 203** and **205**.

8. Possibly **Nos. 198** and **200**.

9. **No. 213** and the enclosure to **No. 198**.

215 | To Charles Townshend

Castle W^m. May 29. 1763.

S^r.

I did myself the honor to write to you a Letter dated the 18th Inst.[1] in which I begd leave to congratulate you on your being placed at the head of the Board of Trade & to make a tender of my especial Services. Since I have recieved the Letter from y^r Lordships, wherein so favorable a notice of the papers I had submitted on the behalf of this Province, is taken,[2] I have turned my thoughts on the very point on which y^r Lordships consider the Question to depend: And I beg leave to submitt to you my Sentiments thereon, drawn up in a hasty manner at this place, to which I have retired to steal a leisure Day from the hurry of Boston, where the Assembly is now sitting.

as I write at a distance from my books & should not have time to turn them over, if I was at Boston, You will excuse such inaccuracies & mistakes as shall occurr: & as I am engaged in the Service of truth only, you will show the like indulgence to the freedom which I have used. The greatest Apology I have to make is for presuming to inform You upon a subject so well known to you. But I dont pretend so much to offer any thing new as to collect detached matters & fix 'em to one point.

There is one political Consideration which I have not taken notice of, as I think it ought not to interfere in this Question: I mean the great extension of the Sea Coast of the Massachusets. If this should be thought to deserve animadversion, it should ~~be~~ not influence the judicial determination of a matter of right, neither would the taking away this bit of land remedy the evil, if it is one. The proper way of treating this matter seems to be by agreement & by exchange of lands lying near Boston for those at a greater distance. I believe such a Convention is not only practicable but might be made agreeable & beneficial to the Province as well as advantageous to the King. I have turned this matter a good deal in my mind, altho'

I have never had occasion to write upon it. If this sh'd become a subject of your consideration I shall be ready to communicate my thoughts upon it: in the mean time I will collect & settle my ideas. For the present I will only say that it seems to me to be by no means advisable to make additions to Nova Scotia, that province is already full large for its powers, & should rather be obliged to confine its settlements within bounds than be encouraged to disperse them.

Boston June 2.

Since I have wrote the foregoing I have recieved an address from the Council & Assembly which is so full of a gratefull sensibility of his Majestys paternal Care of this Country, that I should have begged the favor of you to lay before his Mjesty these expressions of the gratitude & Duty of this his most loyal Province, if I did not apprehend that the general Court, before they rose, would immediately address his Majesty upon the happy Event which fills their hearts with so much Joy. Before I seal this letter, this will probably be determined.

I am &c

The Right Honble Cha[rs] Townshend Esq

L, LbC   BP, 3: 70-73.

In the handwriting of clerk no. 2 with minor scribal emendations. Enclosed **No. 216** and a copy of address of the Council and the House of Representatives to FB, 31 May 1763, for which see *JHRM*, 40: 29-31.

---

1. **No. 210**.
2. **No. 193**.

216 | State of the Facts Bearing on Massachusetts's Title to Sagadahoc

[Apr. or May 1763]

A State of the Facts upon which the Massachusets Title to the lands between Penobscot & St Croix depends.

1621   James the 1 granted to Sr William Alexander the Province of Nova Scotia, of which St Croix is made the western boundary

1664   Charles the 2^d granted to James Duke of York all that part of the main land of New England beginning at a certain place called or known by the name of St Croix next adjoining to New Scotland in America & from thence extending &c to the river of Kennebeck.

The Duke of York in 1676 appointed a Governor over this Country & having not aliened it in 1684 became King.

Charles the second by the Treaty of Breda, ceded that part of Acadia which the French had been before possessed of to France: in which cession The Fort of Pentagoet lying on the East side of Penobscot river is the most westerly place mentioned.[1]

In 1690, War being declared between France & England, The Colony of Massachusets fitted out an armament at their own expence & conquered the whole Territory between Penobscot & St Croix, & entirely removed the few french who were settled there from thence

In 1691 The Massachusets being in the peaceable possession of this Country, by conquest, King William & Queen Mary erected the Colony of Massachusets & the Colony of Plimouth &c into one Province & granted to them among other things all the lands between the River Sagadehock & Nova Scotia (being the same Lands which were before granted by Cha. 2 to the Duke of York, except a small alteration in the inland Western boundary) then called Acadia, & thereafter to be called The Territory of Sagadehock; by which name it is distinguisht to this day.

By the Treaty of Ryswick King William ceded to France all conquered places in America: but this Tract was not named, nor did the French ever take possession of or make any settlement upon it.[2] During Queen Anns War The Massachusets made it a continual object of their Arms, having fitted out two expensive Expeditions against that Country & Nova Scotia, before it was finally conquered by a regular Army assisted by the Massachusets forces[3]

By the Treaty of Utrecht This Country was ceded to England under the Name of Acadia, by which it had been before granted to the Massachusets by King William. The Massachusets immediately resumed their jurisdiction over the Country

& in 1713 received the submission of the Indians thereof as subjects of that Province. In 1717 Govr Shute held a treaty with the Eastern Indians among whom were sevral of the Penobscots, who renewed their subjection to Great Britain under the Massachusets. In 1722 a War broke out with the Penobscot & other Indians which continued 4 years at the expence of the Massachusets much greater than the whole Value of the lands between Penobscot & St Croix. In 1727 Peace was concluded with those Indians, who renewed their submission to the Massachusets. And since that there have been many other instances of such acknowledgements.

The Province has heretofore been prevented settling this Country by the continued intrigues of the french Missionaries among the Indians, but had determined to do it at the end of the War. For which purpose in 1759 Governor Pownall with a large armed force erected a Very respectable fort on the river Penobscot, took a formal Possession of that Country in the right of the Massachusets on the east side of the river, & having called the Penobscot Indians together, declared his intentions of settling that Country & threaten'd them with his resentment if they dared to attempt to interrupt him. And accordingly in 1761 Proposals were made to the General Court for settling 12 Townships of 60 families each on the East side of Penobscot: and 6 of the said Townships have been surveyed & Grants of them have passed to be submitted to his Majesty according to the Terms of the Charter.

Arguments in favour of the Massachusetts Title

~~And [now]~~ ^Upon the aforesaid Grants being tenderd for the Kings Confirmation^ a Question is made whether The Provinces Right under the Charter by the Treaty of Breda, was not originally Void or since evoided by the Treaty of ~~Breda &~~ Ryswick ~~or either of them~~ ? to which another Question may be added, whether if their Title is not good in strictness of Law, it ought not to be perfected upon principles of Equity or of Policy. And taking both these questions as one, We will consider it in four ways 1 Common Law. 2 Civil Law. 3 Equity. 4 Policy.

1 Common Law. Evry Grant contains in it implied Warranty, which Warranty is a perpetual Bar to the Heir of the Grantor. Nor will it alter the Case if the Grantor had no other title but possession. For if a disseisor[4] makes a grant & his heir, as his heir, acquires the legal title, they shall be barred by the implied Warranty of the Grantor. Let K William possessor of this Country by Conquest be considered a Disseisor at common Law, The rest of the Argument follows. The Reason of the Law is that No one shall be allowed to defeat the grant of his Ancestor, under whom he himself claims

2. Civil Law. By the right of Postliminium Where a Country, that formerly belonged to a state, is recovered from the Enemy, all private rights are restored. Or in the Words of Puffendorf Lib 8 ca 6 sec 26[5] "If a part of a people be recoverd by the

people they were for some time divided & torn from, they again incorporate with the old Body and return to the place & rights they had before."

3. Equity. As this Province has for above 70 years acted under a royal grant & in consequence thereof expended in the defence of this land more than ten times the Value of it, if their Title is imperfect, the King ~~is obliged~~ ^ought^ in equity to make it ~~good~~ complete.

4. Policy. The Great Purpose in America is to bring forward the peopling & improving the Wast lands there. If, where Lands lie between two Provinces, One of them is ready to ~~people~~ ^settle^ these lands & really wants them for the use of their supernumerary people, and the other neither can nor ought ~~not~~ in prudence to settle them, having allready much nearer their head quarters lands sufficient to employ them for at least 100 years to come, It surely would not be right Policy to prevent one Province extending its population to add to the allready immense desarts of the other.

ADft, AC   BP, 10: 83-86.

Contains minor emendations. Sawtelle dates the manuscript Apr. 1763, in "Sir Francis Bernard and His Grant of Mount Desert," 217-220, but it is possible that it was composed in May for copies were enclosed in letters to Charles Townshend (**No. 215**) and Richard Jackson (**No. 220**).

The cover to Jackson indicates that this manuscript constitued two parts of a three-piece report justifying Massachusetts's title to Sagadahoc. The first part was "Consideration of an Objection to the right of the Province of Massachusetts Bay" authorized by the General Court; the document printed here comprises the second and third parts and discusses in much more depth some of the points FB raises in the annotations he made to the copy of the "Consideration" that he enclosed in **No. 176**. For the historical background to the province's claim, FB probably relied heavily on Thomas Hutchinson, who had a leading role in the preparation of *Brief State of the Title of the Province of Massachusetts-Bay to the Country between the Rivers Kennebeck and St. Croix* and later discussed the claim in *History of Massachusetts*, 2: 84.

1. The Treaty of Breda (1667) was signed by England, the Dutch United Provinces, France, and Denmark, and ended the Second Anglo-Dutch War of 1665-67 and the first Anglo-French conflict in North America of 1666-67, in which Massachusetts participated; it also returned Acadia—which had been nominally English territory since 1654—to French control.

2. The Treaty of Ryswick (1697) ended France's war of 1688-97 with the League of Augsburg powers— England, Spain, and the Netherlands—and, in North America, King William's War of 1690-97. Nova Scotia was again returned to France.

3. Queen Anne's War of 1702-13 involved several attempts by Massachusetts to capture Port Royal, the Acadian capital, until the successful expedition of 1710 under Francis Nicholson. The Treaty of Utrecht (1713) confirmed France's cession to Great Britain of "Nova Scotia or Acadia."

4. A person who wrongfully evicts another from the possession of lands.

5. Samuel Freiherr (Baron) von Pufendorf (1632–94), *De Jure Naturae et Gentium* (1672).

217 | To Jeffery Amherst

Boston May 30. 1763

S[r]

I have just now received a Letter from Capt Keen Commanding Officer of the Provincials at Halifax informing that on the 1st of May, when the time for which the Men were inlisted expired, they desired to be dismissed, which being refused, they also refused to do duty.[1] Upon which Col Forster stopt their provisions, both officers & privates, & yet will not suffer them to go home, except between 30 & 40 invalides, & even of them He refused to pay for the passage. So there they remain useless & living at their own expence which being beyond their pay or their credit, they must soon be reduced to great misery.[2] I hope however, S[r], that you will give immediate orders for their redress; and if the Men have done their duty & performed their contract, you will direct that they shall have evry thing that is due to them.

I am, with great regard, S[r], Your most obedient & most humble Servant

Fra. Bernard

His Excellency S[r] Jeffry Amherst

ALS, RC   WO 34/26, f 236.

Variant text in BP, 2: 307-308 (L, LbC).

---

1. Letter not found. See **No. 209**. FB had extended the period of enlistment to 1 Jul. Capt. Abel Keen of Pembroke, Plymouth Co., Mass., had been in the Provincials since 1757.

2. See **No. 218**.

218 | To Jeffery Amherst

Castle William June 5 1763

S[r].

I am favoured with yours of the 26th & 27th of May,[1] & I am much obliged to you for your favorable intention towards the L[t] Col Gay. In regard to what you mention of his having no thoughts of entring into the army I know not how to account for it but by supposing that his Modesty might prevent his earnestness in moving for an appointment in that Service, which he might understand you had a multiplicity of engagements for; or he might not be reconciled, after the different commands he had bore (altho under provincial commissions only) in the Kings Service, to be begin, *de novo* at the bottom of the Army. But I am sure, unless some such Objection interfered, He would, if left to his choice, prefer a military Employment to a civil: tho' perhaps, upon account of this difficulty, the latter may be more suitable.

I am very sorry that the Men could not be prevailed upon to stay beyond their Time. I am well assured that the province would not have grudged the expence if the Men could have been made easy. The Worst of these disputes is that it affords matter for popular declaimers:[2] altho' I have nothing to fear of this kind, but as it may affect any extraordinary requisitions, which I may have to make for his Majesty's Service.

I shall be very glad to receive the sketch of the Engineer you mention of Kennebeck river: for I am at a loss in guessing whence the faultiness of the plan I sent you (I mean above Fort Halifax) should arise. The Surveyor, I employed, was the Very best in this Country; His field book, which I have, is apparently very accurate; and M[r] Miller, from my observation of his Working in my presence, is, I think, careful in protracting. I shall lay this before the Assembly & leave it to them whether it shall be continued or not: if they determine in the affirmative, I shall use all possible endeavour to get it done with the greatest exactness: & for that purpose shall be glad to be favoured with all the assistance which the Gentleman you mention can give.

I am, with great regard, S[r] Your most obedient & most humble Servant,

Fra. Bernard

His Excellency S[r] Jeffry Amherst

ALS, RC   WO 34/26, f 237.

Contains minor emendations. Variant text BP, 2: 308-310 (L, LbC).

---

1. Not found.

2. In Sept. disaffection over pay stoppages sparked a mutiny among Regulars of the 40th Regiment. See Peter Way, "Rebellion of the Regulars: Working Soldiers and the Mutiny of 1763-1764," *WMQ* 57 (2000): 761-792.

219 | *To John Pownall*

Boston June 6th. 1763

D[r] S[r],

I hereby enclose an address of the General Court, which as it contains the fullest expressions of their sense of his Majesty's paternal care of this Country, you will be pleased to communicate to their Lordships. I have inclosed herewith my speech to w[ch]. the Address occasionally refers. I should have desired their Lordships to have laid before his Majesty this testimonial of the Duty & Gratitude of this Loyal Province, If the General Court had not intended to have addressed his Majesty upon this occasion: But this was resolved upon last Saturday[1] & a Committee of both houses was appointed Accordingly.

I have the pleasure to inform you that there never was, in the opinion of those who know the Country, an assembly better Composed than the present; and I doubt not but they will effectually eradicate that petulancy of humours which has prevailed here more or less, ever since the General Attack of the Customhouse, soon after I arrived here; & which, altho' it has not obstructed the carrying into effect all necessary public measures, yet it has given a good deal of trouble to those concerned in them. But the present Assembly has shown such a resentment against those who have been concerned in disturbing the internal peace of this Government, that I believe it will be as firmly Established here, as in the universality of the Christian World

I intended this Packet for a ship that was to sail from hence; but I find so much incertainty in regard to the time of her departure, that I have resolved to send these by NYork for the Packet boat; & as this is a sudden resolution, I am obliged to conclude hastily by assuring you that I am S[r].

your Most affect. &c

J. Pownall Esqr.

L, LbC   BP, 3: 77-78.

In the handwriting of clerk no. 1 with minor scribal emendations. Enclosed a copy of address of the Council and the House of Representatives to FB, 31 May 1763, for which see *JHRM*, 40: 29-31.

---

1. 4 Jun. The address to the king was approved on 8 Jun. *JHRM*, 40: 72.

220 | To Richard Jackson

Castle William. June 8. 1763

D^r S^r

The letters of a former date which you will recieve with this have been so long delayd; that I have been able to add this & some more to the packett. Among which is another Letter to Mr Townsend with an enclosure of 3 sheets of more last Words on behalf of the Province right to the Tract Eastward of Penobscot under 3 heads I An enquiry into the Origin of the Terms of Acadia & Nova Scotia, & the use thereof. II A State of the facts upon which Massachusets Title to the Lands between Penobscot & St Croix depends. III Arguments in favor of the Massachusets Title. I shall send to you by another Ship Duplicates of this letter & Papers to be presented to Mr Townshend if this Conveyance should fail. But I will in this send you a Copy of the three head which is but short.

The Settlement at Penobscot promises to be very flourishing if it is not prevented. There is a fresh Spirit rising among them, so that Lots, which some time ago went a begging, now bear a premium; & the 3 most easterly Townships, which I before thought were given up, are now revived & prosecuted as earnestly as the others have been. The Terms of my Township are agreed to, the Plan of the Town is settled, a minister is engaged to supply them with Spiritual food & a merchant with temporal necessaries. And if Permission shall arrive time enough, there will be 60 families settled there before Winter & perhaps 20 or 30 Schooners employed there in fishing this Summer. In the whole, there will be near 800 families settled in a small circle, which at 5 to a family amounts to 4000 Souls. Would it not be a Pity that such a Scheme should be disappointed? What a deal of money has it cost the Government to make such a settlement in other parts? here nothing is askt of it but it's permission.

I shall close this subject with assuring you that I am D^r S^r

Your &c.

R Jackson Esq.

PS.

I closed the letter on the other ^side of as the^ subject was concluded. What I have to write on another I reserved for a PS. In some former letters, I gave you an Account of the violent proceedings of Mr Otis, & in the last of these how he was got to libelling evry respectable Character in the Government, not sparing the Crown itself.[1] These Libells have had raised the abhorrence of all good men, &

opened the Eyes of many who had been deluded. Accordingly the new assembly, which is uncommonly full of men of Ability, & freinds to the Government, showed their resentment against Mr Otis's proceed[ings] by turning off the printer of their Votes[2] who had printed Mr Otis's libells, & by removing their Chaplain,[3] who (tho' a very good ^man^ & I believe quite freindly to me) was supposed to be conn[ec]ted with Otis. His father[4] also was very near being turned out of the Council, being saved only by a leading man among the freinds of Government who was related to him tak[ing] great pains to get him spared.[5] These mortifications with many others made him on [the] third day of the Session by a short Speech resign his seat & pray that they would pursue another Præcept: immediately after which he left the house without waiting for their resolution. But his freinds having prevailed to defer the confirmation of his resignation, He next day came [in] the house & after having made an Apology desired leave to resume his seat, which was granted not without some ~~hesi~~ ^humilia^tion. It is remarkable that on the morning of the day on which he resigned he made the first motion for my salary, which was considered as an overture for a reconciliation, & occasioned some mirth in which he joind.[6] He at present continues pretty quiet, which is sufficiently accounted for by it's appearing upon ~~examination~~ evry trial that the freinds of Government in the Assembly are above 2 to 1. However Care must be taken to prevent his rallying, which I doubt not he will be ready to do upon the first opportunity.

L, LbC   BP, 3: 73-77.

In the handwriting of clerk no. 2 with scribal emendations. The extent and nature of the emendations to the postscript suggest that it might have been dictated by FB. The conjectured readings in brackets are for letters obscured by tight binding. The enclosures FB mentions were copies of **No. 215** and its enclosures, and the enclosures to **No. 176**.

---

1. **No. 191**.

2. Benjamin Edes and John Gill.

3. The Rev. Samuel Cooper (1725-83), pastor at Brattle Street Church, Boston, had been chaplain to the House since 1753.

4. James Otis Sr. (1702-78), politician, farmer, and merchant of Barnstable, Mass., which he represented 1745-56 and intermittently thereafter until 1769; Speaker of the House, 1760-61, and a member of the Governor's Council 1762-65.

5. Harrison Gray, whose daughter was married to Samuel Allyne Otis (1740-1814), brother of James Otis Jr.

6. On 28 May 1762. The Governor's salary bill for £1,300 provincial currency was read and passed to be enacted on 31 May, and was published on 12 Jun. *JHRM*, 39: 15-16, 21. *Acts and Resolves,* 4: 571.

221 | To Jeffery Amherst

Castle William June 11 1763

S^r.

I am favoured with yours of the 5th inst. I am very sorry that any words in my letter concerning the Men at Halifax[1] should give offence: I meant only to express my apprehension of the inconveniences, which will follow Col Forsters detaining the Men; & if I have done it to feelingly, the obligation I am under to take the best care of my provincials will I hope excuse me.

If I had foreseen that the Men would have been wanted beyond the first of May, I could have got the establishment extended for a month or two. But at the time you signify your intention to continue the Men beyond their day, it was impossible for me to do any thing towards it, but to promise to use my endeavours to reconcile the assembly to the expence, if the Men could be prevailed upon to stay.

My best Services are due to the King; and they have never been wanting: but they must be limited by my power. I therefore hope that neither my inability to prevent these inconveniencies nor my concern at their happening will in the least abate the regards, with which I have hitherto been honoured by you. I am, with great regard,

Sr Your most obedient and most humble Servant

Fra Bernard

His Excellency Sr Jeffry Amherst.

ALS, RC　　　　　　　　　　　　　　WO 34/26, f 238.

Variant text in BP, 2: 310-311 (L, LbC).

---

1. **No. 217**.

222 | To Lord Barrington

Boston June 15. 1763

My L^d

When I was at Penobscot last Summer I engaged the Commander of Fort Pownall on that river to employ the best hand he could to make an Indian Canoo, which I entended for y^r Serpentine River at Becket. The Captain afterwards wrote me Word that he had employed a Squaw of the Penob[s]cot Tribe (who are all now our Freinds) esteemed the best hand for a Canoo in America, to exert the utmost of her art on this occasion. But when I came to recieve it, I find I have been mistaken; & instead of a practicable Canoo they have sent me only a Modell of one. I am so disappointed in this, that in order to alleviate it, I have resolved to send y^r Lordship this trifle of trifles, which perhaps may recommend itself as a curiosity: as it is the work of a Lady, perhaps of the first Quality among her own people, & is exactly the same both in materials & Workmanship as a full sized Canoo. I intend however to send y^r Lordship a full sized one, which tho capable of holding three or four at a time is easily carried by one man from river to river.

I propose to reconnoitre this Country this Summer with great accuracy, the assembly having authorised me to employ a mathematician to make observations all along the Coast. I have a very good man for that purpose, the Professor of Mathematics at this College, whom I shall accompany, & assist myself.[1] And I shall make a further progress in surveying mount desart, unless I am ordered off from home. I have concluded with 60 families with a minister at their head & a merchant to supply 'em to settle there this Summer upon a plan already laid out: I want only power to make them a title.[2] There are also 720 families ready to settle upon the continent adjoining to the Islands in 12 Townships already mark't out. I shall greive much (setting aside my own interest) if this settlement should be defeated; as it is compactly planned & laid out to great advantage. And when I consider how much it has Cost the Government of Great Britain to settle 4000 Souls in some other Parts of America, I think it will be a great pity that such a Settlement should be refused when offered to be brought forward at no public expence at all.[3] For my own part I have been drawn into this scheme unperceptibly: & now the People call on me to be their leader, which I shall decline no longer, than till I can learn that my establishing a New Colony in a desert (which will long remain unpeopled if this opportunity is neglected) will be approved

Yours &c

The R Honble the L Viscount Barrington.

L, LbC   BP, 3: 78-81.

In the handwriting of clerk no. 2 with minor scribal emendations.

1. John Winthrop IV (1714-79), Hollis professor of mathematics and natural philosophy and a noted astronomer. The House voted a £90 gratuity for Winthrop. *JHRM*, 39: 199. FB's second voyage is briefly described in **No. 244**.

2. By 1782 there were 235 white adult males on the island. Mass. Archs., 162: 258.

3. FB is referring to recent emigration schemes promoted by Charles Lawrence, former governor of Nova Scotia, with the agreement of the British, intended to displace the Acadians. The province attracted upwards of 5,000 migrants from New England. George A. Rawlyk, *Nova Scotia's Massachusetts a Study of Massachusetts-Nova Scotia Relations 1630 to 1784* (Montréal, 1973), 218-219, 221.

223 | To Jeffery Amherst

Boston June 19.th 1763

S[r]

I had the favor of yours of the 12th inst by last night's post.[1] I did not expect that the Affair would have got into the general Court this Session, as I had observed a strict silence upon it. But on the last day but one of the Session It got into the Council without my having the least notice of it: so that I could do no more than prevent the report of the Committee having any offence in it, which I hope it is free from. I must earnestly desire that the Accounts may be so settled that the Province may not be charged with any part of the billeting, transporting &c, And then this Matter will easily subside.

I hope this Business will be so well settled, before the Assembly meets again, that there will be ^no^ room for it's affecting future requisitions; concerning which I have the greatest reason to expect a ready compliance: as the composition of the present Assembly is Very favorable to Government. But I shall be allways glad to make such Propositions ^rather^ at the usual times of sitting than at extraordinary Sessions, when the House being often Very thin, their resolutions are not allways so much to be depended upon.

I shall be much obliged to you for the plan you have been pleased to promise me & should be glad to have it as exact & extensive as may be. I will in return send a Copy of our Surveyors field book, if it will be acceptable. I have laid aside the continuing the Survey of Kennebec river, as I had proposed, this Summer: and in the room of it have got the Assembly to enable me to employ a good Mathematician to make observation of the Variation of the Needle & the longitude along the

Eastern Coast from Piscataway to Penobscot: This I shall assist in myself, if I can spare time. I am also getting an actual Survey of the East sides of Penobscot & the Coast eastward of it; where We are making a New Settlement of 12 Townships; but wait for his Majesty's approbation of it; which, according to some late letters, We may expect to have soon.

Col Tullikin in a letter I have lately received from him informs me,[2] that He can, without any detriment to the Service, supply me with what coal I shall want for next Winter: but that He should be glad to have your order for it. I am sorry to be repeatedly troublesome to you upon this Subject; and therefore will submit to you, whether it may be proper to give me a general order for coals for my own use, not exceeding 20 chaldrons a year: altho' I shant want above half that quantity this year, as I have considerable remains of my last years stock.

I am, with great regard, Sr Your most obedient & most humble Servant

Fra. Bernard

His Excellency Sr Jeffry Amherst.

P.S.

The inclosed contain an Apology for my troubling you with them

ALS, RC   WO 34/26, ff 239-240.

Endorsed: Governor Bernard. Boston, <u>19</u>th. June 1763. Rec^d.__ 25th. Ditto.__ Ans^d.__ 26th. Ditto__. Variant text in BP, 3: 1-3 (L, LbC). Enclosed copies of the affidavit of Capt. Johnson Moulton, Massachusetts, 15 May 1763, WO 34/26, f 241; a minute of the Massachusetts Council of 15 Jun. 1763, WO 34/26, f 242; and votes of the General Court, 16 Jun. 1763, WO 34/26, f 243.

The reply to this letter is Amherst to FB, 26 Jun. 1763, WO 34/27, p. 295.

FB had to make several requests of Lt. Col. John Tulleken, the commanding officer at Louisburg, before he finally received ten to twelve chaldrons from the Cape Breton mines. The coals were for his personal use, to stock new grates he had had installed in the Province House and the apartments at Castle William. FB to Tulleken, Boston, 18 Aug. 1763, BP, 3: 4.

---

1. Amherst to FB, New York, 12 Jun. 1763, WO 34/27, p. 293.

2. Not found.

224 | *Circular from the Earl of Egremont*

Duplicate.

Whitehall July, 9th. 1763.

Sir,

It having appeared, that the Publick Revenue has been greatly diminished, and the fair Trader much prejudiced, by the fraudulent Methods used to introduce into His Majesty's Dominions, (contrary to the Act of the 12th Charles 2^d, for encouraging and increasing Shipping and Navigation; and that of 15th. Charles 2^d., for the Encouragement of Trade; and the Act of 7th & 8th of William 3^d., for preventing Frauds, and regulating Abuses in the Plantation Trade,) Commodities of Foreign Growth, in National, as well as Foreign, Bottoms, by means of small Vessels hovering on the Coasts; And that this iniquitous Practice has been carried to a great Heighth in America; an Act was passed the last Session of Parliament, intituled, *An Act for the further Improvement of His Majesty's Revenue of Customs; And for the Encouragement of Officers making Seizures, and for the Prevention of the Clandestine Running of Goods into any Part of His Majesty's Dominions*; by which the former Laws, relative to this Matter, are enforced, and extended to the British Dominions in all Parts of the World; And the King having it extremely at Heart to put an End to all iniquitous Practices of this Nature, by a due, punctual, & vigorous, Exertion of the Laws made for this salutary Purpose; And His Majesty having been pleased to order, that the most effectual Steps should be taken for obtaining that End; the Commanders of His Majesty's Ships, stationed in America, will, in Consequence thereof, be vested for the future, with the necessary and legal Powers from the Commissioners of the Customs, for carrying into Execution the several Acts of Parliament relative to the Seizing & Condemning any Ships that shall be found transgressing against the said Acts. I am to signify to you the King's express Pleasure that you do, as far as shall depend upon you, not only co-operate with, and assist, the said Commanders, in the due and legal Execution of the Powers & Instructions given them by the Commissioners of the Customs; but that you do also use your utmost Endeavours, by the most assiduous and impartial Exertion of the Laws enacted for this purpose to put an effectual Stop to the Clandestine Running of Goods into any place within your Jurisdiction; And that you may be fully informed of every particular in an Affair of this Importance, you will find inclosed herewith a Copy of the Act passed last Session of Parliament, refer'd to above; together with His Majesty's Order in Council, made agreable thereto, for the Division of the Seizures: To which I add a List of the Ships stationed in America, distinguishing such as have the Custom House Commissions, from the few which sailed before the Resolution on that Head was taken; And also a Copy of the Instructions, given by the Lords of the Admiralty, to the several Commanders of these Ships.[1]

The Precautions, which, upon perusing the two last mentioned Papers, you will observe to have been taken here, and the strict Orders given, on this Occasion, to the Commanders of all the Ships of War in America, will sufficiently point out to you, how earnestly the King wishes that all possible Means should be used to root out so iniquitous a Practice; a Practice carried on in Contravention of many express & repeated Laws, tending not only to the Diminution & Impoverishment of the Public Revenue, at a Time when this Nation is labouring under a heavy Debt, incurred by the last War for the Protection of America; But also to expose every fair Trader to certain Detriment, and even Danger of Ruin, by his not being able to carry his Commodities to Market, on an equal footing with those, who fraudulently evade the Payment of the just Dues and Customs from the same.

It is the King's Pleasure that you do, by the first Opportunity, acknowledge the Receipt of this Letter,[2] and that you do, from time to time, transmit to me, for His Majesty's Information, exact Accounts of whatever shall happen, within your Government, in an Affair, which the King considers to be of the highest Importance to the Commercial Interest of His Subjects, and the Improvement of the Public Revenue. You will likewise impart to me, for the King's Approbation, such further Hints as may occur to you, as proper for the subject.

I must also inform you, that His Majesty's Resolution to have the most implicit Obedience paid to these His Commands, is so fixed, that, as on the one Hand, your particular Diligence & Attention in the performance of your Duty herein, will not fail to recommend you to His Majesty's Royal Favor, so, on the Other; it is incumbent on me to acquaint you, That the King will not pass over unnoticed any Negligence, or Relaxation, on the part of any Persons employed in His Service, in a Matter on which His Majesty lays so much Stress, and in which the fair Trade of all His faithful Subjects is so essentially interested.

I am with great Truth and Regard, Sir, Your most obedient humble Servant

Egremont

Govr. of Massachusets Bay.

dupLS, RC   BP, 10: 119-124.

Endorsed by FB: 9 July 1763. Secrety of State's letter Concerning Captns of Men of War r Oct 1763. Enclosures not found. The reply to this letter is **No. 240**.

This is the first official notification that FB and the other governors received of Britain's intention to reinvigorate the mercantlist system by improving both enforcement of the trade laws and revenue collection. The ensuing controversy is traditionally regarded as the onset of the imperial crisis that presaged the Revolution.

---

1. There are three contemporaneous virgules in the left margin marking off the enclosures.

2. **No. 240**.

225 | *To John Pownall*

Boston July 25.th1763

S^r.

I have rec^d. your letter inclosing his majesty's disallowance of the Bill for enabling Mary Hunt to sell her lands; but the Cover did not Contain their Lordships representation of the bill, as your letter intimated; I should be glad to have it as a guide for future bills of this Kind.[1]

I have looked over the bills of last Sessions now transmitted, to you & don't see occasion to trouble there Lordships with observations thereupon. The bill for incorporating the Mashbee Indians is in pursuance of orders rec^d. by me above two years ago, in consequence of a Complaint made by one of these Indians who went to England. It has been delayed by some people who had an intrest in the oppressions which these Indians complained of & were not ashamed to endeavour to maintain themselves in it. The Corporation for propagating the Gospel mentioned in the Bill is the London Corporation of which I believe M^r. Jackson is a Member. They Maintain the Missionary at Mashbee & expend about 500 pounds a year in this Country in the like Services.[2] This ^in^ Corporation is a new Experiment, but I believe it will succeed as the Missionary there takes great pains with them & has a considerable Authority over them.

I am S^r. Your most obedient

John Pownall Esqr.
Secretary for trade & Planations

See P.S. hereafter

P.S to the letter to Mr Pownall of July 25

I have now before me my Answers to the Queries sent to me some time ago; but they want a little revising, & there are some blanks to be filled up, which I wait for, So that I don't expect I shall be able to send them by this ship: but you may depend upon their following soon after.[3] I did not succeed in my purpose for which I postponed the return of these Answers; the taking an exact account of the Numbers of the people. I proposed a Method to do this to the General Court last Session: but a jealousy arising in the House concerning this Business & there being no time to remove it the Session then drawing to a Conclusion the Council & House disagreed upon it; & it was postponed to another Session that is another Year in Effect, when it will be resumed.[4] In the mean time I make the best Conjectural acc^t. I can, drawn chiefly from the returns of the Rateable polls.

L, LbC   BP, 3: 82; postscript on p. 88.

In the handwriting of clerk no. 1 with scribal emendations. Endorsed: 9 July 1763. Secretary of State's letter Containing Capt^ns of Men of War r Oct 1763. Enclosure not found.

On 8 Oct. 1761, a joint committee of the Massachusetts House and Council completed a report regarding amendments necessary to the laws "regulating the Indians." The report was read in Feb. 1762 and allowed to lapse; it was revived by the Council on 21 Feb. 1763, and on 30 May another joint committee was formed to bring in a bill. *JHRM*, 38, pt.1: 59; 39: 267; 40: 25, 70-71, 115. The subsequent act removed the white guardians and established the only self-governing Native American community in the province. An act for incorporating the Indians and Mulattos, Inhabitants of Mashpee, 3 Geo. 3, c. 3 (passed 16 Jun. 1763). *Acts and Resolves*, 4: 639-641, 692. The Mashpee's campaign for "self-determination" can be followed in Francis G. Hutchins, *Mashpee: The Story of Cape Cod's Indian Town* (West Franklin, N.H., 1979), 73-74; Jack Campisi, *The Mashpee Indians: Tribe on Trial* (Syracuse, 1991), 84-85; Daniel R. Mandell, *Behind the Frontier Indians in Eighteenth-Century Eastern Massachusetts* (Lincoln, Neb., 1996), 179-183; Daniel R. Mandell, "'We, as a tribe, will rule ourselves': Mashpee's Struggle for Autonomy, 1746-1840," in *Reinterpreting New England Indians and the Colonial Experience,* eds. Colin G. Calloway and Neal Salisbury (Boston, 2003), 299-340.

---

1. Pownall to FB, 27 Apr. 1763, CO 5/920, p. 160.

2. Stephen West (1735-1819), Congregational missionary and minister to the Stockbridge community, 1759-73.

3. **No. 234**.

4. When FB (finally) presented the Board of Trade's queries to the assembly on 2 Jun. 1763, he specifically requested that the assembly authorize the collection of census data from towns; although a committee was appointed no further action was taken, probably because of growing criticism of the prospective census, until FB revived it in a message of 31 Jan. 1764. *JHRM*, 40: 44, 251-252.

226 | To Richard Jackson

Castle William July 26th. 1763

D^r. S^r.

I have now before me of your letters 2 dated Ap. 25; 1 dated Ap 4. & 1 dated May 20th. the two last of which (that is that of *April 4* as well as the last) I received only on Saturday last,[1] In answering of them I shall bring the Several businesses into separate letters: this shall be reserved for the Agency only

I think I am perfectly acquainted with your Sentiments on this Subject & shall guide my self by them. I should be very loth that the Province should lose your service at this Critical time; & therefore shall endeavor to make your appointment as suitable to your dignity & to your convenience as well may be, when your former letters came on the 10th of June, Some of M^r. Mauduit's friends having received letters from him very favourable to you as they said, expresst their willingness that you should be appointed Council of the Province under the Great seal with an Annual salary. But it being at the end of the Session when the house was thin & I supposing, that they would expect at the same time something to be done for Israel Mauduit in the Substituting way, which I don't intend to enter upon again, I declined the offer giving for reason my desire that what Compliment you were to receive should come from a full house.[2] I believe they would be glad now to join you & Israel Mauduit in the Agency with a distinction of functions: but his connections with M^r. Otis would I believe make it difficult on his part.

But this business is not like to come on the Carpet soon, for I do not intend to call the Assembly together till next winter unless some orders from home or something extraordinary here should ~~happen~~ require it: I am sensible of the criticalness of the time & the necessity there is of putting the Agency upon a proper plan: but at present am at a loss how to form it. I am persuaded that the best would be to send a proper person from hence to act under your directions: but I know not where to find one. The Lieut Govr. is by much the fittest Person in the Province for this purpose: but many difficulties would attend such a proposal both with regard to the person & the Measures. M^r. Bollan has sent in such an exorbitant bill of charges (encreased no doubt by his present disgust) that the Assembly will be frighted at the Mention of another Agent from hence. However I shall have time to think & advise about this.[3] The worst is I shan't be able to explain to them the Critical situation in which their Intrests will soon be. If I should find it expedient as a quieting measure to have you & him (Is. M) appointed joint agents, you expressly as Councillor & he as Sollicitor with instructions to him to direct himself by your advice could it be made agreeable to you? Observe that I don't like this myself at present. I am &

R Jackson Esq$_r$[4]

L, LbC   BP, 3: 82-84.

In the handwriting of clerk no. 1, except as noted, with minor scribal emendations.

---

1. Letters not found.

2. The session ended on 16 Jun. and the General Court was prorogued until 3 Aug.

3. The House had approved a letter on 23 Feb. accusing William Bollan of making "diverse Stoppages of considerable Sums" from the parliamentary subsidies, and instructed Jasper Mauduit to demand of Bollan that he produce both an "Account" of the deductions and a "general Account of his Agency." *JHRM*, 39: 268; Timothy Ruggles to Mauduit, Boston, 22 Feb. 1763, Ford, *Jasper Mauduit*, 98-99.

4. This line in FB's hand.

227 | To the Board of Trade

Boston July 28 1763

My Lords

Some of the people usually called French Neutrals residing in this Province have been with me & have shown me sevral letters they have received from their friends now in England; the general purport of which is as follows: The Duke de Nivernois[1] has signified to them that the King (of france) esteems the Acadians as the most faithful of his subjects; and if they will come to France they shall be well provided for. They are therefore required to send a list of all that desire to go to France distinguishing Men Women & children; & Transports will be sent to fetch them. As it has never been determined, in what light these People are to be seen, whether subjects, or Enemies, or Neutrals, I should be glad to receive your Lordships commands how to act, when these french transports arrive.

Many of these People are very industrious & would, I beleive, prefer this Country & become subjects of Great Britain in earnest, if they were assured of liberty of Conscience. I observed in the letters which they Communicated to me that the maintenance of their religion is among the cheif Motives offered to them for their quitting this Country. They are not disposed to go to Canada where a toleration of their religion is promised but cheifly inclined, if they settle at all, to be on the Eastern coast. There is certainly room enough for them & an hundred times their Number, if their settling in a body with the free exercise of their religion under a priest appointed by the English Government should be thought advisable. If your Lordships should take this Matter into your consideration so far as to form any conclusions for encouraging these people to stay here, I should be glad to receive your orders as soon as may be. There are but two things wanting on their behalf; the granting them lands & tolerating their religion: on the other hand it should be required of them that they take the Oaths of Allegiance in as full a manner as Papists can do.

I am, with great respect, My Lords, Your Lordships most obedient & most humble Servant

Fra Bernard

The Right Honble The Lords Commissioners for Trade &c.

ALS, RC   CO 5/755, ff 27-29.

Endorsed (with the wrong date): July 8. 1763. Gov[r]. Barnard concerning French Neutrals R Sep. 10. from the Secry of Board of Trade. Variant text in BP, 2: 83-84 (L, LbC).

FB's letter was transmitted to the secretary of state and acknowledged by the Board. Board of Trade to FB, Whitehall, 17 Oct. 1763, CO 5/920, p. 164.

---

1. Louis Jules Mancini-Mazarini (1716-98), the duc de Nivernais, arrived in London in Sept. 1762 as the French ambassador to negotiate peace, whereupon he learned of the Acadians' plight.

228 | To Richard Jackson

Castle William Aug.st. 2. 1763

Dear S.r

In the close of one of your letters[1] you mention that it was hinted to you that the Crown would consent to the uniting Massachusets Connecticut & Rhode Island; & that you answered that a Consent would not be obtained else where. I would not have made such a proposal to you; but as the first mention of it comes from you & it has really been often talked of here among most sensible men, I would have you consider it well, whether such an Union might not be made advantageous to Connecticut.

In the first place, you can't expect that when the Colonies come to be regulated, Connecticut will preserve it's present Constitution. A British Legislature independent of the King is such a Monster in Politicks that it can only be tolerated for want of time & oppertunity to reform them. Would it not be better for them to form the plan of their own reformation than to leave it to others to do it? Would not they like better to be united to a people connected with them by a similarity of religion & Manners upon a plan of Government as popular as can be hoped to be preserved in this Country, than to run the risk of being made a meer royal Government or added to one that is so & is dissimilar to them in Manners?

As for their Charter; besides that it is under a Sentence which may yet be legally revived,[2] to oppose a modern Grant of the King alone under very confined Views, in bar to the Parliaments providing for the govern.g in the best manner, the people of a large Empire, will surely be a Vain & unsuccessful Work. For my own part I consider Government not to be a Right but a trust, and that the Royal Grants of Jurisdiction in America either to private persons or Corporations are no more than temporary provisions untill the Parliament that is the whole Legislature, shall settle the Govern.mt., Surely this is law now, whatever it was before the Revolution. Observe that I mean there is a Material distinction between Grants of propriety & grants of Jurisdiction; the former creates a durable right the latter only a temporary trust. The Advantages which will arise to Connecticut from such an Union are obvious. The Colony is, at present, as full as it can hold; emigrations are continually made to Countries & People dissimilar to their own. some go to Nova Scotia, to the Eastern parts of this Governm^t., to the NWest parts of the Same & thro' them to the North ^West^ Parts of New hampshire. others more adventurous have settled upon the Susquehannah, from whence they got away but just time to prevent a general Massacre would it not be very happy for these people if they could find Sufficient Settlements near home & bring the same within their own Jurisdiction? the thing is very practicable; as thus:

I would not propose the union of our Province with the two Colonies without including the lands to the Westward of the river Merrimack as far North as the uppermost part of the River Connecticut, which according to Langdons Map of New hampshire would easily join with that of Merrimack.[3] This with our lands on the west side of New hampshire only & the two Colonies would make a noble rich & extensive province exceptionable only on account of it's power & riches, which objections should not come from you nor me. The Lands on the North side of Massachusetts, have been granted away to the Amount of 200 townships (as they say) but it is impossible for the Grantees to perform their Covenants for settling, tho' the utmost allowances should be made; and therefore great part of these Lands must revert to the owners of the fee, or, what is the same, must be saleable for a Very trifle to real settlers. Here alone is a Sufficient resort for all the emigrants of Connecticut; they have it indeed at present: but will it not be much more valuable to them, if, by the Union proposed they consider themselves as not going out of their own Governm^t.?

I will now consider the difficulties that are like to attend this Affair: the most obvious of which is that if Boston is to be the Capital, Connecticut will be plainly disadvantaged by its distance from it. For this, I will only consider the convenience of the Attending the Courts of Justice, & the Grand Court of Parliament or General Court as it is called in this Province. For the first I see no impropriety but that, notwithstanding the Union of the Legislature the Administration of Justice may be kept separate & there may be still two Superior Courts of Justice independant of one another. For the Second, it will become reasonable & therefore no doubt will be readily ordered by the Legislature itself that the meeting of the Assembly shall be at a Place equally suitable, as near as may be to the different parts of the united Province. I am sensible that the towns now enjoying these meeting will except to this;[4] but the General Equity & advantage of the united Province must prevail. As for the intrest of particular persons, who are now in Office, that may be easily provided for

And now S[r]., let me say that if from these loose hints & your improvement of them this Union can be brought about, we shall both of us have some pretension to no little Merit.

I am Sr. Your most faithful &c

R. Jackson Esq[r]

L, LbC   BP, 3: 89-92.

In the handwriting of clerk no. 1 with emendations by FB.

Herein FB refers to two controversial sets of land grants. The first concerns the Wyoming Valley and land along the upper Susquehanna River that had long been coveted by white settlers from Connecticut and Pennsylvania. Settlement was problematic, since these areas had become a refuge for displaced Delawares and around eighteen other fragmented tribes. The community was led by "King" Teedyescung, whom FB had met at the Easton conference of Oct. 1758, and nominally protected by the Iroquois Confederation and the province of Pennsylvania. The aborted "massacre" to which FB alludes refers to the attempted settlement of Wyoming in May 1762 by ninety settlers from Connecticut under the auspices of the Susquehanna Company. The company claimed the valley under a provincial land grant of 1754, but the settlers' designs were temporarily thwarted when threats of reprisals from the resident tribes prompted a withdrawal.

The second set, the "Lands on the North side of Massachusetts," were the so-called "New Hampshire Grants"—land grants in 131 New Hampshire towns issued by the colony's government to over 6,000 persons, many of whom resided in other New England colonies; FB's sons John and Francis were grantees in the town of Barnard, incorporated in Jul. 1761. See George P. Anderson, "New Hampshire Land Grants to Boston Men," *Publications of the Colonial Society of Massachusetts* 25 (1922-1923): 33-38.

---

1. Not found.

2. This may be a reference to James II's attempted consolidation of the New England colonies into the dominion of New England, and Gov. Edmund Andros's infamous failed attempt to obtain possession of Connecticut's royal charter of 1662.

3. Samuel Langdon, *An Accurate Map of His Majesty's Province of New-Hampshire in New England & All the Adjacent Country Northward to the River St Lawrence, & Eastward to Penobscot Bay Containing the Principal Places Which Relate to the Present War on the Continent of North America* (1756), Faden Map Collection, Library of Congress.

4. Thus in manuscript.

229 | *To Richard Jackson*

Boston Aug^st. 3^d. 1763

Dear Sir

I have wrote two letters to you[1] Since my receipt of the last packet:[2] I must make this third contain all I can write now without distinction of Subject, as the Ship which is to carry these is to sail to morrow

In my letter to you dat May 20 I desird you to recommend me to M^r. Townshend, whom I then understood to be the first Lord of Trade.[3] As it is, I must desire now to apply the second paragraph of that letter to Lord Shelburne.[4] It is above a year & a half ago since I wrote to Lord Barrington to offer my Service[5] (in person if thought proper) to represent my Sentiments in regard to what appeared to me to be wanting in the political Constitutions of the Severall Governments in America; as it was a Subject I had much Studied tho' not wrote upon. This was wrote upon a Supposition that there would be a general Reformation in the governments of N America. that if ever this was intended, perhaps it will be postponed, till the Ministry at home is more settled than it seems to be at present. In this letter I represented that if it should be thought that my Attendance would be of use, it should be made unexpensive to me: that in order to save as much of my Salary here as possible, it would be Advisable to keep the Orders for my coming home a secret here, so that I might get my years Salary which is granted at the opening the New Court at the end of May just before I set out. Upon, the appointment of Mr Townshend I reprised Lord Barrington's Memory on this Subject, & have again done it in another letters that accompanies this:[6] and having now mentiond it to you in confidence, I leave it to have Effect or not, as it shall happen, not knowing which will be best for me.

Your Account of the Danger of the Melasses Act being renewed & carried into full execution is Very alarming. The mischeivous consequences of such a Measure, I fear, will not appear so certain on your side of the Water as they do here. What will be more to be regretted upon this occasion is, that by lowering the duty so as not to exceed ½ ^d Ᵽ Gallon, (which, I am told, is the utmost it will bear) a fund might be established sufficient to create a civil list for each colony, which is a provision absolutely necessary for the firm Establishment of government in this Country. On the other hand, if the Northern Colonies are not allowed to import foreign Sugars & Melasses upon Practicable terms, they will, become desperate, for they really wont be able to live. I could write a Volume on this Subject but must defer adding any more at present. I will endeavour some other time to be more particular on this; at present I will only say that I dread the consequences of such a resolution.

I have wrote so much upon the affair of Sagadehock, that I will only now repeat my thank to you.[7] I promist to make a remittance on the behalf of the Settlers of the 6 townships for fees &c: but they have been disappointed in the formality of making thier Collection, so that they were obligd to apply to the generall Court for a further authority to oblige People to pay, which has been granted & the Collections are now making. The principal Proprietor with whom I communicate here, expects that the mony will be sent for, in a few days. The Collection for this purpose is set at dollar a share amounting in the 81 pound Ster^g. If that is not Sufficient more must be raised. The Defence of the Province's Title is to lie upon the Province__ I am &c

R Jackson Esq

L, LbC   BP, 3: 92-94.

In the handwriting of clerk no. 2 with minor scribal emendations.

---

1. **No**. **226** and **228**.

2. Jackson to FB, 25 Apr. 1763, received on 23 Jul. 1763, but not found.

3. **No. 213**.

4. FB to the earl of Shelburne, Boston, 25 Jul. 1763, BP, 3: 84-85.

5. **No. 83**.

6. Thus in manuscript. FB to Barrington, Castle William, 1 Aug. 1763, BP, 3: 86-87.

7. Thus in manuscript.

230 | To Richard Jackson

Boston Augst 6 1763

Dear Sir

I sent you 4 letters 3 in one Cover & 1 in another, all in the cover of the board of Trade,[1] also some New England Pamp[h]letts in a sealed cover: they all went in a Box directed to Mr Mauduit by the Brigg Hannah Capt. Jarvis who sailed for London two days ago__

Since I have sent away these, I have seen Col. Dyer, who is going home from Connecticut to Sollicit leave to proceed in the Connecticut Settlement on the Susquehannah under a purchase from the Six Nations.[2] I have always considered this Settlement as a most vain attempt: but a Conversation I have had with Col.

Dyer has set it in a new Light to me: and as he desires to carry a letter from me to you, I will give you Some of my thoughts upon this Subject.

You know my Opinion concerning the distinction between grants of Jurisdiction & grants of property: that the former are only trusts and not rights; but that the latter are mere rights & ought not to be taken away unless they have been forfeited by non performance of the conditions &c; as in the Cause of Lord Sterling's of Nova Scotia & many others all along this Coast.

To apply this distinction to the present case, If the colony of Connecticut should Offer to extend their Government (leaping over the Province's of New York & New Jersey) by a narrow latitudinal strip to the South Seas, it is inconceivable that the British Government would suffer it: the inconveniences which would arise from thence would be so obvious, that the positive terms of the Charter must be rejected upon Account of the absurdity of their Consequences. And therefore the Government of Connecticut who either do not or will not see the distinction between grants of jurisdiction & grants of property, affraid to appear in support of their property, least they should seem to Claim an improper extension of jurisdiction at the same time, but had they thought proper to claim these lands as property only, they might have been more open & active in the Vindication of this right than they now dare to be__

But if this Matter is made a question of a mere right to lands, Submitting to the King, (as I understand, the grantees under Connecticut are willing to do) the Settling the Government in Such manner as he shall please, The King is no otherwise intrested in this question than 1. Whether Mess[rs]. Penn[3] or Mess[rs]. the grantees of Connecticut have a right to purchase of the Indians & Settle the Country, & 2. which are most likely to do it with effect & to the best advantage to the British Empire. As to the first this Land was certainly granted to the Corporation of Connecticut before it was to M[r] Penn, & therefore the second grant is Void: for the Second, the Connecticut Grantees have allready purchased the right of the Indians & are ready to Settle the lands; Mess[rs]. Penn have neither done one, nor are ready to do the other: indeed they have employment enought elsewhere

If this claim of lands by continuing the latitude of Connecticut should be Valid, I dont see but that the same claim would be good in regard to the latitude of the Massachusets (see Evan's map).[4] And if they should both be willing to quit claim to the jurisdiction & only desire to be allowed to settle the lands with emigrants of their own, under such Government as the King shall please to appoint; I am not sure that the Ministry will not listen to it: It seems to deserve consideration; for which purpose I submit it to yours: It is quite new to me __ I am D[r] Sir &c

R Jackson Esq

L, LbC   BP, 3: 94-96.

In the handwriting of clerk no. 2 with minor scribal emendations. Enclosures not found.

Col. Dyer was unsuccessful in obtaining Crown approval for the Susquehanna Company's attempted occupation of the Wyoming Valley. However, the company purchased the valley from the Iroquois in 1763, forcing the tribes westward to the Ohio River and the Great Lakes, where some participated in Pontiac's Rebellion. Teedyescung, the sachem of the Delawares and other tribes residing in Wyoming, was murdered, probably by company men, in Apr. 1763.

1. FB to the Board of Trade, Boston, 1 Aug. 1763, BP, 3: 86-89.

2. FB is alluding to the aspirations of the Susquehanna Company, whose agent, Eliphalet Dyer (1721-1807), was traveling to England to obtain Crown confirmation of the grant to the Wyoming Valley made by Connecticut in 1754. See **No. 228**.

3. John Penn (1699-1746), Richard Penn (d.1771), and Thomas Penn (1703-75), joint proprietors of Pennsylvania.

4. Lewis Evans, *A General Map of the Middle British Colonies in America; Viz Virginia, Màriland, Dèlaware, Pensilvania, New-Jersey, New-York, Connecticut, and Rhode Island: of Aquanishuonîgy, the Country of the Confederate Indians; Comprehending Aquanishuonîgy Proper, Their Place of Residence, Ohio and Tïiuxsoxrúntie Their Deer-Hunting Countries; Couxsaxráge and Skaniadarâde, Their Beaver-Hunting Countries; of the Lakes Erie, Ontario and Champlain, and of Part of New-France: Wherein Is Also Shewn the Antient and Present Seats of the Indian Nations* (Philadelphia, 1755).

231 | To the Board of Trade

Boston Aug. 13. 1763___

My Lords

I wrote to your Lordships the 28th of last month[1] informing that severall of the Acadians called french Neutrals had been with me to signify their intention to go to Old France, for which purpose they expected transports from France: & I desired your Lordships directions how I should act upon this occasion. They have since brought me a list of the persons who intend to go,[2] which I have analysed & find it stands thus. Families __ 179

Heads of families, Persons__	320
Sons__	363
Daughters__	336
Total	1019

This I take to be very near, if not quite, the whole Number of french Acadians within this Province.

If these people return to France as french Subjects they must be considered as prisoners of War & therefore their Subsistence ought to be paid for. This Government some time ago made out an Account of the Money expended in the maintenance of the french Acadians which has been continued; & by papers now lying before me I find amounts to 9,544 pounds sterling due to this province on that account. I don't find that this has been as yet laid before any of his Majestys Ministers: but this will be thought a proper time to do it & I expect the Agent will be ordered to sollicit it. In this I flatter myself he will succeed, not only because it is justly due to the Province who have had the burthen of these people without being like to reap any benefit from them, but also because the Crown of France, who considers these as it's Subjects & is to demand them accordingly is chargeable with this expence. These Accounts will be transmitted to our Agent in form; at present I only mention the sum total that an early consideration of it may be had.[3]

I have this day received (under a cover directed by M[r] Pownall) a letter from Jacques Robins a french Protestant intending to settle at Miramichy,[4] desiring me to deliver two inclosed letters to Jaqui Maurice, a french Neutral well known to me, tending to persuade him to settle at Miramichy with the rest of the Acadians. I hope it will have effect, notwithstanding it comes rather too late: for I know so much of the industry & frugality of these people, that I have been very desirous that they should not be lost to British America. I have hitherto advised them to suspend their resolution to quit the Country till they know what offers they would have to settle here. I am inclined to think that these letters will still detain some of them.

I informed your Lordships, in a former letter, that if his Majesty should be pleased to confirm to me the Island of Mount desart, It was my intention to set up Works for making Potash on that Island. I have accordingly enquired into that business & have met with a Gentleman[5] who has surmounted all difficulties & has obtained a process different from & more easy & efficacious than any other known. He sent to London last year some potash that was allowed to be better than any heretofore imported. He has now freighted 23 tuns, which he has submitted to the Society for Arts. He is very communicative & has engaged to furnish me, with instructions utensils & an experienced foreman, whenever I shall be at Liberty to pursue it. This Business is very well calculated for clearing of lands: & I dont doubt but when it is more known, it will be generally practised, so as to make a considerable return to Great Britain.

The orders I received for proclaiming peace I executed with all possible Solemnity;[6] for which I beg leave to refer your Lordships to the printed Accounts which are in general true. This was due to the People as well as to the Subject itself; for however they may be divided upon other Matters, they are unanimous (to a Man as far as I can learn in a thankful Approbation of the Treaty of Peace).

I am with great respect, My Lords, your Lordships___ most obedient & most humble Servant

Fra Bernard

The Right Honble The Lords Commissioners for Trade &c

LS, RC   CO 5/891, ff 185-186.

In the handwriting of clerk no. 2. Endorsed by John Pownall: *Massachusets Bay* Letter from Gov[r]. Bernard to the Board, dated 13 Aug[st]. 1763, relative to the Number of the Acadians, & the Expences of the Province in supporting them; & acquainting their Lordships with the Receipt of a Letter from M. Robins, advising the Acadians to settle at Miramichy, with his own Design of making Potash on the Island of Mount Desert, & his Solemn Proclamation of the Peace. Rec[d]. Read Oct. 1763. L.l.62. Variant text in BP, 2: 84-87 (L, LbC); CO 5/755, ff 63-66 (L, LbC).

The "printed account" that was enclosed with this letter was probably a copy of the *Boston Gazette*, 1 Aug. 1763, which contained on p. 1: By His Excellency Francis Bernard, Esq; ... A proclamation for a thanksgiving ... Thursday the eleventh day of August next ... Given at the Council-chamber in Boston, the twenty-seventh day of July, 1763.

This letter was read by the Board of Trade on 24 Oct. 1763. An extract concering the Acadians was referred to the secretary of state on 26 Oct. with a representation from the Board. *JBT*, 11: 399.

---

1. **No. 227**.

2. List of French Neutrals desiring to relocate to France, Mass. Archs., 24: 486-491, enclosed in Andrew Oliver to Jasper Mauduit, 24 Aug. 1763, Mass. Archs., 24: 484-485.

3. Account for the support of French Neutrals in Massachusetts Bay, 1755-1763, Aug. 1763, Mass. Archs., 24: 492-502, of which a copy was enclosed in Oliver to Mauduit, 24 Aug. 1763.

4. Miramachi is in present-day New Brunswick, Canada, and Robins claimed to have been awaiting confirmation of a Crown grant for these lands. *Selections From the Public Documents of Nova Scotia*, 340.

5. Levi Willard (d.1775) of Lancaster, Worcester Co., Mass., who petitioned the General Court for assistance in producing potash on 23 Dec. 1763. *JHRM*, 40: 123. He established a successful mercantile business in partnership with Capt. Samuel Ward, held the provincial rank of Lt. Col., and was a justice of the peace; he became a prominent Loyalist. See **No. 232**.

6. See **No. 204**.

232 | To William Fitzherbert

Boston Aug 13. 1763

Dear S[r]

I beg leave to recommend to the Society through you M[r] Willard of this Province, who with great industry & perseverance has acquired a Process of making potash different from all others & superior both in facility & efficacy. He sent home some last year, which was reported to be the best that ever came to London. He has now shipt 23 Tun with the proper certificates; and hopes that if the Society has not continued their premium this year they will make him a compensation some other Way: especially as he was prevented making a sufficient quantity last year by the burning of some of his Works.

He is very communicative & willing to assist any one who will undertake the same business. As I have intended to set up potash works upon an Island (which has been granted to me by the General Court of this Province & is now submitted to the King for his confirmation) This Gentleman has engaged to give me full instructions to provide Utensils & lend me one of his best hands. I have the greatest hopes that this business will be well understood in this Country: and it is to encourage & propagate it only that I propose to engage in it. I shall write to you soon again on the same subject & am

S[r] Your most faithful & obedient Servant

Fra. Bernard

W[m] Fitzherbert Esq[1]

ALS, RC   Selected Materials Relating to America, 1754-1806, PR.GE/110/14/114, RSA.

Variant text in BP, 3: 97 (L, LbC). The Royal Society does not appear to have taken any special interest in Willard.

---

1. William Fitzherbert (1712-72) of Tissington Hall, Derbyshire, was MP for Derby, 1761-72, and a lord commissioner for Trade and Plantations, 1765-72. Fitzherbert was likely a council member or trustee of the Royal Society for the Encouragement of Arts, Manufactures & Commerce.

233 | To the Board of Trade

Boston Aug 24. 1763

My Lords

By my letter dated July 28[1] I informed your Lordship's that the French Acadians in this Province had signified to me their intention to go to Old France & that they expected transports to be sent to carry them thither. By my letter dated Aug 13[2] I informed that they had delivered me a list of those who intended to go to France, which consisted of 1019 persons in all; & also that I communicated ^to them^ some letters from M⟨r⟩ Robins a french Protestant, inviting them to settle in the Bay of Miramichi & promising them the liberty of their religion. Upon the whole I desired your Lordship's directions in what manner I should act.

Since I sent away the last of these letters I have had an application from 16 families of these Acadians[3] to grant them a passport to go to S⟨t⟩ Peter's the Island lately ceded to France. Altho' I should be loth to part with these people, whilst there was a probability of their settling on British land in good humour & for good purposes, yet I know not how I could refuse them the liberty of going to a french settlement, if they are considered as french prisoners of War or as french subjects of a conquered country and if they are considered as English subjects, the liberty of going out of the Province is absolute, as they stand charged with no crime. For the former distinctions, the sending the Acadians from Liverpool to France in a Cartel is a precedent in point.[4] The only Difficulty I had upon the occasion was, that I had submitted this Matter to your Lordships; & therefore I could not properly send them out of the Province, without your Lordships order: on the other hand I know not how to confine them in it against their Will.

Under these difficulties I this day submitted this Matter to the Council, and in the course of the consideration It was in general agreed that I could not properly open the door nor shut it: and therefore the advice of the Council is conceived in such terms as shall not encourage their departure nor positively prohibit it. In this State it must remain untill I shall receive your Lordships orders.[5]

I hereby enclose a Copy of the Act of the Council & am with great respect

My Lords Your Lordships most obedient & most humble Servant

Fra. Bernard

The Right Honble The Lords Commissioners for Trade & Plantations

ALS, RC   CO 5/891, ff 179-182.

Contains minor emendations. Endorsed: *Massachusets* Letter from Francis Bernard Esqr. Govr. of the Massachusets Bay dated 24. Augst. 1763, relating to the intension of the Acadi-ans in that province to settle under the French at the Island of S^t. Peter & inclosing Reced Read Octr. 13 1763. L.l.59.

Variant text in CO 5/755, ff 45-48 (L, Copy) and BP, 2: 87-89 (L, LbC). Enclosed a copy of a minute of the Massachusetts Council of 24 Aug. 1763, CO 5/891, f 181.

Copies of FB's letter and the enclosure were referred to the secretary of state (*JBT*, 11: 392), whose reply is **No. 237**.

---

1. **No. 227**.

2. **No. 231**.

3. About 90 persons in total were listed. List of French Neutrals desiring to relocate to France, Mass. Archs., 24: 486-491; a minute of the Massachusetts Council of 24 Aug. 1763.

4. In the summer of 1763, over 1,000 Acadian refugees living in England sailed to France from Liverpool. Griffiths, *The Contexts of Acadian History, 1686-1784*, 101.

5. **No. 235**.

234 | *Answer to the Queries of the Board of Trade*

The Answer of Francis Bernard Esq Governor of his Majesty's Province of Massa-chusets Bay to the Queries Proposed by the Right Honorable The Lords Com-missioners for Trade & Plantations.

[*1*]¹ The Province of Massachusets Bay is situated on the continent of North America towards the Atlantick Ocean between the Degrees of latitude 41 & 45² ^reckoning by sea coast only.^ The Soil is inferior to that of England in general, but is Very Suitable to Indian Corn Barley Oats & Rye. It has not as yet produced Wheat enough for its own consumption, being not so easy of tillage as the Soil of the Southern Provinces. It is Very natural to English Grass of all sorts. The Heat in Summer & the Cold in Winter are much more intense than in England. I once observed Farenheits Thermometer³ 3½ degrees below 0 & the Summer following It was 96½ for a short time: But these were both singular & uncommon instances. Last Winter which was very severe it was several times at 2, & never lower, this Summer which has been temperate it has never been higher than 88. So that I would consider those as the general extremities. Notwithstanding the intenseness of the Cold, The Winter is a Very healthy Season; so is the Summer & the Autumn. But the Spring is a dangerous time to uncareful People, upon account of the fre-

quent cold Easterly Wind interfering with the Warmth of the Opening Summer. The Principal Ports, are Boston, Salem, Newberry & Falmouth, each of which has a seperate Custom house: There are several other good harbours. The Principal Rivers that have any considerable inland Navigation are the Merrimack, the Kennebeck & the Penobscot. Boston the Capital by good observations is found to lie in 42°. 25′ North latitude & 71°. 30.⁴ west longitude from London. I cant learn that the longitude has been taken anywhere else by observation; & suppose it is laid down in modern Maps by computation.

2⁵ The Province consists of the Old Colony of Massachusets Bay, the Colony of New Plimouth the Province of Main & the Country between the Province of Main & the River Sᵗ. Croix called the Territory of Sagadehock. The Old Colonys of the Massachusets & New Plymouth being contiguous are bounded on the South by the Colonies of Rhode Island & Connecticut, on ^the West by New York, on the North by New hampshire, on^ the East by the Atlantick. The Province of Main extends from the River Newichewanick along the Sea Coast North Eastward (the Coast lyes nearest North East & South West) to the River Kennebeck & up the Rivers Newichewanock & Kennebeck into the Lands North westward untill 120 miles are finished & a Line to be drawn from the end of the 120 Miles up Newichewanock to the end of the 120 Miles up Kennebeck. By a decree of his late Majesty in Council⁶ settling the Boundaries between the Massachusets & New Hampshire the construction of Northwestward was determined to be North two degrees west, which has altered the formerly conceived Bounds of that Province being then a regular tract about 120 miles Square.⁷ A dispute has subsisted many years between this Province & New York concerning boundaries. The Merits of it having been heard & considered by the Lords Commissioners for Trade & Plantations, & a report having been made thereon the Province humbly waits his Majesty's determination.⁸ A dispute subsisted also between this Province & the Colony of Connecticut untill the year 1713 when the Line was settled & run by Commissioners from both Goverments. Four Towns Woodstock Suffield Enfield & Somers which had been granted & settled by Massachusets fell within Connecticut. By a preliminary agreed between the two Governments,⁹ if any Towns which had been granted by either Government should fall within the other, the Jurisdiction should remain to the Government which granted and an equivalent should be given for the Property: Accordingly an equivalent in other lands was granted by the Massachusets to Connecticut who received & sold the Same; & the Jurisdiction of the Towns remained with the Massachusets without dispute untill the year 1746; when the Province being excessively burthened with a Debt incurred by the Expedition to Cape Breton & an intended Expedition against Canada the Inhabitants of these four Towns refused to submit any longer to the Massachusets Government & applied to Connecticut for Protection who by an Act extended the County of

Windham to the Massachusets Line & have ever since excersised Jurisdiction over them.[10] The Massachusets judging it would be of bad consequence in a time of War by Acts of Power to compel Subjection immediately, exhibited their humble Complaint to his Majesty in Council against the Government of Connecticut for this unfair proceeding; which complaint has not yet been considered. I am humbly of Opinion that if his Majesty should be pleased to order those revolted Towns to return to their subjection to the Massachusets, that it would be for the Peace of both Governments & that the Inhabitants in general of those Towns would like-wise be well satisfyed, provided they might be exempted from paying Taxes to the Massachusets which the Government every year have continued to lay upon them ever since their revolts. It is but equitable they should be exempted for such years as they have paid to Connecticut in the Mean time. But the Taxes for which they were in Arrears at the time of their revolt & which are still unpaid it is equitable they should still be charged with.[11] Some question has lately been made of the Va-lidity of the Title of the Province to the Lands between the Rivers Penobscot & S^t. Croix: the merits of their Claim has been at large laid before your Lordships.[12]

3[13] It is impracticable to take an exact account of the Shipping belonging to this Province & their tonnage, as Shipping itself is a considerable Article of trade; And when a Ship is built for Sale She is registered freighted & cleared in the same manner as if she was to continue in the trade of the Province, and therefore the Entries of the Naval Office & Custom house afford no certain grounds to estimate the quantity of the permanent Shipping of the Province. A List of the Shipping ^from 10 tons upwards^ belonging to the several Towns in the Province was taken by order of the general Court in 1761, & the returns amounted to 57,000 Tons: but this was undoubtedly imperfect. The Shipping of Boston has decreased of late: This is partly owing to the increase of the Trade of other towns in the Province & partly to the illicit trade which is carried on in Rhode Island Connecticut &c with greater Security than it can be here.[14] Ship building is generally a losing trade, but it is a necessary resort to make good the ballance due to Great Britain when other branches fail or prove insufficient. The Whale Fishery has been increased since the reduction of Canada: Many small Vessels have made profitable Voyages in the Gulph of St Lawrence; but I am informed that so little regard has been had to the preserving the Calves or young Whales, & the fishery has been generally pursued with such unremission, that the Want of the regulations to which the french sub-jected that fishery, will be soon felt by the total destruction thereof. The Produce of this fishery, Oyl & Bone is shipped directly for Great Britain, & has for the last year made a considerable part of the returns. The Trade of the Codfishery is carried on at the Towns of Salem Marblehead Glocester & Plymouth, and at some other Towns of lesser Note. It is not an encreasing Trade, the Scarcity of hands & the high Wag-es, which are the Natural Consequences of War having much checked it: but I am in hopes that it will be improved by the Settling the Peace. The best of Cod goes to Spain Portugal & Italy, the produce whereof is chiefly remitted to England; The Worst sort is sent to the West Indies. There are also other lesser fisheries which employ a good many small Vessells. Herrings & Shad are taken in the rivers and in the beginning of the Summer & Mackrell from July to October. These are Salted and Barrelled & sent to the West Indies. These several kinds of fish together with boards staves shingles & hoops commonly called lumber, with some provisions & garden stuff of no great value make up the freights to the West Indies: the returns are made partly in remittances to England & partly in rum Sugar & Melasses. The latter Article (besides what is consumed in Specie by the Inhabitants) is distilled into rum, which is used in the trade to Newfoundland, the whole produce of which is remitted to England & is sent to Maryland & Virginia in return for Corn & Pork: a great part of it is used in the prosecution of the fisheries; & some part (perhaps too much) consumed by the inland inhabitants. But upon the Whole I consider the Melasses distilling as very necessary to the chief part of the trade of this province; and if it should be obstructed either by a severe execution of the present laws or by the enacting of new ones for that purpose, I fear that the consequences would soon be felt by the English Merchants trading to this Country. Indeed there is a succedaneum[15] that this people might resort to, if the Melasses distillery was obstructed, I mean the distilling Spirits from Grain raised in this Country: but the misfortune would be that all the ill consequences of the interruption of the Melasses distillery would take effect before the New Distillery from grain could be brought about. If It was not for the danger of this interval, It might be made a question, whether it would not be better for the province to distill from their own produce: But Innovations in matters of trade are so precarious, that I cannot help recommending the encouragement of the Melasses distillery in this Province. This Province also sends out considerable quantities of Provisions to Nova Scotia & to Newfoundland, the produce of which is remitted to Great Britain. I know of no ^new^ Trades Works or Manufactures that are or may prove hurtful to Great Britain; I rather think that the Province ~~rather~~ wants Trades & Manufactures than abounds in them; for it is certain that within these late years the imports have been greater than the Province can well bear; and they must be lessened, unless New funds can be found out for Answering them. Upon the whole as Great Britain will always have what this Country can spare (at present, I believe, She takes rather more than it can spare) She need not fear trades & Manufactures set up here; since whatever is saved or gained here will be sent to Great Britain to purchase other things. Superfluities are laid out in luxury; American Luxury is almost wholly supplied from Great Britain; therefore all profit in America must centre in Great Britain. Even illegal trade, where the ballance is in favour of the British Subject, makes its final returns to Great Britain. For want of a more certain account of the Shipping I hereto add an

Account of the Ships &c which passed Castle William outward bound from July 1. 1762 to July 1. 1763 viz.[t] Ships 40 Snows 17 Brigs 107 Schooners 178 Sloops 294 total 636. But no conclusion can be formed from hence, as many or most of them are repeated some of them 3 or 4 times.

4[16] The Inhabitants of the trading Towns Men Women & Children have their whole supply of Cloathing from Great Britain. Most of the Women in all other Towns have the Principal part of their cloathing of British Manufactures; the Men have more or less. The poor labouring people in the County Towns wear their common Cloathes principally of coarse homespun linnens & Woolens. Shoes are to be excepted, the Mens being generally manufactured here, the Womens partly only. Most of the Furniture of the Houses in the trading Towns is of British Manufacture. Nails, Glass, Lead, Locks, Hinges & many other materials for Houses are wholly imported from Great Britain. Canvas, Cordage & Ship Chandlery Wares for Vessells & in general such Manufactures as are exported to the Plantations are consumed here & by the best Information I can get the Consumption increases rather than decreases.

5[17] There is a constant Trade carried on with the Dutch & Danish Plantations: in one of the former, Surrinam Many English have considerable Estates. During the War with France and before that with Spain a considerable Trade was carried on with Monto' Christo, the returns chiefly French Sugars; & tho' the exports for this Trade were chiefly Gold & Silver, it was thought to be advantageous to Great Britain. The Trade immediately to the French Settlements called the flag of Truce Trade, this Province was never concerned in. For tho' I believed it to be in general (when provisions & warlike Stores were not exported) very beneficial to Great Britain, yet as I understood that it was not approved of at home, it was never permitted here. In time of peace, A small trade chiefly for Melasses is permitted at some of the french Plantations: but this is very precarious, as sometimes a pretence is made to confiscate Vessells, that have been encouraged to come there, contrary to good faith. The Exports to & imports from foreign plantations are pretty much the Same as with the British. There is a small trade with the Western Islands in about 8 or 10 small Vessells in a year carrying Fish Lumber & Grain & returning with Wines. The Madeira Trade is greatly decreased by reason of the high price those wines are got at, not above one small cargo coming in in a year. A considerable quantity of fish is sent to Spain Portugal & Italy, the returns are chiefly made by remittances to London. Each Vessell generally brings back a load of Salt & from Lisbon some Wine & Lemmons, which latter coming in small quantities & not being in the least injurious to Great Britain, differing, in no respect of trade, from Wine from the Portuguese Islands, is overlookt. Lately two or three Voyages have been made with Logwood to Hamburgh & from thence to Petersburgh,[18] whence they return with Hemp stopping at Scotland to enter & clear. This is a new Experiment; but it is thought that in time of Peace Hemp may be brought cheaper from London. There is very little Trade direct from Holland, as no freights can be made but with Logwood; & that is not imported here in any quantity when it is low in Europe

6[19] The methods used to prevent illegal trade are frequent inspections made by the Naval & Custom house Officers, by whose care the Laws of trade are better supported in this Province than in most others of America. About 2 years ago Great endeavours were made to disable the Officers in carrying the laws into execution, & a public opposition was made in open Court against the Superior Court (which is here Vested with the Powers of the Court of Exchequer) granting writs of Assistance except in special cases. But the Judges overruled the exceptions & Writs of Assistance are now granted in as effectual a form as in England. The greatest difficulty which attends the execution of the Laws of trade here arises from the great liberty which is allowed in some other Colonies. The Merchants here complain, with great show of reason, of the hardship they suffer by being Subject to restraints, which their Neighbours in Ports almost under their Eye are quite Strangers to. The only answer to be given to these complaints is that the negligence of other governments will not justify this in the Same: but that it is hoped that the time is near at hand when these Matters will be liquidated & adjusted; And there will be but one common rule of restraint & indulgence through all the ports in America: a Settlement much to be desired.

7[20] The Soil of the Country being natural to Grass, Black Cattle are one principal part of the Produce. Nothwithstanding the great Supplies made during the War to the Western Army & the new Settlements which are continually making, there is no sensible decrease, except what has been occasioned by the extraordinary drought of the two last Summers which will soon be retrieved by the plenty of the present. About the Year 1740 after a long Peace, Beef in the Season was sold from a penny to five farthings Ster^g _ the pound. The breed of Horses Suitable for the West Indies hath greatly increased. The Province cannot properly be said to have any Staple. If any commodity prevails as to the Value it seems to be Fish. In some years there has been room to suppose the Oyl near equal to it. Manufactures there are none of any consequence except that of Molosses into Rum & Iron into Bars & hollow Ware. There is not sufficient bar Iron manufactured for the use of the Inhabitants; of cast Metal or hollow Ware as it is sometimes called, there is enough made for the Inhabitants & more or less exported every year to the other Colonies. There are divers provincial Acts to prevent frauds & abuses in Boards, Shingles, Staves, Hoops, Fish, the Assize of Casks & in most other Articles exported liable to frauds, which have a good effect. They have been at different times enacted & from time to time as the defects are discovered there appears a good disposition in the General Court to amend them & render them the more effectual

8[21] There are no Mines yet discovered except of Iron. The Iron Oar in general has a mixture of Copper which renders it unfit to work into Bars. some of it has been cast into Cannon shott & Shells. The Bar Iron manufactured here is principally from Piggs imported from New York Philadelphia &c some of an inferior Quality from what is called bogg Oar which lyes in beds in many places of the Province about a foot under the Surface & is found at the bottom of ponds in some parts. From the latter the cast or hollow Ware is commonly manufactured. __ A New Mine of rock Oar has been lately discovered; but it has not been workt as yet.

9[22] I was desirous of answering this Article as exactly as possible & for that purpose had postponed my return for some time in order to have the assistance of the general Court in taking an exact account of the people by returns made in a particular manner upon oath. For this I proposed a Scheme to the general Court at the beginning of last Session: but the Consideration of it having been postponed to near the End of the Session, some objections were started in the house of Representatives, which there was no time to obviate: and the Council & House having disagreed upon the Method, it was of course put off till next Session, when it will be again brought in & I doubt not but it will pass.[23] In the mean time I must answer this Article as well as I can by conjecture from such Materials as I have in my Hands. In the year 1761 a Return was made to the general Court of the rateable Polls vizt. males above 16 which amounted to about 57,000;[24] In this list were excluded not only the Males under 16 but also those who were rendered incapable to pay by poverty. If We reckon these at one third more, the Number will be 76,000 to which adding the Same Number of females the Sum total will be 152,000. Another Method of computing the people will be by the returns of the Militia, which is generally reckoned one fourth part of the Souls. This in 1759 was 41,000 which multiplied by 4 is 164,000. Another method is by the Number of houses which in 1761 was 32,000: this multiplied by 5 makes 160,000 by 5½, 176,000 by 6, 192,000. Upon the whole I cannot help thinking that the Number of the Souls in this Province amounts to near 200,000;[25] for as all the returns beforementioned were taken in order to make a rate of taxes or Personal Duty, they are certainly short of the truth. But I hope to be very exact in this article next Summer. In the Same returns the Slaves, negro & Mulatto, are reckoned at 2,221. The free Negroes & Mulattos are very few; the Indians living within the Settled parts of the Province are not many hundreds: perhaps these latter added to the former may make 3,000 Indians, Negroes & Mulattos. The People here are very much tired of Negro Servants; and It is generally thought that it would be for the Public good to discourage their importation, if it was not at present very inconsiderable, not one Parcell having been imported this year as yet.

10[26] I have not been able to get a Copy of any former return made to these Queries & therefore cannot compare the former Account with the present computation. Undoubtedly the Inhabitants are increased within these 10 years, but not in the proportion of the ordinary encrease of the American Colonies. This Province has had few recruits from other Countries; & therefore it's population must have arisen allmost wholly within itself: And there have been very great drawbacks to that. After the expedition to Louisbourgh in 1745 some thousands of young men were lost by Sickness: this has affected the encrease of the people almost to the present times. In the beginning of the late War Many perished by the Sword, but much more by the diseases incidental to a Campain.

In 1760, and when I came to this Government, I was surprised to see what havock Disease alone made among the Provincial Soldiers in the course of, & especially towards the end of a campain: & yet I remedied this Mischief by three Provisions only; having them well cloathed, keeping them from Rum, & Supplying them plentifully with Spruce beer. If these regulations had been established in the beginning of the War, Many Hundreds (I might say some thousands) of lives would have been Saved. Besides these drawbacks upon natural Population, This Province has suffered much by desertion, if I may so call it: Many families have removed & are continually removing to the neighbouring Provinces, & especially New Hampshire, to take up New Lands. In New hampshire only near 200 Townships have been opened in that Country which was formerly reputed as part of this Province & was allways defended from the common Enemy as such, at the expence of this Province only.

11[27] By a return made in 1759 there appeared to be upon the alarm list about 41,000 fencible Men; but when All Persons exempted from training were deducted, the trainband list did not amount to more than about 35,000. These are divided into 32 regiments each having a Colonel Lieut Col & a Major: some of two battalions having 2 L^t. Colonels & 2 Majors. Most of these Regiments have a troop of horse belonging to each, Some of which are in uniform. There belongs to the Boston Regiment a company of Artillery of 60 Men in uniform of blew & red with four field Pieces. There are belonging to the Castle, besides the Garrison, 4 companies of Artillery of about 300 men in the whole, who are excercised at the great guns 6 times every year, & the two companies of Artillery belonging to the batterys at Boston & one at Charlestown. There are also to attend the Governor a Troop of horse guards consisting of about 80 men in an uniform of blue & red, & a company of Cadets of about 60 gentlemen in an uniform of red & buff Colour. The Governor as Captain-General both by the Charter & his Commission has the whole command of the Militia, appoints & removes officers at pleasure, orders musters & marches as he thinks proper, but cannot march them out of the Province without the consent of the general Assembly. By Law every Man is obliged to train four times a year; defaulters forfeit 5s. lawful money each time: Out of these fines the expence of drums & colours is defrayed. There is no other Expence: when they march in Actual Service, the Province pays them.

12[28] The Principal Fortress in this Province & perhaps throughout his Majestys American Colonies is Castle William situated on an Island on the side of the only Ship Channell about 3 miles from Boston. The Fort is small but well contrived, is a regular Square with 4 bastions & 2 ravelins on the outside: it mounts 38 Guns chiefly nine pounders & two mortars on the ravelins. There are a very considerable Outworks towards the Ship Channel, which have good Communications with the Fort. The Royal Battery mounts 29 guns from twenty four to Thirty two pounders, at the end thereof is a demi bastion with four forty two pounders. Shirleys battery mounts 19 forty two pounders, at the end is an horseshoe with 6 Twenty four pounders. there are some other lesser batteries partly compleated & partly designed only: there is a large block house mounted [with][29] small Cannon to Scour the flatts; and barracks for 1000 Men with a large parade & a picketted breast-work towards the sea. When all the Works intended are finished there will be about 140 Cannon mounted upon the Island. The whole Expence is borne by the Province & for 7 years past, altho' there have been no New Works, has amounted to £2250 Sterling one year with another. The Garrison consists of 60 Men besides the 4 companies of Artillery before mentioned, who live in the Neighbouring Towns, and are excersised at the Castle 6 times in the year. There has lately been built an Armoury for small Arms, of which there are at present about 2500. In the late War many Pieces of Artillery & considerable quantities of Warlike Stores were taken away for the Kings Use. Application has been made for the replacing them & will be renewed, we hope with Success.[30] There is also a Fort on Penobscot river called Fort Pownall garrisoned with 18 men, in which is an Indian Truckhouse; & another called Fort Halifax on Kennebeck river garrisoned with 13 Men where there is another Truckhouse. Fort Western on Kennebeck river, Fort Pemaquid upon Pemaquid river & Fort George upon Georges river have been lately disarmed & are now private dwelling houses; the Artillery & Stores being removed to the Castle. There are small forts or batteries at several of the Sea Ports town[s], capable of repelling a privateer, but as they have no garrisons & have no fund to support them, they are of Very little consequence.

13[31] There is a small number of Indians who were originally of Hudsons River, perhaps 70 or 80 Families, who live upon the Western Frontier of the Province at a place called Stockbridge[32] & who have an English Missionary constantly preaching to them supported by the Society for propogating the Gospel in New England & parts adjacent; about 70 Families more at a place called Mashpee in the County of Barnstable who by a late Act of the General Court have had certain privileges granted them with a view of civilising them & bringing them under good Government & order;[33] and between one & two hundred Families in the two Islands of Nantucket & Martha's Vineyard. All these have Missionaries or Teachers supported by the Same Society. There are about 20 Families more at Natick & a few scattering

Families in several other parts of the Province. The Indians upon the frontiers of the Eastern Parts of the Province are all ranged under the general name, according to the French, of Abenaquis. of these the Arasagunticooks[34] & Wewenocks[35] living on the banks of St Lawrence properly belong to Canada as the St Johns Indians do to Nova Scotia: & yet all these have occasionally treated with this Province. The Indians that more particularly belong to this Province are the Norridgewalks[36] the Penobscots & the Passimaquodies. The two former have been the Subjects of many Wars & many treaties with this Province: In the last War they retired to Canada & joined the Arasagunticooks & Wewenocks. Since the conquest of Canada they have come into these parts again & have renewed the acquaintance with the Provincials. As no formal treaty has been held with them since they were proclaimed Rebels & Traitors, about two months ago to prevent Mischief, I published a proclamation[37] declaring a Cessation of hostilities & requiring the people to treat them as friends. Since which three of the Penobscot Chiefs have, with my leave, come to Boston & in the Name of their own tribe & of the Machias Indians a branch of it, & the Passimaquody Indians a part of the St John's Indians Settled on the west side of St Croix, have desired to be under the Protection of this Government & to have their trade with it regulated in some particulars. Also a Norridgewalk Indian has been here in a private Character & desired to know if they may come to their old Town. I dismissed them all with Satisfactory Answers.[38] These People who have for near a century occasioned so much expence of blood & treasure to this Province are now in a manner reduced to Nothing. The Norridgewalks whose town is about 40 miles above fort Halifax are about 10 families; The Penobscots who live about 50 miles above Fort Pownall with the Machiases who live in a bay of that name are about 40 families & Passimquodies who live on the west side of the Bay of St Croix about 30 families: and yet these People complain of the English settling their Country. The Nature of the Subjection of the Indians [to][39] the English Government, notwithstanding the many Treaties they have had with this Government has never been explained nor rightly understood: nor does it Signify much now whether it ever is,

14[40] By the Terms of the late happy treaty This Province is freed from the neighbourhood of foreign subjects. The nearest foreign Settlement is that of St Peter & Miquelon. What effect that will have on his Majesty's Provinces, time must discover.[41]

15[42] Imposts & Excises have been laid by Temporary Acts of Assembly which are renewed from time to time. The Impost is upon Wine, Rum & other Spirits & 2 Þ Cent upon all goods from Great Britain which are not the produce or manufactures thereof. This brings into the Treasury about £2250 ster^g. Þ Annum. The Excise is upon Wine & spirituous Liquors sold by retail & Lemmons & Limes. This brings in about £1300 ster^g. Þ Annum. There is a farther Excise upon Tea, Coffee & China Ware which brings in about £1500 ster^g. Þ annum. The further charges

The Kennebec River. Drafted by John Small in 1760 before he was accidentally shot and killed by a member of his surveying party, in D/SB MP/25. Courtesy of the Centre for Buckinghamshire Studies. Photograph by Peter Hoare.

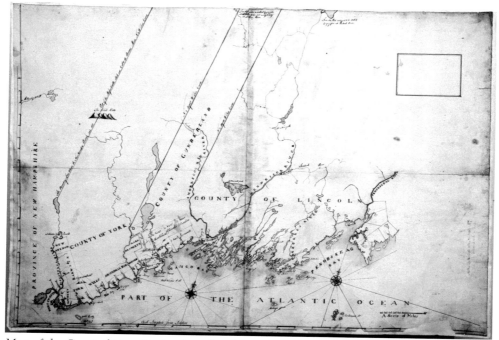

Map of the Coast of New England north of New Hampshire. Francis Miller completed this map after surveying the region in the winter of 1765-66. In D/SB MP/10. Courtesy of the Centre for Buckinghamshire Studies. Photograph by Peter Hoare.

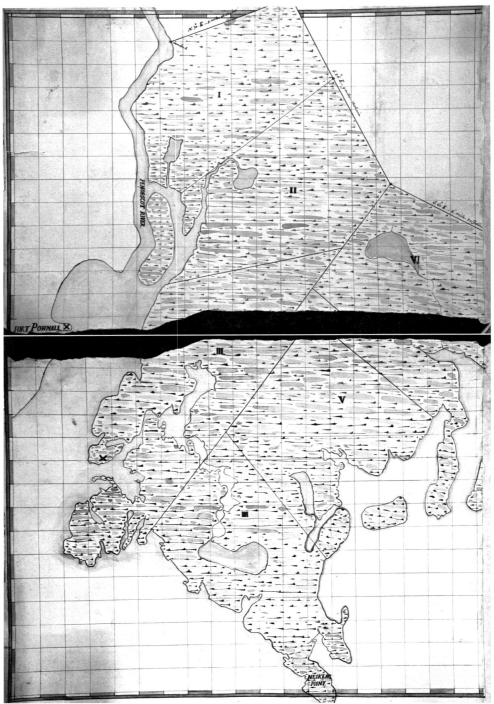

A Plan of the Penobscot River. Made by Capt. John Small, shortly before his death in 1760, in D/SB MP/12. Courtesy of the Centre for Buckinghamshire Studies. Photograph by Peter Hoare.

of Government which in times of Peace may amount to near £20,000 Ster⁸. Þ Ann are raised by a Tax upon Polls & Estates. The Province is in Debt about £220,000 ster⁸. borrowed of the Inhabitants for which the Treasurer gives his notes or Obligations from six pounds to a thousand or upwards upon Interest; which notes are not negotiated or Current as money or Bills of Credit but lye in the proprietors hands as any private Securities would do & upon a transfer they bear a premium. The Revenue is appropriated to such Grants & Services as are or shall be made & ordered by the General Court. The Treasurers Accounts are annually audited by a Committee of the House of Representatives & another of the Council, but he is not discharged without a Vote of the Whole General Court.

16⁴³ The principal officers of the Government are the Governor the Lieut. Governor & the Secretary appointed by the King; The Treasurer the Commissary General & the impost officer elected by the joint ballot of the Council & House of Representatives & consented to by the Governor; but the Commissary, as his office is mixt with the Military Service receives also a commission from the Governor; The Chief Justice & 4 other Judges of the Superior Court & the Attorney general appointed by the Governor with the Advice of the Council. The Governor with the Advice of Council appoints all Judges Justices & Officers belonging to the Courts of Justice. Other Officers especially those belonging to the revenue are elected by the two houses & consented to by the Governor. The Governor with the Council has the cognisance of causes of testacy & intestacy by charter & of causes of Marriages & Divorce by a provincial Law. But the former Jurisdiction is executed by inferior judges of Probate or rather Surrogates who are appointed by the Govʳ. & Council one for each County with a Registrar under him. These inferior Courts of probate are not established by any written Law but by a long usage only; they are in some manner confirmed by being mentioned in several Provincial Acts as legal Courts & the fees being ascertained thereby; & are subject to an appeal to the Govʳ. in Council. These Judges fees are according to the County from £10 to £60 p Stg, the registrars about half as much more. There are also in every County 4 judges of Common pleas from which Court there lies an appeal to the Superior Court: their fees amount to according to the County from five to £45 ster⁸. each. There is also in every County a Sheriff: his fees in the three principal Counties, Suffolk, Essex, & Middlesex amount to from £150 to £200 st⁸. each. In other Counties it is less, decreasing according to the Size or populousness of the County. The Superior Judges hold two terms a year in the three principal Counties & one in each of the other Counties, except Lincolnshire & Berkshire, who upon account of their remoteness join in the business of the superior Court with the Counties next to them; So that they are from home near half the year. Their Salaries which depend upon the Assembly & fees together do not amount to £140 Ster⁸. each; half of which is expended in travelling charges. The Attorney General used to have a salary but of late that has been refused by the Assembly upon a pretence of their having a right to join in his appointment: but they sometimes pay him for public business tho' in a scanty manner. The Principal Officers of the Government are as follows The Governor, Salary £1000, fees under £100 £1,100 Ster. The L[t]. Gov[r]. Tho[s] Hutchinson Esq no salary or fees; when he takes the chair the Assembly makes him a special grant. The Secretary Andrew Oliver Esq Salary & fees £250. the Treasurer Harrison Gray Esq for himself & Clerks salary £375 the Commissary Tho[s] Hubbard[44] Esq Salary £112 10s. the impost Officer James Russell Esq Salary & fees £90 The chief Justice is Thomas Hutchinson Esq the Lieut. Governor; the other Judges are Benjamin Lynde[45] John Cushing[46] Chambers Russell[47] & Peter Oliver[48] Esquires, The Attorney general is Edmund Trowbridge Esq.[49] Their Commission & all others under the Seal of the Province were renewed upon the present kings accession. The inadequateness of the Governors Income to the importance of his charge & the care & trouble attending it has been a subject of frequent observation. This has arisen from the Pains that have been taken in former times by acts of ascertaining fees & by other means to reduce the Governor's perquisites as low as possible, so that they are now under £100 a year & never like to be more: and yet the Salary is no more than what is allowed by his Majesty to the smallest Government paid by him. The insufficiency of the Judges Salaries affords great cause of complaint. To have Gentlemen of the first rank & ability dedicate their whole time to the Service of the public & not have £80 a year clear of expences for their trouble is disgraceful & injurious to the whole Province. And for this, they are dependent every year upon the Assembly, where frequent attempts are made & sometimes successfully, to lower even this poor pittance. To do this, the Very Judgements of the Court, where they have been unpopular, have been used as means to lower the Salaries of the judges. Indeed the present Judges are superior to influence of this kind, but then they suffer for it. The Attorney general has had no Salary allowed him for several years, because the Assembly claim a right to elect him insisting that he is not an Officer belonging to the courts of Justice. Great & many are the inconveniences which arise to the public as well from the insufficiency as from the precariousness of the Salaries of the chief officers; which will never be remedied but by the establishment of a Sufficient & independent civil list, out of which his Majesty may assign to the public officers such Salaries as the Dignity & Duty of their Offices should require: a regulation extremely wanted in America, for which it would be very easy to provide a proper fund.

17[50] The constitution of the Government will appear best from the Charter, which is duly carried into execution. I know of no Colony where the Compact between the King & the People is better observed. The Royal Rights are never openly invaded: the utmost that is done, is to dispute what are royal rights. Whereas in some other Governments the general Assembly in some cases take upon themselves the executive part of Government appointing special receivers disbursers & expenditors of the public money & making them accountable for the same to them only exclusively of the Governor. This is never done here, no money being ever issued but by the Governor with the advice of Council. The chief difference between this Government & the meer royal ones, is in the appointment of the Council or middle part of the Legislature, in the Governor's not excercising the power of Chancellor, & by his being obliged to have the Concurrence of the Council in many acts, which the meer royal Governors can do alone. It was, in my opinion, an unfortunate error in the forming this Government to leave the Council to be elected by the Representatives of the People &c & that annually. Being thus constituted & continually renewed, their complexion is much too popular for them to be, as they ought to be, mediators between the Crown & people. The influence which their reelection is supposed to have on them is so well understood that It is a common practise, whenever any popular business is to be carried through, contrary to the Sentiments of the Government, to bring it into the Court as near as possible before the general Election. It is true that the Gentlemen of the Council give frequent proofs of their steadiness & independence: but it is impossible to say that the reelection may not create some bias, tho' they may not be sensible of it themselves: at least it is highly indecent that they should be publickly threatned to be turned out for what they do in Council, altho they are known to act under the Sanction of an Oath as well as a sense of their duty: This has not been uncommon within my observation. On the other hand it would be objected on the behalf of the People to have a Council appointed & removeable by the Crown: it would be said that such a Council would be no more a proper Mediator between the Crown & People than a Council elected by & removeable by the people. And it has seemed to me that in the meer Royal Governments, the removeability of the Council, altho' so seldom excersised as to be allmost merely nominal, has a tendency to diminish their weight with the People. I cannot but think that the middle legislative power in a provincial Assembly should be made to resemble as near as possible, the house of Lords. The Dignity should be derived from the King, as the fountain of honour, & granted for life defeasible by notorious misdemeanor. It would not be amiss if some title for Life (for this Country is not ripe enough for hereditary honours)[51] such as Baron or Baronet was annexed to it. Such a constitution would add great stability to the Government: These Councellors would naturally support the rights of the Crown, & being independent of it, would not incur the jealousy of the people. It would induce people of consequence to look up to the King for honour & Authority, instead of endeavouring to raise themselves by popular Altercations. I am inclined to think that such an alteration might be made agreable to the people, I am allmost sure it would be for the public good, but I apprehend It would require the Authority of the Parliament to carry it into execution, tho' the consent of the Province should be first obtained for that purpose. At the same time It would deserve consideration whether it would not be proper to make the second Legislative power & the privy Council two distinct bodies as they are in England: in such Case the latter should be wholly appointed & removable by the King. It might have been made a question whether the Governor of this Province has not the power of the Chancellor delivered to him with the great Seal, as well as other royal Governors: but it is impracticable to Set up such a claim now, after a non usage of 70 Years, & after several Governors have in effect disclaimed it by consenting to bills for establishing a Court of Chancery which have been disallowed at home. A Court of Chancery is very much wanted here, many Causes of consequence frequently happening in which no redress is to be had for want of a Court of Equity.[52] I am inclined to think that if a Complainant in a matter of Equity arising within this Province should file his bill in the Court of Chancery in England suggesting that there was no provincial Court in which he could be relieved, that the bill would be retained; in the same manner as I suppose a Libell in the high Court of Admiralty would be admitted, if there was no inferior Court of Admiralty in the province. But this practise would be Very burthensome to the Province, unless it was used only to inforce the Necessity of establishing a Provincial Court of Equity. I have been the more particular upon these Subjects not only to point out what seems to me to be the defects of the Constitution of this Government but also to show how few things are Wanting to make it compleat. If these great Matters were regulated lesser things would mend themselves. In fine, A Civil list, an independent middle legislative power & a Court of Chancery, with a few other regulations which would follow of course, would give this Government as good a constitution as any in his Majesty's American Dominions: especially as the People in general are as well inclined to his Majesty's Government & as well satisfyed with their subordination to Great Britain as any Colony in America; the prejudices which have heretofore occasioned their being represented as otherwise disposed being wholly or allmost wholly wore off.

All which is humbly submitted,

Boston Sep 5. 1763

Ms, RC   CO 5/891, ff 207-220.

In the handwriting of clerk no. 2 with scribal emendations. At 213r and 215v the handwriting style changes slightly, indicating a pause in writing. The author's pagination runs pp. 1-28. There are a few non-contemporaneous annotations in the margins. Variant text in Universities of Minnesota Libraries, James Ford Bell Library, 1763fBe (Ms, Copy); King's, 205: ff 194-211 (Ms, Copy).

   With this report, FB answered a series of questions put to him and other governors by the Board of Trade about the state of their province with particular reference to geography, demography, commerce, industry, agriculture, and government. The queries are summarised in Labaree, *Royal Instructions*, 2: 741-742 and 746-748. The set of "Queries" that FB received in **No. 46** was prepared on 22 Apr. 1761 and approved two days later "with several alterations and additions." *JBT*, 11: 190-192. Unfortunately, this set has not survived. In its absence, the questions supplied in the footnotes are taken from a contemporary set issued to the governor of North Carolina in 1761. William Laurence Saunders, et. al., eds., *The Colonial Records of North Carolina*, 10 vols., (Raleigh, 1886-1990), 6: 605-623.

In the covering letter, FB apologized to John Pownall for the long delay in compiling the document and for the answers being "not as correct as I could wish. They are wrote hastily with a great regard to truth, but with a freedom that in many places will want an Apology, particularly in the last Article." The report may have been written "hastily" prior to FB leaving for eastern Massachusetts, but it was well-researched nonetheless and provides a useful synopsis of the province within the parameters established by Board. It was copied to the king on 1 Oct. 1765 with a representation from the Board of Trade. FB to Pownall, Boston, 12 Sept. 1763, BP, 3: 98-99; *JBT*, 12: 318. The Board acknowledged receipt in a letter to FB dated Whitehall, 29 Nov. 1765, CO 5/920, pp. 206-207.

---

1. Number supplied. "Quere 1. What is the situation of the Province under your Government the Nature of the Country Soil and Climate what are the principal Rivers and Harbours, the Latitudes and Longitudes of the most considerable places in it . . . : Have these Latitudes and Longitudes been settled by good Observations or only by common Computations and from whence are the Longitudes computed?"

2. These latitudes include the disputed territory of Sagadahoc.

3. Daniel Gabriel Fahrenheit (1686-1736), German physicist and inventor of the alcohol (1709) and mercury (1714) thermometers; FB used the latter type, as was noted in a letter to Francis Fauquier, Boston, 7 Feb. 1761, BP, 2: 98.

4. According to US Geological Survey data, the locus of these co-ordinates is near Gleasondale, several miles inland from the site of colonial Boston. Modern State Street, in the heart of old Boston, is -71° 03' longitude and 42° 21' latitude.

5. "Quere 2d What are the Boundaries? Have those Boundaries been settled and ascertained and by what authority? If any parts are disputed by whom, when did the Disputes arise what steps have been taken or in your Opinion ought to have been taken to fix the true Boundary Lines?"

6. 5 Aug. 1740. See Labaree, *Royal Instructions*, 2: 700-703.

7. See illustrations opposite p. 409.

8. Hitherto, Massachusetts and New York had failed to settle their differences over their common boundary. Resolution was made more difficult because of disputes, some of them violent, among frontier settlers and between landowners and tenants. The Board of Trade considered the boundary line in 1757, but neither it nor the Privy Council had resolved the matter by the time FB wrote the this report. In Jun. 1763, the Massachusetts assembly issued a public defence that FB submitted to the Board of Trade. *JHRM*, 40: 38, appendix 277-307; Thomas Hutchinson, *The Case of the Provinces of Massachusetts-Bay and New-York, Respecting the Boundary Lines Between the Two Provinces* (Boston, 1764). Land riots in 1766 ended procrastination on the part of the colonial governments; a joint commission met at New Haven, Conn., in Sept. 1767, and in 1773 the boundary line was finally agreed. Philip J. Schwarz, *The Jarring Interests: New York's Boundary Makers, 1664-1776* (Albany, 1979), 192-207.

9. In 1713.

10. In 1749.

11. William Bollan petitioned the Privy Council on 12 Nov. 1754 requesting that the agreement of 1713 be accorded royal sanction, but without success. *APC*, 4: 274-275. Massachusetts demonstrated its claim of jurisdiction by levying taxes on these Connecticut towns until the Revolution, but these, of course, were never collected. See Hutchinson, *History of Massachusetts*, 2: 151-154; 3: 4-5; Clarence Winthrop Bowen, *The Boundary Disputes of Connecticut* (Boston, 1882).

12. See **Nos. 196, 215**, and **No. 220**.

13. "Third and 4th Queries to be answered by the Collectors Naval Officers and Merchants."

14. The documentation compiled by the naval officers at Boston and Salem is incomplete for FB's administration, and in CO 5/850-CO 5/851.

15. A substitute, *OED*.

16. See note to the third query.

17. "Quere 5th What trade has the Province under Your Government with any foreign plantations or any ports of Europe besides Great Britain; How is the Trade carried on and what Commodities are sent to and received from such foreign Countries or Plantations?"

18. The first voyage from Boston to St. Petersburg was undertaken by the *Wolfe*, captained by William Hayes and owned by wealthy merchant Nicholas Boylston, 26 Mar.-22 Oct. 1763. During this period two other vessels cleared Philadelphia for St. Petersburg. Trade routes to St. Petersburg had been opened up by Britain's commercial treaty with Russia of 1761 and were sustained by British and colonial demand for hemp and sailcloth. See Norman E. Saul, "The Beginning of American-Russian Trade, 1763-1766," *WMQ* 26 (1969): 596-600; *JBT*, 11: 208, 222, and *passim*.

19. "Quere 6th What Methods are there used to prevent illegal Trade, and are the same effectual What Means in your Opinion may be proper for obtaining so valuable an End?"

20. "Qu[e]re 7th What is the natural produce of the Country staple commodities and Manufactures? What Value of Sterling Money may you annually export and to what places? What Regulations have been at any time made for preventing frauds and abuses in the Exportation of the Produce or Manufactures of the Province and at what time did the Regulations take place?"

21. "Quere 8th What Mines are there have these Mines been opened and worked and what may be the reputed Produce?"

22. "Quere 9th What is the Number of the Inhabitants Whites and Blacks?"

23. See postscript to **No. 225**.

24. An act for enquiring into the rateable estates of the province, 1 Geo. 3, c. 24 (passed 31 Jan. 1761), required towns to deliver lists of polls and rateable estates to the province secretary's office by 1 Jun. 1761. *Acts and Resolves,* 4: 422-423.

25. The census of 1764 reported Massachusetts's population at 245,698, which was probably an underestimation. Wells, *Population of the British Colonies,* 79.

26. "Quere 10 Are the Inhabitants increased or decreased within these 10 years how much and for what reason?"

27. "Quere 11 What is the number of the Militia under what Authority and Regulations is it Established what is the Expence of it & how is the Expence defrayed?"

28. "Quere 12 What Forts and Places of Defence are there your within your Government in what Condition and what Garrisons are kept therein? What is the annual Expense of maintaining each fort and out of what fund is it paid?"

29. Smudged.

30. **No. 84**. Castle William and its outworks were destroyed by the British before their evacuation of Boston in Mar. 1776.

31. "Quere 13 What is the number of the Indians inhabiting those parts of America lyeing within or bounding upon your Province? What Contracts or Treaties of Peace have been made with them and are now in force? What Trade is carried on with them and under what Regulations and how have these Regulations been established?"

32. There had been a community of Christianized "Stockbridge Indians" since 1744, including families of the Mahican and Wyachtook tribes, and c.227 members of the Wappinger tribe, that settled in the town in 1756. William C. Sturtevant., ed. *Handbook of North American Indians,* 17 vols.: vol 15: *Northeast,* ed. Bruce Trigger (Washington, 1978), 208.

33. An act for incorporating the Indians and Mulattoes, Inhabitants of Mashpee, 3 Geo. 3, c. 3 (passed 16 Jun. 1763). *Acts and Resolves,* 4: 639-641. Self-government was repealed in 1788 and partially reinstated in 1834, before the common lands were sold and redistributed to families in 1842. Trigger, ed., *Handbook of North American Indians,* vol 15: *Northeast,* 179. See the secondary sources listed in the source note to **No. 225**.

34. Also known as Arosaguntacook.

35. Wawenock or Wewonock are uncommon descriptors and may be synonyms for Wabanaki or Abenaki.

36. Also known as the Kennebec Indians.

37. By His Excellency Francis Bernard, Esq; . . . A proclamation . . . Whereas . . . the Indians . . . inhabiting the Eastern and Northern Parts of New England . . . Given at the Council-chamber in Boston, the Nineteenth Day of Jul., 1763, 1 Aug. 1763, *Boston Gazette,* p. 1.

38. FB and the Council had met with representatives from the Penobscot and other tribes, and the sachem Toma in Boston on 22 and 23 Aug. Their grievances mainly concerned trade, encroachments on their land, and the hunting carried out by the eighty or so provincial soldiers based at Fort Pownall, but an important subtext was their desire to have a Roman Catholic priest. This latter proposal echoed the 1760 treaty made by the St. John's Indians and Nova Scotia, that had allowed priests, and the principle of religious toleration recently espoused by the Treaty of Paris regarding the treatment of Quebec's Catholics. A second conference with the Penobscots was held at Fort Pownall on Saturday 17 Sept. and a third on 26 Sept. 1764, at which the issue of a priest was raised. FB refused, insisting upon an Anglican missionary, which post was briefly held by the Rev. Joseph Bailey. See minutes of a conference with the Penobscot Indians and other tribes on 22 and 23 Aug. 1763, Mass. Archs., 29: 82-489; FB, [Conference with the Penobscot Indians on 17 Sept. 1763, Fort Pownall], Mass. Archs., 29: ff 491-492); [FB,] A Conference held at Fort Pownall on Saturday, Sep. 17 1763 between his Excellency the Governor & Toma, Jo. Hart & Indians of the Penobscot Tribe . . ., Mass. Archs., 29: 489-491; John E. Sexton, "Massachusetts Religious Policy with the Indians under Governor Bernard, 1760-1769," *Catholic Historical Review* 24 (1938-1939): 310-328, at 311-313.

39. The manuscript is torn.

40. "Quere 14. What is the Strength of your neighbouring Europeans French or Spaniards, and what Effect have these Settlements upon His Majesty's Colonies and more particularly upon that under your Government?"

41. The islands of St. Pierre and Miquelon on Newfoundland's southwest coast were ceded to France by the Treaty of Paris, 1763.

42. "Quere 15 What is the Revenue arising within your Government when was it established and by what Laws or other Authority? to what Service is it appropriated how applied and disposed of and in what Manner are the Accounts audited and past?"

43. "Quere. 16. What are the Establishments Civil and Military within your Government, by what Authority do the several Officers hold their places, what are the Names of the present Officers, when were they appointed and what is their reputed annual Value, what Salaries and Fees have they, by what authority are their Salaries and fees paid, and under what Regulations?"

44. Thomas Hubbard (1702-73), a prosperous businessmen and shopkeeper, was a long-serving representative for Waltham, a former Speaker of the House, and a member of the Governor's Council, 1759-72.

45. Benjamin Lynde Jr. (1700-81), originally a merchant of Salem, had been a justice of the Superior Court since 1746 (having replaced his father, who was chief justice) and was a member of the Governor's Council, 1737-40 and 1743-65; he was the presiding judge, between 1769 and 1771, when Thomas Hutchinson was acting governor. He succeeded Hutchinson as chief jusice in 1771 but resigned the following year.

46. John Cushing (1695-1778) of Scituate, Plymouth Co., Mass., was a county judge and justice of the Superior Court, 1748-71.

47. See the biographical note at **No. 29**n3.

48. Peter Oliver (1713-91), a merchant and foundry owner of Middleborough, Plymouth Co., Mass., was a former representative for the town; a county judge; a Superior Court justice, 1756-72; a member of the Governor's Council, 1759-66; chief justice of the Superior Court, 1772-74; and subsequently a prominent Loyalist.

49. Edmund Trowbridge (1709-93) of Cambridge represented the town, 1750-52, 1755, and 1763, and was a member of the Governor's Council, 1764-65. He had been attorney general since 1749, which office he held until his appointment as a justice of the Superior Court in 1767 (and which he relinquished in 1774).

50. "Qu[e]re 17 What is the Constitution of the Government in general and particularly what Courts are there established for the Administration of Justice when were these Courts established and under what Authority; what are their Rules of Proceedings and how are their Judges and subordinate Officers appointed?

51. The phrase in parentheses paraphrases Hutchinson's warning about "hereditary honours" in *History of Massachusetts*, 1: 7, but FB became a firm advocate of a colonial civil list and honors system on the British model for the political reasons stated above. See Jordan D. Fiore, "Governor Bernard for an American Nobility," *The Boston Public Library Quarterly* 4 (1952): 125-136.

52. Courts of equity in English common law, called chancery courts, provide remedies in civil disputes according to the principle of equity administered by a judge; any settlement is enforceable by writs and injunctions, as distinct from common law courts operating under legal precedent, whose remedy is limited to making awards for damages. The chancery courts are a principal division of the law courts in England and Wales, with the High Court of Chancery being under the jurisdiction of the lord chancellor. In 1704, the king's attorney general offered an opinion that the Massachusetts General Court could not establish an equity court in the province as that was a matter for royal prerogative. This did not deter the assemblies in Massachusetts and other colonies from using the legislative process to set up chancery courts. Much of the legislation passed by the American Colonies that was subsequently disallowed by the Privy Council concerned judicial procedure, such as the issuance of writs and the imposition of settlements, that extended the jurisdiction of the inferior or common law courts. Evarts B. Greene, *The Provincial Governor in the English Colonies of North America. Harvard Historical Studies*, vol. 8 (New York, 1898), 137n3-139; Joseph H. Smith "Administrative Control of the Courts of the American Plantations," in *Essays in the History of Early American Law*, ed. David Flaherty (Chapel Hill, N.C., 1969), 281-355, at 284, 296-306, 311. FB's enthusiasm for Anglicizing Massachusetts's legal institutions contrasts with Thomas Hutchinson's informative, traditionalist account of the legal system in his *History of Massachusetts*, 1: 367-383.

235 | From The Earl Of Halifax

S^t: James's. Septem^r. 20th. 1763.

Sir,

Your Letter to the Board of Trade, of the 28th: of July last,[1] concerning the Offers made by The Duc de Nivernois to invite the French Acadians within Your Government to come to France (a Case upon which You ought to have addressed Yourself directly to the Secretary of State) was immediately transmitted to me by Their Lordships; And, having laid it before His Majesty, I am commanded to acquaint You that The King considers those Acadians as His Subjects, exactly in the same State with the rest of His Roman Catholick Subjects in America, and, therefore, cannot suffer them to be brought away from His Dominions, in Shipping sent, for that purpose, by a Foreign Power, in Consequence of a private Negotiation. I have accordingly acquainted Monsieur Le Chevalier D Eon, His Most Christian Majesty's Envoy here,[2] that It will be a fruitless Trouble for His Court to send Transports to Boston to fetch away those People, as You have His Majesty's Commands not to suffer them, or any other of His Majesty's Subjects under Your Government, to be removed in that manner. I have likewise apprized Monsieur D Eon that such French Transports, on their Arrival in the Harbour of Boston, or any other British Port in America, would perhaps be deemed liable to Confiscation under Our Act of Navigation. As such a Measure, however, might be attended with disagreable Consequences, I recommend it to you to use every possible Precaution to prevent the Seizure of such French Vessels (if any should be sent) which may perhaps be best done by preventing their Entrance into Your Port

With respect to that Part of your Letter, in which You desire Directions as to the future Settlement of these Acadians, it is impossible to judge which way of disposing of them is the most eligible, 'till You shall have informed me, what are their Numbers; in what way they have hitherto subsisted since their Arrival in Your Government; what Objections they themselves, or the Province, may have to their continuing in the same State; and whether they are under any, and what Difficulties, or Disadvantages, as to taking up Lands in Your Government, to which they would not be liable in the Government of Quebec. You will, therefore, lose no Time in transmitting to me the fullest Information upon all these Points, together with Your own Opinion as to the best mode of disposing of these Peoples. And, in the mean Time, You will either induce or oblige them to remain in Your Government upon the same Footing as they have hitherto been

For the present, I can only add that it may, perhaps, upon further Information, be judged most expedient to remove these People to Quebec: But I can, by no means, conceive it advisable to collect them in a Body, and plant them, a Papist Colony with an established Priest, on any Part of the Eastern Shore.

I am with great Truth and Regard, Sir, Your most Obedient, humble Servant

Dunk Halifax

Francis Barnard Esqr: Governor of His Majesty's Province of the Massachusets Bay.

LS, RC   BP, 10: 125-130.

Endorsed: Lord Halifax r Jan 7. 1764. Variant text in CO 5/755, pp. 35-39 (L, LbC).

---

1. **No. 227**.

2. Charles-Geneviève-Louis-Auguste-André-Thimothée d'Eon de Beaumont (1728-1810), French minister plenipotentiary and spy when resident in London during 1763. He was recalled in Oct. and subsequently published a volume of secret diplomatic correspondence. He remained in London until 1777, and attracted notoriety because of his transvestism.

236 | *Circular from the Board of Trade*

Whitehall October 11th. 1763.

Sir,

The Lords Commissioners of His Majesty's Treasury having represented to His Majesty, that they find upon a consideration of the present state of the Duties of Customs imposed on His Majesty's Subjects in America, that the Revenue arising therefrom is very small & inconsiderable, having in no degree increased with the Commerce of those Countries, and is not yet sufficient to defray a fourth part of the expence necessary for collecting it, and that through neglect connivance & fraud, not only the Revenue is impaired, but the Commerce of the Colonies is diverted from it's natural course, & the salutary provisions of many wise Laws are in great measure defeated, His Majesty has commanded us to require & enjoin you in the strictest manner to make the Suppresion of the clandestine & prohibited Trade with foreign Nations, & the improvement of the Revenue the constant & immediate Objects of your care; & by a vigorous discharge of the Duty required of you by several Acts of Parliament, and a due execution of your legal Authority, to give the Officers of the Revenue all possible protection & Support; & that you do, from time to time transmit such Observations as occur to you on the state of the illicit & contraband Trade, & on the conduct of all persons, whose duty it is to prevent the same, in order that the necessary Directions may be given for punishing such persons as shall appear to be guilty of any Misbehaviour, and for correcting all Abuses for the future.

We do therefore recommend these His Majesty's Commands to your most serious Attention, not doubting but you will acquit yourself in the execution of them, as becomes a faithfull & vigilant servant of the Crown.

We are, Sir, Your most obedient humble Servants

Hillsborough[1]

Soame Jenyns

E^d. Bacon

John Yorke

Honble Francis Bernard Esqr. Govr. of Massachusett's Bay

LS, RC   BP, 10: 131-134.

In the handwriting of John Pownall. Endorsed by FB: Lords of Trade dat Oct 11 1763 r Dec.

This circular to the colonial governors and Indian agents may have enclosed a copy of the Lords Commissioners of the Treasury, Memorial to His Majesty in Council, Whitehall, 4 Oct. 1763, *APC*, 4: 569-572. The Treasury memorial was approved by His Majesty in Council on 5 Oct. and instructions were issued to the secretary of state, the Admiralty, and the Board of Trade to give directions to address what the Board termed the "defective state of the laws for regulating the Plantation trade." The letter printed here constitutes the substance of the Board's directions to colonial governors. *JBT*, 11: 390; *APC*, 4: 569-572.

---

1. Wills Hill (1718-93), MP for Warwick between 1741 and 1756, when he entered the House of Lords as the earl of Hillsborough; president of Board of Trade, 1763-65 and 1766. He was secretary of state for the colonies at the head of the American Department, 21 Jan. 1768-13 Aug. 1772, and FB's most important point of contact with the policymaking process. He was later created first marquess of Downshire.

237 | *From the Earl of Halifax*

S^t: James's October 15th: 1763.

Sir,

The Lords Commissioners for Trade and Plantations having transmitted to me Your Letter to Them of the 24th. of August last,[1] together with the Opinion of the Council of Your Province, upon an Application made to You by Sixteen Families of the French Acadians for Passports to go to the Island of S^t: Peters, lately ceded to France, I immediately laid the same before The King, and I have the Satisfaction to acquaint You that His Majesty approves the Resolutions You came to upon that Matter, which You, and the Council, have considered in it's true Light. By my Letter to You of the 20th: September last, You will have seen that His Majesty considers those Acadians as upon the same Footing with the rest of His Roman Catholick Subjects in America.[2] It is, therefore, as You rightly judge it to be, Your Duty, on the one Hand, neither to encourage, nor facilitate, their Departure, nor, on the other, to attempt to confine them in the Province against their Wills. It should be the first Object of Your Endeavours to induce them to settle in such Places as may be agreable to themselves, and, at the same Time, most consistent with the Publick Peace and Security, and to become good Subjects, and usefull Inhabitants. But if, as You observe, they cannot be prevailed upon so to settle, in good Humour, and for good Purposes, the Liberty of removing themselves out of the Province, or out of His Majesty's Dominions, cannot be denied to them as Subjects; and it would, perhaps, be no less imprudent than impracticable to prohibit their migration. In that Case, however, His Majesty relies on Your Care, and Vigilance, in discovering their Designs, and in giving Notice thereof to His Majesty's Governors of those Provinces into which they may intend to remove, to the End that proper measures may be taken for preventing such Consequences as might endanger the Security of those Provinces.

I take this Opportunity of acquainting You, that His Most Christian Majesty's Minister here, in Answer to the Letter which in my last I informed You I had written Him in Consequence of Your Letter to the Board of Trade of the 28th. of July,[3] has assured me, that His Court had never had any Intention of sending Transports to bring away the French Acadians from Your Government. I shall, however, expect to receive from You the several Informations required by my said Letter, and depend on Your constant Care and Attention in informing me of every Circumstance, which may happen with respect to the Settlement or Removal of those People.

I am with great Truth and Regard, Sir, Your most Obedient humble Servant,

Dunk Halifax

Francis Bernard Esqr: Governor of His Majesty's Province of the Massachuset's Bay

LS, RC   BP, 10: 135-138.

Variant text in BP, 10: 139-142 (DupLS, RC) and CO 5/755, pp. 53-57 (L, Copy).
    Some 140 Acadians left the province for the islands of St. Pierre and Miquelon. When the British government disallowed emigration to foreign lands in 1764, FB and the Council, in Dec. of that year, refused a petition for four hundred Acadians to go to the French Leeward Islands. In 1766, the province assisted in transporting the remaining Acadians to Quebec. Lowe, "Massachusetts and the Acadians," at 227-228.

1. **No. 233**.

2. **No. 235**.

3. **No. 227**.

238 | *From the Earl of Halifax*

S^t: James's, October 19th. 1763.

Sir,

    His Majesty being informed by Dispatches lately received from Sir Jeffery Amherst, Commander in Chief of His Forces in North America, that the Insurrections of the Indian Nations, which have for some Time been increasing, now bear the Appearance of becoming general, has judged it necessary to require the Assistance of such His Colonies, as are most interested by their Situation, or most able by their Circumstances, to contribute to the general Purposes of Defence, and of Annoyance of the Savages, in order to put the most speedy End to the great Mischiefs, of which this extensive and most barbarous State of War is productive. I am therefore to signify to You His Majesty's Pleasure, that You earnestly recommend it, in His Majesty's Name, to the General Assembly of the Province under your Government, forthwith to make Provision for enabling You to call out a sufficient Number of the Militia, or to raise such a reasonable Number of Troops, as, from the actual State of the Indian War, Sir Jeffery Amherst shall think necessary; and to employ Them not only in defending and protecting the Lives and Properties of His Majesty's Subjects on the Frontiers of your Government, but also in acting offensively against the Indians, at such Places, and in such Manner, as the said Commander in Chief shall judge proper to direct.

And His Majesty trusts, that the Legislature of your Government, from their Zeal and Affection for His Service, as well as from a just Regard to the Safety and Welfare of the Colony, will readily and chearfully concur in exerting Themselves upon this important Occasion, to the End that His Majesty's Subjects in North America may peaceably enjoy the Fruits of the many glorious Successes obtained there by His Majesty's victorious Arms, during the late War, and the extensive Advantages secured to Them by the late Peace.

I am, with great Truth and Regard, Sir, Your most obedient humble Servant.

Dunk Halifax

Governor of the Massachusets Bay.

LS, RC   BP, 10: 143-146.

Endorsed by FB: Lord Halifax r. Jan 15. 1764. Contains minor emendations. An annotation by FB on the last page has been omitted.

239 | To Jeffery Amherst

Boston Oct 22 1763.

S[r].

Upon my return from my Eastern progress I found that you had order'd Hyman to be discharged:[1] I am much obliged to you for this concession; & the more so, as I find it to be more contrary to your purposes, than I had imagined it to be. I did not engage him till June last; and I should not have made him so necessary to my Service, if I had thought at that time, that he would have been called upon to join his former Corps. The Allowance of pay &c is so much beyond his expectation, that as he cannot presume to trouble you with his thanks, I must desire you to accept mine.

In my Eastern Voyage I had some further conference with some of the Penobscot Indian chiefs: and from what I can observe they seem to be well disposed. But if the News which has been circulated here to day, & which is said to come from Lord Colville, viz that 3 french Ships are gone up S[t] Laurence with stores for the Indians, has any foundation, It will be necessary to keep a good look out. The Indians in our Eastern Country are not Very formidable in Numbers: but We know well that a small Number of them can do a great deal of mischeif; and We know not here what resource of allies they may have beyond S[t] Johns River.

Some time ago, you was pleased to promise me a Copy of a survey thro the Rivers Chaudeire & Kennebeck & the Country between them.[2] I should not trouble you now upon this subject, but that I have received an intimation that I may soon expect to receive an order to propose to the Assembly, the settling a boundary Line between the Territory of Sagadahock & the Province of Canada. In such case I shall be glad of all lights which will serve to point out the Geography of the Country: as I presume the Boundary required will be those Hights, from whence on one side the Rivers Kennebeck & Penobscot flow to the Ocean & the Rivers Chaudeire & St Francis on the other side flow to St Laurence. This I suppose the Survey, you have mentioned, may help to explain: but as I have not yet received my orders upon this subject, I would not put you to any inconvenience in hastening this business

I am, with great regard, Sr Your most obedient & most humble Servant

Fra. Bernard

His Excellency Sr Jeffry Amherst.

ALS, RC
WO 34/26, f 246.

Variant text in BP, 3: 5-6 (L, LbC).

---

1. Hyman was one of the British artilleryman brought to Boston from St. John's in Aug. 1762 (**No. 150**). FB evidently took pity on Hyman, who "received no pay nor subsistence" over the winter of 1762-63, and employed him as his gardener, at which job he was likely experienced. FB requested his discharge (since Hyman was strangely not of a mind to claim arrears of pay) in order that the soldier could continue to tend the "large & expensive" garden FB had laid out at Castle William. FB to Amherst, Boston, 11 Sept. 1763, WO 34/26, f 245.
2. See **No. 218**.

240 | To the Earl of Egremont

Boston Oct 25 1763

My Lord

Your Lordships Commands dated July 9 having come to Boston[1] whilst I was absent upon a Visitation of the Eastern parts of this Province, & an immediate acknowledgement of the receipt of them being required, The Lieut Governor acquainted your Lordship that this Letter was arrived.[2] Nevertheless I think it my duty to acknowledge, as soon as possible, my own receipt of these papers & also of the duplicates thereof.

Your Lordship signifies the Kings pleasure that I use my utmost endeavours to prevent the introduction of foreign commodities contrary to the Acts of the 12 Char. 2 the 15th Char. 2 & the 8 & 9 Will. 3. I have the honor to inform your Lordship, that ever since I have been in this Government, I have exerted the best of my powers to maintain a due obedience to the above mentioned Laws; and I can with pleasure add, that I beleive they are no where better supported than they are in this province.

When first I came to this Government, about 3 years ago, Some of the Merchants of this Town, provoked with the liberties allowed at Ports allmost under their Eye, & really injured by them did endeavour to enforce the allowance of the same liberties within this port by divers violent means. But my Resolution & the Steadiness of the Judges of the superior Court defeated this Scheme; & they became content ^to wait^ till Measures should be taken for putting all the Ports in America upon the same footing. Before this Commotion & since The Merchants here in general have acted in such a manner as to intitle themselves to all proper favour.

I do not pretend that this Province is intirely free from the breach of these laws, but only that such breach, if discovered, is surely punished. There has been an Indulgence time out of mind allowed in a trifling but necessary article; I mean the permitting Lisbon Lemons & Wine in small quantities to pass as Ships stores. I have allways understood that this was well known in England & allowed, as being no object of trade, or, if it was, no ways injurious to that of Great Britain. As for Lemons, in this climate, they are not only necessary to the comfort of Life but to health also: And a Prohibition of them would be a great mortification to those who have been accustomed to the use of them. For my own part, I reckon them among the Necessaries of Life & beleive they contribute much to the good health I enjoy here.

In regard to Portugal Wines, there seems to be no material distinction (except as Casus omissions in the letter of Law) between Wines from the Portuguese Islands & wines from the Portuguese continent: nor would the least benefit accrue

THE PAPERS OF GOVERNOR FRANCIS BERNARD

to Great Britain from permitting the one ^only^ & prohibiting the other. Besides, there is sometimes a Want of these little Articles to help to make up a ballance in the Trade between this Country & Portugal; the latter affording no other return hither but Salt. And the Fish Trade of New England is of too great consequence to Old England to run any risk of checking it. Spanish Wines & Fruit, altho at present not in much demand here, are within the same rule of reasoning in regard to promoting the fish trade. But It were to be wished that these were permitted by a positive Law, rather than by an indulgence however reasonable and approved.

The Wine generally used in this Country heretofore has been Madeira: but of late that has grown so extravagantly dear, that few People can afford it. The Wines of the Western Isles are now in the general use of this Country. But some Gentleman prefer Portugal Wines. French Wines can never be an Article of Trade here, as what comes to America is ^in general^ bad & Very perishable; & when it is good, it comes as dear as Madeira, & is not near so much esteemed. And tho' there is now here, under Prosecution, a small Vessel of 130 tuns laden with french Wines said to be bound for Bourdeaux to Eustatia yet this will not conclude for the frequent use of french Wines here. For tho' this Vessel was intended to be unladen on this Coast (as I make no doubt that She was) She would be a singular instance for some years past, and her Cargo would supply the demand for french Wine in New England for 2 or 3 years

I have according to your Lordship's order imparted to your Lordship what alteration of the Laws before mentioned is wanting to the exigencies of this Country; at the same time bespeaking your Lordship's favour that this intimation may not be understood to contain an admission that I myself have been knowingly concerned in or consenting to the aforesaid indulgence. I shall take the like liberty to communicate to your Lordship whatever else shall occur to me on this subject fit for your Lordships consideration

I am with the greatest respect My Lord, Your Lordships most obedient & most humble Servant

Fra Bernard

The Right Honble The Earl of Egremont

ALS, RC   CO 5/755, ff 67-70.

Contains minor emendations. Variant text in BP, 3: 99-102 (L, LbC); *Select Letters*, 1-4.

---

1. **No. 224**.

2. Hutchinson to Egremont, Boston, 15 Sept. 1763, CO 5/755, f 31.

241 | To John Pownall

Castle William Oct[r] 30th. 1763

D[r]. S[r].

Last night a Brig from London brought the Advice of the death of Lord Egremont[1] communicated by M[r]. Mauduit,[2] I had by me a Letter of mine to him sealed ready for dispatch, in answer to his[3] relating to the Appointment of the Captains of the men of War on this Coast to be Custom house officers &c, In mine I endeavoured to show the Expediency of continuing the indulgence, which has been allowed time out of Mind, of Letting Lemmon & Wine in small quantities brought from Lisbon &c by our fish Vessells to pass as ship stores, untill the parliament shall make such importation Lawfull; of which there can be no doubt, if the Case is well understood, My letter is wrote with more freedom than I should have used to I know not who: however I shall let it pass on to the Office let whoever command there

The People here are greatly alarmed at a report that it is determined to carry the Molasses Act into full Execution. I could write a Volume against this measure, If I was at Liberty: but I dont think it prudent to obtrude my advice, especially as it is probable that the contrary to it is resolved upon, So that I will only say, & that in Confidence to you, that I dread the Consequence of such a resolution. It can't be imagined ~~now~~ that NAmerica will be sacrificed at this time of day to the West Indies;[4] and therefore the only motive to such a step is supposed to be the raising a good sum of money. But it is my opinion paradoxical as it may seem, that more mony could be raised by a penny a Gallon than by Six pence And tho' possibly the trade may bear, ~~1½ d.~~ ^three half pence^, it would be better to set out with a penny tho' it was determined to add another half penny soon after; for this reason if there was no other; Every one will readily submit to ~~1d.~~ ^one penny^ tho' it is to be doubted whether ~~1½ d.~~ ^three half pence^ will be so well received. so that by the former you would be sure to learn the utmost of the produce, whereas by the latter perhaps you might not.[5] *once more* I am your &c &c__

J Pownall Esq[r]. q[6]

L, LbC   BP, 3: 104-106.

In the handwriting of clerk no. 1 with emendations by FB.

---

1. On 21 Aug. 1763.

2. Jasper Mauduit to Andrew Oliver, London, 22 Aug. 1763, Prov. Sec. Letterbooks, 1: 421-422.

3. **Nos. 240** and **224**.

4. That is to say, the interests of British merchants trading with the West Indies.

5. With respect to the preferred rate of duty, FB echoes the case made by the speaker of the House of Representatives, Thomas Cushing, in a letter to Jasper Mauduit of 28 Oct. 1763. See Tyler, *Smugglers & Patriots*, 69.

6. Thus in manuscript.

242 | To Dr. William Barnet

Castle William Nov.͏ 7. 1763

Sir.

I have receivd yours of Octr. 22.[1] I should be very glad to promote the practise of inoculation in this Province & encourage the Excercise of it by you. As the Law now stands, I dont see anything more wanting than the allowance of the Select men of the Town where the House proposed to be used stands, with the general consent of the Inhabitants. Our Assembly will sit about Christmas; & if anything will be wanted of them, I will recommend it. But I am satisfyed they will not authorise the setting up of an inoculating Hospital without the Consent of the Town's People: so It will at all events be necessary to obtain that. I am Sir Y͏s

FB.

D.͏ Barnet

L, LbC   BP, 3: 8-9.

In handwriting of clerk no. 2.

Dr. William Barnet, a physician of Philadelphia, had been invited to Boston following the success of his mercury-antimony preparation. Inoculation was prohibited within Boston, and when the House of Representatives in Jan. 1764 refused to authorize Boston's first inoculating hospital, the Governor's Council, the selectmen, and local physicians established the hospital at Point Shirley. The hospital was operational by 20 Feb. and generated such demand that one week later FB permitted the Castle William barracks to be used as a second temporary hospital. Overall, the hospitals markedly reduced the impact of the 1763-64 smallpox epidemic. Philip Cash, "The Professionalization of Boston Medicine, 1760-1803," in *Medicine in Colonial Massachusetts, 1620-1820*: eds. Philip Cash, Eric H. Christianson, and J. Worth Estes (Boston, 1980), 69-100, at 73-75; Blake, "Smallpox Inoculation in Colonial Boston," 289-291; *Reports of the Record Commissioners of the City of Boston*, 16: 102-103.

---

1. Not found.

243 | To Jeffery Amherst

Boston Nov 24. 1763

S^r

I am favoured with yours of the 17th inst[1] informing of your purpose to return to England. I beg leave to wish you a good passage & to thank you for ~~all~~ the many favours I have received from you in the Course of a Constant Correspondence for 5 years.

I am

Sr Jeffry Amherst

AL, LbC   BP, 3: 11.

Haste probably accounts for the brevity of this note acknowledging Amherst's departure. However, the absence of praise for the general's achievements is striking, given that FB has been so effusive in his early correspondence. Their relationship had certainly cooled in the intervening years.

---

1. Not found.

244 | To Welbore Ellis

Boston Novr. 25. 1763

Dear S^r.

I am favoured with yours of July 18th,[1] & cannot sufficiently admire your Sensibility fortitude & prudence. For my own part I have for a long time endeavoured to work up ^in^ myself a high sense of the duty of submitting, with as much ease as we can, to the Accidents of this Life, and yet I was allways aware that there were some strokes, to which I myself am particularly subject, that would quite wither me. In such a case I have often thought to have resorted to dissipation; but you have convinced me that intense business, where it is to be had, forms a more powerful Diversion.

I cannot ask of you an account of the present State of Affairs, knowing what a tender Subject it is, from the quantity of Papers received from England, surely the foulest that ever were defiled by a press. We Americans are at too great a distance to join in the Parties of England: We can only look on & Lament, and pray that Great Britain may not, for ever, be deprived of the advantages of her foreign Acquisitions by domestic dissention.[2]

I have been lately on a Voyage to the N Eastward: for you must know that this Province extends in Coast 300 miles N.E. of this Town. About 240 miles off I am nursing up a new Colony, in the midst of which I have a Very fine Island given me by the Province, as you must have heard. This has afforded me the first opportunity I have yet had of forming the plan of a Town: This I did about 7 Weeks ago with great advantages; & saw the whole markt out by actual Survey: I also built two small houses, in the centre of the Town; & having numbered my People left upon the Island 8 families consisting of 47 Souls, 3 of which were born this Summer, being the first English ~~that were born~~ ^produced^ upon the Island. Some more families are gone down Since: & next year I expect 40 or 50 more families to remove thither: And then the Town will stand upon its own legs.

Another Business in that Country was to look after the Indians there, least they should catch the ill Humours of those in the Southern Parts. Our Indians are so much reduced that if they were to break with us, they would soon be exterminated. But then their first Blow, which they allways contrive to get, would do an infinite deal of Mischief, before they could be sufficiently opposed. I therefore take great care to prevent all real grounds of discontent: I have this Summer done some public ^act^ of Justice on their behalf; among which, I dismissed from the Service, as Commander of a Fort, upon the Indians having made & supported complaints of his injurious treatment of them.[3] I believe I shall find it necessary next Summer to call them together to a general congress & public conference.[4]

You see we little folks mimic you great people; We have our domestic policy & our foreign Negotiations: happily We are not important enough to make any hand of dissension; we leave that to our betters. Now & then a popular blast will arise among us; but with a little explanation or, if wanted, a little amendement, it soon blows over again. At present there is a great noise about seizing a Vessell laden with French Wines; but as soon as the Wine is circulated & the bottles begin to be put about, we shall be in good humour again. I am &c

W Ellis Esq_r Secry at War[5]

L, LbC   BP, 3: 108-109.

In handwriting of clerk no. 2. FB's second voyage to Mount Desert and Penobscot commenced c.15 Sept. and, by the above reckoning, ended c.7 Oct.

---

1. Not found.

2. FB is likely referring to the controversy surrounding the legal pursuit of John Wilkes following publication of *North Britain* No. 45 that had libelled the king and Lord Bute. The *Boston Gazette,* 27 Jun., 1763, reprinted detailed accounts from the London newspapers, from Wilkes's arrest on 23 Apr. to his discharge on 6 May, and his flight to France in Aug. (reported 17 Oct.).

3. Brig. Jedidiah Preble was replaced as commander of Fort Pownall by Capt. Thomas Goldthwait.

4. See **No. 234**n38.

5. Welbore Ellis (1713-1802), a close friend of FB and a longtime associate. Ellis probably met FB at Westminster school, for he entered Christ Church somewhat later than FB in 1732, and graduated B.A. in 1736. An ally of Newcastle, Ellis was an MP for several safe constituencies between 1741 and 1794, including Weymouth, 1747-61, and Aylesbury, 1761-74. He was a lord of the Admiralty, 1747-55, vice treasurer of Ireland, 1755-62 (and again 1765-66), and secretary of war 1762-65. He had been a member of the Privy Council since 1760.

245 | To Richard Jackson

Boston Novr. 26. 1763

Dear S^r.

About a month ago I wrote to you two short letters:[1] in the first of which I gave an Acco^t. of my having remitted £78 11s. 6d. for the proprietors of the ~~said~~ 6 towns, & added some thoughts concerning the forwarding that business. But I forgot one consideration which would have made me urge, more than I have done, the getting these confirmations passed; It would be very agreable to me, if I could inform the Assembly at their Winter Session, which will be in Decr. 21, that the Order of Confirmation is passed. I apprehend that the Affair of Agency &c will be again agitated ~~there~~: But I shall act a different part from what I have done. Having sufficiently established your Character & thereby shown that my motives to engage you in the Service of the province arose from a desire to serve *it* & not you; I shall now consult your dignity & my own, & appear more indifferent about this business than I have been; except that I shall make no doubt of excercising my Negative where I think the good of the Province requires it.

The Merchants here are greatly alarmed at the present proceedings to guard this Coast & especially the appointing the Captains of the men of War to be Customhouse Officers. They are strange People: they are either for ~~taking the government by Storm~~ & enforcing such a remission of the laws of trade as they think fit; or else in a fit of Despondency they give up themselves & their trade to ruin. They never think of a middle way, to remonstrate, with decency, upon the real hardships they lay under & to crave redress, which I cannot think would be hard to obtain. The whole amount seems to be only these: 1 to be allowed to bring Wine & fruit & Oyl Olives &c from such ports of Portugal Spain & the Streights to which they send fish. These imports would amount to very little, & would still leave the great-est part of the Produce of the fish to be remitted to Great Britain; 2 to reduce the duty of Melasses to 1ᵈ Þ Gall. & of Sugars to 1ˢ Þ hund: and if the money it raises is an object, I don't see why yˢ duty may not be extended to all melasses & Sugar withᵗ distinction. I shall say no more on this Subject as I can send a news paper letter that Speaks a good deal of my Sentiments.

I have waited some time for the Arrival of the Sepᵗ. Packet; but expect no news by it, as we have now recieved by private Ships the London papers as far as Octo. 5. However I may possibly learn some of your thoughts upon the present State of Affairs, as far as you dare communicate them. It is reported here with confidence, that you are appointed Secretary to Mʳ Greenville; for what purpose or for what department I must suspend my Curiosity till I hear from you.² If I was well enough acquainted with Mʳ Greenville I would congratulate him on his Acquistion I am, Dʳ Sʳ. &c__

R Jackson Esq.

L, LbC   BP, 3: 106-107.

In the handwriting of clerk no. 2 with scribal emendations.

---

1. FB to Jackson, Boston, 28 Oct. 1763, BP, 3: 102-104; the other has not been found.

2. Jackson was not Grenville's private secretary but secretary to the chancellor of the Exchequer, which office Grenville held whilst first lord of the Treasury.

246 | To [Thomas Pownall?]

Boston Nov. 26. 1763.

My Dear Friend

I had postponed answering your letter¹ which Frank brought me untill his return, which I had intended to have been before now. But as he has defeated my purpose, I find in [it] necessary not only to account to you for the receipt of your letter which I have had now above a year, but also to ~~prevent~~ ^engage^ you to prevent the Deans resenting the abuse of the liberty which He gave to Frank to come hither; which I would never have asked if I had thought I should have been prevented in keeping my word in regard to his return: this I had intended should have been at the beginning of Octo last, & had bespoke a place for him in a good Ship with agreable company.²

About the end of July last, he desird leave to go to New York & Philadelphia in company of a Gentleman whom I entrusted him to. Unluckily that gentleman being prevented going to Philadelphia, Frank takes up mony of him & goes on by himself. When He got to Philadelphia finding himself his own master with some money, not much, in his pocket, He sets out for Maryland, where he rambled about, as long as his money lasted, till Necessity fixed him at Alexandria 524 miles from hence; where he has lived above two months upon credit. As It is above a month since I sent necessary orders for his return, I expect him very Soon: as soon as he arrives I shall put him on board the first ship that sails for England.

I shall not now comment upon this expedition nor express the resentment I have of it. I shall defer to another time the full consideration of his Subject; & at present only Say, that I have not as yet been able to come to, or rather to get him to come to any resolution concerning his future destination. Nothing less than travelling over the whole World will satisfy his Curiosity; and nothing more than residing at Colledge till he has determined for his Batchelor's degree will suit my Concern for him. He will there have better Oppurtunities of acquiring that kind of Knowledge, which his present time of Life requires, than anywhere else. And if He does Nothing, ~~else~~ even Idleness there is more creditable & less dangerous than elsewhere. Besides I dont care that he should loose the gentile appointment, he has in that Society, till he has acquired another. When, or whether ever, he will qualify himself to be a Man of business, I cant foresee. He does not at present promise much: but time makes great alterations & with the help of reflexion, may do much with him. But If he will be nothing but a Pensioner upon my family Stock, He will find the Income of a StudentShip a comfortable addition to the pittance that will come to his Share.

I have carried this Subject further than I Intended: and therefore we will now resort to our selves. I hear, from time to time of Spicer[3] concerning your health: I am aware that it would not be very agreable to you for me to make such frequent enquiries of yourself. His Accounts of late have been good, but the last have so much of dubitation, that I am very impatient for the arrival of his next packet, which is now very late.__

I propose to Inclose with this an original of the Seal & Hand of Oliver Cromwell, which I suppose will be acceptable to you, tho' you have of the same. I have not been able to get you a Massachusets penny: all the rest of that coin you have; groats were never coined. I desire you will present my Compliments to the Dean & such other friends as remember me particularly M[r] Barring[ton];[4] to whom you may communicate what part of this letter you shall think proper I am &c

FB__

M[rs] Bernards compliments are joined with mine__

L, AC   BP, 10: 147-149.

In handwriting of clerk no. 2 with scribal emendations. Enclosures not found.

There is some doubt as to whether Thomas Pownall is the intended recipient. Pownall had been in Germany, having been appointed, on 29 Jun. 1760, a commissary to the British forces there, and evidently wrote FB on his return to England. FB used the salutation "My Dear Friend" only once before in his letterbooks—in a letter to Thomas Pownall of 4 Mar. 1760, BP, 1: 221-223. Their relationship would later deteriorate when Pownall criticised FB's administration in Parliament. Nicolson, *The 'Infamas Govener'*, 190.

---

1. Not found.

2. Thus in manuscript.

3. FB noted that he wrote Mr. Spicer on 18 Jul. 1762 "about Rank." BP, 2: 205.

4. Possibly Shute Barrington.

247 | To John Pownall

Boston. Nov. 28. 1763

Dear S^r

A sensible writer having expressed his thoughts upon the Trade of this province in one of the public papers of this town, in a manner, which it seems intitles him to some regard, I have thought fit to enclose to you a couple of copies for your perusal & the consideration of any one else you sha[ll]¹ think they deserve. I could not, if I would, conceal from you that the Sentiments of this writer in many things coincide with mine, as you have in your power to compare them with papers of mine now in your hands. I must add that I have not the least knowledge or ^even a^ Suspicion ~~of the~~ who is the Author, which will not be Wondered at when I assure you that I so carefully avoid an acquaintance with writers in the Newspapers that pieces of this kind are quite new to me when they appear in the public papers. But as I think the present piece may afford some useful hints, I put it in your way to be used for that purpose, if you see occasion

I am

J Pownall Esq_r

AL, LbC   BP, 3: 110.

The enclosed "piece" has not been found in the Boston newspapers printed between 1 Aug. and 28 Nov. 1763.

---

1. Letters are obscured by tight binding.

248 | *Petition to His Majesty in Council*

[c.Dec. *1763*]

To the Kings most Excellent Majesty in Council

The humble Petition of Francis Barnard Esqr. Captain General and Govr. in Chief in and over His Majesty's Province of Massachusets Bay in New England, & Vice Admiral of the same.

Sheweth

That thier late Majestys King William & Queen Mary, by thier Letters Patent bearing date the 7: day of October in the third Year of thier Reign, did give & Grant unto the Inhabitants of the Province of the Massachusets Bay (among other things) All those Lands and Hereditaments lying between the Territory of Nova Scotia and the River Sagadehock, then, and ever since known and distinguished by the Name of the Territory of Sagadehock together with all Islands lying within ten Leagues of the Main Land within the said Bounds to have and to hold the same unto the said Inhabitants and their Successors to thier own proper use and behoof forevermore. Provided always that no Grant of Lands within the said Territory of Sagadehock made by the Govr: and General Assembly of the said Province should be of any force or effect until their Majestys, their Heirs or Successors should signify their approbation of the same.

That the Govr., Council and House of Representatives of the said Province of Massachusets Bay in the Great and General Court Assembled, by an Instrument in writing bearing date the 27': day of February 1762 (a true Copy whereof is hereunto annexed) Sealed with the publick Seal of the Province at Boston, did give & and Grant to Your Pet^r: All that Island lying North Eastward of Penobscot Bay within the Bounds of the Territory of Sagadehock aforesaid, commonly called and known by the name of the Island of Mount Desart To hold unto and to the use of Your Pet^r:

his Heirs & Assigns for ever Yielding and paying yearly to Your Majesty Your Heirs & Successors one fifth part of all Gold and Silver Oar and precious Stones in the Land of the said Island.

That Your Pet^r: humbly apprehends that the said Grant if confirmed by Your Majesty will be of general publick utility and tend to the Benefit & Security of Your Majestys American Dominions.

Your Pet^r. therefore most humbly prays your Majesty to ratify and confirm the said Grant so made to Your Petitioner in manner & form aforesaid

And Your Pet^r: shall ever Pray &c^a:

Thos. Lise Soll^r. for the Pet^r:

Ms, RC   CO 5/891, f 191.

In the handwriting of Thomas Lise, who evidently was a London lawyer, but of whom nothing else is known. Enclosed **No. 91**.

This petition was prepared as result of the Board of Trade's decision that FB's memorial requesting confirmation of the Mount Desert Island grant must await resolution of Massachusetts's and Nova Scotia's competing claims to Sagadahoc (**Nos. 177** and **193**). The petition was probably composed shortly before it was submitted to the Privy Council's plantation affairs committee on 21 Dec. 1763. On 4 Feb. 1764, the committee referred the petition to the Board of Trade and the Lords Commissioners of the Treasury. The petition and memorial were sent back to the Privy Council on 17 Jul., where they lay until the grant was finally confirmed on 8 Mar. 1771. *JBT*, 11: 338-339; *APC*, 4: 614-615; Sawtelle, "Sir Francis Bernard and His Grant of Mount Desert," 197-254.

249 | *From Thomas Gage*

New York, December, 6th: 1763___

Sir

Sir Jeffery Amherst having found it Indispensably Necessary, for the Effectual Suppression of the Devastations made by the Savages, to Require an Aid of men, from some of the Provinces, for the Service of the next Year; that they might in Conjunction with Such of His Majesty's Regular Troops, as can be Collected, carry the War, into the Heart of the Indian Country, in Order to punish the Savages, who have been guilty of Such Perfidious & Cruel Massacres, & thereby Obtain a Peace which Shall be lasting and Durable.___ The Said Requisition has been laid before the Assembly of New York, who Shew a Readiness to furnish their Quota, of any Number of Men that Shall be thought Necessary, but think it Reasonable that the New England Governments Should be Called upon, to Assist in the manner Constantly practised during the Late War. And in the Interim have Resolved to Raise *Three Hundred Men*, to protect the Communication betwixt Albany & Oswego. The Success of these Measures *now depends on the Resolves of the New England Governments*,[1] & it behoves Me, as having Succeeded Sir Jeffery Amherst in the Command of His Majesty's Forces in North America, in order that a Service so Essential to the future Interest & Happiness of all the Colonies should not be Disappointed, to make Application to Your Province for a Supply of Troops, for the Service of the next Year; that I may be Enabled to Assemble a Respectable Body of Troops, early in the Spring at Niagara, to punish the Savages in those parts, who have so treacherously Commenced, & are now Carrying on Hostilities against Us, & as Sir Jeffery Amherst has also Required a number of men, of the Southward Provinces to act towards the Ohio, I trust they will Raise a Body of Men Sufficient to Chastise the *Shawnese, Delawares*, & Other Tribes on that Side.__

I Doubt not that you will think it Consistent with Sound Policy, Humanity & Brotherly Affection, that Every Province Should in times of Calamity Chearfully Contribute their Quotas, for the mutual assistance of Each other, & that you will, if there's Occasion Enforce these Principles to your Council, & Assembly, from whom I am to hope, a favorable Reception of this Requisition, when I Consider the Readiness your Government has Shewn on former Occasions in forwarding & promoting the Publick Service; and I am to beg of You, that it may be Laid before them, for their Determination thereupon, as soon as possible.__

The Demand I am to make from your Province is of *Seven Hundred men*, Divided into Three Battalions, Each Commanded by a Field Officer, who may be of the Rank of Major; Two Battalions to be Composed of Five Companys, & One of Four, & Each Company to Consist of a Captain, Two Subalterns, & Fifty Men; The Service in which they will be Employed requires a good number of Officers; The men may be Cloathed lightly, a Cloth jacket, Flannel waistcoat, & Leggins; and it will be Necessary, that the whole shall be Raised & ready to proceed to Albany by the first of March next.__

Particular Care should be taken that in Recruiting the Men, None Should be Raised, but such are able Bodied; neither too Young, or too Old, but fit for the most active & Alert Service.__

Altho' by an Order from Home the Regular Troops are Subject to a Stoppage for the Provisions issued to them, belonging to the Crown, yet upon this Occasion, I will take upon me, to Order Provisions to the Provincial Troops, that shall be raised & take the Field; and they shall Likewise be provided with Arms, unless any of them Chuse to bring their Own Arms, for which they shall have the Same allowance, as was made in former Campaigns Should any of them be Lost, or Damaged, in actual service; Tents will also, be furnished to them as formerly.__

The time of Service, may be Limited to the 1ˢᵗ. of November, altho' it is much to be hoped, Every thing will be finished long before that Period, in which Case, the Men will be sent back to their Province.__

I am, with great Regard, Sir, Your most Obedient Humble Servant

Thoˢ. Gage

His Excellency Governor Bernard.

LS, RC   BP, 10: 159-162.

Endorsed by FB: Genl Gage receivd by express Dec 15. 1763. The reply to this letter is **No. 251**.

Thomas Gage deputized for Amherst from 16 Nov., after Amherst returned to England, and was appointed commander-in-chief the following year. Gage's formal request for assistance to crush Pontiac's Rebellion, which had commenced in May 1763 (and would not end until 1766) was triggered by the Battle of Devil's Hole Road, near Fort Niagara, on 14 Sept. when a supply train from the 80ᵗʰ Light Armed Foot and a rescue party were ambushed by a Seneca tribe.

---

1. It is unclear if the underlining in the manuscript was added by Gage or FB, but it appears to be contemporaneous.

250 | *To Benjamin Franklin*

Boston Decʳ. 13. 1763 __

Sir,

The Surveyor General having this day acquainted me that he shall to morrow send an express to Philadelphia, I take this oppurtunity to add to the trouble I have before given you on Account of my Son.[1] By the last Post I received a letter dated Alexandria Novʳ. 16;[2] by which I find he had not then been made acquainted with any orders of yours in his favor, which is well accounted for by his adding that there were then two mails due from Philadelphia.

As the Bearer of this (Mʳ Wyer) is well known to me, & will go to Philadelphia to return hither immediately; if my Son shall not be forwarded to me, when this Messenger arrives, I should like to have him return with him, as Wyer is quite a Master of the road, & can, I suppose, furnish him with a horse from Stage to Stage, & will take due care of him. If He should not be arrived at Philadelphia when Wyer comes, I would have Wyer (with your Approbation, as the expediency will depend upon Circumstances) go on to Alexandria, for which Journey I must be alone an-swerable to him: but this will depend upon the Necessity of his returning from Philadelphia immediately; of which I am not now a Judge. So that upon the whole I must beg the favour of you to order evry thing as you shall think for the best. As I think it greatly against probability that my Son will return with Wyer, as I suppose the Much greater chance will be that he is set out before, I shall not provide Wyer with Money relying upon your goodness, if there should be occasion to furnish him with what shall be Necessary, which will be thankfully repaid whenever you shall order it.

Least my Son should suffer in your opinion by his extravagation,[3] which you may Perceive has not been agreable to me, I will give you my real thoughts of him. He is an uncommon schollar being master of the Latin Greek & Hebrew Languag-es to a greater perfection than I believe allmost any of his age is of all the three. His present Misfortune is that having been worked too much (by Himself) in litteral learning, he now runs riot at the entrance of Science, altho abundant curiosity is among his chief faults. He is therefore impelled by a precipitate desire of hurrying into the Study of Life & manners, altho in my Opinion by no means qualifyed for it as yet: whereas I think it necessary that he should pass thro' the medium of Sci-ence, before he begins to read men. This is at present or rather is to be an interest-ing dispute between us, which must be soon determined by his returning or not to Christ Church at Oxford of which he is a Student, an appointment equivalent to that of a fellow of another Colledge.

I informed you, when at Boston of my thoughts of Sending a Son[4] of mine to the Colledge at Philadelphia; & desired that you would furnish me with advice con-cerning lodging of him & other management. He is a very good Classick Scholar for his age, which is under 14, & will be above the common Pitch by next Summer, as he now remains at School beyond the usuall time of the class he is in, all of which, besides himself, according to usage, went to College last Summer. I should not choose to Spend more of his time than 3 years in Academical Excercises, which I think you told me was all that was required at Pensylvania. I should be glad to have your thought upon this Subject at your own time. I am &c

Benj^m. Franklin Esqr.

L, LbC   BP, 3: 11-13.

In the handwriting of clerk no. 2.

When FB received a letter from his eldest son, Frank, dated Alexandria, 27 Nov., he again requested Franklin's intercession. Frank returned to Boston of his own volition, possibly with some financial help from Franklin. FB to Franklin, Boston, 27 Dec. 1763, BP, 3: 15.

1. FB to Franklin, Boston, 30 Oct. 1763, BP, 3: 8; FB to Franklin, Castle William, 14 Nov. 1763, BP, 3: 9-10.

2. Not found.

3. Meaning "wandering beyond due or prescribed limits; an extravagance." *OED.*

4. Thomas Bernard (27 Apr. 1750-1 Jul. 1818) attended Harvard College, graduating B.A. in 1767 and M.A. (in absentia) in 1770. He became his father's secretary on the family's return to England in 1769, before entering the law and acquiring a considerable reputation as a social reformer.

251 | To Thomas Gage

Boston Dec 15. 1763

S^r.

I have just received yours of the 6th inst.[1] I shall have an opportunity of laying your requisition before our Assembly next week & shall recommend it by all means in my power. It would contribute a good deal to the Success of the motion for me to be made acquainted with what the Colony of Connecticut will do on this occasion; for I suppose Our Assembly will expect to be informed of the resolutions of that Colony before they form their own.[2]

The Principal Objection to this Armament I apprehend will be that when this Province has been engaged in War with the Indians in the Eastern Country, they received no assistance from the Colonies South of them. Indeed I dont know that they ever requested it: If so, there will be less force in this objection. Another Consideration will interfere in this business, which is that I find myself obliged to ask the Assembly for 200 men to march into the Eastern parts of this Province to keep the Indians there in awe: for I have certain advise that they have been solicited to rise; & I have just received fresh advise of the french having imported Warlike stores into the river St Lawrence, the particulars of which I will send you in the Words as they come to me. This expedition will affect your demand no otherwise than in Numbers: for the Assembly will expect that what Men they raise to send to the Eastward shall be reckoned in their proportion of Men, which is but reasonable, as they are raised upon account of the same War.

Upon the whole I will forward this business in the best manner I can; but I cannot at present promise any thing more than my best endeavours to promote the Service.

I am, with great regard, S^r your most obedient humble Servant

Fra Bernard

His Excellency Genl Gage

ALS, RC   Gage.

Contains minor emendations. Endorsed: Gov[r]. Bernard Boston Dec. 15th. 1763. Incloses Intelligence from [Halifax?] Received Dec[r]. 27th Answerd Jan[y] 1st. 1764. Variant text in BP, 3: 14 (L, LbC). Enclosure and Gage's reply have not been found.

FB presented Gage's request for seven hundred men to the assembly on 21 Dec., but the House suspended consideration until a committee had been able to evaluate the strength of the garrisons in Massachusetts's frontier forts. Later, FB presented Gage's letter of 6 Dec. 1763 (**No. 249**) and Lord Halifax's letter of 19 Oct. 1763 (**No. 238**) to the assembly on 18 Jan. 1764, requesting that he be allowed to call out the militia or raise as many new troops as Gage required. To FB's chagrin, the assembly refused. *JHRM*, 40: 118-119, 245, 261-263.

---

1. **No. 249**.

2. See **No. 252**.

252 | *To Thomas Fitch*

Boston Dec[r]. 15. 1763

Sir

I have just received a letter from Gen[l]. Gage,[1] wherein He requires assistance from the Governments of New England to put a speedy end to the Indian War. I shall recommend to the Assembly of this Province to join in giving such Assistance. But as I apprehend our Assembly will want to know the resolution of your Government before they form their own, I should be glad to be informed what you propose to do. Or if you should think it best for these two to act in concert, I would endeavour to promote such a measure. I think it very much the Concern of New England that vigorous measures should be taken for preventing this flame from Spreading

I am &c

The Honble Gov[r] Fitch[2]

L, LbC   BP, 3: 15.

In handwriting of clerk no. 2.

This was probably written after FB had replied to Gage (**No. 251**).

1. **No. 249**.

2. Thomas Fitch (1700-74) of Connecticut. A pious "Old Light" Congregationalist, he was a lawyer by profession and held many public offices before serving as governor of Connecticut, 1754-66.

253 | To John Pownall

Boston Decr. 17. 1763

Dear Sir

I have received their Lordships commands that a more punctual transmission of papers from this Province to their Office may be observed.[1] I have made an enquiry into this matter & cant find out the neglect chargeable upon us. The Secretary sends the Acts of each Session exemplyfied under the great Seal, & the journal of the house of Representatives as soon as they come from the press: he sends also duplicates of them. He sends the proceedings of the general Court which includes the journal of the Council in their legislative Capacity & my consent & dissent to the resolutions, as also the Minutes of the Council in their executive capacity every year at the determination of the general Court. The Treasurers Accounts are sent as soon as they are passed. The Naval Officer says that He sends his Accounts to the board of Trade once a year. I am therefore at a loss to know what is wanting: If it is required to have the proceedings of the general Court & the Minutes of the Council half yearly, it may be done; but then they will not be so compact: besides, the Votes of the House & the Acts show what has come before the general Court. Also if the Naval Officers Account is wanted oftner than yearly, it will be sent. I must therefore wait for further orders. I am &c

John Pownal, Esq;

L, LbC   BP, 3: 118-119.

In the handwriting of clerk no. 2.

1. **No. 188**, which also complained of FB's failure to transmit the "Answers" to the Board's "Queries" (**No. 234**).

254 | To the Earl of Halifax

Boston Dec 20. 1763

My Lord

Altho' I have not been ^particularly^ honoured with ~~particular~~ advice of Lordships having been appointed by his Majesty to the Southern province,[1] yet I have ~~been so certainly informed~~ ^required such ↑a↓ positive [account] ↑confirmation↓ ~~of it by the many~~ ^ that I think it my duty to ~~enga~~ pay my Compliments to your Lordship upon this Occasion. ~~It must give a great pleasure~~ to ^~~the people of North America~~^ ~~this Whole Continent to See it again~~ ↑peo especially↓ ↑thankfully re-~~stored to a relation↓ ~~brought within related to your Lordship, from which~~ ↑whom↓ ~~they have heretofore received such great testimonies of~~ North America must congratulate herself upon being ~~restored~~ again put under your Lordships patronage, from which it has received so many & great benefits. ~~But~~ We who have been placed in the governments of these provinces by your favor, must think ourselves happy in being restored to the liberty of communicating with your Lordship ~~concerning~~ ↑in↓ the execution of Our offices For myself, ~~as~~ I shall allways retain a full Sense of my obligations to your Lordship, ~~so f~~ & shall ~~ever~~ think myself highly honoured by ~~the~~ ↑evry↓ Opportunity ~~you shall~~ given me to express it

I am.

Earl of Halifax

ADft, LbC BP, 3: 115.

This unfinished document is given as an example of a heavily annotated author's draft. Insertions are indicated by carets "^" and substituted text by arrows "↑roman↓". It is the first of two different letters dated 20 Dec. 1763, the other being a draft to the earl of Hillsborough who had been appointed president of the Board of Trade on 15 Sept. (Boston, 20 Dec. 1763, BP, 3: 115-116.)

---

1. Halifax was appointed secretary of state for the Southern Department in Sept. 1763.

255 | *To the Board of Trade*

Boston Dec.[r] 24. 1763

My Lords

Pursuant to the orders I have received I proceed to give your Lordships an Account of the prosecution of the Briggantine lately seized in this port laden with french Wines & other French goods.

The Brigantine Freemason laden with French goods chiefly Wines, at Bourdeaux took her departure for Boston at which place she arrived, (having first touched at Liverpool in Nova Scotia) on fryday the 21st of October, & came to an Anchor within the harbour about 6 miles distance from the Town. There she lay at Anchor all the rest of that & the next day untill the Evening when it was dark; when she went up to town. Being hailed in passing the Castle They answered from Newcastle; & being boarded by the Man of War's barge They answered from Newcastle laden with coals. But it appearing that she had a cargo of Wine, Cap[t]. Bishop commander of the Sloop of War Fortune who had qualified himself in this Province as a Custom house officer seized her.[1] Soon after she was seized They owned that the Brigantine was loaded with french Wines &c & came from Bourdeaux being bound to S[t]. Eustatia. And on the Monday following, being the first time the Custom house was open after the seizures, the Master made a report of his cargo, (which in the course of the trial was falsifyed) & his destination praied that he might be permitted to proceed to S[t]. Eustatia. But the Captain, as a Custom house Officer, by the advice of the Advocate general, libelled the Vessel & Cargo in the Court of Vice Admiralty as forfeited for importing European goods not shipt in great Britain contrary to the Act of the 15th of Char. 2. Upon which the Vessell was claimed by owners living in this province & as for the cargo, a Claim was entered on the behalf of M Belouan a french Merchant at Bourdeaux & M Cossart a Dutch Merchant at S[t]. Eustatia; and it was alledged that these goods were freighted by one to the other, and that leave was given for this Vessell to take Boston in her Way to S[t]. Eustatia: and that they had a right to come into the port so long as they reported & did not break bulk.

This produced a Question Very intresting to the Crown, that is, Whether a Vessell laden with prohibited goods & pretended to be bound from a foreign European port to a foreign American port, might come, ever so much out of their way, into a British American port & there lie at Anchor upon the credit of reporting her cargo & pretended destination. The affirmative of this Question had been pronounced to be law in some popular declamations in the causes which were carried on here against the Custom house officers about 3 years ago: but there never was a cause, that I know, in which this point was adjudged. I therefore determined, whenever a

Case should happen in which this Doctrine should come into question, to oppose it with all my Power: Since it is obvious, that if this question was determined to be law, it would be necessary to apply to Parliament for an amendment of the 15th of Char 2. since it would be impossible to prevent foreign European goods coming into America, if Vessells laden with such goods had a right to come in British American Ports, only by reporting the Cargo & a pretended destination to a foreign Port.

Upon this Account I took upon me the overlooking the conduct of this prosecution in a manner more earnest & public that I have used in other causes of this kind. The Advocate general conducted it with a spirit & Judgement not to be enough commended. The most material Question was whether there could be an importation (so as to forfeit) without landing. The Judge having heard Council for two whole days, gave his Opinion that landing was not necessary to make an importation contrary to that Act, & having shown how effectually the Act would be defeated if a liberty for Vessells laden with prohibited goods to come into British Ports at their own discretion was allowed, & having mark't out several particular Circumstances which showed a fraudulent intention in the present case, decreed the Vessell & Cargo to be forfeited.

From this Decree the Claimers have appealed to the high Court of Admiralty.[2] Upon this occasion I must, in pursuance of the orders I have received to communicate to your Lordships my Sentiments on this Subject, earnestly recommend to your Lordships, that the defence of this Decree against the appeal may be supported at the expence of his Majesty. As one third part of this forfeiture is decreed to his Majesty his intrest in it requires the support of his officers pro tanto.[3] But that is not all: if these extraordinary Custom house officers, whose Service as it is new, is the more invidious, do not appear to have the public support of the Crown in what they do according to the best advice they can procure, I am convinced that a combination will soon be made to distress & embarras them by appeals & Actions at common law for doing their duty in the most plain & positive cases. This I have seen experienced in the confederacy which was formed against the ordinary Custom house officers of this port about 3 years ago, which was effectually discouraged by one instance only of a defence being carried on at the expence of the Crown.

Copies of the proceedings are making out which together with an abstracted state of the case & of the arguments used for the forfeiture, will be sent by the first opportunity.[4] Cap.t Bishop has also seized a Ship for loading with rice without giving bond. I advised & assisted him in this prosecution & the Ship was condemned together with the Rice without any defence.

I am, with great regard, My Lord, your Lordships most obedient and most humble Servant

Fra Bernard

The Right Honble The Lords Commissioners for Trade & Plantations

LS, RC   CO 5/891, ff 203-206.

In the handwriting of clerk no. 2. Endorsed: *Massachusets*. Letters from Fra^s. Bernard Esqr. Govr. of Massachusets Bay, to the Board, dated Decr. 24. 1763, containing an Account of the prosecution of the Brigantine lately seized in the port of Boston laden with French Wines & other French Goods. Rec^d March Read July 2. 1764. Ll67.

The Board of Trade considered FB's letter on 2 Jul. 1764, and John Pownall replied on 12 Jul. *JBT*, 12: 79; BP, 10: 175-178.

---

1. Thomas Bishop (d.1790) was raised to captain on 25 May 1762 and received his customhouse commission under 3 Geo.3, c. 22.

2. Not found in Admiralty Court Series, Early 1-58, 1629-1778, PRO.

3. "So far, to such an extent." *OED*.

4. An account of the seizure and condemnation of the *Freemason* was enclosed in **No. 257**.

256 | *To the Board of Trade*

Boston Dec 26 1763

My Lords

I am honoured with your Lordships orders dated Octr 11th.[1] There has been no neglect that I know of in executing the laws of trade within this province as far as has been practicable. The only indulgences that have been used here I presume have been long well known to your Lordships. That of allowing a small parcell of Wines & fruits to be returned from Portugal &c by the Vessels carrying fish as ship-stores, Your Lordships have been before acquainted with. That this indulgence is not hurtful to Great Britain in the first instance & greatly advantageous to it in the end is to me very certain. The other well known indulgence is in the Act called the Melesses Act which has, I presume never been duly executed; altho' at the same time I must, for my own defence, say, that I never knew an instance of the breach of it. The Custom house officers in this Province are in my opinion good & faithful Officers & have in this case done the best that they could that is, they have got as much money on account of this duty as they could & have brought to account of the King all that they have received. In the last quarters Account of the Collector of this port I observed that the Duties upon this Act amount to between 6 & 700 pounds ster^l, & I am told that the Collector of Salems Account which I have not seen may amount to as much. I therefore conclude, as I can judge by conjecture only, that this Act is not strictly executed: for if it had been, I can't conceive that it could have produced so great a sum in any one quarter. And yet I beleive that if the Duty was lowered so as not to discourage the importation of the goods subject to it, nor make it worth the while to evade the payment of it, it would produce a very much greater Sum.

This Act as been a perpetual stumbling block to Customhouse officers: and it will be most agreable to them to have it anyways removed. The Question seems to be whether It should be an Act of prohibition or an Act of Revenue. It was originally, I beleive, designed for the former; and if it shall be thought advisable to continue it as such, it will want no more than to be fully executed. But if it is meant to be an Act of Revenue, the best means to make it Effectual, that is to raise the greatest Revenue by it, will be to lower the Duties in such a proportion as will secure the entire collection of them & encourage the importation of the goods on which they will be laid. Perhaps a Resolution may be formed allready, or at least before this will come to your Lordships, to continue this Act & enforce the execution of it: in such Case, it may be thought imprudent in me to urge or even to offer my opinion on the subject But, My Lords, in the sincerity of my heart & in the Warmth of my wishes that the Wellfare of this Country may be made advantageous to its Mother Country, I must inform your Lordships, that it seems to me necessary to encourage a trade between North America & the foreign Plantations under proper restrictions: without which the present advantages arising to Great Britain from the trade of North America, I fear, cannot be preserved; much less may an Encrease of them be expected. I founded this Opinion some time ago upon a plain & simple Argument, the fallacy of which I have never been able to discover; and the truth of it has seem'd to be confirmed by frequent observation. It is this: At the time of making the Melasses act, now 30 years ago, It was asserted by the West Indians that as the British West Indian Plantations were capable of taking off all the produce of NAmerica, the sending such produce to foreign plantations ought to be discouraged. To this the North Americans then answerd by denying (I beleive with greater truth) that the British West Indian plantations were capable of taking off all the produce of N America fit for the West Indian Markets. I will suppose however that the ballance was equal. Since that time N America has encreased to above double; the British West Indies remain as they were. What is to become of half the produce of N America, if it is not suffer'd to be carried to foreign Markets upon practicable terms of trade? And how can Great Britain expect that her exports to North America will not keep an equal proportion with the exports of North America to their Markets wherever they lie? It is, in my opinion, a false state of this Question, to consider it as a Contest between the West Indies & N America: it is really a contest between the West Indies & Great Britain; for in the latter will the profit & loss arising from the result of this question determine. The Trade of NAmerica is really the Trade of Great Britain, (prohibited European goods excepted) the profit & loss, the Increase & Decrease of which finally come home to the latter. America will suffer for a time only by being disabled to import from Great Britain what her real or imaginary Wants demand. But her very Necessity will releive her by both obliging & enabling her to resort to her internal powers for what She will not be able to import from abroad. But the Loss to Great Britain will be irretreivable. If this should be exemplified in this Province it will, probably, for the first instance be in the decrease of the fishery; which in the opinion of the most knowing men here, will certainly be the Consequence of a prohibition of foreign Melasses & Sugar.

I have been carried much further upon this subject than I intended; for which I pray your Lordships indulgence: as I mean rather to state the Case to your Lordship's than determine upon it. I am all this while arguing against my own Intrest: Laws that are like to be productive of forfeitures ought to be acceptable to Governors. But for my own part I should be glad, at the expence of all such profits, to see the laws of trade in America so regulated, as to be effectally executed, chearfully submitted to & most conducive to the advantage of Great Britain.

> I am, with great respect, My Lords, Your Lordships most obedient & most humble Servant

> Fra Bernard

The Right Honble The Lords Commrs for Trade & Plantations.

ALS, RC   Dartmouth Papers, American Papers, D(W)1778/II/48.

Contains minor emendations. Endorsed: *Massachusetts*. Letter from Fra[s]. Bernard Esq[r]., Gov[r]. of Massachuset's Bay, to the Board, dated Dec[r]. 26. 1763, relative to the execution of the Laws of Trade in that province, and the necessity of encouraging a Trade between North America & the foreign plantations, under proper restrictions. Rec[d]. March Read July 2[d] 1764. Ll68.
Variant text in BP, 2: 89-92 (L, LbC) and *Select Letters*, 4-8. Considered by the Board of Trade on 2 Jul. 1764. *JBT*, 12: 218.

---

1. **No. 236**.

257 | To John Pownall

Boston De^r. 29. 1763

Dear Sir

I transmit to their Lordships an account of the condemnation of the Free-mason; which being upon the 15th of Cha. 2. one would have thought could have admitted of no doubt as to the execution of it. But Lord Colville Commander in chief, in America, of his Majesty's fleets, having perswaded himself that he is in-titled to a share of whatever his Captains shall seize as Custom house Officers, tho' not subject to the late statute, has, in a letter to the Judge of the Admiralty, made a demand of a share of this Seizure, in terms so indecent & injurious to the Governor the Judge & the Advocate general, that I can't readily submit to it. For I must say that (not excepting myself) the King has no where three Officers of the same kind more attentive to their duty or freer from Corruption than we are. However all the resentment I have shown to this (except a postscript which I have prevailed upon the Judge to add to his Answer to his Lordships letter[1]) is to draw up a state of the Case, on which his Lordships claim is founded: which is done, not to satisfy Law-yers, for Such would have no doubt of this Question, but to explain a Law to those, who will not give themselves the trouble to understand it & yet will judge of it.

I therefore desire leave to put the inclosed paper in your Hands that if this Matter should be stirred in your Office or in any other that your Office has a com-munication with, you would interpose it on the behalf of the American ~~Colonies~~ Governors. I am Sir &c

John Pownall Esq.

P.S. I should be glad if you would communicate the inclosed to Mr Jackson, as also any other of the papers now transmitted to you which the rules of your Office will permit.__ with Enquiry of the 2 Geo 3[2]

L, LbC   BP, 3: 119-120.

In the handwriting of clerk no. 2, except as noted. Enclosures not found.

---

1. Not found. See Chambers Russell to Lord Colvill, 22 Jan. 1764, ADM 1/482, ff 337-338.

2. This line in FB's hand. FB is referring to the act for the further improvement of his Majesty's Revenue of Customs and for the encouragement of officers making seizures and for the prevention of clandestine running of goods into any part of his Majesty's dominions (3 Geo. 3, c. 22).

258 | To John Pownall

Boston Dec.ʳ 30. 1763

Dear Sir

This is the first opportunity I have of acknowledging the receipt of the letters from your Office Sent by the October packet As to what was Sent by the Sepᵗ. Packet, you must before you receive this know that it did not come to hand. The History we have of this Packet is this: She was lost on the flats of North Carolina last, but the Mail was saved; & the Captain with the Mail took his Passage for New York in a Schooner; which Schooner was also lost: But whether the Captain & the Mail, both or either, were lost at this second Shipwreck we know not: but no letters by that mail are arrived here.[1]

As to what I received by the last packet I hope my present dispatches will contain a full answer to your board. As I have been before required to communicate with the Secretary of State concerning the prosecution of the breaches of the laws of trade, I enclose a Copy of a letter Sent to the Secretary of State before I received their Lordships orders, which I must desire you to communicate to their Lordships, if you think there is any thing in it new enough to deserve it. As to the letter relating to the condemnation of the Freemason, I write allmost in the very same Words to the Secretary of State on the same. I have nothing more to add but to desire of you for the real Service of the Crown, which you are never inattentive to, to take care, tho' I know it does not belong to your Office, that the defence of this appeal be supported by the Crown.

As to my letter on the Melasses Act, It is addressed to their Lordships only: but yet I should not be displeasd, if you would communicate it to Lord Halifax; for whatever his Opinion is, I am sure he will perceive, that a love of truth dictates mine. The Merchants of this Town & the whole Province are under the greatest alarm that the Melasses Act will be continued & strictly executed: they have petitioned the General Court, & a Committee of both houses is sitting from day to day to prepare representations against this Act being continued.[2] I wish their results upon this occasion may be so decent & dutiful, (as I doubt not they will) that I may be able to join in them; for there is nothing I am more convinced of than the ~~Expedition~~ Expediency of encouraging a trade (under proper restrictions) between North America & the foreign West India Plantations.

I enclose with this an account of the peregrinations of a young man of this Province among the Ottawas, in which is included part of the History of the War with the Indians so far as relates to the cause & rise of it, But this is only a Matter of Curiosity: for I hope the present Cessation of Arms will produce a peace with the Indians without any more bloodshed.

I am Sir &c

John Pownall Esq.

 with an Enquiry into Act of 2 Geo.3
 with & a Copy of Rand's Declar^n

L, LbC   BP, 3: 116-118.

State paper endorsement: "No. 7". In the handwriting of clerk no. 2 with scribal emenda-
tions. May have enclosed a copy of **No. 240** and Thomas Brown, *A Plain Narrative of the
Uncommon Sufferings, and Remarkable Deliverance of Thomas Brown, of Charlestown, in
New England* (Boston, 1760); other enclosures not found.

---

1. There may not have been any letters from Pownall or the Board to FB, because Massachusetts is
   mentioned only once in the Board journals (on 3 Aug.) between 19 May and 10 Oct. inclusive. *JBT*, 11:
   365-390, at 376-377.

2. A memorial of the merchants and traders of the towns of Boston, Plymouth, Marblehead, and Salem,
   was read by the House on 27 Dec. and sent up to the Council. A committee of both houses reported on
   11 Jan., but a petition was not adopted until the fall, by which time the Revenue Act had been enacted.
   JHRM, 40: 132-182.

APPENDICES

The royal instructions issued colonial governors on their appointment constitute the principal set of rules and guidelines that they were obliged to follow with respect to colonial government and imperial administration. Each set contained two types of instructions: general instructions pertaining to the execution of the governor's commission, and trade instructions pertaining to the enforcement of the Navigation Acts and other trade laws. Bernard received three sets of instructions during his career. The first, dated Court at St. James's, 1 Apr. 1758, was for his administration in New Jersey.[1] The second set, printed below, is dated 18 Mar. 1760, and was one of two issued for his governorship of Massachusetts. The third set, necessitated by the succession of King George III, was drafted on 4 Mar. 1761 and approved on 22 Apr. the trade instructions were signed on 27 May and the general instructions on 30 Jun.[2] There are a few substantive differences between the Massachusetts sets, and these are acknowledged in the footnotes to the transcripts.

Appendix 1 is a transcript of the author's draft of Bernard's general instructions of 1760 (for the **RC** is not extant) while **Appendix 2** is a transcript of the trade instructions (**RC**). This set was prepared by the Board of Trade for the King in accordance with an order-in-council of 27 Nov. 1759. They were considered by His Majesty in Council on 16 Jan. 1760, and were sent to the king himself on 13 Feb. 1760; he signed them on 18 Mar. The Board of Trade noted that this set was consistent with the "usual Form" and "conformable" to those prepared at the same time for other governors; moreover, they contained "no alterations" from the set issued Bernard's predecessor, Thomas Pownall.[3]

---

1. General Instructions as governor of Massachusetts, BP, 13: 1-74; Trade Instructions, BP, 13: 73-140.

2. J. Vernon to the Board of Trade, Court at St. James's, 27 Feb. 1761, CO 5/891, f 21; *JBT*, 11: 172-174; Trade Instructions as governor of Massachusetts, Court at St. James's, 27 May 1761, Nether Winchendon House, Bucks., Eng.; General Instructions as governor of Massachusetts, 30 Jun. 1761, CO 5/920, pp. 54-123.

3. *APC*, 4: 777; CO 5/919, ff 59-60.

Appendix 1

GENERAL INSTRUCTIONS AS GOVERNOR OF MASSACHUSETTS,
18 March, 1760

Instructions to Our Trusty and Well beloved Francis Bernard Esquire Our
Captain General and Governor in Chief in and over Our Province and Territory
of the Massachusets Bay in New England in America. Given at Our Court at
S^t. James's the 18, Day of March 1760 in the Thirty Third Year of Our Reign.

First. With these Our Instructions you will receive Our Commission under Our
Great Seal of Great Britain constituting You Our Captain General and Governor in Chief in and over Our Province of the Massachusets Bay, and likewise
Captain General and Commander in Chief of the Militia and of all Our Forces
by Sea and Land within the Colonies of Rhode Island, Providence Plantation
and the Narraganset Country or Kings Province in New England, and of the
Forts and Places of Strength within the same, You are therefore to fit yourself
with all convenient Speed, and to repair to Our said Province of the Massachusets Bay, and being arrived there, you are to take upon You the Execution of
the Place and Trust We have reposed in You and forthwith to call together the
Members of the Council in that Province.

2^d. You are with all due and usual Solemnity to cause Our said Commission to
be read and published at the said Meeting, and Notification to be also given
to Our Colonies of Rhode Island, Providence Plantation, and the Narraganset Country of the Power wherewith You are intrusted concerning the Militia
Forces and Forts within the said Colonies & Country as aforesaid, which being done you shall then take and also administer unto each of the Members
of the said Council the Oaths appointed to be taken by An Act passed in the
first Year of His late Majesty's Reign Entituled, *An Act for the further Security
of His Majesty's Person and Government and the Succession of the Crown in
the Heirs of the late Princess Sophia being Protestants, and for extinguishing the
Hopes of the pretended Prince of Wales and his open and secret Abettors,*[1] as also
to make and subscribe and cause them to make & subscribe the Declaration
mentioned in An Act of Parliament made in the Twenty fifth Year of the Reign
of King Charles the Second Entituled, *An Act for preventing Dangers which
may happen from Popish Recusants;*[2] And You and every of them are likewise to

---

1. 1 Geo. 1, stat. 2, c. 13.

2. 25 Car. 2, c. 2.

take an Oath for the due Execution of your and their Places and Trusts with regard to your and their equal and impartial Administration of Justice, And You are likewise to take the Oath required by An Act passed in the 7th and 8th. Years of the Reign of King William the third[3] to be taken by Governors of Plantations to do their utmost that the Laws relating to the Plantations be observed.

3. You shall administer or cause to be administred the Oaths mentioned in the aforesaid Act Entituled, *An Act for the further Security of His Majesty's Person and Government and the Succession of the Crown in the Heirs of the late Princess Sophia being Protestants, and for extinguishing the Hopes of the pretended Prince of Wales and his open and secret Abettors,*[4] to the Members and Officers of the House of Representatives, and to all Judges, Justices and all other Persons that hold any Office or Place of Trust or Profit in our said Province, whether by Virtue of any Patent under the Great Seal of Great Britain or the publick Seal of the Massachusets Bay or otherwise, And You shall also cause them to make and subscribe the aforesaid Declaration, without the doing of all which You are not to admit any Person whatsoever into any publick Office, nor suffer those who have been admitted formerly to continue therein.

4. You are forthwith to communicate unto the said Council such and so many of these Our Instructions, wherein their Advice and Consent are mentioned to be requisite, as likewise all such Others from time to time as You shall find convenient for Our Service to be imparted to them.

5. You are to permit the Members of the said Council to have and enjoy Freedom of Debate and Vote in all Affairs of publick Concern that may be debated in Council.

6. You are to observe in the passing of all Laws that the Stile of enacting the same be by the Governor Council and House of Representatives and no other, You are also, as much as possible, to observe in the passing of all Laws that whatever may be requisite upon each different Matter be accordingly provided for by a different Law without intermixing in one and the same Act, such Things as have no proper relation to each other, And You are more especially to take Care that no Clause or Clauses be inserted in or annexed to any Act which shall be foreign to what the Title of such respective Act imports, and that no perpetual Clause be part of any temporary Law, and that no Act whatever be suspended, altered, revived, continued or repealed by general Words, but that the Title and Date of such Act so suspended, altered, revived, continued or repealed be particularly mentioned and expressed in the Enacting Part.

---

3. 7 & 8 Will. 3, c. 27.

4. 1 Geo. 1, stat. 2, c. 13.

7. And Whereas Laws have formerly been enacted in several of Our Plantations in America for so short a time, that the Royal Assent or Refusal thereof could not be had thereupon before the Time for which such Laws were enacted did expire, You shall not therefore give your Assent to any Law that shall be enacted for a less time than two Years, except in the Cases hereinafter mentioned, And it is Our further Will and Pleasure, that you do not re-enact any Law to which the Assent of Us or Our Royal Predecessors has once been refused, without express Leave for that purpose, first obtained from Us upon a full Representation by you to be made, to Our Commissioners for Trade and Plantations, in order to be laid before Us, of the Reason and Necessity for passing such Law, nor give your Assent to any Law for repealing any other Law passed in your Government, altho' the same should not have received the Royal Approbation, unless you take Care, that there be a Clause inserted therein, suspending and deferring the Execution thereof untill Our Pleasure shall be known concerning the same.

8. And Whereas great Mischiefs do arise by passing Bills of an unusual and extraordinary Nature and Importance in the Plantations, which Bills remain in force there from the Time of enacting untill Our Pleasure be signified to the contrary, We do hereby Will and require you not to pass or give your Assent to any Bill or Bills in the Assembly of the said province of an unusual or extraordinary Nature and Importance, wherein Our Prerogative or the Property of Our Subjects may be prejudiced, or the Trade or Shipping of this Kingdom any ways affected, untill you shall have first transmitted to Our Commissioners for Trade and Plantations, in order to be laid before Us, the Draught of such Bill or Bills and shall have received Our Royal Pleasure thereupon, unless you take Care in the passing of any Bill of such Nature, that there be a Clause inserted therein suspending and deferring the Execution thereof untill Our Pleasure shall be known concerning the same.

9. You are to take Care, that no private Act, whereby the Property of any private person may be affected, be passed, in which there is not a Saving of the Right of Us Our Hiers & Successors, all Bodies Politick or Corporate, and all other Persons except such as are mentioned in the said Act, and those claiming by, from or under them, And further you shall take Care, that no private Act be passed without a Clause suspending the Execution thereof untill the same shall have received Our Royal Approbation; It is likewise Our Will and Pleasure, that you do not give your Assent to any private Act, untill Proof be made before you in Council, and entred in the Council Books, that publick Notification was made of the Party's Intention to apply for such Act in the several Parish Churches where the Premises in Question lye for three Sundays at least successively, before any such Act shall be brought into the Assembly, and a Certificate under

your hand be transmitted with and annexed to every such private Act, signifying that the same has passed through all the Forms above mentioned.

10. You are to take Care that in all Acts or Orders to be passed within Our said Province in any case for the levying Money or imposing Fines and Penalties, express mention be made that the same is granted or reserved to Us Our Heirs and Successors for the publick Uses of that Our Province and the Support of the Government thereof, as by the said Act or Order shall be directed, And You are particularly directed not to pass any Law, or do any Act by Grant Settlement or otherwise, whereby Our Revenue may be lessened or impaired without our especial Leave or Command therein.

11. Whereas an unwarrantable Practice hath of late Years been introduced into the Proceedings of the Assembly of the Province of the Massachusets Bay, of raising Money and supplying the Current Service of the Year by a Vote or Resolve, instead of An Act of Assembly, and of reserving thereby to the said Assembly a Power of determining what Accounts shall or shall not be paid, even after the Service performed, which Practice is expressly contrary to the Tenor of the Charter granted to that Province by Our Royal Predecessors King William and Queen Mary, whereby the said Assembly are impowered to raise Monies for the Support of the Government, and for the Defence of the Inhabitants by Act or Acts of Assembly only, And the issuing of the said Money when raised is expressly reserved to Our Governor for the time being, with the Advice and Consent of the Council of Our said Province, Now Our Will and Pleasure is, and We do hereby require you to take Care for the future, that no Money be raised or *Bills of Credit issued* in the Province of the Massachusets Bay but by Act or Acts of Assembly, in which Act or Acts one or more Clauses of Appropriation may be inserted, but that the passing all Accounts for payment, and the issuing of all Monies so raised *or Bills of Credit* be left to Our Governor or Commander in Chief of Our said Province, with the Advice and Consent of the Council, according to the said Charter, subject nevertheless to a future Enquiry of the then present or any other Assembly, as to the Application of such Monies.

12. You are not to permit any Clause whatsoever to be inserted in any Law for levying Money or the Value of Money, whereby the same shall not be made liable to be accounted for to Us and to Our Commissioners of Our Treasury or to Our High Treasurer for the time being, and audited by Our Auditor General of Our Plantations or his Deputy for the time being; And We do hereby particularly require and enjoyn You, upon pain of Our highest Displeasure, to take Care that fair Books of Accounts of all Receipts and Payments of all publick moneys be duly kept, and the Truth thereof attested upon Oath, and that all such Accounts be audited by Our Auditor General of Our Plantations or his Deputy,

who is to transmit Copies thereof to Our Commissioners of Our Treasury or Our high Treasurer for the time being, and that you do every half Year or oftner send another Copy thereof attested by yourself to Our Commissioners for Trade and Plantations, and Duplicates thereof by the next Conveyance, in which Books shall be specified every particular Sum raised or disposed of, together with the Names of the Persons to whom any Payments shall be made, to the end We may be satisfied of the right and due Application of the Revenue of Our said Province, with the Probability of the Increase or Diminution of it under every Head or Article thereof.

13. Whereas several Inconveniences have arisen to Our Governments in the Plantations by Gifts and Presents made to Our Governors by the Assemblies, It is Our express Will and Pleasure, that neither You Our Governor, nor any Governor, Lieutenant Governor, Commander in Chief, or President of the Council of Our said Province for the time being, do give your or their Assent to any Act for any Gift or Present to be made to you or them by the Assembly, and that neither you nor they do receive any Gift or Present from the Assembly or Others on any Account, or in any way whatsoever upon pain of Our highest Displeasure and of being recalled from that Government.

14. And it is Our Express Will and Pleasure that no Law for raising any Imposition on Wines or other strong Liquors be made to continue for less than one whole Year, as also that all other Laws whatsoever for the Supply and Support of Our Government shall be without Limitation of Time, except the same be for a temporary Service, and which shall expire and have their full Effect within the Time therein prefix'd.

15. And Whereas Complaints have been made to Us by the Merchants of Our City of London, in behalf of themselves and of several others our good Subjects of Great Britain trading to Our Plantations in America, that greater Duties and Impositions are laid on their Ships and Goods ^than on the Ships & Goods^ of Persons who are Natives and Inhabitants of the said Plantations, It is therefore Our Will and Pleasure that you do not upon any pretence whatsoever, upon pain of Our highest Displeasure, give your Assent to any Law, whereby the Natives or Inhabitants of Our Province of the Massachusets Bay under your Government may be put on a more advantageous footing than those of this Kingdom, or whereby any Duties shall be laid upon British Shipping or upon the Product or Manufacture of Great Britain upon any pretence whatsoever.

16. You are to transmit authentick Copies of all Laws Statutes and Ordinances which at any time hereafter shall be made or enacted within the said Province, each of them seperately under the publick Seal, unto Our Commissioners for Trade and Plantations within three Months or by the first Opportunity after

their being enacted, together with Duplicates thereof by the next Conveyance, upon pain of Our highest Displeasure and of the Forfeiture of that Years Salary wherein you shall at any Time, or upon any Pretence whatsoever, omit to send over the said Laws, Statutes and Ordinances as aforesaid, within the Time above limited, as also of such other Penalty as We shall please to inflict, but if it shall happen that no Shipping shall come from our said Province within three Months after making such Laws, Statutes and Ordinances, whereby the same may be transmitted as aforesaid, then the said Laws Statutes and Ordinances are to be transmitted by the next Conveyance after the making thereof whenever it may happen, for Our Royal Approbation or Disallowance of the same.

17. And you are to take especial Care that the Copies and Duplicates of the said Acts so to be transmitted as aforesaid be fairly abstracted in the Margins, and that in every Act the several Dates or respective Times when the same passed the House of Representatives, the Council, and received your Assent be particularly expressed, and you are to be as explicit as may be in your Observations to be sent to Our Commissioners for Trade and Plantations upon every Act, that is to say, whether the same is introductive of a new Law, declaratory of a former Law, or does repeal a Law then before in being, And you are likewise to send to Our said Commissioners the Reasons for the passing of such Law, unless the same do fully appear in the Preamble of the said Act.

18. You are to require the Secretary of our said Province or his Deputy for the time being to furnish you with Transcripts of all such Acts and publick Orders as shall be made from time to time, together with a Copy of the Journal of the Council, and that all such Transcripts and Copies be fairly abstracted in the Margins, to the end, the same may be transmitted to Our Commissioners for Trade and Plantations in order to be laid before us, which he is duly to perform upon pain of incurring the Forfeiture of his Place.

19. You are to require from the Clerk of the House of Representatives or other proper Officer, Transcripts of all the Journals and other Proceedings of the said House, fairly abstracted in the Margins, to the end the same may in like Manner be transmitted as aforesaid.

20. Whereas many of the Laws heretofore passed in Our Colonies and Plantations in America respectively have from time to time been either entirely or in part repealed, and Others of them are expired, altered, amended, or explained, by means whereof, Persons not well acquainted with the said Laws may be led into Mistakes, and Great Prejudice and Inconvenience may arise to Our Service, and whereas nothing can more effectually tend to promote Order and good Government, secure the Properties and Possessions of Our Subjects, and prevent litigious Controversies and Disputes than a clear and well digested

Body of Laws, It is therefore Our Will and Pleasure, and We do hereby require and direct you, jointly with the Council and Assembly, of Our Province of the Massachusets Bay under your Government, forthwith to consider and revise all and every the Laws, Statutes and Ordinances which are in force within the said Province, excepting only such as relate to private Property, or are otherwise of a private Nature, and in lieu thereof, to frame and pass a compleat and well digested Body of new Laws for the said Province, taking especial Care, that in the passing of each Law due Regard be had to the Methods and Regulations prescribed by these Our Instructions to you, and that no Law of any kind whatsoever, making a part of such new Body of Laws be passed without a Clause inserted therein suspending and deferring the Execution thereof untill Our Royal Will and Pleasure may be known thereupon, And it is Our further Will and Pleasure that when the said new Body of Laws shall have been so framed and passed as aforesaid, You do forthwith transmit each Law seperately under the Seal of Our said Province, together with my particular Observations thereupon, to Our Commissioners for Trade & Plantations in order to be laid before Us, in Our Privy Council for Our Approbation or Disallowance.

21. And Whereas An Act of Parliament was passed in the 6th: Year of the Reign of Her late Majesty Queen Anne, Entituled *An Act for ascertaining the Rates of foreign Coins in Her Majesty's Plantations in America,*[5] which Act the respective Governors of all Our Plantations in America have from time to time been instructed to observe and carry into due Execution, And whereas notwithstanding the same Complaints have been made that the said Act has not been observed as it ought to have been, in many of Our Colonies and Plantations in America, by means whereof many indirect Practices have grown up, and various and illegal Currencies have been introduced in several of the said Colonies and Plantations, contrary to the true Intent and Meaning of the said Act, and to the Prejudice of the Trade of Our Subjects; It is therefore Our Will and Pleasure, and you are hereby strictly required and commanded under pain of Our highest Displeasure and of being removed from your Government to take the most effectual Care for the future that the said Act be punctually and bona fide observed and put in Execution according to the true Intent and Meaning thereof.

22. You are to examine what Rates and Duties are charged and payable upon Goods imported and exported within our said Province, whether of the Growth or Manufacture of Our said Province or otherwise, And You are to suppress the engrossing of Commodities as tending to the Prejudice of that Freedom which

---

5. 6 Anne, c. 57.

Trade and Commerce ought to have, and to use your best Endeavours in the improving the Trade of those Parts by settling such Orders and Regulations therein with the Advice of the said Council as may be most acceptable to the Generality of the Inhabitants, and to send unto our Commissioners for Trade and Plantations yearly or oftner, as occasion may require, the best and most particular Account of any Laws that have had any time been made, manufactures set up, or Trade carried on in the Province of the Massachusets Bay, which may in any wise affect the Trade and Navigation of this Kingdom.[6]

23. And in the Choice and Appointment of all Judges, Justices, Sheriffs and all other Officers to be by you appointed, you are always to take Care that they be Men of good Life well affected to Our Government, of good Estates, and of Abilities suitable to their Employments.

24. You are to take Care that no Man's Life, Member,[7] Freehold or Goods be taken away or harmed in Our said Province under your Government, otherwise than by established and known Laws, not repugnant to, but as near as may be agreable to the Laws of this Kingdom, and that no Persons for the future be sent as Prisoners to this Kingdom from the said Province under your Government without sufficient Proof of their Crimes, and that Proof transmitted along with the said Prisoners.

25. You shall endeavour to get a Law passed (if not already done) for the restraining of any inhuman Severity which by ill Masters or Overseers may be used towards their Christian Servants and their Slaves, and that Provision be made therein, that the wilful killing of Indians and Negroes may be punished with Death, and that a fit Penalty be imposed for the maiming of them.

26. You are to take Care that all Writs be issued in Our Name throughout Our said Province.

27. You are to take Care by and with the Advice and Assistance of the said Council, that the Prisons there, if they want Reperation, be forthwith repaired and put into and kept in such a Condition as may sufficiently secure the Prisoners that are or shall be there in Custody.[8]

---

6. A revised article was applicable from 1761: "and it is our express will and pleasure that you do not upon any pretence what ever upon pain of our highest displeasure, give your assent to any law or laws for setting up any manufactures or carrying on any trades which are or may be hurtful or prejudicial to this kingdom; and that you do use your utmost endeavours to discourage, discountenance, and restrain any attempt which may be made to set up such manufactures or establish any such trades." Labaree, *Royal Instructions*, 2: 654.

7. Meaning membership of a community, in this case citizenship. *OED*.

8. This article was omitted from the set of instructions issued to FB in 1761. Labaree, *Royal Instructions*, 1: 341.

28. You shall not remit any Fines or Forfeitures whatsoever above the Sum of Ten Pounds, nor dispose of any Forfeitures whatsoever, untill upon signifying to the Commissioners of Our Treasury or Our High Treasurer for the time being, and to Our Commissioners for Trade and Plantations, the Nature of the Offence, and the Occasion of such Fines and Forfeitures or Escheats, with the particular Sums or Value thereof (which You are to do with all Speed) You shall have received Our Directions therein, But you may in the mean time suspend the Payment of the said Fines and Forfeitures.

29. You shall likewise take especial Care, with the Advice and Consent of the Council, to regulate all Salaries and Fees belonging to Places or paid upon Emergencies that they be within the Bounds of Moderation and that no Exaction be made upon any Occasion whatsoever; As also that Tables of all Fees be publickly hung up in all Places where such Fees are to be paid; And You are to transmit Copies of all such Tables of Fees unto Our Commissioners for Trade and Plantations as aforesaid, in order to be laid before Us.[9]

30. And Whereas several Complaints have been made by the Surveyor General and other Officers of Our Customs in Our Plantations in America, that they have frequently been obliged to serve on Juries, and personally to appear in Arms whenever the Militia is drawn out and thereby are much hinder'd in the Execution of their Employments; Our Will and Pleasure is, that you take effectual Care and give the necessary Directions that the several Officers of Our Customs be excused and exempted from serving on any Juries or personally appearing in Arms in the Militia, unless in Cases of absolute Necessity, or serving any Parochial Offices, which may hinder them in the Execution of their Duties.

31. And Whereas the Surveyors General of Our Customs in Our Plantations are impowered, in case of the Vacancy of any of the Officers of Our Customs, by Death, Removal or otherwise, to appoint other Persons to execute such Offices untill they receive further Directions from Our Commissioners of Our Treasury, or Our High Treasurer, or Commissioners of Our Customs for the time being; But in regard the Districts of Our said Surveyors General are very extensive, and that they are required at proper Times to visit the Officers in the several Governments under their Inspection, and that it may happen that some of the Officers of Our Customs in Our Province of the Massachusets Bay may dye at the Time when the Surveyor General is absent in some distant part of his District, so that he cannot receive Advice of such Officer's Death within a

---

9. Omitted from 1761. Labaree, *Royal Instructions,* 1: 371-372.

reasonable Time, and thereby make Provision for carrying on the Service, by appointing some other Person in the room of such Officer who may happen to dye, Therefore that there may be no Delay given on such Occasions unto the Masters of Ships, or Merchants in their Dispatches, It is Our further Will and Pleasure, in case of such Absence of the Surveyor General or if he should happen to dye, and in such cases only, that upon the Death of any Collector of Our Customs within that Province, You shall make Choice of a Person of known Loyalty Experience, Diligence and Fidelity to be employed in such Collector's Room for the Purposes aforesaid, untill the Surveyor General of Our Customs shall be advised thereof, and appoint another to succeed in their Places, or that further Directions shall be given therein by Our Commissioners of Our Treasury or Our high Treasurer, or by the Commissioners of Our Customs for the time being, which shall be first signified, taking Care that you do not under pretence of this Instruction interfere with the Powers and Authorities given by the Commissioners of Our Customs to the said Surveyor General, when he is able to put the same in Execution.

32. And Whereas you will receive from Our Commissioners for executing the Office of High Admiral of Great Britain and of Our Plantations a Commission constituting you Vice Admiral of Our said Province of the Massachusets Bay, You are hereby required and Directed carefully to put in Execution the several Powers thereby granted You.

33. And Whereas We have been informed that the Fees for the Condemnation of a Prize Ship in Our Courts of Admiralty in Our Plantations are considerably greater than those demanded on the like Occasion in Our High Court of Admiralty here; And Whereas We are willing that Our Subjects in the Plantations should have the same Ease in obtaining the Condemnation of Prizes there, as in this Kingdom, You are to signify Our Will and Pleasure to the Officers of Our Admiralty Court in the Massachusets Bay, that they do not presume to demand or exact other Fees than such as are taken in this Kingdom which amount to about Ten Pounds for the Condemnation of each Prize, according to the List of such Fees.

34. And there having been great Irregularities in the manner of granting Commissions in the Plantations to private ships of War, You are to govern yourself whenever there shall be Occasion, according to the Commissions and Instructions granted in this Kingdom, Copies whereof will be herewith delivered you; But you are not to grant Commissions or Marque or Reprizal against any Prince or State, or their Subjects in Amity with Us, to any Person whatsoever without Our especial Command; And You are to oblige the Commanders of all Ships having private Commissions, to wear no other Colours than such as are

described in Our Order in Council of the 7th: of January 1730, in relation to Colours to be worn by all Ships and Vessels to except Our Ships of War a Copy of which Order will herewith be delivered to You.

35. Whereas Commissions have been granted unto several Persons in Our ^respective^ Plantations in America for the trying of Pirates in those Parts pursuant to the Acts for the more effectual Suppression of Piracy, And by a Commission already sent to Our Province of the Massachusets Bay, You (as Captain General and Governor in Chief of Our said Province) are impowered together with Others therein mentioned to proceed accordingly in reference to Our said Province, Our Will and Pleasure is, that in all Matters relating to Pirates, you govern yourself according to the Intent of the said Acts and Commissions.

36. Whereas We have thought it necessary for Our Royal Service to constitute authorize and appoint a Receiver General of the Rights and Perquisites of the Admiralty, It is therefore Our Will and Pleasure, that you be aiding and assisting to Our said Receiver General his Deputy or Deputies in the Execution of the said Office of Receiver General, And We do hereby enjoin and require you to make up your Accounts with him his Deputy or Deputies of all Rights of Admiralty, (Effects of Pirates included) as You or Your Officers have received or shall or may receive for the future, and to pay over to the said Receiver General, his Deputy or Deputies for Our Use, all such Sum or Sums of Money as shall appear upon the foot of such Accounts, to be and remain in your Hands or in the Hands of any of your Officers. And Whereas Our said Receiver General is directed in case the Parties chargeable with any part of such Revenue, refuse, neglect or delay Payment thereof, by himself or sufficient Deputy, to apply in Our Name to Our Governors, Judges, Attorneys General or any other Our Officers or Magistrates, to be aiding and assisting to him in recovering the same; It is therefore Our Will & Pleasure and You Our Governor, Our Judges, Our Attorney General and all other Our Officers whom the same may concern are hereby required to use all lawfull Authority for the recovering and levying thereof.

37. You are to transmit unto Us and to Our Commissioners for Trade & Plantations with all convenient Speed a particular Account of all Establishments of Jurisdictions, Courts and Offices and Officers, Powers, Authorities, Fees, and Priviledges granted or settled within our said Province together with an Account of all the Expenses attending the Establishment of the said Courts and of such Funds as are settled and appropriated for discharging such Expenses.

38. And Whereas We have been graciously pleased to constitute and appoint a Surveyor General of all Our Woods in North America with proper Deputies under him, in order the better to secure and preserve for the Use of Our Royal

Navy, such Trees as shall be found proper for that Service; It is Our Will and Pleasure that you be aiding and assisting to the said Surveyor and his Deputies; And that you give Orders to all Officers Civil and Military, that they in their several stations and Places be aiding and assisting to the said Surveyor or his Deputies, in preventing the Destruction of the Woods in that Province, or in punishing such as shall be found offending therein

39. And Whereas An Act was passed here in the 3ᵈ and 4ᵗʰ: Years of Queen Anne Entituled, *An Act for encouraging the Importation of Naval Stores from Her Majesty's Plantations in America,*[10] and another passed in the Ninth Year of the said Queen's Reign, Entituled *An Act for the Preservation of white and other Pine Trees growing in Her Majesty's Colonies of New Hampshire, the Massachusets Bay and Province of Main, Rhode Island and Providence Plantation, the Narraganset Country or King's Province, and Connecticut in the New England, and New York and New Jersey in America for the Masting Her Majestys Navy;*[11] An also An Act passed in the 8ᵗʰ: Year of his late Majesty's Our Royal Father's Reign Entituled *An Act giving further Encouragement for the Importation of Naval Stores and for other Purposes therein mentioned,*[12] yet nevertheless We have been informed that great Spoils are dearly committed in Our Woods in the Province of Main and other Parts within your Government of the Massachusets Bay, by cutting down and converting to private Use such Trees as are or may be proper for the Service of Our Royal Navy; And it being necessary that all such Abuses which tend so evidently to deprive Us of those Supplies be effectually redressed; It is Our Will and Pleasure that you take Care and give in Charge, that the said Acts, as also that passed in the Second Year of Our Reign Entituled, *An Act for the better Preservation of His Majesty's Woods in America, and for the Encouragement of the Importation of Naval Stores from thence, and to encourage the Importation of Masts, Yards and Bowsprits from that part of Great Britain called Scotland,*[13] and every Clause, Article and Proviso therein be strictly and duly complied with.

40. Whereas the Number of Townships in Our Province under your Government is of late Years very much increased, and may in time prove inconvenient, in case the present Method of splitting and dividing old Towns, and of erecting new ones should continue. And Whereas any future Settlements may be erected into Precincts, Parishes or Villages, with all the Offices and Privileges neces-

---

10. 3 & 4 Anne, c. 11.

11. 9 Anne, c. 22.

12. 8 Geo. 1, c. 12.

13. 2 Geo. 2, c. 35.

sary for their good Government and Security, without the Liberty of sending Representatives to the General Assembly; It is Our Will and Pleasure that you do not give your Assent for the future to any Bill for erecting a new Town or dividing an Old one without a Clause be[*ing*] inserted therein, suspending & deferring the Execution thereof untill Our Pleasure shall be known thereupon.[14]

41. You are to permit a Liberty of Conscience to all Persons (except Papists) so they be contented with a quiet and peaceable Enjoyment of the same, not giving Offence or Scandal to the Government.

42. The Right Reverend Father in God Edmund late Bishop of London having presented a Petition[15] to his late Majesty our Royal Father humbly beseeching him to send Instructions to the Governors of all the several Plantations in America, that they cause all the Laws already made against Blasphemy, Prophaness, Adultery, Fornication, Polygamy, Incest, Prophanation of the Lords Day, Swearing and Drunkenness in their respective Governments to be vigorously executed; And We thinking it highly just that all Persons who shall offend in any of the Particulars aforesaid should be prosecuted and punished for their said Offences, It is therefore Our Will and Pleasure that you take due Care for the Punishment of the aforementioned Vices, and that you earnestly recommend it to the Council and House of Representatives of the Massachusets Bay to provide effectual Laws for the Restraint and Punishment of all such of the aforementioned Vices against which no Laws are as yet provided; And also You are to use your Endeavours to render the Laws in being more effectual by providing for the Punishment of the aforementioned [*Vices by Presentment upon oath*][16] be made to the Temporal Courts by the Church Wardens of the several Parishes, or other proper Officers to be appointed for that purpose; And for the further Discouragement of Vice and Encouragement of Virtue and good living (that by such Example the Infidels may be invited and perswaded to embrace the Christian Religion) You are not to admit any Person to publick Trusts and Employments in the said Province under your Government whose ill Fame and Conversation may occasion Scandal; And it is Our further Will and Pleasure that you recommend to the Assembly to enter upon proper Methods for the erecting and maintaining of Schools in order to the training up of Youth to reading and to a necessary Knowledge of the Principles of Religion.

---

14. This instruction was applicable between 1743 and 1761. Labaree, *Royal Instructions,* 1: 111. See **No. 79**.

15. Edmund Gibson (1669-1748), bishop of Lincoln, 1715-23, and bishop of London, 1723-48. He assiduously upheld the practice of visitations and was an outspoken critic of profanity and impiety.

16. Missing from manuscript. Supplied from General Instructions as governor of Massachusetts, 27 May 1761.

43. You shall send an Account to Our Commissioners for Trade and Plantations in order to be laid before Us, by the first Conveyance, of the present Number of Planters and Inhabitants, Men, Women and Children, as well Masters as Servants, free and unfree, and of the Slaves in Our said Province; As also Yearly Accounts of the Increase or Decrease of them, and how many of them are fit to bear Arms in the Militia of Our said Province.

44. You shall also cause an exact Account to be kept of all Persons, Born, and Christned and buried, and you shall Yearly send fair Abstracts thereof to Our Commissioners for Trade and Plantations as aforesaid.[17]

45. You shall take Care that all Planters and Christian Servants be well and fitly provided with Arms, and that they be listed under good Officers, and when and often as shall be thought fit, muster'd and trained, whereby they may be in a better Readiness for the Defence of Our Province under your Government.[18]

46. But You are to take especial Care that neither the Frequency nor Unreasonableness of remote Marches Musters and Trainings be an unnecessary Impediment to the Affairs of the Inhabitants.

47. You shall not upon any Occasion whatsoever establish or put in Execution any Articles of War or other Law Martial upon any of Our Subjects Inhabitants of Our said Province without the Advice and Consent of the Council there.

48. And Whereas there is no Power given You by your Commission to execute Martial Law in time of Peace, upon Soldiers in Pay, And yet nevertheless it may be necessary that some Care be taken for the keeping of good Discipline amongst those that we may at any time hereafter think fit to send into Our said Province (which may properly be provided for by the Legislative Power of the same) You are therefore to recommend unto the General Assembly of Our said Province that (if not already done) they prepare such Act or Law for the punishing of Mutiny, Desertion and false Musters, and for the better preserving of good Discipline among the said Soldiers as may best answer those Ends.

49. And Whereas by our Commission for the Government of Our said Province of the Massachusets Bay, We have given you all the Powers and Authorities of any Captain General over Our Colonies of Rhode Island, Providence Plantation and the Narraganset Country or Kings Province, Our Royal Pleasure and Intention is, that in Time of Peace the Militia within each of the said Colonies be left to the Government and Disposition of the respective Governors of the

---

17. Omitted from 1761. Labaree, *Royal Instructions*, 2: 747.

18. Omitted from 1761. Labaree, *Royal Instructions*, 1: 392-393.

same, but so as nevertheless in case of apparent Danger or other Exigency You do at all Times take upon yourself the superior Command of those Forces as in the said Commission is directed.

50. Whereas it is absolutely necessary that We be exactly informed of the State of Defence of all Our Plantations in America, as well in relation to the Stores of War that are in each Plantation as to the Forts and Fortifications there, and what more may be necessary to be built for the Defence and Security of the same, You are so soon as possible to prepare an Account thereof with relation to Our said Province in the most particular Manner, And You are therein to express the present State of the Arms Ammunition and other Stores of War belonging to Our said Province, either in any publick magazines or in the Hands of private Persons together with the State of all Places either already fortified or that you judge necessary to be fortified for the Security of Our said Province; And You are to transmit the said Accounts to Our Commissioners for Trade and Plantations, in order to be laid before Us, As also a Duplicate thereof to Our Master General or Principal Officers of Our Ordnance, which Accounts are to express the Particulars of Ordnance, Carriages, Ball, Powder and all other Sorts of Arms & Ammunition in our publick Stores at your Arrival, and so from time to time of what shall be sent to you or bought with the publick Money, and to specify the Time of the Disposal, and the Occasion thereof, and other like Accounts half Yearly in the Same Manner.

51. You are to take especial Care that fit Storehouses be settled in Our Province of the Massachusets Bay, for receiving and keeping of Arms Ammunition and other publick Stores.[19]

52. And Whereas Our Royal Predecessors have been constantly at great Charge in sending thither and maintaining Ships of War to cruize upon the Coasts of that Province in order to their Protection against Enemies by Sea, You are therefore to require and press the Council and House of Representatives vigorously to exert themselves in fortifying all Places necessary for the Security of the said Province by Land, and in providing what else may be necessary in all Respects for their further Defence. In order whereunto You are also to cause a Survey to be made of all the considerable Landing Places and Harbours within the said Province, and with the Advice of the said Council to erect in any of them such Fortifications as shall be necessary for their Security and Advantage.

53. You shall transmit to Our Commissioners for Trade and Plantations by the first Opportunity in order to be laid before Us, a Map with the exact Description of

---

19. Omitted from 1761. Labaree, *Royal Instructions*, 1: 404.

the whole Territory under your Government with the several Plantations and Fortifications upon it, And You are likewise to use you best Endeavours to procure a good map to be drawn of all the Indian Country in the Neighbourhood of Our Plantations in those Parts marking the Names of the several Nations as they call themselves, and are called by the English and French and the Places where they inhabit, and to transmit the same in like manner.

54. You are from time to give an Account as before directed what Strength your Neighbours have (be they Indians or Others) by Sea and Land and of the Condition of their Plantations and what Correspondence you do keep with them.

55. And in case of any Distress of any Others of Our Plantations, You shall, upon Application of the respective Governors thereof to You, assist them with what Aid the Condition and Safety of Our Province under Your Government can permit.

56. Whereas We have been informed that in the Times of War Our Enemies have frequently got Intelligence of the State of Our Plantations by Letters from private Persons to their Correspondents in Great Britain taken on board Ships coming from the Plantations which has been of dangerous Consequence, Our Will and Pleasure therefore is, that You signify to all Merchants Planters and Others, that they be very cautious in time of War in giving any Account by Letters of the publick State & Condition of Our Province of the Massachusets Bay, And You are further to give Directions to all Masters of Ships or other Persons to whom you may intrust your Letters that they put such Letters into a Bag with a sufficient Weight to sink the same immediately in case of imminent Danger from the Enemy, And You are also to let the Merchants and Planters know how greatly it is for their Interest, that their Letters should not fall into the Hands of the Enemy, and therefore that they should give the like Orders to Masters of Ships in relation to their Letters; And You are further to advise all Masters of Ships that they do sink all Letters in case of Danger in the manner before mentioned.

57. And Whereas the Merchants and Planters in America have in Time of War corresponded, traded with Our Enemies and carryed Intelligence to them to the great Prejudice and Hazard of the British Plantations, You are therefore by all possible Methods to endeavour to hinder all such Trade and Correspondence in time of War.

58. You are from time to time to give unto Our Commissioners for Trade and Plantations as aforesaid in order to be laid before Us An Account of the Wants and Defects of Our said Province, what are the Chief Products thereof, what new Improvements are made therein by the Industry of the Inhabitants or Plant-

ers, and what further Improvements you conceive may be made or Advantages gained by Trade, and which way We may contribute thereunto.

59. If any thing shall happen which may be of Advantage or Security to Our said Province under your Government, which is not herein or by Your Commission provided for, We do hereby allow unto You with the Advice and Consent of the said Council to take Order for the present therein, giving to Our Commissioners for Trade and Plantations speedy Notice thereof in order to be laid before Us, that so you may receive our Ratification, if We shall approve the same; Provided always that you do not, by Colour of any Power or Authority hereby given you, commence or declare War without Our Knowledge and particular Command therein, except it be against Indians upon Emergencies, wherein the Consent of the Council shall be had, and speedy Notice thereof given to Our Commissioners for Trade and Plantations in order to be laid before Us.

60. And Whereas by Our Instructions in the third Year of Our Reign to Jonathan Belcher Esqr. Our late Governor of the Province of the Massachusets Bay, We did order and direct our said Governor to acquaint the Council and House of Representatives of Our said Province that as they hoped to recommend themselves to Our Royal Grace and Favour, We did expect that they should manifest the same by establishing a fixed and honorable Salary for the Support of the Dignity of Our Governor there for the time being, and that We deemed One Thousand Pounds Sterling per Annum a competent Sum for that Purpose to be constantly paid out of such Monies as should from time to time be raised for the Support of the Government & Defence of the Inhabitants of the said Province; Now it is Our Express Will & Pleasure that you recommend it in the most pressing and effectual Manner to the Assembly to pass An Act for settling a fixed Salary of One Thousand Pounds Sterling per Annum clear of all Deductions on yourself and your Successors in that Government, or at least on yourself, during the whole time of your Government. But in case the Assembly should not readily comply with this reasonable Recommendation, you may in the mean time, for the Support of Your Dignity as Governor of the said Province, and You are hereby impowered to give your Assent to such Bill as shall be annually passed for paying to you a Salary of One Thousand Pounds Sterling, or the Value thereof in Money of that Province, untill Our Royal Pleasure shall be signified to the contrary; Provided such Act be the first that shall be passed by the Assembly of the said Province before they proceed upon the Other Business of that Session, wherein such Act shall be proposed.

61. Whereas for some Years past the Governors of some of Our Plantations have seized and appropriated to their own Use the Produce of Whales of several

kinds taken upon those Coasts, upon pretence that Whales are Royal Fishes, which tends greatly to discourage this Branch of Fishery in Our Plantations, and prevents Persons from settling there; It is therefore Our Will and Pleasure that you do not pretend to any such Claim, nor give any Manner of Discouragement to the Fishery of Our Subjects upon the Coast of the Province under your Government, but on the contrary that you will give all possible Encouragement thereto.

62. And Whereas great Prejudice may happen to Our Service, and the Security of Our said Province by your Absence from those Parts, Our Will and Pleasure is, that you shall not upon any pretence whatsoever come to Europe from your Government without having first obtained Leave from Us for so doing, under Our Sign Manual and Signet, or by Our Order in Our Privy Council.

63. Whereas We have been pleased by Our Commission to direct that in case of your Death or Absence from our said Province, and in case there be at that Time no Person upon the Place commissionated or appointed by Us to be Our Lieutenant Governor or Commander in Chief, the then present Council of Our aforesaid Province of the Massachusets Bay shall take upon them the Administration of the Government, and execute our said Commission and the several Powers and Authorities therein contained in the manner thereby directed; It is nevertheless Our Will and Pleasure, that in such Case the said Council shall forbear to pass any Acts but what are immediately necessary for the Peace and Welfare of Our said Province without Our particular Order for that Purpose.

64. And Whereas We are willing in the best Manner to provide for the Support of the Government of Our said Province by setting apart a sufficient Allowance to such as shall be Our Lieutenant Governor or Commander in Cheif residing for the time being within the same Our Will & Pleasure therefore is, that when it shall happen that You shall be absent from Our said Province, One full Moiety of the Salary & of all Perquisites and Emoluments whatsoever which would otherwise become due unto You during the Time of Your Absence from Our said Province, be paid and satisfied unto such Lieutenant Governor who shall be resident upon the Place for the time being, which We do hereby Order and allot unto him towards his Maintenance and for the better Support of the Dignity of that Our Government, Provided nevertheless, and it is Our Intent and Meaning that whenever You shall think it necessary for Our Service to go into the Colony of Rhode Island to view and regulate the Militia whereof We have appointed You Our Captain General and Commander in Chief, or whenever You shall be required by especial Order from Us or from Our Commander

in Chief of Our Forces in America, to repair to any other of Our Governments on the Continent of America for Our particular Service, that then and in such Case you shall receive your full Salary, Perquisites and Emoluments as if You were then actually residing within Our Province of the Massachusets Bay, Any thing in these Instructions to the contrary in anywise notwithstanding.

65. And You are upon all Occasions to send unto Our Commissioners for Trade and Plantations only, a particular Account of all your Proceedings, and of the Condition of Affairs within Your Government, in order to be laid before Us, Provided nevertheless when any Occurrence shall happen within your Government of such a Nature and Importance as may require our more immediate Direction by one of Our principal Secretaries of State, and also upon all Occasions, and in all Affairs wherein you may receive Our Orders by one of Our Principal Secretaries of State, You shall in such Cases transmit to Our Secretary of State only, An Account of all such Occurrences and of your Proceedings relative to such Orders.

G.R.[20]

ADft, AC   CO 5/897, pp. 208-242.

Endorsed: Instructions to Francis Bernard, Esqr., Governor of Massachusets Bay.
Flying seal on top left of first page. The handwriting of both the main body of text and the pencil annotations and interlineations is that of John Pownall.

The transcript shown here is a clear version of the draft approximating to how it stood when first prepared by John Pownall for the Board of Trade in 1760. The manuscript contains annotations and emendations by John Pownall when he used it as a boiler plate for the instructions prepared for Gov. Thomas Hutchinson in 1771. The emendations are partly of style, with Pownall substituting "secretary of state" for "Lords Commissioners for Trade and Plantation" in accordance with policy changes implemented in 1766 (for which see above, p. 8). But there are some substantive revisions. Pownall's marginal annotations indicate which particular instructions were to be omitted or updated in Hutchinson's set. The emendations and annotations were cross-referenced to Labaree, *Royal Instructions,* in order to confirm the status of all the instructions in both 1760 and 1771; they were originally recorded in a draft transcript along with appropriate editorial commentaries, which copy has been kept on file for reference.

---

20. Initialed by King George III.

Appendix 2

TRADE INSTRUCTIONS AS GOVERNOR OF MASSACHUSETTS, 18 March 1760

George R.

Orders and Instructions to Our Trusty and Well-beloved Francis Bernard Esq$^r_{//}$ Our Captain General and Governor in Chief in and over Our Province and Territory of the Massachusets Bay in New England in America. In pursuance of several Laws relating to the Trade and Navigation of this Our Kingdom of Great Britain and Our Colonies and Plantations in America. Given at Our Court at S^t. James's the 18. day of March 1760 in the thirty third year of Our Reign.

First. You shall inform yourself of the principal Laws relating to the Plantation Trade, Viz^t: *An Act for the encouraging and increasing of Shipping and Navigation;* made in the twelfth year of the Reign of King Charles the second.[1] *An Act for preventing Fraud and regulating Abuses in the Customs,* made in the thirteenth and fourteenth years of the said King's Reign.[2] *an Act for the Encouragement of Trade,* made in the fifteenth year of the said King's Reign.[3] *an Act to prevent planting of Tobacco in England; and for regulating the Plantation Trade,* made in the twenty second and twenty third years of the said King's Reign.[4] *an Act for the Encouragement of the Greenland and Eastland Trades, and better securing the Plantation Trade,* made in the twenty fifth year of the said King's Reign.[5] *an act for preventing Frauds and regulating Abuses in the Plantation Trade,* made in the seventh and eighth years of the Reign of King William the third.[6] *an Act for the Encrease and Encouragement of Seamen,* made in the same years of the said King's Reign.[7] *an Act to enforce the Act for the Increase and Encouragement of seamen,* made in the eighth year of the said King's Reign.[8] *an Act for raising a sum not exceeding two Millions &c$^a_{//}$ and for settling the Trade to the East Indies,* made in the ninth and tenth years of the said King's Reign.[9] *an*

---

1.   12 Car. 2, c. 18.
2.   14 Car. 2, c. 11.
3.   15 Car. 2, c. 7.
4.   22 & 23 Car. 2, c. 26.
5.   25 Car. 2, c.7.
6.   7 & 8 Will. 3, c. 22.
7.   7 & 8 Will. 3, c. 21.
8.   8 & 9 Will. 3, c. 23.
9.   9 Will. 3, c. 44.

Act to prevent the Exportation of Wool out of Ireland and England into foreign parts, and for the Encouragement of the Woollen Manufacture in the Kingdom of England, made in the tenth and eleventh years of the said King's Reign.[10] *an Act to encourage the Trade to Newfoundland* made in the same years of the said King's Reign.[11] *an Act for the more effectual Suppression of Piracy,* made in the eleventh and twelfth years of the said King's Reign.[12] *an Act to punish Governors of Plantations in this Kingdom for Crimes by them committed in the Plantations,* made in the same years of the said King's Reign.[13] *an Act for granting a further Subsidy on Wines and Merchandizes imported,* made in the third and fourth years of the Reign of Queen Anne.[14] *an Act to permit the Exportation of Irish Linen Cloth to the Plantations &c^a//* made in the same years of the said Queens Reign.[15] *an Act for encouraging the Importation of Naval Stores from Her Majesty's Plantations in America,* made in the same years of the said Queen's Reign.[16] *an Act for an Union of the two Kingdoms of England and Scotland,* made in the fifth year of the said Queen's Reign.[17] *an Act for ascertaining the Rates of Foreign Coins in Her Majesty's Plantations in America,* made in the sixth year of the said Queen's Reign.[18] *an Act for the Encouragement of the Trade to America,* made in the same year of the said Queen's Reign.[19] *an Act for continuing several Impositions &c^a// and to limit a time for Prosecution upon certain Bonds called in the Act Plantation Bonds,* made in the eighth year of the said Queen's Reign.[20] *an Act for the Encouragement of the Trade to America* made in the same year of the said Queen's Reign.[21] *an Act for the Relief of Merchants importing Prize Goods from America,* made in the tenth year of the said Queen's Reign.[22] *an Act for the further preventing Robbery, Burglary and other Felonies &c^a// and for declaring the Law upon some Points relating to Pirates,* made in the 4th year of His late Majesty Our Royal Father's Reign.[23] *an Act against clandestine running of uncustomed Goods, and for the more effectual preventing of Frauds relating to the Customs,* made in the fifth year of His said late Majesty's

---

10. 10 Will. 3, c. 16.
11. 10 Will. 3, c. 14.
12. 11 Will. 3, c. 7.
13. 11 Will. 3, c. 12.
14. 3 & 4 Anne, c. 3.
15. 3 & 4 Anne, c. 7.
16. 3 & 4 Anne, c. 11.
17. 6 Anne, c. 11.
18. 6 Anne, c. 57.
19. 6 Anne, c. 64.
20. 8 Anne, c. 14.
21. 9 Anne, c. 29.
22. 10 Anne, c. 30.
23. 4 Geo. 1, c. 11.

Reign.[24] *an Act for the better securing the lawfull Trade of His Majesty's Subjects to and from the East Indies, and for the more effectual preventing all His Majesty's Subjects trading thither under foreign Commissions,* made in the same year of His said late Majesty's Reign.[25] *an Act for the further preventing His Majesty's Subjects from trading to the East Indies under foreign Commissions and for encouraging and further securing the lawfull Trade thereto,* made in the seventh year of His said late Majesty's Reign.[26] *an Act for giving further Encouragement for the Importation of Naval Stores; and for other purposes therein mentioned,* made in the eighth year of His said late Majesty's Reign.[27] *an Act for Encouragement of the silk Manufactures of this Kingdom &c*[a]*., and for Importation of all Furrs of the Product of the British Plantations into this Kingdom only &c*[a]// made in the same year of His said late Majesty's Reign.[28] *an Act to prevent the clandestine Running of Goods &c*[a]// *and to subject Copper Ore of the Production of the British Plantations to such Regulations as other enumerated Commodities of the like production are subject to,* made in the same year of His said late Majesty's Reign.[29] *an Act for the more effectual Suppression of Piracy,* made in the same year of His said late Majesty's Reign.[30] *an Act for encouraging the Greenland Fishery,* made in the tenth year of His said late Majesty's Reign.[31] *an Act for repealing the Duties laid upon Snuff &c*[a]// *and for giving a further Encouragement to the Greenland Fishery,* made in the twelfth year of His said late Majesty's Reign.[32] *an Act to revive the Laws therein mention'd &c*[a]// *for making Copper Ore of the British Plantations and enumerated Commodity; for making perpetual an Act therein mentioned for Suppression of Piracy, &c*[a]// made in the second year of Our Reign.[33] *an Act for the better Preservation of His Majesty's Woods in America, and for the Importation of Naval Stores from thence &c*[a]// made in the same year of Our Reign.[34] *an Act for reducing the Annuity or Fund of the united East India Company, and for ascertaining their Right of Trade to the East Indies,* made in the same year of Our Reign.[35] *an Act for importing from His Majesty's Plantations in America directly into Ireland, Goods not enumerated in any Act of Parliament,*

---

24. 5 Geo. 1, c. 11.
25. 5 Geo. 1, c. 21.
26. 7 Geo. 1, c. 21.
27. 8 Geo. 1, c. 12.
28. 8 Geo. 1, c. 15.
29. 8 Geo. 1, c. 18.
30. 8 Geo. 1, c. 24.
31. 10 Geo. 1, c. 16.
32. 12 Geo. 1, c. 26.
33. 2 Geo. 2, c. 28.
34. 2 Geo. 2, c. 35.
35. 3 Geo. 2, c. 14.

made in the fourth year of Our Reign.[36] *an Act for granting an Allowance upon the Exportation of British made Gunpowder,* made in the same year of Our Reign.[37] *an Act for further encouraging the Manufacture of British made Sail Cloth by taking off the Duties and Drawbacks therein mentioned, and allowing an additional Bounty &c^a //* made in the same year of Our Reign.[38] *an Act for the more easy Recovery of Debts in His Majesty's Plantations and Colonies in America,* made in the fifth year of Our Reign.[39] *an Act to prevent the Exportation of Hats out of any of His Majesty's Colonies or Plantations in America, and to restrain the Number of Apprentices taken by Hatt Makers in the said Colonies or Plantations; and for the better encouraging the making Hats in Great Britain,* made in the same year of Our Reign.[40] *an Act for encouraging the Growth of Coffee in His Majesty's Plantations in America,* made in the same year of Our Reign.[41] *an Act for encouraging the Greenland Fishery,* made in the same year of Our Reign.[42] *an Act for reviving an Act for better securing the lawful Trade of His Majesty's Subjects to and from the East Indies, &c^a //* made in the same year of Our Reign.[43] *an Act for the further Encouragement of the Whale Fishery;* made in the sixth year of Our Reign.[44] *an Act for encouraging and regulating the Manufacture of British Sail Cloth &c^a //* made in the ninth year of Our Reign.[45] *an Act for laying a Duty upon Apples imported and for continuing an Act passed in the fourth year of Our Reign for granting an Allowance upon the Exportation of British made Gunpowder and for taking off the Drawback upon Exportation of Foreign paper and for the better securing the Payment of the Bounty on the Exportation of British made Sail Cloth;* made in the tenth year of Our Reign.[46] *an Act to continue two several Acts therein mention'd One for encouraging the Growth of Coffee in His Majesty's Plantations in America, & the other for the better securing and encouraging the Trade of His Majesty's Colonies in America,* made in the eleventh year of Our Reign.[47] *an Act for taking off the duties upon Woollen and Bay Yarn imported from Ireland to England and for the more effectual preventing the Exportation of Wool from Great Britain and of Wool and Wool manufactured*

---

36.   4 Geo. 2, c. 15.
37.   4 Geo. 2, c. 29.
38.   4 Geo. 2, c. 27.
39.   5 Geo. 2, c. 7.
40.   5 Geo. 2, c. 22.
41.   5 Geo. 2, c. 24.
42.   5 Geo. 2 c. 28.
43.   5 Geo. 2, c. 29.
44.   6 Geo. 2, c. 33.
45.   9 Geo. 2, c. 37.
46.   10 Geo. 2 c. 27.
47.   11 Geo. 2, c. 18.

from Ireland to Foreign parts; made in the twelfth year of Our Reign.[48] *an Act for granting a Liberty to carry Sugars of the Growth, Produce, or Manufacture of any of His Majesty's Sugar Colonies in America from the said Colonies directly to foreign parts in Ships built in Great Britain and navigated according to Law,* made in the same year of Our Reign.[49] *an Act to rectify a mistake in an Act made in the sixth year of the Reign of of His late Majesty King George the first for preventing Frauds &c^a*_{//} *to obviate a Doubt which has arisen upon an Act made in the seventh year of His said late Majesty's Reign for the further preventing His Majesty's Subjects from Trading to the East Indies under foreign Commissions &c^a*_{//} made in the same year of Our Reign.[50] *an Act to continue several Laws therein mention'd &c^a*_{//} *and for better securing the lawfull Trade of His Majesty's Subjects to and from the East Indies &c^a*_{//} made in the same year of Our Reign.[51] *an Act for the better Supply of mariners and seamen to serve in His Majesty's Ships of War and on Board Merchants Ships and other trading Ships and Privateers,* made in the thirteenth year of Our Reign.[52] *an Act for the more effectual securing and encouraging the Trade of His Majesty's British Subjects to America, and for the Encouragement of Seamen to enter into His Majesty's Service,* made in the same year of our Reign.[53] *an Act for continuing the several Laws therein mentioned relating to the Premiums upon the Importation of Masts, Yards, and Bowsprits, Tar, Pitch and Turpentine, to British made Sail Cloth and the Duties payable on foreign made Sail Cloth, to the Greenland and to the Whale Fishery, and for granting a further Bounty &c^a*_{//} *&c^a*_{//} made in the same year of Our Reign.[54] *an Act for naturalizing such foreign Protestants and others therein mentioned as are settled or shall settle in any of His Majesty's Colonies in America;* made in the same year of Our Reign.[55] *an Act for restraining and preventing several unwarrantable Schemes and Undertakings in His Majesty's Colonies and Plantations in America,* made in the fourteenth year of Our Reign;[56] *an Act for the Encouragement and increase of Seamen and for the better and speedier manning His Majesty's Fleets,* made in the same year of Our Reign.[57] *an Act to revive several Acts &c^a*_{//} *&c^a*_{//} *and for extending the Liberty given by the Act of the twelfth year of the Reign of His present Majesty for carrying Sugar of the Growth of the British Sug-*

---

48. 12 Geo. 2, c. 21.
49. 12 Geo. 2, c. 30.
50. 12 Geo. 2, c. 22.
51. 12 Geo. 2, c. 18.
52. 13 Geo. 2, c. 3.
53. 13 Geo. 2, c. 4.
54. 13 Geo. 2, c. 28.
55. 13 Geo. 2 c. 7.
56. 14 Geo. 2, c. 37.
57. 14 Geo. 2, c. 38.

ar Colonies in America &c^a// to Ships belonging to any of His Majesty's subjects residing in Great Britain, and navigated according to Law &c^a// &c^a// made in the fifteenth year of Our Reign.[58] *an Act for further regulating the Plantation Trade &c^a// made in the same year of Our Reign.*[59] *an Act to continue several Laws for the Encouragement of the making of Sail Cloth in Great Britain;* made in the same year of Our Reign.[60] *an Act for continuing several Laws relating to the Exportation of British made Gunpowder to the Importation of Navall Stores from the British Colonies in America &c^a//* made in the sixteenth year of Our Reign.[61] *an Act to continue the several Laws therein mention'd for preventing Theft and Rapine &c^a// and for granting a Liberty to carry Sugars of the Growth, Produce or Manufacture of any of His Majesty's Sugar Colonies in America from the said Colonies directly to foreign parts &c^a//* made in the seventeenth year of Our Reign.[62] *an Act for the better Encouragement of Seamen in His Majesty's Service and Privateers to annoy the Enemy,* made in the same year of Our Reign.[63] *an Act for giving a public Reward to such Person or Persons His Majesty's Subject or Subjects as shall discover a North West Passage through Hudson's Streights to the Western and Southern Ocean of America,* made in the eighteenth year of Our Reign.[64] *an Act to amend an Act made in the eleventh year of the Reign of King William the third, entituled an Act for the more effectual Suppression of Piracy,* made in the same year of Our Reign.[65] *an Act to continue two Acts of Parliament, one for encouraging the Growth of Coffee in His Majesty's Plantations in America, and the other for the better securing and encouraging the Trade of His Majesty's Sugar Colonies in America,* made in the nineteenth year of Our Reign.[66] *an Act for the more effectual securing the Duties now payable on foreign made sail Cloth imported into this Kingdom and for charging all foreign made Sails with a Duty, and for explaining a Doubt concerning Ships being obliged at their first setting out to sea to be furnished with one compleat set of Sails made of British Sail Cloth,* made in the same year of Our Reign.[67] *an Act for the better Encouragement of the Trade of His Majesty's Sugar Colonies in America,* made in the same year of Our Reign.[68] *an Act for the better securing the Payment of*

---

58. 15 Geo. 2, c. 33.
59. 15 Geo. 2, c. 31.
60. 15 Geo. 2, c. 35.
61. 16 Geo. 2, c. 26.
62. 17 Geo. 2, c. 40.
63. 17 Geo. 2, c. 34.
64. 18 Geo. 2, c. 27.
65. 18 Geo. 2, c. 30.
66. 19 Geo. 2, c. 23.
67. 19 Geo. 2, c. 27.
68. 19 Geo. 2, c. 30.

Shares of Prizes taken from the Enemy to the Royal Hospital at Greenwich and for preventing the Embezzlement of Goods and Stores belonging to the said Hospital, made in the twentieth year of Our Reign.[69] *an Act to extend the Provision of an Act made in the thirteenth year of His present Majesty's Reign intituled, an Act for naturalizing such foreign Protestants and others therein mentioned as are settled or shall settle in any of His Majesty's Colonies in America, to other Foreign Protestants who conscientiously scruple the taking of an Oath,* made in the same year of Our Reign.[70] *an Act to continue several Laws for prohibiting the Importation of Books reprinted abroad &c^a_{//} and for better securing the lawfull Trade of His Majesty's Subjects to and from the East Indies &c^a_{//}* made in the same year of Our Reign.[71] *an Act to continue several Laws relating to the manufactures of Sail Cloth and Silk, and to give further time for the payment of Duties omitted to be paid for the Indentures or Contracts of Clerks and Apprentices, &c. &c^a_{//}* made in the same year of Our Reign.[72] *an Act to continue several Laws &c^a_{//} relating to Rice, to Frauds in the Customs &c^a_{//} and to Copper Ore of the British Plantations &c^a_{//}* made in the same year of Our Reign.[73] *an Act for further regulating the Proceedings upon Courts Martial in the Sea Service; and for entending the Discipline of the Navy to the Crews of His Majesty's Ships wrecked, lost or taken; and for continuing to them their Wages upon certain Conditions,* made in the twenty first year of Our Reign.[74] *an Act for permitting Tea to be exported to Ireland and His Majesty's Plantations in America, without paying the inland Duties charged thereupon by an Act of the eighteenth year of His present Majesty's Reign &c^a_{//}* made in the same year of Our Reign.[75] *an Act for encouraging the making of Indico in the British Plantations in America,* made in the same year of Our Reign.[76] *an Act to continue and amend several Laws for Relief of Debtors &c^a_{//} and to rectify a Mistake in an act passed in the last Session of Parliament for continuing several Laws therein mention'd &c^a_{//}* made in the same year of Our Reign.[77] *an Act for encouraging the People known by the name of Unitas Fraternum or united Brethren to settle in His Majesty's Colonies in America,* made in the twenty second year of Our Reign.[78] *an Act for amending, explaining and reducing into one Act of Parliament the Laws relating to the Government of His Majesty's*

---

69. 20 Geo. 2, c. 24.
70. 20 Geo. 2, c. 44.
71. 20 Geo. 2, c. 47.
72. 20 Geo. 2, c. 45.
73. 20 Geo. 2, c. 47.
74. 21 Geo. 2, c. 11.
75. 21 Geo. 2, c. 14.
76. 21 Geo. 2, c. 30.
77. 21 Geo. 2, c. 33.
78. 22 Geo. 2, c. 30.

Ships, Vessels and Forces by sea, made in the same year of Our Reign.[79] *an Act for the further Encouragement & Enlargement of the Whale Fishery, and for continuing such Laws as are therein mentioned relating thereto, and for the naturalizing of such foreign Protestants as shall serve for the time therein mentioned on Board such Ships as shall be fitted out for the said Fishery,* made in the same year of Our Reign.[80] *an Act for encouraging the Growth and Culture of Raw Silk in His Majesty's Colonies or Plantations in America,* made in the twenty third year of Our Reign.[81] *an Act to encourage the Importation of Pig and Bar Iron from His Majesty's Colonies in America, and to prevent the Erection of any Mill or other Engine for slitting of rolling Iron, or any plateing Forge to work with a Fill Hammer, or any Furnace for making Steel in any of the said Colonies,* made in the same year of Our Reign.[82] *an Act for regulating the Commencement of the year, and for correcting the Calendar now in use,* made in the twenty fourth year of Our Reign.[83] *an Act for the more effectual securing the Duties upon Tobacco,* made in the same year of Our Reign.[84] *an Act for encouraging the making of Pott Ashes and Pearl Ashes in the British Plantations in America,* made in the same year of Our Reign.[85] *an Act for continuing several Laws therein mentioned relating to the Præmiums upon the Importation of Masts, Yards and Bowsprits, Tar, Pitch and Turpentine, to British made Sail Cloth and the Duties payable on foreign sail Cloth, and to the Allowance upon the Exportation of British made Gunpowder,* made in the same year of Our Reign.[86] *an Act to regulate and restrain Paper Bills of Credit in His Majesty's Colonies or Plantations of Rhode Island and Providence Plantation, Connecticut, the Massachusetts Bay and New Hampshire in America, and to prevent the same being legal Tender in payment of Money,* made in the same year of Our Reign.[87] *an Act to continue several Laws therein mentioned, and for granting a Liberty to carry Sugars of the Growth, Produce or Manufacture of any of His Majesty's Sugar Colonies in America from the said Colonies directly into foreign Parts in Ships built in Great Britain, and navigated according to Law &cᵃ. &cᵃ⁄⁄* made in the same year of Our Reign.[88] *an Act for avoiding and putting an end to certain Doubts and Questions relating to the At-*

---

79. 22 Geo. 2, c. 33.
80. 22 Geo. 2, c. 45.
81. 23 Geo. 2, c. 20.
82. 23 Geo. 2, c. 29.
83. 24 Geo. 2, c. 23.
84. 24 Geo. 2, c. 41.
85. 24 Geo. 2, c. 51.
86. 24 Geo. 2, c. 52.
87. 24 Geo. 2, c. 53.
88. 24 Geo. 2, c. 57.

testation of Wills and Codicils concerning real Estate in that part of Great Britain called England, and in His Majesty's Colonies and Plantations in America, made in the twenty fifth year of Our Reign.[89] *an Act to restrain the making [of] Insurances on foreign Ships bound to or from the East Indies,* made in the same year of Our Reign.[90] *an Act to amend an Act made in the last Session of Parliament, intituled; an Act for regulating the Commencement of the year, and for correcting the Calendar now in use,* made in the same year of Our Reign.[91] *an Act for continuing the Act for encouraging the Growth of Coffee in His Majesty's Plantations in America; and also for continuing under certain Regulations so much of an Act as relates to the Præmiums upon the Importation of Masts, Yards and Bowsprits, Tar, Pitch and Turpentine,* made in the same year of Our Reign.[92] *an Act for continuing several Laws relating to the Punishment of Persons going armed or disguised in Defiance of the Laws of Custom or Excise &c^a. &c^a// and for encouraging the Trade of the Sugar Colonies in America, &c^a &c^a//* made in the twenty sixth year of Our Reign.[93] All which Laws you will herewith receive, and you shall take a solemn Oath to do your utmost that all the Clauses, Matters and things contained in the before recited Acts and in all other Acts of Parliament now in force or that hereafter shall be made relating to Our Colonies or Plantations, be punctually and bona Fide observed according to the true Intent and meaning thereof.

2.   And as by the aforesaid Act, made in the seventh and eighth years of King William the third[94] the Officers appointed for Performance of certain things mentioned in the aforesaid Act for the Encouragement of Trade,[95] commonly known by the name of the Naval Officers, are to give Security to the Commissioners of Our Customs in Great Britain for the time being, or such as shall be appointed by them for Our Use for the true and faithful Performance of their Duty, you shall take Care that the said Naval Officers do give such Security to the said Commissioners of Our Customs, or the Surveyor General of the Customs for the Northern District, who is empower'd to take the same in the manner thereby enjoin'd; and that he or they produce to you a Certificate from them of his or their having given Security pursuant to a Clause in the said Act, and you are not to admit any Person to act as naval Officer, who does not within

---

89.   25 Geo. 2, c. 6.
90.   25 Geo. 2, c. 26.
91.   25 Geo. 2, c. 30.
92.   25 Geo. 2, c. 35.
93.   26 Geo. 2, c. 32.
94.   7 & 8 Will. 3, c. 22.
95.   15 Car. 2, c. 7.

two months, or as soon as conveniently may be, after he has entered upon the Execution of his Office, produce a Certificate of his having given such Security as aforesaid.

3. And whereas it is necessary for the more effectual Dispatch of Merchants and others that the naval Officer and the Collectors of the Customs should reside at the same Ports or Towns, you are therefore to take Care that this Regulation be observed, and to consult with the Surveyor General of Our Customs in what place it may be most convenient to have the Custom House fix'd in each part of his District, and to take Care that the Collector and naval Officer reside within a Convenient Distance of the Custom House for the dispatch of Business.

4. Whereas by the said Act of Navigation[96] no Goods or Commodities whatsoever are to be imported into or exported out of any of Our Colonies or Plantations in any other Ships or Vessels whatsoever, but in such as do truly and without Fraud belong only to Our People of Great Britain or Ireland, or are of the Built of and belonging to any of Our Lands, Islands or Territories as the Proprietors and right Owners thereof, and whereof the master and three fourths of the Marines at least are British, under the penalty of the Forfeiture and Loss of all the Goods and Commodities, which shall be imported into or exported out of any of the said Places in any other Ship or Vessel, as also of the Ship or Vessel, with her Guns, Furniture, &c[a] And whereas by a Clause in the aforesaid Act of Frauds,[97] no foreign built Ship, that is to say, not built in any of Our Dominions of Asia, Africa or America, shall enjoy the Privilege of a Ship belonging to Great Britain or Ireland, altho' owned and manned by British Subjects, (except such Ships only as shall be taken at Sea by Letters of Mart or Reprizal and Condemnation thereof made in Our Court of Admiralty as lawful Prize;) but all such Ships shall be deemed as Aliens Ships, and be liable to all Duties that Aliens Ships are liable to by virtue of the aforesaid Act for the encouraging and encreasing of Shipping and Navigation;[98] and whereas by a Clause in the aforesaid Act for preventing Frauds and regulating Abuses in the Plantation Trade,[99] it is enacted that no Goods or Merchandizes whatsoever shall be imported into or exported out of any of Our Colonies or Plantations in Asia, Africa or America, or shall be laden in or carried from any one Port or Place in the said Colonies or Plantations to any other Port or Place in the same or to Our Kingdom of Great Britain, in any Ship or Bottom, but what is, or shall be

---

96. 12 Car. 2, c. 18.
97. 13 & 14 Car. 2, c. 11.
98. 12 Car. 2, c. 18.
99. 7 & 8 Will. 3, c. 22.

of the Built of Great Britain or Ireland, or of the said Colonies or Plantations, and wholly owned by the People thereof or any of them, and navigated with the Master and three fourths of the Mariners of the said Places only, (except such Ships only as shall be taken Prizes and Condemnation thereof made in one of the Courts of Admiralty in Great Britain, Ireland, or the said Plantations, to be navigated by the Master and three fourths of the Mariners British, or of the said Plantations as aforesaid, and whereof the Property doth belong to British Subjects,) on pain of Forfeiture of Ship and Goods; and whereas by another Clause in the said Act for the more effectual Prevention of Frauds, which may be us'd by colouring foreign Ships under British Names, it is further enacted, that no Ship or Vessel whatsoever shall be deemed or pass as a Ship of the Built of Great Britain, Ireland, Guernsey, Jersey, or any of Our Plantations in America, so as to be qualified to trade to, from or in any of the said Plantations, until the Person or Persons claiming Property in such Ship or Vessel shall register the same in manner thereby appointed; you shall take Care and give in Charge that these Matters and Things be duly observed within Our said Province under your Government, according to the True Intent and Meaning of the said Acts, and the Offences and Offenders prosecuted according to the Directions thereof, and where it is required that the Master and three fourths of the Mariners be British, you are to understand, that the True Intent and Meaning thereof is, that they shall be such during the whole Voyage, unless in case of Sickness, Death or being taken Prisoners in the Voyage, to be proved by the Oath of the Master or other Chief Officer of the Ship, and none but Our Subjects of Great Britain, Ireland or the Plantations are to be accounted British.

5. Whereas by the said Act of Navigation,[100] as the same stands amended and altered by the aforesaid Act for regulating the Plantation Trade,[101] it is enacted that for every Ship or Vessel which shall set Sail out of or from Great Britain for any British Plantation in America, Asia or Africa sufficient Bond shall be given with one surety to the Chief Officer of the Customs of such Port or Place, from whence the said Ship shall set sail, to the Value of one thousand pounds, if the Ship be of less Burthen than one hundred Tons, and of the sum of two thousand pounds, if the Ship shall be of greater Burthen, that in case the said Ship or Vessel shall load any of the Commodities therein enumerated, Viz^t. Sugar, Tobacco, Cotton, Wool, Indigo, Ginger, Fustick or other Dying Wood of the Growth, Production or Manufacture of any British Plantation in America, Asia or Africa, at any of the said British Plantations, the said Commodities shall by

---

100. 12 Car. 2, c. 18.
101. 7 & 8 Will. 3, c. 22.

the said Ship be brought to some Port of Great Britain, and be there unloaden and put on Shore, the Danger of the Seas only excepted, and for all Ships coming from any Port or Place to any of the aforesaid Plantations, which by this Act are permitted to trade there, that the Governors of such British Plantations shall, before the said Ship or Vessel be permitted to load on Board any of the said Commodities, take Bond in manner and to the Value aforesaid for each respective Ship or Vessel, that such Ship or Vessel shall carry all the aforesaid Goods that shall be loaden on Board the said Ship or Vessel to some other of the said British Plantations or to Great Britain, and that every Ship or Vessel, which shall load or take on Board any of the aforesaid Goods until such Bond be given to the said Governor or Certificate produced from the Officers of any Custom House of Great Britain, that such Bond hath been there duly given, shall be forfeited, with her Guns, Tackle, Apparel and Furniture, to be employed and recovered as therein is directed; And whereas by the Two aforementioned Acts passed in the third & fourth years of Queen Anne, the one, entituled, *an Act for encouraging the Importation of Naval Stores from Her Majesty's Plantations in America,*[102] and the other, *an Act for granting to Her Majesty a further Subsidy on Wines and Merchandizes imported,*[103] and by two other aforementioned Acts passed in the eighth year of His said late Majesty's Reign, the one entituled, *an Act for Encouragement of the Silk Manufactures of this Kingdom, and for taking off several Duties on Merchandizes exported, and for reducing the Duties upon Beaver Skins, Pepper, Mace, Cloves and Nutmegs imported, and for Importation of all Furs of the Product of the British Plantations into this Kingdom only,*[104] the other entituled, *an Act to prevent the Clandestine running of Goods, &cᵃ⁄⁄ and to subject Copper Ore of the Production of the British Plantations to such Regulations as other enumerated Commodities of the like Production are subject,*[105] continued by an Act passed in the eighth year of Our Reign,[106] and is still in force, all Rice (except under the Regulations prescribed in the beforementioned Acts of the third and eighth years of Our reign,) Molasses, Furs, Hemp, Pitch, Tar, Turpentine, Masts, Yards, Bowsprits, and Copper Ore are under the like Securities and Penalties restrain'd to be imported into this Kingdom as the other abovementioned enumerated Commodities; you are therefore to take particular Care, and give the necessary Directions, that the true Intent and Meaning of all the said Acts be strictly and duly complied with.

---

102. 3 & 4 Anne, c. 11.
103. 3 & 4 Anne, c. 3.
104. 8 Geo. 1, c. 15.
105. 5 Geo. 1, c. 11.
106. 8 Geo. 1, c. 18.

6. You shall carefully examine all Certificates which shall be brought to you of Ships giving Security in this Kingdom to bring their lading of Plantation Goods hither, as also Certificates of having discharged their Ladings of Plantation Goods in this Kingdom pursuant to their Securities. And whereas the better to prevent any of the aforesaid Certificates from being counterfeited, the Commissioners of Our Customs have thought fit to sign the same, it is therefore Our Will and Pleasure, that no such Certificates be allowed of, unless the same be under the Hands and Seals of the Customer, Collector & Comptroller of the Customs in some Port of this Kingdom, or two of them, as also under the Hands of four of Our Commissioners of the Customs at London, or three of Our Commissioners of the Customs at Edinburgh, and where there shall be reasonable Ground of Suspicion, that the Certificate of having given Security in this Kingdom is false & counterfeit, in such Case you or the Person or Persons appointed under you shall require and take sufficient Security for the Discharge of the Plantation Lading in this Kingdom, and where there shall be cause to suspect, that the Certificate of having discharged the Lading of Plantation Goods in this Kingdom is false and counterfeit, you shall not cancel or vacate the Security given in the Plantations, untill you shall be informed from the Commissioners of Our Customs in Great Britain, that the matter of the said Certificate is true; And if any Person or Persons shall counterfeit, raze or falsify any such Certificate for any Vessel or Goods, or shall knowingly or willingly make use thereof, you shall prosecute such Person for the Forfeiture of the sum of five hundred pounds, according to a Clause of the aforesaid Act for preventing Frauds and regulating Abuses in the Plantation Trade; and pursuant to the said Act you shall take Care, that in all such Bonds to be hereafter given, or taken in the Province under your Government, the Sureties therein named be Persons of known Residence and Ability there for the Value mentioned in the said Bonds, & that the Condition of the said Bonds be within eighteen Months after the Date thereof, the Danger of the Seas excepted, to produce a Certificate of having landed and discharged the Goods therein mentioned in one of Our Plantations or in this Kingdom, otherwise to attest the Copy of such Bonds under your hand and Seal, and to cause Prosecutions thereof. And it is Our further Will and Pleasure, that you do give Directions to the Naval Officer or Officers not to admit any person to be Security for another who has Bonds standing out undischarged, unless he be esteemed responsible for more than the Value of such Bonds.

7. And you are also to give Directions to the said Naval Officer or Officers to advise with the Collector of the Port or District in taking Bonds, and not to admit any Person to be Security in any Plantation Bond, untill approved by the said Collector. And whereas Lists of all Certificates granted in South Britain for

the Discharge of Bonds given in the Plantations are every Quarter sent to the Collectors of the Districts where such Bonds are given, the said Naval Officer or Officers is or are to take Care, that no Bond be discharged or cancelled by him or them without first advising with the Collector and examining the said List to see that the Certificate is not forged or counterfeited. And whereas the Surveyors General of Our Customs in America are directed to examine from time to time, whether the Plantation Bonds be duly and regularly discharged, you are to give Directions, that the Surveyor General for the Northern District be permitted to have recourse to the said Bonds as well as the Book or Books in which they are or ought to be entred, and to examine as well whether due Entry thereof be made, as whether they are regularly taken and discharged, and where it shall appear that Bonds are not regularly discharged you are to order that such Bonds be put in Suit.

8. You are to understand that the Payment of the Rates and duties imposed by the aforesaid Act for the Encouragement of the Greenland and Eastland Trades, and for the better securing the Plantation Trade,[107] on the several Plantation Commodities therein enumerated, doth not give Liberty to carry the said Goods to any other Place than to some of Our Plantations or to great Britain only; and that notwithstanding the Payment of the said Duties, Bond must be given to carry the said Goods to some of the said Plantations, or to Great Britain, and to no other Place.

9. You shall every three Months or oftner, or otherwise as there shall be Opportunity of Conveyance, transmit to the Commissioners of Our Treasury or Our High Treasurer for the time being, to Our Commissioners for Trade and Plantations, and to the Commissioners of Our Customs in London, a List of all Ships and Vessels trading in the said Province according to the Form and Specimen hereunto annexed, together with a list of the Bonds taken, pursuant to the Act passed in the twenty second and twenty third years of King Charles the second's Reign, entitled, an Act *to prevent planting Tobacco in England, and for regulating the Plantation Trade;*[108] and you shall cause Demand to be made of every Master at his clearing, of an Invoice of the Content and Quality of his Lading &cᵃ// according to the Form hereunto also annexed, and to inclose a Copy of thereof by some other Ship, or, for want of such Opportunity, by the same Ship under Cover sealed and directed to the Commissioners of Our Treasury or Our High Treasurer for the time being, to Our Commissioners for Trade and Plantations, and to the Commissioners of Our Customs in London,

---

107. 25 Car. 2, c. 7.
108. 22 & 23 Car. 2, c. 26.

and send another Copy of the said Invoice in like manner to the Collector of that Port in this Kingdom for the time being, to which such Ship shall be said to be bound.

10. Whereas by the aforesaid Act for the Encouragement of Trade,[109] no Commodities of the Growth, Production or Manufacture of Europe, except Salt for the Fishery of New England and Newfoundland, Wines of the Growth of the Maderas, or Western Islands or Azores, Servants and Horses from Ireland and all Sorts of Victuals of the Growth & Production of Ireland, and Salt to the Provinces of Pennsylvania and new York in pursuance of two Acts, the one passed in the thirteenth year of His said late Majesty's Reign,[110] & the other in the third year of Our Reign[111] shall be imported into any of Our Colonies or Plantations, but what shall be bona fide & without Fraud laden & shipp'd in Great Britain, & in Ships duly qualified, you shall use your utmost Endeavour for the due Observance thereof; & if contrary hereunto, any Ship or Vessel shall import into Our said Province under your Government any Commodities of the Growth, Production or Manufacture of Europe but what are before excepted, of which due Proof shall not be made that the same were Ship'd or laden in some Port of Great Britain by producing Cocquet or Certificates under the Hands & Seals of the Officers of Our Customs in such Port or Place where the same were laden, such Ship or Vessel, & Goods shall be forfeited; & you are to give in Charge that the same be seized and prosecuted accordingly.

11. And in order to prevent the Acceptance of forged Cocquets or Certificates, which hath been practised to Our great Prejudice, you are to give effectual Orders, that for all such European Goods as by the said Act are to be ship'd and Laden in Great Britain, Cocquets for [blank] the same from hence be produced to the Collectors or other Officers of Our Customs in Our foresaid Province under your Government for the time being before the unlading thereof, and you shall give order that no European Goods be landed but by Warrant from the said Collector in the Presence of an Officer appointed by him. And for the better Prevention of Frauds of this kind, you shall take Care that, according to the said Act of Trade, no Ship or Vessel shall be permitted to Lade or Unlade any Goods or Commodities whatsoever, until the Master or Commander thereof shall first have made known to you or such Officer or other Person as shall be thereunto Authorized and appointed, the Arrival of such Ship or Vessel, with her Name and the Name and Sir Name [surname] of

---

109. 15 Car. 2, c. 7.
110. 13 Geo. 1, c. 4.
111. 3 Geo. 2, c. 14.

the Master, and hath shewn that She is a Ship duly Navigated and otherwise qualified according to Law, and hath delivered to you or such other Person as aforesaid a true and perfect Inventory of her Lading, together with the Place or Places in which the said Goods were Laden and taken into the said Ship or Vessel, under Forfeiture of such Ship and Goods.

12. You shall not make or allow of any Law, By Laws, Usages or Customs in Our said Province under your Government, which are repugnant to the Laws herein before mentioned, or any of them; or to any other Law already made or hereafter to be made in this Kingdom, so far as such Laws relate to and mention the said Plantations; but you shall declare all such Laws By Laws, Usages or Customs in Our said Province under your Government, which are any wise repugnant to the said Laws or any of them, to be illegal, null and void to all Intents and purposed whatsoever.

13. You shall be aiding and assisting to the Collectors and other Officers of Our Admiralty and Customs appointed or that shall hereafter be appointed by the Commissioners of Our Customs in this Kingdom by and under the Authority and Direction of the Commissioners of Our Treasury or Our High Treasurer of Great Britain for the time being, or by Our High Admiral or Commissioners for executing the Office of High Admiral of Great Britain for the time being, in putting in execution the several Acts of Parliament before mentioned; and you shall cause due Prosecution of all such Persons as shall anyways hinder or resist any of the said Officers of Our Admiralty or Customs in the Performance of their Duty, It is likewise Our Will and Pleasure, and you are hereby required by the first Opportunity to move the Assembly of Our said Province, that they Provide for the expence of Making Copies for the Surveyor General of Our Customs in Our said Province for the time being of all Acts and Papers which bear any Relation to the Duty of his Office; and in the meantime you are to give Orders, that the said Surveyor General for the time being as aforesaid be allowed a free Inspection in the Publick Offices within your Government of all such Acts and Papers without paying any Fee or Reward for the same.

14. Whereas the Commissioners appointed for Collecting the Six Pence Per Month from Seamens Wages for Our Royal Hospital at Greenwich pursuant to an Act of Parliament passed in the second Year of Our Reign, entitled, *An Act for the more effectual Collecting in Great Britain, Ireland and other Parts of his Majesty's Dominions the Duties granted for the Support of the Royal Hospital at Greenwich*,[112] have given Instructions to their Receivers in foreign Parts for their Government therein; It is therefore Our Will and Pleasure, that you be aiding

---

112. 2 Geo. 2, c. 7.

and Assisting to the said Receivers in your Government in the due Execution of their Trusts.

15. And whereas by an Act passed in the sixth Year of Our Reign, entitled, *an Act for the better securing and encouraging the Trade of His Majesty's Sugar Colonies in America*,[113] a Duty is laid on all Rum, Melasses, Syrups, Sugar & Paneles[114] of the Produce and Manufacture of any of the Plantations not in Our Possession or under Our Dominion, which shall be imported into any of Our Colonies or Plantations; Notwithstanding which We are informed, that great quantities of foreign Rum, Melasses, Syrups, Sugar and Paneles are clandestinely landed in Our Plantations without Payment of the said Duty, Our Will and Pleasure is, that you be aiding and Assisting to the Collectors and other Officers of Our Customs in your Government in Collecting the said Duties, and seizing all such Goods as shall be so clandestinely landed or put on Shore without Payment of the Duty; and you shall cause due Prosecution of all such Rum, Melasses, Syrups, Sugar and Paneles, as shall be seized for Non-Payment of the Duty, as well as the Persons Aiding or Assisting in such unlawfull Importations, or that shall hinder, resist or molest the Officers in the Due Execution of the said Law.

16. You shall take care that upon any Actions, Suits and informations that shall be brought, commenced or Entred in Our said Province under your Government upon any Law or Statute concerning Our Duties, or Ships or Goods to be forfeited by Reason of any unlawful Importations or Exportations, there be not any Jury but of such as are Natives of Great Britain or Ireland or are born in any of Our said Plantations.

17. You shall take Care that in all Places of Trust in the Courts of law, or in what relates to the Treasury of Our said Province under Government, be in the hands of Our native Born Subjects of Great Britain, or Ireland or the Plantations.

18. And that there may be no Interruption or Delay in matters of Prosecution, and Execution of Justice in Our Courts of Judicature within Our said Province under your Government by the Death or Removal of any of Our Officers employed therein, until We can be advised thereof and appoint others to succeed in their Places, You shall make Choice of Persons of known Loyalty, Experience, ^Diligence and^ Fidelity, to be employed for the Purposes aforesaid, until you shall have Our Approbation of them or the Nomination of others from hence.

---

113. 6 Geo. 2, c. 13.
114. Brown unpurified sugar from the Antilles.

19. You shall from time to time Correspond with the Commissioners of Our Customs in London for the time being, and advise them of all Failures, Neglects, Frauds, and Misdemeanours of any of the Officers of Our Customs in Our said Province under your Government, and shall also advise them, as Occasion shall offer, of all Occurrences necessary for their Information, relating either to the aforesaid Laws of Trade and Navigation, or to Our Revenue of Customs, and other Duties under their Management both in Great Britain and the Plantations.

20. If you shall discover that any Persons or their Assigns claiming any Right or Property in any Island or Tract of Land in America by Charter or by Letters Patents, who shall at any time hereafter Alien, Sell or dispose of such Island, Tract of Land, or Propriety, other than to Our Natural born Subjects of Great Britain, without the Licence or Consent of Us, Our Heirs or Successors, signified by Our or their Order in Council first had and obtained, you shall give notice thereof to Us, and to Our Commissioners of Our Treasury, or to Our High Treasurer of Great Britain for the time being.

21. Whereas by the aforesaid Act for preventing Frauds and regulating Abuses in the Plantation-Trade,[115] it is provided for the more effectual Prevention of Frauds, which may be used to elude the Intention of the said Act by Colouring foreign Ships under British Names, that no Ship or Vessel shall be deemed or pass as a Ship of the Built of Great Britain or Ireland, Guernsey, Jersey or any of Our Plantations in America, so as they be qualified to trade to, from or in any of Our said Plantations, until the Person or Persons claiming Property in such Ship or Vessel shall Register the same in manner thereby directed, you shall take care that no foreign built ship be permitted to pass as a Ship belonging to Our Kingdom of Great Britain or Ireland, until Proof be made upon Oath of one or more of the Owners of the said Ship before the Collector or Comptroller of Our Customs in such Port to which she belongs, or upon like Proof before your self with the Principal Officer of Our Revenue residing in Our aforesaid Province under your Government, if such Ship shall belong to the said Province; which Oath you and the Officers of Our Customs respectively are Authorized to administer in manner thereby directed, and being Attested by you and them so administring the same, and registered in due form according to the Specimen hereunto annexed, you shall not fail immediately to transmit a Duplicate thereof to the Commissioners of Our Customs in London, in order to be entred in a general Register to be there kept for that purpose, with Penalty upon every Ship or Vessel trading to, from or in any of Our said Plantations

---

115. 7 & 8 Will. 3, c. 22.

in America, as aforesaid, and not having made Proof of her Built and Property, as by the aforementioned Act is directed, that she shall be liable to such Prosecution and forfeiture as any foreign Ship, (except Prizes condemned in Our High Court of Admiralty) would for Trading with Our Plantations by the said Law be liable unto; with this Proviso, that all such Ships as have been or shall be taken at Sea by Letters of Mart or Reprizal, and Condemnation or thereof made in Our High Court of Admiralty as lawfull Prize, shall be specially registered, mentioning the Capture and Condemnation instead of the time and place of Building, with Proof also upon Oath that the entire Property is British, before any such Prize be allowed the Privilege of a British built Ship according to the meaning of the said Act: and that no Ships Name registred be afterwards changed without registring such Ship de Novo, in which by the said Act is required to be done upon any transfer of Property to another Part, and delivering up the former Certificate to be Cancelled, under the same Penalties of and in like method; and in case of any alteration of Property in the same Port by the Sale of one or more Shares in any Ship after registring thereof, such Sale shall always be acknowledged by endorsement on the Certificate of [*blank*] Register before two Witnesses, in order to prove that the entire Property in such Ship remains to some of Our Subjects of Great Britain, if any Dispute shall arise concerning the same.

22. Whereas by the Act passed the Twenty first Year of Our Reign *for encouraging the making of Indigo in the British Plantations in America*,[116] a Premium of Six pence per Pound is allowed on the importation of Indigo of the growth of the British Plantations, and there are likewise contained in the said Act several Provisions to prevent Frauds by importing foreign Plantation-made Indigo, or any false Mixtures in what is made in the British Plantations with a view to recover the said Premiums; It is therefore Our Will and Pleasure, that, if there now are or here shall be any Plantation of Indigo within Our said Province under your Government; you do not take particular Care, that the said Provisions be duly and punctually complied with, and do likewise from time to time transmit to Our Commissioners for Trade and Plantations, in order to be laid before Us, an Account of all such Plantations of Indigo, with the Names of the Planters and the quantity of [*blank*] Indigo they make, as also the quantity of such Indigo Exported from the said Province, distinguishing the time when exported and the Port where shipped, the Name of the Vessels, and the Port to which bound, and if there be any foreign Indigo imported into the said Province, it is Our further Will and Pleasure, that you do in like manner transmit

---

116. 21 Geo. 2, c. 33.

an Account of such ^foreign^ Indigo Imported, distinguishing the time when and the place from whence imported, together with an Account of such foreign Indigo exported, and the Port where Shipped, the Names of the Vessels, and the Ports to which bound.

23. Whereas by the Act passed in the tenth Year of the Reign of King William the third *to prevent the Exportation of Wool out of the Kingdoms of Ireland and England into foreign Parts, And for the Encouragement of the Woollen Manufactures in the Kingdom of England,*[117] It is among other things therein enacted, that no Wool, Woolfels, shortlings, Mortlings, Wool flocks, Worsted, Bay or Woolen Yarn, Cloth, Serge, Bays, Kerseys, Says, Frizes, Druggets, Cloth-Serges, Shalloons, or any other Drapery Stuffs or Woolen Manufactures whatsoever, made or Mixed with Wool or Wool Flocks, being of the Product or Manufacture of any of the British Plantations in America, shall be laden or laid on board in any Ship or Vessel in any Place or Port within any of the said British Plantations upon any Pretence whatsoever: As also that no such Wool or other the said Commodities, being of the Product or Manufacture of any of the said British Plantations, shall be loaden upon any Horse, Cart or other Carriage, to the Intent and Purpose to be exported, transported, carried or conveyed out of the said British Plantations to any other of Our [*blank*] Plantations or to any other Place whatsoever, upon the same and like Pains, Penalties and Forfeitures to and upon all the Offender and Offenders therein within all and every of Our said British Plantations respectively, as are provided and prescribed by the said Act for the like Offences committed within Our Kingdom of Ireland, You are to take effectual Care, that the true Intent and Meaning thereof, so far forth as it relates to you, be duly put in Execution.

24. In the Act made in the Twenty fourth Year of Our Reign *for the more effectual securing the Duties upon Tobacco,*[118] there is a Clause to prevent Frauds in the Importation of Bulk Tobacco, enacting that no Tobacco shall be imported into this Kingdom otherwise that in Cash, Chest or Case containing Four hundred and fifty Pounds Weight of Tobacco each, under Penalty of Forfeiture thereof; You shall take Care that this Part of the said Act be made publick, that none may pretend Ignorance, And that the true Intent and meaning thereof be duly put in Execution within your Government.

25. And whereas His said late Majesty was informed, that a Clandestine Trade had been carried on as well by British as foreign Ships from Madagascar and

---

117. 10 Will. 3, c. 16.
118. 24 Geo. 2, c. 41.

other Parts beyond the Cape of Bona Esperanza[119] within the limits of [*blank*] Trade granted to the United East India Company, directly to Our Plantations in America to the great Detriment of these Realms and in breach of the Several Laws in force relating to Trade and Navigation; Our Will and Pleasure is, that you the said Francis Bernard or in your Absence the Commander in Chief of Our said Province of Massachusets Bay for the time being do duly and Strictly observe and Cause to be Observed the several good Laws and Statutes now in force for the regulating of Trade and Navigation, particularly the several Acts of Parliament already mentioned in your General and in these Instructions; and in order to the better Execution of the Laws and Statues abovementioned, upon the first Notice of the Arrival of any Ship or Ships within the Limits of any Port of or belonging to Your Government, which have or are suspected to have on board any Negroes, Goods or Commodities of the Growth, Produce or Manufacture of the East Indies, Madagascar, or any other Parts or Places beyond the Cape of Bona Ezperanza within the Limits of Trade granted to the United East India Company, pursuant to the aforementioned Act of the Ninth and tenth of King William,[120] you shall immediately cause the Officers of Our Customs in your Government, and any other Officers or Persons in Aid of them to go on board such Ship or Ships, and to visit the same, and to examine the Masters or other Commanders the Officers and Sailors on board such Ship or Ships, and their Charter Parties, Invoices, Cocquets and other Credentials, Testimonials, or Documents; and if they find that such Ship or Ships came from the East Indies, Madagascar, or any other Parts or Places beyond the Cape of Bona Ezperanza, within the Limits of Trade granted to the said United East India Company, and that there are on board any such Goods, Commodities or Negroes as is above mentioned, that they do give Notice to the Master or other Person having then the Command of such Ship or Ships forthwith to depart out of the Limits of your Government, without giving them any Relief, Support, Aid, or Assistance, altho' it should be pretended that such Ship or Ships were, or the same really should be in Distress, Want, Disability, Danger of Sinking, or for or upon any other Reason or Pretence whatsoever; And that you Our Governor or Commander in Chief do by no means suffer any Goods, Merchandize or Negroes from on board such Ship or Ships to be landed or brought on Shore upon any Account or Excuse whatsoever. And it is Our further Will and Pleasure, that if any such Ship or Ships being foreign having on board any such Goods, Merchandize or Negroes, do not, upon No-

---

119. The Cape of Good Hope.
120. 9 Will. 3, c. 44.

tice given to the Master or other Persons having the Command thereof, as soon as conveniently may be, depart out of the Limits of your Government and from the Coasts thereof, without Landing, Seeing or Bartering any of the said Goods or Negroes, You Our Governor or the Commander in Chief for the time being shall cause the said Ship or Ships, and Goods and Negroes to be seized and proceeded against according to Law. But if such Ship or Ships having such Goods or Negroes on board, and entring into any Port or Place, or coming upon any of the Coasts or Shores of the said Province under your Government, do belong to Our Subjects, & do break Bulk, or Sell, barter, exchange, or otherwise dispose of the said Goods or Negroes or any Part thereof, contrary to Law, you are to take Care that such Ship or Ships with the Guns, Tackle, Apparel and Furniture, thereof, and all Goods and Merchandizes laden thereupon and the proceed[s] and Effects of the same be immediately seized, and that the Laws in such Case made and provided be put in Execution with the greatest Care, Diligence and application. But if any Ship belonging to the Subjects of any foreign State or Potentate, having on board any Negroes or East India Commodities, shall be Actually bound to some place or port in the West Indies belonging to any foreign Prince or State from some European Port, and such Ship shall happen to be driven in by Necessity, and be in real distress, the same may be supplied with what is absolutely necessary for her Relief: But you shall not take, have or receive, nor permit or suffer any Person to take, have or receive any Negroes or other the said East India Commodities in payment or satisfaction for such Relief; that if any Officer of Our Customs or other Officer employed by you Our Governor or Commander in Chief in visiting, Searching or Seizing such Ship or Ships, Goods, Merchandizes or Negroes be Corrupt, Negligent or remiss in the discharge of his Duty therein, We do hereby require you to suspend him from the Execution of his said Office, and that you do by the first Opportunity send an Account of such Officer's Behaviour to Our Commissioners for Trade and Plantations, that Care may be taken that such Officer be removed from his Employment, and further punished according to his Demerit. And Our further Will and Pleasure is, that you Our Governor or Commander in Chief do constantly from time to time and by the first Opportunity that shall Offer, send to Our Commissioners for Trade and Plantations, a true, full and exact Account of your Proceedings, and of all other Transactions and Occurrences in or about the Premises or any of them, in order to be laid before Us.

26. And whereas notwithstanding the many good Laws made from time to time for preventing of Frauds in the Plantation Trade, which have been enumerated in these and former Instructions, it is manifest, that very great Abuses have been and continue still to be practised to the prejudice of the same; which Abuses

must needs arise from the insolvency of Persons who are accepted for Security, or from the Remissness or Connivance of such as have been or are Governors in the several Plantations, who ought to take care that those Persons who give Bond should be duly Prosecuted in case of non-performance, You are to take Notice that We take the Good of Our Plantations and the Improvement of the Trade thereof by a Strict and punctual Observance of the several Laws in Force concerning the same, to be of so great Importance to the Benefit of this Kingdom, and to the advancing the Duty of Our Customs here, that if We shall hereafter be informed that at any time there shall be any Failure in the due Observance of those Laws and of these present Instructions by any Wilful Fault or Neglect on your Part, We shall esteem such Neglect to be a Breach of the aforesaid Laws. And it is Our fixed and determined Will and Resolution, that you or the Commander in Chief respectively be for such Offence not only immediately removed from your Employments, and be liable to the Fine of one Thousand Pounds, as likewise suffer such other Fines, Forfeitures, Pains, and Penalties as are inflicted by the several Laws now in force relating thereunto; but shall also receive the most rigorous Marks of Our Highest Displeasure, and be prosecuted with the utmost Severity of the Law for your Offence against Us in a Matter of this Consequence that We now so particularly charge you with.

G. R.

MsS, RC   BP, 13: 149-222.

Docket: Orders and Instructions to Francis Bernard Esqr Governor of Massachusets Bay. Contains minor emendations.

Massachusetts

A List of Ships and Vessels which have entered in the Port of [*blank*] in the Province of [*blank*] between the [*blank*] Day of [*blank*] and the [*blank*] day of [*blank*] following being the Quarter ended at [*blank*] with the particular Quantity and Quality of the Loading of each Vessel.

| Time of Entry | Ships Name | Masters Name | Built | Number | | | Where & when built | Where & when registered | Owners Names | General Cargo | | | From Whence | Where and when Bond given |
				Tons	Guns	Men								
										NB The particular Quantity and Denomination of Goods frequently imported must be mentioned in Columns and the rest in the last Column left for other Goods still being as particular as [to] Quantity & Specie as the Acc.ts will allow.				

Massachusetts

A List of Ships and Vessels which have cleared outwards in the Port of [*blank*] in the Province of [*blank*] between the [*blank*] day of [*blank*] and the [*blank*] day of [*blank*] following being the Quarter ended at [*blank*] with the particular Quantity and Quality of the Loading of each Vessel.

| Time of Clearing | Ships Name | Masters Name | Built | Number | | | Where & when built | Where & when registered | Owners Names | General Cargo | | | Whither Bound | Where & when Bond given |
				Tons	Guns	Men								
										N.B. The particular Quantity and Denomination of Goods frequently exported must be mentioned in the Columns and the rest in the last Column left for other Goods, still being as particular as to Quantity and Specie as the Accounts will allow.				

In the Register of Prize Ships the Capture and Condemnation must be absolutely mentioned in Stead of the time and Place of Building

List of all Ships trading to and from the Plantations, or from one Plantation to another are to be prepared Quarterly by the Collectors of the Customs and the Naval Officers in the respective Plantations in Order to be transmitted by you to the Lord High Treasurer or Lords Commissioners of the Treasury for the time being, or to the Commissioners. for Trade and Plantations, & to the Commissioners of His Majestys Customs at London by the first Opportunity of Shipping every Quarter.

Appendix 3

LIST OF CORRESPONDENCE

The following list itemizes in chronological order extant correspondence pertaining to Gov. Bernard's administration in Massachusetts, 1759-63. It excludes enclosures, unless they are printed here, and all material concerning New Jersey.

From the Earl of Halifax, Downing Street, 13 Nov. 1759. BP, 9: 71-72 (ALS, RC). **No. 1.**
From the Board of Trade, Whitehall, 14 Nov. 1759. CO 5/998, pp. 141-142 (L, LbC). **No. 2.**
From John Pownall, [*London*], 14 Nov. 1759. BP, 9: 76 (ALS, RC). **No. 3.**
From Lord Barrington, Cavendish Square, 14 Nov. 1759. BP, 9: 73-76 (ALS, RC). **No. 4.**
From Jeffery Amherst, New York, 13 Dec. 1759, BP, 9: 81-84 (LS, RC).
To the Earl of Halifax, Perth Amboy, 16 Feb. 1760. BP, 1: 192-194 (L, LbC). **No. 5.**
To Lord Barrington, Perth Amboy, 18 Feb. 1760. BP, 1: 194-196 (L, LbC). **No. 6.**
To Thomas Boone, Perth Amboy, 18 Feb. 1760. BP, 1: 216-218 (L, LbC).
From Jeffery Amherst, New York, 21 Feb.1760. BP, 9: 89-92 (LS, RC).
To Thomas Pownall, Perth Amboy, 4 Mar. BP, 1: 221-223 (L, LbC).
General Instructions as Governor of Massachusetts, Court at St. James's, 18 Mar. 1760. CO 5/897, pp. 208-242 (ADft, AC). **No. 7.**
Trade Instructions as Governor of Massachusetts, Court at St. James's, 18 Mar. 1760. BP, 13: 149-222 (Ms, RC). **No. 7.**
To Andrew Oliver, New London, 14 Apr. 1760. BP, 1: 246-247 (L, LbC).
To Lord Barrington, New York, 19 Apr. 1760, BP, 1: 201-203 (L, LbC).
To Andrew Oliver, Perth Amboy, 11 May 1760. BP, 1: 248-250 (L, LbC).
To Andrew Oliver, Perth Amboy, 2 Jun. 1760. BP, 1: 251 (L, LbC).
From Lord Barrington, Cavendish Square, 3 Jun. 1760. BP, 9: 107-110 (ALS, RC). **No. 8.**
From John Pownall, [*Whitehall*] 13 Jun. 1760, BP, 9: 111-114. (ALS, RC).
To Thomas Hutchinson, Perth Amboy, 15 Jun. 1760. BP, 1: 264 (L, LbC).
From Cadwallader Colden, New York, 4 Aug. 1760. *The Colden Letterbooks, 1760-1775.,* 2 vols., *Collections of the New-York Historical Society* vols. 9-10 (New York, 1876-1877), 1: 1-2 (PC).
To Jeffery Amherst, Boston, 5 Aug. 1760. WO 34/26, f 77 (ALS, RC).
To Lord Barrington, Boston, 7 Aug. 1760. BP, 1: 272-274 (L, LbC). **No. 9.**
From Jeffery Amherst, River St. Lawrence below the Ilse Royale, 22 Aug. 1760. BP, 9: 119-120 (LS, RC).
To Lord Barrington, Boston, 23 Aug. 1760. BP, 1: 275-276 (L, LbC). **No. 10.**
Circular From William Pitt, Whitehall, 23 Aug. 1760. BP, 9: 121-124 (dupLS, RC). **No. 11.**
——Prov. Sec. Letterbooks, 2: 287-288 (L, Copy).
From Jeffery Amherst, River St. Lawrence below the Ilse Royale, 26 Aug. 1760. BP, 9: 125-128 (LS, RC).
To William Pitt, Boston, 29 Aug. 1760. BP, 1: 277 (L, LbC).
To Cadwallader Colden, 6 Sept. 1760. Colden Papers (ALS, RC).
From Jeffery Amherst, Camp at Montréal, 9 Sept. 1760. BP, 9: 137-140 (LS, RC).
To William Pitt, Boston, 9 Sept. 1760. BP, 1: 278 (L, LbC).

To Cadwallader Colden, 12 Sept. 1760. Colden Papers, (LS, RC).

From Jeffery Amherst, Camp at Montréal, 13 Sept. 1760. BP, 9: 141-142 (LS, RC).

To the Board of Trade, Boston, 17 Sept. 1760. CO 5/891, ff 11-12 (ALS, RC). **No. 12.**

From Cadwallader Colden, Fort George [*New York*], 22 Sept. 1760. *Colden Letterbooks*, 1: 20-21 (PC).

To Horatio Sharpe, Boston, 22 Sept. 1760. *Correspondence of Governor Horatio Sharpe, 1753-1771,* 4 vols: vol. 2, 1757-1761 (1890). *Maryland Archives,* vol. 9, ed. William H Brown (Baltimore, 1888-1911), 3: 574 (PC).

To Jeffery Amherst, Boston, 27 Sept. 1760. WO 34/26. f 79 (ALS, RC). **No. 13.**

To Lord Barrington, Boston, 29 Sept. 1760. BP, 1: 282-283 (AL, LbC).

To the Earl of Halifax, Boston, 29 Sept. 1760. BP, 1: 282 (L, LbC). **No. 14.**

From Jeffery Amherst, Lake Champlain, 14 Oct. 1760. BP, 9: 143-144 (LS, RC). **No. 15.**
——WO 34/27, f 207 (L, LbC).

From Lord Barrington, Cavendish Square, 15 Oct. 1760. BP, 9: 145-148 (ALS, RC). **No. 16.**

From John Pownall, [*Whitehall*], 18 Oct. 1760. BP, 9: 149-152 (ALS, RC).

Circular from the Board of Trade, Whitehall, 31 Oct. 1760. BP, 9: 153-156 (dupLS, RC). **No. 17.**

From Thomas Goldthwait, Albany, 7 Nov. 1760. Mass. Archs., 56: 359-362 (ALS, RC).

To William Pitt, Boston, 8 Nov. 1760. CO 5/19, pt.2, f 298 (dupALS, RC). **No. 18.**
——BP, 1: 284 (AL, LbC).

To the Earl of Halifax, Boston, 17 Nov. 1760. BP, 1: 283 (AL, LbC). **No. 19.**

Circular from William Pitt, Whitehall, 17 Dec. 1760. BP, 9: 157-162 (dupLS, RC). **No. 20.**
——CO 5/214, pp. 183-186 (L, LbC).

To Jonathan Belcher, Boston, 10 Jan. 1761, BP, 2: 94-95 (L, LbC).

To Cadwallader Colden, Boston, 10 Jan. 1761. Colden Papers, (ALS, RC).
——BP, 2: 93 (L, LbC).

To John Pownall, Boston, 11 Jan. 1761. BP, 1: 285-286 (L, LbC). **No. 21.**

To William Bollan, Boston, 12 Jan. 1761. BP, 1: 286-288 (L, LbC). **No. 22.**

To John Pownall, Boston, 13 Jan. 1761. BP, 1: 289-291 (L, LbC). **No. 23.**

To Lord Barrington, Boston, 17 Jan. 1761. BP, 1: 292-295 (L, LbC). **No. 24.**

From Jeffery Amherst, New York, 17 Jan. 1761. BP, 9: 163-166 (ALS, RC).
——WO 34/27, p. 209 (L, LbC).

To [John Pownall], Boston, 19 Jan. 1761. BP, 1: 296 (L, LbC). **No. 25.**

To Thomas Boone, Boston, 2 Feb. 1761. BP, 2: 97-98 (L, LbC). **No. 26.**

To Jeffery Amherst, Boston, 7 Feb. 1761. WO 34/26, ff 80-81 (ALS, RC). **No. 27.**

To Francis Fauquier, Boston, 7 Feb. 1761. BP, 2: 98 (L, LbC).

To Jeffery Amherst, Boston, 8 Feb. 1761. WO 34/26, f 84 (ALS, RC).
——BP, 2: 99 (AL, LbC).

Account of the Coast of Labrador, 16 Feb. 1761. *Collections of the Massachusetts Historical Society,* 1st ser., 1 (1792), 233-237 (PC). **No. 28.**

To [John Pownall], Boston, 21 Feb. 1761. BP, 1: 296-298 (L, LbC). **No. 29.**

From Randle Wilbraham, Lincoln's Inn, 21 Feb. 1761. BP, 9: 167-168 (ALS, RC). **No. 30.**

From Jeffery Amherst, New York, 22 Feb. 1761. BP, 9: 169-172 (LS, RC). **No. 31.**
——WO 34/27, pp. 210-211 (L, LbC).

To Francis Fauquier, Boston, [*Mar.*] 1761. BP, 2: 100-101 (AL, LbC).

To John Pownall, Boston, 2 Mar. 1761. BP, 1: 299-301 (AL, LbC). **No. 32.**

From Jeffery Amherst, New York, 2 Mar. 1761. WO 34/27, p. 212 (L, LbC).
To the Earl of Halifax, Boston, 3 Mar. 1761. BP, 1: 301 (AL, LbC). **No. 33.**
To Lord Barrington, Boston, 3 Mar. 1761. BP, 1: 302-303 (AL, LbC). **No. 34.**
Trade Instructions as Governor of Massachusetts, 4 Mar. 1761. CO 5/920, 7-31 (Dft, LbC).
To Jeffery Amherst, Boston, 9 Mar. 1761. WO 34/26, f 85 (ALS, RC).
——BP, 2: 101 (AL, LbC).
From Jeffery Amherst, New York, 15 Mar. 1761. BP, 9: 173-174 (LS, RC).
——WO 34/27, p. 213 (L, LbC).
From Jeffery Amherst, New York, 15 Mar. 1761. BP, 9: 175-178 (LS, RC). **No. 35.**
To Cadwallader Colden, Boston, 21 Mar. 1761. Colden Papers (ALS, RC).
——BP, 2: 102 (L, LbC).
To Jeffery Amherst, Boston, 23 Mar. 1761. WO 34/26, f 86 (ALS, RC).
——BP, 2: 102-103 (L, LbC).
From Jeffery Amherst, New York, 29 Mar. 1761. BP, 9: 179-180 (LS, RC). **No. 36.**
——WO 34/27, p. 214 (L, LbC).
To Jeffery Amherst, Boston, 30 Mar. 1761. WO 34/26, f 87 (ALS, RC).
To John Pownall, Boston, 30 Mar. 1761. BP, 1: 305-306 (L, LbC). **No. 37.**
To Jeffery Amherst, Boston, 4 Apr. 1761. WO 34/26, ff 88-89 (ALS, RC). **No. 38.**
From Jeffery Amherst, New York, 5 Apr. 1761. BP, 9: 181-182 (LS, RC).
——WO 34/27, p. 215 (L, LbC).
To William Pitt, Boston, 6 Apr. 1761. CO 5/20, ff 109-110 (ALS, RC). **No. 39.**
To John Pownall, Boston, 6 Apr. 1761. BP, 1: 306-307 (L, LbC). **No. 40.**
To Timothy Ruggles, Boston, 6 Apr. 1761. BP, 2: 105 (L, LbC).
From Jeffery Amherst, New York, 9 Apr. 1761. BP, 9: 183-185 (LS, RC). **No. 41.**
——WO 34/27, p 216 (L, LbC).
To Jeffery Amherst, Boston, 18 Apr. 1761. WO 34/26, ff 91-92 (ALS, RC). **No. 42.**
——BP, 2: 106-108 (L, LbC).
From the Board of Trade, Whitehall, 21 Apr. 1761. BP, 9: 186-189 (dupLS, RC). **No. 43.**
——CO 5/920, pp. 44-46 (L, LbC).
From Jeffery Amherst, New York, 26 Apr. 1761. BP, 9: 190-193 (LS, RC). **No. 44.**
——WO 34/27, p. 217 (L, LbC).
To the Board of Trade, Boston, 28 Apr. 1761. CO 5/891, ff 27-28 (ALS, RC). **No. 45.**
——BP, 2: 39-40 (L, LbC).
Circular from the Board of Trade, Whitehall, 28 Apr. 1761. BP, 9: 194-197 (LS, RC). **No. 46.**
To John Pownall, Boston, 28 Apr. [1761]. BP, 1: 315-316 (L, LbC).
To Governor in Command of Newfoundland [Thomas Graves], Boston, [May] 1761. BP, 2: 111 (AL, LbC).
To Jeffery Amherst, Boston, 3 May 1761. WO 34/26, f 95 (ALS, RC).
——BP, 2: 109 (AL, LbC).
To Jeffery Amherst, Boston, 4 May 1761. WO 34/26, ff 96-97 (ALS, RC). **No. 47**
——BP, 2: 110-111 (L, LbC).
To Jeffery Amherst, Boston, 5 May 1761. WO 34/26, f 98 (ALS, RC). **No. 48.**
——BP, 2: 112 (L, LbC).
To William Pitt, Boston, 5 May 1761. CO 5/20, ff 123-124 (ALS, RC). **No. 49.**
——BP, 1: 309-311 (L, LbC).

To John Pownall, Boston, 9 May 1761. CO 5/891, ff 31-32 (ALS, RC).

From Jeffery Amherst, New York, 11 May 1761. BP, 9: 198-201 (LS, RC).

——WO 34/27, p. 218 (L, LbC).

To John Pownall, Castle William, 12 May 1761. BP, 1: 316-317 (L, LbC).

From Jeffery Amherst, New York, 17 May 1761. WO 34/27, p. 219 (L, LbC).

To Robert Hale, Boston, 21 May 1761. BP, 2: 113 (L, LbC).

Trade Instructions as Governor of Massachusetts, 27 May 1761. Nether Winchendon House, Bucks., Eng. (Ms, RC).

To Thomas Lechmere, Province House, 2 Jun. 1761. BP, 2: 113 (L, LbC).

From William Warburton, Prior Park [*Bath*], 3 Jun. 1761. BP, 9: 202-204 (ALS, RC). **No. 50.**

To Lord Barrington, Boston, 6 Jun. 1761. BP, 1: 313-314 (Dft, LbC).

To John Pownall, Boston, 6 Jun. 1761. BP, 1: 314-315 (L, LbC).

From Lord Barrington, Cavendish Square, 6 Jun. 1761. BP, 9: 209-212 (ALS, RC).

——BP, 9: 205-208 (dupALS, RC).

To Jeffery Amherst, Castle William, 14 Jun. 1761. WO 34/26, f 99 (ALS, RC). **No. 51.**

——BP, 2: 117-118 (L, LbC).

To John Pownall, Boston, 15 Jun. 1761. BP, 1: 317-320 (L, LbC). **No. 52.**

From Jeffery Amherst, Albany, 25 Jun. 1761. BP, 9: 213-215 (LS, RC).

——WO 34/27, p. 220 (L, LbC).

To Jeffery Amherst, Boston, 27 Jun. 1761. WO 34/26, f 100 (ALS, RC).

——BP, 2: 114 (L, LbC).

To [John Pownall?], Boston, 28 Jun. 1761. BP, 1: 320-323 (L, LbC).

General Instructions as Governor of Massachusetts, 30 Jun. 1761. CO 5/920, 54-123 (Dft, LbC).

From Jeffery Amherst, Albany, 1 Jul. 1761. BP, 9: 217-220 (LS, RC).

——WO 34/27, p. 221 (L, LbC).

To Artemas Ward, Boston, 2 Jul. 1761. Ward-Perry Papers, MHS (LS, RC).

To Israel Williams, 2 Jul. 1761. Israel Williams Papers, MHS (LS, RC).

To Jeffery Amherst, Castle William, 5 Jul. 1761. WO 34/26, f 101 (ALS, RC). **No. 53.**

——BP, 2: 115 (L, LbC).

To John Pownall, Boston, 6 Jul. 1761. BP, 1: 322-323 (L, LbC). **No. 54.**

To William Pitt, Boston, 6 Jul. 1761. CO 5/20, f 137 (ALS, RC).

To Thomas Gage, Boston, 7 Jul. 1761. BP, 2: 116 (L, LbC).

To Jeffery Amherst, Boston, 11 Jul. 1761. WO 34/26, f 102 (LS, RC). **No. 55.**

To Jeffery Amherst, Boston, 11 Jul. 1761. Prov. Sec. Letterbooks, 2: 306 (L, Copy).

To Jeffery Amherst, Boston, 12 Jul. 1761. WO 34/26, f 103 (ALS, RC). **No. 56.**

To [Thomas Pownall], Boston, 12 Jul. 1761. BP, 2: 6-8 (dupL, LbC). **No. 57.**

To unknown, Boston, 12 Jul. 1761. BP, 2: 116-117 (dupL, LbC).

To John Pownall, Boston, 13 Jul. 1761. BP, 1: 323-324 (L, LbC).

From Jeffery Amherst, Albany, 16 Jul. 1761. WO 34/27, p. 222 (L, LbC).

From John Pownall, London, 22 Jul. 1761. BP, 9: 221-224 (ALS, RC). **No. 58.**

To Jonathan Belcher, Boston, 29 Jul. 1761. BP, 2: 118 (L, LbC).

To John Henry Bastide, Boston, 29 Jul. 1761. BP, 2: 119 (L, LbC).

To the Board of Trade, Boston, 3 Aug. 1761. CO 5/891, ff 53-55 (ALS, RC). **No. 59.**

——BP, 2: 41-43 (L, LbC).

To the Board of Trade, Boston, 6 Aug. 1761. CO 5/891, ff 41-45 (ALS, RC). **No. 60.**

——BP, 2: 45-50 (L, LbC).

To Jeffery Amherst, Boston, 9 Aug. 1761. WO 34/26, f 104 (ALS, RC). **No. 61.**
To Lord Barrington, Boston, 10 Aug. 1761. BP, 2: 2-4 (L, LbC). **No. 62.**
To Lord Sandys, Boston, 17 Aug. 1761. BP, 2: 1 (L, LbC). **No. 63.**
To Robert Wood, Boston, 17 Aug. 1761. CO 5/20, ff 169-170 (ALS, RC).
——BP, 2: 1 (L, LbC).
From Jeffery Amherst, Albany, 20 Aug. 1761. WO 34/27, p. 223 (L, LbC).
To Jeffery Amherst, Castle William, 22 Aug. 1761. WO 34/26, f 105 (ALS, RC).
——BP, 2: 119 (L, LbC).
To the Board of Trade, Boston, 27 Aug. 1761. CO 5/891, ff 51-52 (ALS, RC). **No. 64.**
——BP, 2: 51-52 (L, LbC).
To Lord Barrington, Boston, 28 Aug. 1761. BP, 2: 4-5 (L, LbC). **No. 65.**
To William Pitt, Boston, 28 Aug. 1761. BP, 2: 6 (L, LbC). **No. 66.**
To Thomas Pownall, Boston, 28 Aug. 1761. BP, 2: 9-11 (L, LbC). **No. 67.**
From Jeffery Amherst, Staaten Island, 28 Aug. 1761. BP, 9: 225-228 (LS, RC).
——WO 34/27, p. 225 (L, LbC).
To Jeffery Amherst, Castle William, 30 Aug. 1761. BP, 2: 119-120 (L, LbC). **No. 68.**
From Jeffery Amherst, Staaten Island, 30 Aug. 1761. WO 34/27, p. 226 (L, LbC).
To Jeffery Amherst, Boston, 4 Sept. 1761. WO 34/26, f 107 (ALS, RC). **No. 69.**
——BP, 2: 121 (L, LbC).
——BP, 2: 123-124 (L, LbC).
To Nathaniel Thwing, Richard Saltonstall, and Jonathan Hoar, Boston, 4 Sept. 1761. Prov.
  Sec. Letterbooks, 2: 321-323 (L, LbC).
From Jeffery Amherst, Staaten Island, 6 Sept. 1761. WO 34/27, p. 227 (L, LbC).
To Nathaniel Thwing, Boston, 15 Sept. 1761. BP, 2: 124-125 (L, LbC).
To Nathaniel Thwing, Castle William, c.15 Sept. 1761. BP, 2: 120 (ADft, LbC).
To [Nathaniel Thwing], 16 Sept. 1761. BP, 2: 125-126 (L, LbC). **No. 70.**
To Colonels Nathaniel Thwing, Richard Saltonstall, and Jonathan Hoar, Castle William, 16
  Sept. 1761. BP, 2: 126-127 (L, LbC). **No. 71.**
From Jeffery Amherst, Staaten Island, 17 Sept. 1761. WO 34/27, p. 228 (L, LbC).
To Jeffery Amherst, Boston, 20 Sept. 1761. WO 34/26, f 108 (ALS, RC). **No. 72.**
——BP, 2: 123 (L, LbC).
To the Rev. Edward Bass, Boston, 21 Sept. 1761. BP, 2: 123 (L, LbC). **No. 73.**
To Lord Barrington, Boston, 27 Sept. 1761. BP, 2: 11-13 (L, LbC). **No. 74.**
To William Bollan, Boston, 28 Sept. 1761. BP, 2: 13 (L, LbC).
To Jeffery Amherst, Boston, 2 Oct. 1761. WO 34/26, f 109 (LS, RC).
From Jeffery Amherst, Staaten Island, 4 Oct. 1761. WO 34/27, p. 229 (L, LbC).
To William Pitt, Boston, 5 Oct. 1761. BP, 2: 14-16 (L, LbC). **No. 75.**
——BP, 9: 229-232 (ADftS, AC).
To Jeffery Amherst, Boston, 12 Oct. 1761. WO 34/26, ff 111-112 (ALS, RC). **No. 76.**
——BP, 2: 128-129 (L, LbC).
From Jeffery Amherst, Staaten Island, 18 Oct. 1761. Prov. Sec. Letterbooks, 2: 328-329
  (L, Copy).
——WO 34/27, p. 230 (L, LbC).
To Nathaniel Thwing, Boston, 19 Oct. 1761. BP, 2: 129-130 (L, LbC).
To Lord Barrington, Boston, 20 Oct. 1761. BP, 2: 16 (L, LbC). **No. 77.**
From Jeffery Amherst, Staaten Island, 27 Oct. 1761. WO 34/27, p. 231 (L, LbC).

To William Bollan, Boston, 16 Nov. 1761. BP, 2: 17 (AL, LbC). **No. 78.**
From Jeffery Amherst, New York, 16 Nov. 1761. WO 34/27, p. 233 (L, LbC).
From the Board of Trade, Whitehall, 25 Nov. 1761. CO 5/920, pp. 130-133 (L, LbC). **No. 79.**
To Jeffery Amherst, Boston, 28 Nov. 1761. WO 34/26, f 113 (ALS, RC). **No. 80.**
——BP, 2: 130-131 (L, LbC).
From Jeffery Amherst, New York, 6 Dec. 1761. WO 34/27, p. 234 (L, LbC).
To Jeffery Amherst, Boston, 9 Dec. 1761. WO 34/26, f 114 (ALS, RC).
——BP, 2: 131-132 (L, LbC).
To Nathaniel Thwing, Boston, 9 Dec. 1761. BP, 2: 132 (L, LbC).
Circular from the Earl of Egremont, Whitehall, 12 Dec. 1761. BP, 9: 241-244 (dupLS, RC). **No. 81.**
——CO 5/214, pp. 247-251 (L, LbC).
——CO 5/214, pp. 252-254 (Dft, LbC).
——Prov. Sec. Letterbooks, 1: 348-349 (L, RLbC).
From Lord Barrington, Cavendish Square, 12 Dec. 1761. BP, 9: 233-236 (ALS, RC).
To Lord Barrington, Boston, 14 Dec. 1761. BP, 2: 18-20 (L, LbC). **No. 82.**
To the Earl of Egremont, Boston, 14 Dec. 1761. CO 5/755, f 1 (dupALS, RC).
——BP, 2: 20 (L, LbC).
To Josiah Hardy, Boston, 14 Dec. 1761. BP, 2: 133 (AL, LbC).
To Lord Barrington, Boston, 15 Dec. 1761. BP, 2: 21-23 (AL, LbC). **No. 83.**
To Jeffery Amherst, Boston, 28 Dec. 1761. WO 34/26, f 115 (ALS, RC). **No. 84.**
——BP, 2: 133 (L, LbC).
To Lord Barrington, Boston, 12 Jan. 1762. BP, 2: 24-26 (AL, LbC). **No. 85.**
From Lord Barrington, Cavendish Square, 14 Jan. 1762. BP, 9: 245-248 (ALS, RC). **No. 86.**
To Benning Wentworth, Boston, 16 Jan. 1762. BP, 2: 134 (AL, LbC).
From Jeffery Amherst, New York, 22 Jan. 1762, WO 34/27, p. 236 (L. Copy)
From Jeffery Amherst, New York, 1 Feb. 1762. Prov. Sec. Letterbooks, 1: 346-348 (L, Copy).
From the Board of Trade, Whitehall, 4 Feb. 1762. BP, 9: 249-253 (LS, RC). **No. 87.**
——CO 5/920, pp. 134-138 (L, LbC).
To [John Pownall], Boston, 13 Feb. and 1 Mar. 1762. BP, 2: 29-31 (L, LbC). **No. 88.**
To Lord Barrington, Boston, 20 and 27 Feb. 1762. BP, 2: 27-29 (L, LbC). **No. 89.**
From Jeffery Amherst, New York, 21 Feb. 1762. Prov. Sec. Letterbooks, 1: 352-353 (L, Copy).
To William Bollan, Boston, 2 Mar. 1762. BP, 2: 32-33 (L, LbC).
To John Pownall, Boston, 4 Mar. 1762. BP, 2: 33-34 (L, LbC).
To the Earl of Egremont, Boston, 4 Mar. 1762. BP, 2: 34-35 (L, LbC). **No. 90.**
Mount Desert Island Grant, [*Boston*], 27 Feb. 1762. CO 5/891, f 193 (Ms, Copy). **No. 91.**
——PC 1/60/7: (Ms, Copy).
To the Earl of Egremont, Boston, 5 Mar. 1762. BP, 2: 179 (L, LbC).
To Jeffery Amherst, Boston, 6 Mar. 1762. WO 34/26, ff 119-120 (ALS, RC). **No. 92.**
——BP, 2: 134-135 (L, LbC).
To John Pownall, Boston, 10 Mar. 1762. BP, 2: 36 (L, LbC). **No. 93.**
From Jeffery Amherst, New York, 14 Mar. 1762. BP, 9: 259-262 (LS, RC). **No. 94.**
——WO 34/27, f 238 (L, LbC).
To Israel Williams, Boston, 16 Mar. 1762. BP, 2: 136 (L, LbC). **No. 95.**
To Jeffery Amherst, Boston, 20 Mar. 1762. WO 34/26, ff 121-122 (ALS, RC).
——BP, 2: 137-138 (L, LbC).

From Jeffery Amherst, New York, 28 Mar. 1762. BP, 9: 263-266 (LS, RC). **No. 96.**
——WO 34/27, f 239 (L, LbC).
To the Board of Overseers of Harvard College, 31 Mar. 1762. Records of the Board of Over-
seers, II, 1744-1768, Harvard Archives, UAII 5.5.2, pp. 119-120 (L, RbC). **No. 97.**
To Jonathan Belcher, Boston, 3 Apr. 1762. Prov. Sec. Letterbooks, 2: 336 (L, Copy)
——CO 5/891, f 152 (L, Copy).
To Jeffery Amherst, Boston, 8 Apr. 1762. WO 34/26, f 125 (ALS, RC).
——BP, 2: 139 (L, LbC).
To the Board of Trade, Boston, 12 Apr. 1762. CO 5/891, ff 70-72 (ALS, RC). **No. 98.**
——BP, 2: 53-56 (L, LbC).
To the Board of Trade, Boston, 13 Apr. 1762. CO 5/891, ff 75-76 (ALS, RC). **No. 99.**
——BP, 2: 58 (L, LbC).
From Jeffery Amherst, New York, 15 Apr. 1762. BP, 9: 267-268 (LS, RC). **No. 100.**
To Robert Monckton, Boston, 16 Apr. 1762. BP, 2: 141-142 (L, LbC). **No. 101.**
To the Earl of Egremont, Boston, 16 Apr. 1762. CO 5/755, ff 5-7 (dupALS, RC). **No. 102.**
——BP, 2: 180-181 (L, LbC).
To Jeffery Amherst, Boston, 17 Apr. 1762. WO 34/26, ff 123-124 (AL, RC). **No. 103.**
——BP, 2: 181-182 (L, LbC).
From Jeffery Amherst, New York, 18 Apr. 1762. BP, 9: 269-272 (LS, RC).
From Jeffery Amherst, New York, 21 Apr. 1762. BP, 9: 273-276 (LS, RC).
——WO 34/27, f 241 (L, LbC).
To John Pownall, Boston, 25 Apr. 1762. BP, 2: 183-184 (L, LbC). **No. 104.**
To John Pownall, Boston, 25 Apr. 1762. BP, 2: 184-186 (L, LbC). **No. 105.**
To Randle Wilbraham, Boston, 25 Apr. 1762. BP, 2: 186-187 (L, LbC). **No. 106.**
To Jeffery Amherst, Boston, 29 Apr. 1762. WO 34/26, ff 126-127 (ALS, RC). **No. 107.**
——BP, 2: 139-141 (L, LbC).
To Cadwallader Colden, 1 May 1762. Colden Papers, f (LS, RC). **No. 108.**
To the Board of Trade, Boston, 3 May 1762. CO 5/891, ff 73-74 (ALS, RC). **No. 109.**
——BP, 2: 56-57 (L, LbC).
To Jeffery Amherst, Boston, 5 May 1762. WO 34/26, ff 128-129 (ALS, RC). **No. 110.**
——BP, 2: 142-144 (L, LbC).
To Jeffery Amherst, Boston, 6 May 1762. WO 34/26, f 130 (ALS, RC). **No. 111.**
To Jeffery Amherst, Boston, 6 May 1762. Prov. Sec. Letterbooks, 2: 341 (L, Copy).
From Jeffery Amherst, New York, 6 May 1762. BP, 9: 277-280 (LS, RC). **No. 112.**
——WO 34/27, pp. 242-243 (L, LbC).
From Jeffery Amherst, New York, 10 May 1762. BP, 9: 281-284 (LS, RC).
——WO 34/27, f 244 (L, LbC).
From Cadwallader Colden, New York, 14 May 1762. *Colden Letterbooks*, 1: 207-208
(PC).
To Jeffery Amherst, Boston, 17 May 1762. WO 34/26, ff 132-133 (ALS, RC). **No. 113.**
To the Board of Trade, Boston, 17 May 1762. CO 5/891, ff 81-82 (ALS, RC). **No. 114.**
——BP, 2: 58-59 (L, LbC).
To Jeffery Amherst, Boston, 17 May 1762. Prov. Sec. Letterbooks, 2: 341-342 (L, Copy).
To Jeffery Amherst, Boston, 18 May 1762. WO 34/26, ff 135-136 (ALS, RC). **No. 115.**
——BP, 2: 144-145 (L, LbC).
To Sir William Johnson, Boston, 21 May 1762. BP, 2: 146 (L, LbC).
To William Shirley, Boston, 21 May 1762. BP, 2: 147 (L, LbC). **No. 116.**

To Jeffery Amherst, Castle William, 22 May 1762. WO 34/26, ff 138-139 (ALS, RC). **No. 117.**
——BP, 2: 148-149 (L, LbC).
To Jeffery Amherst, Castle William, 23 May 1762. WO 34/26, ff 140-141 (ALS, RC). **No. 118.**
——BP, 2: 150-151 (L, LbC).
From Jeffery Amherst, New York, 23 May 1762. BP, 9: 285-286 (LS, RC).
——WO 34/27, p. 246 (L, LbC).
To Lord Barrington, Castle William, 24 May 1762. BP, 2: 190-192 (AL, LbC).
From Jeffery Amherst, New York, 24 May 1762. BP, 9: 287-290 (LS, RC). **No. 119.**
——WO 34/27, p. 247 (L, LbC).
To Jeffery Amherst, Boston, 25 May 1762. WO 34/26, f 142 (ALS, RC). **No. 120.**
——BP, 2: 152-153 (L, LbC).
To Jeffery Amherst, Castle William, 25 May 1762. WO 34/26, f 144 (ALS, RC).
——BP, 2: 152 (AL, LbC).
To Jeffery Amherst, Boston, 30 May 1762. WO 34/26, ff 145-147 (ALS, RC). **No. 121.**
——BP, 2: 153-156 (L, LbC).
From Jeffery Amherst, New York, 30 May 1762. BP, 9: 291-294 (LS, RC).
——WO 34/27, p. 248 (L, LbC).
To Jeffery Amherst, Boston, 2 Jun. 1762. WO 34/26, f 148 (ALS, RC).
——BP, 2: 156-157 (L, LbC).
To Jeffery Amherst, Boston, 4 Jun. 1762. WO 34/26, f 161 (ALS, RC).
——BP, 2: 158 (L, LbC).
From Jeffery Amherst, New York, 6 Jun. 1762. WO 34/27, p. 250 (L, LbC).
To the Earl of Egremont, Boston, 7 Jun. 1762. CO 5/755, f 9 (dupALS, RC). **No. 122.**
——BP, 2: 192 (L, LbC).
To John Pownall, Boston, 7 Jun. 1762. BP, 2: 193 (L, LbC). **No. 123.**
To Lord Barrington, Boston, 7 Jun. 1762. BP, 2: 193-194 (AL, LbC).
To Jeffery Amherst, Boston, 7 Jun. 1762. WO 34/26, f 162 (ALS, RC).
From Jeffery Amherst, New York, 10 Jun. 1762. BP, 9: 295-298 (LS, RC).
——WO 34/27, p. 251 (L, LbC).
To Jeffery Amherst, Boston, 10 Jun. 1762. WO 34/26, f 167 (ALS, RC).
——BP, 2: 159 (L, LbC).
From the Board of Trade, Whitehall, 11 Jun. 1762. BP, 9: 307-314 (LS, RC). **No. 124.**
——CO 5/920, pp. 139-143 (L, LbC).
From Jeffery Amherst, New York, 13 Jun. 1762. BP, 9: 315-318 (LS, RC). **No. 125.**
To Jeffery Amherst, Boston, 14 Jun. 1762. WO 34/26, f 164 (ALS, RC). **No. 126.**
To Jeffery Amherst, Boston, 17 Jun. 1762. WO 34/26, f 165 (ALS, RC).
To Jonathan Belcher, Boston, 17 Jun. 1762. CO 5/891, f 153 (L, Copy). **No. 127.**
——Prov. Sec. Letterbooks, 2: 343 (L, Copy).
To Jeffery Amherst, Boston, 19 Jun. 1762. WO 34/26, f 168 (ALS, RC). **No. 128.**
——BP, 2: 160 (L, LbC).
To Thomas Boone, Boston, 21 Jun. 1762. BP, 2: 161 (L, LbC).
To Thomas Fitch, Boston, 23 Jun. 1762. BP, 2: 161 (L, LbC).
From Jeffery Amherst, New York, 24 Jun. 1762. BP, 9: 319-320 (LS, RC).
——WO 34/27, p. 255 (L, LbC).
From Jonathan Belcher, Halifax, 30 Jun. 1762. Prov. Sec. Letterbooks, 1: 359-360 (L, Copy). **No. 129.**

To the Earl of Egremont, Boston NE., 1 Jul. 1762. CO 5/755, ff 15-18 (ALS, RC). **No. 130.**
——BP, 2: 201-202 (L, LbC).
To Jeffery Amherst, Castle William, 5 Jul. 1762. WO 34/26, f 169 (ALS, RC).
——BP, 2: 161-162 (L, LbC).
To Richard Jackson, Castle William, 6 Jul. 1762. BP, 2: 194-197 (L, LbC). **No. 131.**
To William Bollan, Castle William, 7 Jul. 1762. BP, 2: 197-198 (L, LbC). **No. 132.**
To Richard Jackson, Castle William, 10 Jul. 1762. BP, 2: 198-200 (L, LbC). **No. 133.**
To the Board of Customs Commissioners, Boston, 10 Jul. 1762. BP, 2: 200 (AL, LbC).
To Jeffery Amherst, Castle William, 11 Jul. 1762. WO 34/26, f 171 (ALS, RC). **No. 134.**
——BP, 2: 162 (L, LbC).
To Edmund Affleck, Castle William, 11 Jul. 1762. BP, 2: 163 (L, LbC).
From Jonathan Belcher, Halifax, 11 Jul. 1762. Mass. Archs., 5: 473.
To Jeffery Amherst, Boston, 14 Jul. 1762. BP, 2: 164 (AL, LbC).
To Richard Jackson, Castle William, 14 Jul. 1762. BP, 2: 201 (L, LbC).
To Jeffery Amherst, Boston, 15 Jul. 1762. WO 34/26, f 174 (ALS, RC)
——BP, 2: 164 (L, LbC).
To Sir George Pocock, Boston, 16 Jul. 1762. BP, 2: 164-169 (dupL, LbC). **No. 135.**
To Jeffery Amherst, Boston, 16 Jul. 1762. WO 34/26, f 175 (ALS, RC). **No. 136.**
——BP, 2: 164 (AL, LbC).
To Lord Barrington, Castle William, 17 Jul. 1762. BP, 2: 203-204 (L, LbC).
To William Shirley, Castle William, 19 Jul. 1762. BP, 2: 163 (L, LbC). **No. 137.**
To Jeffery Amherst, Castle William, 19 Jul. 1762. WO 34/26, f 178 (ALS, RC).
——BP, 2: 164 (L, LbC).
From Jeffery Amherst, New York, 20 Jul. 1762. BP, 10: 1-2 (LS, RC). **No. 138.**
——WO 34/27, p. 261 (L, LbC).
To Jeffery Amherst, Cambridge, 22 Jul. 1762. WO 34/26, f 181 (ALS, RC).
——Prov. Sec. Letterbooks, 2: 325 (L, Copy).
To Jeffery Amherst, Castle William, 25 Jul. 1762. WO 34/26, ff 184-185 (ALS, RC). **No. 139.**
——BP, 2: 165-166 (L, LbC).
To William Shirley, Castle William, 26 Jul. 1762. BP, 2: 167 (L, LbC).
To Sir George Pocock, Boston, 26 Jul. 1762. BP, 2: 167-168 (L, LbC). **No. 140.**
To Benning Wentworth, Boston, 29 Jul. 1762. BP, 2: 169 (AL, LbC). **No. 141.**
To Jeffery Amherst, Boston, 1 Aug. 1762. WO 34/26, f 187 (ALS, RC). **No. 142.**
——BP, 2: 170-171 (L, LbC).
To Sir George Pocock, Castle William, 1 Aug. 1762. BP, 2: 170 (L, LbC). **No. 143.**
To William Shirley, Castle William, 1 Aug. 1762. BP, 2: 171 (L, LbC).
From Jeffery Amherst, New York, 1 Aug. 1762. BP, 10: 3-4 (LS, RC).
——WO 34/27, p. 261 (L, LbC).
From Jeffery Amherst, New York, 4 Aug. 1762. Mass. Archs., 4: 190-191 (LS, RC).
To Jonathan Belcher, Boston, 5 Aug. 1762. BP, 2: 172 (L, LbC). **No. 144.**
To Jeffery Amherst, Boston, 9 Aug. 1762. WO 34/26, f 191 (ALS, RC). **No. 145.**
——BP, 2: 171-172 (L, LbC).
To William Bollan, Castle William, 11 Aug. 1762. BP, 2: 205-206 (L, LbC).
From Jeffery Amherst, New York, 12 Aug. 1762. BP, 10: 5-6 (LS, RC).
——WO 34/27, p. 267 (L, LbC).
From Jonathan Belcher, Halifax, 13 Aug. 1762. Prov. Sec. Letterbooks, 1: 364-365 (L, Copy).

To Jeffery Amherst, Castle William, 5 pm. 16 Aug., 1762. WO 34/26, f 192 (ALS, RC).
——BP, 2: 173 (L, LbC).
To Jeffery Amherst, Boston, 18 Aug. 1762. WO 34/26, f 195 (ALS, RC). **No. 146.**
——BP, 2: 174-175 (L, LbC).
To Sir George Pocock, Boston, 19 Aug. 1762. BP, 2: 175-176 (L, LbC). **No. 147.**
To Jeffery Amherst, Boston, 20 Aug. 1762. WO 34/26, f 196 (ALS, RC). **No. 148.**
——BP, 2: 176 (L, LbC).
From Jeffery Amherst, New York, 22 Aug. 1762. BP, 10: 7-8 (LS, RC).
——WO 34/27, p. 272 (L, LbC).
To Jeffery Amherst, Boston, 23 Aug. 1762. WO 34/26, f 197 (ALS, RC). **No. 149.**
From Jeffery Amherst, New York, 25 Aug. 1762. BP, 10: 9-10 (LS, RC)
——WO 34/27, p. 273 (L, LbC).
From Jeffery Amherst, New York, 29 Aug. 1762. WO 34/27, p. 274 (L, LbC).
To Jeffery Amherst, Castle William, 29 Aug. 1762. WO 34/26, f 198 (ALS, RC). **No. 150.**
——BP, 2: 177-178 (L, LbC).
Account of the Surrender of St. John's, Newfoundland, [*c.29 Aug. 1762*]. WO 34/26, ff
    202-203 (Ms, RC). **No. 151.**
From Jeffery Amherst, New York, 30 Aug. 1762. BP, 10: 11-14 (LS, RC). **No. 152.**
——WO 34/27, p. 275 (L, LbC).
To [Lord Barrington], Castle William, 30 Aug. and 14 Sept. 1762. BP, 2: 207-208 (L, LbC).
    No. 153.
To Jeffery Amherst, Boston, 2 Sept. 1762. WO 34/26, f 204 (LS, RC).
From Jonathan Belcher, Halifax, 4 Sept. 1762. Mass. Archs., 5: 474-478 (ALS, RC). **No. 154.**
To Jeffery Amherst, Castle William, 5 Sept. 1762. WO 34/26, ff 206-207 (ALS, RC). **No. 155.**
——BP, 2: 269-270 (L, LbC).
From Jeffery Amherst, New York, 5 Sept. 1762. WO 34/27, p. 276 (L, LbC).
To James Murray, Boston, 8 Sept. 1762. BP, 2: 270 (L, LbC).
To Jeffery Amherst, Boston, 10 Sept. 1762. WO 34/26, f 209 (ALS, RC).
——Prov. Sec. Letterbooks, 1: 370-371 (L, Copy).
——BP, 2: 272 (L, LbC).
From Jeffery Amherst, 10 Sept. 1762. WO 34/27, p. 277 (L, LbC).
To Jeffery Amherst, Boston, 11 Sept. 1762. WO 34/26, ff 210-211 (ALS, RC). **No. 156.**
——BP, 2: 270-271 (L, LbC).
From Lord Barrington, Cavendish Square, 11 Sept. 1762. BP, 10: 15-18 (ALS, RC).
To Jeffery Amherst, Boston, 13 Sept. 1762. WO 34/26, ff 213-214 (ALS, RC). **No. 157.**
——BP, 2: 273-274 (L, LbC).
To Jeffery Amherst, Boston, 16 Sept. 1762. WO 34/26, ff 215-216 (ALS, RC). **No. 158.**
——BP, 2: 274-276 (L, LbC).
To Jeffery Amherst, Boston, 17 Sept. 1762. WO 34/26, f 217 (ALS, RC).
——BP, 2: 276 (L, LbC).
To John Tulleken, Boston, 18 Sept. 1762. BP, 2: 277 (L, LbC).
To the Earl of Halifax, Boston, 20 Sept. 1762. BP, 2: 209 (L, LbC).
To Jeffery Amherst, Castle William, 20 Sept. 1762. WO 34/26, f 219 (ALS, RC).
——BP, 2: 277 (L, LbC).
From Jeffery Amherst, New York, 21 Sept. 1762. BP, 10: 19-20 (LS, RC). **No. 159.**
——WO 34/27, p. 280 (L, LbC).

To Jeffery Amherst, Boston, 23 Sept. 1762. WO 34/26, f 220 (LS, RC).
——Mass. Archs., 56: 405 (L, Copy).
To Thomas Hancock, Castle William, 26 Sept. 1762. BP, 2: 278-279 (L, LbC).
To Capt. Brookes, Castle William, 26 Sept. 1762. BP, 2: 279 (L, LbC).
The Officer commanding at Louisburg, Castle William, 26 Sept. 1762. BP, 2: 281-282 (L, LbC).
To Jeffery Amherst, Castle William, 26 Sept. 1762. WO 34/26, f 221 (ALS, RC). **No. 160.**
——BP, 2: 279-280 (L, LbC).
To [John?] Elliot, Castle William, 26 Sept. 1762. BP, 2: 281 (L, LbC).
To Capt. Brookes, Castle William, 27 Sept. 1762. BP, 2: 282 (L, LbC).
Journal of a Voyage to Mount Desert Island, 28 Sept.-15 Oct., 1762, BP, 10: 21-28 (AMs, AC). **No. 161.**
To John Tulleken, Castle William, 19 Oct. 1762. BP, 2: 283-284 (L, LbC).
To John Pownall, Castle William, 20 Oct. 1762. BP, 2: 209-211 (L, LbC). **No. 162.**
To Lord Barrington, Castle William, 20 Oct. 1762. BP, 2: 219-221 (L, LbC). **No. 163.**
To the Board of Trade, Boston, 21 Oct. 1762. CO 5/891, f 94 (tripLS, RC). **No. 164.**
——BP, 2: 60-62 (L, LbC).
To John Pownall, Castle William, 21 Oct. 1762. BP, 2: 211 (L, LbC). **No. 165.**
To Lord Barrington, Castle William, 21 Oct. 1762. BP, 2: 223-224 (L, LbC). **No. 166.**
To Jeffery Amherst, Castle William, 25 Oct. 1762. WO 34/26, f 225 (ALS, RC).
——BP, 2: 283 (L, LbC).
To Richard Jackson, Castle William, 29 Oct. 1762. BP, 2: 214-219 (L, LbC). **No. 167.**
To Lord Barrington, Castle William, 30 Oct. 1762. BP, 2: 221-223 (L, LbC). **No. 168.**
To John Pownall, Castle William, 31 Oct. 1762. BP, 2: 211-214 (L, LbC). **No. 169.**
From Jeffery Amherst, 31 Oct. 1762. WO 34/27, p. 283 (L, LbC). **No. 170.**
To Jeffery Amherst, Castle William, 6 Nov. 1762. WO 34/26, f 228 (ALS, RC). **No. 171.**
——BP, 2: 284-285 (L, LbC).
To Jasper Mauduit, Castle William, 6 Nov. 1762. BP, 2: 224-225 (L, LbC). **No. 172.**
To John Stevens, Castle William, 8 Nov. 1762. BP, 2: 285-286 (L, LbC). **No. 173.**
To Jeffery Amherst, Boston, 11 Nov. 1762. WO 34/26, f 229 (ALS, RC). **No. 174.**
——BP, 2: 287-288 (L, LbC).
To William Shirley, Boston, 12 Nov. 1762. BP, 2: 286-287 (L, LbC).
To Thomas Boone, Boston, 16 Nov. 1762. BP, 2: 289-290 (L, LbC). **No. 175.**
To John Tulleken, Boston, 22 Nov. 1762. BP, 2: 246-247 (L, LbC).
To Jeffery Amherst, Boston, 23 Nov. 1762. WO 34/26, f 230 (ALS, RC).
——BP, 2: 290 (L, LbC).
To John Pownall, Boston, 1 Dec. 1762. CO 5/891, ff 104-105 (dupLS, RC). **No. 176.**
——BP, 2: 226-228 (L, LbC).
——BP, 10: 45-48 (ADftS, AC)
Memorial to the Board of Trade, 1 Dec. 1762. CO 5/891, ff 106-109 (MsS, RC). **No. 177.**
——BP, 10: 49-56 (ADft, AC).
To the Earl of Egremont, Boston, 1 Dec. 1762. BP, 2: 228-230 (L, LbC). **No. 178.**
To John Pownall, Boston, 5 Dec. 1762. BP, 2: 230-234 (L, LbC). **No. 179.**
To Richard Jackson, Boston, 6 Dec. 1762. BP, 2: 234-240 (L, LbC). **No. 180.**
To Richard Jackson, Boston, 10 Dec. 1762. BP, 2: 240-243 (L, LbC).
To Jeffery Amherst, Boston, 13 Dec. 1762. WO 34/26, f 231 (ALS, RC).
——BP, 2: 291 (L, LbC).

From Jeffery Amherst, New York, 20 Dec. 1762. WO 34/27, p. 286 (L, LbC).
From the Board of Trade, Whitehall, 24 Dec. 1762. BP, 10: 41-44 (LS, RC). **No. 181.**
——CO 5/920, pp. 146-147 (L, LbC).
From the Board of Trade, Whitehall, 24 Dec. 1762. CO 5/920, p. 148 (L, LbC). **No. 182.**
To John Stevens, Boston, 27 Dec. 1762. BP, 2: 291-292 (L, LbC). **No. 183.**
To John Pownall, Boston, 3 Jan. 1763. BP, 2: 244 (L, LbC).
To Richard Jackson, Boston, 6 Jan. 1763. BP, 2: 244-246 (L, LbC). **No. 184.**
To Benjamin Acquart, Boston, 18 Jan. 1763. BP, 2: 292 (L, LbC).
To Richard Jackson, Boston, 23 Jan. 1763. BP, 2: 248-252 (L, LbC). **No. 185.**
To Richard Jackson, Boston, 25 Jan. and 1 Feb. 1763. BP, 2: 252-257 (L, LbC). **No. 186.**
To Benjamin Acquart, Boston, 29 Jan. 1763. BP, 2: 293 (AL, LbC).
To the Earl of Halifax, Boston, 7 Feb. 1763. BP, 2: 258 (AL, LbC).
To Richard Jackson, Boston, 7 Feb. 1763. BP, 2: 260-262 (L, LbC). **No. 187.**
From the Board of Trade, 8 Feb. 1763. CO 5/920, pp. 151-153 (L, LbC). **No. 188.**
From Lord Barrington, Cavendish Square, 13 Feb. 1763. BP, 10: 57-58 (ALS, RC).
To the Earl of Egremont, Boston, 16 Feb. 1763. CO 5/755, ff 19-22 (ALS, RC). **No. 189.**
——BP, 2: 258-259 (L, LbC).
To the Board of Trade, Boston, 19 Feb. 1763. CO 5/891, ff 132-133 (ALS, RC). **No. 190.**
——BP, 2: 62-64 (L, LbC).
To John Pownall, Boston, 19 Feb. 1763. BP, 2: 259 (AL, LbC).
To Richard Jackson, Boston, 21 Feb. 1763. BP, 2: 262-263 (L, LbC). **No. 191.**
To John Pownall, Boston, 22 Feb. 1763. BP, 2: 264-265 (L, LbC). **No. 192.**
To Alexander Colden, Boston, 28 Feb. 1763. BP, 2: 293 (AL, LbC).
From the Board of Trade, Whitehall, 11 Mar. 1763. BP, 10: 63-66 (LS, RC). **No. 193.**
——CO 5/920, pp. 154-156 (L, LbC)
——Prov. Sec. Letterbooks, 1: 379 (L, Copy).
To Jeffery Amherst, Boston, 14 Mar. 1763. WO 34/26, f 232 (ALS, RC).
——BP, 2: 294 (L, LbC).
To Benning Wentworth, Boston, 14 Mar. 1763. BP, 2: 294-295 (L, LbC). **No. 194.**
To Theodore Atkinson, Boston, 25 Mar. 1763. BP, 2: 295 (L, LbC).
To William Popple, Boston, 26 Mar. 1763. BP, 2: 295 (L, LbC).
From the Earl of Egremont, Whitehall, 26 Mar. 1763. Prov. Sec. Letterbooks, 1: 387 (L, Copy).
To James Murray, Boston, 7 Apr. 1763. BP, 2: 296-299 (L, LbC). **No. 195.**
To Jonathan Belcher, Boston, 7 Apr. 1763. BP, 2: 299-300 (L, LbC). **No. 196.**
To the Board of Trade, Boston, 8 Apr. 1763. CO 5/891, ff 136-138 (ALS, RC). **No. 197.**
——BP, 2: 64-68 (L, LbC).
To John Pownall, Boston, 8 Apr. 1763. BP, 2: 265-267 (L, LbC). **No. 198.**
To Richard Jackson, Castle William, 9 Apr. 1763. BP, 3: 45-49 (L, LbC). **No. 199.**
To John Pownall, Boston, 17 Apr. 1763. BP, 3: 49-50 (L, LbC). **No. 200.**
——BP, 10: 67-73 (ADft, AC).
Apology to the Board of Trade, Boston, [*16-17 Apr. 1763*], BP, 3: 51-56 (Ms, LbC). **No. 201.**
——BP, 10: 69-73 (ADft, AC).
To John Barbarie, Boston, 22 Apr. 1763. BP, 2: 300-301 (L, LbC).
To John Stevens, Boston, 23 Apr. 1763. BP, 2: 302 (L, LbC).
To James Parker, Boston, 23 Apr. 1763. BP, 2: 304 (L, LbC).
To William Franklin, Boston, 23 Apr. 1760 [*1763*]. BP, 2: 303 (L, LbC).

To the Board of Trade, Boston, 25 Apr. 1763. CO 5/891, ff 146-149 (ALS, RC). **No. 202.**
——BP, 2: 69-74 (L, LbC).
——BP, 10: 75-82 (ADft, AC).
From John Pownall, 27 Apr. 1763. CO 5/920, p. 160 (L, LbC).
——Prov. Sec. Letterbooks, 1: 419 (L, Copy).
To the Board of Trade, Boston, 29 Apr. 1763. CO 5/891, ff 154-157 (ALS, RC). **No. 203.**
——BP, 2: 78-82 (L, LbC).
Circular From the Board of Trade, Whitehall, 29 Apr. 1763. Prov. Sec. Letterbooks, 1: 418
  (L, Copy). **No. 204.**
To the Board of Trade, Boston, 30 Apr. 1763. CO 5/891, ff 174-176 (ALS, RC). **No. 205.**
——BP, 2: 74-78 (L, LbC).
To the Earl of Egremont, [c.*May-Jun. 1763*]. BP, 3: 81 (L, LbC).
To Richard Jackson, Boston, 4 May 1763. BP, 3: 56-60 (L, LbC). **No. 206.**
From Jeffery Amherst, New York, 8 May 1763. WO 34/27, p. 289 (L, LbC).
To Jeffery Amherst, Boston, 14 May 1763. WO 34/26, ff 233-234 (ALS, RC). **No. 207.**
——BP, 2: 304-306 (L, LbC).
To James Cockle, Boston, 16 May 1763. BP, 2: 306 (AL, LbC). **No. 208.**
To Jeffery Amherst, Boston, 18 May 1763. WO 34/26, f 235 (ALS, RC). **No. 209.**
——BP, 2: 307 (L, LbC).
To Charles Townshend, Boston, 18 May 1763. BP, 3: 60-62 (L, LbC). **No. 210.**
From the Board of Trade, Whitehall, 18 May 1763. CO 5/920, pp. 161-162 (L, LbC).
  No. 211.
To Lord Barrington, Castle William, 21 May 1763. BP, 3: 62-65 (L, LbC). **No. 212.**
To Richard Jackson, Castle William, 21 May 1763. BP, 3: 65-68 (L, LbC). **No. 213.**
To John Pownall, Castle William, 22 May 1763. BP, 3: 69-70 (L, LbC). **No. 214.**
To Charles Townshend, Castle William, 29 May 1763. BP, 3: 70-73 (L, LbC). **No. 215.**
State of the Facts Bearing on Massachusetts's Title to Sagadahoc, [*Apr. or May 1763*], BP,
  10: 83-86 (ADft, AC). **No. 216.**
To Jeffery Amherst, Boston, 30 May 1763. WO 34/26, f 236 (ALS, RC). **No. 217.**
——BP, 2: 307-308 (L, LbC).
To Jeffery Amherst, Castle William, 5 Jun. 1763. WO 34/26, f 237 (ALS, RC). **No. 218.**
——BP, 2: 308-310 (L, LbC).
To John Pownall, Boston, 6 Jun. 1763. BP, 3: 77-78 (L, LbC). **No. 219.**
To Richard Jackson, Castle William, 8 Jun. 1763. BP, 3: 73-77 (L, LbC). **No. 220.**
To Jeffery Amherst, Boston, 11 Jun. 1763. WO 34/26, f 238 (ALS, RC). **No. 221.**
——BP, 2: 310-311 (L, LbC).
From Jeffery Amherst, New York, 12 Jun. 1763. WO 34/27, p. 293 (L, LbC).
To Lord Barrington, Boston, 15 Jun. 1763. BP, 3: 78-81 (L, LbC). **No. 222.**
To Jeffery Amherst, Boston, 19 Jun. 1763. WO 34/26, ff 239-240 (ALS, RC). **No. 223.**
——BP, 3: 1-3 (L, LbC).
From Benning Wentworth, Portsmouth [*NH*], 1 Jul. 1763. Prov. Sec. Letterbooks, 1: 418
  (L, Copy).
Circular from the Earl of Egremont, Whitehall, 9 Jul. 1763. BP, 10: 119-124 (dupLS, RC).
  No. 224.
To Jeffery Amherst, Boston, 15 Jul. 1763. WO 34/26, f 244 (ALS, RC).

To John Pownall, Boston, 25 Jul. 1763. BP, 3: 82, 88 (L, LbC). **No. 225.**

To the Earl of Shelburne, Boston, 25 Jul. 1763. BP, 3: 84-85 (L, LbC).

To Richard Jackson, Castle William, 26 Jul. 1763. BP, 3: 82-84 (L, LbC). **No. 226.**

To the Board of Trade, Boston, 28 Jul. 1763. CO 5/755, ff 27-29 (ALS, RC). **No. 227.**

——BP, 2: 83-84 (L, LbC).

To John Pownall, Boston, 29 Jul. 1763. BP, 3: 87-88 (L, LbC).

To the Board of Trade, Boston, 1 Aug. 1763. BP, 3: 86 (Dft, LbC).

To Lord Barrington, Castle William, 1 Aug. 1763. BP, 3: 86-87 (L, LbC).

To Richard Jackson, Castle William, 2 Aug. 1763. BP, 3: 89-92 (L, LbC). **No. 228.**

To Richard Jackson, Boston, 3 Aug. 1763. BP, 3: 92-94 (L, LbC). **No. 229.**

To Richard Jackson, Boston, 6 Aug. 1763. BP, 3: 94-96 (L, LbC). **No. 230.**

To the Board of Trade, Boston, 13 Aug. 1763. CO 5/891, ff 185-186 (LS, RC). **No. 231.**

——BP, 2: 84-87 (L, LbC).

——CO 5/755, ff 63-66 (L, RC).

To William Fitzherbert, Boston, 13 Aug. 1763. Selected Materials Relating to America, 1754-1806, PR.GE/110/14/114, RSA (ALS, RC). **No. 232.**

——BP, 3: 97 (AL, LbC)

To John Pownall, Boston, 15 Aug. 1763. BP, 3: 98 (L, LbC).

To John Tulleken, Boston, 18 Aug. 1763. BP, 3: 4 (AL, LbC).

To the Board of Trade, Boston, 24 Aug. 1763. CO 5/891, ff 179-181 (ALS, RC). **No. 233.**

——BP, 2: 87-89 (L, LbC).

——CO 5/755, ff 45-48 (L, Copy).

Answer to the Queries of the Board of Trade, Boston, 5 Sept. 1763. CO 5/891, ff 207-220 (Ms, RC). **No. 234.**

——King's, 205: ff 194-211 (Ms, Copy).

——1763 fBe, (Ms, Copy).

To Jeffery Amherst, Boston, 11 Sept. 1763. WO 34/26, f 245 (ALS, RC).

——BP, 3: 4-5 (L, LbC).

To John Pownall, Boston, 12 Sept. 1763. BP, 3: 98-99 (L, LbC).

From the Earl of Halifax, St. James's, 20 Sept. 1763. BP, 10: 125-130 (LS, RC). **No. 235.**

——CO 5/755, pp. 35-39 (L, Copy).

Circular from the Board of Trade, Whitehall, 11 Oct. 1763. BP, 10: 131-134 (LS, RC). **No. 236.**

From the Earl of Halifax, St. James's, 15 Oct. 1763. BP, 10: 135-138 (LS, RC). **No. 237.**

——BP, 10: 139-142 (dupLS, RC).

——CO 5/755, pp. 53-57 (L, Copy).

From the Board of Trade, Whitehall, 17 Oct. 1763. CO 5/920, p. 164 (L, LbC).

From the Earl of Halifax, St. James's, 19 Oct. 1763. BP, 10: 143-146 (LS, RC). **No. 238.**

To Jeffery Amherst, Boston, 22 Oct. 1763. WO 34/26, f 246 (ALS, RC). **No. 239.**

——BP, 3: 5-6 (L, LbC).

To Montague Wilmot, Boston, 22 Oct. 1763. BP, 3: 7 (AL, LbC).

To the Earl of Egremont, Boston, 25 Oct. 1763. CO 5/755, ff 67-70 (ALS, RC). **No. 240.**

——BP, 3: 99-102 (L, LbC).

——*Select Letters*, (PC). 1-4.

To John Tulleken, Boston, 26 Oct. 1763. BP, 3: 7 (AL, LbC).

To Richard Jackson, Boston, 28 Oct. 1763. BP, 3: 102-104 (L, LbC).
To Benjamin Franklin, Boston, 30 Oct. 1763. BP, 3: 8 (L, LbC).
To John Pownall, Castle William, 30 Oct. 1763. BP, 3: 104-106 (L, LbC). **No. 241.**
To Dr. William Barnet, Castle William, 7 Nov. 1763. BP, 3: 8-9 (ALS, LbC). **No. 242.**
To John Penn, Castle William, 12 Nov. 1763. BP, 3: 9 (L, LbC).
To Benjamin Franklin, Castle William, 14 Nov. 1763. BP, 3: 9-10 (L, LbC).
To Lord Colvill, Boston, 18 Nov. 1763. BP, 3: 10-11 (L, LbC).
To Jeffery Amherst, Boston, 24 Nov. 1763. BP, 3: 11 (AL, LbC). **No. 243.**
To Welbore Ellis, Boston, 25 Nov. 1763. BP, 3: 108-109 (L, LbC). **No. 244.**
To Richard Jackson, Boston, 26 Nov. 1763. BP, 3: 106-107 (L, LbC). **No. 245.**
To [Thomas Pownall?], Boston, 26 Nov. 1763. BP, 10: 147-149 (ALS, AC). **No. 246.**
To John Pownall, Boston, 28 Nov. 1763. BP, 3: 110 (AL, LbC). **No. 247.**
Petition to the Privy Council, [c.Dec. 1763]. CO 5/891, f 191 (Ms, RC). **No. 248.**
From Thomas Gage, New York, 6 Dec. 1763. BP, 10: 159-162 (LS, RC). **No. 249.**
To Benjamin Franklin, Boston, 13 Dec. 1763. BP, 3: 11-13 (L, LbC). **No. 250.**
To Thomas Gage, Boston, 15 Dec. 1763. Gage (ALS, RC). **No. 251.**
——BP, 3: 14 (L, LbC).
To Thomas Fitch, Boston, 15 Dec. 1763. BP, 3: 15 (L, LbC). **No. 252.**
To John Pownall, Boston, 17 Dec. 1763. BP, 3: 118-119 (L, LbC). **No. 253.**
To the Earl of Halifax, Boston, 20 Dec. 1763. BP, 3: 115 (ADft, LbC). **No. 254.**
To the Earl of Hillsborough, Boston, 20 Dec. 1763. BP, 3: 115-116 (ADft, LbC).
To the Board of Trade, Boston, 24 Dec. 1763. CO 5/891, ff 203-206 (LS, RC). **No. 255.**
——BP, 2: 114 (extract, LbC).
To the Earl of Halifax, Boston, 24 Dec. 1763. CO 5/755, ff 71-76 (ALS, RC).
——BP, 3: 111-114 (L, LbC).
To the Board of Trade, Boston, 26 Dec. 1763. D(W)1778/II/48, (ALS, RC). **No. 256.**
——BP, 2: 89-92 (L, LbC)
——*Select Letters*, (PC). 4-8.
To Benjamin Franklin, Boston, 27 Dec. 1763. BP, 3: 15 (AL, LbC).
To John Pownall, Boston, 29 Dec. 1763. BP, 3: 119-120 (L, LbC). **No. 257.**
To John Pownall, Boston, 30 Dec. 1763. BP, 3: 116-118 (L, LbC). **No. 258.**

INDEX

The editor prepared the index with two principal objectives in mind: to help readers find people, places, events, and topics discussed or mentioned in the transcripts, and to facilitate searches by correspondence and their contents.

The main index entries can be used to conduct standard searches for people, places, and so on, but four features should be noted. (a) Entries for individuals who corresponded with Bernard, such as Sir Jeffery Amherst, have subentries pertaining to their correspondence (and in which Bernard is designated "FB"). (b) There are two principal entries for Bernard himself: "Bernard, Francis, ABOUT" is essentially biographical, while his views on the issues of the day are grouped under "Bernard, Francis, OPINIONS ON." (c) Italicised locators indicate pages where, generally, people are mentioned for the first time in a transcript and where biographical information is provided in an endnote. (d) There are separate entries for legislative acts passed by the English and the British (from 1707) parliaments and by the Massachusetts General Court: "Legislation, English," "Legislation, British," and "Legislation, Massachusetts." Each of these entries has subentries of short-titles of acts referring the reader to the main body of transcripts and also to the governor's instructions printed in **Appendices 1** and **2**.

Searches by correspondence require a little more guidance, for there are five headings for Bernard's papers. Four of them concern the epistolary history of the transcripts printed in this volume—"Bernard, Francis, CORRESPONDENCE," "Bernard, Francis, IN-LETTERS," "Bernard, Francis, LETTERS RECEIVED FROM,"and "Bernard, Francis, OUT-LETTERS." One other heading, "Bernard, Francis, PAPERS," lists non-epistolary material. The remaining heading, "Bernard, Francis, LETTERS TO," arranges Bernard's out-letters by correspondent with subentries for the matters raised by him. These headings have been arranged alphabetically with the other index entries and should therefore be read as standard entries.

For example, readers wishing to find information about Sir Jeffery Amherst will find that Amherst, as with all people mentioned in the volume, has an individual entry—"Amherst, Sir Jeffery." Several subentries allow the reader to locate

Amherst's views on particular issues, such as the deportation of the Acadians. Readers will also see that Amherst's correspondence with Bernard is catalogued under the subentry "letters to FB about" and accompanying sub-subentries. The subentry "replies to FB" concerns the occasions—not the actual transcripts—when Amherst replied to Bernard; finally "letters to FB listed" directs the reader to items calendared in **Appendix 3** while "writes to" (which is missing from Amherst's entry) also relates to the epistolary record. Conversely, Bernard's letters to Amherst can be found under the heading "Bernard, Francis, LETTERS TO," the subentry "Amherst, Jeffery, about," and appropriate sub-subentries, such as "Acadians".